HISTORY
of the
NORWEGIAN PEOPLE
in
AMERICA

✳ ✳ ✳

by

Olaf Morgan Norlie

Professor of Psychology
Luther College, Decorah, Iowa

"AMERICANS ALL"

HERITAGE BOOKS
2012

AMERICA, MY COUNTRY

THE NEW NATIONAL ANTHEM

1. A - mer-i-ca, my coun-try, I come at thy call, I plight thee my troth and I give thee my all; In
2. A - mer-i-ca, my coun-try, brave souls gave thee birth, They yearned for a ha - ven of free-dom on earth; And
3. A - mer-i-ca, my coun-try, now come is thy hour,— The Lord of hosts counts on thy courage and pow'r; Hu-

peace or in war I am wed to thy weal— I'll car - ry thy flag thru the fire and the steel. Un-
when thy proud flag to the winds was un-furled, There came to thy shores the oppressed of the world. Thy
man - i - ty pleads for the strength of thy hand, Lest lib - er - ty per - ish on sea and on land. Thou

sul - lied it floats o'er our peace-lov-ing race, On sea nor on land shall it suf - fer dis-grace; In
milk and thy hon - ey flow free - ly for all— Who takes of thy boun-ty shall come at thy call; Who
guard-ian of free-dom, thou keep-er of right, When lib - er-ty bleeds we may trust in thy might; Di-

rev-'rence I kneel at sweet lib - er-ty's shrine: A - mer - i - ca, my coun-try, com-mand, I am thine.
quaffs of thy nec-tar of free-dom shall say: A - mer - i - ca, my coun-try, com-mand, I o - bey.
vine right of kings or our free-dom must fall—A - mer - i - ca, my coun-try, I come at thy call.

CHORUS.

A - mer - i - ca, my coun-try, I an-swer thy call, That freedom may live and that tyrants may fall; I

owe thee my all, and my all will I give — I do and I die that A - mer - i - ca may live.

(By Jens K. Grondahl, editor, born in Norway).

TO NORWAY

Thou land of our sires, where the northlight is gleaming
In frostbitten, quivering ray,—
And yet where the balmiest sunshine is beaming
Its glories by night and by day,—
Where mermaid and nøck in the billows are dreaming
Or charmingly chanting their lay,—
Old Norway, thou mother of song,
Our tenderest mother so long,—
Some never have met you,
Yet cannot forget you,
And therefore they greet you in song!
In song, in song, in heartiest song,
We greet mother Norway in song!

Thou land that with continents bravely art vying
In all that is noblest and best,—
Whose banner of freedom as proudly is flying
As that of the Queen of the West—
Thou land where our fathers and mothers are lying
In slumbering grave-yards at rest,—
Old Norway,—in right or in wrong—
You were our dear mother so long;
Some here never met you,
Yet cannot forget you,
And therefore they greet you in song!
In song, in song, American song,
We greet mother Norway in song!

(By Knut Martin O. Teigen, M.D., Ph.D., born in America).

PREFACE

At the Second General Convention of the Norwegian Lutheran Church of America held in St. Paul, Minnesota, June 8-15, 1923, a resolution was adopted providing for the proper celebration of the centennial of the sailing of the sloop, "Restaurationen," from Stavanger, Norway, July the Fourth, 1925, with fifty-two emigrants on board, constituting the first contingent of the nineteenth century emigrations to America. The President, the Right Rev. H. G. Stub, D. D., was authorized to appoint a committee of five members to make arrangements for the centennial celebration to be held in the summer of 1925. The President appointed the following Centennial Committee: Rev. George Taylor Rygh, Chairman; Rev. R. Malmin, Secretary; Rev. C. S. B. Hoel, Treasurer; Rev. O. S. Reigstad, Professor G. M. Bruce.

The Committee was given three definite instructions, as follows: (a) to make provision for the universal and simultaneous celebration of the centennial in all the parishes of the Church throughout the United States and Canada; (b) to secure the production of a centennial cantata; (c) to provide for the publication of a scholarly, comprehensive and authoritative history of the Norwegian people in America. The present volume by Professor O. M. Norlie is the result of the effort of the Committee to meet the third item in its instructions.

Dr. Norlie is a prolific author, having a large number of books, pamphlets and brochures to his credit. He is well known as a Church statistician and as an authority on data connected with the Lutheran Church in America. Among the numerous degrees conferred upon him by various institutions of learning may be mentioned the following: Ph.D., Pd.D., S.T.D., Litt.D. Dr. Norlie is as modest and unassuming as he is scholarly and studious. A few of his best known works are: *The Open Bible, Elementary Christian Psychology, Principles of Expressive Reading, The School Calendar,* 1824-1924. The present History is the product of a lifetime of research, giving ample evidence of the author's untiring energy and painstaking accuracy. It will prove a mine of information, from which future historians of America will produce many nuggets of historic worth. His elucidation of the discovery of America by the Norsemen is quite enough to determine the opening chapters of any future history of our country worthy of the name.

Dr. Norlie has for all time fixed the place of the Norwegian element in the making of the American nation, than which no other component holds a worthier place. For good citizenship, industry, thrift, enlightenment, and character, the Norwegian element ranks second to none, and this History is the demonstration of that fact. In peace and war, the American of Norwegian ancestry knows but one loyalty, loyalty to the principles and ideals of America.

The Church Committee is proud to have had some little share in the production of this History by Dr. Norlie. It desires, however, to make clear that the volume is the sole work of the author whose name is attached to it. We believe that it will prove a notable contribution to the history of our beloved country.

The Centennial Committee of the Norwegian
Lutheran Church of America.

ACKNOWLEDGMENT

The author is under great obligations to a great number of people who have aided him in making this book and wishes hereby to express to them his sincere thanks:

1. The Centennial Committee.

2. President Calvin Coolidge, Governor General Lord Byng and King Haakon VII, who sent greetings to the Norse-Americans in honor of their Centennial.

3. T. T. Colwick, Norse, Texas; Jacob Olson, Clifton, Texas; Ivan Doseff, artist, St. Paul, Minn., for making the crayon drawing of Cleng Peerson, said to be the only portrait of Cleng ever made.

4. The Sloopers, especially Georgiana Larson, Rochester, N. Y.; Inger M. Johnson, Detroit, Mich.; John L. Atwater, Jane Sara Atwater and Mabel Truesdell, Chicago, Ill.; Caroline C. Bower, Sheridan, Ill.; Daniel Rosdail and Emily Fruland, Norway, Ill.; Jacob Rosdail, Sr., Norway, Iowa; B. F. Stangland, Morton, N. Y.; Mettie Larson and Malinda Larson, Marseilles, Ill.; and Emily Jane Raymond, Hollywood, Cal., for important information, photographs, books and relics from the Sloop. Also Mrs. Anna D. Parker, Kendall, N. Y., and Lieut. Joseph M. Johnson, relatives of Ole Johnson; Capt. Louis Larson, Chicago, relative of Lars Larson; Rev. Helmer T. Haagenson, Seneca, Ill., Fox River pastor, who helped to catalog the Sloopers.

5. Dr. Oscar L. Olson, president of Luther College, Decorah, Ia.; Edith Hexom, artist, Decorah; Prof. J. J. Skørdalsvold, proofreader, Minneapolis; A. M. Sundheim, publisher, Minneapolis; Hon. G. N. Haugen, congressman, Northwood, Ia.; Hon. O. J. Kvale, congressman, Benson, Minn.; Hon. H. H. Bryn, minister from Norway, Washington, D. C.; Dr. E. A. Ross, author of "The Old World in the New," Madison, Wis.; The Century Co., publishers of Ross' book, New York; John Anderson Pub. Co., Chicago; B. Anundsen Pub. Co., Decorah; Normanden Pub. Co., Grand Forks, N. Dak.; United States Census Bureau; Rev. J. M. Hestenes and Mrs. Ellen Runden, Waterford, Wis.; American Scandinavian Foundation and Henry Holt, New York; G. B. Joergensen, Stanwood, Wash.; J. S. Illeck, Harrisburg, Pa.; R. H. Coats, Ottawa, Can.; B. T. Jenson, Toano, Va.; Th. Johannesen, Portland, Ore.; Wm. H. E. Ludwig, Springdale, Ark.; Cora Bangerter, Los Angeles, Cal.; Dr. Knut Gjerset, Decorah, Ia.; all of whom have assisted in various ways.

6. A long list of others, including presidents of institutions and associations, secretaries, authors, editors and publishers.

O. M. NORLIE.

December 23, 1924.

My dear Mr. Norlie:

Honorable Gilbert N. Haugen has been good enough
to hand me your letter regarding the centennial observance, which is to be held in 1925, by the American
community of Norwegian descent in celebration of a century
of Norwegian immigration to this country.

It was particularly pleasing to learn that an
adequate history of Norwegian people and their descendants in this country is being prepared, for it will be
of great interest and value, illuminating one of the
important phases of the national development. The
Norwegians who have in such great numbers cast in their
lot with our country have represented one of the most
important elements in the national community. Springing
from the race which made the first conquest of the
unknown Atlantic, they have borne a great part in the
settlement and growth of many among the states in the
union. By habit and tradition as lovers of freedom,
they have been readily assimilated into the body of
American citizenry, because they have so fully understood and sympathized with our institutions of liberty
and equal opportunity. They have given generously to
every department of national advancement, and I am
gratified to know that a fitting observance of this
centennial year is to be held.

Very truly yours,

(signature)

Mr. O. M. Norlie,
Decorah,
Iowa.

CALVIN COOLIDGE
President of the United States

In connection with the celebration of the
Norse-American Centennial in June next, I desire to
send my personal greetings to all the Norwegian people
who have settled and are living in the Dominion of
Canada.

I heartily wish them continued prosperity and
success.

Byng of Vimy.

Gov Gen' of Canada.

LORD BYNG OF VIMY
G. C. B., G. C. M. G., M. V. O., Governor General and Commander in Chief of the Dominion of Canada

Med, hilsen til u Gamdad
Herdmand,

HAAKON VII
King of Norway

"'Mong the rocks by the North Sea's blue waters"

CHAPTER I

THE NORWEGIANS

1. THE HOME LAND

Norway has been the homeland of the Norwegians for two thousand years or more. It is a wonderful little land, beautiful and beloved, illustrious in story and song.

Norway forms the northwestern part of the Scandinavian peninsula. It lies as far north as Labrador and Greenland, as Alaska and Siberia. It extends from $57^0 59'$
Location N. Lat. (at Mandal) to $71^011'$ N. Lat. (at North Cape), a difference in latitude of over 13 degrees, equal to that between San Diego and Seattle, between New Orleans and Decorah, between Palm Beach and New York.

East and west, the country extends from $4^0 30'$ E. Long. (at Utvær, in Sognefjord) to $31^011'$ E. Long. (at Nornö, near Vardö).

The area is only 124,495 sq. miles. Norway is, then, three-fourths the size of Sweden and eight times that of Denmark. It is a trifle larger than the British Isles, but
Size and Shape the British Isles have 18 times as large a population. Norway is twice as large as New England, one-half as large as Texas. It is nearly as large as.Minnesota and Iowa combined, but has less than one-half the population of these two states.

Its length from Lindesnes to Vardö is 1100 miles in a straight line, but along the coast round the outer belt of rocks the distance is 1700 miles. The entire shore line, including the fjords in and

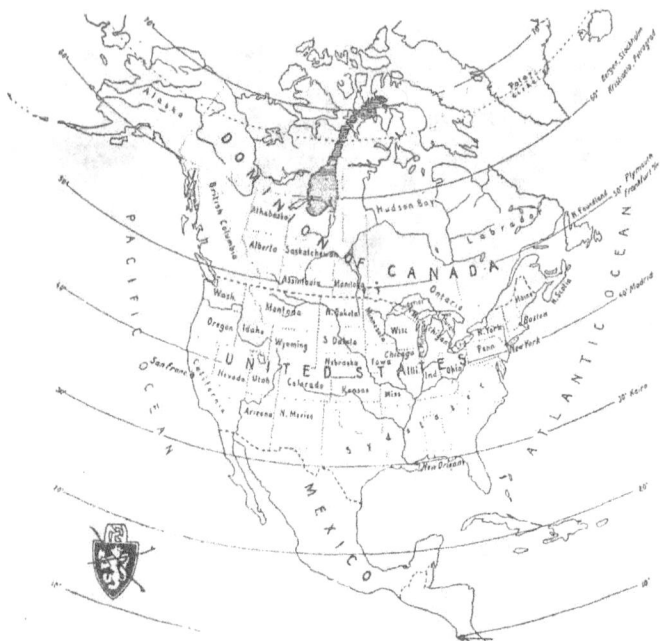

Relative Size and Position of Norway (if moved 120⁰ farther west)

out, is 12,000 miles, a line that would stretch half way around the globe.

Its width in the south is about 250 miles; in the north, 60 miles, often less. At Rombaken, at the head of Vestfjorden, the width is only five miles.

It will thus be seen that Norway, as a whole, is a long, narrow coast-country on the North Atlantic. It looks on the map like a big bag slung over the shoulders of Sweden. It is fringed along the coast by countless rocky islands that resemble a vast flock of sea birds flitting along the shore.

Norway is a land of mountains, with majestic, snow-covered tops rising 6,000 to 8,000 feet in places. Its glaciers are the largest in Europe. Jostedalsbræ, for exam-
Surface   ple, is 330 sq. miles in extent, while the mightiest glaciers of Switzerland are only 20 sq. miles. The mountains of Norway comprise 65 per cent of the whole land. Another 21 per cent is occupied by heavy for-

ests, and 4 per cent is occupied by marshland and lakes. Hence, only 10 per cent of the land is habitable; only 3 per cent is arable; only 1 per cent is tilled.

It might seem that nothing would grow and nobody would care to live in a land so far north. But such is not the case. The climate, indeed, is bracing, but not impossi-
Climate   ble. In the same latitude in which Franklin, the explorer, lost his life in the Arctic regions of America, and in which lies the inhospitable plains of frozen Siberia, the waters of the fjords of Norway never freeze except at their upper ends. "One would expect," says John L. Stoddard, "the climate of Norway to be that of Greenland; but Nature saves it, as a habitation for the race, by sending thither the mysterious Gulf Stream, which crosses the Atlantic for 5,000 miles, and, although far spent on that distant shore, fulfills its mission, transforming, by its warm breath, an otherwise barren region to a fertile land."

The mean temperature of Norway, therefore, is somewhat like that of the northern half of the United States and the southern provinces of Canada, and the vegetation
Vegetation   of Norway is rich for so northern a region. The Norway pine, cited by Milton in his "Paradise Lost," is the most common forest tree. Oaks, birches, elms, beeches, and other trees also abound in places. The apple tree, the plum and the cherry occur far north of Trondhjem, while currants, marsh berries, gooseberries and strawberries thrive as far north as the North Cape. Wheat, rye, barley, oats and potatoes are successfully cultivated in the lower valleys. It is a curious fact that barley takes the same time (90 days) to ripen at Alten (70^0 N. Lat.) as at Oslo (60^0) and in southern France (45^0). The reason for this is, that the summer days are so much longer farther north. At Alten the sun does not set at all during the summer months. Norway is the Land of the Midnight Sun.

Although only 3 per cent of the land can at present be cultivated, farming is, nevertheless, the chief occupation of the people, nearly one-half of the population (48.65 per
Other Resources   cent) being dependent upon agriculture for their support. The land is rich also in other resources. There are rich mineral deposits in the mountains and unlimited power in the many mountain streams and waterfalls. God has richly provided the land with the necessities of life. He never forgets anything. He remembers the lilies of the field and notes the sparrow's fall. He has given the Norwegians houses and homes, food and fuel aplenty. The forests furnish timber

for home-building and ship-building and wood for fuel. There are peat bogs providing fuel, and coal is mined in Svalbard (Spitzbergen before 1925). The great fishing banks, particularly at Lofoten, annually yield millions of pounds of cod fish, herring, lobsters and seal. The maritime trade dates back to the piratical Vikings, and the commercial fleet of Norway today in absolute tonnage ranks next to those of Great Britain and the United States, and in relative tonnage (per capita) is far in the lead of all the nations of the earth.

Why should not Norwegians everywhere love Norway? It is a land of marvellous beauty, rivalling Switzerland as the summer resort of Europe and the playground *Natural Scenery* of the world. Travelers never tire of sounding its praises. J. B. Putnam, for instance, writes: "A traveler may here find the grandest of snow-covered mountains, from which tumble innumerable waterfalls of striking beauty, the most charming stretches of fjords or inland seas, the wildest and most desolate of fields, a wealth of color which in its intense brilliancy can scarcely be matched in any other part of the world, and a kindly-hearted and supremely honest people."

No one has perhaps more fully appreciated the grandeur of Norway and its people than the poets, and their verses outlive the bravest deeds of men. Listen a moment to Ole Vig when he tunes his harp and sings:

> Of all the lands in the East or West
> I love my own native land the best;
> Its rocky towers
> And leafy bowers
> My heart arrest.

> Alone in Norseland spite darkness 'tis
> That sunlight reaches its highest bliss.
> There eve reposes
> 'Mong dawn's red roses,
> And gets a kiss.

We therefore join sympathetically with Bjørnson in his patriotic hymn:

> Yes, we love with fond devotion
> Norway's mountain domes,
> Rising storm-lashed o'er the ocean,
> With their thousand homes;
> Love our country while we're bending
> Thoughts to fathers grand,
> And to saga-night that's sending
> Dreams upon our land.

2. THE PEOPLE

By far the greater part (98.5 per cent) of the population of Norway is of Teutonic, or Germanic, origin. The remainder (1.5%) consists mainly of Lapps and Finns. How long the Norwegians have lived in Norway it is impossible to say with any certainty. The history of Norway stretches back only about 1100 years—to 800 A. D. Previous to that date, in the prehistoric era, the Scandinavian North is at times given a passing notice by the historians and geographers of Greece and Rome. The earliest mention of Norway is perhaps that of Pythias, an enterprising Greek explorer, who visited the land and called it Thule. Hence the name Ultima Thule in ancient times meant the lands to the Farthest North. The name Norway (*Norvegr*, the North Way) seems not to have been in use before the historic era.

The Norwegians are, then, Teutons. The Teutons are descendants from Japheth, one of the three sons of Noah. Noah once made a prophecy that God would enlarge Japheth, and Japheth should dwell in the tents of Shem, and Canaan (Ham) should be his servant. This prophecy is one of the most far-reaching and important facts in history, for it has been in fulfillment until this day. Japheth has been enlarged. For example, at the present time his descendants own about 90 per cent of the land area of the earth, and they profess Christianity, the faith once delivered to the Jews, descendants of Shem. For 3,000 years the Japhetics have been the dominant race of the world. For 1500 years the Teutons have been the most progressive of the Japhetics. At the present date, the Teutonic peoples—the English and Americans, the Germans and Hollanders, the Danes, Swedes, Icelanders and Norwegians—control about 35 per cent of the earth's land surface. The Norwegians are Teutons, of the same blood as Danes and Swedes, as Englishmen and Germans.

Race

Physically, the Norwegians are the most typical of the Teutons. Anthropological investigations have been made of all the principal nationalities. It has been shown that the Norwegians are the tallest of all Europeans and in breadth of chest they are excelled by none. Scandinavians, and with them Norwegians, are found to be the fairest among the so-called white races, since fully 85 per cent of them have light complexions, with light hair and blue eyes. Only 71 per cent of the English and the Germans are fair-skinned and light-haired. Of the French, 55 per cent have a dark complexion; of the Italians, 78 per cent are dark. The Norwegians are physically as well as otherwise a strong and hardy race. " A Hardy Norseman," Edna Lyell calls her

Physical Characteristics

Norwegian hero. "Any nation," says Samuel J. Beckett, "might well envy the people of Norway with their upright, manly bearing and their fair complexions and blue eyes. This simple, honest, hospitable people are the modern descendants of those victorious Vikings who ravaged the coasts of Britain and later settled there—bringing with them that love of freedom which these men of the North have ever considered their most cherished possession. The progress made during the last fifty years is nothing short of wonderful; in it is found national spirit at its best, singularly united and advanced, and producing as fine a race, both physically and intellectually, as is found in any country." Compared with other countries, the number of old people in Norway is very great, exceeded by only a few countries, as, for instance, Sweden and France. The average age in Norway is 50 years, but for Italy it is only 35.

The Norwegians are distinguished for their intelligence and literacy. The Icelandic saga "Heimskringla," the history of the kings of Norway, says that Odin, the god *Intellectual Traits* of wisdom, the highest god of the Norsemen, and the chief who led the Teutonic tribes from Asia into Europe, taught his people the science of war and the art of writing. Already at the dawn of the historic era the Norwegians were far advanced in civilization. They have ever since kept pace with the educational progress of their day and age. Today Norway shares with Denmark and Sweden the honor of being the most literate country in the world. A surprisingly large number of Norwegians are engaged in intellectual pursuits and win for Norway a fame quite out of proportion to the population. Norway has a smaller population than Iowa, but so far Iowa has not produced any Ibsens, Björnsons, Garborgs and Lies, nor any Ole Bulls or Edvard Griegs, or Kjerulfs or Nordraaks. One-third of the engineers that built the Panama Canal are said to have been Norwegians. There is no occupation in which Norwegian brain and brawn are not employed.

Throughout all the ages the typical Norwegian has been upright and honest and clean. He has loved righteousness and truth and morality. He has been conscientiously *Moral Character* trying to obey his native sense of right and the laws of the land. He does not laugh at vice. There are exceptions to the rule, of course, but these exceptions are notably few and far between. On this point comparisons are not odious as far as the Norwegians are concerned. The United States, for example, in the period 1891-1895 had no less than 39,612 murders and homicides, one murder to every 6,600 people. During the same period Norway had only 38 murders, one murder to 266,600 people. There are 40 times as many murders per capita in the United States as in Norway. There were only 10 robberies in Norway in five years. Norway consumes less intoxicating liquors than any other country except Finland. The modern Viking is a temperate man, temperate in all things.

The Norwegian character is deeply religious. His religion in ancient times is that outlined in Norse mythology, a very sturdy sort of religion, with many noble ideals, pre-
Religion cepts and examples. The Norwegians had this religion in common with other Teutons, and kept it no doubt at a higher level than any other Teutonic tribe. At any rate, they were the last of the Teutonic peoples to put aside the religion of Odin and Thor and to accept Christianity, and they preserved in the Icelandic literature the best and fullest account of the religion of the ancient Teutons. As soon as the Norwegian accepted the Christian faith, he took it as seriously as he had taken the old Asa faith, as the old Norse religion is called. For 500 years Norway was a Roman Catholic country and maintained a very high type of Catholicism. Witness, for example, the religious zeal of King Olaf in trying to make his people Christians.

> Olaf here the cross erected
> While his blood he shed.

Witness also the bold defiance of King Sverre, when he and his people were excommunicated by Pope Innocent III. He promptly told the Catholic hierarchs that the Norwegian people were politically and religiously independent of any and every foreign tyrant.

> Sverre's word the land protected
> 'Gainst the Roman dread.

During the 400 years that Norway has been a Lutheran land, it has been notably steadfast in its loyalty to the Lutheran confessions. True, it has been under the influence of larger movements in the world of thought, and has suffered from the inroads of rationalism, sectarianism and indifferentism. Nevertheless, the people as a whole have been God-fearing and church-going, with a profound respect for the Word of God and the Christian Church. "High up stands the Church in the thoughts of the Norwegian peasant." Like a city set on a hill that can not be hid. Norway has had religious reformers of note, giants in the land. Such was, for example, Hans Nielsen Hauge (1771-1824), the peasant lay preacher that awoke Norway from a rationalistic sleep and brought in a new day of Christian living, with political, social, industrial and intellectual progress in its train. At present 99 per cent of the Norwegian population is Lutheran. The Norwegian has always been tolerant in religious matters, as in all matters of conscience and personal freedom. He has not been willing to force anybody to accept his views, even though he himself has been willing to give his life for the faith that is in him.

There was a time when the Norwegians were very warlike; when, as Tacitus says of their kinsmen, the Germans: "They deemed it a disgrace to acquire by sweat *Social Qualities* what they might obtain by blood." In those days, the Norsemen, or Northmen, as they were also called, went on long viking raids into the neighboring lands, plundering and killing. The English chroniclers describe them as stinging wasps and savage wolves. The French monks prayed daily to God to deliver them from the fury of the Northmen. But the modern Norwegian is different. He is probably not a bit less brave than his warlike ancestor. He has been tempered by Christianity and made to see that it is the meek that shall inherit the earth and that peacemakers shall be called the children of God. Norway has not had a war for over 100 years. When war clouds threatened in 1814, the brave Norwegians went to church and prayed for peace, and they got peace, and independence along with it. When war was imminent again, in 1905, the country was again on its knees in prayer before the Throne of Grace, and war was again averted, resulting in the separation of Sweden and Norway, without a drop of blood having been shed. Besides being naturally warlike and yet peace-loving, the Norwegians have many noteworthy emotional traits. They have a feeling of reverence for womanhood. Woman is man's equal. She has full suffrage, and Norway was the first land in the world to grant women the right to vote and hold office. The wife is the queen of the home. The Norwegian home is well provided with children, the average being 4.7, the greatest in Europe. Cruelty, desertion and divorce occur very seldom in Norway. The Norwegian is tender and true, faithful unto death, as in "Njaal's Saga." Njaal was besieged by his enemies, who threatened to burn him up in his house. They informed him that his wife would be spared and ordered her to come out. But she said no. She had stayed by him throughout a long life and therefore she would stay by him to the end. So the old couple, with their grandchild between them, lay down on their bed and were consumed by the flames.

The Norwegians are a race of workers. They all learn to work in Norway and all are set to work who are physically and mentally able. They are willing to work and rejoice *Industry* in their task. About 56 per cent are engaged in farming and fishing; about 24 per cent are engaged in manufacturing; 15 per cent in trade and transportation, including shipping; and 5 per cent are occupied with intellectual work. Formerly, they preferred the outdoor life and occupations that called for the exercise of strength, courage and endurance; but with the growth of the cities and the demand for manufactures, they have taken to mechanical and intellectual pursuits. There are few who are very rich, and few very poor. The pauper class represents only 1.2 per cent of the population; only 2.9 per cent of the population are independently rich. Norway is the most thinly settled land in Europe, having only 18 to the square mile. This is due in part to the fact that only 10 per cent of the land is habitable and also to the fact that the population is constantly drained through a large emigration of young people. But, in spite of such fearful handicaps the tendency of the Norwegian people is upward, socially and industrially, in culture and in wealth. Speaking of this, Curtis remarks: "The population of the kingdom not only holds its own, but shows a slight increase, which seems remarkable because of the continual drain of young, able-bodied men and women who have removed to our western states. In all public movements, in all social, intellectual and commercial activities, in art, science and literature, in wealth and prosperity, Norway stands abreast of the most advanced nations of Europe; but its progress is not won without greater effort than any other people put forth and the application of thrift and industry elsewhere unknown, but which is required in a climate so bleak and inhospitable and by a soil so wild and rocky. None but a race like the Norsemen could have kept a foothold here, but as I have suggested, this constant struggle against nature has been the strongest factor in framing the character of the Norwegian."

Politically, the typical Norwegian is an ardent champion of democracy and personal independence. "He would endure the rigid climate of the North, the burning sun **Political Aspects** of the South. He would sleep beneath no other roof than the arch of heaven, use bark for bread, drink rain-water as a beverage, make the forest his habitation, and have the wild beasts for his companions. But he would never give up one inch of his rights as a free man. The people of classical countries were free men, because they belonged to a powerful and free state; they boasted of their citizenship. The Northman was a free man because he was a *man*—he boasted of *himself* and the deeds he performed." This passion for freedom runs throughout Norwegian history. It accounts for the exodus of the Norwegians to Iceland and Normandy. It accounts for the fact that Norway has really never had any nobility. The Norwegians were the last people in Europe to submit to the Catholic yoke and the first to throw it off. Kings were kings by grace.

In the saga days, if the crops failed or bad weather destroyed
the herds, sometimes the peasants sacrificed their king to the gods.
In modern days the king is expected to sacrifice himself as the
servant of his people. For over 400 years Norway was a province
of Denmark and suffered many humiliations. Still, the desire for
freedom was never extinguished and the spirit of independence
was never quenched. There came a day, in 1814, when Norway
drew its sword against all Europe and demanded national independence. Norwegian Vikings had in years past settled in England
and had established law and order there, with Magna Charta and
the Bill of Rights. From the Norwegian sections of England had
come the deep protests against the English kings and their misrule. From these parts of the land are the Pilgrim Fathers who
came to settle the American shores and the ancestors of George
Washington, who, according to Albert Welles' "Pedigree and
History of the Washington Family," had at one time, for 300 years,
lived in Norway before moving to England. Norwegian Vikings
had likewise established strong governments in other lands—in
Iceland, France, Russia, etc. In short, the Norwegians have been
political and religious Protestants; they have been exponents of
individual freedom and constitutional rights. Henrik Anker Bjer-
regaard sings in his "Sons of Norway":

> Pride of the Norsemen, the temple of freedom
> Stands like a rock where the stormy wind breaks,
> Tempests howl 'round it, but little he'll heed them;
> Freely he thinks, and as freely he speaks.
> Birds in their motion,
> Waves of the ocean,
> Poorly can rival his Liberty's voice;
> *Yet he obeys, with a willing devotion,*
> *Laws of his making and kings of his choice.*

The Norwegians resemble the other Teutonic peoples in language as well as in looks, original religion, customs, laws, etc.

Language
Somewhere, away back in time, the Teutons
were no doubt one people, living together
and speaking the same language. Even now
Danes, Norwegians and Swedes can easily converse together
without learning one another's language. A thousand years ago
the Anglo-Saxons and the Northmen talked together without
interpreters. Says "Gunnlaug's Saga": "In those days was the
same language in England as in Norway and Denmark; but the
speech changed when William the Bastard conquered England."
The Old Norse, still spoken in Iceland in its old-time purity,
with only slight modifications, is the purest of the Teutonic languages, freest from admixture with other languages. The Old
Norse is still pretty strong in some of the Norwegian dialects and
in the Norwegian "landsmaal." Modern Norwegian, a dialect of

Danish, is almost entirely a Teutonic language. In this it is unlike English, which has borrowed so much from the French, Latin and Greek. But it has thousands of words almost identical with the English, and is like the English simple in its sentence structure and analytical in character. Norwegians readily learn to use the English language. They are good linguists, and a large per cent of the people of Norway speak English as well as German and other languages.

A nation's culture is measured in many ways—by its institutions and laws, its music, paintings, sculpture and architecture, its philosophy, science and literature, and in *Culture* other ways. Measured by any of these standards, the Norwegians have culturally been a great people throughout their history. Let a word or two about their literature suffice. The actual beginning of writing no one knows for sure. But we all feel certain with Carlyle, sometimes called "that old Scotch-Norseman," that "the art of writing is one of the most miraculous things man has devised." No wonder that the old Norsemen attributed its origin to their god of wisdom, Odin. He is said to have invented the runic alphabet of the Scandinavians. Runic inscriptions have been found wherever Teutonic peoples have dwelt, but they are especially numerous in Scandinavia and Great Britain. Many of these are in stone and go back as far as 300 A. D. The language is everywhere the same at this age. These inscriptions are the oldest remains of Norse literature; in fact, they are the oldest specimens of Teutonic writings, being older than Ulfilas' translation of the Bible into Gothic and "Beowulf," the Anglo-Saxon epic. During the Middle Ages the Norwegian settlers in Iceland carried on a most brilliant literary activity. Darkness, intellectual and spiritual, brooded heavy over the other nations of Europe. But way up in Iceland, "with frost and mist around it," the sun was at high noon. Men were making history and writing it.

F. Metcalfe, in his "Comparisons of Anglo-Saxon and Old Norse Literature," says: "Scandinavian literature is very attractive in itself, very sparkling, full of nerve and energy, like the people themselves. . . . . Anglo-Saxon literature, on the other hand, is not so attractive. Good, solid, honest work it is, but of no great brilliancy." Says Mary W. Williams, in her "Social Scandinavia in the Viking Age": "The literature produced and preserved by the Scandinavian North is a real national body of writing, unequalled by any other literary compositions of the Middle Ages. . . . . In consequence, it is a contribution which deserves the deep gratitude of subsequent generations. At a time when interest in things intellectual and literary scarcely extended beyond the monastic walls and when the literary output of the Continent was in the form of dreary church chronicles of saints and martyrs, tiresomely told, these virile inhabitants of the Far North created a literature original in form, narrating in prose the deeds of real, red-blooded men and women living in a natural secular world and meeting and giving battle to the problems which the Fates sent their way; or singing in meter their own hopes and fears, joys and sorrows, or the praise of the valor and wisdom of the sturdy gods of Northern heathendom."

Norwegian literature may be divided into three sections—the Ancient Period, mainly Icelandic, from 800 to 1319; the Union Period, during which time Norway had its literature in common with Denmark, from 1319 to 1814; the Modern Period, from 1814 until the present day. The first of these periods has already been described as one of unique brilliancy, the richest in mediæval Europe. The literary activities of the second period are blended with the glory of Denmark. "When Norway was separated from Denmark (in 1814) it was as if all the literary forces in the country had awakened from a long trance with fresh life and energy, and there sprang forth with almost violent strength, a literature the importance of which reached far beyond the boundaries of Norway, and influenced the intellectual life of the whole of Europe." Again it can truly be said that the Norwegians, during the last century, have been active in making history and writing it. They have beaten their swords into plow shares and pen points. Henrik Wergeland, who died in 1845 when only 37 years of age, was a lyric poet, who typifies the poetical and national expansion of the race itself after centuries of repose. His sister, Camilla Collett, was a great novelist and champion of woman's emancipation. Aasen and Vinje were ardent nationalists. Jonas Lie and Alexander Kielland were novelists of high rank. Arne Garborg was a fine lyric poet and novelist in "landsmaal." Head and shoulders above their fellows in the literary field were Bjørnson and Ibsen. Bjørnson (1832-1910) was equally productive as lyric poet, dramatist and novelist, in all of which, as well as in platform oratory, he took up with mighty energy the questions of the day, particularly those that concerned Norway. His influence has been tremendous. For example, through the local color of his peasant stories, every hill and valley and fjord of Norway has had its own author. Ibsen (1828-1906) excelled in the drama, romantic, realistic and social. He is called the greatest of modern dramatists and his works have been translated into the chief modern languages. There is a host of younger writers of note, such as, Heiberg, Hamsun, Prydz, Bojer, Olaf Bull, Herman Wildenwey, etc. These writers, as a rule, no matter how secular and gay in tone, have a serious vein and an uplifting influence. Like the scalds and saga-writers of old, they picture the Norwegian as a man of high ideals and a seeker after the truth, imaginative, with deep convictions and sincere emotions, a toiler, a fighter, conscientious in moral influence and profoundly religious.

The English interest in the Norwegian language and literature has never been very wide-spread or intense. Englishmen have made Norway their summer resort and expect the Norwegians to use the English language if they would have the honor of their visits. An American minister to Denmark resided at Copenhagen seven years and, upon his return to America, proudly declared that he had not learned to speak Danish. Professor C. B. Burchardt of Oxford University, in his "Norwegian Life and Literature," traces the development of the English interest in Norwegian matters. He finds that Ibsen is practically the only Norwegian author that is read to any considerable extent in English translation. At present there is a flurry of interest over Hamsun and Böjer, but at best the English are careful to deny themselves the privilege of getting an inspiration from Norse literature. William Archer, the great English critic and translator of Ibsen, was a half Norwegian.

3. Their History

The Norwegians came upon the historical arena relatively late. But when they did come they played a leading part, contributing on a large scale to the highest idealism and the soundest material welfare of the world. It is truly remarkable that general histories, as a rule, have so little to say about Norway and its part in the world's work. Norway gets in the average general history almost as little mention as Palestine. It is remarkable, too, that the two lands that have been most signally benefitted by Norwegian idealism and labor, namely, Great Britain and America, should be content with histories that never say one word about the Norwegians and their contribution to the material progress and the pursuit of happiness in these English speaking lands. This indifference to the story of Norway and all Scandinavia, for that matter, is also seen in the fact that, until recently, there have been very few histories of the Scandinavian North in the English language.

In this book it is not possible to give even a brief catalog of important events in Norwegian history. We simply call attention to the fact that Norway has a history, and that this history, as well as the people who made it, is of special interest to those who pride themselves on being of English descent and American citizenship. Metcalfe says in his "An Oxonian in Norway": "But Norway is not only interesting for its unique scenery, but also for its blood-relationship with Great Britain."

The "New York Journal of Commerce" is quoted by P. S. Sinding as saying: "There is a nation, even now extant (!), possessing as brave a history as that of the Romans, as poetic as that of the Greeks; a nation that controlled the world's history in many things, and at many times, and whose achievements in war and in letters, are worthy the most heroic age of Rome and the most finished period of Greece; a nation whose philosophy outran their age, and anticipated results that have been slowly occurring ever since. This reference can be true of but one people, and that people is the Norsemen, who lived as heroes, lords and conquerors; who, sailing out of the ice and desolation in which they were born and nurtured, conquered England, Scotland and Ireland; ravaged Brittany and Normandy; discovered and colonized Iceland and Greenland; and they can be said, with confidence, to have crossed the Atlantic in their crazy barks, and to have discovered this very continent, before Columbus. And then their religion—what a wild, massive, manly mythology! With nothing of the soft sentimentalities of more southern peoples, but containing much that revelation has assured us to be true of doctrine—preaching ever the necessity of right, and doing right—of manliness, honesty and responsibility, rewards and punishments."

It is not necessary for an American to be ignorant about this people. There are books now, such as Knut Gjerset's "History of the Norwegian People" and his "History of Iceland," which give in plain English a truthful and sober account of the Norwegians, and it should be possible in the writing of American histories, to give due credit to the Norwegians and the other nationalities who have helped to make America.

The story of Norway can be divided into two periods, of about equal duration—the Prehistoric (from 300 B. C. to 872 A. D.) and the Historic (from 872 A. D.). The Historic Period falls into six sub-periods—independence (800-1319), union with Sweden (1319-1380), union with Denmark and Sweden — the Calmar Union (1380-1523), union with Denmark (1523-1814), union with Sweden (1814-1905), and independence (1905—).

There is, of course, much obscurity hanging over this era. The historical sources are only fragmentary and incidental—a few runic inscriptions and relics, a poem or two, like "Widsith" and "Beowulf," and an occasional mention by a Greek and Roman historian, as Plutarch, Livy, Ptolemy, Tacitus.

Prehistoric Era (ca. 300 B. C.— 872 A. D.)

The world empire of Rome never extended as far north as Scandinavia. It was eventually (in 476 A. D.) crushed by the Teutonic tribes, particularly the Goths and the Germans. But the first Germanic people that crossed into the Roman Empire were the Cimbri, in 113 B. C., who came from

Denmark. From Denmark and its immediate vicinity came also the Angles, Saxons and Jutes, who in the latter half of the fifth century invaded Britain and made it England (after the Angles). The Norsemen were kinsfolk of these Cimbri, Angles, Saxons and Jutes, and no doubt took part in their expeditions. They had well-built boats, fitted with mast and sail. Their call was to the sea, if they would win fame and fortune. So the sea became their highway from coast to coast, and Viking expeditions were carried on in search of booty, conquest and adventure. The "Anglo-Saxon Chronicle" mentions the coming of the Vikings to England as early as 787 A. D.

The ancient Norsemen had always been independent. There is no record to the contrary. But they had not been unified into a distinct nation before 872, when Harald *Independence* the Fairhaired defeated the last of the rival *(872-1319)* petty kings of Norway in a naval battle at Havrsfjord near Stavanger. After his death the kingdom was again broken up and reunited time and again. In 995 Olaf Trygvasson, a great-grandson of Harald, reunited the kingdom. He had been baptized in England and sought to Christianize his people, but he met with opposition and was defeated and slain at Svolder by the united forces of Denmark, Sweden, and Eric, son of Jarl (Earl) Haakon of Norway. Another descendant of Harald, St. Olaf, again reunited the kingdom, besides trying to evangelize it. He attempted to force Christianity on his people, and naturally met with bitter opposition. He was killed in the battle at Stiklestad, in 1030. Soon he was regarded as a martyr and declared a saint by the national assembly.

Among the more important kings who came after him may be mentioned the following: Magnus the Good (1035-1047), Harald Sigurdsson (1047-1066), Olaf the Peaceful (1066-1093), Magnus Erlingsson (1161-1184), Sverre Sigurdsson (1177-1202), Haakon Haakonsson (1217-1263), Magnus Law-Mender (1263-1280), and Haakon Magnusson 1299-1319.) Magnus the Good established peace in the land. Harald Sigurdsson attacked England in 1066, the year of the Norman Conquest, and fell at Stamford Bridge. Olaf the Peaceful framed a constitution and organized the Christian Church. Magnus Erlingsson granted the Roman Catholic Church too large concessions, which brought on the bitter and bloody "Birkebeiner-Bagler" war between the common people and the episcopal party. Sverre Sigurdsson defeated Magnus and the papal party. Haakon Haakonsson, a grandson of Sverre, further deprived the clergy of their undue political influence, and annexed Greenland. Magnus Law-Mender subdued Iceland and reformed the laws. Haakon Magnusson was the last male descendant of the Harald-the-Fairhaired line.

King Haakon had a daughter, Ingeborg, who was married to Duke Erik of Sweden. Magnus Eriksson, the son of Duke Erik and Ingeborg, was only three years old when *Union with Sweden* his grandfather died. Over in Sweden a rebel-*(1319-1380)* lion had broken out against King Birger, and Magnus Eriksson was proclaimed king. Thus Norway and Sweden were for the first time united under one ruler. The union was only nominal, as the two countries had separate laws and administrations, with nothing in common except the king. It was arranged that Erik, the king's oldest son, should reign in Sweden, and Haakon, the second son, should rule over Norway. Haakon married Margaret, a Danish princess. The most important event during his period was the coming of the Black Death, a terrible pestilence which ravaged most of the European countries, reaching Norway in 1349. In many districts it swept away the entire population. Centuries elapsed before the country recovered from this terrible calamity.

In 1375 Queen Margaret succeeded in getting her son Olaf Haakonson elected king of Denmark. On the death of his father in 1380 he became king of Norway also. On *Union with Sweden* Olaf's death in 1387 Margaret was proclaimed *and Denmark* regent of Denmark and Norway and in 1389 *(1380-1523)* Sweden was also included in her regency. In 1397 her great-nephew, Erik of Pomerania, was formally elected king of the three Scandinavian states at the Diet of Calmar. Margaret continued to rule until her death in 1412. As each of the three kingdoms jealously maintained its own form of government, the prospects of a lasting peaceable union were not very bright. The Danish kings had the utmost difficulty in maintaining the union. The outcome of the century-long struggle was that Norway, not having any nobility, was made a vassal province, and Sweden, through its aristocracy, with the backing of the peasantry, regained its independence. In 1523 Gustavus Vasa was proclaimed king of Sweden, and the Calmar Union was at an end.

It has been said that during the union with Denmark, Norway had no history. In 1537, the year in which the Lutheran Reformation was introduced into Norway, Nor-*Union with Den-* way was formally declared to be a province of *mark (1523-1814)* Denmark, and the decree was accepted without a protest. The country had been reduced to a state of poverty and dependence. Commerce had been destroyed; taxation without representation consumed the people's substance. The Danish language supplanted the Old Norse. The literature of Norway from the Reformation to the end of the union is inseparable from that of Denmark. There was no university in

Norway before 1811, therefore the young Norwegians had to go to Copenhagen to get their higher and professional training. Ludvig Holberg, the great "Danish" poet, is an example of a Norwegian, born in Norway, but trained in Denmark, hence reckoned as a Dane.

As long as Norway was a mere appendage to Denmark it could not escape being involved in the consequences of Denmark's foreign policies. When the Danes desired to maintain an armed . neutrality in the Napoleonic wars in 1800-1801, England objected and attacked Copenhagen. Six years later, the English fleet again bombarded Copenhagen and forced the surrender of the Danish and Norwegian fleets. At the same time Norway was entirely cut off from Denmark by the British blockade, and reduced to the point of starvation. In the midst of these calamities the old love of freedom and independence awoke again in the Norseman's breast and he demanded his birthright. His night of political servitude was at an end. This was in 1814. Only a few years before the spiritual darkness which had for a century or more rested over Norway, was also dispelled by the Gospel preaching of the peasant-reformer, Hans Nielsen Hauge.

On May 17, 1814, the Norwegians held a representative assembly at Eidsvold, where they adopted a new constitution and
Union with Sweden (1814-1905)
elected Christian Frederick, heir to the Danish throne, as king of Norway. This show of independence did not suit the great powers of Europe—England, Prussia, Austria and Russia, which had decided at the Peace of Kiel that Norway should belong to Sweden. The powers demanded fulfilment of their decree. A Swedish army proceeded to occupy Norway as far as Glommen. Christian Frederick quickly resigned and set sail for Denmark, where he afterwards reigned as Christian VIII (1839-1848). The Norwegians prepared to defend their rights, and would no doubt have done so to the last man, in case war had been declared. As stated before, they laid their case before the Lord of Hosts, Who answers prayer. They called also a "storthing," or parliament, accepted the resignation of Christian Frederick and elected Charles XIII of Sweden as king of Norway, on condition that Norway should be an independent country and that the king would govern it in accordance with its new constitution. On these terms he accepted the crown of Norway and withdrew his troops. His successors were: Charles XIV John (1814-1844), Oscar I (1844-1859), Charles XV (1859-1872), and Oscar II (1872-1905). These Swedish rulers were all noble-minded men, who, with the exception of Charles John, scrupulously sought to observe the constitution of Norway and to promote the material and spiritual welfare of the country.

Under this system of dual monarchy, Norway was really just as independent as Sweden. But to the world it did not seem so, because the king was a Swede and the consular service was united. In the eyes of the world Norway was a province of Sweden, and this was a constant source of grievance to the Norwegians. The desire of the Norwegians to gain complete separation increased from year to year and came to a head in 1905. The Norwegian Storthing had passed a bill for a separate consular service, and this bill the king vetoed. The Norwegians promptly voted that he had forfeited their confidence and declared him "out of office." This resolution was confirmed by a popular vote—362,980 votes against 182. An unofficial poll of women votes registered an additional 278,000 for dissolution. War clouds threatened, but arbitration and prayer averted the scourge of war. King Oscar abdicated the Norwegian throne, and the Norwegians offered it to a prince of his house, an offer that was refused.

History is a record of what man has done, and should teach the nations of the world how to live together in peace and mutual helpfulness. In this selfish and war-mad world there is perhaps no finer example of national honor and justice than that of Sweden and Norway during the dissolution of their union. Norway wanted to be free; Sweden wanted to be fair. They settled all their disputes without war, according to the principles of Christianity. They continue to regard each other as friendly neighbors, kinsfolk, of equal rank and worth, with a right to a place in the sun.

When King Oscar denied a Swedish prince the right to accept the throne of Norway, the Norwegian Storthing offered the vacant

Independence (1905—)

throne to Prince Carl of Denmark, on the basis of an election, which gave 259,563 in favor of a king and 69,264 in favor of a republic. Prince Carl accepted the offer and took the name of Haakon VII, taken from the saga period. He made his entry into Christiania Nov. 25, 1905, accompanied by his wife, Queen Maud (an English princess) and their son, Alexander, who had now been named Olav. In 1906 the king was formally crowned at Trondhjem. Thereby, after nearly 600 years, Norway again existed as an independent nation in its own consciousness and in that of its contemporaries.

The country has passed through stirring times since it became independent. It lived close to the scenes of the World War, sailed the seven seas, and kept out of the war. The growth of manufacturing is perhaps the most far-reaching of the changes in the land, bringing in its wake many changes in the life of the people. They are passing from a rural to a city population. Hence they have many new problems—industrial, social, moral, religious and intellectual—with which they now are grappling.

In 1914 Norway celebrated the centennial of its constitutional independence. What stupendous progress during the century! What dreams had been fulfilled and how quickly!

4. Their Place in History

The Land

The land is small, approximately 1-450th of the earth's land surface. That is all. Siberia and Sahara are much larger, but count for less. Palestine and Greece are much smaller, but have counted for more. In any event, Norway has great resources and marvellous scenery, and has a place in history that can not be exactly measured in square miles. Norway occupies a larger place in history than it does on the map.

The People

The population is small, only 1-650th of the population of the earth. Just a handful. The Norwegians are not multitudinous as are their cousins, the Germans and the English. The immigration to Norway has always been small, the emigration has been great. Ethnographically, the Norwegians are Teutons, the most typical of Teutons. Physically, they are tall and lank, healthy and hardy, a vigorous, handsome race. Intellectually, they are like the other Teutons, highly endowed, with a boundless capacity for civilization. Morally, they are a clean, chaste race, with the highest standards and most tender conscience. Religiously, they are God-fearing—in olden days, according to their Norse mythology, they had the highest type of natural religion recorded; and in our day, according to the Lutheran faith, the purest type of Christianity ever formulated. Socially, they are a friendly, hospitable, thrifty, home-loving race, reverencing womanhood and respecting conjugal ties. Industrially, they love to work at any honest calling, and, as R. L. Stevenson says, "They know what pleasure is, for they have done good work." Politically, they are independent and democratic, anxious to make their own laws and willing to abide by them, loyal to their chosen rulers and magistrates, patriotically living for their country in times of peace and dying for it in times of war. Linguistically, they are Teutons of the purest type, and their written language as well as its dialects, is clear, strong, beautiful, extremely simple, yet fully adequate to express the widest range of thought and feeling. Culturally, they have from the dawn of their history been far advanced in civilization and have contributed liberally to art, science and literature, affecting the spiritual uplift and the material progress of the world.

The history of Norway is a record of war as well as peace, of course; but it is to be noted that most of the wars are either

Their History

in behalf of personal independence and democracy or in behalf of laws and institutions that safeguard individual rights and the stability of the nation. Norway's place in history is, then, a little land, putting up a great fight for individual freedom, democratic government, protection of fundamental institutions and loyal obedience to constituted authority.

We do not want to say that the Norwegian is perfect and that he has no weaknesses. He has weaknesses aplenty, and his very strength has often become a weakness to such a degree as to prevent him from making the mark in the world that he should make. For example, his love of independence has frequently prevented him from uniting with others in greater undertakings. It was a long and bloody task, that of uniting Norway under one king. Many a brave Viking, many a hardy emigrant, has left Norway for good, in order to give his strength to some other land, just because he would not give up any of his personal freedom in Norway. But for the petty quarreling and extreme individuality of the Norwegians, Norway might early have been one of the largest and mightiest empires of the world. Norway is not counted as one of the great world powers, not only because it is small in size, but because it does not develop any great enterprise. It has prided itself too much on past achievements. On the other hand, the excessive respect for constituted authority has not been an unmixed blessing for Norway and the Norwegians. They have in consequence often been too modest and submissive. They submitted to a foreign yoke 600 years, sweetly dreaming about better days coming. They had so much respect for law and order that they did not like to protest at unjust laws and tyrannical governments. Norway has therefore never had a real riot or revolution, and it often happens that the Norwegian in his heart has the moral firmness of a Brand, but in his life he has the moral inertia of a Peer Gynt.

In spite of its shortcomings, Norway has secured an honorable place in history, and the sons and daughters of Norway everywhere should be justly proud of their lineage.

Concerning the place of Norway in history, DeChaillu says: "This country, embracing nearly sixteen degrees in latitude, is inhabited by a flaxen-haired and blue-eyed race of men—brave, simple, honest and good. They are descendants of the Norsemen and of the Vikings, who in the days of old, when Europe was degraded by the chains of slavery, were the only people that were free, and were governed by the laws they themselves made; and, when emerging from their rockbound and stormy coasts for distant lands, for war or conquest, were the embodiment of courage and daring by land and sea. They have left to this day an indelible impression of their character in the countries they overran, and in which they settled; and England is indebted for the freedom she possesses and the manly qualities of her people—their roving disposition, their love of the sea, and of conquest in distant lands—to this admixture of Scandinavian blood, which, through hereditary transmission, makes her prominent as descended chiefly from Anglo-Scandinavians and not Anglo-Saxons."

Boyesen writes in his "Story of Norway": "It is these conquering Vikings who have demonstrated the historic mission of Norway, and doubly indemnified the world for the misery brought upon it. The ability to endure discipline without loss of self-respect, voluntary subordination for mutual benefit, and the power of orderly organization, based upon these qualities, these are the contributions of the Norse Vikings to the political life of Europe . . . . The breath of new life which the Vikings infused into history lives today in Norway, in England and in America."

A Viking Boat

CHAPTER II

THE VIKING EXPEDITIONS

For the first eight centuries of the Christian era the Norseman is practically hid from our view, quietly attending to his own business way up there in his remote mountain home. Then suddenly, in the role of a Viking, he burst upon the rest of Europe, like a tornado, spreading destruction in his path. The Viking Age had come. It lasted for three hundred years or more (800-1100).

The name Viking is thought by some to mean sea-king, from the fact that many of the chiefs of these expeditions were of royal birth—petty kings who refused to submit to Harald the Fairhaired and his successors in their attempts to unify Norway under one head. The name is more properly derived from their habit of leaving their boats in the viks, or inlets, along the coast when they pounced down upon a countryside to plunder it.

What caused the Viking movement? There were various causes, some of them immediate, others more deep-seated. There were several kinds of Viking cruises. Some of them were irregular plundering expeditions, caused by the desire for adventure and booty. It was hard at best to make a living in Norway, and it seemed much easier to go off on a Viking raid and come back rich in plunder. Besides, such a trip was very interesting and thrilling—it came to be considered perfectly honorable and a necessary part of one's education. Some of the expeditions were well-planned military campaigns, numbering hundreds of ships, for the purpose of conquest. Other expeditions were peaceable commercial ventures, transporting goods of merchandise from one port to another. Still others represent an exodus from Norway, an exodus of people who were unwilling to submit to an overlord. Rather than give up their personal independence, they would leave their beloved country and go to some far-off land of their own choice. "The chief cause," says Haskins, "was doubtless that which lies back of the colonizing movements in all ages—the growth of population and the need of room." "Overpopulation," thinks Leach, "is the simplest explanation of the Viking madness." Coman and Kendall write thus: "In the course of the ninth century the people seem to have grown too numerous for the resources of the scant coast-lands, and the more enterprising spirits set out to seek their fortunes in the richer realms to the south."

Gjerset concludes: "In the Scandinavian countries, with their limited area of tillable soil, and their extensive seacoast, a seafaring life was necessitated from the start, which produced a hardy and energetic race, and fostered the spirit of daring and adventure which expresses itself in the whole movement . . . . . . The young men were partly encouraged, partly driven by necessity, to seek fortune on expeditions to foreign countries. Led by love of adventure, and encouraged by the prospects of wealth and fame, they flocked to the standards of the Viking chieftains in such numbers that the movement soon became a migration, and extensive campaigns were waged for conquest and colonization. . . . . It is an error often repeated that the Vikings came to foreign lands as bands of adventurers, married women there, and soon forgot their customs and language. As a rule they brought their families with them, and settlers, both men and women, came to the new colony as soon as it was safely established. The social organization of the home country was reproduced in the colonies, and there is ample evidence to show that the Vikings clung to their own customs and national identity with a tenacity not unworthy of so proud a race."

The Viking movement affected all Scandinavia, not Norway only. The Swedes naturally directed their attention mainly to the east; the Norwegians and Danes, mainly to the south and west. In the chronicles of the times little distinction was made between these free-booters. There were Danes and Swedes as well as Norsemen in the raids on France, still in the French litanies they are all called by one name—Northmen. There were Norsemen and Swedes as well as Danes in the raids on England, yet the English chroniclers generally call them all Danes. With respect to England it should be remembered that England had

twice been conquered and governed by people from Denmark.
The Angles and Jutes came from Denmark in the fifth century—
the Angles (after whom England is named) came from southern
Denmark, and the Jutes came from northern Denmark. Saxo
Grammaticus, in the twelfth century, begins his history of the
Danes by relating that Denmark was founded by two brothers,
Dan and Angul, and that Angul was the father of the English. "It is evident," says Mallet in his "Northern Antiquities," "that two-thirds of the conquerors of Great Britain came from Denmark; so that when the Danes again infested England about three or four hundred years after, and finally conquered it toward the latter end of the tenth century, they waged war with the descendants of their own ancestors." This will illustrate why the English preferred to apply the name Dane to the Vikings, even in instances when they came from Norway instead of Denmark.

Norse Settlements in Great Britain

(From L. M. Larson's "History of England and the British Commonwealth." Copyrighted by Henry Holt and Co., New York.)

1. Great Britain

The expeditions of the Norsemen took two main directions—
to the south and to the west. The southward expeditions touched
along the eastern coasts of Scotland and England and the western
shores of the continent, as far south as Africa and Italy. The
westward expeditions stopped at the Shetland and Orkney Islands,
and then either went on south to the Hebrides and Scotland, and
then on to England, Wales, Ireland, and even to France, Portugal,
Spain, and the Mediterranean; or, it went west to the Faroes, Iceland, Greenland and Vinland.

The Shetlands are an island group of 117 islands about 175 miles to the northeast of Scotland. They have a total area of 560 sq. miles and a population of about 30,000.

Shetlands, Orkneys, Hebrides and Man   They were discovered and settled by the Norwegians as early as 700 A. D., and belonged to them until 1471, when they were sold to Scotland by the Danes for a song. Old Norse was spoken on the islands for over 1100 years. According to Jakob Jacobsen, the English dialect now in use on the islands has in it an admixture of not less than 10,000 Norse words. The population is still mainly Norwegian in race and customs.

The Orkneys are an island group of approximately 75 islands just off the northeast coast of Scotland. They have a total area of 390 sq. miles and a population of over 25,000. They were settled by the Norwegians as early as the Shetlands. They were governed as a dependency of Norway by Norwegian jarls (earls) until 1471 when they were pawned by Christian I of Denmark to Scotland, but never redeemed. The people of these islands have also maintained until the present day their Norse character, race, language, customs, etc. Their English dialect is strongly marked by Norwegian words and accentuation. They say, for example: "luk the grind" for "shut the gate." One of the earls of the Orkney Islands was Thorfinn, who settled in Yorkshire, England, in 1030. He was founder of the Washington family in England, from which George Washington sprang. Welles' genealogy traces Washington 18 centuries. In Denmark, 70 B. C.—735; in Norway, 735-900; in the Orkneys, 900-1030; in England, 1030-1659; in America, 1659-1799.

The Hebrides are an island group of 521 islands to the west of Scotland, comprising 2,812 sq. miles and about 100,000 people. The Norwegians colonized the islands in the ninth century. They were annexed to Norway by Harald the Fairhaired and ruled by local chiefs, jarls and petty kings. In 1263 they were wrested from Norway by Alexander III of Scotland, and in 1471 they were formally ceded to Scotland by Christian I of Denmark.

The Isle of Man lies between England and Ireland, is 22 sq. miles in area, and numbers a little over 50,000 inhabitants. It was early settled by Celts, chiefly Welshmen, but the Norwegians were in the ascendency during the Viking Age. Harald the Fairhaired made an expedition to the island and annexed it to Norway. Magnus Law-Mender ceded it to Scotland in 1266. The influence of the Vikings in the island can be seen in the fact that the present constitution of the island dates back to the Viking occupancy.

The Norsemen early made settlements in Scotland, especially along the northern and western coasts. They entered the land also from the east, by sea, and from the south, where they had mighty settlements in northern England. When the Norsemen first began to settle in Scotland, that country was not yet organized into a central kingdom. There were several Celtic tribes, with a political organization that resembled a rude confederacy. The coming of the Vikings forced the Picts and Scots to form a more perfect union for the common defence of their country. The Norwegians had a good foothold in Scotland for over 1,000 years, and their language was spoken there during that period. Margaret, "Maid of Norway," was the heiress of the crown of Scotland, but she died as she was enroute to Scotland (1284). Another Margaret, daughter of Christian I of Denmark, king of Norway, became the wife of King James III of Scotland (1468). The Danish king was supposed to give a marriage dower, amounting to $24,000. As he was unable to pay this amount, he borrowed the money, giving the Shetlands, Orkneys and Hebrides as security. Thereby Norway lost these ancient dependencies. The Norsemen have left a deep and lasting imprint on Scotland—on the race, language, literature, art, customs, beliefs. According to George Henderson, in his "Norse Influence on Celtic Scotland," this influence has often been overlooked and belittled. "Carlyle once called the Highlanders a Norse breed," says Henderson, "and he was in a rough way nearer the truth than many imagine."

Scotland

In Ireland they appeared as early as 803, plundering churches and monasteries. In 826 they made their first permanent settlement, soon to be followed by numerous other colonies in many parts of the island, especially along the east coast. In 836 Torgils became king of the Norsemen in Ireland. In 840 he founded Dublin (Dyflinn) and soon afterward Limerick (Hlymrik) was also established as a thriving Norwegian city. Norse kings reigned in Dublin in unbroken succession for nearly 400 years, until 1200. There was a good deal of fighting with the Irish, and at times the whole land was in the hands of the Norsemen. The Norsemen established in Ireland their social order and laws, and in return accepted Christianity. From Ireland they made warlike expeditions into England and France and carried on a peaceable commerce with the lands of southern Europe. According to Gjerset, the downfall of the Vikings in Ireland is connected chiefly with the name of Brian Borumba, the greatest of Irish kings. He slew King Ivar of Limerick and made himself king over the southern half of the land. Later he defeated King Olav Kvaar-

Ireland

an of Dublin and made himself high-king of all Ireland. In the Battle of Clontarf, known as the Brian battle, April 23, 1014, the last great conflict between the two races was fought, in which 4,000 Irish and 7,000 Norsemen lost their lives. The Norsemen continued to rule in Dublin and to occupy the same cities and territories as before, but their political power had been destroyed in the Brian battle. Meanwhile, during the 300-400 years of their stay in Ireland, they had been gradually intermarrying with the Irish and becoming part and parcel of the Irish people. When the Anglo-Norman armies came to Ireland in 1169-1171, they met with little resistance, except in the fortified Norse towns. But as there was no national government and no general leadership, the conquest was easily accomplished. Viking dominion in Ireland was at an end after 400 years of varied success. Traces of the Norwegian occupancy of Ireland are still numerous in the names of places and persons, and in the customs of the people. It has been claimed that all the red heads in Ireland are descended from Norse stock. Our own William Jennings Bryan, thrice a candidate for the presidency of the United States, is thought to be a descendant of Viking Norwegian stock that came to Ireland possibly via Iceland. He himself says he does not know.

There was an almost uninterrupted stream of Norsemen to England and Wales from 787, when they sacked Lindisfarne, to 1066, when King Harald of Norway fell at *England and Wales* Stamford Bridge. Like the Danes, they came first to plunder, later to possess, and, if possible, to rule. They invaded the land from all sides and, together with their Danish kinsmen, pressed the natives, both Celt and Anglo-Saxon, hard. They forced the Welsh into their mountain fastnesses and the Anglo-Saxons into the forests of southern Britain. Alfred of Wessex and Rhodri of Wales, both surnamed the Great, tried to organize the native forces against the invaders. In 876 Rhodri was a fugitive in Ireland; in 878 Alfred was in hiding in Athelney, and was forced to make the treaty of Wedmore. By the terms of this treaty the invaders withdrew from southern England, and secured the right from Alfred to govern the northern half of England according to the laws of the Danes, hence, this part of England was called Danelaw. This gave peace to the land, so that the Anglo-Saxons were left to grow strong and united, able in time to defeat the invaders and rule the whole land. But a century after Alfred the Great, a new series of Viking invasions began which ended in a complete conquest of England, by Sweyn, King of Denmark, in 1012. He was succeeded by Canute the Great, greatly beloved in England and Denmark alike. After Canute's death, in 1035, two of his sons reigned briefly, and then the crown went back to the Saxon rulers, in 1042. In 1066 they were in turn forced to hand it over to the Norman conquerors.

It is quite customary even for historians to overlook or belittle the influence of the Danes and Norsemen in England and Wales. Edwards, in his "Story of Wales," calls these light-haired Scandinavians the "black Norse nations." These Scandinavians in the course of 1,000 years or more of close contact, at times hostile, oftener neighborly and friendly, gradually mingled with the Welshmen and contributed much to the race and its culture. Yet Edwards does not give them one word of credit. Larned, in his "History of England," says: "England was little affected by anything which the Danes brought in; since the two peoples were substantially of one blood, and their institutions, customs and language were closely alike." But the influence of the invaders was not small. Their presence united the Anglo-Saxons. The Anglo-Saxons were invigorated by them. They contributed much to the language and the laws of the land. Bradley, in his "Making of English," (56) points out that the place names and modern dialects in England tell us that in some districts of England the population must at times have been far more largely Scandinavian than English. The Pilgrim Fathers and John Washington, ancestor of our first president, came from the Danelaw.

It is quite customary also for historians to magnify the influence of the Normans on England. Welles has traced the genealogy of George Washington through the English Records (the Common Pleas Rolls) back to a Norseman who came from the Orkney Islands. The pedigree which he has published he could establish by legal evidence. Washington Irving, on the other hand, in his "Life of Washington," thinks that Washington came originally from Normandy. But, the Normans also were Norsemen, the name Norman being a softening of the name Northman. Normandy was peopled by Norse Vikings in the same way as England was, and it makes very little difference whether these Vikings came directly to England or by the way of Normandy.

As an example of what the historians say regarding the results of the Norman conquest, the following from Montgomery is given as one of the most modest summaries: "1. It was not the subjugation of the English by a different race, but rather a victory won for their advantage by a branch of their own race. It brought England into closer contact with a higher civilization of the continent, introduced fresh intellectual stimulus, and gave to the Anglo-Saxons a more progressive spirit. 2. It modified the English language by the influence of the Norman-French element, thus giving it a greater flexibility, refinement and elegance of expression." Montgomery adds also the following results from the Norman conquest: It improved architecture, established the feudal system, re-organized the people, put an end to the Viking invasions, created a strong monarchial government, and enforced a partial obedience to law.

2. CONTINENTAL EUROPE

During the Viking Age practically all Europe was made to feel that the Scandinavian Vikings were to be reckoned with. On the continent, as in Great Britain, the lands were first ravaged for plunder and then colonized for permanent habitations. The Elbe, the Weser, the Rhine, the Scheldt, the Meuse, the Somme, the Seine, the Loire, the Garonne, the Guadalquivir, the Rhone, and other streams were open highways by which the long boats of the Norsemen approached the rich farm lands and populous cities of the interior. Smoking houses and bloody battlefields marked their track. They frequently pillaged and even burnt Paris, Amiens, Orleans, Poitiers, Bordeaux, Toulouse, Nantes and Tours. It is told of Charlemagne (742-814), ruler of all the Christian lands in western Europe, that he wept when he heard of the havoc the Vikings were already causing and predicted the ruin of his empire. In the litany service, as stated, the terrified clergy inserted a special prayer for protection from the fury of the Northmen.

Normandy was an ancient province of France, a trifle larger than Massachusetts. This fell into the hands of the Norsemen so completely as to take from them its name. *Normandy* The first mention of their coming to Normandy was in 841, when they sailed up the Seine to Paris. In 911 King Charles the Simple granted the province to Rolf Ganger, leader of the Northmen. At the same time he gave Rolf permission to plunder Brittany. Rolf accepted Christianity and became a good ruler. It is related that Rolf, according to feudal custom, should kiss the king's foot as a token that he would be the king's vassal. But he refused, and ordered one of his followers to do so in his stead. This man lifted the king's foot to his mouth so that the king fell backward, and great merriment resulted.

Under Rolf's successors Normandy became the most prosperous and progressive land in the Feudal Era. Feudalism, chivalry, literature, learning, pilgrimages, crusades, Christianity and civilization, all seemed to thrive better in Norman soil than anywhere else on the continent. In 1066, William, a Norman duke, crossed the Channel and conquered England. In 1154, the Norman Empire, consisting of England, Ireland and western France, was established; in 1130, a Norman kingdom was established in Sicily and southern Italy. In the First Crusade (1096-1099) Robert II, Duke of Normandy, was easily one of the greatest leaders. The Latin Kingdom of Jerusalem was founded and at its head was placed the Norman Godfrey, the most valiant and devoted of the crusader knights. Tancred, another famous Norman knight, was placed in charge of other parts of Palestine. Richard, the Lion Hearted, King of England, of Norman descent, was the central figure in the Third Crusade (1189-1192). In all these exploits they still bore the stamp of their original Norse character—physical strength, ready wit, loyalty, rugged virtue, religious zeal, independence, submission to chosen, constituted authority, ability to rule, surpassing courage.

Myers gives the Normans the following tribute: "The history of the Normans is simply a continuation of the story of the Northmen. . . . . . When first we met them in the ninth century they were pagans; now they are Christians. Then they were rough, wild, danger-loving corsairs; now they are become the most cultured, polished and chivalrous people in Europe. But the restless, careless, daring spirit that drove the Norse sea-kings forth upon the waves in quest of adventure and booty, still stirs in the breasts of their descendants. They have simply changed from heathen Vikings, delighting in the wild life of sea-rover and pirate, into Christian knights, eager for pilgrimages and crusades."

The Norse Vikings pressed on farther south. The Norsemen in Ireland traded with western France and established a permanent colony on the Loire in A. D. 877, under **Southern Europe** the rule of Dublin. They sailed along the coasts of Spain and the Mediterranean lands, sometimes plundering, at other times trading. For example in 853, as they sailed along the west coast of Spain (now Portugal), they attacked Lisbon, plundered Cadiz, captured the suburbs of Seville, and fought many battles with the Saracens. In 866, a Norse fleet sailed around Spain to the mouth of the Rhone and then made an attack on the coast of Italy, where they captured Luna, mistaking it for Rome itself. Again in 1107, when Sigurd the Crusader, King of Norway, with ten thousand volunteer countrymen at his command, was on his way to Palestine, he defeated a Moorish fleet on the west coast of Spain, and on two Mediterranean islands, Formentera and Majorca, and eventually reached Palestine. The Norsemen in Palestine were as mighty in battle as their brothers, the Normans. Mention has already been made of the Norman kingdom of Sicily, which was really a Norse kingdom. When King Sigurd visited Duke Roger of Sicily, who was married to the widow of

Canute the Great, king of Denmark and England, he was treated as a kinsman.

Norsemen often joined the Swedes in their expeditions to the East, and often they went alone. They approached Finland and *Eastern Europe* Russia from the north, and forced the Finns to pay yearly tribute in walrus, seal, whale and fur. All the lands along the Baltic were visited by the Vikings. In 862, Rurik, a Swede, organized a Russian kingdom, with his capital at Novgorod. To this place many a Viking came, plying his trade. Two of the kings of Norway spent a considerable part of their youth here in the service of the Russian king. One of these was Olaf Trygvasson, who later when on Viking trips to Germany, Denmark, Holland and England, became converted to Christianity, and then returned to Norway to evangelize it. The other was Harald Sigurdsson, who first held command of the Russian armies against the Bulgarians and Greeks, then was captain of the Varangians, the foreign body-guard of the Greek emperors at Constantinople, then returned to Norway and won the title "Hard-Ruler" on account of his ruthlessness in breaking the power of the tribal aristocracy, and finally was killed at the battle of Stamford Bridge in England, in 1066. That Norway was favorably known in far-off Greece may be seen from the fact that as late as 1195 the Greek emperor, Alexius, sent a Norseman to Norway for more troops to help him out. In 1222 a Norwegian pilgrim followed the well-beaten route through Russia and the Black Sea to Constantinople and the Holy Land.

3. The Faroes and Iceland

The great colonial empire of Norway extended westward to the Faroe Islands, Iceland and beyond—to Greenland and Vinland the Good. Iceland may well be considered the most important of the Old Norse colonies. Here grew up an active civilization, fostering the idea and ideals of independence, learning, literature, religion and brave deeds. Here the Old Norse race, language and spirit have been preserved to this day in their purest forms. The Icelanders are to this day Norwegians, and their literature is Norwegian. As Samuel Laing, the Icelandic scholar, says: "The sagas, although composed by natives of Iceland, are properly Norwegian literature. The events, persons, manners, language, belong to Norway; and they are productions which are strongly stamped with the nationality of character and incident."

The Faroes are a group of twenty-one islands, one hundred ninety miles northwest of the Shetland group and two hundred fifty miles southeast of Iceland. The area

The Faroes   is five hundred and forty square miles. The population is eighteen thousand. The islands are mountainous, with thin, scanty soil and slight vegetation. Trees can not grow there on account of the prevalent hurricanes. The islands were discovered and settled by the Norsemen in the middle of the ninth century. They were held by Norway until 1380 and have been a Danish possession ever since. "The people are of Norse descent—a vigorous, laborious, loyal and religious race, belonging to the Lutheran Church." They speak a dialect only slightly different from the Old Norse spoken by the original colonists one thousand years ago.

Iceland is an island lying up to the Arctic Circle, six hundred miles west of Norway and two hundred miles east of Greenland. It is reckoned as a part of Europe,

Iceland   but geographically it belongs rather to America. It has an area of 39,756 sq. miles, and, at present, about 100,000 people. It is a land of high mountains, great volcanoes, frequent earthquakes, vast lava deserts and glacial snowfields, mighty waterfalls, hot springs and geysers, cold climate and rocky soil. Only one-sixth of the land is habitable.

According to Sturla's "Landnamabok," Naddod, a Norseman, discovered Iceland in 860 A.D., having lost his way while on a voyage to the Faroes. According to Hauk's "Landnamabok," Gardar, a Swede, first discovered the island (in 864). According to Ari Thorgilsson's "Islendingabok," Floke Vilgerdsson, a Norseman, sailed to Iceland from the Hebrides in 870 and gave the island its present name. When Harald the Fairhaired in 872 became sole master of Norway, many of the dissatisfied chieftains sought new homes. Some went to Normandy, others to Great Britain, while perhaps the greater number went clear to Iceland.

> First to that wonderful island went
> Norsemen breaking the fetter;
> With them from Norway was liberty sent,
> There to establish it better.

The island had already been occupied by a few Celtic Christians, who fled at the coming of the Vikings. That the immigration to Iceland was popular can be seen from the fact that King Harald was forced to place a heavy tax in gold upon everyone who set sail for Iceland, fearing that Norway might be depopulated. For nearly a century the colony received fresh additions from Norway. Anderson and Bryce estimate that the population at the close of the period of settlement (about 950) was 50,000; Hermann places it at 60,000; while Gjerset, Munch and Sars place it more conservatively at 25,000.

The story of Iceland is very interesting. There were many settlements, each one at first independent of the others. They tried naturally to reproduce as far as possible the Norwegian social organization and laws, with such modifications as they found necessary. They founded a constitutional republic, "a home of the brave and a land of the free," nine centuries before the American Declaration of Independence. In 1874 Icelanders celebrated a millennial of their republic just as we in 1876 celebrated a centennial of ours. They had their legislative assemblies, notably the Althing, in which all took part. They had their courts and codified laws. They were small in numbers, but great in organized freedom. King Olaf Trygvasson, with true crusading zeal, tried to make Norway and its colonies accept Christianity, and succeeded, in the year 1000, the year of his death. In 1262, after nearly four centuries of freedom, the island was annexed by Norway. In 1380, it became a Danish possession. During the Napoleonic wars it was captured by Great Britain, but ceded back to Denmark in 1815. Since 1814 there has been a constant agitation and struggle for home rule and complete independence. In 1874, the Icelanders obtained a new constitution, and in 1918, by the Danish-Icelandic Act of Union, Iceland was made a free and sovereign state united with Denmark by a common king. Since 1550 the Lutheran faith has prevailed.

The Icelanders are especially noted for their discovery and colonization of Greenland and their unique literary output. Concerning their work in Greenland, a word will be said in another place. As to their work in literature, their glory is like that of the morning sun. From 875 to 1100 there was a great outburst of oral literature. "Most of the military and political leaders were also poets, and they composed a mass of lyric poetry . . . . much of which has been preserved. Narrative prose also flourished, for the Icelander had a passion for story-telling and story-hearing. After 1100 A.D. came the day of the writers. These saga-men collected the material that for generations had passed from mouth to mouth, and gave it permanent form in writing. After 1250 came a rapid and tragic decline. Iceland lost its independence, becoming a Norwegian province. Later Norway, too, fell under alien rule. . . . . Pestilence and famine laid waste the whole North; volcanic disturbances worked havoc in Iceland. Literature did not die, but it fell upon evil days."

The chief collectors and saga-writers were Sæmund Sigfusson (1056-1133) and Snorri Sturlason (1178-1241.) Sæmund collected the poems that floated among the people, catching many of them from the lips of the scalds. His collection is known as the Elder or Poetic Edda. Snorri wrote a Younger, or Prose, Edda, which is a scientific treatise of scaldic versification and a survey of Norse mythology. Both of these men were also historians—saga-men. Of Sæmund's historical work nothing has been preserved. Snorri's "Heimskringla" is a collection of sagas, telling the story of the kings of Norway from the earliest times to 1177. It is one of the greatest history books in the world, masterful in outline and perspective, exact in description and reliable in details.

The saga literature treats not only of Norway and Iceland, but also of the Norse settlements in France, England, Scotland, Ireland, the Shetlands, Orkneys, Hebrides, Faroes, in Greenland and America. "It is in these Norwegian sagas," says Samuel Laing, "not in Tacitus, that we look for the origin of the political institutions of England." And it is in these sagas that we find the first accounts of the coming of the Norwegians to America.

4. THEIR PLACE IN HISTORY

The Viking expeditions occupy at least one-sixth of the centuries since Christ. During these centuries the Scandinavians were everywhere. They ventured out upon the surging main; in open boats, without compass, they sailed across the untried seas. Wherever they went they scattered seeds of independence and industry, liberty and law, vigorous literature and refined culture. No country today has a higher percentage of literacy than have the Scandinavian lands. In Scandinavia there is full religious toleration, yet nearly everyone is a Protestant; 99 per cent are Lutheran.

Norway has never seriously tried to establish a far-reaching empire with far-flung battle lines. It has been the peculiar genius of the Norwegians to give themselves to the countries which they have colonized rather than to make these colonies a part of a Norwegian empire. In Russia, therefore, the Norwegians have become Russians; in Italy, Italians; in Spain, Spaniards; in France, Frenchmen; in England, English; in Scotland, Scotch; in Ireland, Irish; in Iceland, Icelanders; in Canada, Canadians; in the United States of America, Americans. Everywhere they have given themselves wholly, and of their culture freely, to the lands of their adoption.

It is impossible to escape noticing that the countries that were settled by Norsemen assumed leadership—Great Britain and France, in particular. Again, it is noticeable that within these countries it is the sections occupied by the Norsemen that came to the front. Thus, Normandy in France, Northumbria in England, Dublin in Ireland, etc. William the Conqueror was a great-grandson of Rolf Ganger, the Norwegian founder of

Normandy. When he made a conquest of England, he met with a most serious opposition from the men of Northumbria, colonists of his own race. He drove them by fire and sword over the border into Scotland, where their influence has been felt in the heroic struggles of a William Wallace, and a Robert Bruce, and is reflected in the persevering character of the people.

The influence of the Normans upon Great Britain is admitted by all historians to have been very great. The Normans were Northmen, their character like their *In Great Britain* name being somewhat softened by intermingling with the French. Concerning the influence of the other Northmen on Great Britain, Samuel Laing, an Englishman, says in part: "All that men hope for of a good government and future improvement in their physical and moral condition, all that civilized men enjoy at this day of civil, religious and political liberty—the British constitution, representative legislature, the trial by jury, security of property, freedom of mind and person, the influence of public opinion over the conduct of public affairs, the Reformation, the liberty of the press, the spirit of the age—all that is, or has been, of value to man in modern times as a member of society, either in Europe or in America, may be traced to the spark left burning upon our shores by the Norwegian barbarians." Aug. J. Thebaud, an Irishman, says: "Endowed with all the characteristics of the Scandinavian race, deeply infused with the blood of the Danes and the Northmen, she (England) has all the indomitable energy, all the systematic grasp of mind and sternness of purpose, joined to the wise spirit of compromise and conservatism of the men of the far North. She, of all nations, has inherited the great power of expansion at sea, possessing all the roving propensities of the old Vikings, and the spirit of trade, enterprise and colonization of those old Phoenicians of the Arctic Circle."

Paul H. Mallet, a Frenchman, writes: "Is it not well known that the most flourishing and celebrated states of Europe owe originally to the Northern nations whatever liberty they now enjoy, either in their constitution *In Continental Europe* or in the spirit of their government? . . . Is not this, in fact, the principal source of that courage, of that aversion to slavery, of that empire of honor which characterized in general the European nations; and of that moderation, of that easiness of access, and peculiar attention to the rise of humanity, which so happily distinguish our sovereigns from the inaccessible and superb tyrants of Asia? The immense extent of the Roman Empire had rendered its constitution so despotic and military, many of its emperors were such ferocious monsters, its Senate was become so mean-spirited and vile, that all elevation of sentiment, everything that was noble and manly, seems to have been forever banished from their hearts and minds. . . . But Nature has long prepared a remedy for such great evils, in that unsubmitting, unconquerable spirit with which she has inspired the people of the North; and thus she made amends to the human race for all the calamities which, in other respects, the inroads of these nations and the overthrowing of the Roman Empire produced. The great prerogative of Scandinavia, and what ought to recommend its inhabitants beyond every people upon the earth, is, that they afforded the great resource to the liberty of Europe, that is, to almost all the liberty that is among men. The North of Europe is the forge of mankind. It is the forge of those instruments which broke the fetters manufactured in the South. It was there those valiant nations were bred who left their native climes to destroy tyrants and slaves, and so to teach men that Nature having made them equal, no reason could be assigned for their becoming dependent but their mutual happiness."

In speaking of the Icelandic literature, Pliny Miles says: "When we consider the limited population of the country and the many disadvantages under which they lived, their literature is the most remarkable on record." W. Fiske says: "All other early Teutonic literatures are in comparison with the Icelandic as a drop in a bucket of water." He adds: "For the English-speaking races especially there is nowhere, so near home, a field promising to the scholar so rich a harvest." Says William Howitt: "There is nothing besides the Bible, which sits in a divine tranquillity of unapproachable nobility, like a king of kings among all other books, ... which can compare in all the elements of greatness with the Edda."

In Iceland

Let B. F. DeCosta, an American scholar, say a final word: "Let us remember that in vindicating the Northmen we honor those who not only gave us the first knowledge possessed of the American Continent, but to whom we are indebted for much beside that we esteem valuable. For we fable in a great measure when we speak of our 'Saxon' inheritance; it is rather from the Northmen that we have derived our vital energy, our freedom of thought, and, in a measure that we do not yet suspect, our strength of speech. . . . . It is to be hoped that the time is not far distant when the Northmen may be recognized in their right social, political and literary characters, and, at the same time, as navigators, assume their true position in the Pre-Columbian discovery of America."

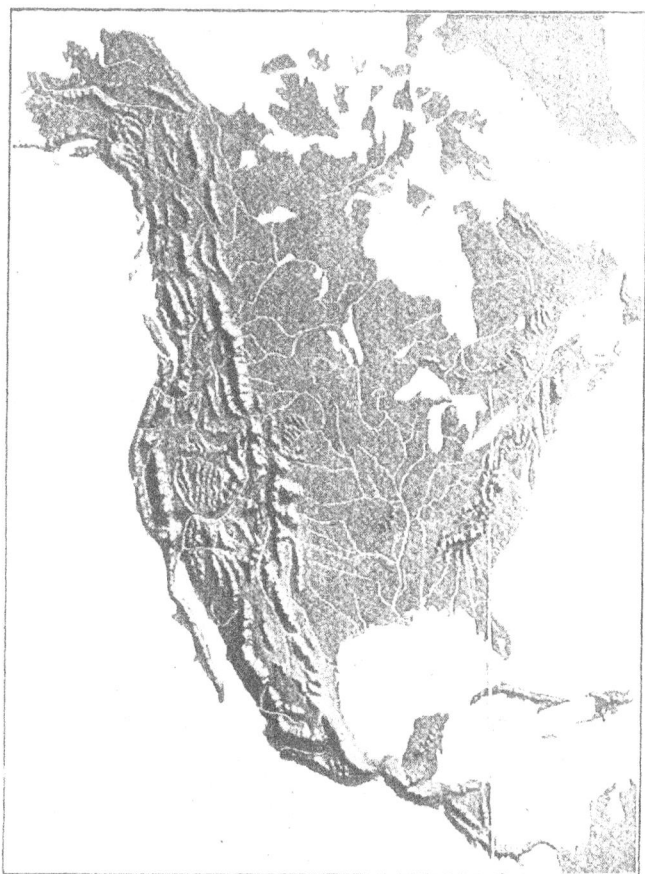

Physical North America

Chapter III

THE NORSE DISCOVERIES OF AMERICA

Christopher Columbus discovered America in 1492. His discovery was the result of patient and persevering study of all the geographical references within his reach, besides an extraordinary ability and perseverance in carryng out his plans. We would not detract in any way from his well-deserved fame. Nevertheless, he was not the first European to discover America, and it is reasonable that some credit should be given also those who had been to America before him and shown him the way. The first Europeans to discover America were the Norsemen. By way of Iceland they settled Greenland and Vinland, and by way of Ireland, they settled Great Ireland.

1. Greenland

Greenland is the largest island in the world. Nelson calls it an"island-continent" in the Arctic Seas. It lies between 59⁰

N. Lat. (at Cape Farewell) to 83⁰ N. Lat. (at Cape Jessup), and is the most northern known land. It is 1600 miles north and south, and 700 miles east and west, and has an area of 850,000 sq. miles, seven times as large as Norway, sixteen times as large as Wisconsin. Its interior is covered with an immense shield-shaped mantel of ice rising from 4000 to 11,000 ft., is uninhabitable and is appropriately called by Hayes, "The land of desolation." It has many monster fjords, very steep and very deep, its sides rising perpendicularly from the sea from 4000 to 9000 ft. and discharging numberless icebergs, some of them ten miles long and one mile deep. The temperature is arctic. Stefansson calls the polar regions "The Friendly Arctic."

The habitable coast constitutes a thin fringe along the southeastern and southwestern coasts with an area of 46,740 sq. miles. The present population of about 15,000 souls consists mainly of Eskimos, with a considerable sprinkling of Danes and half-breeds. The exports are oil, seal, walrus, whales, skins, feathers and fish.

Greenland lies midway between Iceland and Labrador. The greatest distance between Iceland and Greenland is about 250 miles; the shortest is less than 100 miles. It
Gunnbjørn, 876   was inevitable that the settlers of Iceland should find Greenland and the North American continent. Thus it is recorded that Gunnbjørn, Ulf Krage's son, was driven by a storm to the coast of Greenland. His ship became ice-bound, so he was compelled to winter there, returning to Iceland in the spring. This was in 876, shortly after Iceland had been settled.

The memory of Gunnbjörn's discovery did not die. There lived a man in Iceland by the name of Erik the Red, who had left his home in Jæderen, Norway, to es-
Erik the Red, 983   cape a feud. In Iceland a landslide had damaged his neighbor's land, whereupon the neighbor blamed two of Erik's slaves and killed them. Erik flared up and killed the slayer. Erik was outlawed and made his home on Ox Island in the great Southwestern Broadfirth. There he got into trouble with a friend who borrowed a pair of doorposts and would not return them. Finally he went to fetch them himself, and the result was there was a battle in which Erik cut down a man or two. For this offence he was again outlawed and driven to hide in outlying islands, while his enemies hunted diligently to find him and slay him. While a fugitive and an exile he came to think of the island to the west that Gunnbjørn had found. He sailed out in search of it and found it. For three years—the length of his sentence into exile —he was lost to the world and busy exploring this island. Rink

thinks that his exploration of Greenland was so thorough that it left hardly anything for later explorers to find. Nansen ranks him as one of the greatest explorers of all time. After three years Erik returned to Iceland. He called the land Greenland, hoping to attract settlers. He returned the same year, in 986, and established two colonies, the Vestbygd and the Østbygd, both located in southwestern Greenland. From that time until 1409, for over 400 years, there was an uninterrupted communication between Greenland, Iceland and Norway, and the American mainland, too, for that matter.

Says William Hovgaard: "Considering that the Norse colonies in Greenland existed more than four hundred years, . . . and that during this period trade was kept up, at least intermittently, between these colonies and Iceland and Norway, it must be admitted that the chances of such accidental discovery (of the mainland) were very great. Moreover, the Norse Greenlanders, who habitually sailed far to the north along the west coast of Greenland, may at times have been driven across the Davis Strait, which at Holstenborg is only 165 miles wide. Once this region was discovered, the intrepid and enterprising explorers would hardly hesitate to push southward along the milder climates, where navigation was far simpler and less dangerous than about Greenland, and where it was easier to obtain means of sustaining life. The coasts of America, even of Labrador and Newfoundland, with their wealth of timber, berries, fish, birds and mammals, must have appeared an Eldorado to the Greenlanders, who there found in abundance most of the natural products in which Greenland was lacking. We may, therefore, assert that, even had the sagas not contained one word of reference to such discovery, we should still be justified in concluding that . . . . . they could hardly help discovering America."

Gardar became the capital of Greenland and the seat of a bishopric. The first Christian missionary to Greenland was a son of Erik the Red, the famous Leif the Lucky, discoverer of Vinland. He bore the name Lucky because he had saved some men on a shipwreck. In 999 Leif made a visit to Norway and there was induced to accept Christianity. King Olaf Trygvasson commissioned Leif to Christianize the people in Greenland. This became his life work, broken only by a voyage of discovery to Vinland in 1000. He had along with him priests from Norway. It is known that in 1112 Pope Paschal II appointed Eric Knutsson, "Bishop of Greenland and Vinland in partibus infidelium." In 1121 this bishop went in search of Vinland. The bishops after him are mentioned in the Icelandic vellums by name in succession down to 1409.

The intercourse with Greenland, including Vinland, was terminated in the beginning of the fifteenth century, principally for three reasons: The Black Death, which desolated all Europe and eventually reached Greenland; the transfer of the Norwegian crown to Denmark, by which act the Danes obtained a monopoly of the Norwegian shipping, and traffic to Greenland was stopped, causing the colony to languish; the massacre of the colonists by Eskimos in 1348, 1379 and possibly also after 1409.

The latest record that we have of the Norwegian settlements in Greenland is that of a marriage ceremony in 1409 performed by Endrede Andreasson, the last bishop. In a letter from Pope Nicholas V to the bishops of Skalholt and Holar, Iceland, dated September 30, 1448, he speaks of Greenland as having received the faith six hundred years before. He mentions the attacks of the barbarians and urges the Icelanders to serve them again with the Gospel. In a letter from Pope Alexander VI, dated 1492, the year Columbus discovered San Salvador, the sad condition of Greenland is reviewed and Matthias, a Benedictine monk, is appointed Bishop of Gardar.

When Hans Egede, a Norwegian, came in 1721 to Greenland, bringing the Gospel to the descendants of the colonists,
Hans Egede, 1721 "who had become heathen," he found only the ruins of their villages and farm houses. The settlements had vanished. Only Eskimos remained to occupy the land. Though they were hostile, he settled among them, enduring severe treatment and extreme hardships. He laid the foundation for the present Church of Greenland, which is Lutheran. Greenland is thoroughly Christianized, with schools and native ministry under the care of the Bishop of Zealand, Denmark. On July 31, 1921, the 200th anniversary of Egede's landing at Greenland was celebrated, this being one of the earliest events and most successful undertakings in the history of modern foreign missions.

2. VINLAND

Vinland (Wineland) is the old Norse name for America; or rather, it is that part of America which Leif Erikson and other colonists from Greenland attempted to settle. The chief historical sources concerning the voyages to Vinland are: "The Saga of Erik the Red" and the "Flat Island Book," compiled by Hauk Erlendsson about 1334. These sagas are quite detailed, but still not sufficiently so to identify the places mentioned. There is therefore much division of opinion as to where Vinland lay. J. Leslie, R. Jameson, and H. Murray, for example, thought that Vinland was merely a more southern point of Greenland, while J. P. MacLean suggests the northwestern regions of Greenland. J. Filson, J. R. Forsteer and P. H. Mallet located Vinland in Labrador. D. Crantz, W. Robertson and W. D. Cooley thought that Vinland was in Newfoundland. Andrew

Fossum and H. J. Steenstrup located Vinland in the St. Law-
rence Valley. Gustav Storm, Juul Dieserud and Knut Gjerset
locate it in Nova Scotia. R. B. Anderson, N. L. Beamish and
E. N. Horsford represent the view that Vinland was in New-
England. J. V. N. Yates, J. W. Moulton and Alexander Hum-
boldt believed that New York was a part of Vinland. Benjamin
Franklin, M. C. Sprengel and J. G. Fritsch think that the
Vikings went south of New England, probably as far south
as the Carolinas. It is plain from this that the doctors disagree.
They are sure that Vinland was in America, but just where they

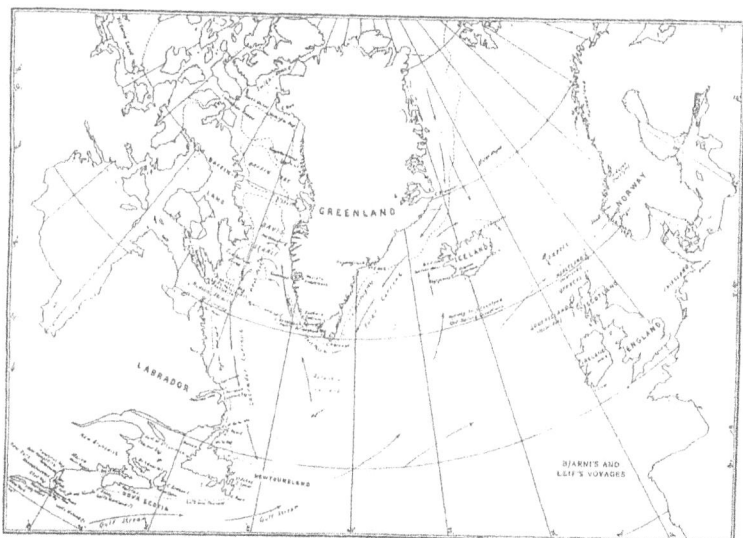

The Vinland Voyages showing Bjarni's voyage from Iceland to New
Foundland and New England and Leif Erikson's from Norway to Greenland and following the coast to New England.

(From Hovgaard's "Voyages of the Norsemen to America." Copyright, 1914, by
American-Scandinavian Foundation).

do not know. The older critics favored the view that Vinland
was in Massachusetts and Rhode Island; later scholars prefer a
little more northern or a more southern locality.

Erik the Red had a friend by the name of Herjulf. Herjulf
had a son by the name of Bjarni; hence Bjarni Herjulfson was
his name. Bjarni chanced to be in Norway
when his father moved from Iceland to Greenland. When he returned to Iceland with a cargo
of merchandise he did not unload his ship, but
resolved to follow a good old custom to take up his abode with
his father. His men were all willing, so they sailed for Greenland. On account of a north wind and a fog they lost sight

Bjarni Herjulfson,
986

of their course and sailed many days until they came to a land without mountains, covered with woods. He was too far south. C. R. Damon thinks that the land which he now discovered was either Cape Cod or Nantucket. Bjarni turned his boat to the north again and sailed for two days, when he again spied land. When his men asked him if it was Greenland, he said "No, for in Greenland there are great snowy mountains, but this land is flat and covered with trees." This place, thinks R. B. Anderson, was Nova Scotia. Again he sailed to the north and kept the sea with a fine breeze from the southwest for three days, when a third land was seen, no doubt Newfoundland. Bjarni would not go ashore, so on he sailed farther north, driven by a violent southwest wind, and after four days he reached Greenland.

Statue of Leif Erikson at Boston

Erik the Red and wife Thorhild lived at Brattahlid, West Greenland, with their three sons, Leif the Lucky, Thorvald and Thorstein. When Leif heard of the ad-

Leif Erikson, 1000 venture of Bjarni he determined to find the land which Bjarni had sighted, and explore it. He bought Bjarni's ship from him, set sail with 35 picked men and found the lands just as Bjarni had described them far away to the southwest of Greenland. He landed at three places. The first he called Helluland, meaning stoneland. It has been variously located in Labrador and Newfoundland. The second place he called Markland, meaning woodland, possibly in Nova Scotia. The third place he called Vinland, because one of his party, a German, by name Tyrker, had found some grapes and became so excited that he began to talk German.

Leif Erikson was the first to cross the Atlantic without a stop, since he did not stop at Iceland on his way to Greenland from Norway. He was the first Christian missionary to America. He was the first to set out to find America and one of the first to set his foot on the American continent.

Leif Erikson returned to Greenland in the following spring. His brother Thorvald listened with rapture to the tale of adventure and thought that the land had been too little explored. So he set sail with thirty men for Vinland in 1002. He found Vinland to be a fair country, and after a good deal of exploration he concluded to make it his home, but he and his party were attacked by the Indians, or Skrellings (weaklings), as they called them, and Thorvald was killed. His companions buried him there in Vinland and two crosses were erected on his grave, one at his head and one at his feet. When the Norsemen had buried their chief, they loaded their ships with grapes and wood, and returned to Greenland in the year 1005.

Thorvald Erikson, 1002

Thorstein, the youngest son of Erik the Red, was seized with a desire to go and fetch the body of his brother Thorvald. He set out with Thorvald's ship with a crew of twenty-five men of good stature and strength and, taking with him his wife Gudrid, he sailed for Vinland. Through the whole summer his ship was tossed about on the deep and he lost all reckoning. Finally, they made land and discovered that they were on the western coast of Greenland. Here Thorstein and several of his men died of disease, and his widow and the rest of the party returned to Eriksfjord from whence they had departed.

Thorstein Erikson, 1005

In 1006 Karlsefne came from Norway to Eriksfjord with two ships. While there he married Gudrid, widow of Thorstein Erikson. She persuaded Thorfinn to undertake an expedition to Vinland. This he did in the year 1007 with the intention of colonizing the new found land. His party consisted of one hundred and fifty-one men and nine women. He carried along on this occasion also a number of cattle and sheep. They arrived safely at Leif's Booths, and remained there three years, when hostilities with the Indians compelled them to give up their colony. In 1008 a son was born to Thorfinn and Gudrid. He was called Snorri Thorfinnson. He was the first white child born on the American continent, of which we have any record. From him the famous sculptor, Bertel Thorvaldsen, is lineally descended, besides many other distinguished men. After Thorfinn's death, which occurred some years later in Greenland,

Thorfinn Karlsefne, 1007

Gudrid made a pilgrimage to Rome, after which she returned to the home of her son Snorri, who had caused a church to be built at Blaumbør. Gudrid then took the veil and remained a Catholic nun until the end of her days. There is in Bristol County, Massachusetts, the Dighton Rock, on which is an inscription, which it has been claimed dates from the occupancy of Thorfinn in this neighborhood. The rock with its inscription was there when the Pilgrim Fathers landed in Massachusetts.

There was much talk about another Vinland voyage, and in 1011 two ships set sail for Vinland. One was commanded by
Freydis, 1011   Freydis, Erik's daughter, and the other by the brothers, Helgi and Finn Bogi, whom she had invited to go along with her. The story of this expedition is very sad, for it concerns the massacre of thirty men and five women of the party at the instigation of Freydis herself. After the massacre she returned to Greenland and bribed her party to screen her guilt. Nevertheless, "murder will out," and the story got abroad at last. At this point the sagas for a time are silent about Vinland and its colonization. The saga-man was a historian and, as such, wrote about events which were considered important events in Norway and Iceland mainly. Not very much was written about Greenland and Vinland because they were considered less important. More attention was paid to the Vinland voyages of Leif, Thorvald, Thorstein, Thorfinn and Freydis, because they belonged to the family of Erik the Red, who was considered an outstanding man.

The sagas report that a few of Thorfinn Karlsefne's men remained in Vinland. Later, two Icelandic chieftains joined them
and established a colony there. In 1059
Bishop John, 1059   they were joined by yet another Icelander, Bishop John, a man of English or Irish descent, who had preached in Iceland for four years. In Vinland he preached not only to the Norsemen, but also to the Indians. Some of the Indians he succeeded in converting to Christianity; nevertheless, he suffered martyrdom at the hands of the Red Men.

Eric Upsi was, according to some accounts, the first bishop of Greenland. The "Lawman's Annals" records under date of
1121 these brief words: "Bishop Eric of
Eric Upsi, 1121   Greenland went in search of Vinland." There is no indication anywhere why he went or whether he ever returned. The Norse-Greenlanders applied for a new bishop, and according to the "Annals," they got one in the person of Bishop Arnold, who was consecrated in 1124 as Eric's successor.

In 1261, Iceland and Greenland, for the first time in their history acknowledged the overlordship of the king of Norway and promised to pay taxes. In 1380 Erik Priest-hater came to the throne of Norway. He appointed as governor of Iceland Arne Thorlaksson, a man not very friendly to the clergy. On this account two of the Icelandic pastors, Adelbrand and Thorvald Helgesson, set out for Vinland in the year 1285. The sagas report that they "found a new land," which some suppose was the island of New Foundland. Cabot, in 1497, gave the island its present name, which is remarkably like the saga report.

Adelbrand and Thorvald Helgesson, 1285

The "Skalholt Annals" are a manuscript found in southern Iceland. They contain a record, dated 1347, as follows: "There came also a ship from Greenland, less in size than small Icelandic trading vessels. It came into the outer Stream-firth (on the western coast of Iceland). It was without an anchor. There were seventeen men on board, and they had sailed to Markland, but had afterwards been driven hither by storms at sea." That is, this ship, on its homeward voyage to Greenland, had been driven by adverse storms over to Iceland.

Skalholt Annals, 1347

There is a good deal of documentary and circumstantial evidence to prove that in or about 1476 an expedition was sent by Christian I of Denmark-Norway to America. The expedition was sent on the suggestion of the Portuguese government. The object of the expedition was to find the "Cod Fish Country" of Labrador and Newfoundland. The venture was successful. It was commanded by a Dane, Dietrik Pining, and was piloted by a Norwegian, John Scolvus.

John Scolvus, 1476

Two Portuguese noblemen, Cortereal and Homen, went along as representatives of Portugal. Cordeyro therefore credits these men with the discovery of the codfish country, and the King of Portugal gave them official appointments in the Azores in recognition thereof. It is interesting in this connection to note that in 1476 Columbus made his home in Lisbon, Portugal. In 1477, when he was enroute to Iceland, he wrote a letter from Bristol, England, to his son. This expedition to America by Scolvus occurred nearly 500 years after Bjarni's first land-sighting.

3. GREAT IRELAND

Another part of America that was settled by the Norse Vikings was Hvitramannaland, or White Man's Land, also called "Irland itt Mikla," or Great Ireland. It was called White Man's Land, because two native boys, captured by Thorfinn Karlsefne, in Markland in 1007, had told of a country beyond their own (to the south) where people wore white garments. It was called Great Ireland because it was conceived to be nearest to Ireland across the ocean, southwestward. An old manuscript says: "Thither was sailing formerly from Ireland; there Irishmen and Icelanders recognized Ari, of whom nothing had been heard for a long time and who had been made a chief there by the inhabitants." Ari Frodi (1067-1146), the first compiler of "Landnamabok," states that this land lay to the west, in the sea, near to Vinland the Good. "VI days' sailing from Ireland." According to Carl Christian Rafn, the figure VI was written by mistake for XI, XV or XX, by the transcriber of the original manuscript which is now lost. The mistake, R. B. Anderson thinks, might easily have been caused by a blot or defect in the manuscript. Great Ireland is supposed to have been some part of the Atlantic coast, from Virginia to Florida.

Ari Marson, an Icelandic chieftain, was, in the year 983, driven by storms far out of his course, until he finally landed at what the chroniclers called Irland itt Mikla. *Ari Marson, 983* The story of this voyage was first told by Rafn, Ari Marson's contemporary. Rafn was surnamed the Limerick-trader, because he lived at Limerick, Ireland, for a number of years. Ari Frodi, the historian, was a great-grandson of Ari Marson. He relates that Thorfinn Sigurdsson, Jarl of Orkney, claimed that Ari Marson was held in great respect in his new home and could not get away from there. In those days there seems to have been an occasional intercourse between the British Isles and Great Ireland.

Bjørn Asbrandsson was also an Icelander. On account of a love affair with Thurid, a married woman, he had been banished from Iceland for three years. He went to Denmark, joined the celebrated Jomsborg warriors, *Bjørn Asbrandsson, 999* and fought in the Battle of Fyrisal, Sweden. In 999 he returned to Iceland and again took up his unfortunate love affair. For this breach of ethics he had to leave the country again. He set sail from Iceland with a northeast wind, and no one knew what became of him until Gudleif returned from his voyage to Great Ireland.

Gudleif Gudlaugsson was a brother of Thorfinn, the ancestor of Snorri Sturlasson, the historian. Gudleif undertook a voyage to Dublin, at that time a Norwegian city. On *Gudleif Gudlaugs-* leaving Ireland he set sail again for Iceland, *son, 1027* but was driven by adverse winds far to the west and southwest. He and his crew sent up many prayers that they might find land. Finally, they saw land to the west and resolved to go ashore. As they did so, people came down to meet them, laid hands on them, and bound them. While the natives were debating what to do with them, another company of men approached, at the head of which rode a man of distinguished appearance, old and gray. He spoke to Gudleif in the Old Norse, for he was no other than Bjørn Asbrandsson. Bjørn asked many questions about Iceland, set Gudleif and his men at liberty, sent a present along to his sweetheart Thurid and a sword for her son Kjartan, and directed them to set sail again, as the natives were not to be trusted. Gudleif sailed back to Dublin, and then returned to Iceland, bringing with him the greetings and presents.

B. I. Jensen, Toano, Va., writes concerning the ruins of an old stone house in Virginia, in part as follows:

"Near the junction of Weir Creek and the York River in James City (this) County, are the ruins of an old stone house, the history of which is a matter of conjecture. Some believe it was an outpost erected by Capt. John Smith. There are no stone at all in this section, so all used in building this house must have been brought in, presumably by water, may have been brought from the New England states. . . . . . My father was of the firm conviction from the evident age of the ruin that it antedated Smith and the English settlement and that it must have been the work of the Vikings. . . . . . I believe the Vikings built this old house six hundred years before Smith was born."

4. INLAND

Even though the old Norsemen were good chroniclers and saga-men, it is reasonable to presume that they did not record everything. "The half has never yet been told." Besides, much that has been written has been lost. Nothing has been preserved, for example, of the historical works of Saemund Sigfusson, who established the Norse chronology up to 1047. The originals of Ari Frodi's "Islendingabok" and Karl Jonsson's "Sverrirssaga" have been lost; we possess only copies and versions of these. Many manuscripts have been destroyed—some by reformers in the 16th century, some by the Algerine and English pirates in the 17th and 18th centuries, some by the burning of the Royal Library at Copenhagen in 1728, etc. Most manuscripts were at first privately owned, and possibly not all have been discovered yet. In 1837 Carl Christian Rafn, a Danish scholar, published his "Antiquitates Americanae" (American Antiquities), a collection of sagas and other historical references to the Pre-Columbian discovery of America by the Norsemen. One of the chief sources on the Vinland story is the "Flateyarbok" owned by a family on an island, Flat Island, off the coast of Iceland. This precious book is now in the possession of the Royal Library at Copenhagen, where it is jealously guarded. The United States wished to place it on exhibit at the Chicago Columbian Exposition in 1893. The American minister at Copenhagen promised to convey the book here in an American warship, to keep it constantly under guard and accompanied by a Danish scholar, but the request was refused.

It is plain, then, that we do not have all the sources, also that many events were not chronicled. Men did not record all the voyages back and forth between Norway and Iceland, Ireland and Iceland, Greenland and Iceland, etc., and it is hardly to be expected that they should keep track of every trip to the mainland. During the 12th and 13th centuries the Norsemen in Greenland used to make their fishing expeditions up and down what is now known as Baffin Bay and Davis Strait, just as their kinsmen in Norway have from time immemorial fished at Lofoten and Finmarken. From Davis Strait they could easily make their way into Hudson Bay—and Hudson Bay is in the heart of America, far inland. This did actually happen to the Jens Munk Expedition in 1619. If the Kensington Stone is genuine, then we are assured that such an event took place also in 1362. The Kensington Stone and the white Eskimos and white Indians are indications that the Norsemen penetrated far inland.

In the fall of 1898 Olaf Ohman, a Swedish farmer living three miles northeast of Kensington, Minn., in clearing a timber tract of stumps, discovered a stone with an in-

The Kensington Stone   scription in the runic characters of the Old Norse tongue carved upon it. The stone lay deep down entwined by the roots of the tree. The tree was native and much older than the settlement. The inscription said that eight Swedes and twenty-two Norsemen were on a journey of discovery from Vinland westward. Ten of their men had been killed. They were 14 (or 41) days' journey from their vessel, where ten men were stationed. Year 1362. The stone at once attracted much attention. It was sent to Minneapolis and Chicago to be examined by experts, most of whom declared it a fraud. It was returned to the owner, who used it for a doorstep to his granary for eight years. Then in 1908, Hjalmar R. Holand got interested in it, exhibited it in this country and Europe, and for a time practically reversed the opinion that it is of modern origin. In the line-up denouncing the stone as a fraud are such men as: O. J. Breda, H. Gjessing, R. B. Anderson, Gisle Bothne, J. Dieserud, Geo. T. Flom, Horatio Gates, G. N. Gould, Julius E. Olson and Knut Gjerset; among its defenders are such men as: H. R. Holand, Anders Daae, Olaf Huseby, P. P. Iverslie, Andrew Fossum, N. A. Grevstad, Knut Hoegh, O. L. Kirkeberg, O. A. Normann, A. E. Petterson, F. C. Schaefer, Warren Upham, N. H. Winchell and Louis H. Roddis. A look at the map shows probable routes the Kensington Norsemen took—down the Hudson Bay, the Nelson River, Lake Winnipeg, and the Red River of the North, a distance of one thousand miles, or by way of the St. Lawrence and the Great Lakes. According to Gustav Storm's "Studier over Vinlandsreiserne," an expedition was sent by King Magnus from Bergen in 1355, under the command of Paul Knutson, into American waters. In 1349 the Eskimos had attacked the western settlement (Vestbygd), hence this expedition was to defend the Greenland settlements against the Eskimos. This expedition, or a part of it, returned to Norway in 1364. This is but another indication to show that the intercourse between Norway and America was still kept up at the time of the Kensington expedition.

"For nearly four centuries," says Roddis, "Greenland remained a place with five or six thousand people apparently prosperous and with considerable commercial re-

White Eskimos lations with Iceland and Norway. There were a number of churches, and ecclesiastical relations with Rome existed, as is shown by the mention of Greenland and Vinland in papal letters as well as in monastic records. During this time it is known that a number of voyages were made to Vinland and Markland, and no doubt the record of many more are lost. Then in 1406 all mention of Greenland and its settlement ceases."

What became of the Greenland settlements? When Hans Egede came to Greenland in 1721 he found only Eskimos, but no Norsemen. What had become of the hardy Norsemen? The Black Death had visited the island and the Eskimos are said to have made attacks on the weakened settlements. Still, it is not quite reasonable to suppose that every man, woman and child was exterminated by these two enemies. There have been tales of blond and blue-eyed Eskimos, and they have led to many interesting speculations and explorations. A recent explorer, Vilhjalmur Stefansson, an Icelandic-American, has made a careful study of the blond Eskimos. He reports that in Victoria Land and Prince Albert Island, to the north of Canada, seven per cent of the Eskimos are blonds, with blue eyes. Sir John Franklin said of these

people that they were like Europeans; Thomas Simpson, that they were "of a distinguished appearance and much like Scandinavians." "No one," says Stefansson, "who has any familiarity with the history of the North (Canada) can imagine that these light characteristics have come since the beginning of modern exploration or of whaling." These white Eskimos are no doubt descendants from the Greenland colony.

There have been rumors also of blond and blue-eyed Indians. Where there is much smoke there must be some fire. G. B. Joergenson, Stanwood, Wash., set out to invest-
White Indians   igate this question. He has found considerable concrete evidence of the intermixture of the Norse and the Indian races. He has listed a thousand or more words in the Indian languages of Washington and western Canada, derived from the Old Norse. "Elva," for example, is the Indian name for a river in Alaska, just as "kona" is the Eskimo name for wife in Greenland. He has also discovered a number of Indian traditions about the coming of the Norsemen, their intermarriage with the Indians, and the warfare between the white Indians and the Red Men.

5. Their Place in History

History is a record of what man has done. Historians manifestly cannot keep a record of everything that has been accomplished. Therefore, they choose what they consider the most important material. The choice may be according to bias or the fashion of the day. Now they emphasize the deeds of war and then again the works of peace. One school of historians will stress one view; another school will fight for another opinion. With regard to the Norse discoveries of America, most historians in every land have commonly disregarded the whole subject as being beneath their notice. Still, there is plenty of evidence of the fact that the discoveries were made, and plenty of opinion by good men at that, that these discoveries had important and far-reaching influence on world events.

It is everywhere accepted as a fact that Greenland was discovered by Norsemen as early as 876; furthermore, that the Norsemen settled Greenland in 983, and
Greenland   that thriving settlements were maintained until the Black Death visited Denmark-Norway and its colonies. After 1409 the communication with Greenland was practically cut off until 1721, when it was resumed. The story of Greenland is not to be despised. The reports, for instance, with regard to foreign missions, as already stated, point to one of the first and most successful mission conquests in mod-

ern history. The whole world sings Bishop Heber's famous mission hymn: "From Greenland's Icy Mountains." It cannot be denied that Greenland is a part of North America; it is not denied that the Norsemen discovered Greenland in 876, therefore they did discover North America in 876.

An examination of thirty-three works on United States history, taken at random, scattered over one hundred years of time as to publication, making eighty-seven volumes, and covering 39,179 pages, reveals the following facts: Only forty-five pages of the eighty-seven volumes are devoted to the Norsemen in America. Not one word is said about the recent immigration of Norwegians to America, and their part in the making of this country. One would never know from United States history that there are any Norwegians here.

Vinland

Twelve of the thirty-three books do not mention the Norse discoveries at all. Twenty of the thirty-three do mention their coming, but do not consider the event as significant. Only one of the thirty-three,—C. R. Damon,—accepts the story of the Norsemen on a par with other historical data.

Bancroft, for example, says: The claim "rests on narratives mythological in form and obscure in meaning." He speaks about Snorri, one of the world's greatest historians, as having a "zealous curiosity that could hardly have neglected the discovery of a continent." Snorri, by the way, devotes only one sentence to Vinland: "Thereafter he found Vinland the Good." It is a safe bet that Bancroft had never read the great Snorri and here passed a snap judgment. Hildreth says: "Greenland they certainly discovered and colonized; but their alleged visit to North America, though not without warm advocates, rests on events of too mythic a character to find a place in authentic history." This evidence, by the way, is exactly of the same kind as the evidence for the discovery of Greenland. Barnes says: "Admitting the claims of the Northmen, the fact is barren of all results." Armstrong says: "The discoveries did no good, except to satisfy their love of adventure." Johnston thinks: "Their discoveries were little heard of and were soon forgotten altogether." Channing maintains that: "The whole matter of the Vinland voyages is one of those curious academic puzzles which are interesting on account of the absurd theories that have clustered around them. The history of America would have been what it has been if Leif Ericson had never been born." A. B. Hart has written a "Source Book of American History," 1900, in which he does not mention the Norsemen at all. He has written also a book entitled "American History Told by Contemporaries," 1920, in which he says about the sagas which he quotes: "The narrative is trustworthy, but does not go into detail enough to identify the places mentioned." C. R. Damon, in his "American Dictionary of Dates," says that Gunnbjørn sighted a western land in 876, Erik the Red discovered Greenland in 983, Bjarni came to Cape Cod or Nantucket in 986, and Leif Erikson in 1000 sought the land reported by Bjarni. Several other of the Norse discoveries are listed in chronological order by Damon.

The historians are particularly interested in trying to show that, even if the Norsemen had discovered America, Columbus knew nothing about it. But this is discrediting the intelligence of Columbus, as well as the importance of the Norsemen in the Viking Age. The first Icelander to make mention of Vinland was Ari Frodi in his "Islendingabok," about 1120. But over 50 years previous to the writing of "Islendingabok," Adam von Bremen, a German, wrote, in 1067, a church history, in which he says that he had gotten information from the Danish king, Svenn Estridsson, about Vinland. Having given an account of Iceland and Greenland, Adam continues: "Besides these there is still another region, which has been visited by *many*, lying in that ocean (the Atlantic), which is called Vinland, because vines grow there spontaneously, producing very good wine; corn likewise springs up there without being sown. This we know, not by fabulous conjecture, but from positive statements of the Danes."

The oldest known literary mention of Vinland was found on a runestone at Hønen in Ringerike, Norway. The inscription was copied in 1823, but the stone has since disappeared. Sophus Bugge estimates that this record was cut in 1050, or at an earlier date.

It is important to know that other peoples in Europe besides the Norsemen attempted voyages to the west before Columbus. A Prince of Wales, Madoc by name, is said to have sailed to America in 1170, and returned. He sailed again, but never returned. Pizigani, an Italian, published a map in 1367 showing islands in the Atlantic. In 1394, Niccolo Zeno, a Venetian, visited Greenland and presumably Vinland also. In 1427 the Claudius Clavus map of Greenland and Vinland was published, just eight years before Columbus was born. In 1476 Portugal tried to rediscover the "Cod Fish Country," and that year Columbus settled in Portugal. The next year he made a trip to Iceland and one hundred leagues beyond. It must be remembered that Gudrid, who had twice been in Vinland, after her return to Iceland made a visit to Rome, and later took the veil as a Catholic nun. Also that the popes knew about Greenland and Vinland, as is shown from the fact that they appointed bishops of Greenland and Vinland for the space of at least three hundred years. It seems plain, therefore, that Europe had considerable knowledge of the lands to the west.

Europe, thinks Paul L. Ford, was busy with its own affairs, felt no pressure of population, and therefore did not care to give heed to tales about western lands. It needed men, not lands. Europe enjoyed a lucrative trade with India,—by water, across the Mediterranean; and by caravan, across Asia Minor and Persia. But when the Turk blocked the way to India, then Europe began to listen to the possibility of a western route. Certain it is that the air was full of stories about the lands to the west and the map-makers persisted in locating strange lands out in the Atlantic, all the way from Greenland to Brazil. Columbus himself was a map-maker by profession. In the few maps that have been preserved, no less than 27, made between 1351 and 1492, by different geographers working in different cities, locate islands and continents in the western Atlantic, of which no account or mention is to be found in the writings of the same time. Of course many of the rulers and schoolmen would not believe the accounts of the Norsemen, nor of Columbus either. King John of Portugal would not believe until he saw the Indians and treasures that Columbus took along with him.

That the voyage of Columbus produced more results than those of the Norsemen is due to various causes: The monarchs of southern Europe were interested in the enterprise; vast mines of gold and silver were reported; the modern age had begun, with awakening everywhere and in every direction. Nevertheless, it took Europe another century to decide that it would try to colonize America.

Columbus was an earnest student, and the best geographer and map-maker of his day. He was in close touch with the pope at Rome, with the scholars and rulers of his day, and with the seamen from every port. He was a diligent reader of Aristotle, Seneca, Strabo and other authorities on geography, and had made extensive travels. He agreed with the ancient and mediaeval scholars that the world is round as a ball and not flat as a pancake. He could, therefore, not have been ignorant of the works of Adam von Bremen, the sagas, the papal records and the many maps which showed that there were islands and lands to the west.

In his contract with Ferdinand and Isabella of Spain, who financed his undertaking, he makes plain that he intends to discover new lands. He demands five things: 1. He wishes to be "admiral of the seas and countries which he is about to discover," and that this dignity "shall descend to his heirs forever." 2. He wishes to be made viceroy of all the continents and islands that he may discover. 3. He wishes to have a share, amounting to one-tenth part, of all the exports from said countries. 4. He wishes to be made sole judge of all mercantile matters in said countries. 5. He wishes to receive the eighth part of all the profits from all ships which traffic with the new countries. He wishes to be called Admiral of the Seas, Admiral, Viceroy and Governor of the Indies. All these rights, titles, offices, percentages and privileges were granted him by the Spanish monarchs, as he set out on his first voyage of discovery in 1492, and were repeated in 1497 and 1501.

Columbus did not want much, it seems, but it was a good deal more than the Norsemen were asking. At any rate, he did not give the Norsemen any credit for having shown him the way to the western world. In that respect he is in a class with the average writer of United States history. Thus Spencer says: "There is not the slightest reason to believe that the illustrious Genoese was acquainted with the discovery of North America by the Normans five centuries before his time, however widely authenticated that fact now appears to be by the Icelandic records." And Thomas says: "The Northmen must have carried home news of their discoveries . . . . . Their stories would hardly have been believed even if carried to other Europeans." Garner and Lodge venture the following judgment: "While, therefore, Leif Ericson and his followers were probably the first Europeans to visit America, their discoveries had no permanent result, and the history of the country would have been what it is had they never left their native shores." Such statements are ridiculous. The Norsemen contributed their share to making Columbus realize that there was an American continent and they should be given credit for this contribution in the school histories of our land. History should not be a juggling of facts. It is a record of what man has done.

The story of Great Ireland is often dismissed as mythical for the reason that the sagas as a body of literature discuss matters ranging from dry chronicle to romantic myth.
Great Ireland The sagas which give the most elaborate accounts of the Great Ireland discoveries are the "Landnamabok" and the "Eyrbyggja" saga and they bear marks of being sober history.

There is nothing so stubborn as facts. It may be that the Kensington Stone and other runic inscriptions, particularly in Canada, are fraudulent, but it is hard to account for the white Eskimos and white Indians, except on the theory that a very long time back there had been an intermixture of the races. The data for such a theory is easily at hand if we admit that the Norsemen penetrated inland. Again, if the Kensington Stone is a fraud, the mystery deepens: who perpetrated the fraud, and how, and when, and why?

Chapter IV

THE NORWEGIANS IN AMERICA

The Norwegians have been in America since 876 A. D., 1049 years. Their occupancy of America may be divided into three periods, as follows:

1. The Viking Period, 876-1476, 600 years.
2. The Colonial Period, 1476-1825, 349 years.
3. The Modern Period, 1825-1925, 100 years.

1. The Viking Period

The Viking Period was one of discovery and of interrupted colonization. The Norsemen discovered Greenland and the American continent. They explored America from Greenland as far south as Florida and as far west as Minnesota. They made settlements in Greenland, New England (Vinland), the Chesapeake country (Great Ireland), and possibly in other localities.

Greenland was discovered by Gunnbjørn by chance, just as the continent was accidentally discovered by Bjarni, both of them speeding before the gale. But Erik the Red intended to find Greenland and Leif Erikson planned to discover the land that Bjarni reported having seen.

It was the intention of the Norsemen to settle these lands and live there. Therefore Erik the Red called his land Greenland, hoping, as he said, to attract settlers. Therefore Leif would not sell the huts that he had built in Vinland, but was willing to lend them. When Thorvald came to Vinland, he said: "It is a fair region here, and here I should like to make my home." When he was shot by an Indian arrow, he picked out a pleasant spot for his grave, saying: "Ye shall bury me there, with a cross at my head and another at my feet, and call it Crossness hereafter for ever." It is said of Thorfinn Karlsefne that he brought with him a company of 160, besides "all kinds of cattle, for it was their intention to settle there, if they could." There is pretty good circumstantial evidence to show that there were Norse settlements in Vinland as in Greenland long after Thorfinn Karlsefne had to leave on account of the hostilities of the Indians. It was, for example, considered both honorable and profitable to go to Vinland to fetch timber and other supplies. The pope kept on appointing bishops of Greenland and Vinland from 1112 to 1492. The Greenland colony existed until it was wiped out by the Black Death and the Eskimos. It is said to have had upward of six thousand Norsemen. But the records are meagre. An examination of three hundred modern text books in United States history reveals the fact that not one of these books, by one word, gives any information about the presence of Norwegians in America since 1825. And yet they are found in every state and almost every county of the United States.

There are many reasons why the early Norse settlements were hard to establish and maintain. Norway was far away. Iceland was far away. Greenland was far away. Greenland had no timber from which to build ships. It was difficult to cross the stormy seas in open boats, without compass. Norway became a province of Denmark and her communication with her colonies ceased. The Black Death ravaged here and there. Indians and Eskimos were hostile.

2. THE COLONIAL PERIOD

No one knows how many Norwegians came over during the Colonial Period or when they began to come. They did not come in collective bodies as in the good old Viking Age. Norway, being subject to Denmark, was not in a position to enter the race with Spain, France and England to come to America first and claim the land.

King Christian IV in 1619 sent an expedition to find a northwest passage to Asia. The captain of this expedition was the Norwegian Jens Munk. He sailed from Copenhagen May 9, 1619, with two ships and 66 men. He entered Hudson Bay and had to winter there at the mouth of the Churchill River. He took possession of the country and gave it the name of Nova Dania. But sickness visited them and all died except Jens Munk and two of his crew, who returned to Norway Sept. 25, 1620. Munk kept a diary, which is in the Royal Library at Copenhagen.

In his "First Chapter of Norwegian Immigration" R. B. Anderson mentions two Norwegians who served under Admiral John

Paul Jones, namely, Thomas Johnson and Lewis Brown, both born in Norway. A biography of Johnson written by John Henry Sherburne was published at Washington in 1825.

In his "Norske Settlementers Historie" H. R. Holand sets forth a number of interesting instances of Norwegians in America during the 17th and 18th centuries; as, for example: John Vinje, a Norwegian, born in 1614, was the first white child born in New York. His sister was married to Dirck Volkertson, a Norwegian in the Dutch colony at New Amsterdam (New York). "Hans Hansen van Bergen in Norwegen" was the name of a prominent Norwegian in the Dutch colony. One of his descendants is Dr. John Bergen, pastor of the First Presbyterian Church, Minneapolis, author of "Evidences of Christianity," published by Augsburg Publishing House in 1923. In a private letter Pastor Bergen says that there is no doubt as to his remote Norwegian nationality, but he adds: "I ban ein gemixter." At Bethlehem, Pa., is a Moravian cemetery, with a printed list of burials during the 18th century. Nine out of the 2600 names are listed as born in Norway. One of the prominent physicians in the early history of North Carolina was Dr. Hans Martin Kalberlahn, born in Trondhjem in 1722. A Scandinavian Society was organized in Philadelphia in 1769 and continued active until 1802. It was reorganized in 1868 and is still in existence. The first president was Capt. Abraham Markoe, a Dane. George Washington became an honorary member of this organization in 1783.

In his "Nordmaend in Nieuw Nederland," Torstein Jahr presents a list with documentary evidences, of Norwegians who lived and labored in the Dutch colony. For example, at Troy, New York, Claes Claesz and Jacob Goyversen from Flekkerø, Roelof Jansz from Marstrand, who came over on the ship "De Eendracht" in 1630. In 1631 the Dutch patroon, Van Rensselaer, made a three years' contract with four Norwegians to work for him as builders, farmers, etc., at Ft. Orange, New York. The names of the men are: Andries Christensen and Cornelius Goverts of Flekkerø, Barent Thoniz of Hellesund, and Laurens Laurensz Noorman. The contract is found in the "Van Rensselaer Bowier Manuscripts," pages 186-189. In 1636 the ship "Rensselaerswyck" brought over from Holland 38 passengers, of whom seven were Norwegians. One of these was a child born at sea on a stormy day. His parents were Albert Andriessen of Fredrikstad and wife Annetje Barents. The child was appropriately baptized Storm van der Zee, in honor of the day and place. One of the leading pioneers i Schenectady, New York, was Arent Bratt, a descendant of Bishop T. O. Bratt of Trondhjem, and of the ancient Norse jarls. Arent is the ancestor of a numerous race that have been active in the making of New York State.

One of the interesting bits of information in G. T. Flom's

"History of Norwegian Immigration to the United States" is this: A Norwegian sailor, Captain Iverson, settled in Georgia some time about the close of the 18th century. United States Senator Alfred Iverson from Georgia was a grandson of this sailor pioneer. In June, 1808, Frank Peterson, a Norwegian enlisted in the United States Army. He was stationed at Fort Dearborn, Ill., and fell in 1812 in an attack by 500 Pottawattomie Indians. He was one of the "first martyrs of the West."

J. O. Evjen's book, "Scandinavian Immigrants in New York, 1630-1674," gives biographies of thirty-four Swedes, ninety-seven Danes and fifty-seven Norwegians who lived in New York during that period. Among the Norwegians listed is Anneken Hendricks, the first wife of Jan Arentzen Vander Bilt, the ancestor of the Vanderbilts. He married her in New Amsterdam, Feb. 6, 1650. She came from Bergen, Norway; he was from Utrecht, Holland. They had three children.

Concerning the Norwegians in America during the Colonial days Jahr cites the words of Linne: "Ea quae scimus, sunt pars minima eorum, quae ignoramus (The things that we know are only a very small part of what we do not know). Jahr's own comment is strikingly true: "Om de allerfleste har Saga glemt hvad hun visste" (Concerning most of them Saga has forgotten what she knew). Halvdan Koht estimates that over one-fourth of the immigration to the Dutch colony at New Amsterdam consisted of Norwegians. Rev. Justus Falckner, the first Lutheran minister to be ordained in America, kept a church record, still in existence, which contains an occasional Norwegian name. For example: On October 12, 1707, he married Peter Johansen, born at Bergen, Norway; on October 10, 1708, he baptized Johannes Norman; on April 18, 1710, he baptized Catharina Noorman, etc.

3. THE MODERN PERIOD

The Norwegian immigration to America during the last century can best be understood as a part of a world movement. Such migratory movements occur now and then in the course of the centuries, the chief cause being land-hunger.

Since the Confusion of Tongues at Babel and the first dispersion of families in consequence thereof, the world has beheld many a migration of the races, here and there, back *Norwegian Immigra-* and forth, from one land to another. Witness, *tion Part of a* for example, the Patriarch Abraham and his *World Movement* household setting out for the Promised Land, and the Children of Israel, several millions strong, under Moses making an exodus out of Egypt. Or, take the pressing of the Huns into Europe in the 4th century of our era, and the invasions of the restless Teutonic tribes in the 5th century—Goths, Franks, Vandals, Burgundians, Lombards, Germans, Angles, Saxons, Jutes—, pouring south and west with irresistible force and fury, seeking new homes in the crumbling Roman Empire. The Saracens in the 8th century, the Scandinavians in the 9th, the Hungarians in the 10th, the Mongols in the 13th, the Turks in the 15th, are further examples of the periodic phenomena of whole races suddenly starting to migrate, almost after the fashion of De Quincy's "Flight of a Tartar Tribe."

These sudden and vast migrations, however, are not more stupendous and awe-inspiring than the immigration of the Europeans and other peoples to America during the last hundred years, though quite different. The great migrations of the early centuries were nearly always accompanied by violence and bloodshed, by conquest and subjugation of the native population. The immigration to America has been peaceful. The immigrants came to America, not to conquer the country by force and to change its language and laws, but to find here greater freedom in religious, political and economic matters and better opportunities to make a living. They have willingly worked hard to transform deserts into gardens; they have vied with one another in the making of America. Each national group has contributed its quota of citizens, and, in the blending of the races through intermarriage, has a part in the creation of a brand new race, the American people. Each people that came here brought along with it some of the culture of its home land, and some of this has been transplanted to American soil.

Norway has never sent her criminals or paupers to America; she strives to take care of these unfortunates herself. She has given to America a goodly share of the strongest and most ambitious young men and women that she has been able to foster. In olden days it was chiefly the ruling classes that emigrated, for the reason that they did not wish to submit to an overlord. In modern times it has been chiefly the working classes that have left for America. Says the United States Immigration Commission in its report, giving a statistical review from 1820 to 1910: "Norway has sent a larger per cent of its population to America than any other country excepting Ireland. Considering the smallness of its population, but little over 2,000,-000 (in 1910), as compared with the 72,000,000 of Germans and 40,000,000 of English, Scotch and Irish, it has done its full share in populating America."

Relative Position of the Norwegian Immigration

As compared with Denmark and Sweden, sister Scandinavian countries, the emigration from Norway from 1821 to 1920 was as follows:

Country	Population 1920	Immigration 1821-1920	Per Cent of Scandinavian Immigration
Sweden	5,847,637	1,144,607	63.5
Norway	2,691,855	693,450	32.4
Denmark	3,268,907	300,008	14 1
Total.	11,808,399	2,138,065	100.0

Out of every 1000 Scandinavian immigrants, 141 have been Danes, 324 Norwegians, and 535 Swedes.

As compared with the total immigration to the United States during the period 1821-1920, the part Norway has played is quite small, being only a trifle over 2% of the whole. This century of immigration is in point of numbers, really the greatest migration of peoples in the history of mankind. Over 33 millions of people

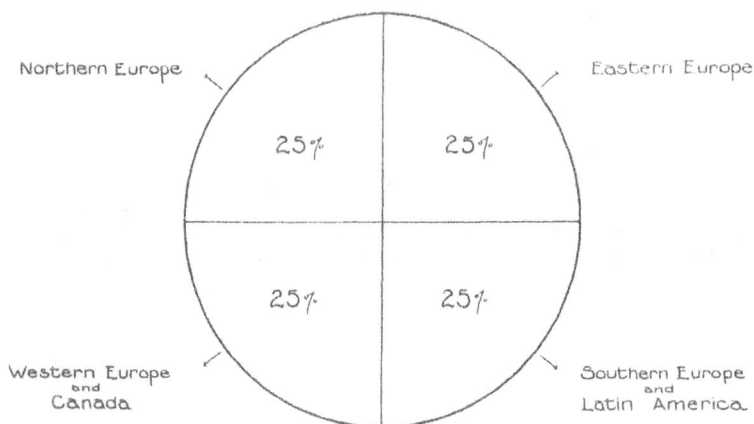

Northern Europe 25% Eastern Europe

Western Europe and Canada 25% 25% Southern Europe and Latin America

Sources of Immigration to U. S.
1820 - 1920

came to the United States in this period, an average of over 330,000 a year. The bulk of the immigration during the first 80 years came from western and northern Europe; during the last 20 years it has come from eastern and southern Europe. The following table gives a comparison of the six principal sources of this immigration:

Country	Population	Immigration 1821-1920	Per Cent of Immigration
Great Britain	47,157,749	8,333,710	24.6
Germany	60,900,197	5,533,493	16.4
Scandinavia	11,808,399	2,138,065	6.4
Total W. and N.	119,866,345	16,005,268	47.4

Italy	36,120,118	4,199,653	12.2
Austria-Hungary	50,000,000	4,073,143	12.1
Russia	175,000,000	3,437,102	10.2
Total E. and S.	261,120,118	11,709,898	34.5
All Other Countries	1,300,000,000	6,088,108	18.1
Grand Total	1,680,986,463	33,803,274	100.0

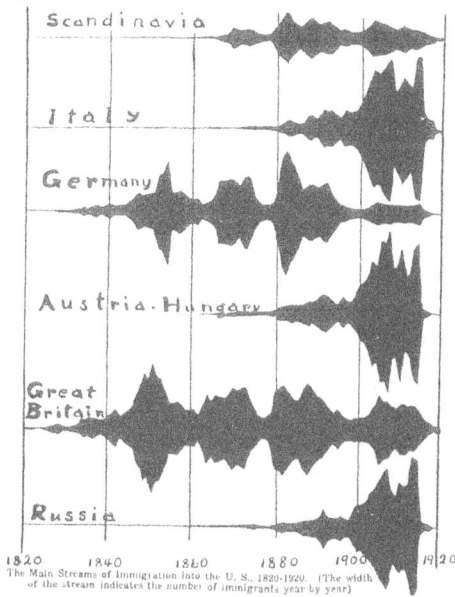

The Main Streams of Immigration into the U. S., 1820-1920. (The width of the stream indicates the number of immigrants year by year)

Main Streams of Immigration, 1820-1920

Some of the causes of the Norwegian immigration may be called general; others, specific. The most pronounced general causes were: The immigration to America *Causes of the Nor-* was a world movement, and this movement was *wegian Immigration* mainly an economic one.

The immigration was a world movement. Never before in history, except at the first dispersion at Babel, has there been such a wide-spread and general migratory movement as in the 19th century. A century ago the United States consisted of hardly more than a narrow fringe of settlements along the Atlantic. The population in 1820 was only 9,638,453, of whom 77% lived east of the Alleghany Mountains. The task that lay before the original settlers was immense. There was in front of them to be subdued

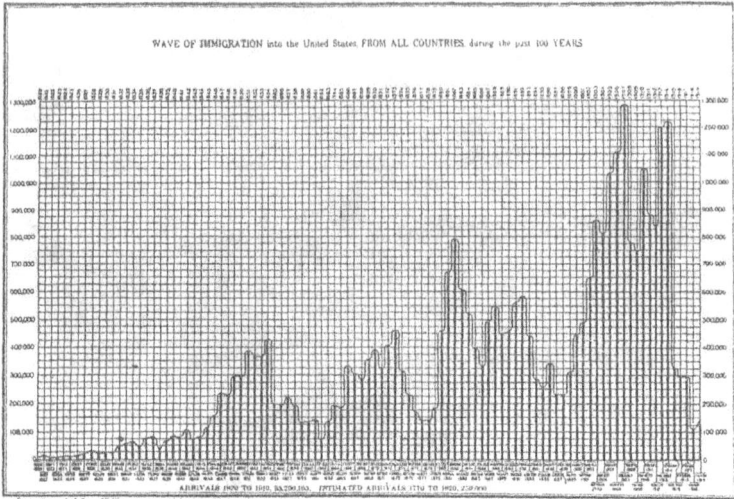

Curve of Immigration, 1820-1920

a vast wilderness over 3,000 miles long and 2,000 miles wide. America called for men to develop its seemingly limitless domains, and the call was heard to the ends of the earth by horny-handed sons of toil. But it was not only the United States of America that needed men. Also the rest of North America and South America—Canada, Mexico, Brazil, Argentina, in fact, every country of the new world, besides Australia and South Africa. The United States did not make any vigorous efforts to induce immigration either, and did not legislate much concerning immigration before 1883, when it was found necessary, on account of the change in the character of the immigration, to make laws controlling and restricting immigration. The so-called "Old Immigration," from 1820 to 1880, came mainly from western and northern Europe, and, with the exception of the Irish, consisted of Protestant stock; the "New Immigration," from 1880 to 1925, has come mainly from eastern and southern Europe, and consists mainly of Catholic stock.

According to the estimate of the United States Bureau of Statistics, only 250,000 immigrants were received from 1776 to 1820, or only 10,000 per annum. From 1820 down to the present the immigration stream has constantly increased, without fluctuating to any great extent except when it has been checked by natural and artificial barriers. The great financial panics which this country has experienced, and the wars, have been powerful natural barriers in stemming the tide of immigration. The United States laws against the admission of criminal, pauper, defective and diseased aliens and against contract labor and ticket agents as means of securing immigrants, the application of literacy tests, the exclusion of the Chinese and the limiting of the quota of immigrants that may come each year, are artificial barriers against immigration. It is clear, then, that during the 19th century there was a

A Modern Steamship

world movement toward the United States, and the Norwegians naturally took part in it. The movement took the form of an epidemic and is often characterized as the "America Fever."

This world movement was mainly economic, at least as far as the Norwegians were concerned. It is true that in Norway, too, there was some cause for religious and political discontent. The State Church in the 18th century had become rationalistic and resented the activities of pietistic reformers like Hauge, and the sectarians that began to get a foothold in Norway, as, for instance, the Quakers. It is true that the leaders of the famous Sloop "Restaurationen" were Quakers and that they looked for greater religious freedom in America than in Norway. Still, it must be noted that there were only ten (or twelve) Quakers in Norway in 1825, and some of these never emigrated at all. It is true also that some emigrated from Norway so as to escape military service, which was obligatory. Nevertheless, it is generally agreed that the Norwegians came to America to improve their living. They found this a good land, and, like Thorvald, the brother of Leif the Discoverer, they have said: "And here I should like to make my home."

Of more specific causes, and minor influences, there have been many, varying with time and place. As, for example: Letters from relatives and friends in America, with possibly an inclosure of money or a ticket to America, and a promise of a job at good pay; the visit to Norway of Norwegian-Americans and their colorful accounts of America; the study of geography and history; the publication of books on America; the emigrant societies and missions; the activity of steamship ticket agents and sub-agents in selling tickets; the introduction of machinery and steam and electric power; the improved means of transportation and communication; at times, the cut-rate fares for steerage passengers; the Homestead laws; the discovery of gold; the hope of greater freedom and better prospects in America; the desire for adventure and the call of the far-away; the assurance that they would find good neighbors in America.

The way to get friends is to be one yourself, and the way to get good neighbors is to be a good neighbor. The Norwegians have been good neighbors to the other Amer-

The Neighbors in America

icans, and they have found them good neighbors, as dear as their own kith and kin. The story of the Norwegian people in America could not be adequately or truthfully told without some reference to the sterling character and considerate helpfulness of these kind neighbors.

First of all, the Americans of English descent, the so-called Anglo-Saxons, often called "*The* Americans." Through early colonization and conquest they laid claim to

The English

the whole of the Atlantic seaboard, and later through war, purchase and treaty extended their possessions from the Atlantic to the Pacific. They determined the language of the country, its form of government and most of its institutions and opportunities for advancement. During the 17th and 18th centuries they were the main contributors to the population of America. During the 18th century the Scotch-Irish and the Germans migrated in almost equal numbers, and their combined migration was nearly that of the English for the century. But these newcomers were compelled to settle down as frontiersmen, and to leave to their English-sprung predecessors the more prominent occupations of politics, the professions, education, literature, trade, commerce, army and navy. From 1820 to 1920 only 2,591,231, or 7.4%, of the total immigration, came from England. Still, the English have easily maintained their position as the most eminent and influential people in America. They are not handicapped by language or other foreign "taint." They occupy, as a rule, controlling positions in every walk of life. Nearly all the presidents have been of English lineage; most of the governors. They have furnished most of the editors of the great dailies and the heads of school systems and universities. The great American authors are nearly all English, and the captains of industry. The culture of the American schools and the ideals of America, as a whole are mainly from England, by way of New England. The English have been, as a rule, kind masters; the other races faithful servants.

Second in importance in the making of this nation are the Scotch-Irish-Welsh—the Celtic branch of the British race. In the century 1820-1920, 4,670,805 Irish immigrated to the United States, 748,788 Scotch and 262,921 Welsh—a total of 5,682,514 for the group, over twice as many as from England. It has been estimated that in 1920 the combined strength of the Scotch, Irish and Welsh in America was a little greater than that of the English —18,132,344 Celts to 17,501,165 Englishmen out of a population of 105,710,620.

The Celts

Ireland has the distinction of sending more of her people here than she kept at home. The governor of Pennsylvania in 1728 complained that: "It looks as if Ireland were to send all her inhabitants hither." Having come from the British Isles and speaking the English language, the Irish were from the start more on a par with the English element and were at once admitted into the controlling governmental and social circles. Out of their midst have, therefore, come some of the presidents of the United States, as, Andrew Jackson, Zachary Taylor, Ulysses S. Grant, William McKinley and Woodrow Wilson, and hundreds of men famous in politics, army, navy, business, education, etc. Commons says of the Scotch-Irish: "They were very little Scotch and much less Irish. They were called Scotch because they lived in Scotia and they were called Irish because they moved to Ireland. They were a mixed race through whose blood ran the Celtic blood of the primitive Scot and Pict, the primitive Briton, the primitive Irish, but with a larger admixture of the later Norwegian, Dane, Saxon and Angle." Burr says: "It is difficult to say whether the Englishman, Scotchman, Welshman or Irishman has the greater degree of Nordic blood in his veins."

The Dutch settled in New Amsterdam (now New York) as a business venture, although some of them were Walloons fleeing oppression in the Spanish Netherlands. Cap-
The Dutch   tain Hendrick Hudson discovered New York Harbor in 1609 and Dutch traders built some huts on the Manhattan Island in 1613. About one-fourth of the early colonists were Scandinavians. In 1664 an English fleet came to anchor in the harbor and took possession of the city in the name of the Duke of York. The town was named New York after him. The Dutch soon lost their language and assimilated with the English readily, being of close kin as to race, language and institutions. During the century 1820-1920, 339,639 Dutch were admitted to the United States. In 1920 the estimated number of people of Dutch descent in America was 2,233,503. Two of our presidents have come from this stock—Martin Van Buren and Theodore Roosevelt.

In the period 1820-1920, France gave to the United States only 352,752 of her sons and daughters and the estimated French population in the United States in 1920 was
The French   only 703,590. France had naturally been eager to share with Spain in the profits which the new discovery of America brought. She sent out Verrazano and Cartier to explore. Ribaut, Laudonniere, Champlain, Marquette, La Salle, Hennepin and Nicollet are names of well-known French explorers and colonizers.

In 1562 Admiral Coligny of France sent Ribaut to plant a colony for his persecuted Huguenot brethren, at that time still known as Lutherans. A settlement was made at Port Royal, S. C. In 1564 another settlement was made at Ft. Caroline, Fla. A Spaniard named Menendez fell upon this peaceable colony in 1565 and massacred every one. According to Challeaux and Parkman, Menendez hanged his prisoners on trees and placed over them the inscription: "I do this, not as to Frenchmen, but as to Lutherans."

In the next two centuries following this massacre the French occupied the St. Lawrence and Mississippi valleys and the English were held down to a narrow strip along the Atlantic Coast. Eventually there was a war between the English and the French (the French and Indian War), in which France was defeated, and Canada and the French territory east of the Mississippi in 1763 were ceded to England.

In 1803 Thomas Jefferson purchased from France the territory west of the Mississippi, known as Louisiana, for $15,000,000 —about 2 cents per acre.

The early French settlers of the United States are of special interest to the Norwegians because of kinship by way of Normandy. Commons calls them "a select class of people, the most intelligent and enterprising people in the 17th century." Says Ross: "Probably no stock ever came here so gifted and prepotent as the French Huguenots. They have the same affinity for ideals and the same tenacity of character as the founders of New England, but in their French blood they brought a sensibility, a fervor and artistic endowment all their own." Burr shows that the French Huguenots who came to America were "recruited from among the gentry who were preponderantly of Nordic blood," but, on the other hand, the French Catholics who settled in Quebec did not have the Norse strain.

According to Douglas Campbell, A. B. Faust, E. A. Ross, and J. R. Commons and the census reports, every fourth white person in the United States is a German. The Ger-
The Germans mans came here early—there was a German —Tyrker—along with Leif Erikson in the year 1000. There were Germans along with the Dutch, and the first governor of New Netherlands was Peter Minuit, a German. William Penn shrewdly mixed business with religion. In his trip to the Rhineland in 1677, he made converts and induced them to buy land in Pennsylvania, the first band reaching Germantown in 1683. Francis II of France used harsh measures against the Lutherans in his realm. He employed every refinement of cruelty, such as, burnings and hangings as after dinner entertainment for the ladies. This led to an exodus of Lutherans. Most of them came to America. Angry at the Germans and Dutch for sheltering his hunted subjects, Louis XIV of France invaded the Palatinate which became the scene of French fire, pillage, rapine and slaughter. The people were expected to change their religion to suit their rulers. At the same time they were forbidden to emigrate on pain of death. Tired of these long-endured miseries, the French and German Lutherans, under the protection and aid of England, came to America. They settled in New York, Pennsylvania, Maryland, Virginia, the Carolinas and Georgia. Pennsylvania especially attracted them, on account of which it has been called the German-American's Holy Land. In 1790, 176,707, or 5.6% of the people in the United States had German surnames. During the past 100 years they have come to America for religious, political and economic reasons. Between 1839 and

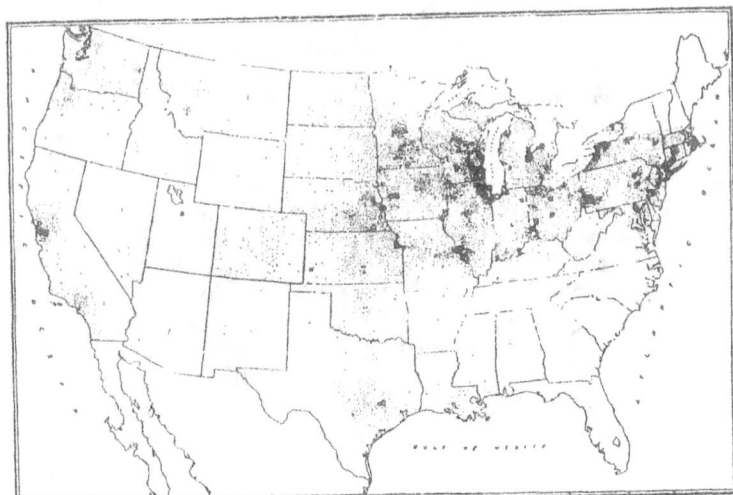

Distribution of Germans

(From E. A. Ross' "The Old World in the New." Copyright, 1914, by The Century Co., New York)

1845 many Lutherans left their Fatherland because they resented the attempts of their leaders to unite the Lutherans and Reformed faiths. Here in America their conservatism in doctrine and practice has created the Missouri and Wisconsin Synods and the Synodical Conference.

The chief reason why Germans have come to America has been the economic one—America needed men to open up the West and America paid better wages than did Germany. When Germany began to develop her own industries, the migration from Germany began to fall off. Over 90% of the German immigrants have come from the poorer classes, who settled on the frontiers and worked in the humbler stations in the cities, factories and mines. Political exiles, who came here after the revolutions of 1830 and 1848, were mainly from the upper classes. Among them were university professors, professional men, journalists, and aristocrats, who have been influential in creating a sentiment for German culture, political idealism, social radicalism and religious skepticism. The great body of Germans have been God-fearing, law-abiding, hard-working and thrifty, loyal to this country in war and peace. They have been rather slow to give up the German language and ways entirely, but this is no evil trait, and America has richly gained thereby. The Germans have given America, not only willing workers on

Distribution of Scandinavians

(From E. A. Ross' "The Old World in the New." Copyright, 1914,
by The Century Co., New York)

farms and in factories, but large contributions in education,
science, music, art and religion.

The German is of close kin to the Englishman and the Scandinavian; originally these peoples were of the same race and
language. He had the same spirit and ideals as they.

From the time of Charlemagne Germany has been rather too
much under the influence of Rome, on account of which the
real Teutonic spirit as shown by the Norwegian Vikings, has at
times been suppressed. It broke out in Luther and the Reformation, but not as completely as in Scandinavia and Great Britain.
Hence 40% of Germany is still Roman Catholic.

The Germans make good neighbors and excellent citizens,
but they have never taken a leading part in politics to the extent
of furnishing the country with its chief executives.

"In the colonial period," says John W. Burgess, "almost the
entire western border of our country was occupied by Germans.
It fell to them, therefore, to defend the colonists from the attack of the French and Indians." Had it not been for Germans
like Conrad Weiser this country might still have been French
instead of English. The Germans were the first to protest against
English misrule. Washington had a German bodyguard. Baron
Steuben and Peter Muhlenberg were two of Washington's most
trusted generals. The first speaker of the House of Representatives was F. A. Muhlenberg. The first protest against human

slavery on American territory was made by Germans at Germantown, April 18, 1688. Lincoln seems to have had a German
ancestry, his family name being Linkhorn. Thirty per cent of
the soldiers in the Union Army were German, although at that
time the Germans comprised less than 20% of the people. The
first ten Amendments to the Federal Constitution providing for
religious freedom and other natural rights, have their roots in the
German Reformation. In the recent World War when nearly all
the powers of the world fought against their Fatherland, German-
Americans were loyal to the United States despite a propaganda
of suspicion and uncalled for persecution.

The Swedes and Danes are in race, language, history, customs, religion, etc., more like the Norwegians than any of the
other peoples in America. They have as a
The Swedes   rule occupied the same sections of the country,
worked at the same tasks, been equally suc-
cessful. They have been on good terms, often working hand
in hand. In church matters, for example, there has been
much cooperation. Of the Norwegian men who do not take
Norwegian girls to wife, 55.1% marry Swedish girls, 10.8%
marry Danish, 4.5% marry Finnish, 8.5% marry German, and
14.8% marry British and Canadian, whereas only 6.3% marry
non-Teutons. Of the Norwegian women who do not take Norwegian men as husbands, 52.4% marry Swedes, 18.0% marry
Danes, 2.6% marry Finns, 8.6% marry Germans, 12.9% marry
Britishers and Canadians, whereas only 5.5% marry non-
Teutons. The Norwegians, then, seem to be closer to the
Swedes and Danes than to any of their other neighbors. This
is, at least, the case with the first generation, concerning which
these statistics apply.

The Swedes in America, as also in Europe, are as numerous as both the Norwegians and the Danes put together. Sweden
was one of the great European powers in the 17th century, and
her king, Gustavus Adolphus, called the "Lion of the North"
and the "Snow King," intended to compete with England and
Holland in the colonization of the New World. But there was
being waged at that time a most bitter and bloody struggle, the
Thirty Years' War, between the Catholic and Protestant forces
in Germany. The Swedish king took his army into Germany
and saved Protestantism, although at the price of his own life,
for he was killed at the Battle of Lützen in 1632. It was not
until 1637 that the plan to establish a colony in America could
be taken up in earnest, and, unfortunately it had soon to be
abandoned. The first expedition of Swedes to reach America
arrived at Fort Christina (now Wilmington), Delaware, in
March, 1638. The west bank of the Delaware as far north as

Philadelphia was at once bought of the Indians; forts, churches and other buildings were erected and arrangements were made for farming, trading with the Indians and doing missionary work among them. New Sweden, as the colony was called, was to include Delaware, New Jersey and parts of Maryland and Pennsylvania. In 1655 the Dutch made war on these peaceable neighbors and laid claim to the territory. In 1664 the English took possession of the land. Meanwhile the Swedes developed their colony as best they could under Dutch and English supremacy, and are in many respects the finest of the early colonists. They issued an edict of toleration the very first year of their stay, and were, in fact, with the exception of Pennsylvania, the only colony that practiced toleration. They were the first to treat the Indians fair and square and to try to Christianize them. When William Penn in 1682 sailed up the Delaware looking for a site for a city, he chose a spot where stood a Lutheran church and a Swedish village. The Swedes had been there almost fifty years when he arrived and took possession. He called the village Philadelphia. Two of the early Swedish churches are still standing, the Wilmington, dating from 1699, and the Gloria Dei Church, in Philadelphia, dating from 1700. On July 4, 1776, the Liberty Bell was rung by a member of the Lutheran Church. The first American flag was made by Betsy Ross and the women of the Swedish Gloria Dei Church. Between 1642 and 1779 Sweden sent to this colony 41 pastors. After the Revolutionary War the missionaries were recalled and the Episcopal Church gradually took over all the Lutheran congregations of the early Swedes as their brothers, and on various occasions the Indians state that they were unlike the white people of Virginia, "who always shoot the Red Man dead when they find him in the woods." William Penn said of them: "They have fine children and almost every house full; rare to find one of them without three or four boys and as many girls; some six, seven and eight sons. And I must do them right—I see few young men more sober and industrious." In the colonial period John Hanson, a Maryland Swede, was the first president of the "United States in Congress assembled," and John Morton, a Pennsylvania Swede, was one of the signers of the Declaration of Independence. J. Fenimore Cooper, the novelist, was of combined English and Swedish descent. The Swedes of more recent immigration have all the good qualities of the settlers on the Delaware and have made good in many conspicuous ways. The country still talks of Jenny Lind and .Christina Nilsson, Swedish singers who sojourned in America for a season. The country will not soon forget the services of John Ericsson and John A. Dahlgren during the Civil War. Ericsson was the inventor of the Monitor, which defeated the Merrimac, and Dahlgren was the inventor of the Dahlgren gun. These two inventions revolutionized naval warfare.

Citizens of Swedish lineage have contributed in great share to the material progress of America and have made valuable additions to its cultural life. They have cleared and cultivated over 12,000,000 acres of land, a little over 4% of the total cultivated area. They gave 12.5% of their total population to the United States in the World War. On the same basis, if all nationalities, including the native-born, had contributed an equal share, our armies during the war would have totaled 12,500,000 men. They have built over 2,000 churches and contributed more to church schools per capita than any other nationality. They have a good record as authors, editors, musicians, artists, inventors and manufacturers. They have held many political offices, including six governorships. In an article under the caption "Minnesota," by George Fitch, copyrighted in 1912 by the "Globe," the author writes in part as follows about Gov. John A. Johnson: "But Minnesota's greatest feat in citizen-producing was John A. Johnson, who would have mixed up the Democratic convention in Baltimore more than ever had he lived. Minnesota mourns his death sincerely, but has 100,000 more Johnsons in training and will yet produce a president of that name." Thomas F. Bayard, who had lived in a Swedish community, said in 1888, at the 250th anniversary of the Swedish immigration: "I make bold to say that no better stock has been contributed (in proportion to its numbers) towards giving a solid basis to society under republican forms, than these hardy, honest, law-abiding, God-fearing Swedish settlers."

The Danes comprise a relatively small group, their total number being only about 1% of the white population in the United States. They rank in point of numbers

The Danes   eleventh among the white races in America, the Germans being No. 1, the English No. 2, the Irish No. 3, the Canadians No. 4, the Austria-Hungarians No. 5, the Russians No. 6, the Italians No. 7, the Swedes No. 8, the Scotch No. 9, the Norwegians No. 10, the Danes No. 11, the Dutch No. 12, the Welsh No. 13, the Mexicans No. 14, the French No. 15, etc. While the Scandinavians are found in all parts of the United States they are not distributed everywhere in the same proportion. In the eight New England and Middle Atlantic States, for example, the foreign-born Scandinavians in 1920 were distributed as follows: Danes 16.7%, Norwegians 12.1%, Swedes 24.2%. In the 16 Southern states for that year 2.8% of the Danes were located, 1.4% of the Norwegians, 1.9% of the Swedes. In the eleven Mountain and Pacific states were to be found 25.2% of the Danes, 18.2% of the Norwegians, and 17.5% of the Swedes; and in the twelve North Central, also called Northwestern, states we find 65.3% of the Danes, 68.3% of the Norwegians, and 56.4% of the Swedes. As to the ranking states, California had 9.9% of the Danes, Iowa 9.5% and Illinois 9.0%; Minnesota had 24.8% Norwegians, Wisconsin 12.5%, North Dakota 10.5%; Minnesota had 17.9% Swedes, Illinois 16.9% and New York 8.5%.

The Danes were early interested in America. It will be remembered that King Christian I of Denmark sent the John Scolvus expedition to America in 1476 to discover the "Cod Fish Country." In 1568 King Frederick II sent an expedition to rediscover Greenland. In 1579 he sent another expedition to find Greenland, and after that various parties were sent in 1605, 1607, 1612, 1652, 1653, 1654, etc. In 1721 Hans Egede, a Norwegian pastor, was sent to Greenland to take up missionary work, and in 1619 the Norwegian captain Jens Munk was sent by King Christian IV to find the Northwest Passage. Munk rediscovered the Hudson Bay, only eight years after Hudson himself, and took possession of Canada naming it New Denmark. He had along a Lutheran pastor, Rev. Rasmus Jensen (Aarhus), who was the first Lutheran pastor in America. In 1724 King Frederick IV sent Vitus Bering on an exploring expedition, which resulted in the discovery of the Bering Strait between Asia and North America. In 1733 Denmark bought the Virgin Islands in the West Indies from France, and in 1916 these Islands were sold to the United States.

It has been claimed that Henrik Hudson was a Dane. However that may be, it is certain that there were Danes with him when he discovered the Hudson River, which he at that time called Mauritius Floden. There were many Danes in those days that made the trip between the Danish West Indies and Denmark and many who were in the service of Holland. Captain Henrik Christiansen, for instance, made ten trips between New York and Holland in the years 1611-1614. In 1614 he was killed by his friend, the Indian chief Orson at Ft. Nassau. There were many prominent Danes in the Dutch colony at New York; perhaps the most noted of these was Jonas Bronck, whose name is perpetuated in Bronx Borough of New York, Bronx Park and Bronxville. Bronck came to New York in 1639 and died in 1643. Another Dane who has given his name to a section of our country was Peter Lassen, who in 1841 founded the first permanent American settlement in California. Mt. Lassen, the only volcano in the United States, is named after him; also Lassen County, California, Lassen Pass and Lassen's Big Meadows of Feather River. The Danes were distinctive in Washington's army and in all the more recent wars. The Danish farmers, dairymen and buttermakers are famous in this land. The first creameries, the first cow-testing association, the first co-operative dairy-farming on a large scale, were established by Danish farmers. Qualities of good citizenship are highly developed in the Danes. Recognition of this was given by Theodore Roosevelt in referring to his friend Jacob Riis as "the best American citizen." Riis was a social worker in the slums of New York, and is the author of "How the Other Half Lives" and "The Making of an American."

The population of Iceland is hardly 100,000, so small in numbers as apparently to be of no importance in immigration, but viewing the history of this remarkable people, *The Icelanders* one can truly use the current expression: "Little, but oh my!" It was through Iceland that Greenland was settled and America was discovered. It was Iceland that wrote the eddas and sagas of the Middle Ages. It is in Iceland that we find the Teutonic race and language and spirit in its purest forms. Icelanders have, of course, immigrated to this country, but until recently they have been included with the Danes. They have settled in the northwestern states, particularly North Dakota and Minnesota, and in the Canadian province of Manitoba, besides Washington and Alaska. Most of them are engaged in agricultural pursuits and fishing. They have a fair sprinkling of literary men, professional men, statesmen and artists.

There are, of course, contrasts among the Scandinavian peoples. The Danes are the most sociable and pleasure loving, and they run to moderation in virtues as in vices. The Norwegians are the most unsociable and independent in their ways. The Swedes are the most refined and aristocratic. O. N. Nelson called the Danes, the Germans of the North; the Norwegians, the Englishmen of the North; and the Swedes, the Frenchmen of the North.

Finland, called by the natives Suomi (Marshland), is a land of a thousand lakes,—"du tusen sjøars land," as Runeberg calls it. The Finns were originally a Mongolian *The Finns* race, but through intermixture with the Swedes, Norwegians and Russians, they are Caucasian in appearance. Christianity was forced on them in the 12th and 13th centuries by Swedish steel. From 1157 to 1809 Finland was a province of Sweden, during which time Swedish was made the official language. In 1524, under Gustavus Vasa, king of Sweden, the country became Lutheran. Under Sweden the land enjoyed most of the privileges of a free state and made rapid progress in industry, religion, literature, art and science.

In 1743 a part of the land had to be surrendered to Russia; in 1809, the whole land. For 100 years Finland was the freest part of the Russian Empire. The late Czar, about 30 years ago, began the policy of Russianizing Finland. The Russian language took the place of Swedish and Finnish as the official medium. A severe censorship of the press was enforced. The Lutheran religion, claiming 99% of the people, was subordinated to the Russian Catholic. The Finnish army was disbanded. A Russian governor with absolute authority displaced the Finnish parliament and officials. There was no need for this change, for the Finns were peaceable and loyal to Russia. They were as honest and intelligent as any people in the world, and their patience and industry had extorted a livelihood out of a cold and sterile soil. So when Russia began to rob them of their ancient rights, they began to leave for America. Finland had in 1897 a population of 2,352,000. In the 13 years from 1893 to 1905 Finland lost 128,000 by emigration. All except 37 came to America. From 1906 to 1914, 105,146 emigrated. After the World War Finland obtained her independence, on account of which only a few Finns are emigrating—only 26,105 from 1915 to 1922.

In 1920 the Finnish population in the United States was as follows: Finns born in Finland, 150,770; Finns born here, 1st generation, 145,506; Finns born here, second generation, 75,842; total 372,118. They generally take to the occupation of their homeland, as farmers, fishermen, lumbermen and miners. They are located in greatest numbers in Upper Michigan (23.7%), Northern Minnesota (20.8%), Massachusetts (8.8%), Washington (7.1%), and New York (6.1%). The remaining one-third is scattered over the other 43 states. Except for their race and language they can be considered Scandinavians. In race they are about one-fourth Scandinavian. Those Finns who do not marry within their own race prefer to marry Swedes or Norwegians.

The neighbors thus far mentioned have been in the main Teutonic—hence related in blood, language, literature, religion, customs, ideals, history, government, etc. They *The Other White Races* have therefore understood each other pretty well and have been readily assimilated by the American Republic. They began to settle America first and are known as the "Old Immigration."

The other white races—especially from southern and eastern Europe; from Russia, Poland, Hungary, Rumania, Bulgaria, Greece, Italy, etc.—have been coming here in great numbers only the last thirty or forty years, but during this time they have supplied America with over three-fourths of the immigrants. These are called the "New Immigration." And, since they are remote from the original American stock as to race, language, religion, ideals, history, government, etc., they are found not to assimilate so readily and rapidly as the "Old Immigration." Therefore they are much feared and many laws are made to restrict and regulate their coming. They are considered a menace to American labor and standard of living, are often declared to be criminal, degenerate and hostile to democratic institutions.

It is true that southern and eastern Europe is mainly Catholic, while northern and western Europe is mainly Protestant. It is also true that northern and western Europe has been more literate, progressive and free than southern and eastern Europe. The eleven countries of northern and western Europe, for example, in the period 1899-1910 had only sixteen persons in a thousand above 14 years old that were unable to read and write, while southern and eastern Europe in this period had, in eleven countries, not less than 415 in a thousand unable to read and write. Scandinavia leads the world in literacy, with only .4% who cannot read and write; Portugal is at the tail end in Europe with 68.2% illiterate.

But the danger from southern and eastern Europe is probably not so great as it is thought to be. The people from these lands came here because of oppression or poverty at home. They appreciated the greater political and religious freedom that America offered them, and the better wages for the labor of their hands. So they came, in ever swelling numbers, until the World War held them in check. The migration from the northern and western parts began to fall off when the "New Immigration" began to set in. There were three reasons why the "Old Immigration" was falling off: The best American land had been taken; the home countries were advancing industrially and giving about as good wages as America; and the people from northern and western Europe could not compete in salary with the people of southern and eastern Europe, whose living standards were much lower. There were three reasons why the "New Immigration" was on the increase: America began an industrial expansion, has changed from an agricultural to a manufacturing and commercial nation, and needed cheap labor; the people from southern and eastern Europe could make more money here than they could at home; and they had begun to long for the freedom of a democracy.

Meanwhile, the Americans, especially those of English descent, looked upon these last newcomers with much concern. The best students of immigration do not think that America is able to assimilate them and remain English in web and woof. Hunter thinks that the newcomers are inferior and degenerate and that, by intermingling and intermarrying with the natives, they will lower the standards of American manhood and ultimately annihilate the English stock. Elwood urges that we avoid "introducing into our national blood the degenerate strains in the suppressed peoples of southern and eastern Europe." Burr, Hall, Jenks and Lauck, Roberts, Ross, and Warne, each leans strongly toward restricting the "New Immigration" to a minimum. The legislation of Congress is decidedly in the direction of restriction. The Ku Klux Klan has declared war on this immigration. Other organizations and agencies work for restriction and suspension. America must be for Americans and those who will quickly become Americans. This is the burden of their cry.

Still, we are not convinced that the "New Immigration" is a menace. These "new" immigrants are trying to be good citizens. They love America and obey the laws of the land. They are less criminal as a group than the native-born, public-school-trained Americans. In 1904 one out of 6,404 native-born Americans was in prison but only one out of 6,500 of the dreaded "degenerates" from southern and eastern Europe.

There has always been an unwarranted fear of the foreigner, especially if he speaks a foreign language. As far back as 1817 Niles' "Register" urged that the immigrant be shoved into the interior. In 1819 a Society for the Prevention of Pauperism bewailed the menace of the foreigner. In 1845 the native American National Convention expounded loud and long on the imminent peril of the Irish immigration. In 1852 the American Party, better known as the Know-Nothing Party, terrified by the swelling tide of immigration from Germany and Ireland, set up the slogan: "Americans must rule America." The name "American Party" was adopted because its members as 100% Americans advocated that only Americans should hold office. The name "Know-Nothing" was applied to the party because the meetings of the party were secret, and the members, when asked the aims and work of the organization, invariably answered: "I don't know." The Civil War put an end to this party, for the German, Irish and Scandinavian foreigners responded to the call of Abraham Lincoln and saved the Union. Thus there have always been writers and speakers who fear the foreigner.

On the other hand, there have been good men who have pleaded for the foreigner. Thus Hourwich and Steiner, for example. In an address before the National Conference of Charities and Corrections, at Cleveland, in 1912, Cyrus L. Sulzberger, a Russian Jew, said: "On the Fourth of July, 1876, the Centennial of American Independence, every cell in a Siberian prison was decorated with scraps of red, white and blue.

For months these exiles and prisoners had saved every scrap of suitable color, and on the morning of our Independence Day, their cells blossomed forth with this expression of admiration and love for American freedom. . . . .In all generations, the saviors of mankind have come from among the poor. Let us not have it on our conscience that we have closed the door of opportunity to one of these."

Up to the close of 1919 the United States had issued five "liberty loans"—two in 1917, two in 1918 and one in 1919, the last being known as the Victory Liberty Loan. In these five loans $18,500,000,000 was called for. Over $24,000,000,000 was actually subscribed. 21,000,000 people subscribed for the Fourth Loan. One of the posters in the Victory Liberty Loan of April, 1919, was drawn by Howard Chandler Christy, entitled "Americans All!" It had the picture of an American flag, a woman in front of it placing a laurel wreath above the honor roll of men who had given their lives for the United States. There were five names of men from northern and western Europe: Smith, O'Brien, DuBois, Haucke and Knutson; there were nine names of men from southern and eastern Europe: Gonzales, Villotto, Andressi, Pappandrikopolous, Chriszanevicz, Kowalski, Turovich, Cejka and Levy. These were all Americans—"Americans All!" Here were both Jew and Gentile, Greek and Barbarian; all were, as Gavit calls them: "Americans by choice." America had been to them, as Craig puts it: "God's Melting Pot." The massing here of representatives from many lands should not hinder them from becoming one nation. They all have something to supply and something to surrender for the making of an ideal people. "Stop calling the immigrant a problem," says Shriver. "How would you like somebody to call you a problem?" Among the interesting things in Shriver's book, "Immigrant Forces," is a table showing the proportion of immigrant employees in various industries. For example: 94% per cent of the people engaged in making clothing are immigrants; 53% of those engaged in the manufacture of boots and shoes; 71% of the iron and steel workers; 79% of the copper miners; 72% of the coal miners; 89% of the oil refiners; 80% of the furniture makers; 76% of the meat packers; 93% of the sugar refiners.

The variety of races in America is astonishing. America is a Babel. A newspaper reporter observed that in New York City, 66 languages are spoken by as many groups, 49 newspapers are published in foreign languages, and the school at Mulberry Bend has children of 29 nationalities. Yet all these eventually become one people, with one language and one flag.

For mankind is one in spirit, and an instinct bears along,
Round earth's electric circle, the swift flash of right or wrong;
Whether conscious or unconscious, yet Humanity's vast frame
Through its ocean-sundered fibers feels the gush of joy or shame,—
In the gain or loss of one race all the rest have equal claim.

The language problem is no doubt the most important and difficult of the problems that confront any immigrant to America who can not speak English when coming here.

The Language Problem

The native language is the chief medium by which an immigrant can hold on to the cultural heritage of the people from which he sprang; the English language is the chief medium by which he can gain recognition and make progress in this country. At first he struggles hard to learn the English, and then, if he loves his heritage, he will have a still harder struggle on his hands, to keep up the use of his native tongue in his new home. In itself it is no impossible task to learn to speak two languages readily. The difficulty lies especially in this, that in this country the bi-lingual situation is regarded as an evil that may be tolerated, but should not be encouraged. Those who use two languages in their homes are branded as "hyphenates" and "foreigners" and are often handicapped in the race for position or power. The little children at school pledge themselves, not only to one nation and one flag, but also to one language. During the recent World War the foreign-language population suffered much humiliation and persecution at the hands of those who could speak only English. In at least one state (Iowa) it was forbidden even to preach in a foreign language; conversation over the telephone could be carried on in English only. It was urged to prohibit the printing of books and papers in foreign languages. Men were actually killed on the streets for using a foreign language. The language problem has, of course, affected the Norwegians, and that in a variety of ways, for weal or woe.

In studying the language problem it is well to have in mind the general laws of language rivalry in the case of race mixture. According to George Hempl, there are four conditions under which language rivalry takes place. Under two of these conditions the foreign language wins over the native, and under two the native wins over the foreign.

When vast hordes of foreigners come into a country and conquer it, their language displaces that of the natives. Examples of this condition are the Anglo-Saxons in England and the English in America. English is now the language of America, enriched by a few native Indian words of things, as: tomahawk, toboggan, wigwam, squaw; and many place names, as: Illinois, Wisconsin, Iowa, Minnesota, Dakota, Decorah, Winona, Minnehaha, Mississippi, Missouri, etc.

When the conquerors are neighbors who reduce the conquered territory to a province, which they colonize and denationalize, the language of the conquerors prevails in time, but is apt to be learned by sound substitution and to be considerably mixed with the native language. Examples of this situation are: The Romans in France, Spain and Portugal, and the Danes in Norway. During the Danish supremacy in Norway, Danish became the official language of Norway, but with Norwegian pronunciation and a good supply of Norwegian words. Since 1814, and especially since 1905, the Norwegians have been striving to make their language like the modern dialect offshoots of the Old Norse.

When the conquerors are a comparatively small body, their language in time dies out, but implants upon the native language its terms pertaining to government, army, navy, and all spheres of life that the conquerors control. Examples are the Northmen in France and the Normans in England. Skeat mentions thirty-four words which the Normans in England had brought with them to France from Norway. Thus bondage, from the Norwegian "bonde," a small farmer. Scott, in his "Ivanhoe," makes one of his characters say: "Swine is good Saxon. And so when the brute lives, and is in charge of a Saxon slave, she goes by her Saxon name, but becomes a Norman, and is called pork (Lat. porcus, swine), when she is carried to the castle-hall to feast among the nobles."

When the foreigners are immigrants and come in scattered bands and at different times to make their homes in a new country, then the native language wins out over the foreign language. As a class immigrants become servants and follow the humbler callings. As long as they have the marks of the foreigner, they can not expect to occupy many ruling positions in their adopted country. The immigrant came here to better his economic position and to live here. It is to his advantage in a financial and social way to learn English as fast as possible. He is given to understand that it is also to his advantage to remove from himself as much as possible every taint of foreign speech, or otherwise, which may keep him from making headway as an American. The language of the immigrant is, according to this stern condition, this relentless law, bound to die out sooner or later, making, as a rule, little or no impression on the native language. There are more Germans than English in America, but German is the language of an immigrant people, while English is the language of the ruling class, therefore English must prevail. Though German has been spoken in the United States for 300 years and by great numbers of people, and though it has been taught extensively in the public schools, it has scarcely added a word to the English dictionary of words. English is the dominant language in America.

In the light of these laws, then, the Norwegian language in the

United States is doomed. Individuals and groups may keep it up, and even speak it better than the English, but English will nevertheless go marching on as the dominant language of the land. The public schools of the land encourage the study of foreign languages—a little Latin and less of something else—but they do not see, or want to see, the pedagogical value of encouraging and aiding each child to keep up the language of his immigrant parents or grandparents. It is through this language, more than anything else, that the child can keep in touch with his forefathers and their culture. Without this language tie, a person does not, as a rule, seem to know, or care to know, what his ancestors stood for.

Norwegian	Norwegian - American	American
Period	Period	Period
1825 - 1860	1860 - 1890	1890 - 1925

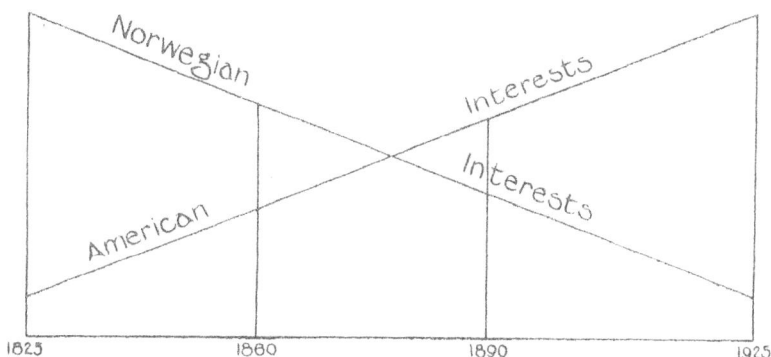

Periods of Norwegian-American History

The story of the Norwegians in America may be divided into three periods—the Norwegian Period, 1825-1860; the Norwegian-American Period, 1860-1890; and the American Period, 1890-1925.

The Historical Periods

In the Norwegian Period the Norwegian-Americans were more Norwegian than American. They were more Norwegian than English, in language, ideas, ideals, worship and ways.

In the Norwegian-American Period they were as much American as Norwegian. They spoke both languages readily, kept pace with the events in both countries, built their own higher schools and supported the public schools with holy zeal, celebrated the Seventeenth of May and the Fourth of July with equal fervor, and loved to float the two flags of Red, White and Blue side by side.

In the American Period most of them speak English only, though many of these understand Norwegian well enough and can, if hard pressed, also talk it. Most of the Norwegian higher schools have been dismantled; the Norwegian summer schools are dying, and Norwegian in the Sunday School and young people's society is of the past. English services are supplanting the Norwegian. Associations are formed to save the Norwegian—literary, cultural, religious, national. Both press and pulpit try by fits to revive and maintain the interest of the young in Norwegian and things Norwegian. The Norwegian language is introduced into many universities, high schools and even common schools, but it is fast disappearing from the home and the pulpit. The home is the best language training school in the world, and the cheapest. In the American Period English becomes the language of the home. The Norwegian-American has become an "American" in the sense that he can speak only one language and looks with disfavor upon the "foreigners," or "hyphenates," who try to keep up a bi-lingual existence.

4. THEIR PLACE IN HISTORY

The Norwegians *Discovered* America first:

In 876 Gunnbjørn discovered Greenland and stayed there over the winter.

The Viking Period   In 983 Eric the Red rediscovered Greenland and made it his home.

In 983 Ari Marson discovered Great Ireland (the Chesapeake country) and made it his home.

In 986 Bjarni Herjulfson discovered the New England coast, but did not land.

In 1000 Leif Erikson set out to find the land that Bjarni had seen, and found it.

In 1476 John Scolvus made an expedition to find the "Cod Fish Country" (Newfoundland) and found it.

In 1477 Christopher Columbus visited Iceland.

In 1492 Christopher Columbus discovered San Salvador, an island 400 miles to the southeast of Florida.

The Norwegians *Settled* America first:

Greenland is a part of North America and Erik the Red was not only a colonist, but a promoter of colonization. He called the land Greenland in order, as he said, to attract settlers. Babcock says of Erik the Red: "No one who follows the career of Eric, as outlined by the often unsympathetic saga-men, will grudge him this hardly won triumph. Few characters, if any, are more clearly presented in history; few are stronger and more interesting. A sea-king who never marauded; a just man, careful of what was confided to him, yet insisting promptly on his rights at every cost; a conservative, who could turn explorer off hand with better results than the work of the very best; a deadly fighter who fought defensively only; a man of hospitality, cordiality, cheerfulness, who never complained except when his Christian wife turned against him for remaining a pagan. He made the Norse Greenland, which stood as his monument for nearly five hundred years. He gave the name by which we know it still. If Greenland be America, he was the first explorer of any part of America, so far as we know. He may have been the first white man to view the more immediate American shores. At any rate he gave to the world, and sent forth upon his ventures, the historic Leif who is first of record as making that discovery. He also aided in sending forth the expedition which bore Thorfinn Karlsefne and Gudrid to these shores, giving Gudrid in marriage from his house and seeing his son Thorvald sail off to death in their company."

Great Ireland was a part of North America and was settled by Ari in 983, Bjarni in 999, Gudleif in 1027, and possibly others.

Vinland was a part of North America and Norsemen from Greenland attempted at various times to settle it. History tells of Thorvald's attempt in 1002, and Thorfinn's in 1007. Bishops of Vinland were regularly appointed from 1112 to 1409.

There were Norwegians in America throughout the Colonial Period, not many, but up and doing. A Norwegian captain, Jens Munk, under Danish colors, tried to find the **The Colonial** Northwest Passage, later, in 1912, discovered **Period** by another Norwegian, Roald Amundsen, also the discoverer of the South Pole. The Norwegians numbered about one-fourth of the early Dutch colony of New Amsterdam and have for 300 years been contributing to the upbuilding of these United States.

This book will try to show in part what the Norwegians have been doing in the last one hundred years. The whole story can not be told within the covers of any one **The Modern Period** book. At this point, we shall let the editor of the "Chicago Daily Tribune" speak in an editorial September 25, 1924, on "Leif Erikson's Day" (Sept. 29) He is speaking of the Scandinavians, and not of Norwegians alone, and the other members of the group deserve these kind words as much as do the Norwegians. "Swedes make good citizens; Danes and Norwegians make good citizens. They have settled in large numbers in the Northern Middle West. They have given the new country social stability, hard work, and a well developed countryside. In Chicago there are 90,000 born in Scandinavia. In Illinois there are 150,000. In the United States there

are more than a million. There are few Scandinavians in the
jails and poorhouses. Their stock adapts itself well to American
conditions and American life. Saturday is Leif Erikson's Day. He
was the first Scandinavian immigrant. He came in the year 1000.
His people built a tower or so and drifted out again into nowhere.
But Leif Erikson gave all Scandinavians a proper introduction to
America. He made the first trans-Atlantic trip. The other day,
Eric Nelson, along with Smith, Harding and Arnold, arrived by
air from around the world. The Norsemen are up to their old
stunts. Scandinavians are born pioneers and fighters. America can
never have too many of them. They are builders, whether it be
a farmstead or a nation, and when the time for building stops they
move along to other fields. We may hope that America never will
be satisfied. If it can offer always something to build and a new
hope there always will be good men around with yellow hair to
do the job."

August Weenaas   David Lysnes   Bjug A. Harstad

Three Norwegian Church Pioneers

NOTE ON THE NORSE-AMERICAN CENTENNIAL MEDAL.

(As soon as Congressman O. J. Kvale of Minnesota was assured by the Post Office Department that the two special postage stamps would be issued he prepared and introduced in the House of Representatives a bill authorizing the striking of a medal at the United States Mint at Philadelphia in commemoration of the Centennial. This bill was in-

The Norse-American Centennial Medal, Front View

troduced in the House February 4, 1925, and later introduced in the Senate by Senator Peter Norbeck of South Dakota.

When the bill had passed both the Senate and the House Mr. Kvale was authorized by the Centennial Committee to secure an artist, and to make all arrangements connected with the coining of the medal. According to the bill the medal was to contain "appropriate emblems and inscriptions." Mr. Kvale made a rough sketch of what he considered proper for the obverse and the reverse side of the medal, with the inscriptions

to be placed on it, and took these to New York, where he secured the
services of James Earle Fraser, considered the foremost medalist in the
United States. Mr. Fraser at once accepted the suggestions both as to
the emblems and the inscriptions, and put other work aside to design the
medal. Mr. Fraser himself considers it "one of the best medals he has
ever done." And The National Commission of Fine Arts, in passing on

The Norse-American Centennial Medal, Back View

the medal, not only approved it, including the date, "A. D. 1000," but
went out of their way to say it had "especial artistic merit."

The medal will be coined to the number of 40,000. As the photograph
shows, it is octagonal in shape. It is made of silver identical with that
used in the Nation's silver coins, and approximating a half dollar in size.

It is worthy of note that this is the first commemorative medal to be
issued in the history of the United States Mint. Other medals have been
coined, but these have been for awards in the case of expositions and
similar events.)

Statue of Liberty

CHAPTER V

THE NORWEGIAN PERIOD, 1825-1860

The Norwegian Period covers approximately the 35 years from 1825 to 1860. It begins with the coming of the Sloop "Restaurationen." It ends with the outbreak of the Civil War.

1. THE HISTORICAL BACKGROUND

The Norwegian immigration, being a part of a world movement, can best be understood in the light of contemporary world events. A few such events are accordingly herewith set forth.

Marvellous, indeed, is the 19th century. During this century Europe was able to give to North America about 25,000,000 of her sons and daughters, besides many millions to South America, Africa and Australia, and at the same time she more than doubled her population at home. In 1800 the population of Europe was 175,000,000; in 1900, it had increased to 400,600,000.

The century was an age of invention. Invention is stimulated by the increased contacts between men and the needs of great masses of people. Necessity is the mother of invention. Invention, in turn, helps to bring about still greater intercourse among men and adds to their wants. Among the inventions of the first half of the 19th century was the application of steam power to transportation and to industry. In 1807 Robert Fulton built a steamboat and sailed it up the Hudson. In 1838 ocean travel by steam was also accomplished, in that the "Great Western" crossed the Atlantic in 15 days' time, thus shortening the voyage by about eight weeks. In 1851 the time had been reduced to eight days. In 1825 George Stephenson perfected a locomotive that could pull passenger cars on rails at the speed of eight miles an hour; he improved it so that in 1829 he could move along at the rate of 35 miles an hour. In addition to this change in transit and transportation there were many improvements in the mail service, and other methods of communication. The postage stamp came into use. Mail routes and regular schedules were instituted. Express companies were established, as, for example, the Adams, dating from 1840. In 1844 Samuel Morse conceived the idea of the electric telegraph. In 1854 Cyrus W. Field began to lay a submarine cable and in 1866 he had one laid across the Atlantic. The first message sent over the cable was: "What wonders God hath wrought." The cable had revolutionized methods of trade, for by it the market prices of the world are daily reported in the newspaper press.

The 19th century was an age of machine-made, instead of hand-made, wares. It was a factory age. Water power was harnessed. Coal was mined. Steam, electricity, gas, oil, were applied in a thousand ways to run the factories. Machines were invented, one after the other, to do the work formerly done by hand. The invention of Portland cement in 1825, friction matches in 1827, the reaping machine in 1834, rubber boots in 1839, daguerrotype photography in 1839, the steam hammer in 1842, the typewriter in 1843, ether as anesthetic in 1846, the sewing machine in 1846, Bessemer steel in 1855, are a few out of hundreds of epoch-making inventions in the first part of the 19th century. In 1790 only three patents were taken out in the United States; in 1860 the number of patents issued was 4,778. Between 1790 and 1860 the total number was 43,431; between 1790 and 1916 the total was 1,125,000.

These inventions promoted immigration. Distance did not mean what it formerly did. The continents were brought closer together. The crossing of the sea had lost much of its danger and terrors.

Besides, there were going on great changes within the people themselves, which affected them even more profoundly than the external changes. Compulsory education at public expense was gaining a foothold in all the more progressive lands. The era of popular education, the day of the public school, was being ushered in. The greater intercourse among the nations and between the people within a nation, resulted in a growth of fellow-feeling, not strong enough indeed to end wars, but yet strong enough to live through wars and increase in spite of wars. Politically, the keynote of the 19th century was democracy; but the democracy that was obtained was in most cases purchased at great cost, on account of injustice, persecution and suffering, through riot, revolution and war. These educational, social and political changes all gave an impetus to obeying the call of America: "Come over and help us." America needed workers. Here were dense forests to be cleared, rich mines to be developed, fertile prairies to be cultivated. Here was a land that had an open door policy and welcomed the stranger warmly.

Great Britain was in the midst of an industrial revolution following immediately upon the wars with Napoleon and with **Europe** the United States (1812-1814). The newly invented machinery put men out of work and yet increased production. The returning soldiers added to the crowds of idle and hungry men. The

Ole Paulson   Knut Bjørgo   Elias Harbo

crops were poor; the prices were high. High protective tariffs (Corn Laws) made it well-nigh impossible to get food supplies from abroad. Distress and discontent stalked throughout the land. Out of this wide-spread and deep-felt misery came a cry for redress, a cry that took on the form of a persistent agitation for legislative reform. Happily many reforms were instituted. Among these may be mentioned: The working day was shortened from 15 hours to something less; child labor was prohibited; slavery in the colonies was abolished; Dissenters and Catholics were given the right to vote; free trade was established; the House of Commons was made supreme, with the sovereign as a figure head. During this period England adjusted herself to the new order of things and settled down to become a manufacturing and commercial nation. She therefore sought to strengthen her colonial possessions and power, a policy that led to the Opium War, the Crimean War and the East Indian War (Sepoy Rebellion). In the years 1820-1860, 744,285 emigrated from England to the United States, 47,622 from Scotland, and 1,952,943 from Ireland, a total of 2,744,850 from Great Britain. A disease called "potato rot" destroyed the potato crop of Ireland in the years 1845-1849, causing much suffering. 300,000 starved to death. Over 1,500,000 came to America.

On the Continent there was even more restlessness than in Great Britain. At the Congress of Vienna, in 1814-1815, the map of Europe had been readjusted. The commissioners at this Congress seemed to have but one aim—to put everything back as nearly as possible in the shape it was before the French Revolution. They had no care for the people; the princes were their only concern. France was made a monarchy. Italy and Germany were divided among a horde of petty tyrants. The partition of Poland was ratified. And so forth. But the day of democracy had arrived, and there were many uprisings which upset the decrees of the Vienna autocrats. In 1814 Norway declared herself a free nation. In 1830 and 1848 there were revolutions in France, which lighted the signal fires of liberty throughout Europe. A new republic was established in France in 1848, only to be overturned again in 1852. Belgium broke lose from Holland in 1831 and established a constitutional kingdom. Italy had uprisings in 1820, 1830, 1848 and 1859, which resulted both in political freedom and national unity for the Italian states. Of all the European states, Germany had suffered most under Napoleon's cruelty and was most dismembered, but was reviving again and striving towards a more perfect union of the German people. The rivalry between the German states of Prussia and Austria led inevitably to war, in which Prussia came out as victor. There was a revolution in Greece in 1828, in Poland in 1830, in Hungary in 1848, out of which came some measure of greater liberty, especially in Greece, which was freed from Turkish rule. In 1584 serfdom had been legalized in Russia. Peasants were bought and sold with the land they worked. The land belonged to the nobility and the peasants had to stay there from generation to generation. In 1858-1863, yielding to the urgent cry for redress and the spirit of the times, Czar Alexander II emancipated the serfs of Russia, by which these semi-slaves could, under certain conditions, acquire land and move from place to place. From 1820 to 1860 the total number of emigrants from the continent was 1,899,833—from Germany 1,555,508; France, 207,692; Scandinavia, 45,957; and from all other lands, 90,676. Of the total immigration to the United States during the period 1820-1860, 54.3% came from Great Britain, 30.7% from Germany, 4.1% from France, .9% from Scandinavia, and the remaining 10% from the other lands of the earth. America was the haven for freedom and the land of opportunity for all that were poor and oppressed.

Norway and Sweden became a dual monarchy in 1814. Their first king was Bernadotte, a French marshal under Napoleon.

Norway

The Swedes had chosen him as heir to the throne, hoping thereby to gain the friendship of Napoleon, and that thus through his help they might regain possession of Finland, which they had lost to Russia in 1809. They reckoned, however, without their host, for Napoleon and Bernadotte did not long remain friends after Bernadotte's elevation. Hardly had Bernadotte, or Charles John, as he called himself in Sweden, come into power, when he joined with Russia, Prussia and England in a new (sixth) confederacy against Napoleon. Denmark sided with Napoleon and against England, because England had in 1807 bombarded Copenhagen· and taken the Dano-Norwegian fleet. The Powers promised Charles John Norway as the price for his aiding them against Napoleon. Napoleon went out to fight the Allies and met them at Leipzig in 1813, where he met defeat (the "Battle of Nations"). At the Peace of Kiel (Jan. 14, 1814) the Powers gave Norway to Sweden. As stated in another place in this book, Norway objected to being given away by anybody to anybody. Norway declared herself free and, on the Seventeenth of May, 1814, adopted a constitution. When Norway finally accepted Charles John as her king, she did it with the understanding that she was a free country and in no sense a province.

Charles John remained a Frenchman all his days. He never learned to speak Norwegian, not even Swedish, although he lived at Stockholm 32 years. The peace conference at Vienna had tried to restore the power and dignity of the monarchs as they were before the French Revolution, and Charles John, though himself not of royal birth, had caught the spirit of the old school and was jealous of his authority. Yet he was, on the whole a good king. There was, naturally, some friction between him and the democratic Norwegians. He and the Norwegian Storthing, for example, differed on a number of questions, as: The payment of the war debt, the celebration of the Seventeenth of May, the equality of the kingdoms, the naval flag, the treatment of diplomatic matters, amendments to the constitution, etc. He took upon himself in 1828 to forbid the celebration of the Seventeenth of May as the national holiday. In answer to this tyrannous act the poet Wergeland sang hymns to liberty so effectively that the people in 1829 were determined at all costs to celebrate. The king sent his troops to disperse the multitudes, but without avail. Fortunately, he did this only once—in 1829. Since that date, the day has been celebrated in peace. In 1836 the king proposed constitutional changes, but the Storthing promptly tabled the proposal and passed a law as to a Norwegian merchant flag. The king therupon rashly dissolved the Storthing; the Storthing brought the case before the courts and had the action declared unconstitutional. The king, awestruck by their boldness, made concessions, and, by appointing a Norwegian, Wedel-Jarlsberg, as viceroy, became justly popular. From this it appears that the Norwegians of this period were fearless in asserting their rights, moderate and persistent in their demands. Eventually they obtained every right and privilege they asked for.

In 1844 Oscar I, son of Charles John, came to the throne. He tried to conciliate the Norwegians. He gave them their own flag. Under his reign many good laws were passed and many reforms in the means of communication and in trade were carried into effect. In 1859 Oscar I was succeeded by his son Charles XV.

During this period Norway was very poor. England had destroyed or seized her ships and had blockaded her ports. It took many years to overcome this handicap. The financial panics which swept over Europe in the '30s and '50s affected also Norway. Norway's poverty was the main cause for the emigration from Norway at this time. The emigration going on from the rest of northwestern Europe was also felt as a stimulating factor in Norway. Cleng Peerson, who had been in Germany, France, England and America, became the apostle of immigration to America, and the Sloop "Restaurationen," setting out from Stavanger on July 4, 1825, was the first boatload of Norwegian immigrants to the United States in modern times.

In 1825, when the Sloop "Restaurationen" came, this nation was scarcely fifty years old. The Revolutionary War began in 1775, the Declaration of Independence was made July 4, 1776, the Articles of Confederation were agreed upon by the Continental Congress in 1777, the Constitution of the United States was written in 1787. It was a document of compromises. Some men, for example, wanted a strong central government—these came to be known as Federalists; others believed that the states should have as much power as possible—these came to be known as Anti-Federalists, or Democratic-Republicans. George Washington became the first president, the unanimous choice of both factions. He served from 1789 to 1797 and was succeeded by John Adams, the nominee of the Federalist Party. Adams' term was from 1797 to 1801. The third president was Thomas Jefferson, candidate of the Democratic-Republicans. He served eight years, from 1801 to 1809. The fourth president was James Madison, twice elected by the Republicans; and after him came James Monroe, the fifth president, also Republican, whose term of office extended from 1817 to 1825. Up to this time—1825—the Federal Constitution had been tried out only thirty-six years. The administration of Washington was a period of organization. The administrations of John Adams and Thomas Jefferson were periods of experimentation in foreign and domestic policy, ending in a second war with Great Britain (1812-1814). The purchase of Louisiana, in 1803, was one of the most notable events in this period. Then came the Era of Good Feeling, which lasted ten years—from 1815 to 1825. The Monroe Doctrine, first announced on December 2, 1823, has since been one of the fundamental rules of America with respect to European interference in American affairs.

The Norwegian Sloopers arrived in America just as the Era of Ill Feeling began to set in. The new era lasted from 1825 to 1861, which are the years marking the beginning and end of the first period of the story of the Norwegians in America. It might seem that this era should be one of Good Feeling. The country had made great progress from 1775 to 1825 and was about to witness a growth which had never before been paralleled. In 1775 the population was less than 3,000,000; in 1825 more than 11,000,000. And in 1860 it had increased to more than 31,000,000. In 1775 there were 13 colonies; in 1825 there were 24 states; and in 1860, 33 states. The country had grown from about 350,000 sq. miles in 1775 to about 2,000,000 sq. miles, most of it uninhabited and untilled, in 1825. In 1860 the area was over 3,000,000 sq. miles, most of it occupied and partly tilled. Alongside of the political and territorial growth there had been much progress in agriculture, mining, manufacturing, commerce, invention and internal improvement. Europe had begun to look to America for supplies of cotton and grain. American factories had begun to supply domestic needs and even to offer their wares in foreign markets. American ships flying the American flag could be seen in every principal port. To the poor and oppressed immigrant from Europe, America seemed a haven of peace, a land of prosperity and freedom. Nevertheless, this period is rightly called the Era of Ill Feeling, politically, socially, economically and otherwise.

One of the causes of ill feeling was the question of internal improvements by the Federal Government at national expense. The Democratic-Republicans opposed such a system. The Federalists advocated it. John Quincy Adams, president in 1825-1829, boldly recommended appropriation for national observatories, a university, and scientific enterprises of various kinds, as well as for public roads, canals and defences. The country was not ready for such liberal views, and Adams became very unpopular. He was succeeded by Andrew Jackson, who sternly opposed such improvements as unconstitutional. With

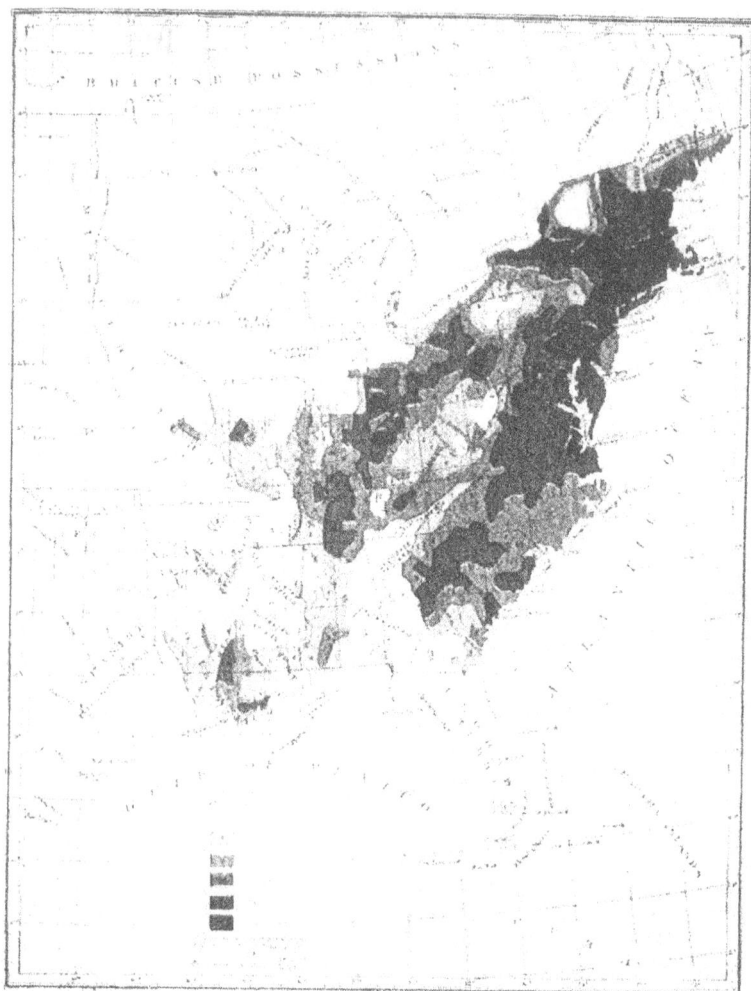

Settlements in 1820

(An attempt to reproduce the U. S. Census Color Plates by the camera
—not very successful. The population west of the Alleghanies is considerably lighter than indicated in this reproduction.)

Settlements in 1860

(An attempt to reproduce the U. S. Census Color Plates by the camera
—not very successful. The population west of the Alleghanies is considerably lighter than indicated in this reproduction.)

the introduction of railroads it was necessary to give them a grant of land along the line of their route. This grant was managed in this way, that Congress gave the land to the states in order to enable them to give the land to corporations within their boundaries. The first grant for railroad purposes was made in 1850, when the state of Illinois gave 2,500,000 acres to the Illinois Central Railroad.

Another bone of contention was the Protective Tariff. The trouble over this question began also with John Quincy Adams. New England favored protection to aid her growing manufactures, especially that of woolens. The cotton-growing states of the South did not have factories and did not want any tariff. A tariff law was passed in 1828, which was called "The Tariff of Abominations." Under Jackson it was modified, but was so unpopular even at that, that South Carolina passed an ordinance of nullification declaring the tariff acts of 1828 and 1832 void. President Jackson acted with energy, ordering General Winfield Scott to collect duties by force of arms.

The United States Bank was a third source of trouble. It was a part of Hamilton's financial scheme. It had been opposed by Jefferson, Madison and other advocates of state rights. Andrew Jackson was an enemy of the bank, and would not permit its rechartering in 1836. From 1833 to 1836 he withdrew the government money and placed it in state banks. This was at a time when the West was opening up and there was a great boom everywhere. It became easy to borrow money and a wild orgy of speculation ensued. New banks, called "wild cat banks," were formed on little or no capital, since paper money could be issued with little or no specie back of it. The madness in money and speculation could not go on forever. In 1837 occurred a terrible financial panic which paralyzed all industries, one of the most painful and prolonged crises in our financial history.

It seems to have been the intention of the founders of our government that civil officers should retain their positions during good behavior. Andrew Jackson introduced the "Spoils System," making a clean sweep of all who differed with him in politics. Since his day public office has been considered a reward for party service, except in so far as civil service reform has been introduced.

The great political parties during this period were the Democratic-Republicans, now called Democrats, and the Federalists, now called Whig. The Democrats elected Jackson, Van Buren, Polk, Pierce and Buchanan, a total of 24 years in office. The Whigs elected Harrison and Tyler, Taylor and Fillmore, a total of 8 years in office. John Quincy Adams was elected by the House of Representatives for one term. He was a Federalist. The campaign of Harrison was the first political campaign, since so familiar, having mass meetings, political speeches, songs, torch lights and slogans. "Tippecanoe and Tyler too" won his election.

There were several smaller parties advocating this or that reform measure. Thus, in 1826-1835, the Anti-Masonic Party opposed Free Masonry. A prohibition movement was on foot, which made Maine a prohibition state in 1846, Vermont in 1852, New Hampshire in 1855, Connecticut in 1854-1872. New York in 1855-1857, and restricted the sale of liquor in Ohio, Michigan and other places. The Know-Nothing Party in 1856 confined itself to vigorous opposition to aliens and Catholics. Texas, originally a part of Mexico, from which it declared its independence, was annexed to the United States in 1845. This brought on the War with Mexico, won by the United States. Mexico ceded to the United States in 1848 522,568 sq, miles of land, including California, and in 1853, through the Gadsden Purchase, the United States obtained an additional 45,535 sq. miles of territory. Gold was discovered in California in 1848, resulting in a wild rush of adventurers and settlers to California. The northeastern boundary difficulties with Great Britain were settled in 1842. The northwestern boundary question was settled in 1846.

The chief source of ill feeling during this period was the subject of slavery. The South wanted slaves because it was profitable to the South. The North had originally favored slaves, but had found it unprofitable, and slavery died a natural death. The moral side of the question was early recognized and boldly proclaimed, but the matter was hushed and compromised at the framing of the Constitution. The South wished to introduce slavery into new territory. The North tried to prevent it. The Missouri Compromise of 1820 recognized the power of Congress to exclude slavery from new territory. The Compromise of 1850 admitted California as a free state, but gave the other territories the right to decide for themselves as to slavery. The Kansas-Nebraska Bill likewise left the states to decide the question. The Fugitive Slave Law made it the duty of Congress to protect slavery. The Dred-Scott Decision declared slaves to be property, not people. Mrs. Stowe's "Uncle Tom's Cabin," a story of slave life in the South, published in 1852, had an immense sale, and was largely instrumental in changing the political question to a moral one.

Garrison started a newspaper in 1829 advocating immediate abolition of slavery. He was fined and his paper was suppressed. He started another paper, "The Liberator," declaring the United States Constitution, because of its compromising attitude on the slavery question, to be a "covenant with death, and an agreement with Hell." He had many followers. They were often persecuted. Lovejoy, an Illinois abolition editor, was mobbed and killed in 1838. The Liberty Party, organized in 1840, opposed slavery. It was succeeded by the Free Soil Party, in 1848, and this in turn was succeeded by the Republican Party, in 1856. Its first candidate was John C. Fremont, and the slogan of the party was "Free Soil, Free Speech, Free Men and Fremont." The second candidate, in 1860, was Abraham Lincoln, who was elected. The German and Scandinavian vote put him into office. His election brought on the secession of the South and the Civil War, in which struggle slavery perished.

2. The Norwegian Immigration, 1825-1860

We have learned that the brave and adventurous Norsemen found their way to America during the Colonial Days and as

Cleng Peerson

far back as the Viking Age. Gunnbjørn came to Greenland in 876; Leif Erikson, to Vinland, in 1000. But to Cleng Peerson belongs the honor of having started a steady stream of im-

Stavanger in 1825

migration to America. He was the Pathfinder of Norwegian Settlements in the Northwest and Southwest.

Peerson was born on the farm Hesthammer, in Tysvær Parish, north of Stavanger, Norway, May 17, 1782. He went originally by the name Kleng Pedersen Hesthammer, but in later years he came to be known by the shorter name. He is reported to have married a rich widow considerably older than himself and to have traveled in Scandinavia, Germany, France and England. He is said to have acquired some speaking knowledge of the languages of the countries through which he journeyed. He returned to Norway, and was sent to America in

(Copyrighted by O. M. Norlie)

Cleng Peerson

(Drawn by Ivan Doseff and approved by five of Cleng Feerson's friends as a reasonably good likeness)

1821, as an advance agent for a group of Quakers in Stavanger. They wanted more freedom than they were having in Norway, and hoped to find a place where they could live and worship as they pleased, without suffering any persecutions or restrictions at the hands of anybody.

Quakerism was a new movement in Norway. It had been

brought to Norway by Norwegian sailors who had been held prisoners of war in England during the Napoleonic Wars. The leader among these was Lars Larson i Jeilane, who in 1807 attempted to ship a cargo of lumber to France, but was captured by an English man-of-war and held prisoner until 1814. Upon his release he worked one year for Mrs. Margaret Allen, a Quakeress, who had visited him in prison. He accepted the Quaker faith, returned to Norway and organized at his house in Stavanger the first Society of Friends in Norway. In 1818, two Quaker missionaries from England visited Stavanger. They

Cleng Peerson's Dream Fulfilled: A Typical Norwegian Farm Home in 1925

were William Allen, a son of Larson's benefactress, and Stephen Grellet, a Frenchman who had lived twelve years in the United States. Grellet no doubt had told the Norwegian Quakers about the greater religious freedom in America, to which country he himself soon afterward returned.

While the history of Norway is relatively free from religious persecutions, the State Church naturally has not welcomed dissenters and separatists, and has at times called upon the civil government to restrict their interference in church matters. In the case of Hans Nielsen Hauge, the great Lutheran revivalist, the Church and State joined hands to suppress the revival movement. Hauge was imprisoned from 1804 to 1814 and his followers were subjected to various kinds of annoyance by the regular clergy and the state officials. Hauge remained a Lutheran until his death, in 1824, but the Quakers were thorough-going separatists and wanted nothing to do with Lutheran doctrines and practices. They would not baptize and confirm their children, which were church requirements, and they objected to military service, which was a state requirement. When the church and civil authorities began to insist on the observation of these demands, the Quakers were much annoyed and longed for a land where they could worship according to the dictates of their own conscience. Besides, the Quakers of Stavanger were humble and poor and would appreciate the economic advantages offered by America. So it was decided to send Cleng Peerson over here, together with one companion, Knud Olson Eide, and funds were raised among the Friends and given the travelers to defray their expenses.

Cleng Peerson came to the United States in August, 1821, and remained three years. His companion took sick and died. "Peerson," says a writer in the "New York American" for Oct. 22, 1825, "procured the best medical attendants, still laboring with his own hands for his support, and debarring himself of the comforts of life to administer to the necessities of his friend. After the decease of his friend, the survivor . . . proceeded on foot to examine the country, the character of the soil, our mode of agriculture, engaged without any hesitation at any kind of employment to meet the current expenses of the day, by which means he obtained a knowledge of our customs, laws, language and agriculture. In this manner he scoured the vast regions of the West and left a journal from day to day." He returned to Norway in 1824, reported to his Stavanger friends as to conditions in America and urged them to emigrate. As a direct result of his report and stay in Stavanger the Sloop "Restaurationen" set sail the next summer for America.

Peerson hastened back to America to prepare for the arrival of the immigrants, this time too with a companion—Andrias Stangeland. In a letter written at New York Dec. 20, 1824, a copy of which is in the Minnesota Historical Society Library, Peerson says: "Dear father, brother, sister, brother-in-law and friends: This will inform you that I have arrived in America, happy and well. After a voyage of six weeks, we reached New York where we found all my friends in good health."

In this letter he tells furthermore that he had gone to Albany by steamboat, and then, by way of the Erie Canal, as far as Farmington, in western New York. "I then went overland to Geneva, where the land commissioner lives, in order to purchase land, both for myself and you. . . . . . The land commissioner is very friendly and has promised to aid us as much as he can. We reached an agreement in regard to six pieces of land which I

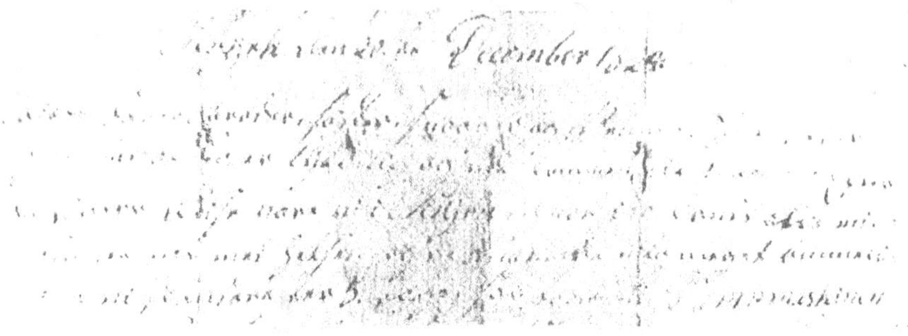

The Beginning of Cleng Peerson's Letter

have selected, and this agreement will be in force until next fall. I already have a house in process of construction, 24 ft. long by 20 ft. wide, which I hope to complete by New Year's Day. . . . . .When I was in Rochester I bought a stove for $20.00. It is fully equipped, with such things as pans, pots for meat, a baking oven, etc. . . . . ."

He says further: "I am very much concerned in my mind about your coming to America . . . . . How happy I should be to receive word that you were coming to New York and I might meet you there . . . . . . I must entrust everything to Providence. You also would do the same. You must not allow yourselves to be frightened away by talk. I have experienced the help of Providence as long as I remain steadfast in my faith. More than that we can not do. I have told you everything orally and I will stand by my promises. Do not fail to write me in good

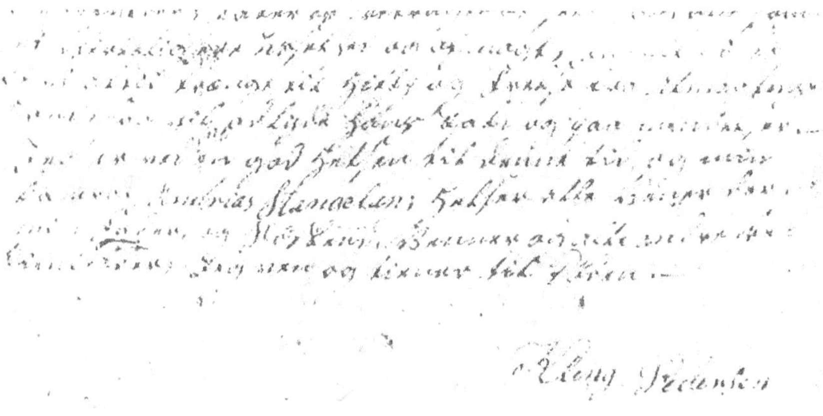

The Closing of Cleng Peerson's Letter

(Photostat used by permission of Prof. Theodore C. Blegen, Minnesota State Historical Society.)

season and I shall do my best. . . . . . My friends in New York
have promised to do all in their power to sell the vessel as advantageously as possible. On the other hand, if you could invest your money in Swedish iron and hire a vessel, that would
accomplish the same end. . . . . I hope that you will write me
a letter as soon as you are ready, to acquaint me with your
plans. Above all, deal with one another in a brotherly spirit.
Do not fail to love one another. . . . . Let us see ourselves as we
really are, wretched and feeble, then we shall understand that
we always have need of help and salvation from the hand of
the Almighty. Then we will obey His call and heed His admonitions. Up to the present I have been in good health, as has my
comrade, Andrias Stangelan. . . . .

Your friend and servant unto death,

Kleng Pedersen."

"This letter," says Theodore C. Blegen, the biographer of
Cleng Peerson, "proves clearly that Cleng Peerson was the advance agent of the immigrants of 1825, that he was directly
urging the enterprise and encouraging its backers, that he
arranged in 1824 for the purchase of land for his friends, that
he was attempting to arrange for the sale of their ship should
they purchase one for their journey. . . . . That he was indeed
the trail-blazer and advance agent for the Sloop Folk, and that
his name stands properly at the head of the Norwegian immigration leaders of the last century, can no longer be disputed."

Cleng Peerson was not only the Father of Norwegian Immigration to America, but he was also the Pathfinder of the Norwegian settlements in the West. He was not satisfied with the
conditions in the Kendall Colony. The great Mississippi Valley
was now opening up. People were moving westward, some by
way of the Erie Canal and the Great Lakes, others by the
prairie schooner, trekking slowly toward the setting sun. Aided
largely by this stream of settlers, Ohio increased its population
in the decade of 1820-1830 by 256,469, Indiana by 195,853, Illinois by 102,234, and Michigan by 22,743. Peerson caught the
spirit and started for the West to find a new site for his colonists. He walked as far as Chicago, which was then, in 1833,
a little village of only 20 huts. A French half-breed offered him
an 80 acre farm in what is now the Loop district for a pipe and
a change of clothing, but Cleng would not take the bargain. The
marshes of Chicago did not appeal to him. He proceeded on
to Milwaukee, then a hamlet of only three rude huts, surrounded
by deep and dark forests.

Returning to Chicago, he set out across the open plains of

Illinois, almost due west. After some days' wandering, weary one day he lay down on top of a hill under a tree to rest. "He slept and dreamed," says Anderson, "and in his dream he saw the wild prairie changed into a cultivated region, teeming with all kinds of grain and fruit most beautiful to behold; that splendid houses and barns stood all over the land, occupied by a rich, prosperous and happy people. Alongside the fields of waving grain large herds of cattle were feeding. Cleng interpreted this as a vision and as a token from Almighty God that his countrymen should come there and settle. He forgot his pain and hunger and thanked God that He had permitted his eyes to behold this beautiful region and he decided to advise his countrymen to come west and settle there. He thought of Moses, who, from the mountain, had looked into the land of promise. Refreshed and nerved anew by his dream, he went back to Kendall and persuaded his friends to emigrate to La Salle Co., Ill." Cleng's dream has been fulfilled. And on the spot where he dreamed this dream, at Norway, Ill., there should be placed a proud monument in memory of his great services to the Norwegian people in America. Every one with Norwegian blood in his veins should contribute his mite to this memorial.

Just a word or two about his later life, full both of realistic and romantic incident. In 1834 he brought the main body of the Sloopers to La Salle Co., Ill. In 1837 he founded the Shelby County settlement in Missouri. In 1838 he made a second visit to Norway. In 1839 he returned to America. In 1840 he made a settlement in Lee County, Iowa. In 1842 he made a third trip to Norway. In 1847, having sold his farm lands in Missouri and Iowa, he joined the Erik Janson colony at Bishop Hill, Henry Co., Ill. This was a Swedish communistic settlement, established in 1846. He contributed all his possessions to the colony, and, though 65 years old, he married a young Swedish woman, a member of the Jansonite sect. Shortly after his marriage he departed from the colony and left his wife, never to return to her, "stripped," as he said, "of everything except his honor." The next two years he spent in the Fox River Settlement, La Salle Co., which he had been instrumental in founding, and which now had become populous and prosperous. A man past 65, he could now have lived here at Fox River, among friends, to the end of his days. But he was still the restless seeker after new fields. In 1849 he went to Texas to investigate as to a new site for a Norwegian settlement. In 1850 he went back to Illinois, only to return to Texas, with a company of immigrants. He lived near Dallas, Texas, from 1850 to

1854, and in Bosque County, Texas, from 1854 to the day of his death, Dec. 16, 1865. According to T. T. Colwick, postmaster at Norse, Texas, the Texas Legislature presented Peerson with a gift of 320 acres of land in Neils, Bosque County, Texas, as an appreciation of his services as a pioneer leader. He was a carpenter by trade and a sample of his skill is seen in the picture of his chair which was furnished for this book by Cleng's friend, Jacob Olson, Clifton, Texas. Though twice married, he had no children. In his first marriage he took to wife an elderly woman, Catherine————who gave him

Cleng Peerson's Chair

(Made by Cleng himself, now owned by Jacob Olson, Clifton, Texas)

wealth. In his second marriage he married a girl at least 40 years his junior, and her sect got his last cent. Her name was Charlotte Marie ————. She died of the cholera in 1849. He never had any children.

A monument on his grave, erected in 1876 at a cost of $300.00, bears an inscription in Norwegian on one side and in English on the opposite side, which reads:

Cleng Peerson
the first Norwegian immigrant
to
America, .
born in Norway, Europe,
May 17, 1782,
came to America in 1821,
and died in Texas, Dec. 16, 1865.
Grateful countrymen in Texas erected this
monument to his memory.

In 1921 a centennial was held at Norse, Tex., at his grave, O. M. Norlie delivering the anniversary address. A similar celebration was held also at two of the chief Norwegian cultural centers in America, at Decorah, Ia., with Gisle Bothne as the chief speaker, and at Minneapolis, Minn., with Theodore C. Blegen as the centennial orator.

There has been considerable controversy as to Cleng Peerson's character and historical importance. He has been called a shiftless tramp, and it must be admitted that he had some of the characteristics of a vagabond. He was a rover, but not an aimless one. Blegen is right in his characterization of his person and work: "In truth, he appears to have been actuated constantly by the high aim of searching out favorable places for settlement by Norwegian immigrants, and he served again and again as leader and guide and instigator of movements of immigration to America and to the settlements in the West in the future of which he had faith. He usually owned land, even though he did not actually cultivate it . . . . Never content to remain in one place and win the ordinary rewards of patient work, he traveled back and forth across the Atlantic, and trudged from frontier to frontier, always searching for desirable lands, and leading to these lands groups of settlers who possessed the qualities which he lacked, who founded settlements, who built homes, and, conquering the wilderness to which they came, achieved that prosperity which was the lode-star that had drawn them to the West. Professor Svein Nilssen, who published in 1869 and 1870 the results of numerous interviews and extensive researches in the old settlements, declares without qualification that Cleng Peerson exercised a greater influence upon the early Norwegian immigration and settlement than any other man." Says Nilssen: "Despite his faults and shortcomings, Cleng Peerson was certainly the right man to head the movement. Unsteady though he was, none could deny him honor and uprightness. He was good-hearted and always prepared to help others. . . . . . He was always a faithful friend of the needy and suffering. His goal was to work for the temporal happiness of his fellow-beings."

His Texas friends, who knew him well, all accord him high tribute. T. T. Colwick writes: "His inherent honesty, nobility and benevolence were expressed in the mild and pleasant features of his face. . . . . Suffering was repugnant to him in any form. He believed in the power of love instead of force. He was the most unselfish man I have known. His chief ambition was to promote the welfare of his countrymen and fellow-men." The history of the Norwegians in America can not be written without giving him an honored place as the first leader.

On July 4, 1825, occurred one of the most important events in the history of Norway, an event which at the time was scarcely noted by public officials and the press and *The Sloopers* which the Norwegian historians have hardly yet considered worthy of mention in their voluminous writings. This event was the sailing of the first emigrant boat to America.

When Cleng Peerson returned to Stavanger in 1824 he had much to tell and there were many willing ears to listen to him. Lars Larson, the Quaker leader, determined to emigrate and began to organize a company of emigrants. Together with five other men he purchased a small ship to take them across the Atlantic to that wonderful land from whence Peerson had just come. This ship was only a large boat, a 54-foot long sloop of only 38 or 40 tons, and costing 1,800 Norwegian "specie"

The Sloop "Restaurationen"

dollars, approximately $1,350.00 in American coin. Some of the present-day boats are over 1,000 times as large and costly. The Sloop had been built in Hardanger in 1801 and went by the name "Restaurationen" (The Restoration). Larson hired a captain, Lars Olson Helland, and a mate, Nels Erikson. Larson himself was a ship carpenter and most of his party had had experience on the sea as fishermen. They freighted their little bark with iron, which they intended to market in New York, and all told they numbered 52 passengers when they departed from Stavanger on July 4th, and 53 when they arrived at New York on Oct. 9, 97 days later, a girl baby having been born to Mr. and Mrs. Larson on Sept. 2nd. This child was named Margaret Allen Larson, in honor of Mrs. Allen, the Quakeress, of London, already mentioned.

The party consisted of 9 married couples, with 21 children, of whom 4 are known to have been boys, and 13 girls, while four are simply listed as children. There were also 13 single men and 1 single woman. The names of these Sloop Folk, together with the years of their birth and death, are given herewith, based largely on R. B. Anderson's "First Chapter of Norwegian Immigration :"

Family Heads:

(1) Larson, Lars (1787-1845).
(2) Larson, Martha Georgiana, nee Peerson (1803-1887).
(3) Hersdal, Cornelius Nelson (1789-1833).
(4) Hersdal, Caroline, nce Peerson (-1848).
(5) Hersdal, Nels Nelson (1800-1886).
(6) Hersdal, Bertha, nee Hervig (1804-1882).
(7) Hervig, Henrick Christopherson (-1884).
(8) Hervig (Harwick), Martha, nee — — — (-1868).
(9) Lima, Simon.
(10) Lima, — — —
(11) Madland, Thomas (1778-1826).
(12) Madland, — — — (1768-1829).
(13) Rossadal, Daniel Stenson (1779-1854).
(14) Rossadal, Bertha, nee Stavøson (-1854).
(15) Stene, Johannes (1779-   ).
(16) Stene, Martha (nee Kindingstad) (1780-   ).
(17) Thompson (Thorson), Oyen (1795-1826).
(18) Thompson, Bertha Caroline, nee — — — (1790-1844).

Children:

(19) Larson, Margaret Allen (1825-1916). Mrs. John Atwater.
(20) Nelson (Hersdal), Ann (1814-1858). Not married.
(21) Nelson (Hersdal) Nels (1816-1893). Married Catherine Iverson.
(22) Nelson (Hersdal), Inger (1819-1896). Married John S. Mitchell.
(23) Nelson (Hersdal), Martha (1823-   ). Married Beach Fellows.
(24) Lima, — — —
(25) Lima, — — —
(26) Lima, — — —
(27) Madland, Rachel (1807-   ). Mrs. Lars Olson Helland.
(28) Madland, Julia (1810-1846). Mrs. Gudmund Haugaas.
(29) Madland, Serena (1814-   ). Mrs. Jacob Anderson Slogvig.
(30) Rosdail (Rossadal), Ellen (1807-1884). Mrs. Cornelius Cothren.
(31) Rosdail (Rossadal), Aave (Ovee) (1809-1890). Married Gertrude Jacobs (1); Mrs. Martha Haagenson (2).
(32) Rosdail (Rossadal), Lars (1812-1837). Not married.
(33) Rosdail (Rossadal), John (1821-1893). Married — — — Quam (1); Caroline Peerson (2).
(34) Rosdail (Rossadal), Helga Hulda (1825-1914). Mrs. Erasmus Olson.
(35) Stene, Helene Cora (1812-   ).
(36) Stene, ——.
(37) Thompson, Sara (1818-   ). Mrs. George Olmstead (1); Mrs. Wm. W. Richey (2).
(38) Thompson, Anna Marie (1819-1842). Mrs. Wm. W. Richey.
(39) Thompson, Caroline (1825-1826).

Single Men:

(40) Bjaadland, Thorstein Olson (1795-1874). Married Guro Olson.
(41) Dahl (Dall), Endre (Andrew). Married Mrs. Sven Aasen.
(42) Erikson, Nels.
(43) Haugaas (Hogas), Gudmund (1800-1849). Married Julia Madland
(1); Caroline Hervig (2).
(44) Helland, Lars Olson. Married Rachel Madland.
(45) Hettletvedt, Ole Olson (-1849). Married — — — Chamberlain
(1); — — — (2).
(46) Iverson, Halvor.
(47) Johnson, George (-1849). Married — — — Nordboe.
(48) Johnson, Ole (1798-1879). Married Mrs. Malinda Frink (1);
Ingeborg ——— (2); Ingeborg Iverson (3).
(49) Slogvig, Jacob Anderson (1807-1864). Married Serena Madland.
(50) Slogvig, Knud. Married — — — Olson Hettletvedt.
(51) Stangeland, Andrew. Married Susan Cary.
(52) Thompson, Nels (-1863). Married Mrs. Bertha Caroline
Thompson.

Single Woman:

(53) Larson, Sara. Deaf and dumb sister of Lars Larson. Not married.

Thorkild Johannesen, bookkeeper, Portland, Oregon, writes that his grandfather, Johannis Stene (John Sten), had two children, Svend and Helena Cora, and that only the daughter went along to America. Svend remained to get confirmed and had instructions then to take a boat and come to America. As he did not hear from his folks any more, he stayed in Norway and died in 1867 as a sea captain. B. F. Stangland says that his father, Andrew Stangeland, came over before the Sloop, and did not, as far as he knows, return to Norway and come back on the Sloop. If these two statements are correct then the question is, Were there 53 or only 51 that came on the Sloop? If 53, who were the other two taking the place of Svend Stene and Andrew Stangeland? In a letter dated May 8, 1925, C. B. Olmstead, Springdale, Arkansas, grandson of Oyen Thompson, follows the order of all the Sloopers except B. F. Stangland in insisting that Andrew Stangeland came over on the Sloop. Though 81 years of age Olmstead is going to be at the Norse-American Centennial. He is a member of the German Missouri Synod.

It has often been claimed that the whole party was made up of Quakers, but such can not have been the case, since there were not more than 10 or 12 Quakers in the whole country of Norway in 1825. This sect has never made much headway in Norway. "In 1846," says Tverteraas, in his "Stavanger, 1814-1914," "these Quakers numbered 58 members and 107 adherents." In 1920 the official census reported only 88 Quakers in the whole land. It is sufficient to say that this expedition was started by Quakers and under the leadership of Quakers.

The Sloopers landed at Funchal, Madeira, and were kindly treated by the natives and the American consul, John H. March. In the "New York Daily Advertiser," Oct. 15, 1825, the captain and passengers of the Sloop publicly acknowledge their thanks to the American consul for his hospitality to the company when they touched the island.   After a three days' stop at Madeira, in which they replenished their provisions, they set sail again, on July 31st for the New World, and arrived ten weeks later in New York Harbor, every one hale and hearty.

Concerning their reception at New York, Rynning says: "It created universal surprise in New York that the Norwegians had ventured to sea in so small a vessel, a feat hitherto unheard of. Either through ignorance or misunderstanding the ship had carried more passengers than the American laws permitted, therefore the skipper and the ship with its cargo were seized by the authorities.   Now I can not say with certainty whether the government voluntarily dropped the matter in consideration of the ignorance of the law and child-like conduct of our good country-

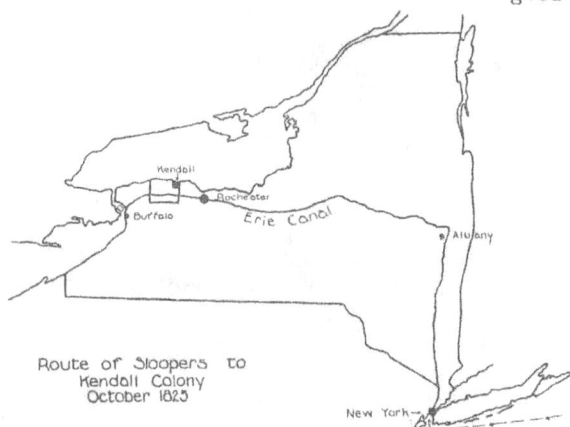

Route of Sloopers to
Kendall Colony
October 1825

men, or whether the Quakers had already at this time interposed for them; all I am sure of is that the skipper was released, and the ship and its cargo were returned to their owners."   They received some contributions from the Quakers and were led by Cleng Peerson by way of Albany to Rochester and Kendall, N. Y. The party passed through Albany on October 22nd, and attracted the attention of a reporter on the "Albany Patriot," who remarked in his issue for Oct. 24th that the newcomers "appear to be pleased with what they see in this country, if we may judge from their good-humored countenances.   Success attend their efforts in this asylum of the oppressed." Lars Larson remained behind in order to sell the boat.   He finally disposed of it at a considerable loss, receiving only $400.00 for it, after which he made his way to his party, from Albany to Rochester, on skates.

Two of the party remained in New York—the captain, Lars Olson Helland, and the mate, Nels Erikson. Lars Larson was a ship carpenter by trade and settled down at Rochester as a builder of canal boats. The rest of the Sloopers moved on to Kendall, Orleans Co., N. Y., about thirty-five miles northwest of Rochester. There, by the shore of Lake Ontario each man purchased 40 acres of land at $5.00 per acre and started with might and main to clear the forest primeval: It was no sweet task and for many years these poor pioneers suffered great need. They had no money and work was scarce. It is said that 24 of them lived in a single log house, having only one room. At the end of the second summer they were able to harvest two acres of wheat. This gave them renewed courage, and they attacked the forest

Clara Larson (Millits), Martha Larson (Patterson)
Elias Larson, Martha Peerson-Larson, Margaret Larson (Atwater)
Photo of Some of Lars Larson's Family, ca. 1858
(From a Daguerrotype owned by Jane S. Atwater)

with new vigor. And yet, during the first years, they often wished themselves back to Norway. But they had no money to get there and were too proud to return as beggars. And so they toiled on, with a helping hand now and then from well-to-do neighbors. With such help and by their own industry and thrift, they at last got their land in such condition that they could make a living from it, and could live better than in their native land.

As a result of their growing prosperity and adjustment to American conditions, their letters home to Norway began to be happier and more encouraging, and in consequence many of their

friends over there began to feel the call of the far-away and to
venture out upon the deep, determined to make their fortunes
in America. Soon other boats, much larger than the Sloop, set
out from Norway, filled with hopeful passengers, who in due
time landed at New York and hastened on to Rochester, and then
on again to the Far West, which Cleng Peerson in 1833 had discovered and made known to his Norwegian countrymen.

The story of the Sloopers has not yet been told. By the term
"Sloopers" is here meant those who came over on the Sloop
in 1825 and all their descendants. In 1895, R. B. Anderson pub-

George Larson, Georgiana Larson
Inger Larson (McFaden), Ole Johnson, Lydia Larson (Whittelsey)
Photo of Some of Lars Larson's Family and Uncle Ole Johnson,
ca. 1858
(From a Daguerrotype owned by Jane S. Atwater)

lished his "First Chapter of Norwegian Immigration," in which
he devotes about 75 pages to these very interesting people. He
describes with considerable detail the original 53 and 153 of their
descendants, in all 206. But his list was not complete. Besides,
in the thirty years since Prof. Anderson made his investigation the
Slooper tribe has multiplied fast, so that for the 100-year period
it numbers at least 1000 names. An intensive study of the whole
group for the whole period would no doubt make a fairly good
picture of the character of the Norwegian people in America.

The present writer has been on the trail of the Sloopers for five years and has already discovered 500 of the tribe, many of whom he has talked with personally. They are all at work and are found in every representative occupation. About two-thirds of them are on the farm. They are literate, most of them trained exclusively in the public schools. A number of them have college and professional degrees. Some of them can still understand Norwegian and a few can speak it. Five of them have attended Lutheran colleges; fully as many have attended Reformed institutions of learning. Most of the Sloopers are now of mixed blood due to frequent intermarriages. Nearly one-half of them live in Illinois, but they are found in goodly numbers also in Iowa, Utah, New York, Minnesota, Kansas, California and Michigan, with here and there a Slooper in Colorado, Idaho, Louisiana, Mississippi, Missouri, New Mexico, Ontario, South Dakota, Texas, Oregon, Washington and Wisconsin. Nearly one-half of them are known to belong to some Christian church—15% Lutheran, 1% Catholic, 12% Methodist, 6% Congregationalist, 5% Baptist, 2% Adventist, 1% Episcopalian, 1% Campbellite, 2% Quaker. Quite a few are members of the Mormon Church; a few are followers of Christian

Georgiana Larson and Lars Larson's House, Built in 1827

Science. Not one of them has been imprisoned for crime. They are thrifty and prosperous, law-abiding and patriotic. Many of them bear old American names; all of them are full-fledged Americans.

A few names, by way of illustration: Lars Larson, the leader of the Sloopers, was a highly respected citizen of Rochester until the day of his death, November 13, 1845. He built a house, in 1827, which still stands at 41 Atkinson St., Rochester. At this house Larson received thousands of Norwegians who were on their way from Norway to Illinois or beyond. He is known to have housed over 100 at one time and fed and entertained them for days at his own expense while giving them valuable information and advice about America. One of his children, Georgiana, still owns this house, although she lives in a statelier mansion close by. His daughter, Margaret Allen, born on the Sloop, mar-

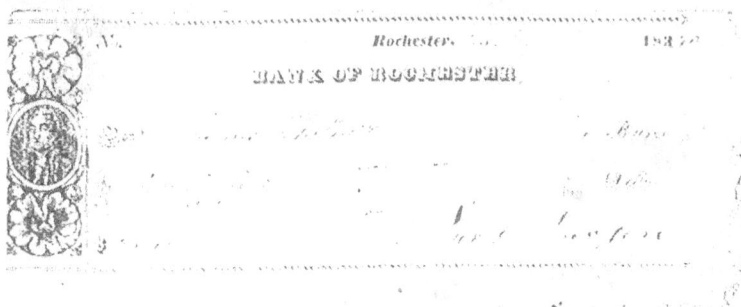

Lars Larson's Check
(Presented to Luther College Museum by Captain Louis Larson.)

ried John Atwater, city superintendent of schools at Rochester, later a physician in Chicago. One of Margaret Atwater's sons, John Larson Atwater, was a Baptist pastor at Western Springs, Ill., and the inventor of the Vive cameras, which for many years competed with the Kodaks. He is now retired, a strong man of

John L. Atwater   Jane Sara Atwater   Mabel A. Truesdell
                       Three Larson Children

73, living with two of his sisters, Jane Sara Atwater, a teacher in the Chicago Public schools nearly fifty years and principal of the Parkside School, and Mrs. Mabel Truesdell, whose daughter Charlotte is taking her A. M. in biology at the University of Chicago this year. Elias Tastad Larson, a son of Lars Larson, was a gold miner in California, one of the '49ers. A daughter of Larson, Martha Jane, began to teach private school in 1844, though only 12 years of age. She was the first Norwegian to teach English school in America, the first of a thousand Misses Larson who have labored in the school room or are still teaching the young in the way they should go. She married Elias Clark Patterson, a New York inventor of milling and threshing machinery. One of her sons, Elmore Clark Patterson, is the in-

| Cecilie Miller
(Granddaughter) | Svend Johannesen
(Son) | Martha Andersen
(Granddaughter) |

| Thorkild Johannesen
(Grandson) | Svend Johannesen
(Grandson) |

Some Descendants of Johannes Stene, Slooper

ventor of an auto shade lens, a manufacturer of auto accessories, at Chicago, and is rated as a millionaire.

Ole Johnson, half-brother of Mrs. Lars Larson, returned to Norway in 1827 to secure a wife. He lived on his farm at Kendall nearly 50 years and spent his latter years at Rochester, N. Y. One of his daughters, Inger Marie, born in 1839, is still owner of the Johnson home at Rochester. A great niece, Mrs. Anna Danielson Parker, is still living at Kendall, and is the only relative of the Sloopers there who is a full-blooded Norwegian. A grand-nephew, Joseph M. Johnson, is police lieutenant at Chicago. A grandson, Frank Edward Raymond, was employed

Ole Johnson's Bible Brought Over on the Sloop
(Owned by Emily Jane Raymond, Great-granddaughter)

for many years as assistant general manager of the Santa Fe
Railroad. Another grandson, Ole Johnson Raymond, is a phy-
sician at Wichita, Kans. A third grandson, Edmund Desire
Colon, is a shop efficiency engineer of the Pere Marquette, at
Detroit, Mich. Miss Emily Jane Raymond, a great-grand-
daughter, is an instructor in English at the high school in Holly-

Caroline C. Bower

Benjamin Franklin
Stangland

wood, Cal. She has in her possession Ole Johnson's Bible, which
he had along with him on the Sloop in 1825. Her brother Edward is taking his B. S. in chemistry at Knox College this coming
June.

The family of Cornelius Nelson Hersdal has distinguished

Inger Marie Johnson

Emily Jane Raymond

itself in many ways. Mrs. Cornelius Nelson Hersdal was a
sister of Cleng Peerson. The oldest son, Nels, born in 1816,
became a farmer at Norway, Ill. He died Aug. 29, 1893, and
was the last male survivor of the Sloop party. A daughter,
Sarah, born in 1827, began to teach district school at Fox River,
Ill., in 1845, and is the first Norwegian girl to teach public
school. She married Canute Peterson Marsett, who came from
Norway in 1837, and who afterwards became a Mormon bishop

at Ephraim, Utah. In 1852-56 Bishop Peterson acted as Mormon missionary in Norway, and brought with him to Utah about 600 Scandinavian immigrants. In 1895 she had seven children and thirty-two grandchildren. A son of Cornelius Nelson Hersdal, Peter C. Nelson, was a farmer at Larned, Kans., having, in 1895, nine children and twenty-three grandchildren living. One of Peter Nelson's daughters married Judge Henry W. Johnson, president of the Illinois Central Life Insurance Co. of Chicago. He died April 4, 1925. Another daughter married J. A. Quam, a banker at Sheridan, Ill. There are in all 212 names in the Cornelius Nelson family.

Nels Nelson Hersdal, brother of Cornelius, was the progenitor of a large and prosperous family, located in La Salle County, Ill. Rev. Helmer T. Haagenson has located 106 of the Nels Nelson offspring. In La Salle County lived also Daniel Stenson Rossadal, as do most of his descendants to this day, 255 strong. Thomas Madland had three daughters, and all three married Sloopers—Rachel married Lars Olson Helland, the captain; Julia married Gudmund Haugaas, who became a Mormon preacher and practised medicine in La Salle Co., dying of cholera during the epidemic of 1849; Serena married Jacob Anderson Slogvig, who later died as a man of wealth at San Diego, California. One of Dr. Haugaas' daughters, Caroline Cecilia, married Dr. Reuben W. Bower, in 1867. She is still living. Among her children are: Dr. George S. Bower, Galesburg, Illinois; Mrs. Dr. George C. Poundstone, Chicago; and Dr. Willis H. Bower (dentist), Sheridan, Illinois. A. S. Anderson, a son of Andrew Dahl, was a member of the Utah Constitutional Convention in 1895. Haugaas is the progenitor of 203 descendants.

Earl Nelford Larson, 1924
(6th generation of Daniel Stenson Rossadal's race)

Knud Anderson Slogvig went back to Norway in 1835 to find a wife. He not only found one in the person of a sister of Ole Olson Hettletvedt, but he was also the main cause of the great exodus from Norway in 1835. Ole Olson Hettletvedt was the first Norwegian layman to preach the Lutheran doctrine in America, the first to teach Norwegian parochial school and to act as Bible colporteur. He is said to have preached even on the

Top Row: Eric, Jesse, Gertrude, Lee Roy, Jacob, Jr.
Bottom Row: Jacob, Sr., Calvin, Orvil, Glenn, Mrs. Jacob, Sr.

The Jacob Rosdail, Sr., Family
(Jacob's father, Aave Rosdail, came over on the Sloop)

Nels Nelson (Hersdal)
(Came over on the Sloop)

Mrs. Emily Rosdail-
Fruland
(Daughter of Aave Rosdail)

Daniel Rosdail
(Son of Aave Rosdail)

Sloop. He was married twice, both times to American women.
He had three sons and a daughter. The three sons enlisted in
Co. F., 36th Regiment, Illinois Volunteers, in the Civil War.
Their names were James Webster Olson, Soren L. Olson and
Porter C. Olson. James Webster came home again without a

scar. Soren L. had his head blown off at the Battle of Mur-
freesboro, Tenn., in 1862. He was a good sergeant. Porter C.
was killed in the Battle of Franklin, Tenn., Nov. 30, 1864. He
had been a student at Beloit College, and at the opening of the
Civil War he was teaching school at Lisbon, Ill. Through his
efforts a company was recruited at Newark, made up largely of
Norwegians. He was elected captain and later promoted to
colonel. A monument to his memory has been erected at the Newark-Millington Cemetery, Ill. A centennial service was held January 11, 1925, at Newark, Ill., in honor of his father as the first Norwegian lay preacher in America. The address was made in Norwegian by O. M. Norlie. As one result of the celebration a monument will be placed over the resting place of Ole Olson Hettletvedt. His grave is on Lot 17, Block 3, Newark - Millington Cemetery. Mr. Howard W. Derby, a great-grandson of Ole Olson Hettletvedt, is a senior at the College of the Pacific, Stockton, Cal. He has written a "Sketch of the Hettletvedt Family" for his aunt, Mrs. Chas. J. Platten, Highwood Park, St. Paul, Minn. Sven Miller, in the employ of the Chicago, Milwaukee and Puget Sound Railway, is a great-grandson of Johannes Stene. The wife of President C. J. Eastvold of the Southern Minnesota District of the Norwegian Lutheran Church is a grand niece of Ole Olson Hettlevedt. She writes about the Slooper and her grandfather Knud, his brother, in "Visergutten," May 7, 1925.

Monument of Col. Porter Olson
(Son of Ole Olson Hettletvedt, Slooper)

Like Hettletvedt, Andrew Stangeland also married an American lady—Susan Cary. This was in June, 1827, before he had learned to speak English. He lived at Kendall, but later sold his land to Ole Aasland and got in exchange some land at Wolf Lake, in Noble Co., Ind. The Aaslands, now calling themselves Orslands, still live in Kendall, N. Y. One of Andrew Stangeland's sons, Benjamin Franklin Stangland, is a mechanical engineer of New York City, with homes at Morton and Rochester. B. F. Stangland (note the spelling) is the eighth of nine children. The other children are: Elezar (1829), Lydia (1830), Talock (1832), Bela (1834), Rosetta (1836), Maria (1839), Mary E. (1844), and Andrew (1849). Rosetta married Rev. A. D. Olds, is still alive and on Feb. 22, 1925, celebrated her dia-

A "Kubberulle"
(Home-made wagon used by Norwegian pioneers. Made by L. D. Reque, Koshkonong, Wisconsin. Now in Luther College Museum)

Anders A. Kloye
Leland, Ill.

Andrew Jensen
Edgerton, Wis.

James M. Wahl
Worthing, S. D.

Norwegian Pioneer Farmers
(Prominent also in local and state politics, church and school work)

mond (75th) wedding anniversary. He is the only descendant of the Sloopers who has succeeded in getting a place among the notables in "Who's Who in America." He is a cousin of Charles Emil Stangeland, Ph. D., listed in "Who's Who" as a political economist, a graduate of Augsburg Seminary, 1898, secretary to the American Legation at La Paz, Bolivia (1912-1913), at London (1914-15), and secretary of the Nonpartisan League, Bismarck, N. D., during the World War.

The Sloop "Restaurationen" reached our hospitable shores in 1825. Over a decade passed before the next boatload of Norwegians came to America. Then, in 1836, two Norwegian brigs, "Norden" (the North) and "Den Norske Klippe" (The Norwegian Rock), left Stavanger July 12th with a total of approximately 160 passengers. Meanwhile every year had brought some Norwegians to America. According to the United States Bureau of Immigration the number of immigrants from Sweden-Norway from 1820 to 1835 was as follows:

Later Arrivals, 1825-1860

1820	3	1828	10
1821	12	1829	13
1822	10	1830	3
1823	1	1831	13
1824	9	1832	313
1825	4	1833	16
1826	16	1834	42
1827	13	1835	31

The total number of immigrants from Sweden-Norway during these 16 years was 509. Some of them were no doubt Swedes; most of them were surely Norwegians. In many ways the census figures are puzzling. Only four immigrants are reported for 1825, and yet there is overwhelming evidence to prove that 53 came over on the Sloop. In 1832 313 are reported as having arrived. So far we have no other evidence to prove this.

Knud Langeland, who came to America in 1843, on the boat with which Cleng Peerson returned from his last visit to his fatherland, writes in his work on Norwegian immigration that individuals in those days who wished to come to America went by way of Gothenburg, Hamburg or Havre. R. B. Anderson lists among the immigrants of this period the following: Christian Olson and Gudman Sandsberg, 1829; Knut Evenson, Ingrebret Larson Narvig, and Gjert Gregorius Hovland, 1831; and Johan Nordboe, 1832. Flom adds the name of David Johnson as having arrived in 1832. With the exception of Johnson they all stopped for a season at Kendall, N. Y. Christian Olson moved to La Salle Co., Ill., in 1837. His son Erasmus married Helga, one of the daughters of Daniel Rossadal, the Slooper. Gudman Sandsberg made his home at Mission, Ill., in 1836. His daughter married M. B. Mitchell, a cigar dealer in Ottawa, Ill. Knut Evenson settled in Kendall, where he died. His daughter Catherine married Nels Nelson (Hersdal), Jr., the last male survivor of the Sloop. Ingrebret Narvig joined Cleng Peerson on his journey to Illinois in 1833. He tired of the march and went to work for a farmer at Erie, Monroe Co., Mich., where he remained until 1856. Then he moved to Green Lake Co., Wis., where he resided until 1885, and finally he moved to Tyler,

Minn., where he died in 1892. He was married twice, to American women, and had twelve children. He was the first Norwegian to settle in Michigan. He practised medicine as a side calling, but did not ask for fees.

Gjert Hovland was probably the first emigrant from Hardanger. After a four years' stay at Kendall he moved to La Salle Co., Ill., in 1835. He wrote letters home to friends urging emigration, and hundreds of copies of his letters were circulated far and wide and were no small factor in leading many people in southwestern Norway to emigrate. Johan Nordboe came from Ringebu in Gudbransdal in eastern Norway and is one of the first to come from some other region of Norway than Stavanger. He settled in Kendall in 1832; in La Salle Co, Ill., in 1836; in Shelby Co., Mo., in 1837; and in Dallas, Tex., in 1838, where he lived on a farm of 1920 acres and practised medicine. He was the first Norwegian to settle in Texas. David Johnson had been a sailor. In New York he secured work as pressman. In 1834 he went to Chicago as operator of the newly installed cylinder press of the "Chicago Democrat." He was the first permanent Norwegian settler of Chicago.

In 1835 Knud Anderson Slogvig, the Slooper, returned to Norway to get married. For ten years the people had been reading the letters from America, and with growing interest. Some of the letters were sad and discouraging, telling of hard times and advising people to stay at home; most of the letters were joyful and optimistic, portraying victory after struggle and recommending emigration. These letters had been read with the deepest interest, but here was a man who had spent ten years in the New World. The news of his arrival spread like wildfire and he was the hero of the day. People came from far and near to see Slogvig and to interview him. Through him Norway got its first real taste of the "America Fever," and he unwittingly became one of the chief promoters of emigration. The two ships, "Norden" and "Den Norske Klippe," which left Stavanger in 1836, were a direct answer to his tale. Most of the passengers on these boats went directly to La Salle Co., via Larson's home in Rochester. Larson's patience in dealing with the newcomers never waned and his generosity in helping them never was withdrawn.

The next year, 1837, witnessed two more ships depart from Norway with passengers that could not be accommodated in 1836. One of the ships was called "Enigheden" (Harmony) and sailed from Stavanger with 93 passengers, from the city and county of Stavanger. The other ship bore the name of the sea-god Aegir. It departed from Bergen on July 4th, carrying eighty-four passengers from Hardanger, Voss and Bergen, with also one man, the famous Ole Rynning, from Trondhjem. Thereby a new movement in immigration was inaugurated, in that other sections of Norway than Stavanger began to contribute their quota of immigrants to America.

There are many names out of the 337 on these four ships in 1836 and 1837 that are worthy of special mention. Bjørn Anderson Kvelve, for example, one of the passengers on the "Norden," was the first settler in the town of Albion, Dane Co., Wis., and a very active and useful man in Norwegian-American history. He lived through the hardships of pioneer life at a time when the nearest town was 70 miles distant and the fastest conveyance was the oxcart through a trackless wilderness. And just as fortune began to smile upon his labors, the cholera came and ended his life. He had 10 children: Andrew Anderson became a farmer; Bernt, a merchant; Abel, a Lutheran pastor; two girls married Lutheran pastors; two girls married farmers; two children died before maturity; and Rasmus B. Anderson is internationally known as university professor, author, editor, lecturer, business promoter, diplomat and authority on things Norwegian-American.

Another notable in this group was Hans Valder, a passenger on the "Enigheden." Valder lived one year in Michigan, then moved to Mission, Ill., in 1838. In 1844 he became a Baptist preacher, the first Norwegian Baptist preacher in the world. In 1853 he retired from the ministry and became a farmer and hotel keeper at Newburg, Minn. In 1871 he served as a member of the Minnesota State Legislature. In 1892 he had sixteen children and more than 150 descendants living in six different states. His son Charles was the proprietor of the Valder Business College and Normal School, Decorah, Iowa., 1888-1922.

Another important character who emigrated with "Enigheden," was Hans Barlien, a native of Overhalden, Trondhjem. He had been a member of the Norwegian Storthing. A radical in politics and a liberal in religion, he had as editor of a paper in Norway provoked the enmity of the ruling classes and was subjected to considerable persecution. Therefore he emigrated. Barlien was a member of Cleng Peerson's party that settled in Shelby Co., Mo., in 1837, and in 1840 he was a member of the party that settled at Sugar Creek, Lee Co., Ia. This was the first Norwegian settlement in Iowa, and Barlien is considered as its real founder.

A number of important men came over on the Aegir, notably the following: Mons Adland, Nels Frøland, Anders Nordvig and Ole Rynning. Adland came from Samnanger, near Bergen. He settled at Beaver Creek, Iroquois Co., Ill., and together with his wife was the last to abandon that marshy and malarial settlement. He then moved to Racine Co., Wis., becoming the founder of the Yorkville Settlement. His daughter Martha became the wife of Rev. Adolph C. Preus, one of the early patriarchs of the Norwegian Synod. Adland was a brother of Knud Langeland, well known journalist. Nels Frøland also came from Samnanger and settled in Beaver Creek. His son, Lars Fruland, born March 15, 1831, is still alive and resides at Newark, Ill., spry as a man of 60, in spite of his 96 years of hard labor. He has seven children and 18 grandchildren. Anders Nordvig was a brother-in-law of Mons Adland. He died in the Beaver Creek Settlement. His daughter Malinda married Iver Larson Bø, who emigrated from Voss, Norway, in 1844. Victor F. Lawson, editor and publisher of the "Chicago Daily News," the largest newspaper in the world, is her son, born 1850. He has been president of The Associated Press, is Father of the Postal Savings Bank in America, established Daily N e w s Fresh Air Fund and Lincoln Park Sanitarium for sick poor children and has been active i n philanthropic work.

Ole Rynning was a graduate of the University of Christiania, class of 1830. He settled in the B e a v e r C r e e k marshes, south of Chicago, and like the rest

Facsimile Picture of First Page Rynning's Book

of the colony, took sick. While he lay confined to his death bed he wrote a small book about America, which one of his companions, Ansten Nattesta, took with him to Norway in 1838 and had it printed in Christiania (now Oslo). The title page of the book reads: "True Account of America for the Information and Help of Peasant and Commoner. Written by a Norwegian who arrived there in the month of June, 1837. Christiania, 1838." It is the first book written by a Norwegian-American and the first book written about the Norwegian-Americans. It is simple, clear, accurate, scholarly, and might have been written by a man who had spent a long life in America, instead of a newcomer fighting fever in a swamp. The book is in the form of questions and answers, questions which he asked himself about America before coming here, and answers which he had been able to make after having come here. The questions cover such ground as: Location, distance, history, topography, climate, population, government, Norwegian settlements, cost of land and living, wages, religion, schools, language, dangers from disease, wild beasts and Indians, kind of people who should emigrate, dangers on the sea and as to slavery, and guiding advice for travelers. The book had a wide distribution and a profound influence for over a decade, and Rynning has been considered second in importance only to Cleng Peerson, as one of the fathers of Norwegian im-

Ole K. Nattesta   H. O. Nattesta   Charles Orrin Solberg

Three Generations of Nattestas

migration. Rynning was not married, but he had a sister, whose son, Rev. Bernt J. Muus, immigrated in 1859 and distinguished himself as one of the most energetic and stalwart of Lutheran pastors in the pioneer days, numbering among his achievements also the founding of St. Olaf College, Nov. 6, 1874.

Some of the immigrants from this year (1837) came by way of Gothenburg. They came from Numedal and Telemarken in south central Norway and are a sort of advance guard from those districts. From Vaegli in Numedal came two brothers, Ole and Ansten Nattestad, and from Tinn in upper Telemarken came Erik Gauteson Midbøen, Mrs. Thorsten Thorson Rue, and several others.

The Nattestad brothers, known as Nattesta in this country, were also members of the ill-fated Beaver Creek Settlement in 1837. Ole Nattesta wrote an account of his journey, beginning April 8, 1837, with his departure from home, until Feb. 21, 1838, just before leaving Beaver Creek. From Beaver Creek the brothers went to La Salle Co., Ill. In July, 1838, Ole Nattesta entered Wisconsin and made his home at Jefferson Prairie, also known as Clinton, thus becoming the first Norwegian settler in Wisconsin. His brother Ansten returned to Norway with the two manuscripts about America, Rynning's "True Account of America" and Ole Nattesta's "Day Book." The latter was printed in Drammen in 1839. The original manuscript was recovered by a son, James Nattesta, on a trip to Norway in 1900. A printed copy of the first edition is in the possession of the youngest son, Henry O., who still occupies the original homestead, a farm that has so far never failed of a crop. A grandson of Ole Nattesta is Dr. Charles Orrin Solberg, president of Augustana College and Normal School, Sioux Falls, S. D. The

Rev. N. E. Boe　　　Hon. Oley Nelson　　　Gen. Alfred Wm. Bjornstad

Veterans of Three Wars

significance of Nattesta was that he led the stream of Norwegian migration into Wisconsin. The direction of the stream was uncertain until he took the step he did.

One of the leaders from Tinn was Erik Gauteson Midbøen. "He had a large family," says Anderson, "and settled in La Salle County, but fortune does not appear to have smiled on him. He became a Mormon, and in the capacity of a Mormon preacher, he made a visit to Norway and died soon after his return to America." That is, he was one of the first Mormon missionaries to Norway, if not the very first. Mrs. Thorsten T. Rue was a widow with two sons, Thorstein and John. They made their home at first in La Salle County, Ill.; then moved to Shelby County, Mo., in 1838; in 1840 they departed for Lee County, Ia.; and in 1846 they became a part of the Blue Mounds Settlement in Dane County, Wis. John Rue took the name

John Thompson, better known as "Snowshoe" Thompson from the fact that for twenty years (1856-1876) he was the U. S. mail carrier from Carson Valley, Ida., to Placerville, Cal., over the Sierra Nevada Mountains, covering the ninety mile route on skis. He had gone to California as a gold hunter in 1851 and is said to have worked faithfully for the postal department twenty years without any other pay than fine promises. His life was filled with heroic adventure. Only once in his life was he afraid, he is reported to have said, and that was when he had to pass six hungry, howling wolves. Thompson's skis are on exhibit at the capitol at Sacramento—silent witnesses of a day that is gone forever.

It is impossible to list all the ships and representative men that came from Norway after 1837. It is also impossible to say just how many immigrants did come. The immigration statistics of the U. S. Bureau of Immigration places Norwegians and Swedes in one rubric until 1869. It has been estimated that during this period at least two-thirds of the arrivals from Sweden-Norway were Norwegians. The statistics of immigration kept by the U. S. officials do not agree with those kept by the officials of Norway. The two lists, for the period 1836-1860, are as follows:

IMMIGRATION STATISTICS, 1836-1860

Year	As reported by the U. S. Census Swedes-Norwegians Number	As reported by the Norw. Census Norwegians only Number
1836	57	200
1837	200	200
1838	60	100
1839	324	400
1840	55	300
1836-1840	786	1200
1841	195	400
1842	553	700
1843	1748	1600
1844	1311	1200
1845	928	1100
1841-1845	4735	5000
1846	1916	1300
1847	1307	1600
1848	903	1400
1849	3473	4000
1850	1569	3700
1846-1850	9168	12000

	As reported by the U. S. Census Swedes-Norwegians Number	As reported by the Norw. Census Norwegians only Number
1851	2424	2640
1852	4103	4030
1853	3364	6050
1854	3531	5950
1855	821	1600
1851-1855	14243	20270
1856	1157	3200
1857	1712	6400
1858	2430	2500
1859	1091	1800
1860	208	1900
1856-1860	6688	15800
1836-1860	35620	54270
1825-1860	36094	54323

The United States Census for 1860 enumerates 43,995 Norwegians born in Norway and 18,625 Swedes born in Sweden, 2.3 times as many Norwegians as Swedes. On the basis of this report the immigration figures of the United States Bureau are too small and those of Norway are too large.

3. The Norwegian Population, 1825-1860

The Sloop Folk comprised nine married couples whose average age was thirty-two years. They had twenty-one children whose average age was about eight years. And there were thirteen single men and one single woman, the average age of these fourteen being about 24 years. The average age of the whole group was 20.4 years. There were therefore several children born to these young married couples before 1830 and thereafter. Lars Larson, for example, had, in addition to the Sloop baby, Margaret Allen, several other children:

Inger Marie, born Feb. 18, 1827, married Wm. F. McFaden, 1872.

Lydia Glazier, born Nov. 18, 1828, married Fred C. Whittelsey.

Elias Tastad, born July 9, 1830, married Effie ———.

Martha Jane, born July 30, 1832, married Elias C. Patterson, 1879.

Clara Elizabeth, born July 30, 1834, married Alfred E. Willets.

George Monroe, born July 8, 1841, married Louise ———.

Georgiana Henrietta, born July 19, 1845, not married.

The other families had as a rule large families The young bachelors married as soon as they could get around to it. Andrew

Stangeland met Susan Cary and it proved to be a case of love at first sight, so they married, in 1827. He had two children by 1830 —Elezar, Jan. 11, 1829; Lydia, Feb. 20, 1830. Ole Johnson went back to Norway to find a bride in the person of Mrs. Malinda Frink. He married three times and had in all ten children, born between 1827 and 1850. Oyen Thompson died in 1826 and his brother Nels married his widow in 1827. Nels had three children: Serena, born March 18, 1828; Abraham, born Dec. 23, 1830; and Caroline, born July 15, 1833. The children that came over on the Sloop soon were of age and got married. Julia Madland, for instance, married Dr. Gudmund Haugaas, in 1827, and had ten children by him before her death in 1846; her sister, Serena Madland, married Jacob Anderson Slogvig in 1831. Rachel, the oldest, married Captain Lars Olson Helland, possibly in 1825. Ellen Rosdail married Cornelius Cothren in 1832 and had six children, twenty-three grandchildren, thirty-nine great-grandchildren, and twenty-five great-great-grandchildren (sixth generation from Daniel Rossadal, Slooper). Caroline Rosdail was born April 1, 1829; she married Jens Jacobs, and had six children by him. She had fourteen grandchildren and twenty-eight great-grandchildren.

Margaret Allen Larson married John Atwater, in 1851, and had nine children, five of them within this period:

John Larson, born August 7, 1852, married Emma F. Scranton, 1874.

Margaret Elizabeth, born Nov. 12, 1854, died Sept. 25, 1855.

Jane Sara, born March 3, 1858, not married.

Lydia Eva, born Oct. 12, 1860, died August 27, 1861.

Clara Josephine, born Feb. 5, 1863, died Dec. 6, 1866.

Mary Anna Lincoln, born May 6, 1865, died Dec. 11, 1866.

Emma Mabel, born Oct. 4, 1868, married Chas. Harvey Truesdell, 1895.

Grace Lillian, born Nov. 6, 1870, died Sept. 15, 1872.

Sarah Nelson, daughter of Cornelius Nelson Hersdal, was born Feb. 16, 1827, and on July 2, 1849, married Canute Peterson (Marsett), afterwards a Mormon bishop. Her first son, Peter Cornelius, was born June 2, 1850, at Salt Lake City. In 1895 she had seven children and thirty-two grandchildren. All this is written to illustrate that the Norwegian-Americans were a prolific race. 106 Nels Nelsons have been traced, 203 Haugaases, 212 Cornelius Nelsons, 255 Rosdails, etc. In the absence of full facts as to the second and third generations the following conservative estimate has been made:

Year	1st Generation	2nd Generation	3rd Generation	Total
1830............	*100	*5	0	*105
1840............	*1,000	*100	0	*1,100
1850............	12,678	*1,902	*2	*14,582
1860............	45,995	*10,999	*64	*55,058

* Estimate.

4. NORWEGIAN SETTLEMENTS, 1825-1860

Birds of a feather flock together. So do immigrant new-comers from foreign lands, whenever possible. Thus our Sloop-er friends found it expedient to settle down together at Kendall, N. Y. Later, most of these moved farther west and made new settlements, similar to the one they forsook. In 1830 there was as yet only one Norwegian settlement. In 1840 there were seventeen, located in six different states. In 1850 there were fifty-three or more, distributed throughout a dozen states. In 1860, more than 110 counties, scattered over fifteen states, had one or more Norwegian settlements. In addition to this there were Norwegians who for valid reasons did not live in a Nor-wegian settlement. Thus, Lars Larson, the leader of the Sloopers, did not go to Kendall, but preferred to remain at Rochester, where he could ply his trade as boatbuilder. The U. S. Census of 1850 shows that there were Norwegians in 26 states, that is, in fourteen states besides those that had Norwegian settlements. The U. S. Census for 1860 shows that there were Norwegians in thirty-six states, that is, in twenty-one states besides those that had Norwegian settlements. The Nor-wegian foreign-born population had increased from about 100 in 1830, to about 1000 in 1840, to 12,678 in 1850 and 43,995 in 1860.

The following table, with accompanying map, gives a bird's eye view of the progress in settlement making during this period.

NORWEGIAN SETTLEMENTS BY COUNTIES

No.	Year	State	County
1.	1825.....................	New York	Orleans
2.	1834.....................	Illinois	La Salle
3.	1835.....................	Indiana	White
4.	1836.....................	Illinois	Cook
5.	1837.....................	Illinois	Iroquois
6.	1837.....................	Missouri	Shelby
7.	1837.....................	Illinois	Stephanson
8.	1838.....................	Indiana	Nobles
9.	1838.....................	Illinois	Boone
10.	1838.....................	Wisconsin	Rock
11.	1839.....................	Illinois	Kendall
12.	1839.....................	Illinois	Grundy
13.	1839.....................	Wisconsin	Waukesha
14.	1839.....................	Wisconsin	Racine
15.	1839.....................	Wisconsin	Milwaukee

No.	Year	State	County
16.	1840	Wisconsin	Dane
17.	1840	Iowa	Lee
18.	1841	Wisconsin	Iowa
19.	1841	Wisconsin	Lafayette
20.	1842	Wisconsin	Walworth
21.	1843	Wisconsin	Dodge
22.	1844	Wisconsin	Green
23.	1845	Wisconsin	Columbia
24.	1845	Wisconsin	Fond du Lac
25.	1845	Iowa	Clayton
26.	1845	Texas	Henderson
27.	1846	Illinois	Jo Davies
28.	1846	Wisconsin	Osaukee
29.	1846	Wisconsin	Manitowoc
30.	1846	Wisconsin	Winnebago
31.	1847	Utah	Salt Lake
32.	1847	Michigan	Muskegon
33.	1848	Wisconsin	Brown
34.	1848	Wisconsin	Crawford
35.	1848	Wisconsin	Jackson
36.	1848	Wisconsin	Jefferson
37.	1848	Wisconsin	Vernon
38.	1848	Texas	Kaufman
39.	1849	California	....
40.	1849	Iowa	Fayette
41.	1849	Wisconsin	La Crosse
42.	1849	Wisconsin	Monroe
43.	1849	Wisconsin	Pierce
44.	1849	Wisconsin	Portage
45.	1849	Wisconsin	Richland
46.	1850	Minnesota	Ramsey
47.	1850	Wisconsin	Adams
48.	1850	Wisconsin	Juneau
49.	1850	Wisconsin	Waushara
50.	1850	Wisconsin	Waupaca
51.	1850	Iowa	Allamakee
52.	1850	Iowa	Winneshiek
53.	1850	Minnesota	Ramsey
54.	1850	Minnesota	Goodhue
55.	1851	Michigan	Manistee
56.	1851	Wisconsin	Door
57.	1851	Minnesota	Fillmore
58.	1852	Wisconsin	Burnett
59.	1852	Iowa	Mitchell
60.	1852	Minnesota	Carver
61.	1852	Minnesota	Winona
62.	1852	Pennsylvania	Potter
63.	1853	Iowa	Worth
64.	1853	Minnesota	Dakota
65.	1853	Minnesota	Houston
66.	1853	Iowa	Clinton
67.	1854	New Hampshire	Coos
68.	1854	Wisconsin	Kewaunee
69.	1854	Wisconsin	St. Croix
70.	1854	Wisconsin	Trempealeau
71.	1854	Texas	Bosque
72.	1854	Iowa	Benton
73.	1854	Iowa	Chickasaw
74.	1854	Iowa	Iowa
75.	1854	Iowa	Story

No.	Year	State	County
76.	1854	Minnesota	Dodge
77.	1854	Minnesota	Olmsted
78.	1854	Minnesota	Steele
79.	1854	Minnesota	Mower
80.	1855	Wisconsin	Grant
81.	1855	Illinois	Livingston
82.	1855	Iowa	Hamilton
83.	1855	Minnesota	Faribault
84.	1855	Minnesota	Freeborn
85.	1855	Minnesota	Rice
86.	1855	Minnesota	Sibley
87.	1855	Minnesota	Waseca
88.	1856	Wisconsin	Buffalo
89.	1856	Iowa	Winnebago
90.	1856	Michigan	Oceana
91.	1856	Minnesota	McLeod
92.	1856	Minnesota	Meeker
93.	1856	Minnesota	Watonwan
94.	1857	Minnesota	Blue Earth
95.	1857	Minnesota	Chippewa
96.	1857	Minnesota	Red Wood
97.	1857	Nebraska	Dixon
98.	1857	Kansas	Greenwood
99.	1858	Illinois	Lee
100.	1858	Minnesota	Kandiyohi
101.	1858	Minnesota	Wright
102.	1858	Kansas	Atchison
103.	1859	Wisconsin	Polk
104.	1859	South Dakota	Clay
105.	1860	South Dakota	Yankton
106.	1860	South Dakota	Union
107.	1860	Minnesota	Jackson
108.	1860	Kansas	Brown
109.	1860	Kansas	Doniphan
110.	1860	Iowa	Woodbury

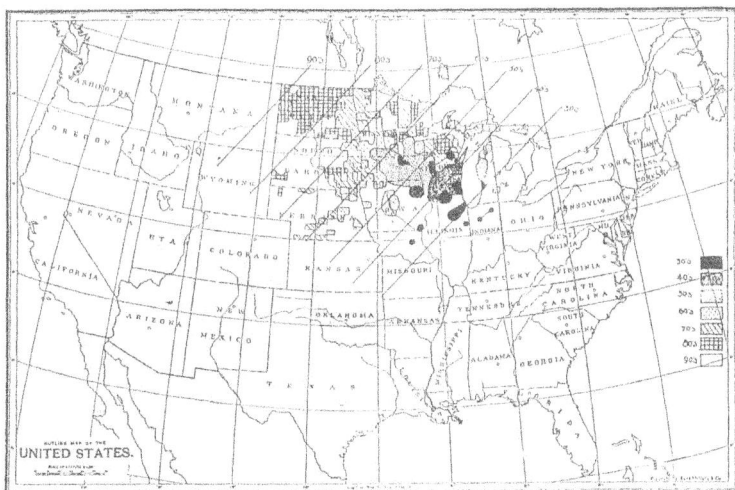

Settlements by Decades

(The diagonal lines represent decades beginning with the '30s. For every 10 years the line moves northwestward about 100 miles)

NORWEGIAN SETTLEMENTS BY STATES

State	No. Settlements	Foreign-born Norwegians, 1850	Foreign-born Norwegians, 1860
Wisconsin..........	37	8651	21442
Minnesota	27	7	8425
Iowa	·15	361	5688
Illinois	10	2415	4891
Kansas	4	....	223
Michigan	3	110	440
Dakota (S. D.) ...	3	....	129
Texas	3	....	326
Indiana	2	18	38
New York	1	392	539
New Hampshire ...	1	2	5
Missouri	1	155	146
Nebraska	1	....	.....
California	1	....	715
Utah	1	....	.....
Total—			
these 15 states....	110	12111	43007
Total—other states	0	567	988
Grand total	110	12678	43095

In the above list it will be seen that 37 of the settlements were located in Wisconsin, 27 in Minnesota, 15 in Iowa, 10 in Illinois, four in Kansas, three in Michigan, three in Texas, three in South Dakota, two in Indiana and one each in New York, New Hampshire, Missouri, Nebraska, California, and Utah. In 1860 nearly fifty per cent of the Norwegians were located in Wisconsin.

It should be noted that these early Norwegian settlements were all pioneer settlements, and that they were on the very outskirts of civilization at the time they were made. They lacked practically all the modern conveniences in the home and on the farm; they had no church, school or market awaiting them. Neighbors were few and far between. There were no roads; the prairies were trackless. The rivers and marshes were difficult to ford. The woods and forests were almost impassable. Even the matter of reaching their destination was a work of no small concern, because the steamboat and the railroad were as yet only in the earliest pioneer stage of their development. Wild beasts and hostile Indians were their neighbors; destructive prairie fires and death dealing plagues made their annual visits.

The Erie Canal had just been opened in 1825, the year in which the advance guard of Sloopers came. In Pennsylvania, the opening of this canal caused great excitement, and well it might, for traffic would now go by water through New York for about one-third what it would cost over land. The people of

Pennsylvania demanded canals and roads at state expense to meet the competition. The energy of Pennsylvania alarmed the neighbors in Maryland, who now demanded a speedy and cheap route to the West, which all felt was now opening up. It was decided to build the Baltimore and Ohio Railroad, and on July 4, 1828, the work of construction began. In 1830 the road was opened—a distance of fifteen miles. The rails were of wood and the cars were drawn by horses. An era of railroad building began. In 1835 there were twenty-two railroads in the United States, but only two were west of the Alleghanies, and not one was 140 miles long. Steam engines began to come into use in 1830, and after 1836 became the sole locomotive power. In 1840

Prairie Schooner

the railroad mileage had increased to 4,026 miles for the whole country. In 1850 to 9,021 miles, and in 1860 to 30,626 miles. The Norwegian people, however, went on ahead of the railroads in the making of the 110 settlements listed above and others not listed. Most of the immigrants went by the canal route through New York and then by steamboat on the Great Lakes to Milwaukee and Chicago. Some stepped off at Detroit and then proceeded by ox cart the rest of the way, while others journeyed the whole distance, from New York to the Mississippi Valley in their prairie schooners.

The first Norwegian settlement, as already stated, was at Kendall, Orleans County, New York, in the northeastern corner of the county on the shores of Lake Ontario *New York, 1825* in northwestern New York. The land here was heavily wooded and the clearing of the forests required hard work, but no income. The people naturally suffered great privations and often longed to get back to the Old Country, a fact shown very plainly in some of the letters home, which have been preserved, and in the traditions which have been handed down to their descendants.

In 1923-1924 Gunnar Malmin was sent by the Carnegie Foundation and the American-Scandinavian Foundation to Scandinavia to make researches concerning immigration. Malmin found a large number of interesting letters and newspaper accounts, some of which have been published serially in "Decorah Posten" under the title "Norsk Landnam i U. S." (Norwegian Landtaking in the U.S.). A number of these letters are bright and cheerful; others are gloomy and sorrowful. "Fruitful land," remarks Torsten Gaarden, Racine, October 28, 1843, but he tells a sad tale of 31 who died of the cholera that fall. Wisconsin is best, thinks Gunder Misbø; Texas is best, is Halvor Aslakson's dictum. Jørgen A. Wibelve writes from Pein Lek (Pine Lake), Weskontien (Wisconsin), October 12, 1841, that he made the trip in eight weeks. John N. Gjøsdal relates that 68 from Tinn were already dead of the swamp fever, in 1844. One man writes from Decorah, Eovei (Iowa), August 1, 1857, saying that he was bid $2,000.00 for his 120 acres. An anonymous writer from Milwaukee, August 12, 1853, complains: "Woe is me, that was so foolish as to leave Norway, and I surely have been punished for my folly." "Glorious land!" writes Halvor H. Bjornestad of Chicago, January 4, 1844, "my advice is: Come here." Halvor J. Nymoen of Modum tells, January 9, 1840, that he left Gothenburg on an American boat May 25, 1839. The immigrants on this boat, "The Constitution," were badly mistreated. "We were kept as prisoners," he writes. "The captain had a vicious dog on board who went about loose and bit both adults and children many times, but the crew just laughed at this. They called us devils. The sailors threatened to hit me with a hammer in order to force me to drink whiskey. Many of us were beaten up." Another one writes that he had his collar bone broken by the captain of his boat. He had not understood the captain. Most interesting and judicious of all the letters are those by Munch-Ræder, a law graduate, who wrote for the "Norske Rigstidende," November 6, 1847-July 3, 1848, 20 letters in all. He prophesies that the United States will become one of the greatest of nations and that the Norwegians will contribute largely to its making.

In 1871 Arad Thomas published a pioneer history of Orleans County in which he speaks about the first Norwegian settlement, in part, as follows: "They came from Norway together and took up land in a body. They were an industrious, prudent and worthy people, held in good repute by people in that vicinity. After a few years they began to move away to join their countrymen who had settled in Illinois, and but a few of that colony are still in Kendall. They thought it very important that every family should have land and a home of their own. A neighbor once asked a little Norwegian boy, whose father happened to be too poor to own land, where his father lived, and was answered: 'Oh, we don't live nowhere. We hain't got no land.'"

Concerning the progress of this colony, interesting information is

Lewis Parker and Wife, nee Anna Danielson, Kendall, N. Y.

Northeast Corner of Orleans County Kendall Settlement

given in three letters found in Anderson's "First Chapter." One is a letter by H. Harwick, being the Henrick Hervig, Slooper. He says: "After the land was cleared, we found the soil to be very good, and a crop grows here as good as in few places in the vicinity." At the time of his letter, January 20, 1871, the land was worth from $50.00 to $100.00 an acre. Now (in 1925) it is the best Baldwin apple tract in the world. The main part of his letter relates to the church conditions in the colony. He says that they have many churches and various denominations, but he does not mention either Quakers or Lutherans. It seems that they never had either Quaker or Lutheran congregations in this colony. For that reason, Ole Johnson, a Quaker, finally left the colony and moved to Rochester where he could attend Quaker meetings. He was a Hicksite Quaker, whereas Lars Larson was an Orthodox Quaker. A well-thumbed copy of Hicks' "Sermons" published in 1826, owned by Ole Johnson, is now in the Luther College Museum, presented by Ole Johnson's daughter, Inger. A letter from Canute Orsland dated January, 1895, shows that the colony had at least seventeen Norwegians at the time, 16 of whom had moved in at various times after the founding of the settlement— 1838, 1840, 1852, 1853, 1857, 1858, 1870, 1871, 1882, 1883, 1887, and as recently as 1891.

The only direct descendant of the Sloopers living in the colony in 1895 was Andrew J. Stangeland, whose father was Andrew Stangeland, Slooper. The third letter dated February 28, 1895, and written by Anna Danielson, now Mrs. Lewis Parker of Kendall, gives a good deal of information about the early times and the condition in 1895. She still resides in Kendall, has been a seamstress, raises strawberries, writes for the papers, and is proud of her Norwegian lineage. "When I was little," she writes, "I used sometimes to hear the people say: 'Oh, they are Norwegians,' in a tone as though we did not count for much. They made fun of the Norwegians and it cut so deep the wounds have never healed exactly. The scars are very tender." Kendall should have a proud monument in memory of the Sloopers.

Illinois was made a territory in 1809; a state, in 1818. Its population in 1800 was 2,358, largely French. La Salle County received its name from the French explorer, La *Illinois, 1834* Salle, who sailed down the Mississippi in 1682 and proclaimed the Mississippi and all the land it drained, the property of France. La Salle County was organized in 1830 and the first settlers were a mixed class from New York, Ohio, Kentucky, Virginia, and immigrants from Germany, Ireland and Norway.

(a) *La Salle*

The Norwegians settled along the Fox River in the northeastern part of the county, in Rutland, Mission and Miller townships. The land had not yet been surveyed into sections. The newcomers on their arrival selected claims and squatted on them until they were placed on the market. The records at Ottawa, the county seat, reveal that when the land was put on the market in 1835 the following Norwegians purchased land: On June 15th Jacob Slogvig, 80 acres in Rutland; and Gudmund Haukaas (Haugaas), 160 acres in Rutland. On June 17th, Cleng Peerson, 80 acres in Mission; and his sister, Carrie Nelson, widow of Cornelius Nelson Hersdal, 80 acres in Mission. On June 25th, Peerson bought 80 acres more for himself. On June 17th, Gjert Hovland, who immigrated in 1835, bought 160 acres in Miller; and on the same date Thorstein Olson bought 160 acres, of which he sold, on Sept. 5th, 80 acres to Nels Nelson Hersdal. On June 17th, Nels Thompson bought 160 acres in Miller; and on Jan. 16, 1836, Thorstein Olson purchased 80 acres more. This was the beginning of the Fox River settlement in

Northeast Corner of LaSalle County
Fox River Settlement

La Salle County, in point of time the second settlement, and in point of interest, perhaps the first, in Norwegian-American history.

(b) *Chicago*

Chicago is the second Norwegian settlement in Illinois. The first Norwegian settler in Chicago was the sailor David Johnson,

Lars Fruland at 96

who came to Chicago to run the new press of the "Chicago Democrat," Chicago's first newspaper. This was in 1834, and Chicago was then a very small village. It was not yet incorporated, and no man could have foretold its marvellous growth, which surpasses any of the fictitious tales of the Arabian Nights. The progress of Chicago truly amazes mankind. Think of it: A dismal swamp, surrounded by water on the one side and a trackless desert on the other, within the span of a single life, has been transformed into one of the mightiest cities on the globe, with a population of nearly 3,000,000 busy people from all parts of the world. Lars Fruland, still hale and hearty, living within the shadow of Chicago's sky scrapers, came to Chicago in 1837, the year it became incorporated, and has beheld all this fabulous growth within his own lifetime. The rapid growth of the city ceases to be an enigma when one studies intelligently the conditions which have led to it. It has in reality only kept pace with the country of which it is the natural commercial center.

The Norwegians have been pioneers in opening up this west country whose commerce is drained by Chicago, and they have been prominent also as citizens of Chicago in its building. In 1925 Chicago has about 100,000 citizens of Norwegian birth or descent —20,481 born in Norway, 24,480 born here of foreign-born parentage, and over 50,000 belonging to the third, fourth and fifth generations. It is the largest Norwegian settlement in America.

It would be impossible to name all the prominent Norwegians in Chicago, even during the period 1825-1860. Suffice it to say, that in 1836 there came a number of Norwegian immigrants who settled in Chicago. Among these were Johan Larson from Kobbervik, Svein Lothe from Hardanger, Nils Rothe from Voss, and Halstein Torrison from Fjeldberg. Torrison worked as gardener for W. L. Newberry, the founder of the Newberry Library. Torrison built himself a fine house on the spot where the Northwestern Depot now stands. In 1840 Iver Larson, the father of Victor Lawson, the present publisher of the "Chicago Daily News," landed in Chicago. Also Jens Olson Kaasa, a master mason and builder of Our Savior's Church at Erie and May Streets. He and the pastor, Rev. Jens Krohn, were the most generous givers to the building of this house of worship. Kaasa donated $3,230.00 and Krohn $2,370.00, magnificent sums in those pioneer days. John Anderson from Voss arrived in Chicago in 1846, then a ten-year-old lad. His father died of the cholera in 1849, and thereby John's school days were at an end. He peddled apples and sold newspapers on the streets, got a job in a printing office and became the best compositor in the city. Then, in 1866, he founded "Skandinaven," now in its 60th year, one of the best newspapers in the country, and organized the John Anderson Publishing Co., which is still doing business at 511 N. Peoria Street. Paul Anderson, one of the earliest Norwegian pastors in Chicago, was the first Norwegian pastor to use the English language in his pulpit and Sunday School. There could hardly have been a call for it at that time, but Paul Anderson believed in the use of English to the extent that he did not teach his own children Norwegian. There are others equally foolish even in our enlightened day.

(c) *Beaver Creek*

Brief mention will here be made of only one more Norwegian colony in Illinois—the ill-fated Beaver Creek Settlement. It was located in the northeast part of Iroquois County, near the present town of Beaverville, about 60 miles due south of Chicago. It had been founded in the summer of 1837 by the party of immigrants that came over on the Aegir in June of that year. At Detroit they had been joined by the Nattesta brothers, Ole and Austen. At Chicago they met Bjørn Anderson Kvelve who then lived at Fox River in La Salle County, but advised them not to settle there because they would all die of the malarial fever which raged there. They paused in despair. Ole Rynning, their leader, could talk English and was advised by two Americans, with whom he conferred, to go south to Beaver Creek. A delegation of four— Ole Rynning, Ole Nattesta, Ingebrit Brudvig and Niels Veste— was sent down there to explore the country. These returned with a favorable report. And so these people—eighty-six in number— went to Beaver Creek. When the rains came, it was discovered, too late, that the settlement was situated in a vast marsh. In this low and unhealthy climate most of the party died next spring. Also Ole Rynning died, this great and good man, who on his death-bed wrote "A True Account of America," already referred to. The settlement disappeared the next year. The last one to leave it was Mons Adland (Aadland), who staid on until 1840. Later, the marshes were drained and Frenchmen ploughed the sod under which the Norsemen of 1837-1838 lay buried. Visiting the Beaver Creek region in 1917, the author found that boys and girls on the streets of Beaverville conversed in French in preference to English.

Indiana was the third state to be settled by the Norwegians. The first European visitor to these parts was La Salle, who *Indiana, 1837* coasted along the Ohio River in 1669. Indiana was taken from the English in 1778. It became a territory in 1800 and a state in 1816. Indiana is an unbroken, undulating plain and has rich alluvial soil, which should have been attractive to the land-hungry Norwegians.

Our first information about Norwegian settlements in Indiana is that by Ole Rynning, who, in answer to the question, "In what part of the country have the Norwegians settled?" answers: "Norwegians are to be found scattered about in many places in the United States. One may meet a few Norwegians in New York, Rochester, Detroit, Chicago, Philadelphia and New Orleans, yet I know of only four or five places where several Norwegians have settled together." He then names Orleans County, N. Y., La Salle County, Ill., White County, Ind., Shelby County, Mo., and Iroquois County, Ill., as the only Norwegian settlements at that time (1838). Concerning the Indiana settlement he says: "There are living in this place as yet only two Norwegians from Drammen, who together own upwards of 1100 acres of land; but in the vicinity good land still remains unoccupied." R. B. Anderson tried, but was unable, to discover anything further about these two Norwegians.

Another Norwegian settlement in this state was in Nobles County, dating from 1838. In that year Ole Aasland, a wealthy farmer of Flesberg, Numedal, Norway, sold out and came to America, via Gothenburg. He stopped at Kendall and got into the hands of a speculator who sold him 600 acres of land in Nobles County, Ind., near Fort Wayne, at a good price. Aasland, or Orsland, as he called himself, had paid the passage of twenty of his countrymen on condition that they should work for him here until their debt was paid. They accompanied him to Indiana, but, as the land was swampy and the people took sick of swamp fever and many of them died, he returned to Kendall. He traded his 600 acres in Indiana to Andrew Stangeland, Slooper, for 50 acres of Kendall property. There, along the Norwegian Road, some of his descendants have been living in peace and prosperity to this day. The Stangelands moved to Indiana, but later returned to Kendall. B. F. Stangland, above mentioned, was born in Nobles Co., Jan. 20, 1848.

In spite of its good soil, Indiana has never attracted the Norwegians. The number of foreign-born Norwegians within the state in 1850 was 18; in 1860, 38; in 1870, 123; in 1880, 182; in 1890, 285; in 1900, 384; in 1910, 531; and in 1920, 544.

Missouri (Indian name, meaning Big Muddy) was discovered by Marquette and Joliet in 1673 and claimed for France. The Louisiana Purchase made by President Thomas Jefferson from Napoleon in 1803 included Missouri. Missouri became a territory in 1812; a state, in 1820. As to surface, soil, climate and products, it is one of the most diversified of the great western states.

Missouri, 1838

Cleng Peerson explored Missouri and planted a colony in Shelby County, in March, 1837. The first colonists were Jacob Anderson Slogvig, the Slooper, Anders Askeland, and 12 others. To recruit the Shelby Settlement Peerson went to Stavanger, Norway, in 1838, returning in 1839 with a company of immigrants.

A good description of the Shelby Colony and its troubles is found in Peter Tesman's "Short Description," printed in Stavanger in 1839. Peter Tesman, together with his two brothers, William and Hans, and three other persons, emigrated in 1838 by way of Bremen. After an eight weeks' voyage they reached New York and there met Cleng Peerson, who persuaded them to follow him to Missouri. They took the Erie Canal-Lake Erie route as far as Cleveland, but stopped at Rochester to add a few more Norwegians to their company, making a total of twenty-two. From Cleveland they followed the Ohio Canal down to Portsmouth, from whence they transferred their belongings to

Ohio River boats. Eventually they reached St. Louis and the Shelby homesteads. The situation so far had not been very inviting—summer heat, hard labor and death-dealing sickness, and the money going fast. The settlement was a wilderness and was far from town. Sickness and poverty stalked in every household. The squatters had an opportunity to buy their land at the public auction that year, but they were all too poor to take advantage of it. Others then bought the land, and the Norwegians had to leave house and home and squat again on some unoccupied spot. Peter Tesman paid for his land, and in consequence he had so little money that he would either have to go out as a day laborer or go back home. He decided to go back home. Peerson had gone by the Ohio River route because Slogvig and Askeland had returned to La Salle County dissatisfied, and he feared that if he went by the La Salle Settlement, his new recruits would refuse to go to Missouri. Tesman returned by way of La Salle and found that people there, too, had their full share of pioneer hardships, including the ravages of the cholera.

The Shelby County Settlement was short lived. The settlers were dissatisfied. It was too much of a wilderness and too far to market. One of the settlers, Peter Gjilje, once walked for nine days before he found a human habitation. During these days he lived on wild strawberries. Cleng Peerson is said to have chosen a new place for settlement at Sugar Creek, about eight miles west of Keokuk, Lee County, Iowa. Most of the Shelby County settlers, following the lead of Andrew Simonson, moved in 1840 to Sugar Creek, but Peerson remained behind and did not sell his Missouri farm until 1847, when he was about to join the Swedish Communistic Colony at Bishop Hill, Ill. At Sugar Creek Barlien and others were already coming in from the east.

It has been said that the Shelby Settlement was badly chosen, but Andrew Simonson gave this testimony in 1879: "No settlement ever founded by Norwegians in America had a better appearance or better location than this very land in Shelby County, of which the Norwegians took possession at that time, and which they in part still own." In 1920, according to the U. S. Census, Shelby County had four foreign-born Danes and two foreign-born Swedes, but no foreign-born Norwegians.

Missouri has never been a Norwegian state. In 1850 it had 155 foreign-born Norwegians; in 1860, 146; in 1870, 297; in 1880, 373; in 1890, 526; in 1900, 530; in 1910, 660; and in 1920, 610. Missouri was a slave state, and Norwegians hated slavery. Besides, the state lay too far south. The Norwegians preferred the North.

The Norwegians entered Wisconsin in 1838 and came there to stay. Wisconsin was visited by the French explorer Nicollet as early as 1634. In 1763 it was ceded to *Wisconsin, 1838* England; in 1783, to the United States. It became a territory in 1836; a state in 1847. Rock County was organized in 1838, that is, the same year in which Ole Nattesta captured it for the Norwegians. Wisconsin had been from time immemorial one of the best happy hunting grounds of the Indians and an Eldorado for the French traders. Southern Wisconsin supplied the French and Indians with lead, and in 1821 the Americans opened operations, until the output reached 25,000 tons of lead a year. In developing the lead mines the lands of the Indian tribes of the Winnebagoes, Sacs and Foxes were overrun. The Indians protested and began what is known as the Black Hawk War, from the name of the Indian leader. At the close of the war, in which Captain Abraham Lincoln took part, the Indians were forced to give up 10,000,000 acres of land and to move further west. In this way, Rock County was fairly cleared of its Indians.

Americans who had seen the beautiful landscapes in Rock County, took part in that great frenzy of speculation, which ended in the panic of 1837. There were many towns on paper, in which there was not a house or a citizen, and the town lots thereof were sold at fabulous prices. In 1837, for example, Newburg, one of these "wild cat" towns, was sold for $20,000.00 and shortly afterward resold at $95,000.00. Luckily, the panic came, with much suffering in its train, after which people came to their senses again.

(a) *Rock County*

The Norwegians found the land delightful in every way and cheap in price. The speculation boom was over. In place of speculation now came a season of settling and building, the like of which Wisconsin had so far never seen. Rock County became, as far as Norwegians are concerned, a doorway, not only to Wisconsin, but to all the Northwest. Thousands of immigrants had in view Rock County as their first objective, if not their last, and throughout the Northwest will still be found hundreds of settlers who came first to Rock County before deciding on where to go further. Some of them settled at Jefferson Prairie; others at Rock Prairie; still others at Beloit, Janesville, Brodhead, etc. P. O. Langseth, in his history of the Norwegians in Rock County, calls it the "Inexhausible Rock County."

In this county many of the great Norwegians of America have been nurtured; many of the most vital historical events have there taken place. The first three Norwegian Lutheran pastors in America—Eielsen, Clausen and Dietrichson—each

Illustrating Location of Norwegian Lutheran Congregations and Settlements

lived and labored in this county at about the same time. Three
synods first saw the light of day in this county—the Evangelical
Lutheran Church in America (Eielsen Synod), 1846; the
Norwegian Evangelical Lutheran Church in America (Norwegian
Synod), 1851; and the Scandinavian Augustana Synod, 1860.

(b) *Muskego*

Muskego was the second Norwegian settlement in Wisconsin.
In the summer of 1839, 40 people from Tinn, Telemarken, took a
Gothenburg boat for America, together with twenty from Stavanger. They came up through Rochester and the Great Lakes.
Their boat on the Lakes was a miserable, unseaworthy craft,
carrying a cargo of powder. It might have been blown up. Twice
the boat came near sinking. At last they reached Milwaukee and
were about to depart for La Salle County, Ill., but were prevented from doing so by the enterprising business men of Milwaukee, who pleaded eloquently against the open, storm-swept
plains of Illinois and the terrible malarial epidemic down there.
Finally, the newcomers were persuaded to settle in Muskego, a
low, marshy place, about 20 miles southwest of Milwaukee. In
the summer, when everything was dried up, Muskego looked good
to them, but when the fall rains came, the poor immigrants found
that they lived in a swamp and that for several months a year
they were visited by the dreaded cholera and malaria. In 1843
every home but one was visited by the cholera. In 1849 the
cholera came like the angel of death in Egypt, ending lives in
every hut and house. Strong men, retiring at night, often were
found stiff in death in the morning. The pastor, H. A. Stub,
sometimes buried a dozen or more a day. Few settlements, if any,
thinks H. R. Holand, have seen so much struggle and privation,
sickness and poverty, sorrow and blasted hopes, and yet no
settlement can present a brighter picture of victories won and
great things accomplished during the early pioneer days than can
Muskego.

Muskego is located in the southwestern corner of Milwaukee County, the southeastern corner of Waukesha County,
but mainly in Yorkville, Raymond and Waterford townships in
Racine County. The eastern Part of Racine County is often
referred to as North Cape and Yorkville Prairie; the western
section is usually called Norway or simply Muskego. There were
many accessions to the settlement, notwithstanding the severe
hardships it had to undergo. Every one bragged of his own
settlement, of course, and tried to discourage immigrants from
going to other fields. Johan R. Reierson, for example, settled in
Texas in 1847. He wrote a book, "Veiviseren" (The Pathfinder),
in which he specifically warns immigrants against Muskego.
Consequently, many parties of immigrants made it a point to avoid

Muskego. Still Muskego kept on growing, and is today one of the finest and richest parts of Wisconsin. Big ditches have drained the swamps. The heavy forests have been felled. The land is a garden, in the midst of which stand numerous substantial residences and barns in the place of the dug-outs and log sheds the pioneers occupied.

Here is a partial list of the pioneers: John Luraas was the leader of the first party that settled at Muskego. He was a good man. John Evenson Molee, a member of Luraas' party, has given in Anderson's "First Chapter" an interesting account of the three months' journey from Tinn to Muskego. In 1855 Molee moved to Blue Mounds, Wis.; in 1873, to Bloomfield, Fillmore County, Minn. His son, Elias J. Molee, of Tacoma, Wash., has tried to create a universal language, which he calls "teutonish."

In 1840, the settlement had important accessions in the persons of Søren Bache, Johannes Johanneson and Elling Eielsen, the first two from Drammen, the last from Voss. These three had come over together on the same boat in the summer of 1839 and had made their way to the Fox River Colony in La Salle. Johanneson did not like the Illinois prairies, so he and Bache walked up along the Fox River until they came to Wind Lake, and settled down there in the black forests, near the present Norway postoffice. Eielsen came later. Bache was a rich man, and very generous. He accidentally killed a woman when out hunting and, almost crazed with grief, he returned to Norway. Johanneson died in 1845 of the cholera.

Eielsen was a lay preacher of the Haugean school in Norway. In 1841 he built at Fox River the first Norwegian house of worship in America. That same year he walked to New York to get the Lutheran catechism printed. He succeeded in getting it printed in English. Again, in 1842, he footed it to New York, and got Pontoppidan's "Sandhed til Gudfrygtighed" and the Augsburg Confession printed in one volume in Norwegian, "in Gothic type." On Oct. 3, 1843, he was ordained, thus becoming the first Norwegian Lutheran pastor in America. On April 13-14, 1846, he organized the first Norwegian Lutheran synod in America, of which he was president until his death, Jan. 10, 1883.

Of other immigrants to Muskego, let it suffice to mention Mons Adland (Aadland), Claus L. Clausen, Anund Drotning, Hans Friis, Jens O. Hatlestad, Even Heg, John Homme, Peter Jacobson, Nels Johnson, Knud Langeland, Johan R. Reymert, Hans Andreas Stub and Hermo N. Tufte.

Adland has already been mentioned as being the last man to leave the Beaver Creek settlement.

Clausen was a Dane. He had accepted a call to come to Muskego as parochial school teacher. When he came, his people wanted him as their pastor and he was regularly ordained,

Oct. 18, 1843. His first wife was Martha Rasmussen, the author of the well known hymn: "Saa vil vi nu sige hverandre farvel" (And now we must bid one another farewell). In 1845 Clausen accepted a call to Koshkonong, Wis.; in 1846, to Rock Prairie, Wis.; in 1853, to St. Ansgar, Ia. He helped to organize four synods and was editor of two papers. He was a member of the Iowa Legislature and a commissioner of immigration. He was a chaplain in the Civil War. Through his influence Luther College was not made merely a preparatory school for ministers. Luther College therefore welcomes any youth who desires a higher Christian education as well as those who intend to prepare for the ministry. C. W. Clausen, his son by his second wife, Bergette Brekke, was the state auditor at Olympia, Washington, for many years.

Anund Drotning reared a good son in Edwin, for many years postmaster at Stoughton, Wis., an exemplary American citizen in every sense, though a pacifist.

Hans Friis was a sea captain who had brought nine emigrant ships across the Atlantic between 1837 and 1847. In 1847 he became an American citizen and sailed the Great Lakes. He enlisted in the Civil War, was wounded, and spent his old age on his farm in Muskego. He died in 1886, at the age of 75.

Jens O. Hatlestad was the father of Rev. Ole J. Hatlestad, Norwegian Lutheran pastor, 1854-1892. Ole Hatlestad has distinguished himself as one of the first editors and publishers among Norwegian-Americans. The very first Norwegian paper was called "Nordlyset," published in Muskego, 1847-1849. "Nordlyset" was purchased by Hatlestad and his brother-in-law, Knud Langeland. Its name was changed to "Democraten," and it was issued during 1849-1850. Hatlestad served thirteen years as president of the Norwegian Augustana Synod, 1870-1881, 1888-1890, and wrote in 1887 one of the first histories of the Norwegian people in America.

Even Heg was a sort of Lars Larson in Muskego. His place was the haven and hospice of all immigrants who came through or to Muskego. His son, Hans C. Heg, was the colonel of the Fifteenth Wisconsin, a volunteer regiment of soldiers in the Civil War, whose membership was over 90% Norwegian. Col. Heg was born at Drammen, Dec. 21, 1829, and emigrated in 1840. He was one of the Norwegian '49ers on the California gold fields. He was a brave soldier and a good commander. He was killed in action at the Battle of Chickamauga, Tenn., Sept. 20, 1863. A fitting monument to his memory is soon to be erected at Madison. The money has been raised mainly through the efforts of Waldemar Ager, Heg's chief biographer. His sister Andrea was one of the first Norwegians to teach school in Wisconsin. She married Dr. Stephen O. Himoe (Høimo), a surgeon in the Fifteenth Wisconsin.

John Homme was the father of Rev. Even Homme, the founder of the first Norwegian orphanage and the first home for the aged, and one of the first to issue Sunday School papers for children and youth. The town of Wittenberg, Wis., was founded by Homme.

Peter Jacobson was the progenitor of a large tribe of Jacob-

The Samuel Jacobson Family
(Relatives of Peter Jacobson, with home at Port Washington, Wis., and Kenyon, Minn.)

sons who now have a good place in the sun in many counties. From 1846 to 1906 there was in Ozaukee County, Wis., near Port Washington, a large settlement of Jacobsons, whose worth and work can hardly be overstated. Nels Jacobson, the patriarch of the settlement, was the unofficial arbitrator in every dispute for many miles. Germans, Americans and other nationalities used to say: "Let's ask the Jacobsons." About the year 1906 most of these good people moved to Goodhue county, Minn., in order to get closer to the Norwegian people. Peter Jacobson, the Muskego patriarch, built the Muskego Church in 1843. His sons moved and rebuilt it on the grounds of the United Church Seminary, St. Paul, in 1904, now called the Luther Theological Seminary. Their cousin, Axel Jacobson, has been superintendent of the

Indian School of the Norwegian church, and the American Government, at Wittenberg, since 1888. Axel's daughter Carolyn is a graduate of the American Conservatory, Chicago, and the wife of Prof. L. A. Moe, Decorah.

Nels Johnson arrived in 1839. In 1855-1857 he was a Norwegian Methodist pastor at Cambridge, Wis. From 1857 to his death in 1882, he lived in Winneshiek county, Ia. He was the father of Martin N. Johnson, congressman, 1891-1899, and U. S. senator from North Dakota, 1899-1911.

Knud Langeland is best known as an editor. He edited "Democraten" in 1849-1850; "Skandinaven," in 1866-1872; "Amerika," 1872-1873; "Skandinaven," 1873-1881; also "Den Norske Amerikaner," in the early fifties. He was a member of

James D. Reymert   Knud Langeland   Hans C. Heg

the Wisconsin Legislature in 1860. Before his death, in 1888, at Milwaukee, he published a short history of the Norwegians in America. His son Peter is a practising physician in Milwaukee. Another son, Leroy, is news editor of the "Evening Wisconsin," Milwaukee.

James Denoon Reymert was the first editor of a Norwegian paper in America, "Nordlyset" (The Northern Light), published at Muskego, 1847-1849. Even Heg furnished the money to run the paper. Ole Torgerson was the typesetter. The paper had 200 subscribers the first year. As to politics it supported the Free Soilers. Ole J. Carlson, a pioneer at Colton, S. D., contracted to deliver it to the settlers in Muskego, and should get as pay a pair of overalls the first year and thereafter $10.00 a year. The paper brought Reymert into public notice. He was made a member of the Wisconsin Constitutional Convention in 1847, of the State Legislature in 1849, of the Senate in 1854-55 and 1857, and was the first Norwegian in America to hold a state office. He built a plank road over the Muskego marshes. He established saw mills. He was justice of peace, superintendent of schools, vice-consul for Swe-den - Norway, presidential elector, receiver and tax collector, U. S. disbursing agent, and Democratic candidate for Congress. In 1861 he moved to New York and established a law office with large practice. In 1873 he went to Chili, South America, and engaged in business. In 1876 he moved back to the United States and organized the Reymert S i l v e r

Where the First Norwegian Newspaper in America Was Printed

Mining Company at Pinal, Ariz. President Grover Cleveland appointed him a judge. He died in Los Angeles in 1896. One of his sons, and three of his nephews, through his influence became lawyers. Lake Denoon is named after him.

Hans G. Stub at Age of 12 and His Sister Bolette Marie (later Mrs. Rev. J. E. Bergh)

Hans A. Stub heeded the call of the Norwegian settlers: "Come over and help us." Full of faith and youthful enthusiasm he began to serve the Norwegian Congregation at Muskego as Lutheran pastor in 1848. In 1855 he was transferred to Coon Prairie, Wis. On June 27, 1907, Pastor Stub was called to his reward after a long life of blessed service in the Master's kingdom. In 1849, during the most frightful epidemic of cholera in the history of the Norwegian settlements, a son was born to H. A. Stub and

Søren Bache's Log Hut

wife, destined to rear head and shoulders above his fellows. This son is Hans Gerhard Stub, D.D., Litt. D., LL.D. Stub was educated at the Bergen Cathedral School, Norway; Luther College, Iowa; Concordia Seminary, St. Louis; and Leipzig University, Germany. He speaks and writes English, Norwegian and German with equal facility. He has been pastor at Minneapolis, 1872-78; professor of systematic theology and Old Testament at Luther Seminary, 1878-96; pastor and college professor, Decorah, Iowa, 1896-1900; professor of theology, Luther Seminary, 1900-17; president of Luther Seminary; president of the Norwegian Synod, 1911-17; president of the Norwegian Lutheran Church of America, 1917——; president of the National Lutheran Council, 1919-22; etc. He has been editor of "Theologisk Tidsskrift" and "Kirketidende" and has written several books. He has been thrice knighted by the King of Norway, Haakon VII: In 1908, created Knight of St. Olav; in 1912, made Commander of St. Olav; in 1923, decorated with the Grand Cross. His life has been most closely identified with the story of the Norwegians from the days of the most primitive beginnings to the present with its manifold successes. He has tasted poverty, hardships, aspiration, toil, self-denial, victory. In him are harmoniously blended a true love of the country of his fathers and of this his native land, together with a just appreciation of the free institutions and opportunities of each. He has been a faithful servant. His life is inspiring.

Hauling Grain to Market

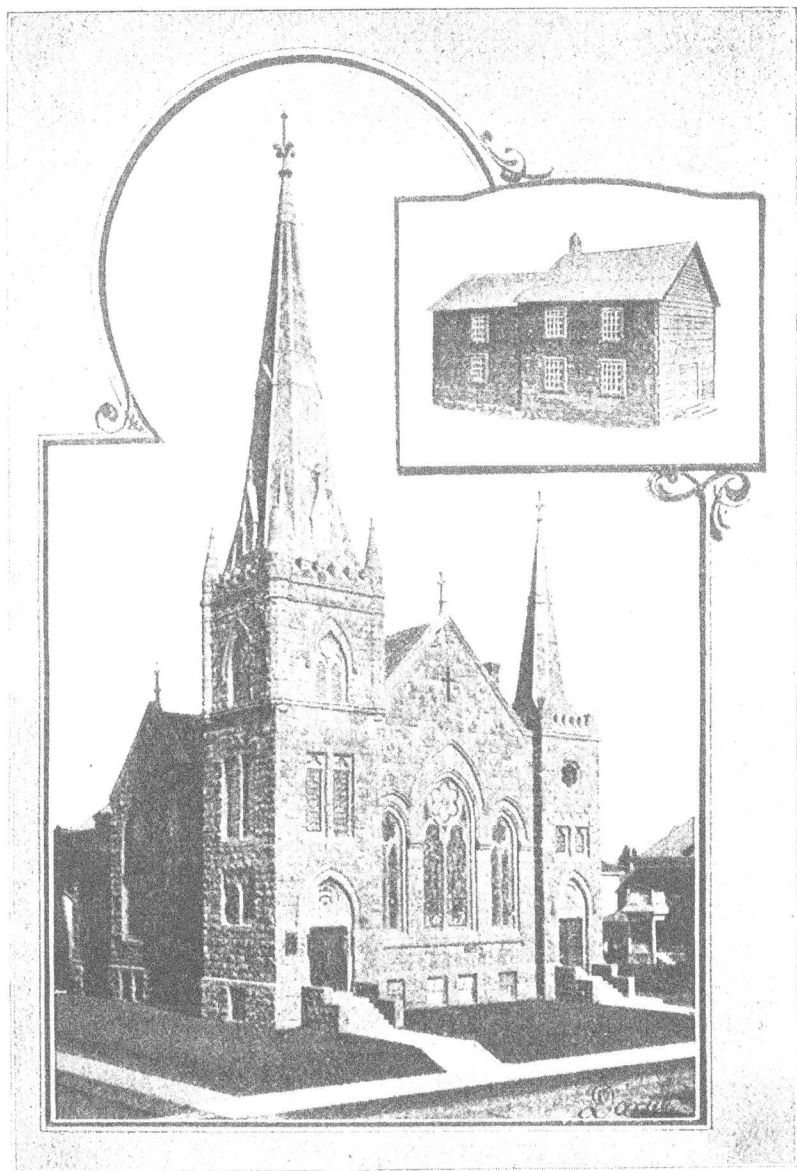

Muskego Church (1843), Rev. J. M. Hestenes, Pastor (1925), and
Bethlehem Church, Minneapolis (1893), Olin S. J. Reigstad, Pastor (1925)

Hermo N. Tufte was the first immigrant from Hallingdal. Now there are surely over 25,000 Hallings in America, over twice as many as dwell in the old valley. Tufte was a devout Haugean. His family turned out well. One of his sons is said by Holand to have been the most lovable man in Racine County. Three of his daughters made notable marriages—Sigrid married Rev. Elling Eielsen, the far-famed revivalist and pioneer missionary; Julia married Thomas Adland, son of Mons Adland, himself like his father, one of Muskego's best men; and Betsey married O. B. Dahle, a wealthy merchant of Mt. Horeb, Wis. father of Congressman Herman B. Dahle.

(c) *Koshkonong*

Only one more of the Norwegian settlements will be noticed, and that very briefly. Koshkonong was the third and mightiest of the Norwegian settlements in this great Norwegian state. Koshkonong lies in the southeastern part of Dane County. The first Norwegians located there in the spring of 1840. They were Gunnul Olson Vindeg, Bjørn Anderson Kvelve, Nels Larson Bolstad, Lars Olson Dugstad, Anders Finnø, Nels Severson Gilderhus, Amund Anderson Hornefjeld and Thorstein Olson Bjaadland, one of the Sloopers. Also Magny Buttelson, Lars Davidson and Foster Olson. Bolstad, Buttelson and Severson were the first to record in the land office the land they had purchased,— May 5, 1840. Vindeg was the first to build a house.

Most of the settlers in Koshkonong have hailed from southern and southwestern Norway—from Telemarken, Numedal, Stavanger, Hardanger and Sogn. Few settlements have been more prosperous. Perhaps no other settlement has turned out so many eminent men. Here at Koshkonong lived Rev. Johannes W. C. Dietrichson, the first preacher ordained in Norway, who came here to serve his countrymen as pastor. He came in 1844, organized ten congregations, returned to Norway in 1845 to get more help, then came back to Koshkonong, 1846-1850. In 1846 he wrote a book about his experiences in America. His successors in the pastorate, A. C. Preus, 1850-1860, and J. A. Ottesen, 1860-1885, were learned, stalwart, zealous men, who left a deep impress on that neighborhood. East Koshkonong Church, though the third church edifice to be built, was the first one to be dedicated by Norwegian-Americans. In this church the Norwegian Synod was organized Feb. 5, 1853, by seven pastors and forty-five delegates, representing thirty-eight congregations—thirty-one in Wisconsin, three in Illinois, and four in Iowa.

Among the famous sons of Old Koshkonong (Kaskeland, the pioneers called it) may be mentioned the following 77 :

R. B. Anderson, U. S. minister to Denmark.

Lars S. Reque, U. S. Consul General, Holland, and Lutheran professor.

Andrew E. Lee and Charles N. Herreid, governors of South Dakota.

Knute Nelson, U. S. Senator from Minnesota.

Halvor Steenerson, congressman from Minnesota.

John Mandt Nelson, congressman from Wisconsin.

Fred P. Brown, secretary of state, Minnesota.

John L. Erdall, insurance commissioner, Wisconsin.

Canute R. Matson, sheriff in Chicago.

N. O. Falk, J. J. Holman, L. L. Hulsather, Christopher Jerdee, N. A. Ladd, William Nelson, lawyers.

J. L. Johnson, judge.

N. C. Amundson, Andreas Holo, G. M. Johnson, Albert Kittleson, G. M. J. Lee, Alfred B. Olson, and K. M. O. Teigen, physicians.

J. A. Johnson, T. G. Mandt and N. O. Stark, inventors and manufacturers.

Knute Reindahl, violin maker.

Edwin Drotning and Levi Kittelson, tobacco commission merchants.

Erik S. Gjellum, Knud Henderson, Peter Hendrickson, Nels Holman, Per Røthe, Aslak Teisberg and A. A. Trovaten, authors and editors.

J. J. Anderson, Knute E. Bergh, Ole G. Felland, Jacob D. Jacobsen, C. A. Naeseth and E. J. Onstad, professors in Lutheran colleges.

Andrew O. Johnson, Adventist professor.

J. T. Flom, professor at University of Illinois.

J. E. Olson, professor at University of Wisconsin.

Henry Johnson, Albert Olson, Andrew Olson, Edvard Olson, Martin Olson and Ole A. Olson, Adventist pastors.

Bendix Ingebretson and J. H. Johnson, Methodist pastors.

A. O. Aasen, Abel Anderson, N. B. Berge, Knut Bjørgo, G. M. Erdall, N. A. Giere, N. O. Giere, H. B. Hustvedt, O. O. Klevjord, G. A. Larsen, A. J. Lee, G. T. Lee, O. T. Lee, A. E. Lien, Olaf Mandt, O. A. Normann, Otto Ottesen, N. A. Quammen, Peter S. Reque, S. S. Reque, A. K. Sagen, T. K. Thorvilson and Ole K. Vangsnes, Lutheran pastors.

For about thirty years, 1845-1875, Wisconsin was the greatest Norwegian state in America. Then Minnesota took the lead and has kept it ever since. The number of foreign-born Norwegians in Wisconsin in 1850 was 8,651; in 1860, 21,442; in 1870, 40,046; in 1880, 49,349; in 1890, 65,696; in 1900, 61,575; in 1910, 57,000; in 1920, 45,453.

Father Marquette and Joliet visited Iowa in 1673 and claimed it for France. In 1763 it was ceded to Spain; in 1803 it was

Iowa, 1840

ceded back to France and then sold to the United States as a part of Louisiana. It became a territory in 1838; a state in 1846. The "Iowa State Song" says about Iowa: "Best in all the land, Here's where the tall corn grows." Hon. O. M. Oleson, the enterprising merchant, philanthropist and song veteran, of Fort Dodge, Ia., has written an Iowa song, entitled, "Come to Iowa."

Iowa is well-watered, has rich soil and a healthy climate. Almost every foot of it is tillable, and in 1919 the value of its crops was nearly one billion dollars, only surpassed by one other state, Texas, which has nearly five times the area of Iowa. The railroads of Iowa now make her map look like a piece of intricate lace-work, but in 1840 there was, of course, not even a thought of building railroads in this vast wilderness, designated in the old geographies as a part of the "G r e a t American Desert."

Primitive Plowing

(a) *Sugar Creek*

The first settlement was at Sugar Creek, Lee County, eight miles west of Keokuk. Cleng Peerson had explored it. Hans Barlien was the first settler. His colony was fed by migrations from La Salle County, Ill., Shelby County, Mo., and more recent immigrations. In 1843, according to Reierson's "Veiviser," the settlement had between thirty and forty families, 200 to 300 souls. In 1856 the number had dwindled down to 56; in 1885, to 31; in 1920 there were only twenty-seven foreign-born Norwegians in that county. Flom gives as reasons why Sugar Creek did not grow as did the later settlements to the north and west, that the land in Sugar Creek was not of the best, that the tide of immigration was toward Wisconsin and the Northwest, and it was impossible to stem the tide, and that Mormons and Quakers were very active in the neighborhood of Sugar Creek, and, finally, that the Norwegians at Sugar Creek found it difficult to secure title to the land upon which they had settled.

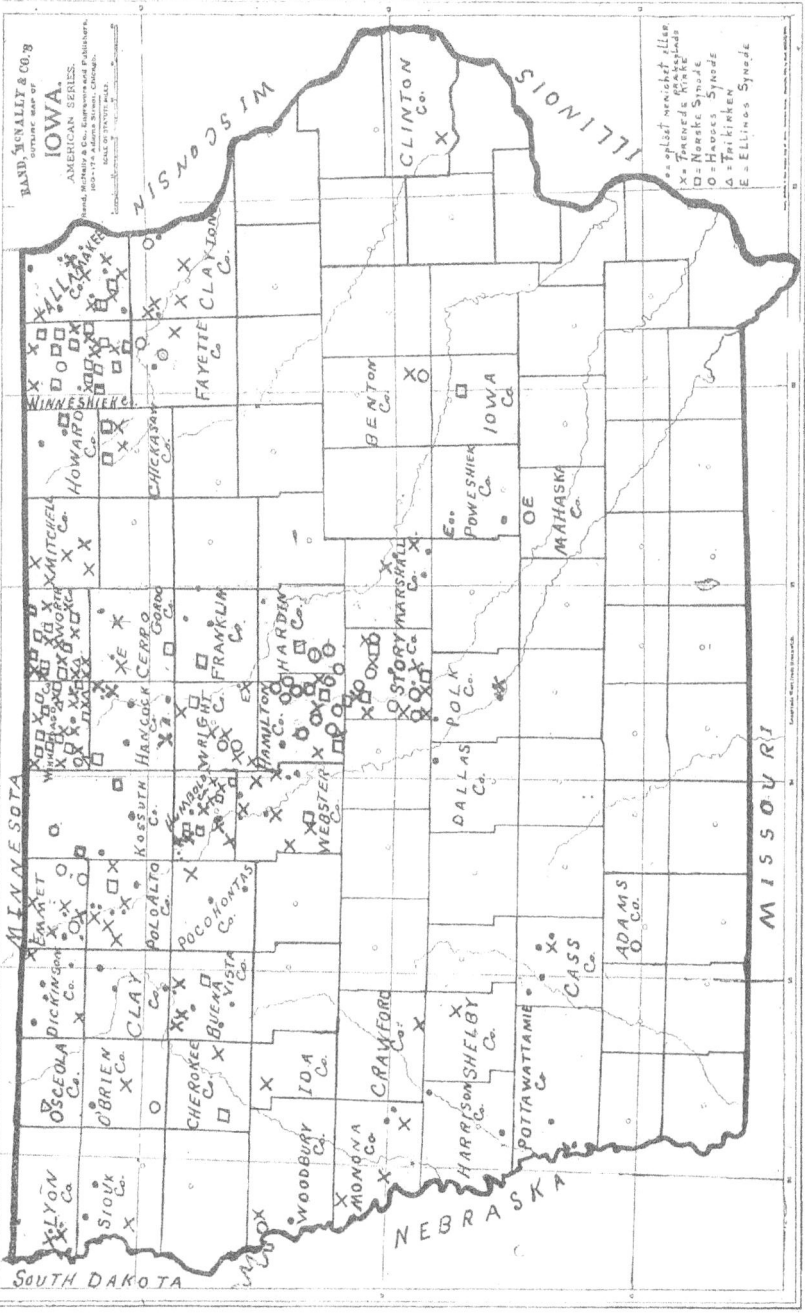

Norwegian Settlements

(b) *Fort Atkinson*

The second settlement in Iowa was made at Fort Atkinson, Winneshiek County, in 1843. Fort Atkinson was at that time a real fort. It had been built by the government with a double object in view—to protect the white man against the Indians and to teach the Indian the white man's method of agriculture. Two Norwegians from Numedal, Ole Halvorson Valle and Ole Tollefson Kittilsland, hired out to Uncle Sam at $12.00 per month and arrived at the fort in the early spring of 1843 on skis. As an Irishman put it: "The two first white men in Winneshiek County were two Norwegians, who came clear from the Old Country on a pair of snow shoes."   In 1846 Valle quit his posi-

Rev. U. V. Koren   Mrs. U. V. Koren

Koren Parsonage, 1853, Washington Prairie, Iowa
(See Mrs. Koren's "Fra Pioner Tiden," being selections from her diary)

tion and was replaced by his cousin, Søren Olson Sørum from S. Land, Norway.   In 1847, Valle obtained employment at the fort for another cousin, Miss Ingeborg Nilsen.   The next year, 1848, the government decided to remove the Indians to Long Prairie, Todd County, Minn., and the Norwegians of Fort Atkinson followed their Indian charges into Minnesota.   Søren Olson and Ingeborg Nilsen became man and wife in 1850.

(c) *Clayton County*

Meanwhile, in 1846, Valle had made his home in Clayton County on a farm three miles southeast of the present village of St. Olaf.   There his first child was born, Sept. 20, 1846—Jorund Halvorson, now Mrs. Lars Thovson, St. Olaf, Ia.   She is the first Norwegian child born in northern Iowa.   St. Olaf is the old home of Rev. Ole Glesne, the author's good pastor. Pastor Glesne's father staked his claim at St. Olaf in 1850.

(d) *Westward Ho*

Once begun, the settlements in northern Iowa were made in rapid succession. Fayette was entered in 1849; Allamakee and Winneshiek received their fair share of Norwegians in 1850 and every year thereafter for many years. In 1852 the pioneer line had reached to Mitchell County; in 1853 to Worth County;

A Sod Church at Hemingford, Box Butte Co., Neb., 1903. Student (now Pastor) T. A. Johnson and His Parochial School.

in 1854, to Story County; in 1855 to Hamilton County; and in 1860, as far as Woodbury County, on the Nebraska-Dakota boundaries. Another line of march approached Iowa at the center, entering Clinton in 1853. This line had gotten to Benton and Iowa counties in 1854, but for lack of reinforcements did not push on farther west. Norway in Benton County, is the home of some of the Rosdails, Sloopers.

(e) *Decorah*

The Norwegians have always been numerically strong in northern Iowa, ever since they discovered it. Their influence has no doubt been far out of proportion to their numerical strength. This is due in large measure to the personal influence

of the great church leaders who lived in Iowa, for example, U. V.
Koren, Laur. Larsen and C. K. Preus; also to the work of
Luther College, founded in 1861, probably so far the most influential school that the Norwegians have had; also to the high
character of its Norwegian press, as, "Decorah Posten," founded
in 1874, the largest Norwegian newspaper in the world.
They tell almost as many good stories about this paper as they
do about the Ford auto. Here is one just off the bat. Dr. Otto
O. Svebakken had been out in the country on a sick call. An
old Norwegian woman was dying. Nothing could save her. Dr.
Svebakken is a pious man and as concerned about the soul's
welfare as a preacher is. He inquired about her religious state.
He chanced to ask if she had been a "reader," meaning Bible
reader, as Norwegians call the converted. "Jau, me har lest
'Decorah Posten.'" Yes, she had read "Decorah Posten."
Decorah, the Norwegian capital of Iowa, is a beautiful little city
of about 4,000 people, but that its fame far exceeds its size can be
seen from this true story: An intelligent Norwegian lady in
Brooklyn, N. Y., remarked that she had heard so much about
Decorah. She wondered how large it really was. "How large
do you suppose?" "It is not as large as New York, is it?" she
innocently guessed. In "Decorah Posten" for April 14, 1925, is
an account of Professor C. A. Tingelstad's recent visit to the
little, ancient town of Southport, Connecticut. He wanted to see
the Pequot Library. The librarian said: "Where are you from?"
"From Decorah." The librarian smiled: "Ah, that's where the
gladioli came from." Editor Prestgard and Dr. Hoegh have some
of the finest gladioli in the world and number among their patrons
even the great wizard Luther Burbank himself.

In 1850 Iowa had 361 foreign-born Norwegians; in 1860,
5,678; in 1870, 17,554; in 1880, 21,583; in 1890, 27,078;
in 1900, 25,634; in 1910, 21,924; and in 1920, 17,344.

Texas was founded by the Spaniards. After the United
States bought Louisiana, it became a great question as to where
that territory ended on the west. Spain
Texas, 1843   claimed the Sabine as the boundary line; the
United States claimed the Rio Grande. Texas
thus became a No Man's Land made almost a desert by revolutionary forays from both sides. Mexico began the policy of inviting American immigrants; by 1830 about 20,000 hardy
American adventurers had pitched their tents on Texan soil.
This led to a demand for statehood for Texas, among the Mexican commonwealths. Gen. Austin, the spokesman, was thrown
into prison for his presumption, and civil war ensued. Texas
declared itself free, hence it is called the Lone Star State. After

ten years of national life Texas joined the American Republic (in 1845). With the annexation of Texas the United States succeeded to a quarrel with Mexico, which was settled in favor of the United States by the Mexican War (1846-1848).

Johan Nordboe came to Dallas, Tex., in 1838. He was the first Norwegian from Gudbrandsdalen, the first Norwegian in Texas and one of the first Norwegian doctors in America. Nordboe did not found a settlement in Texas.

(a) *Henderson County*

The first one to do that was Johan Reinert Reierson who left Norway in 1843 by way of Havre for New Orleans. From New Orleans he proceeded north to Illinois and Wisconsin and then down to Texas. There he had gone to Austin, the capital, and had been presented to the governor, who was anxious to get Norwegians to occupy the Texan prairies. He returned to Norway, published in 1843 his famous book, "Veiviseren," rounded up his family and a few others, and set sail again for America. He located in Henderson County and called the colony Normandy, but it was later changed to Brownsboro. He died at Prairieville, Tex., Sept. 6., 1864, but his widow was still living there in 1895. One of his sons was then a hotel keeper at Kaufman, Tex.; another son was a bank cashier at Key West, Fla.

(b) *Kaufman County*

Prairieville, founded in 1847 by Reierson, is the second Norwegian settlement in Texas. It was known also as Four Mile Prairie. One of the most remarkable Norwegians in Texas was Mrs. Elise Wærenskjold. She came to Four Mile Prairie in 1847 as Mrs. Foyen, then married Wærenskjold in 1848 and lived with him until he was assassinated on account of his anti-slavery views. She had been an editor in Norway and wrote many articles for the Norwegian press from her far western home. They give much first hand reliable information about pioneer life. She organized a temperance society in her community; also a Lutheran congregation, taught school and prevailed on her husband to preach until a trained pastor could be secured. Through her Rev. Elling Eielsen made a missionary journey to Texas in 1849 and Emil Frederichsen was called as minister of the Gospel at Four Mile Norwegian Lutheran Congregation, 1854-1857.

(c) *Bosque County*

The third Norwegian settlement in Texas is in Bosque County, stretching from Clifton westward to Cranfills Gap, with Norse as the center. Ole Canuteson was the founder of this settlement, in 1853. Canuteson had gotten the America Fever in 1842.

when as a ten-year old boy he listened to Cleng Peerson's stories
about America. In 1850 his parents resolved to go. They
reached New York, Buffalo and Chicago, but on the way to
Ottawa on a canal boat his good mother died of the cholera.
Cleng Peerson was at La Salle, just back from Texas and full
of its praises. So the Canutesons and some others followed
Cleng to Texas. They bought land at fifty cents an acre.
In 1852 the Texas Legislature resolved to give land to actual
settlers. Ole Canuteson found vacant land in 1853 in Bosque
County, near the Bosque River, and in that rich and beautiful
spot a Norwegian settlement was then established which flour-
ishes to this day. Down there they still speak the Norwegian
language. They have Norwegian congregations and a Norwegian college, Clifton College, founded in 1896, whose president is
Carl Tyssen, A. M. Cleng Peerson lies buried there—at Norse.
T. T. Colwick is the postmaster at Norse; J. K. Rystad, the
Lutheran pastor.

The Norwegian foreign-born population of Texas has never
been very large. According to the census, there were no Norwegians there in 1850. There must have been nearly 75 in 1850.
In 1860 the census reports 326 born in Norway; in 1870, 403;
in 1880, 880; in 1890, 1,313; in 1900, 1,356; in 1910, 1,785;
in 1920, 1,740.

Utah is the Holy Land of the Mormons. In the spring of
1847, after their expulsion from Nauvoo, Ill., 12,000 Mormons
lay in camp on the site of Council Bluffs, Ia.
Utah, 1847   Brigham Young and 142 picked men then
marched westward to spy out a home beyond
the power of the United States. They came to Salt Lake and
dedicated it to the Lord. July 4, 1847, 1,653 persons and 580
wagons started on the long trek from Iowa to Utah. Thos. Rosdail was a Mormon. He and wife started in 1851 to walk from
Norway, Ill., to Salt Lake, each one lugging a child. They trudged
along with their dear burdens as far as the Mississippi. There
they lost courage and returned to La Salle.

There were Norwegians in that band of religious enthusiasts. A number of the La Salle county Norwegians had become
Mormons. Canute Peterson Marsett had become a Mormon
bishop. He was sent as a missionary to Norway in 1852 and
came back in 1856 with 600 Scandinavian immigrants bound for
Salt Lake City. Ole Heier had been made a bishop, but withdrew
when the Mormons in 1843 proclaimed polygamy legal, and
joined the Close Communion Baptists. Dr. Gudmund Haugaas,
the Slooper, became a high priest of the Order of Melchizedek
and was a Mormon preacher at the time of his death, in 1849.
His son Thomas became his successor as Mormon pastor in

La Salle. The congregation there still exists. A. H. Lund was made an apostle. In the Sugar Creek Colony most of the Norwegians became Mormons. So, from the very start in Utah, there have been Norwegian Mormons. Prof. John Andreas Widtsøe, Ph. D., president of the University of Utah, 1916-1921, one of the greatest experts on dry-farming, is a member of the Council of Twelve Apostles of the Latter Day Saints.

The first census for Utah, 1870, gives 613 foreign-born Norwegians; in 1880, 1,214; in 1890, 1,854; in 1900, 2,128; in 1910, 2,305; in 1920, 2,109.

Michigan (Chippewa Indian name for Great Lake) was explored by French Jesuits as early as 1641. It was taken from the French in 1763 and Detroit was made the capital of England's Northwest Territories. England did not evacuate Detroit until 1796. Michigan became a territory in 1805 and a state in 1835. Its people are engaged in farming, lumbering, mining, shipping and the manufacture of furniture, autos, breakfast foods and health cures.

Michigan, 1848

The first Norwegian to settle in Michigan was Ingebret Larson Narvig, already mentioned as having been Cleng Peerson's traveling companion to the West in 1833. On the way to Illinois he went to work for a farmer six miles north of Erie, Monroe County, Mich., where he married. About two years later he moved into the neighborhood of Adrian, Lanawee County, and there he dwelt until 1856.

According to Martin Ulvestad, in his "Nordmændene i Amerika," the first permanent Norwegian settlement in Michigan was at Muskegon in 1848. Østen Andersen of Ulefos, Telemarken, and Lars Larson of Arendal, were the first settlers. In 1851 Oliver Thompson, another Telemarken emigrant, settled down near Onekoma, Manistee County. In 1856 a third settlement was started at Shelby, Oceana County, by the arrival of Hendrik Hendriksen of Fossum, Bratsberg.

The Norwegian settlements in Michigan are small and scattered. In 1850 there were 110 foreign-born Norwegians in the state; in 1860, 440; in 1870, 1,516; in 1880, 3,520; in 1890, 7,795; in 1900, 7,582; in 1910, 7,638; in 1920, 6,888.

California was discovered by the Spanish officer Mendoza in 1542 and by the Englishman Drake in 1590. It became a Mexican territory in 1824. During our war with Mexico, 1846-1848, it became the possession of the United States. On Jan. 24, 1848, a piece of native gold was found by Marshall at Coloma, Eldorado County. The news electrified the world. By the close of that

California, 1849

year miners assailed the foothills from the Tuolumne to the Feather River. They came from everywhere, adventurers and outlaws, good men and bad, and wild speculation, gambling, robbery, murder, and every other crime was openly committed, unhindered by other form of law higher than lynch law and self defense. In 1849, 100,000 men crossed the American continent to search for gold. In 1850, when California became a state, its registered population was only 92,597.

The Norwegians were among the first to set out for the gold fields. Elias Tasted Larson, oldest son of Lars Larson, Slooper, went there in 1849 and came back alive to tell the story. "Snowshoe" Thompson was the first mail carrier across the Sierras, a most hazardous position, which he faithfully held from 1856 to 1876. In 1860 there were no less than 715 Norwegians born in Norway recorded as citizens of the state. There were probably that many in 1850 trying to pick up a fortune. There is a letter in the "Bratsberg Amtstidende" from Christian Høier, dated Nevada City, Cal., Nov. 25, 1850. He had just crossed the desert—a frightful ordeal. He had met Norwegians at Salt Lake City, members of the Mormon Church—an outlawed sect. He had begun to dig—no sweet task.

California, with its unusually varied and rich natural resources, scenery and climate, had always attracted Norwegians. But, strange to say, it has never developed any large and prominent Norwegian colonies. The Norwegians of California are widely distributed. The census of foreign-born Norwegians is as follows: 1850—no report; 1860—715; 1870—1,000; 1880—1,765; 1890—3,702; 1900—5,060; 1910——9,952; and 1920—11,460.

Minnesota (Indian name, meaning Sky-tinted Water) is the chief Norwegian state in America. It was originally the home of the Chippewas and the Sioux, or Dakotas. The French fur-traders and missionaries began to come here in 1659. Duluth established trading posts in 1678. Hennepin ascended the Mississippi in 1680. In 1803 Minnesota became the property of the United States. It was made a territory in 1849; a state, in 1858. The first number of "Nordlyset," July 17, 1847, discusses the advisability of its being made a territory. "Nordlyset" was the first Norwegian newspaper, right up-to-date in its contents.

Minnesota, 1850

Mention has already been made of the fact that four Norwegians came to Todd County in 1848. Rev. C. L. Clausen came pretty near becoming a citizen of Minnesota in 1849. He was out on an exploring expedition, hunting for a new site for a Norwegian settlement. St. Paul was then a village only eleven years old and consisted of only thirty huts. Clausen took the first steam boat that ever went as far north as St. Paul. The territory of Minnesota had just been created by Congress and St. Paul was its capital city. The boat brought the good news, which was received with wild acclaim. Clausen was not much impressed with the hills of St. Paul as a prospective settlement. So he proceeded on to the Minneapolis side. There was no town on the west side of the river, not a house. On the east side lay the little village of St. Anthony, now a part of Minneapolis. Clausen might have preempted Minneapolis, but did not do so, for the Minneapolis plain was too small and too sandy for the settlement he had in mind. An Indian told him about land some ten miles to the east of St. Paul. Thither he went and found what he wanted in Pierce County, Wisconsin. Thus, writes Holand, Clausen barely escaped becoming t h e founder of one of the world's l a r g e metropolises.

Minneapolis is n o w the capital city of the Norwegian country in America.

The Knitter of the Johnson Self Binder, the First Twine Binder in the World

(a) *St. Paul and Minneapolis*

The second governor of Minnesota was Alexander Ramsey. He had a Norwegian servant girl, Ingeborg Levorsen Langeteig, who, together with her brother Amund, came to St. Paul in 1850. They were from Hallingdal and had stopped off at Rock County, Wisconsin, for a season. Ingeborg Langeteig worked for Governor Ramsey one year, then moved to Fridley, just north of St. Anthony. In 1854 she married an Irishman by the name of Clark. After his death, in 1864, she married Mikkel Johnson, from Selbu, Norway, and settled down in North Minneapolis, where he reigned as a patriarch for many years. He was one of the first settlers of Meeker County, Minn., in 1856. His younger brother, John P. Johnson (Moen), a brave soldier in the Civil War, became the inventor of the first self binder in the world.

(b) *Goodhue County*

In 1850 a number of Norwegians from Rock Prairie, Wis., set out for St. Paul. There were two men who stepped off at a steamboat landing place before reaching St. Paul and, finding the

Self Binders at Work Using J. P. Johnson's Idea

spot to their taste, settled there. They were Halvor H. Peterson (Haugen) and Østen Burtness, both from Numedal, and the place they selected as their home was Red Wing, Goodhue County, where they started to manufacture and ship charcoal. In 1852 Goodhue County was opened for settlement. Strange enough, the general opinion was, that it would take 100 years to settle the whole county. It did not take ten years. In 1851 Matthias Peterson Ringdahl located also at Red Wing, which then boasted three or four houses. In 1854 the immigration caravans began to come in, one after the other, hardy Norsemen from Koshkonong, Rock County, and elsewhere. The first lot to arrive consisted of Henrik Nelson Talla and his brother Tøge and four other families. Henrik Talla had been a gold miner in California. Tøge had found gold in Australia. A son-in-law of Henrik Talla was the well known Hon. Osmund Wing, a noble and philanthropic soul. A son-in-law of Osmund Wing is the professor of church history at Luther Theological Seminary, St. Paul, Rev. Carl M. Weswig, D. D., famed for eloquence. Tøge Talla bore witness to the charms of Goodhue County in these words: "I have lived in three continents and have traveled through many lands, but never have I seen such a beautiful sight as this. Here will I live and here will I die."

Hardly had the first caravan settled down when a second one came into sight. This one consisted of Andreas Bonhus, Erik Gunhus, and about ten other families. Andrew G. Bonhus, a grandson of Andreas Bonhus, is a St. Olaf graduate, a law graduate from the University of Minnesota and has served as mayor of Valley City, N. D., 1920-1924. Andrew's sister, Louise, married one O. M. Norlie, at the time of the nuptials a high school instructor at Stoughton, Wis. A grandson of Erik Gunhus is a man bearing the same name, Rev. Erik H. Gunhus, president of the Lutheran Brethren Synod. No doubt the greatest man who has lived and labored in Goodhue was the Rev. Bernt J. Muus, pastor at Holden from 1859 to 1899. He is buried near the Trondhjem Cathedral, Norway, and a little wooden cross marks his grave telling the story that here lies B.J. Muus, 1832-1900. Some day a more fitting monument will mark the resting place of this tall and noble son of the Lutheran Church, a pioneer among the pioneers of America. Meanwhile St. Olaf College rears up high and pleasant to behold as one of the memorials to his faith.

(c) *Southern Minnesota*

In Southern Minnesota, too, large and thrifty Norwegian settlements were made in the early fifties. Fillmore County was entered in 1851. Even Ellertson started farming that year near Mabel and is the first Norwegian farmer in the state. Carver and Winona counties received Norwegian settlers in 1852; Dakota, Houston and Nicollet counties in 1853; Dodge, Olmsted, Steele and Mower counties in 1854; and so on. Minnesota land had been discovered, dearer to the hearts of Norwegians than the gold of California.

According to the census, the number of foreign-born Norwegians in Minnesota in 1850 was 7; in 1860, 8,425; in 1870, 35,940; in 1880, 62,521; in 1890, 101,169; in 1900, 104,895; in 1910, 105,303; and in 1920, 90,188.

Swedish ships entered the Delaware in 1638 and the first towns founded in Pennsylvania were Swedish. The land was then called New Sweden. Its progress alarmed *Pennsylvania, 1852* the Dutch in New York, who swooped down on the Swedes in 1655 and made captives of them. Nine years later the Dutch had to surrender to the English.

Pennsylvania was given to William Penn to cancel a debt. In 1682 he came to his principality. Pennsylvania was one of the original thirteen states. In the colonial days it was the haven of German refugees and is still the most German of the American commonwealths.

The first Norwegian settlement in this state was that in Potter County, in 1852. Potter County lies in north central Pennsylvania, among the foothills of the Alleghanies, a wild and romantic country, "far from the maddening crowd's ignoble strife." This settlement was conceived and projected by Ole Bull, the master violinist. In his first concert trip to America, 1843-1845, he had studied with sympathetic interest the toil and troubles of the early pioneers. The thought came to him that he could find a better spot to live in than he had seen in Illinois and Wisconsin and that he himself could build a colony which could stand as a monument to his day's work. He got into the hands of some landsharks who sold him 120,000 acres of wild hill and dale at twice the market price. He tried to raise the $300,000.00 to pay for the land by giving "Farewell Concerts," that is, n o t a farewell t o America, but a farewell to his fiddle. His work from now on would be to build the colony. The enterprise might have succeeded except for t h e f a c t that the deeds that he and his settlers received for their money were not worth five cents. The w h o l e transaction was a swindle. The immigration was encouraging. Within a short time he had 1,000 Norwegians in his New Norway and several towns were established—Oleana, Odin and New Bergen.

Ole Bull (insert) and Ole Bull's Castle (1852)
(By permission of Pa. Dept. of Forest and Waters)

A Coudersport paper, "The People's Journal," has an editorial dated Sept. 10, 1852, entitled "Good News for Potter County." This announces the coming of Ole Bull and the Norwegians. It relates that 105 are on the way to the proposed colony at Kettle Creek (now Oleana), and adds: "Let them come. The more, the better." This paper contained poems to the colonists, of which the following lines are a sample:

Lo! Forest and valley and mountain lie spread
Untouched save by sunlight and wandering breeze,
Awaiting to welcome the Northmen's free tread
To their echoing slopes and their shadowing trees.

To make a long story short, the project failed. The settlers could not get their warranty deeds and began to pull out. Ole Bull hastened away to raise money by his concerts, from the proceeds of which he sent load after load of provisions to his people to meet their needs. The latest survivor of the colony

Autos Visiting Ole Bull's Castle in 1924
(By permission of Pennsylvania Department of Forest and Waters)

who remained there as long as he lived was Ole Olsen, who died at New Bergen in 1903, fifty years after the hopes of the colonists were shattered.

In "Oleana," a very interesting work on the Ole Bull Colony, by Thorstein Jahr, a library expert at the Library of Congress, the story of the colony is related and a number of survivors are located. As, for example:

John N. Holfeldt established the firm Holfeldt and McDonald, Quebec, 1853-1863, and then a shipping business at Stavanger, 1863-1873. Bertel V. Suckow became a bookbinder at Rock Prairie, Wis., 1854, the publisher of "Billed Magasin," Madison, 1868-1870 (Prof. Svein Nilssen, editor), and finally he worked for the "Milwaukee Sentinel," until 1885. Christian F. Solberg became editor of "Emigranten," 1857-1868, studied law, was postmaster in the Wisconsin Legislature, 1869-1871, edited "Minnesota," 1872, was appointed commissioner of statistics, 1872-1876, railroad commissioner, 1876-1881, was with the Chicago, Milwaukee and St. Paul Railroad, 1881-1883, with the New York Life until his death. A daughter of Jens Jacobsen, of Oleana, became the wife of Charles Kittleson, state treasurer of Minnesota, 1879-1883, and president of Columbia National Bank,

Minneapolis. Johan S. Irgens was a soldier in the Fifteenth
Wisconsin and the first Norwegian to hold the office of secre-
tary of state in Minnesota, 1875-1879. Burt Olson was editor of
the "McKean County Miner," Pa., and died in Chattanooga,
Tenn., Nov., 1902. Ole Snyder, the first child born at Oleana,
is a lawyer at Buffalo, N. Y. Knud Olsen lived at Stoughton,
Wis. Ole Teppen and Syver Iversen were farmers at Coon
Valley, Wis.

The foreign-born Norwegians of Pennsylvania for the decennial years are: 1850—27; 1860—83; 1870—115; 1880—
381; 1890—2,238; 1900—1,393; 1910—2,320; 1920—2,446.

New Hampshire was founded by Englishmen in 1623 and
was one of the original thirteen states. The state has only one
real Norwegian settlement—at Berlin Mills,
New Hampshire,   Coos County. This was founded in 1854 by
1854   Johannes L. Osvold, immigrant from Oslo,
Norway. The next to join his colony were
Carl Olson, Herman Olsen and Nils Holje. Osvold was postmaster at Berlin Mills for many years. Osvold, Even A.
Nøttestad, Hans C. Johnson and Anton L. Petterson, all Norwegians, have been members of the New Hampshire State Legislature. In 1890 Rev. G. T. Rygh organized a Norwegian Lutheran Congregation at Berlin Mills with 87 members. In 1915
this congregation had 538 members.

New Hampshire has never figured as a Norwegian state. In
1850 it registered only two born in Norway; in 1860, five; in
1870, 55; in 1880, 79; in 1890, 251; in 1900, 295; in 1910, 491;
and in 1920, 427.

Nebraska was a part of French Louisiana. It became a territory in 1854; a state in 1867. The name is an Indian word,
meaning "Shallow Water." There are no
Nebraska, 1857   mountains in the state, but wide, rolling prairies, cut by slow, shallow streams. Both the
valleys and the uplands provide rich soil. It is a great farming
country.

The first Norwegian settlement was at Lime Grove, Dixon
County, in 1857. Mons Nilson, from Vossevangen, was the first
Norwegian settler. In 1920 there were foreign-born Norwegians
in 88 of the 93 counties in Nebraska, but the settlements were
all small. Dixon County ranked fifth in Norwegian population.
It has had four Norwegian Lutheran congregations. The first of
these was the Lime Creek Church, three miles south of Maskell,
organized September 25, 1873, with 34 souls, Rev. E. G. A.
Christensen, first pastor.

The Norwegians of the first generation located in Nebraska

by census years are as follows: 1850—no report; 1860—no report; 1870—506; 1880—2,010; 1890—3,632; 1900—2,833; 1910—2,750; 1920—2,165.

Kansas is the geographical center of the United States. Coronado marched through Kansas in 1541 and says that he traversed "mighty plains and sandy heaths, smooth and wearisome, and bare of wood." In describing the buffalo then roaming over the limitless plains, he says: "All that way the plains are as full of crooked-backed oxen as the mountain Serena in Spain is full of sheep." Kansas became a part of the United States by the Louisiana Purchase in 1803. It was made a territory in 1854 and a state in 1861. The Kansas-Nebraska Bill of 1854 left it to each commonwealth to settle whether it should be slave or free. Two

Kansas, 1857

Hunting the Buffalo

great hostile tides of immigration began to flow into Kansas, the one Pro-slavery from Missouri and the South, the other Free-Soilers from the North. A terrible civil war ensued, and "Bleeding Kansas" aroused the pity of the world. John Brown was the leader of the Freedom party, later a martyr to the cause. "His soul is marching on." The settlers of Kansas were some of the bravest men from the North and South, met here to fight for a principle.

The hardy Norseman was also in Kansas, and, though a newcomer, he was in the thick of the fight—for freedom. Charles Christianson, from East Toten, Nels Ladd from Sogndal, and Mathias Johnson from Biri, moved from Dane Co., Wis., to Greenwood Co., Kans., in 1857. Their address was Eureka; their market, Kansas City, Mo., was 150 miles distant. In 1858 they were joined by six other countrymen from Dane Co. In 1870 Rev. G. M. Erdahl organized a Norwegian Lutheran congregation for them. In 1858 a second settlement was planted at Lancaster,

Atchison County, by Harold O. Tvedt, a Valdris, coming down from La Crosse, Wis. Brown and Doniphan Counties were peopled by Norwegians about 1860. In 1920 88 of the 105 counties in the state had Norwegians born in Norway. None of the settlements is large.

The immigrant Norwegians in Kansas are listed by the census as follows: 1850—no report; 1860—223; 1870—588; 1880—1,358; 1890—1,786; 1900—1,477; 1910—1,294; 1920—970.

In 1859 there were no Dakotas. The territory of Dakota was created in 1861 out of Nebraska and Minnesota. In 1889 Dakota Territory was made two states—South Dakota *South Dakota, 1859* and North Dakota. South Dakota is a farming state essentially, with gold and silver mining in the Black Hills in the southwest corner of the state. The seal of the state bears a river with a steamboat, and on the right a farmer at the plow, with a herd of cattle and a field of corn. On the left stands a smelting furnace and a range of hills. The Norwegians came to South Dakota early in great numbers and have worked hard to make it a good state. Four of the nine governors have been Norwegians—A. E. Lee, C. N. Herreid, P. Norbeck, and Carl Gunderson; 3 of the lieutenant governors—Herreid, Norbeck and Gunderson; 3 of the secretaries of state—A. O. Ringsrud, Thomas Thorsen and O. C. Berg; 1 state auditor—H. B. Anderson; 2 state treasurers—George G. Johnson and G. H. Helgerson; 2 state superintendents—H. A. Ustrud and C. G. Lawrence; 1 U. S. Senator—Peter Norbeck; 2 congressmen—C. A. Christopherson and William Williamson.

Clay County was the seat of the first Norwegian settlement in South Dakota, founded in 1859. South Dakota was entered from the Nebraska, not the Iowa side, by these first land seekers. Lars A. Torblaa, from Hardanger, Sjur H. Myran, from Hallingdal, Ole O. Gjeitli, from Voss, and Elling O. Engum, from Sogn, were the first to cross over into Dakota. They came from Koshkonong. Torblaa has the honor of being the first Norwegian to place his feet on Dakota soil. Soon there came other delegations from the eastern settlements. Three of the Norwegian governors of South Dakota—Andrew E. Lee, Peter Norbeck, and Carl Gunderson—have lived in this county. Norbeck was born in Clay County. According to Martin Odland, the newspaper man, born in Clay Co., the first white child born in Dakota was a Norwegian, Ole Olson, also a Clay Co. product. In 1894 Ole Olson ran for senator against Carl Gunderson, the present governor, and defeated him. Olson now lives in Oregon.

In 1861 Rev. Abraham Jacobson, of Decorah, Ia., accompanied a company of eight to these Dakota settlements at Vermilion, Clay Co., and the adjoining counties to the east and west, Union and Yankton. The town of Yankton was the capital city. Jacobson was pleasingly surprised to find that he was acquainted with

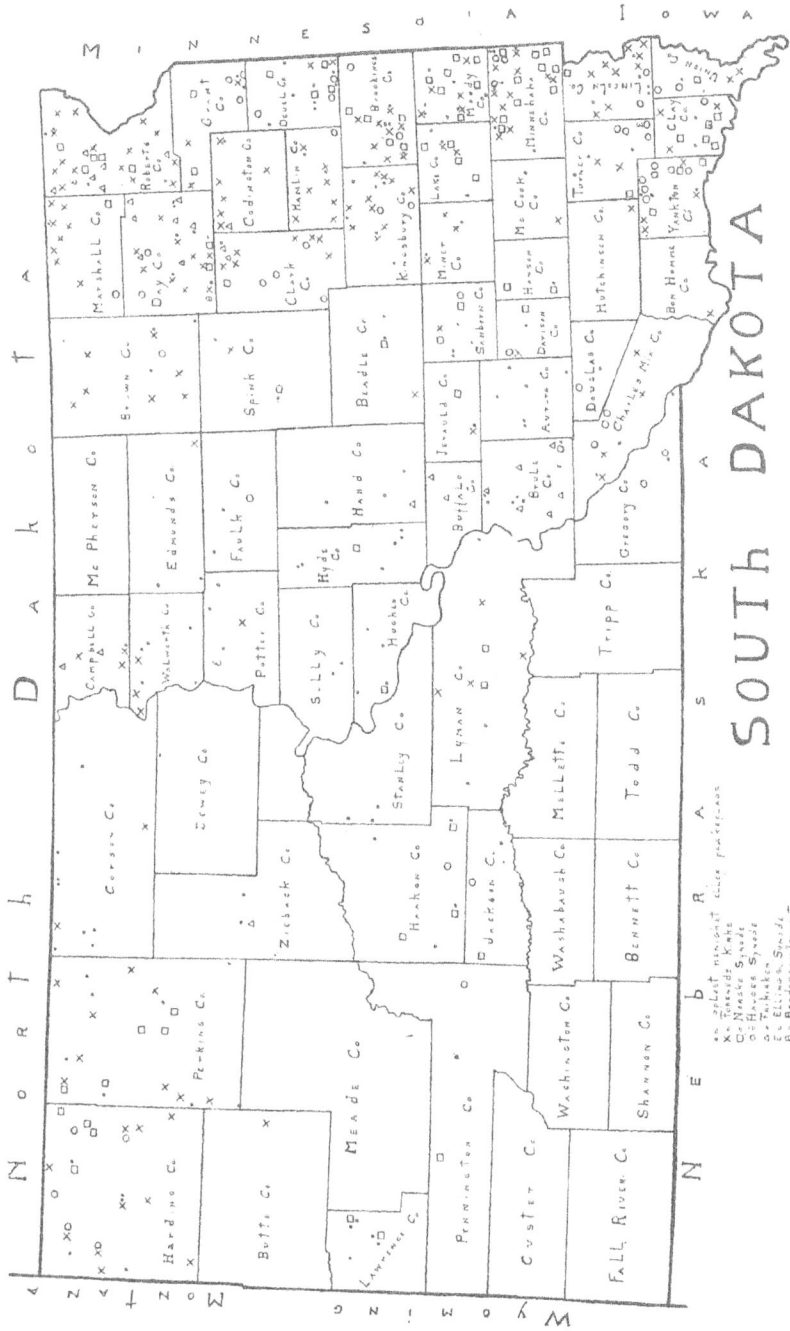

SOUTH DAKOTA

Shows Where the Norwegian Lutheran Congregations Are Located.

the newly appointed governor, his wife and other functionaries. They all hailed from Springfield, the home of Lincoln, then just elected president of the United States. Jacobson had attended the Illinois State University, Springfield, 1852-1860, and had been a school mate of Robert Todd Lincoln, who attended that school. Jacobson describes the primitive conditions—the slow ox cart, the sod cellars without windows or roofs, the open prairies and prairie fires, the Indians and their ways, the political tension, the hunger for God's Word. During a rain, Jacobson had to seek shelter at a shack. The husband was not at home. The wife and children slept in the wagon box, for there was no other bed. So Jacobson sat on a bench in the corner of the cellar, holding an umbrella over his head all night, to ward off the cold November rain. Hospitality was freely shown in those days. Everyone was willing to share his last morsel with a traveler. And these settlers were young and full of faith and hope and charity. When asked if she did not think the situation looked rather hopeless out there on the cold, bleak prairies, a woman replied: "Better times are coming." They came.

South Dakota has been a favored state with regard to the Norwegians. Of Norwegians born in Norway it had in 1850, none; in 1860, 129; in 1870, about 800; in 1880 about 8,000; in 1890, 19,257; in 1900, 19,788; in 1910, 20,018; and in 1920, 16,813.

5. Churches, 1825-1860

Since 1536 the Lutheran Church has been the State Church in Norway. At the time of the departure of the Sloop, in 1825, the whole country was nominally Lutheran except about a dozen dissenters. Even today nearly 99% of the people belong to the Lutheran Church, in spite of the fact that there is complete religious toleration and that Roman Catholics, Methodists, Baptists, Adventists, Salvation Army people, Mormons, Quakers, and other denominations have carried on a very active propaganda in Norway for many years. The American Methodists, for example, began work in Norway in 1853, in Sweden in 1854, in Denmark in 1857, and in Finland in 1883. From 1851 to 1920 they contributed $2,636,141.00 to establish themselves in Scandinavia and $746,760.00 among the Scandinavian immigrants to the United States. In 1920, according to the Report of the Board of Foreign Missions of the Methodist Church North, there were 27,688 Methodists in Scandinavia, of whom 6,406 were in Norway. Nearly all the sectarian movements have come from England and America, and, while they have not caused much of an exodus out of the Lutheran Church, they have nevertheless in places profoundly affected the thought, life and literature of the Norwegian Lutherans. Thus, the Quaker movement which began in 1816 with Lars Larson, Elias Tastad, and a half dozen others, had increased outwardly to only 86 in 1920, but inwardly it had affected many of the

Lutherans so that they were dissatisfied with the Lutheran Church and bore a spirit of dissent against it.

The Norwegian immigrants to America carried with them as religious heritage from Norway, not only the Lutheran faith, but also the religious tendencies within the Lutheran Church over there. There were three marked tendencies which can possibly be expressed by the terms high schurch, low church and broad church.

Religious Situation in Norway

The high church tendency was one that highly respected the Church as a divine institution, the Word and the Sacraments as the Means of Grace, and the ministry as a holy office. The pastors of Norway and the upper classes generally were high churchly. Now, unfortunately, during the 18th century Rationalism came like a black shroud over the State Church of Norway. Under cover of this darkness there was much indifference both to pure doctrine and Christian living. The high churchly view then came to be associated with worldliness in teaching and practice.

The low church view came as a protest to this worldliness. It demanded that men should repent and believe. It called for personal experience in the power of the Gospel to save sinners and the privilege of every man, nay, even the duty, to bear witness of the fact that he has himself found peace with God and that God can save sinners. It called for Bible reading and prayer, prayer meetings and lay preaching, in addition to the regular work by the pastor. But, unfortunately, since the pastors and official classes as a rule opposed the low church movement, the men who held the low church views began to look upon everything connected with the high church as dangerous—the Church, the ministry, the ritual, the ordinances, the ministerial training. They regarded seminaries as spiritual cemeteries. Hans Nielsen Hauge, the great reformer, was clear in his own mind as to the value of the Church and the ministry, but some of his followers, called Haugeans, were more extreme in their opposition to the high church party.

The broad church view saw the need, on the one hand, of law and order, of ministry and ceremonies, and, on the other hand, they acknowledged also that there must be Christian living according to the true teaching of the Word and that lay people must have the privilege, as they have the duty, to bear witness and "show forth the excellencies of Him Who called them out of darkness into His marvellous light" (1 Pet. 2:9). But, unfortunately here, too, the men of the broad church view were apt to include the bad as well as the good in the other two tendencies. These tendencies were found in Norway in 1825. The leaders were high church people. The Haugeans were low church. The majority of the people were broad church, tolerant and easy going.

In addition to these three movements within the Lutheran Church there was the sectarian movement which refused to conform to Lutheran doctrines and practices. The Quakers of Stavanger were such dissenters and schismatics. And while possibly not more than five of the Sloopers were Quakers, the members on the boat were to a large extent affected by the Quaker spirit of dissent.

Norway had only one recognized church in 1825; America had over 100, most of them of the Reformed group. Here was
Religious Situation in America
perfect religious freedom with high churchly, low churchly and broad churchly groups of every description. Here you could belong to church or not, as you pleased. What a strange world to these newcomers of ours who had been compelled to baptize their children and confirm them in the Lutheran faith! But there was some difficulty in knowing just what to do here. Should they join the great throng who did not belong to any church? Should they join one of the American churches? If so, which one? Even the Quakers in the party found it difficult to agree as to whether they should be Orthodox, Hicksite, Wilburite or Primitive. Lars Larson remained Orthodox Quaker; Ole Johnson chose the Hicksite brand. Their children became Baptists. The Adventists made a strong bid for their support; they put up a school right in the heart of the Fox River Settlement, which is still standing as a witness of missionary zeal. The Baptists and Methodists labored among them both long and faithfully, but there were a dozen kinds of Baptists and as many Methodist denominations, so it was rather difficult to know which one was in the right. Campbellites and Congregationalists, Presbyterians and Episcopalians, all looked upon the Norwegian immigrants as their rightful possession and added to the religious confusion. Possibly the boldest of all, and the most successful, were the Mormons. In La Salle County Mormon and Methodist congregations are still at work. whose membership is to a large extent drawn from the descendants of the Sloop Folk and later arrivals from Norway. As a concrete illustration of the effects of the religious confusion in America the case of the Rossadal family is typical. Daniel Rossadal was a good man and a good Quaker. He had a large family and no doubt tried to bring them up in the Quaker faith. His descendants are numerous—255—and representative citizens and churchmen. But they are distributed among a great number of denominations. in the following order, beginning with the denomination that has had most of them as members,—Lutheran, Methodist, Congregational-

ist, Adventist, Catholic, Quaker, Campbellite, Mormon. And in addition 40% of them are not known to belong to any church. Such are the conditions in America.

And yet, in the midst of all the preaching, it seemed to many that there was a famine in the land, "not a famine of bread, nor a thirst for water, but of hearing the *Lay Preachers*   words of the Lord" (Amos 8:11). The words of their friends in Norway came true, that "they would feel like a people in captivity among the heathen people, when they could not gather about the Word of God according to their custom; they would think of the ringing of the church bells in their home valley; they would remember the festive march to church on a clear, glorious Sunday morning, call to mind the singing, the sermon, the communion, the chanting at the altar, and feel so unutterably forsaken and poor." So great would their want and longing be, that their wail of woe, as A. O. Vinje had predicted, would be likened to that of the children of Judah in captivity: "By the rivers of Babylon, there we sat down, yea, we wept, when we remembered Zion. We hanged our harps upon the willows in the midst thereof" (Ps. 137:1-2). That many of the immigrants felt such a hunger and sorrow is really a fact, as can be seen from the letters which they wrote home and from the personal witness of men and women who have lived through the pioneer days before the Lutheran Church came to feed their hungry souls. And this situation was perfectly natural, for the Word of God has been taught in its truth and purity in the Old Country, and His Word does not return void unto Him (Isa. 55:11).

It was especially the Norwegian Lutherans of high churchly leanings that felt that it was a great hardship not to have a Norwegian Lutheran Church in their midst. The low churchly group had recourse to prayer meetings, by means of which they strengthened one another. Practically everyone took along his Bible and hymn book and possibly also his catechism and postil. Occasionally, of course, this had been neglected. Still, most of the goodbyes had been said amidst prayers by the old folks and admonitions to read the Bible and follow its precepts to watch and pray. John W. Arctander, in his book, "Trøst for Tvivlere" (Comfort for Doubters), relates that when he left his home, his pious parents duly prayed with him and admonished him to be a child of God. Then, with these parental blessings, he set out. As soon as he came out in the harbor, he went to his trunk, for he was sure to find a Bible there. And there it was, a brand new one. At that time, and for many years afterward, he hated all this talk about Christianity, so his object was to get a hold of the Bible and throw it away. He took the Good Book, spit into it and then

A Haugean Meeting: Lay Preaching
(Painted by Herbjørn Gausta, Minneapolis)

heaved it into the sea. But there came a day when he had to have it again to get peace for his troubled soul.

The immigrants of the low church group held prayer meetings. At these devotional gatherings, some one acted as leader. He would read a Bible selection, which he then proceeded to expound and to apply. Sin and grace was the general theme of every lay sermon, and exhortations to repent and believe were as much a part of the sermon as the amen was a part of their prayers. Anyone in the gathering could take part in prayer, praise, personal witnessing or song. The prayer meetings were serious occasions, at which sinners came to the throne of mercy for pardon and peace.

Ole Olson Hettletvedt was the first lay preacher among the Norwegian settlers. He preached on the Sloop and was engaged in preaching until his death in 1849, 24 years later. There are men still living who can testify to having heard him and to having been edified by his glad tidings. O. J. Hatlestad writes about him these words of fitting tribute: "He was the first one in the Fox River Settlement to gather the people about the Word of God. This humble and serious-minded man later became known in wider circles among our countrymen, in that he was sent out by the American Bible Society as a Bible agent. In that capacity he visited the Norwegian settlements in Illinois, Wisconsin and parts of Iowa." Hatlestad mentions also a number of other laymen in Illinois and Wisconsin who served their people as lay preachers. His list, which is not exhaustive, includes: Aslak Aae, Endre Osmundsen Aagerbø, Herman Osmundsen Aagerbø, John Brakestad, Bjørn Hatlestad, Even Heg, Peder Asbjørnson (Mehus), and Kleng Skaar. Asbjørnson became ordained in 1856.

The people felt the need of more fixed forms and regular services than they were getting through the prayer meetings and lay preachings. Jørgen Pedersen was called by the Haugean Lutherans to administer the Sacraments as well as to preach the Word. He accepted the call, and once administered the Lord's Supper at Indian Creek, near Leland, Ill. Shortly afterward he joined the Mormon Church. In 1837, Ole Olson Heier came to La Salle. He had been a school teacher in Norway and was an earnest Haugean of fine presence and great ability as a speaker. He was then called to take Pedersen's place. He accepted. For a time he warned against the heresies of the Mormons, but not long afterward he also joined them. He became an elder in their church and then a bishop, but eventually he joined the Baptists. The third layman to be called as minister was the greatest of all Norwegian lay preachers in those days, and perhaps since. He remained faithful to the Lutherans to the end. This man was Elling Eielsen.

Eielsen was born at Voss, Norway, September 19, 1804. He was just 35 years old when he arrived in America. Trained as a blacksmith and carpenter, when he "got religion" he dropped his profession and began to witness. In the footsteps of Hauge he traveled as a revivalist back and forth all over Norway, from North Cape to Lindesnes. He had suffered under the cross— had been mocked and threatened, and cast into prison. Still he kept on undaunted, bearing testimony to the faith that was within him. He was assured that a disciple was not above his Master. In his sermons he was true to Scripture. His sermons were exposi- tions and exhortations, well seasoned with quotations from the Bible and the hymn book and illustrations from life. He had little use for the established order of things in church work, especially with regard to rituals, vestments, scholastic training and the like. He was suspicious of the regular clergy because they had perse- cuted him and defended the sham and hypocrisy of the Church. He was therefore often intolerant and hard to cooperate with.

Rev. Mr. and Mrs. Elling Eielsen

He came at the right time, and he came to work while it was day. He preached in Chicago the day he arrived there. He preached in Fox River and at all places where he went. At Fox River he built a house of oak, with two rooms on the ground floor to be used as a hospice for immigrants and one room on the sec- ond floor as a church auditorium for his services. This house was actually used as a church from 1841 to 1847 and as hospice for many more years. It is the first Norwegian Lutheran church edi- fice in America. When he discovered that there was a shortage in Norwegian school books he secured a supply by going to New York to get them printed. This he did twice, in 1841 and in 1842. In 1841, when he was in New York, the good ship "Emilia" came in with another boatload of immigrants. Eielsen went on board, caused the people to pause a few minutes before landing, and then he conducted a devotional meeting as a fitting entrance to this land of promise. On that boat he met a young woman, Sigrid Nelson Tufte, who two years later became his wife. The cane which Eielsen used and which comforted him in his long pilgrimages he gave to his friend, Rev. Ole E. Hofstad; Hofstad gave it to his favorite deacon, Mathias J. Aus, Canton, S. D.; Aus gave it to O. M. Norlie, reared on the Dakota prairies as his neighbor; Norlie gave it to the Luther College Museum, the greatest depository of Norwegian pioneer articles in America. See "Ellings Stav" in "Visergutten," October, 1920.

He came at the right time, and his influence is felt to this day. Drinking, dancing and other forms of worldliness were getting the upper hand in the Norwegian settlements. His was a voice in the wilderness, calling to repentance. The work of the sects, as stated, was bewildering. Eielsen was a dissenter, but not a sectarian. He knew what he wanted, and proceeded in a bold, uncompromising manner to get it. He wanted people to be converted Christians according to the Lutheran doctrines. He established congregations. He organized the first Norwegian synod in America. In the constitution of this synod he makes provision for the teaching of the young in both languages (Norwegian and English). He was the first Norwegian to publish books in America. He was the first home mission superintendent. He helped to found three higher schools—Lisbon Seminary, Lisbon, Ill., 1855-56; Eielsen Seminary, Cambridge, Wis., 1865-68; and Hauge College and Eielsen Seminary, Chicago, Ill., 1871-1878. He advocated doing mission work among the American Indians, a "foreign" mission work that his synod still is engaged in. He intended to build an orphans' home in memory of his son Elias, who was killed while working as a carpenter on the Palmer House, Chicago. His greatest influence is perhaps in this, that he got the Norwegian people to start doing definite congregational work and, by his uncompromising attitude in favor of lay preaching and conversion, he kept the extreme high churchmen from becoming too much like the State Church. Blessed be his memory.

It is written: "How beautiful are the feet of them that preach the Gospel of peace, and bring glad tidings of good things" (Isa. 52:7; Rom. 10:15). This Bible passage ap-

Pastors, 1825-1860 plies with peculiar fitness to the pioneer pastors among the Norwegian settlers. In the period 1825-1860 there were 38 Norwegian Lutheran pastors. The honor roll is given on Page 196.

These 38 ministers averaged 26 years of service in the Norwegian Lutheran Church of America. Eielsen, Clausen, Andrewson, Anderson, Scheie, Hatlestad, Asbjørnsen, Olsen, Boyum, Strand, Johnson, Scheldahl, Amlund and Fjeld were parochial school teachers and lay preachers who had been pressed into the service as preachers. J. W. C. Dietrichson, Stub, A. C. Preus, Brandt, G. F. Dietrichson, H. A. Preus, Ottesen, Koren, Duus, Munch, Thalberg, Brodahl, Claussen, Larsen, Jensen, Magelssen, and Muus, held the degrees of Master of Arts and Candidate

NORWEGIAN LUTHERAN PASTORS, 1843-1860

Name	Age	Birthplace	Years of Ministry	Synod
Eielsen, Elling	1804-1883	Voss	1843-1883	Eielsen
Clausen, Claus Lauritz	1820-1892	Denmark	1843-1885	Norwegian
Dietrichson, Joh. W. C.	1815-1883	Fredrikstad	1844-1845	
Andrewson, Ole	1818-1885	Telemarken	1846-1850	Northern Illinois
Anderson, Paul	1821-1891	Valdres	1846-1885	Northern Illinois
Scheie, Andreas A.	1818-1885	Rofylke	1848-1884	
Stub, Hans A.	1822-1907	Midthordland	1848-1880	Northern Illinois
Preus, Adolph C.	1814-1878	Trondhjem	1848-1891	Norwegian
Brandt, Nils O.	1824-1921	Valdres	1850-1872	Norwegian
Dietrichson, Gustav F.	1813-1886	Christiansand	1851-1882, 1851-1859	Norwegian
Larsen, Hans	...-1853		1851-1853	Norwegian
Preus, Herman A.	1825-1894	Christiansand	1851-1894	Northern Illinois
Johannesen, Johs.	1826-1902	Karmsund	1852-1856	Norwegian
Ottesen, Jacob A.	1825-1904	L. Romerike	1852-1896	Northern Illinois
Koren, U. Vilhelm	1826-1910	Bergen	1853-1910	Northern Illinois
Duus, Olaus F.	1824-1893	Bamle	1854-1859	Norwegian
Hatlestad, Ole J.	1823-1892	Karmsund	1854-1892	Norwegian
Munch, Johan S.	1827-1908	Christiansand	1855-1859	Norwegian
Rasmussen, Peter A.	1829-1898	Stavanger	1854-1896	Northern Illinois
Thalberg, Hans L.	1824-1901	Skjeberg	1855-1860, 1882-1890	Norwegian
Brodahl, Peter M.	1823-1900	Egersund	1855-1868	Eielsen
Asbjörnsen, Peder L.	1824-1891	Stavanger	1856-1882	
Claussen, Fredrik C.	1810-1870	Trondhjem	1857-1870	Norwegian
Larsen, Laur.	1833-1915	Christiansand	1857-1915	Northern Illinois
Norem, Lars H.	1829-1910	Haugesund	1857-1865	Norwegian
Olsen, Nils F.	1815-1884	S. Söndhordland	1857-1884	Norwegian
Petersen, P. H.	...-1873		1857-1862	Northern Illinois
Boyum, Arne E.	1833-1913	Sogn	1858-1913	Northern Illinois
Strand, Gudmund	1794-1864	N. Söndhordland	1858-1864	Northern Illinois
Jensen, Nils E. S.	1824-1875	Bergen	1859-1873	Eielsen
Johnson, Lars A.	1810-1875	Toten	1859-1875	Eielsen
Magelssen, Claus F.	1830-1904	Nordfjord	1859-1904	Norwegian
Muus, Bernt J. I.	1832-1900	Namdalen	1859-1899	Eielsen
Scheldahl, Osmund	1824-1900	S. Söndhordland	1859-1896	Norwegian
Amlund, Nils	1830-1902	Toten	1860-1893	Norwegian
Duborg, Hans P.	1855-?	Denmark	1860-1871	Eielsen
Fjeld, John N.	1818-1888	Valdres	1860-1888	Norwegian
Jacobson, Abraham	1816-1910	Telemarken	1860-1862	Augustana

in Theology from the University of Christiania. Duborg had attended the universities of Copenhagen and Kiel. Larsen and Johannesen were graduates of Hartwick Seminary, New York, founded in 1798 as a Lutheran school. Hartwick Seminary belonged to the Hartwick and Franckean synods. Rasmussen was a graduate of Concordia Seminary, Ft. Wayne, Ind., a school belonging to the Missouri Synod. Norem, Petersen and Jacobson were graduates of the Illinois State University. This was the name of the college and theological seminary of the Illinois Synod and the Northern Illinois Synod of the English Lutherans. Anderson had attended Beloit College, but no seminary. Just 50% of these pastors were college-trained men, but this percentage is higher than for the Norwegian Lutheran pastors for the 70-year period 1843-1913. In this 70-year period only 40% of the ministers had college degrees.

It should now be noted that the university-trained men from Norway all except Thalberg joined the Norwegian Synod, while the lay preachers were at first followers of Eielsen. The Norwegian Synod represented a high church type of Lutheranism; Eielsen, a low church type. Eielsen's ministerial followers deserted him in 1848 and in 1851 took part in the organization of the Northern Illinois Synod, a broad church synod. In 1850 he obtained a valuable ally in P. A. Rasmussen, but Rasmussen and Eielsen parted in 1856. In 1858 Arne E. Boyum became an "Ellingianer," but in 1876 he became president of the Hauge Synod.

A word or two about a few of these pastors:

Claus Lauritz Clausen was a Dane, born Nov. 3, 1820, at Aerø, Fyen. He had studied business, law and theology, but was not a graduate from any school. He had wanted to go to Zululand as a missionary, took to lay preaching, went to Norway, received a call to come to America as parochial teacher, and came. Shortly after his arrival he was examined by Rev. L. F. E. Krause of the Buffalo Synod and ordained at the wish of the Muskego Congregation. He lived at Muskego; Eielsen was his neighbor at North Cape. They often met, but they could not exactly agree. They agreed to disagree. Eielsen was too extreme. When Dietrichson, a high church extremist, arrived in 1844, Clausen joined him, although at heart he was really a broad church man. In 1845 Clausen became pastor at Koshkonong; in 1846, at Rock Prairie, ill health compelled him to resign and seek a new climate. In 1853 he removed to St. Ansgar, Ia. Here he founded congregations that he served several years, 1853-1856, 1861-1872, resigning again on account of sickness. He was a member of the Iowa Legislature, 1856-57, and a commissioner of immigration, 1857-60. He was a chaplain in the Fifteenth Wisconsin, 1861-62. In 1851, H. A. Preus, A. C. Preus and Clausen met at Rock Prairie, and organized the Norwegian Evangelical Lutheran

Church in America. The constitution of this body, which it was claimed contained too much leaven of Grundtvigianism, was revoked next year, and the Norwegian Synod arose in 1853 on its ruins. Clausen was made the president of the former in 1851. In 1868 he withdrew from the Norwegian Synod on account of a resolution, adopted in 1862, relating to slavery. In 1870 he was one of the leaders in establishing the Norwegian-Danish Conference, a broad church synod. In 1890 he assisted in organizing the United Norwegian Lutheran Church. In 1872 he removed to Virginia to regain his health. He was pastor at Philadelphia, Pa., 1875-77; at Austin, Minn., 1877-85. He spent the last years of his memorable life at Paulsbo, Washington, with his son, who for several years was auditor of Washington. Says J. C. Roseland of him: "His name is woven into the principal events of the history of the Norwegian Lutherans of this country, down

C. L. Clausen   J. W. C. Dietrichson   H. A. Stub

to recent years. Zealously and faithfully he administered to the spiritual wants of the pioneers, traveling continually between the small and scattering settlements throughout the Northwest." He died Feb. 20, 1892.

Johannes Wilhelm Christian Dietrichson was 31 years old when he came to America as a missionary among his people who were literally scattered as sheep without a shepherd. He was a disciple of Bishop N. F. S. Grundtvig and succeeded in swinging Clausen over to his views. A zealous man he was, with a firm hand, and a mighty exponent of the high church view. He had great respect for the office of the ministry and performed his official duties with authority and in full regalia. U. V. Koren said of him: "There is in the 'Ordinance of Christian the Third' a rule, saying that 'Pastors shall always be dressed in the proper vestments.' Dietrichsen observed this command literally, and it is related of him that, even when he hauled wood, water or other stuff, he was clad in his long preacher's gown and with a clerical ruff about his neck." Eielsen, on the other hand, did not use any uniform to distinguish him from others. He was terrified at Dietrichson's high church manners and especially his Grundtvigian doctrines. Grundtvig was a Danish reformer who had awakened the Danish Church out of a rationalistic sleep, but he himself had promulgated some heresies. He strangely declared the Apostles' Creed to be the living Word and the Bible to be a dead word and that there was a possibility for conversion and salvation after death. Eielsen declared war on Dietrichson and Dietrichson on Eielsen. "With Dietrichson's arrival," declares Norelius, "commenced the great church war, which has raged among the Norwegians up to the present time." Dietrichson made a trip to Norway in 1845 to get more men to come to his assistance. He and Clausen could by no means serve the multiplying and growing settlements. In 1850 he returned to Norway for good, where he labored as pastor until 1874, and then as postmaster until 1882. Dietrichson was a worthy exponent of the high church view, a Christian man with both knowledge and zeal. He shared pioneer life with his people without a murmur. He preached his first sermon at Amund Anderson's barn in East Koshkonong on August 30, 1844, and his second service he held under a large oak tree on Knud Aslakson's farm in West Koshkonong. He wanted cleancut rules to go by; his aim was to transplant the Norwegian Lutheran Church to American soil. He was a good husbandman.

Paul Anderson represented another element in the life of the Norwegian Lutheran Church in America. He had attended a Congregational College (Beloit), and had seen and heard things there which he thought worth taking along. He favored the use of English. He was much wrought up about the slavery question. In 1848 he joined the Franckean Synod of New York, chiefly because of the vigor with which this Synod combatted slavery. The name Franckean sounded good to him and the one Franckean pastor he knew was a fine Lutheran. That this Franckean Synod was rather weak on the Augsburg Confession he at that time knew little or nothing about. In 1851 Anderson joined in the movement to establish a Northern Illinois Synod. Swedish, Norwegian, German and English Lutherans joined hands in the venture. Anderson served both as secretary and president of this new synod. The new synod was to be a part of the General Synod, whose leading theologian at the time was S. S. Schmucker, a man of liberal tendencies. The English Lutherans of the N. Illinois represented Schmucker's views all too well, for they wrote a constitution in which the Augsburg Confession was referred to as only "mainly correct." In 1852, upon motion by Paul Anderson, the words "mainly correct" were stricken, but the spirit which had put them there remained as strong as before. It finally caused the Scandinavians to withdraw and organize a more staunch Lutheran synod, the Scandinavian Augustana, in 1860. Anderson translated the Illinois Constitution into Norwegian in 1847 and the United States Constitution, in 1854. He wanted the Norwegian people quickly to become Americanized and Anglicized.

Hans Andreas Stub was a much-beloved pastor, whose name is still a household word. Adolph Carl Preus was an energetic president of the Norwegian Synod during many trying years, 1853-1862. Nils O. Brandt was the first pioneer pastor west of the Mississippi, a teacher at Luther College, 1865-1882, and a man of long and inspiring influence. His wife, nee Didrikke Ottesen, was a wonderful mother in Israel, of blessed memory. She never tired in behalf of students at Luther College; thousands enjoyed her hospitality. Hundreds of the great Norwegians, as well as those not so famous, have had their stockings darned and their pantaloons mended by this kind woman and her ladies'

P. A. Rasmussen   Knud Henderson   L. M. Bjørn

aids. Her brother, Jakob Aall Ottesen, was one of the most learned of the early pastors. Herman Amberg Preus was the man who reorganized the Norwegian Synod and commanded it through thick and thin, from 1862 to 1894. And those were strenuous days, with doctrinal controversies and practical problems every day. Ulrik Vilhelm Koren, pastor at Washington Prairie, Iowa, 1853-1910, succeeded Preus as president of the Norwegian Synod, 1894-1910. A staunch Lutheran, a learned scholar, an excellent writer, a wise administrator, mighty in debate, inspiring in his contacts with men. Ole J. Hatlestad added much to our knowledge of pioneer conditions by his "Historiske Meddelelser" (Historical Communications) based on 40 years' experience as church worker, a man among men. Peter Andreas Rasmussen, at first a disciple of Eielsen, then a member of the Norwegian Synod, then, again, a leader among the Anti-Missourians who fought the Norwegian Synod, and finally, one of the organizers of the United Norwegian Lutheran Church. Pastor at Lisbon, Ill., 1854-96; president of Lisbon Seminary, 1855-56; founder of the Lisbon Norwegian Lutheran Society for the Publication of Norwegian School Books and Devotional Literature, 1856; publisher of "Kirkelig Tidende" (Church Times), 1856-61; "Opbyggelsesblad" (Devotional Paper), 1877-1887; printer of many books; friend of foreign missions; father of four sons in the ministry—Gerhard (1883—), Henry Edmund (1890—), Wilhelm Augustin (1890—) and Halbert Jacob (1898—). Laur. Larsen, the grand old man and Nestor among Norwegian educators, pastor, 1857-1915, professor, 1859-1915; and president of Luther College, 1861-1902. Arne E. Boyum, a Haugean, faithful unto death, pastor, 1858-1916, first president of Hauge Synod, 1876-1887. Bernt J. I. Muus, pastor at one time of 28 pioneer congregations, in a district as large as Denmark, and which now numbers over 150 self-supporting Norwegian Lutheran congregations.

Whole books might be written about each of these men and also about the other pastors of this period. Their lives are epics. Two books have already been written about Eielsen—Brøhaugh and Eisteinsen's in 1883 and E. O. Mørstad's in 1917. There are good sketches of him in various other books, as: one by John Johnson, in 1887; J. C. Roseland, in 1890; O. M. Norlie, in 1915; and M. O. Wee, 1919. R. Andersen has published the Life of Clausen, 1924; L. M. Bjørn wrote one on P. A. Rasmussen in 1905. Mrs. Elisabeth Koren's "Fra Pioneertiden" (From the Pioneer Days), extracts from a daybook and letters in 1853-1854, was published by her children in 1914. The historical magazine "Symra" contains spirited accounts about some of these heroes: Svein Strand writes about C. L. Clausen (1913); H. G. Stub, about H. A. Stub (1907); A. Bredesen, about N. O. Brandt (1907), and H. A. Preus (1910); C. K. Preus, about H. A. Preus (1906); L. S. Swenson, about Laur. Larsen (1909); Th. Eggen, about B. J. I. Muus (1910); Clara Jacobson, about A. Jacobson (1912); also one on "Nogle Gamle Minder" (Some Old Recollections), by Laur. Larsen, 1913.

In his speech before the House of Representatives, February 24, 1925, Congressman O. J. Kvale, himself a Norwegian Lutheran pastor (1894-1923), says about the pioneer pastors:

"An inspiring thing it is to recall the stories of the lives of the young men, many of them university graduates, who had been ordained to the ministry in Norway, with splendid openings and careers ahead of them there, but who, nevertheless, at great sacrifice, were willing to abandon these confident hopes and throw their lot with their countrymen who so sorely needed their services in the New World. Of these there were many; more than could be enumerated here. But the roster of their names includes, among others, the names of Eielsen, Clausen, Dietrichson, Anderson, Stub, Preus, Brandt, Ottesen, Koren, Hatlestad, Rasmussen, Larsen, Magelssen, Muus, Hanson, Dahl, Homme, Lysnes, Weenaas, Ylvisaker, Wright, Hoyme, Mohn, Oftedal, Sverdrup. Surely these names are chiseled in adamant by the Recording Angel of God. Their work lives forever in the hearts of their blood brethren, in the history of this Nation."

Pastoral calls were extended to Jørgen Pedersen in 1836 by the Fox River Lutherans; to Ole Heier, in 1837. Ole Nattesta, on behalf of the Jefferson Prairie Lutherans, sent a letter of call to Norway in 1839. Elling Eielsen was called in 1843 at Fox River, although he had previously served the Lutherans there four years and had built them a church there in 1841. C. L. Clausen was called to serve Muskego in 1843. J. W. C. Dietrichson tells in his book on the settlements ("Reiser blandt de norske Emigranter") just how he proceeded to organize the congregations at Koshkonong in 1844. These were the first attempts at gathering the Norwegians into organized congregations and securing regular pastoral care. The following is a list of the congregations organized before 1850. There were also preaching stations, but they are not included. For a description of the congregations see "Norsk Lutherske Menigheter i Amerika, 1843-1916".

Congregations, 1825-1860

The first Norwegian Lutheran Synod was the Evangelical Lutheran Church in America, commonly called the Eielsen Synod or the Elling Synod. It was organized in 1846 at Jefferson Prairie, Wis., "where a few of the widely scattered believers were assembled at a publicly called church meeting." A constitution was then and there drawn up. "Eielsen dictated and Andrewson wrote" that constitution which has since been called the "Gamle Konstitution" (Old Constitution). It was quite polemical. In Paragraph 1 it refutes the charge that the followers of Eielsen are a sect—they are true Lutherans. In Paragraph 2 conversion is demanded as a condition for membership — Clausen and Dietrichson accepted nominal Lutherans as members. Paragraph 6 is an attack on the "papal authority" and the clerical gowns of the State Church pastors and a warning is put on record against the "scribes which desire to walk in long robes, and love greetings in the markets, to be seen of men" (Luke 20:46). Paragraph 6 rejects the laying on of hands in Communion, practised by the Norwegian Synod.

Synods, 1825-1860

The second synod with which the Norwegians were connected was the Franckean Synod of New York. It was organized in 1837 by four German-English Lutheran pastors and four delegates. In 1908 it united with the Hartwick Synod (1830) and the Synod of New York and New Jersey (1872) to form the New York Synod, since 1918 one of the constituent synods of the United Lutheran Church in America. Paul Anderson was the only Norwegian pastor who officially belonged to the Franckeans. Andrewson supported it in 1848-1851.

NORWEGIAN LUTHERAN CONGREGATIONS, 1843-1850

Year	Location	Congregation	Synod	1st pastor	1st membership
1843-1847	Middlepoint, Illinois	Fox River	Eielsen	Eielsen	53
1843-....	Muskego, Wisconsin	Norway	Norwegian	Clausen	230
1843-1883	North Cape, Wisconsin	North Cape	Eielsen	Eielsen	?
1844-....	Cambridge, Wisconsin	Østre Koshkonong	Norwegian	Dietrichson	200
1844-....	Stoughton, Wisconsin	Vestre Koshkonong	Norwegian	Dietrichson	150
1844-....	Palmyra, Wisconsin	St. Mattæus	Norwegian	Dietrichson	160
1844-....	Milwaukee, Wisconsin	Norsk Lutherske	Norwegian	Clausen	?
1844-....	Orfordville, Wisconsin	Luther Valley	Norwegian	Clausen	250
1844-....	Clinton, Wisconsin	Jefferson Prairie	Eielsen	Eielsen	?
1844-....	Whitewater, Wisconsin	Heart Prairie	Norwegian	Dietrichson	37
1844-....	Hartford, Wisconsin	St. Olaf's	Norwegian	Unonius	355
1844-....	Oconomowoc, Wisconsin	St. Johannes	Norwegian	Unonius	120
1844-1853	Capron, Illinois	Long Prairie	Norwegian	Dietrichson	?
1844-1863	Woodstock, Illinois	Queen Anne Prairie	Northern Illinois	Scheie	75
1844-1848	Chicago, Illinois	Menigheden		Clausen	?
1844-....	Wiota, Wisconsin	Wiota Norsk	Norwegian	Dietrichson	?
1845-....	Ixonia, Wisconsin	St. Lukas	Norwegian	Dietrichson	350
1845-....	Keyser, Wisconsin	Lodi	Eielsen	Eielsen	53
1846-....	Chicago, Illinois	Trefoldigheds	Eielsen	Eielsen	?
1847-....	De Forest, Wisconsin	Norway Grove	Norwegian	Dietrichson	104
1847-....	Norway, Illinois	Hauges	Eielsen	Eielsen	50
1847-1872	Norway, Illinois	1ste Frie	Eielsen	Andrewson	23
1847-....	Rio, Wisconsin	Bonnet Prairie	Augustana	Dietrichson	102
1848-....	Chicago, Illinois	Evang. Luth.	Norwegian	Andrewson	?
1848-1910	Pt. Washington, Wisconsin	Holden	Augustana	Stub	70
1848-....	Clinton, Wisconsin	Evang. Luth.	Norwegian	Hatlestad	41
1849-....	Elkhorn, Wisconsin	Sugar Creek	Augustana	Clausen	37

A. C. Preus, N. S.   H. A. Preus, N. S.   Dr. U. V. Koren, N. S.
  1853-62   1862-94   1894-10

The Northern Illinois Synod is the third attempt of the Norwegians to establish synodical connections. Paul Anderson was the Norwegian leader in the movement; Lars P. Esbjørn was the Swedish leader. This synod had 8 pastors, 20 congregations and 653 souls in 1851, and in 1859 it had 5,316 souls; while in 1860, after the Swedes and Norwegians withdrew, it had only 1,551 souls. In doctrine and practice, largely through Reformed influence, the English members of the Northern Illinois Synod were rather liberal. Esbjørn desired to have included in the minutes of the organization meeting a note showing the doctrinal position of the Swedish churches, to the effect that the Bible is the infallible Word of God and the highest authority and rule of faith and practice, and that the symbolical books of the Lutheran Church contain a correct summary and exposition of the Bible. The reason why he did this was, that Article 2 of the constitution of the N. Illinois Synod referred to the Augsburg Confession as only "mainly correct." Anderson moved the objectionable words struck out, and this was done, without changing the views of the English members. Esbjørn became the Scandinavian professor of theology at the Illinois State University, at $700.00 a year. The first president, Francis Springer, 1852-1855, was an ultra-liberal. The sec-

Paul Anderson, N. I.   O. J. Hatlestad, A. S.   A. Wright, A. S.
  1857-58   1870-81, 1888-90   1885-88

Synodical Presidents

Østen Hanson, H. S.
1887-93

M. G. Hanson, H. S.
1899-05, 1910-17

Johan Olsen, N. C.
1872-81

ond president, Simon W. Harkey, 1855-1858, was mediating. The third president, Wm. M. Reynolds, foolishly opposed the theology, the practices and the languages of the Scandinavians at his school, and the results were as sudden as they were emphatic. The Scandinavians picked up their hats and books and departed. The rupture came in 1860, the year in which Dr. Reynolds resigned his post. He joined the Episcopal Church in 1864, to get, as he said, something to do.

The fourth synod, organized in 1851, by C. L. Clausen, H. A. Stub and A. C. Preus, was dissolved in 1852 on account of H. A. Preus's objection to Paragraph 2 of the constitution. This paragraph read as follows: "The doctrine of the Church is that which is revealed through God's Holy Word in our Baptismal covenant, also in the canonical books of the Old and New Testaments." As this paragraph, according to the constitution, could never be altered, it was found necessary to dissolve the organization and to start anew. This was done.

The fifth synod, usually called the Norwegian Synod, was officially named the Synod for the Norwegian Evangelical Lutheran Church in America. It was organized February 3, 1853, under the direction of H. A. Preus. Six other pastors were present at the

L. M. Bjørn, A. M.
1886-90

Dr. T. H. Dahl, U. C.
1902-17

E. E. Gynild, L. F.
1899, 1905, 1909, 1912-14, 1923—

Synodical Presidents

organization meeting—C. L. Clausen, H. A. Stub, A. C. Preus, N. O. Brandt, G. F. Dietrichson, and J. A. Ottesen. A. C. Preus became the first president, 1853-1862; H. A. Preus, the second, 1862-1894; U. V. Koren, the third, 1894-1910; and H. G. Stub, the fourth and last, 1910-1917. Of the 38 congregations represented at the first meeting 31 were located in Wisconsin. Since this synod for several decades had its main strength in Wisconsin, is was often called, by friend and foe alike, the Wisconsin Synod. Purity of doctrine was its slogan. It has fought for purity of doctrine, sometimes on the offensive, oftener on the defensive, and has been the bulwark of conservatism among the Norwegian Lutherans. It early formed friendships and connections with the Missouri Synod, the most conservative and exclusive of the German synods in America. The chief among the theological giants of Missouri was Dr. Carl F. W. Walther, rated as the greatest Lutheran in American history. German immigration to America was heavy. Nearly 1,000,000 came over from Germany in the fifties; nearly 500,000 had come in the forties. They came on account of economic, religious and political oppression at home. Walther came because of religious oppression. He was intensely pious and strictly Lutheran. The Union movement was on; Rationalism and Indifferentism held honored places in nearly all church circles. Walther became involved in difficulties with his rationalistic superiors and cast his lot with the Saxon emigrants who left the Fatherland in 1839. He rallied them here, founded congregations, synod, schools, publishing plant, church periodicals, missions; he called his people to the banner of the pure doctrine and left a deep impress, not only on his own synod, but on the remotest Lutheran bodies. The impress on the Norwegian Synod was indeed great. Beginning with 1859 the Norwegian Synod sent its prospective ministers to the German theological seminary at St. Louis, Mo. At this school—Concordia Seminary—Rev. Laur. Larsen that year began work as Norwegian theological professor. In their controversies with the other Norwegian Lutherans—on questions such as Donatism, the Sabbath, slavery and predestination—the Norwegian Synod often sought advice or support from the German brethren.

The sixth synod was the Scandinavian Augustana, founded in 1860. It was called Augustana to show that it stood firm on the Augustana, or Unaltered Augsburg Confession. It was organized by Swedes and Norwegians who had belonged to the Northern Illinois Synod and had left that body on account of its halting attitude in doctrinal matters. It was a conservative synod, but not extreme as was the Norwegian Synod. It had large sympathies for lay preaching, but not in a pronounced degree, as did the Eielsen Synod. It was a broad church synod, a middle-of-the-road church party.

Norway is one of the most Lutheran, if not *the* most Lutheran of all countries in the world. The Lutheran faith is the most

Lutheran Doctrine

evangelical of all the systems of religion based on the Bible. The Lutheran Church gets its name from Martin Luther, the Hero of the Reformation. As a separate and distinct church, it dates from 1530, when the Augsburg Confession was read before the Emperor Charles V at the Diet of Augsburg. In doctrine it is as old as the original Church which came into being on the Day of Pentecost.

In its doctrines, the Lutheran Church is a staunch champion of the Bible as the Word of God, inspired by Him, preserved by Him, authoritative, perfect, clear and efficacious. It believes in the verbal inspiration of the Bible. "Firm in the faith Immanuel taught, she holds no faith besides." It accepts the ecumenical creeds of Orthodox Christianity— the Apostolic, the Nicene and the Athanasian Creed. It holds also the Unaltered Augsburg Confession to be a correct exhibition of the faith and doctrine of the Lutheran Church, founded upon the Word of God. Every Lutheran congregation and synod accepts this as the fundamental confession. By the side of the Augsburg Confession is Luther's Smaller Catechism, in use throughout the Lutheran Church in the instruction of the young. No Lutheran

Christ Church, Chicago, Illinois,
J. H. Meyer, Pastor

body rejects the other confessional books in the Book of Concord (1580). Many accept all. The Lutheran Church is thus seen to be a Bible-loving and creed-loving Church. It is both conservative and progressive, peace-loving and militant, a Mary learning at the feet of Jesus, a Martha serving Him. The Norwegian Lutheran synods have suffered less from the inroads of rationalism and sectarianism than any other branch of the Lutheran Church.

As to worship, there may be differences in details, because the Lutheran Church grants great liberty in such matters. But in the essential things Lutheran worship is practi-
Lutheran Worship   cally the same everywhere. The typical Lutheran building has an evangelical symbolism. The tall, slender steeple, for example, points heavenward and summarizes the Gospel of Atonement, God's plan of salvation. The ground plan of the church building is in the form of a cross. The furniture includes a pulpit, a baptismal font and an altar, representing the three Means of Grace—the Word, Baptism and the Lord's Supper. The Lutheran congregation

First Lutheran Church, Albert Lea, Minnesota
Dr. Martin Anderson, Pastor

assembles in God's house to meet God, and the congregation and pastor as God's ambassador are two equally important elements. Most congregations follow a beautiful, but simple, liturgy, in which the two principal elements of worship——the sacramental and the sacrificial—appear in splendid balance. In the sacramental, God comes to the worshiper and offers him grace. In the sacrificial, man goes to God and offers Him prayer and praise and thanksgiving. The church year is observed, with its stated pericopes, and the sermon is made a vehicle for the expounding of the Scripture without fear or favor. The whole congregation sings; the choir is of secondary importance. The minister is the shepherd of God's flock, the servant of all. Everyone has a right to approach the throne of grace; everyone has a duty to proclaim His praises. There is room for men and women, for young and old, in this ministry. The Norwegian Lutherans regard the Church as a divine institution and the ministry as a holy calling. The old Muskego Church indicates in its structure what a great regard the pioneer Norwegians had for the Means of Grace. One-third of the building was occupied by the pulpit, font and altar.

Scandinavian Zion Church, Richmond, Staten Island,
R. O. Sigmond, Pastor at Time of Building

Organically, there is no such body as the Lutheran Church of America. Not yet, and perhaps there never will be. The Lutheran Church does not stress organic union very much, if at all. It believes in doctrinal unity, rather than external union. The form of government, it believes belongs to the human side of the Church, in which liberty is granted. It has thrived under every type of polity—episcopal, presbyterial, congregational and synodical. The synodical is the favorite one among the Norwegian Lutheran synods of America. The individual congregation has the

Lutheran Organization and Polity

right to govern itself, possessing all the privileges granted by the Gospel, and governed only by the Word of God. It can unite with other congregations of the same faith into larger units, such as synods, in order to promote the unity of doctrine and practice, and carry out the program of the Church. Hence, there is much striving also in the Lutheran Church, not only to promote church unity, but also church union, though, as stated, the duty of creating church unions is regarded as a practical measure, not as a doctrinal tenet. Among the early Norwegian Lutheran congregations and church leaders there were therefore attempts to form synods and to unite the synods into one Norwegian Lutheran Church of America. And ever since, such efforts toward a more perfect union have been going on, and there have been mergers of synods into new synods, and the organization of associations, federations, conferences, commissions, councils and inter-synodical corporations. In this way the Norwegian Lutheran Church has better been able to do its work at home and abroad, in the fields of publication, education, foreign missions, home missions, inner missions or charity, as well as the regular work of the pastor.

It is difficult to tell just how much work was done by the non-Lutheran denominations among the Norwegian settlements for the reason that the greater part of this work *Non-Lutheran* was done in English. Even the history of the *Denominations* work conducted in Norwegian is hard to write about because it has not been adequately recorded. A complete history of the non-Lutheran activities among the Norwegians would involve most of the denominations and fill many volumes.

a. *Quakers*

The Quakers, or Friends, own as their founder George Fox, who began to preach holiness of life in 1647. They have no creed, no liturgy, no sacraments. Their most distinctive doctrine is spiritual baptism. Periods of silence occur in their meeting, when no one feels called on to speak, while waiting for direct inspiration from the Holy Ghost. They are opposed to war and emphasize brotherhood in all human relationships. They came to Norway in 1815 through Lars Larson, Elias Tastad, Ole Frank and Even Samuelsen, Norwegians who had been held prisoners of war in England. They gave to Norway its first and greatest temperance advocate, Asbjørn Kloster, and made Stavanger the open door into Norway for sectarians. They were the immediate cause of the coming of Cleng Peerson and the Sloop in 1825. They had a hold on the first company of immigrants, whose leaders were Quakers, and who settled at Kendall through Quaker influence. But gradually this hold was lost, and the number of Quaker congregations among Norwegians have dwindled down to one (in 1916), with a membership of 92.

b. *Mormons*

The Mormons call themselves the Church of Jesus Christ of Latter Day Saints. This sect was founded in 1830 by Joseph Smith at Seneca, N. Y. It began an active propaganda but met with an equally active opposition, especially after 1843, when Smith announced a revelation in favor of plural marriages. He was shot by a mob in 1844 and Brigham Young became his successor. In 1847 there was a general migration from Illinois, where they then had their stronghold, to Utah, where they in 1916 numbered 91.8 per cent of the total church population. In 1916 there were 1,530 Mormon congregations, of which 463 were in Utah. There were 462,329 Mormons, of whom 258,282 lived in Utah. They claim to accept the Bible and the "Book of Mormon," both of equal authority. As to their doctrines read the expositions by O. L. Kirkeberg and I. G. Monson. The Mormons and the Sloopers came to Illinois about the same time and the Mormons soon convinced many of the Fox River Norwegians that Mormonism was the true religion. Jørgen Pederson, Ole Heier, Canute Peterson, Dr. Gudmund Haugaas, and others became Mormon preachers. A Mormon congregation was established near Norway, Ill., which still is flourishing. Some of the branch presidents, or pastors, at Norway have been: Yonce (Jens) Jacobs, 1862-63; Thomas Hougas, 1863-1900; John Midgorden, 1902-07; Thomas Hougas, 1907-19; and O. T. Hayer, 1919——. Missionaries were sent to Norway. Canute Peterson was one of them, returning with 600 converts bound for Utah. Some of the greatest men of Utah today are of Norwegian blood and Mormon faith. Reed Smoot, United States Senator since 1903, an apostle in the Mormon Church, had a Norwegian mother—Anna K. Mauretz. John Andreas Widtsoe, one of the Twelve Apostles of the Latter Day Saints, has been president of the Utah State Agricultural College and the University of Utah and the International Dry-farming Congress.

c. *Baptists*

The Baptists appear in history as early as 1523. Persons who had been baptized in infancy, on professing conversion and applying for admission to Baptist churches, were baptized again, hence they were often called Anabaptists. Roger Williams of Rhode Island fame, was the first American Baptist. The first Norwegian Baptist convert and preacher in America, and in the world, was Hans Valder, La Salle Co., Ill. He was converted through the instrumentality of Elder Harding, June 22, 1842. In August, 1844, he was ordained as Baptist minister. He was earnest, aggressive, a gifted and winsome speaker, and was able, after four years of zealous work to baptize seven adult Norwegians in January, 1848—the first fruits. They organized a congregation at Norway, Ill., and took up a subscription of $13.00 as pastoral salary. In view of the fact that they were not able to earn more than 25 cents a day at splitting cord wood, this subscription was considered very liberal, and it was. An application was made to the American Baptist Home Missionary Society for an annual assistance of $50.00 from its treasury. Later it was found expedient to unite Valder's Norwegian congregation with the nearest English Baptist congregation. A goodly share of the Sloopers became English Baptists. The further work of the Baptists will be dwelt on in the succeeding chapters.

d. *Methodists*

Methodism is the result of a movement begun in 1729 at Oxford University by John and Charles Wesley. John Wesley's conversion was occasioned by his reading Luther's "Introduction to Romans." Subsequently he made a journey to Germany, but he did not become a Lutheran. The Moravians whom he met there were too quiet to suit his militant nature. Men could not be saved without holiness. God's people must be a holy people. The cause was urgent; the time was short. He must be up and doing, inviting, inciting, compelling men to come to the marriage feast. Naturally, the Methodist preachers would feel concerned about the spiritual welfare of the Norwegian immigrants. They have also been the most successful in converting Norwegians from Lutheranism to Methodism. Methodism was first planted in Norway in 1853 when Rev. O. P. Peterson, a Norwegian who had been converted in New York, was sent as missionary to his native land. The first Norwegian Methodist congregations in America were organized in 1853 at Norway and Leland, Ill., by John Brown, a Danish convert to Methodism. The pastoral appointments of the Norway Congregation have been: John Brown (Dane), 1853-1854; Halvor H. Holland (Norwegian), 1854-1859; Nels O. Westergren (Swede), 1859-1860. The Leland charge was served by John Brown and Halvor H. Holland.

e. *Episcopalians*

At Nashotah, 30 miles west of Milwaukee, Wis., the Protestant Episcopal Church had erected a theological seminary as early as 1842. It is still in operation under the name Nashotah House and has a school plant and endowments valued at upwards of

$1,000,000.00. One of the first students, if not the very first, was Gustaf Unonius, a Swedish Lutheran, who had come to Pine Lake, Wis., in 1841. The Pine Lake Swedes hold a position among Swedish-Americans somewhat similar to that of the Sloopers, being the vanguard of the Swedish immigration to the United States. Unonius graduated in 1845 and was ordained, first as deacon and then as pastor in the Episcopal Church, being the first Episcopalian ordained in Wisconsin. He organized Episcopalian congregations at Pine Lake and elsewhere among the Swedes and Norwegians. Thus the Norwegian St. Johannes or Pine Lake Congregation, located six miles northeast of Oconomowoc, Waukesha County, was organized in 1844 by Unonius as an Episcopalian congregation, but through the efforts of Dietrichson, Stub and Clausen it was won back to the Lutheran fold. Rev. J. C. Walledom is the pastor in 1925. St. Olaf Congregation, sometimes called Ashippun, ten miles south-southwest of Hartford, Dodge County, Wisconsin, also owes its origin to Unonius. This congregation, too, is under the spiritual care of J. C. Walledom. Unonius took up a new field of labor in 1849, at Chicago, posing both as a Lutheran and an Episcopalian. Through the aid of Jenny Lind, who gave him $1,500.00, he built St. Ansgar Episcopal Church in Chicago. In 1858 he returned to Sweden. His book "Minnen" (Recollections) give a true account of his 17-year stay in America and is a valuable source book of pioneer history. The success of the Episcopalians among the Norwegian Lutherans has never been very conspicuous. From the first, the Episcopal Church has been friendly and has urged amalgamation, due mainly to the fact that the Scandinavian State Churches live under an episcopal organization. The Lutherans do not stress episcopal succession, but justification by faith, and therefore have not desired an organic union or federation with the Episcopalians.

6. Education

The "Report of the Immigration Commission, 1820-1910" speaks in the highest terms of the literacy of the Norwegians. An illiterate in census statistics is a person at *Literacy* least ten years of age who can not read and write any language. In the United States it is considered very necessary for the well-being of democracy that all citizens be able to read and write. A literacy test is applied to immigrants and compulsory school laws exist in every state. Nevertheless, the census returns show an uncomfortably large per cent of illiterates. Thus: In 1880—17 per cent were illiterate; in 1890—13.3 per cent; in 1900—10.7 per cent; in 1910—7.7 per cent; and in 1920—6 per cent. Illiteracy is not a problem in Norway. Says the "Report of the Immigration Commission" just referred to: "The character of the Norse element in America is well enough known to need no detailed description. In Norway the rate of illiteracy is the lowest in Europe. In religion the Scandinavians are Protestant almost to a man—over 99 per cent, according to the censuses of these countries." In the "Report of the Commissioner General of Immigration for 1923," as in all other years, the Scandinavians are rated the most literate. In 1923, 37,630 Scandinavians were admitted, of whom 3 were illiterate, less than 1-10 of 1 per cent. Mother Norway had taught her children the importance of letters. Norwegian children had to be confirmed, and that meant that they had first to be instructed in the catechism, Bible history, Bible and hymnal. To receive such instruction they had to learn to read. Hence, in Norway, as in all other Lutheran lands, it became a practical necessity to learn to read and write. The early immigrants were literate. On the fly-leaf of his New Testament Daniel Stensen Rossadal writes: "Jeg denne bog eier, Til lykke og seier; Den give mig Gud Frimodigt at stræbe Alt syndigt at dræbe Min levetid ud." Also the inscription: "Daniel Stensen og hustru Berthe Stavødatter, Sluppen Resteration den 28 juli, 1825. Liggende i — — — Spanske Søe — — —" (Dashes indicate matter too faint to decipher).

The universal passion for letters which the Norwegian inherited from Norway was not lost in this country. In fact, in this country all immigrant groups vie with
Public Schools   one another to give their children a good education. In the Census for 1920, for example, 2.5 per cent of the native white are illiterate, 22.9 per cent of the native Negroes; 13.1 per cent of the foreign born whites are illiterate, but only .8 per cent of their children. There is no class in America more anxious to get an education than the children of the foreign-born, and there is no class of foreign-born more eager than the Norwegians. The average per cent of illiteracy among the people of foreign-born parentage in the states where the Norwegians are quite numerous is a trifle over .4 per cent. The actual average for the Norwegians is possibly not over .1 per cent. These Norwegians have been faithful patronizers of the public schools, both elementary and higher, from the kindergarten to the university. They have promoted the public schools in every possible way. They have built them and paid taxes for their support. They have sent their children to them and urged their sons and daughters to teach in them. They have tried to keep the schools non-sectarian and free from anti-Christian doctrines and practices. The history of the public schools show that

they have had their greatest relative strength and progress in the Northwest, where the light-haired Scandinavians have come to stay.

In Norway it was customary for the parents to teach the children the rudiments of reading and the essentials of the cate-

Church Schools
chism at home. The Norwegian children could as a rule read before they began to go to school. They received aid from father and mother, particularly from mother, every day they attended the elementary school until they were confirmed. Confirmation took place about the years 14-16. This home instruction was most fundamental, in that it included both religious and secular instruction, both the common house duties of every sort as well as book learning.

a. *Parochial Schools*

In America they had to adjust themselves to new conditions and provide for new emergencies. Life was more strenuous here, and there was less time for home instruction. Besides, it was not customary in this land to pay so much attention to parental teaching. The public schools were secular; they could not teach religion there if they would, and they would not if they could, on account of the many creeds represented in this country, all on an equal footing before the law. Furthermore, the language of the public schools was exclusively English, and the parents could not keep pace with the children in acquiring it. In this way the parents could not very easily assist the children in their school work, and the religious instruction was bound to be neglected even in the best of families.

The congregations, therefore, made provision for maintaining parochial schools, in a very few cases to supplant the public schools, in nearly all cases to supplement them. These schools were held at the most convenient times, whenever the public schools were not in session and the farmers could most easily spare their children, for in those days all children had to work side by side with father and mother, and there was no talk about getting an amendment to the Constitution of the United States to forbid the employment of children under 18. So these schools were held, in the heat of summer or the cold of winter, as the case might be, from a month to three months at a time. The subjects were mainly religious, along doctrinal, historical, Biblical and practical lines. The Smaller Catechism by Luther and some Explanation of it—Pontoppidan, Sverdrup, Synodens—were learned by heart. The Bible history, with a taste of church history, was carefully mastered. The Bible became a familiar book through much reading and discussion. The most select hymns and tunes in the hymn book were committed to memory. A masterful system of education, this; a truly liberal education. School masters were chosen almost as carefully as were the pastors Parochial school teaching became a profession, not well paid, but respected. Ole Olson Hettletvedt, Slooper, was a parochial teacher. Elling Eielsen no doubt would have been one, had he not been too busy with finding the lost sheep. His wife was an excellent parochial teacher, and her fame still lingers. C. L. Clausen was called to come to Muskego as a parochial teacher, not as a preacher, and answered: "Lord, here am I."

Illinois State University: The "Coffee Mill"

b. *Illinois State University*, 1852-1860 (1867)

But it was manifestly hard to secure teachers and pastors. They had to be Norwegian; they had to be Lutheran. It was clear to all that the harvest truly was great, but the laborers few. It was equally clear that the State Church of Norway was not going to send a sufficient supply of workers. Those that had come, had come of their own initiative or at the call of the Norwegians here. The Norwegian Lutheran synods therefore discussed the problem of building higher schools whose aim should be to train teachers and pastors.

The first synod to take definite action was the Northern Illinois. There had been a Lutheran academy at Hillsboro, Illinois, since 1839. In 1847 this school became a college—Hillsboro College. In 1852 the school was moved to Springfield, the capital of the state, and was made a university—the Illinois State University. This Illinois State University was not a state institution but a Lutheran academy, college and seminary, the property of the Illinois and Northern Illinois synods. The English members of these synods were not particularly concerned about the Scandinavians and their need of men to teach and preach in the Scandinavian tongues. They elected men of prominence in state politics, to membership on their board of trustees, good men withal, but most of them non-Lutherans. Even Abraham Lincoln was a patron of the school, gave of his money to its support, and sent his son Robert to study there for a number of years, 1853-1859. A letter from Robert Lincoln to the author testifies that it was a good school. The school had a faculty of about 10 men. In 1852 the attendance was 79 in the academy, and 3 in the college; in 1858 it was 101 in the academy, 41 in the college, and 4 in the seminary. Only boys in attendance. In 1853 there were seven Norwegians in attendance: Abraham Jacobson, Decorah, Iowa; John G.

Lars P. Esbjørn

Johnson, Decorah; Knud Knudson, Mission Point, Illinois; Nelson Lawson, Chicago; Lars H. Norem, Chicago; Christian Olson, Chicago; and P. H. Peterson, Clay, La Salle County, Illinois. Most of the students were in attendance because the school was near at hand. In 1852, 77 per cent of the students came from Springfield; in 1859, 63 per cent. Abraham Jacobson, whose daughter Helga is wife of Dr. L. W. Boe, president of St. Olaf College, the largest Norwegian college in America, was the first Norwegian student at the University. The first Swede to enroll was A. Andreen, the father of Dr. G. A. Andreen, president of Augustana College, Rock Island, the largest Swedish school in America. The courses were standard. The college had four years of Greek and Latin and mathematics through calculus, no subject elective. The financial support came mainly from the constituent congregations. The school stranded in 1867 on account of the withdrawal of the Scandinavians in 1860 and the lack of sufficient support by the remaining congregations. The buildings in 1874 became the property of the Missouri Synod, which has since that date conducted there the Concordia Theological Seminary.

c. *Lisbon Seminary*, 1855-1856

The second Norwegian synod to establish a higher school was the Eielsen. It is known as the Lisbon Seminary and was located at Lisbon, Illinois. It had only one teacher, Rev. P. A. Rasmussen, the Lisbon pastor. Rasmussen had arrived in America in 1850, a bright 21 year-old youth. He came directly to Muskego intent on meeting Rev. H. A. Stub in order to get his bearings in this new land. Stub was about to set out for his congregations at Whitewater and directed Rasmussen to take the road to Mons Adland. Rasmussen set out for Adland's, but met Elling Eielsen on the way, who picked up a conversation with him and convinced him that he ought to join his party. Rasmussen did so. He taught parochial school at Neenah, Jefferson Prairie, Fox River and other places, 1850-1852. He attended Concordia Seminary, a Missouri Synod school at Ft. Wayne, Indiana, from which he graduated in 1854. That year, at the synodical meeting at Lisbon, the Eielsen Synod determined to erect its own school and appropriated $2,000.00 for a suitable building. An old hotel at Lisbon was purchased for $1,800.00 and Lisbon Seminary began work in October, 1855, with three students in attendance. The names of these men are Bjørn and Syver Holland, Hollandale, Wisconsin, and Olaus Landsvaerk. In "Ungdommens Ven" for 1910 Bjørn Hol-

Bjørn Holland

Lisbon Seminary

land gives a spirited account of his year at this school. He studied "church history, penmanship, composition, etc." The Augsburg Confession was committed to memory in toto. At Primrose, Wisconsin, June, 1855, Professor Rasmussen attacked Paragraph 2 in the constitution of the Eielsen Synod as containing Donatistic leaven. Donatists held that a holy church must consist only of holy members. Eielsen would not yield to the criticism, and the controversy forced Rasmussen to withdraw from the Eielsen Synod. His withdrawal stopped the activity of the school. The building still stands and is used as a dwelling.

d. *Augustana College and Seminary,* 1860

The third higher school to see the light of day was Augustana College, the child of the Augustana Synod. The formal organization of the synod was on June 5, 1860, at Jefferson Prairie, Wisconsin. The Norwegian contingent consisted of 13 congregations, 8 churches, 1,220 communicant members and 8 pastors. The purpose of the school was "to educate young men for the Gospel ministry in the Lutheran Church, and also to prepare young men for the profession of teaching." It was located at Chicago, L. P. Esbjörn and Abraham Jacobson were the first teachers. Instruction was given in the following subjects the first year: Arithmetic, algebra, geometry, trigonometry; geography, history; English grammar, Norwegian grammar, Swedish grammar, German, Latin, Hebrew, Greek New Testament; rhetoric, logic; sacred history, church history; dogmatics, symbolics; pastoral theology, homiletics. The attendance for 1860-1861 was 21 boys. One of the students that year was Ole Paulson, of Carver, Minnesota, who makes brief mention of his experiences at the school in his "Erindringer." Paulson enlisted and rose to the rank of captain in the Civil War. He became pastor at Minneapolis and was instrumental in locating Augsburg Seminary there and is lovingly referred to as the Father of Augsburg. He died April 20, 1907, with 39 years in the ministry to his credit.

The oldest higher school among the Norwegian immigrants was not a Lutheran institution. It was founded in 1850 at Green Bay, Wisconsin, by Nils Otto Tank. Tank *Other Schools* was born in 1800, at Fredrikshald, Norway. Trained at continental universities and at Herrnhut, Germany, he married a Dutch girl and departed for Dutch Guiana as a missionary in 1825. His wife having died, he again sought a wife among the Dutch damsels. Through this second marriage and careful business enterprise in South America, he is said to have been in possession of $1,500,000.00 when he came to Milwaukee. In 1846 a Norwegian Moravian congregation was started in Milwaukee by John Olson, a lay preacher from Farsund, Norway. In 1849 Andreas M. Iverson, a graduate of Stavanger Mission School, was ordained a Moravian missionary among the Norwegians. Hav-

Nils Otto Tank

ing heard of this venture in North America, Tank resolved to
come here too and lend a hand. He arrived in 1850. Like the
Swede Erik Janson in Henry County, Illinois, Tank was a Com-
munist and determined now to carry out a communistic experiment. He purchased 969 acres of forest at Green Bay, platted
it like a city, and 9,000 acres adjoining the town. He thereupon invited the Norwegian Moravians to come and get free
land. They came together with Pastor Iverson and a German,
Pastor Fett. He erected a two-story school building, and, with
five students in attendance, he conducted an academy during
the year 1851-1852. Mr. Ingebretson, merchant, Green Bay,
was one of the five. Tank lived in a palace and had a library
of 5,000 Dutch books, which in 1868 was donated to the University of Wisconsin. H. R. Holand has written an epic on this
romantic figure in "Nordmandsforbundet," December, 1924. He
relates that Fett sowed seeds of suspicion which bore plenteous
fruit. The people demanded warranty deeds to their land. They
were refused these papers because this was a communistic colony.
They departed and established a new colony and called it Ephraim,
which name it bears to this day. Tank's old home is now a museum and his town is called Tank Town.

7. Publications, 1825-1860

The literary beginnings of the Norwegian pioneers in America
are humble, yet noteworthy. They will be listed under four heads:
Books published in Norway; books published in America; secular
papers; religious papers.

These books are all written to serve as guide books for emigrants or to warn them against leaving the Fatherland. Rynning
was a graduate of the University of Christiania
Books Published and his book was written on his death bed.
in Norway It is the first, and perhaps the best, literary
effort by a Norwegian during this period.
Nattesta was the first Norwegian settler in Wisconsin. His account of his trip to America is quite charming in its simplicity.
He was much surprised to find the buildings in New York five
to six stories high. They are now ten times as high as in 1837.
Testman had tried a year of pioneer life and, finding it too
strenuous, he returned to Norway and published this account to
warn people against coming here. Haalim had emigrated in
1836. He had tried farming at Medelport (Middle Point?),
Illinois, and Shelby County, Missouri; had met with one dis-
appointment after another—the huts were miserably poor, land
was hard to get, work was killing and sickness raged everywhere.
He had tasted sickness and dire want and warned his countrymen
to stay away from America. Knudsen tells about the trip from

Drammen to New York and Detroit, June 6 to September 30, 1839. Reierson was a very competent editor who had explored the Norwegian settlements and had chosen Texas as his home. His book is, as it aims to be, a pathfinder for the immigrant. He advises to keep away from Wisconsin. Dietrichson was the first State Church pastor from Norway to the Norwegian colonies. He writes about his journeys in and out among his countrymen and his efforts to establish congregations and bring order out of apparent religious chaos. Fribert was a Dane who had lived here several years as a farmer. His book has 45 instructive chapters. In Chapter 7 he advises all to settle in Wisconsin. Løvenskjold was a consul general to the Norwegian Government. This is a report, dated October 15, 1847, describing his visit to the Norwegian settlements in the summer of 1847. A very judicious and enlightening book. Schytte was a Norwegian physician who had practised medicine here from 1843 to 1848. The title of Bollin's book indicates that it was a geographical and political handbook for emigrants.

Eleven small books belong to this class, namely:

Author	Title of Book	Year	Place of Publication
Rynning, Ole	"Sandfærdig Beretning om Amerika"	1838	Christiania
Nattesta, Ole	"Dagbog: Beskrivelse"	1839	Drammen
Testman, Peter	"Kort Beskrivelse over de Vigtigste Erfaringer under et Ophold i Nord-Amerika"	1839	Stavanger
Knudsen, Knud	"Beretning om en Reise til New York"	1840	Drammen
Haalim, Sjur J.	"Oplysninger om Forholdene i Nordamerika"	1842	Christiania
Reierson, J. R.	"Veiviser for Norske Emigranter til de Forenede Nordamerikanske Stater og Texas"	1844	Christiania
Dietrichson, J. W. C.	"Reise blandt de Norske Emigranter i de Forenede Nordamerikanske Stater"	1846	Stavanger
Fribert, L. J. (a Dane)	"Haandbog for Emigranter til Amerikas Vest"	1847	Christiania
Løvenskjold, Adam ..	"Beretning om de Norske Settlere i Nordamerika"..	1848	Bergen
Schytte, Theodor A...	"Vägledning för Emigranter"	1849	Stockholm
Bollin, J.	"Geografisk Politisk Beskrivelse over de Forenede Nordamerikanske Stater, i Særdeleshed for Emigranter"	1853	Christiania

---

DOCTOR MARTIN LUTHER'S

SMALL CATECHISM,

WITH

PLAIN INSTRUCTION

FOR CHILDREN,

AND SENTENCES FROM THE WORD OF GOD

TO STRENGTHEN THE FAITH OF THE MEEK.

Translated from the Danish, and published by

Elling Eielsen.

Suffer little Children to come unto me, and forbid them
not, for of such is the kingdom of heaven.—Matt. x. 14.

PRINTED AT 176 BOWERY,

1841.

(A Photograph, exact size, of Title Page of First Book
Printed in America by a Norwegian.)

The books published in this country, with the exception of
one, a veterinary book ("Dyrlægebog", 1859, by Chr. Krug), were
all reprints of religious books—school books,
Books Published   hymnals and devotional works—for use in the
in America   school room, church and home. Bibles were
secured through the New York Bible Society
and the American Bible Society. These associations handled Norwegian books printed in Christiania. In 1848 the American Bible
Society published its own first edition of the New Testament in
Norwegian; in 1857 the whole Bible was issued in Norwegian—

Danish. Many of the pioneer Norwegians acted as Bible colporteurs. As, for example, Ole Olson Hettletvedt, Slooper, Andreas A. Scheie, Peder L. Asbjørnsen, Lars H. Norem, Nils Olsen Fjeld. The American Tract Society issued Bunyan's "Pilgrim's Progress" as early as 1850, and some devotional books by Richard Baxter and Ph. Doddridge even earlier. These books were sold by book agents. Krug's "Dyrlægebog" was the first scientific treatise published by a Norwegian-American. It sold at $1.00.

Elling Eielsen was the first one to have any book printed in this country. It is interesting to note that, just as the first book written by a Norwegian-American and printed in Norway, is entitled "A True Account of America," so the first book published by a Norwegian in America was printed in the English language. A copy of the book is in the possession of Mrs. Ellen Serine Runden, a daughter of Eielsen. Its title page is reproduced herewith. Note that Eielsen's name, through poor proof reading, is misspelt. Note also that the book was translated by Eielsen into English and that it was printed in 1841, at 176 Bowery, New York. Through the kindness of J. M. Hestenes and Mrs. Ellen Runden the present writer has secured the loan of this precious book and is reprinting the book, using photograph copies of each page. The original Pontopidan's "Sandhed til Gudfrygtighed" which Eielsen had reprinted in 1842 is now at the Lutheran Theological Seminary, having been placed there by Rev. J. A. Bergh, church historian. He secured it from Rev. J. C. Roseland, formerly pastor at Jefferson Prairie, Wis.

Books were published as individual enterprises, as association efforts or as synodical undertakings. Eielsen issued his catechism on his own initiative; also Pontoppidan's "Sandhed til Gudfrygtighed" (Truth unto Godliness) and the Augsburgske Konfession. Ole Andrewson had a printing press in Norway, Illinois, on which he printed Guldberg's "Psalmebog" (Hymn Book) in 1854 and Pontoppidan in 1856. As an example of Norwegian publication societies may be mentioned the Scandinavian Printing Association and the Lisbon Society. The Scandinavian Association was organized at Inmansville (now Orfordville), Wisconsin, in 1851, by Revs. C. L. Clausen, A. C. Preus and H. A. Stub and a number of other shareholders. This society published two editions of Pontoppidan, 1853 and 1856, Linderot's "Prædikener," 1853, Wexels' "Bibelhistorie," 1854, Guldberg's "Psalmebog," 1854, "Luthers Bekjendelse," 1856, "Fader Vor" (short stories), 1856, "Symbolske Bøger," 1856, etc. The Lisbon Society published the "Symbolske Bøger" in 1855 and other works. In 1857 C. F. Solberg published Luther's "Kirke- og Huspostille" in Madison. This is a very large book, but paper, print, ink, binding and gilt edges are of excellent quality, fully equal to the best in Europe.

Haldor Hanson, specialist in old books, thinks that this monumental work printed for a small band of impoverished newcomers, must show the great faith which these publishers had in their Lutheran religion and their Norwegian countrymen.

The Norwegians waited 23 years before they attempted to publish a Norwegian newspaper. Their first venture was called "Nordlyset" (Northern Lights), 1847-1849, *Secular Periodicals* and was published in Heg's log barn at Muskego, with J. D. Reymert as editor. A full set of this rare paper is now on file at the Wisconsin Historical Library, and partial sets are in safekeeping at the Koren Library, Luther College, and the Luther Theological Seminary, St. Paul. It was a political newspaper. It favored the Free Soil Party, the forerunner of the Republican Party. The first issue

Elling Eielsen's Home, Jefferson Prairie, Wis.

bears the announcement that the price is $2.00 a year, or 6 cents a copy. The opening editorial states the aim of the paper to be to enlighten those of the Norwegian nationality who cannot read English, by giving news of general interest, and particularly news of interest to Norwegians. An editorial is written in praise of Jørgen Pedersen, a Norwegian of Chicago, who under the name of George Pilson had enlisted in the Mexican War which was then raging, and who had met his death at the Battle of Buena Vista. An American flag appears at the head of the column. A portion of the Declaration of Independence is printed in Norwegian version. There is, furthermore, considerable war news, market news, local news and advertisements. There is also a sample of church controversy to give the paper its proper pep.

In the following list of papers it will be noted several of the papers were Democratic in politics. When the Republican Party was formed, and war was imminent, the Norwegian editors and the Norwegian settlers everywhere in the North were found on the side of the Union and Honest Abe. In the South the Northern sympathizers were handled—like the Pro-Germans and the Pacifists in the recent World War—rough. Wærenskjold was murdered because he favored the North. Langeland and Hatlestad bought up the "Nordlyset" in 1849 and changed the name of the paper to "Democraten," in order, as they thought, to get more subscribers. Editor Reymert was a Democrat, but edited a Free Soil paper; Langeland was a Free Soiler, but edited a Democratic sheet. Later on, Langeland became the most ardent advocate of the Republican Party.

The secular papers are nine in number, eight political and one an organ of the people from Voss. See Page 215.

The first church paper appeared four years in the wake of "Nordlyset." It was edited by Norwegian Synod pastors in support of their synod and its growing work. The name of the periodical was "Maanedstidende for Den Norsk Lutherske Kirke i Amerika." It was published in 1851-1853. It resumed publication in 1856 under the name "Kirkelig Maanedstidende" and continued under that name until 1874, when it again was rebaptized, this time being called "Evangelisk Luthersk Kirketidende," 1874-1917. In 1851 O. J. Hatlestad began the publication of "Den Norske Lutherske Kirketidende," 1851-1853, as organ for the Norwegians of the Northern Illinois Synod. From 1856 to 1866 Eielsen published a paper in Chicago which bore the name "Organ," the aim of which was to promote the cause of his synod.

Religious Periodicals

Fox River Church, 1841

EARLY NORWEGIAN SECULAR PERIODICALS

Periodical	Place of Publication	Years	Party	Editor
"Nordlyset"	Muskego, Wisconsin	1847-1849	Free Soil	J. D. Reymert
"Democraten"	Racine, Wisconsin / Janesville, Wisconsin	1849-1850	Democrat	K. Langeland
"De Norskes Ven"	Madison, Wisconsin	1850	Whig	Ole Torgerson
"Skandinaven"	New York, N. Y.	1851-1853	Republican	Anders G. Obom
"Frihedsbanneret"	Chicago, Illinois	1851-1852	Republican	Joh. Mauritson
"Emigranten"	Inmansville, Wisconsin	1852-1857		K. J. Fleischer
	Madison, Wisconsin	1857-1868	Independent	C. L. Clausen
"Den Norske Amerikaner"	Madison, Wisconsin	1854-1856	Democrat	Elias Stangeland
"Wossingen"	Leland, Illinois	1857-1859	Bygdelag	Nils Bakkethun
"Nordstjernen"	Madison, Wisconsin	1857-1858	Democrat	C. M. Reese

As cold waters to a thirsty soul, so is good news from a far country. —Prov. 25:25.

"I fear three newspapers more than 100,000 bayonets."—Napoleon.

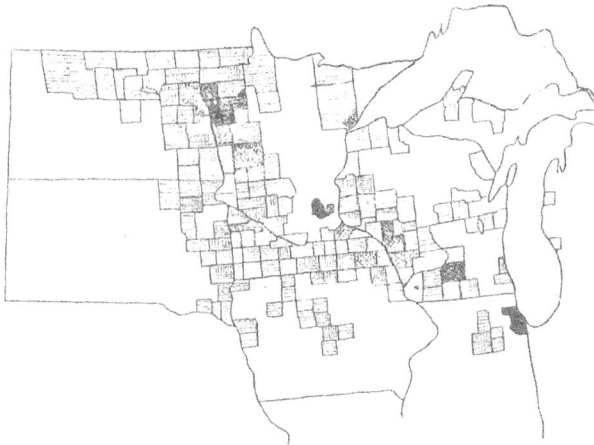

Principal Norwegian Counties in the Northwest.

Chapter VI

NORWEGIAN-AMERICAN PERIOD, 1860-1890

The Norwegian-American Period covers approximately 30 years. It begins with the Civil War, which called the Norwegians to the American colors, and ended with the organization of the United Church, which marked the beginning of a new day in Norwegian Lutheran church history.

1. Historical Background

The events of this period are best understood in the setting of European and American history. The inventions and discoveries of the first half of the century have taken a new and more practical turn. People no longer are hostile to inventions as something that takes the bread and butter from the toiler; they look upon them now as work-saving and money-making devices. Men are adjusting themselves to the new conditions. There is plenty of work and food for all. Crowded Europe hears the call from America still sounding: "We need you to conquer our great plains; we welcome you and will give you a homestead."

In England two opposing policies are conspicuous—an imperial and a reform. Disraeli was an exponent of imperialism; Gladstone, of reform. Ireland especially was

Europe crying out for needed reform. The Fenians demanded complete separation from England and demonstrated their wants by insurrections. Gladstone was elected to redress Irish grievances. He dis-established the Episcopal Church in Ireland and proposed new land laws and a restoration of the Irish Parliament. He would give the poor farmers fair rents, fixity of tenure and free sale of their interest in improvements made as renters. He went farther in his reforms than the English people could stand, and so he was succeeded by Disraeli. Disraeli wanted new worlds to conquer. His policy was:

> That they should take who have the power,
> And they should keep who can.

In brief, during this period, through the advocacy of reform, there was much internal progress and improvement, and through the advocacy of imperialism, England extended her world power immensely. By defending the Turk against Russia she got possession of Cyprus and a foothold in the Near East and Egypt. By the partition of Africa, she got the lion's share of that continent. She entertained opposing opinions as to our Civil War. The common people favored the North; the wealthier classes and the government wanted to aid the South. Queen Victoria was neutral. In March, 1867, the British provinces of North America, with the exception of New Foundland, became united into one dominion, with the constitution of a substantially independent state.

On the continent there were wars and rumors of wars, strivings toward freedom and some advances. The unification of the German states and the establishment of the German Empire were the most significant events. Prussia was the leader. Bismarck was her chief statesman, and his policy was blood and iron. There was a controversy with Denmark about Schleswig-Holstein. It ended very abruptly in the Danish War in 1864, in which Denmark was promptly defeated and stripped of the disputed territory. Austria was jealous of Prussia's growing power and, being much more powerful than Prussia, sought every pretext for a dispute with her northern rival. Prussia quickly settled the dispute in the Seven Weeks' War, in which Austria was completely humbled. After the debate with Austria was over, Prussia formed the North-German Union in 1867. In 1870 the vacant throne of Spain was offered to Leopold, a member of the reigning Prussian family (Hohenzollern). Leopold refused the crown so as not to offend France, but France, like a cock on the walk, rudely demanded that no member of the Hohenzollerns should ever become a candidate for the Spanish throne. The demand was refused and a French army rushed into Germany. The result of the Franco-Prussian War was a sudden and decisive defeat of France. Germany established an empire in 1871. The empire in France was overthrown and a republic was built on its ruins. The Turk was busy with his outrages in the Balkans and Asia Minor.

F. A. Schmidt, D.D.　Johs. T. Ylvisaker, D.D.　M. O. Böckman,
(53)　　　　　　　(40)　　　　　　　D.D., LL.D. (38)

Sven Oftedal, A.M.　Georg Sverdrup, A.M.　O. E. Brandt, D.D.
(34)　　　　　　　(33)　　　　　　　(27)

E. Kr. Johnsen, D.D.　Elling O. Hove, A.B.　A. A. Helland, A.M.
(27)　　　　　　　(26)　　　　　　　(23)

Hans H. Bergsland　C. M. Weswig, D.D.　G. M. Bruce, S.T.D.
(20)　　　　　　　(19)　　　　　　　(17)

Lutheran Theological Professors
(Figure after name stands for years teaching)

England supported him and urged on the massacres. Russia protested and plunged into a new war, 1877-1878, with Turkey. England prevented Russia from ousting the Turk, but, at the Treaty of Berlin, Turkey was stripped of some of its territory, and the Balkan states of Servia, Montenegro and Rumania were made independent of the sultan. The oppression in Russia was great, and men longed for freedom. This longing took the form of Nihilism, and was a fierce, though smothered, volcanic fire in the breasts of the lowly.

With Europe in such turmoil, and America offering so many advantages to the poor and oppressed, it is no wonder that immigration during the years 1860-1890 should increase by leaps and bounds. The immigration to the United States in the 30 years, 1830-1860, was 4,910,590; and for the 30 years, 1860-1890, it was 10,373,628, more than twice as great.

Norway was, on the whole, more happily situated from 1860 to 1890 than the European nations just mentioned. She enjoyed domestic peace and progress. Her merchant *Norway* marine, flying the Norwegian flag, was visiting the remotest ports. Lumbering, manufacturing and trade quickened everywhere the pulses of life. The law against Dissenters was abolished in 1843; the law excluding Jews was repealed in 1851. The telegraph was extended; railroads were built. The Storthing met annually after 1869 and its demands for full sovereignty and equal rights were being granted one by one. The consular question was about the only one unsolved. Norway brought forth great sons in literature, art, science and statesmanship. Ibsen, Bjørnson, Kielland, Lie, Aasen, Vinje, Arne Garborg, Gustav Storm, C. P. Caspari and Gisle Johnson, are names of representative literary heroes of this period, Behrens, Bull, Grieg, Kjerulf, Lindeman and Nordraak are names of representative musicians. The poets, orators, musicians and painters were aggressive, even declamatory, in their patriotism. The Norwegians seemed to be proud of their past, contented with their present and hopeful of the future. Still, there was a deep-felt longing in the heart of many a Norseman to see his people in Vinland the Good; he listened to the call of the prairies and said goodbye to Mother Norway.

The war which Ole Rynning in his "True Account of America" in 1838 clearly foresaw, came. It had long been abrewing. It was fierce and destructive when it came. It *The United States* called for men as cannon fodder, many men — strong men, young men. The North furnished 2,269,588, 95 per cent of them under 21 years of age; the South furnished almost as many. The result of the War was that the United States remained a united and free country, with freedom for the black man as well as for his white brother. After the war came a period of reconstruction. The troubles attending reconstruction were aggravated by the Ku Klux Klan, whose purpose was to terrify the Negro and the foreigner. The Atlantic Cable was successfully laid in 1866. The Union Pacific Railroad was opened in 1869. Alaska was purchased in 1867. A financial crisis took place in 1873. Frances Willard began the Woman's Christian Temperance Union in 1873. A centennial celebration was held in Philadelphia in 1876. This brought the results of industry and invention before the people to a degree impossible by any other means, instructed them in the knowledge of their own and other countries, and greatly educated the taste of the whole community. There were many labor troubles, strikes and riots. The land was filling with people, the West was being dotted with farm homes and villages. The railroads were extending their lines in every direction, increasing their mileage from 30,626 in 1860 to 163,597 in 1890; the Western Union Telegraph Company increased its miles of wire from 183,832 in 1876 to 678,997 in 1890. The Brooklyn Bridge was completed in 1883. The Chinese Exclusion act was passed in 1883 and other immigration restriction laws were enacted. The Census of 1890 gave a population of 62,947,714, of whom 60 per cent lived west of the Alleghanies. People were taking the advice of Horace Greeley: "Go West, young man."

2. Norwegian Immigration, 1861-1890

According to the American statistical authorities 334,340 Norwegian immigrants came to the United States from 1861 to 1890; according to the Norwegian census authorities, 346,477 left Norway from 1866 to 1890. That means that Norway gave the United States nearly one-fifth of her population during these 24 years. Nearly 80 per cent of this army was under 30 years of age, men, women and children in their best years, strong, healthy, vigorous, full of life and hope. It was quite a drain on the vitality of the nation, and it never met with the hearty approval of Norwegian statesmen and patriots.

About 22 per cent of the immigrants came from the towns, 78 per cent came from the rural parts. Stavanger and its contingent territory (Rogaland), had furnished approximately one-half of the immigration during the period 1825-1860; during 1860-1890 it furnished only 24,559 out of 346,477, or barely seven per cent of the total stream. Opland, consisting of the great Gudbrandsdalen and Valdres valleys together with Toten and Land near Lake Mjøsen, was the banner district. It contributed 50,140, or 14 per cent of the exodus. Norway is divided into 20 "fylker," or counties. The emigration by counties from 1866 to 1890 is as follows:

No.	County	Emigration	No.	County	Emigration
1.	Oslo City	24,610	11.	Rogaland	24,559
2.	Østfold	12,301	12.	Hordaland	16,962
3.	Akershus	18,305	13.	Bergen City	4,936
4.	Hedemark	31,681	14.	Sogn & Fjordane	18,409
5.	Opland	50,140	15.	Møre	12,211
6.	Buskerud	27,047	16.	Sør-Trøndelag	21,893
7.	Vestfold	7,752	17.	Nord-Trøndelag	16,729
8.	Telemark	19,161	18.	Nordland	9,901
9.	Aust-Agder	9,655	19.	Troms	4,395
10.	Vest-Agder	11,135	20.	Finmark	4,685

Total.... 346,477

3. Norwegian Population, 1860-1890

Below is a tabulation of the population by decades, genera-tions, states and mixed marriages. The United States Census figures are used. The inquiry as to country of birth of the foreign-born has been made at each census, beginning with 1850. The foreign-born Norwegians here comprise all Norwegians born out-side of the United States. The earliest complete statistics pertain-ing to the number of children of the foreign-born are those of 1890. The United States Census makes no attempt to determine the national origins of its people beyond the first generation (for-eign-born) and the second generation (children born of foreign or mixed parentage). The third and fourth generations will have to be estimated.

BY DECADES

Census	1st Generation	Increase
1860	43,995	31,317
1870	114,246	70,251
1880	181,729	67,483
1890	322,665	140,936

BY GENERATIONS

Census	1st Generation	2nd Generation	3rd Generation	4th Generation	Total
1860	43,995	10,999	64	....	55,058
1870	114,246	45,698	1,261	1	161,206
1880	181,246	109,037	9,503	32	300,301
1890	322,665	273,466	48,651	673	645,455

NORWEGIAN POPULATION BY STATES, 1st Generation

State	1860	1870	1880	1890	Rank 1860	Rank 1890
Alabama	51	21	24	47	18	41
Arizona	..	7	45	59	..	40
Arkansas	5	19	33	60	35	10
California	715	1,000	1,765	3,702	5	10
Colorado	12	40	354	893	30	20
Connecticut	22	72	168	523	23	23
Delaware	..	..	6	14	..	47
District of Columbia	1	5	19	70	40	47
Florida	11	16	79	179	31	30
Georgia	13	14	23	88	29	35
Idaho	..	61	276	741	..	21
Illinois	4,891	11,880	16,970	30,339	4	3
Indiana	38	123	182	285	20	27
Iowa	5,688	17,554	21,586	27,078	3	4
Kansas	223	588	1,358	1,786	9	17
Kentucky	10	16	21	120	32	33
Lousiana	63	76	78	136	17	32
Maine	27	58	99	311	22	26
Maryland	7	17	108	164	34	31
Massachusetts	171	302	639	2,519	10	12
Michigan	440	1,516	3,520	7,795	7	9
Minnesota	8,425	35,940	62,521	101,169	2	1
Mississippi	15	78	56	54	27	40
Missouri	146	207	373	526	12	22
Montana	..	88	174	1,957	..	15
Nebraska	103	506	2,010	3,632	14	11
Nevada	16	80	119	69	26	37
New Hampshire	5	55	79	251	36	29
New Jersey	65	90	229	1,317	16	18
New Mexico	2	5	17	42	39	42
New York	539	975	2,185	8,602	6	7
North Carolina	4	5	10	13	37	48
North Dakota	..	....	....	25,773	..	5
Ohio	10	64	178	511	25	24
Oklahoma	..	....	....	36	..	45
Oregon	43	76	574	2,271	19	13
Pennsylvania	83	115	381	2,238	15	14
Rhode Island	38	22	56	285	21	28
South Carolina	4	....	5	23	38	46
South Dakota	129	....	....	19,257	13	6
Tennessee	14	37	25	41	28	43
Texas	326	403	880	1,313	8	19
Utah	150	613	1,214	1,854	11	16
Vermont	..	34	10	38	..	44
Virginia	8	17	29	102	32	34
Washington	22	104	580	8,324	24	8
West Virginia	..	1	3	7	..	49
Wisconsin	21,442	40,046	49,349	65,696	1	2
Wyoming	..	28	74	345	..	25

Mixed marriages are of infrequent occurrence among the immigrants from Norway—less than 0.2 per cent; among their children—the second generation—in 1890 they reached 14 per cent. Among the descendants of the third, fourth and later generations they are increasingly higher.

4. Norwegian Settlements, 1860-1890

During this period the Norwegians entered every state in the Union and the eastern provinces of Canada. Following is a tabulation to show how widely the Norwegian newcomers were distributed. They were planting themselves in the Far East as well as the Far West; in the sunny South as well as in the invigorating North.

DISTRIBUTION OF SETTLEMENTS

Geographical Division	State	Total Counties	Counties with Norwegian Immigrants
New England	6	67	64
Middle Atlantic	3	148	125
East North Central	5	434	303
West North Central	7	612	531
South Atlantic	6	438	111
East South Central	2	194	65
West South Central	3	369	161
Mountain	5	126	112
Pacific	3	124	124
	40	2,512	1,596

Alabama, Arizona, Delaware, Nevada, New Mexico, Oklahoma, Tennessee and West Virginia in 1890 had a combined total of 260 counties. They are not included in this tabulation, because the census does not indicate how many of them had foreign-born Norwegian settlers. Of the other counties 63.5 per cent are listed as having Norwegian immigrants. New Hampshire and Rhode Island in the New England states had foreign-born Norwegians in every county; Wisconsin in the East North Central division likewise; Minnesota in the West North Central; Montana and Idaho in the Mountain division; and Washington, Oregon and California in the Pacific group of states, all had Norwegians in every county.

No less than 80 counties had more than 1,000 foreign-born Norwegian citizens. Minnesota had 29 such counties out of 80; Wisconsin 19 out of 68; Iowa 8 out of 99; North Dakota 8 out of 53; South Dakota 5 out of 68; Illinois 3 out of 102; New York 2 out of 60; Washington 2 out of 35; Pennsylvania 1 out of 67; Oregon 1 out of 36; and California 1 out of 53 counties. According to rank these counties are:

LARGEST NORWEGIAN COUNTIES: 1890
(Foreign-born only)

Rank	County	State	Norwegian Immigrants
1	Cook	Illinois	22,365
2	Hennepin	Minnesota	13,014
3	Polk	Minnesota	6,861
4	Dane	Wisconsin	6,728
5	Ottertail	Minnesota	5,955
6	Kings	New York	5,002
7	La Crosse	Wisconsin	4,371
8	Fillmore	Minnesota	4,171
9	Trempealeau	Wisconsin	4,118
10	Eau Claire	Wisconsin	3,897
11	Norman	Minnesota	3,821
12	Ramsey	Minnesota	3,636
13	Traill	North Dakota	3,572
14	Grand Forks	North Dakota	3,518
15	Goodhue	Minnesota	3,485
16	Vernon	Wisconsin	3,387
17	Winneshiek	Iowa	3,347
18	Dunn	Wisconsin	3,167
19	St. Louis	Minnesota	3,038
20	Minnehaha	South Dakota	2,953
21	Clay	Minnesota	2,700
22	Lac qui Parle	Minnesota	2,641
23	St. Croix	Wisconsin	2,638
24	Pope	Minnesota	2,623
25	Freeborn	Minnesota	2,600
26	Kandiyohi	Minnesota	2,562
27	Walsh	North Dakota	2,523
28	Jackson	Wisconsin	2,507
29	Cass	North Dakota	2,428
30	Yellow Medicine	Minnesota	2,384
31	Barron	Wisconsin	2,373
32	King	Washington	1,999
33	Chippewa	Minnesota	1,995
34	Pierce	Washington	1,992
35	Renville	Minnesota	1,980
36	Woodbury	Iowa	1,947
37	Houston	Minnesota	1,934
38	Worth	Iowa	1,910
39	Milwaukee	Wisconsin	1,904
40	Winnebago	Iowa	1,871
41	Richland	North Dakota	1,837
42	Pierce	Wisconsin	1,835
43	Story	Iowa	1,824
44	Swift	Minnesota	1,822
45	Mower	Minnesota	1,787
46	Grant	Minnesota	1,770
47	La Salle	Illinois	1,718
48	Marshall	Minnesota	1,711
49	Rock	Wisconsin	1,632
50	Hamilton	Iowa	1,613
51	Day	South Dakota	1,582
52	New York	New York	1,575
53	Douglas	Minnesota	1,569
54	Brookings	South Dakota	1,540

Rank	County	State	Norwegian Immigrants
55	Becker	Minnesota	1,527
56	Philadelphia	Pennsylvania	1,500
57	San Francisco	California	1,396
58	Chippewa	Wisconsin	1,379
59	Lincoln	South Dakota	1,324
60	Polk	Wisconsin	1,311
61	Rice	Minnesota	1,283
62	Allamakee	Iowa	1,283
63	Waupaca	Wisconsin	1,270
64	Faribault	Minnesota	1,264
65	Jackson	Minnesota	1,232
66	Buffalo	Wisconsin	1,165
67	Barnes	North Dakota	1,150
68	Steele	North Dakota	1,118
69	Muskegon	Michigan	1,116
70	Kendall	Illinois	1,099
71	Bayfield	Wisconsin	1,085
72	Douglas	Wisconsin	1,058
73	Yankton	South Dakota	1,054
74	Rock	Minnesota	1,049
75	Portage	Wisconsin	1,048
76	Dodge	Minnesota	1,044
77	Watonwan	Minnesota	1,042
78	Humboldt	Iowa	1,031
79	Multnomah	Oregon	1,014
80	Nelson	North Dakota	1,008

The old Kendall Settlement in Orleans County, New York, is not in the above honor roll. It had only 25 foreign-born Norwegians in 1890. There were 18 settlements in New York considerably larger than that of Orleans County, in 1890. La Salle County is

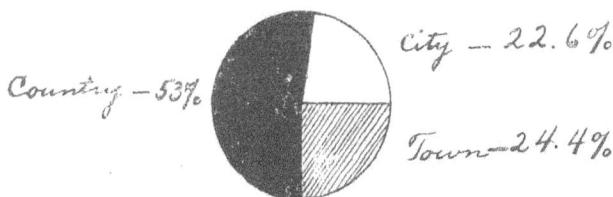

City — 22.6%

Country — 53%

Town — 24.4%

Distribution of Norwegians as to City, Town and Country

way down to the 47th place; Rock County, Wisconsin, is 49th. There were over one hundred settlements more populous than Muskego. This tells the story of the steady advance westward. County by county, state by state, the land is laid under the plow, and every year ushers out upon the western plains a brand new regiment of Norse immigrants, eager to conquer the wilderness for Uncle Sam.

The city begins to make a stronger appeal to the Norsemen. In 1890 there were 85 cities having 25,000 inhabitants or more. There were foreign-born Norsemen in 83 of these cities, an army of 61,302 people, nearly 20 per cent of the foreign-born Norsemen in America.

Space does not permit even a catalog, not to say a description, of the thousand and one settlements made by the Norwegians during 1860-1890. But a few words must be *North Dakota, 1869* devoted to North Dakota and her neighbors to the west.

North Dakota was not discovered by the Norwegians before 1869, but when they did discover it they claimed it for themselves and their children and children's children. It is relatively the strongest Norwegian state; 30 per cent of its inhabitants are Norwegians. The state is a perfect network of Norwegian farms. It is said that a man can cross the state in almost any direction without stepping off Norwegian land. In 1914 Alfred Gabrielsen prepared a map showing the land holdings of the Norwegians in North Dakota. The map is reproduced in this book by permission of the Normanden Publishing Company, Grand Forks.

Like South Dakota, North Dakota was a part of the French province of Louisiana, bought from Napoleon in 1803. It had been the familiar haunts of the Red Man for ages before the French traders came. The first trader located at Pembina in 1780. North Dakota was a part of Dakota Territory from 1861 to 1889; it became a separate state in 1889, with Bismarck as capital. Up to 1875 there were less than 1,000 whites in all North Dakota, but after that a great flood of immigration came in, favored by the advance of the railways—the Northern Pacific, the Great Northern and the Soo (Minneapolis, St. Paul and Sault Ste. Marie R. R.). Another factor that aided the rapid settling of North Dakota and other western states was the homestead law of 1862. Under this law a citizen, or an alien having declared his intention of becoming a citizen, has the right to 160 acres of land free after actual residence and cultivation for five years. In addition to a homestead, under the timber culture law, he might acquire an additional 160 acres tree claim by cultivating ten acres of trees for eight years.

The first Norwegian to reach North Dakota and to become a permanent settler there was N. E. Nelson, appointed a tax collector at Pembina in 1869. That same year Paul Hjelm Hansen was sent by the Minnesota Board of Immigration to explore the Red River Valley and write it up in the Norwegian press. Hjelm Hansen was born in 1810. He had studied law, but had spent most of his life in journalism. He came to America with the intention of getting first-hand information by means of which he could in some measure check the heavy emigration from Norway, which was sapping the country of its best man power. But he found this country, with its freedom and vast possibilities, exactly to his liking and could not speak against it. So he settled down

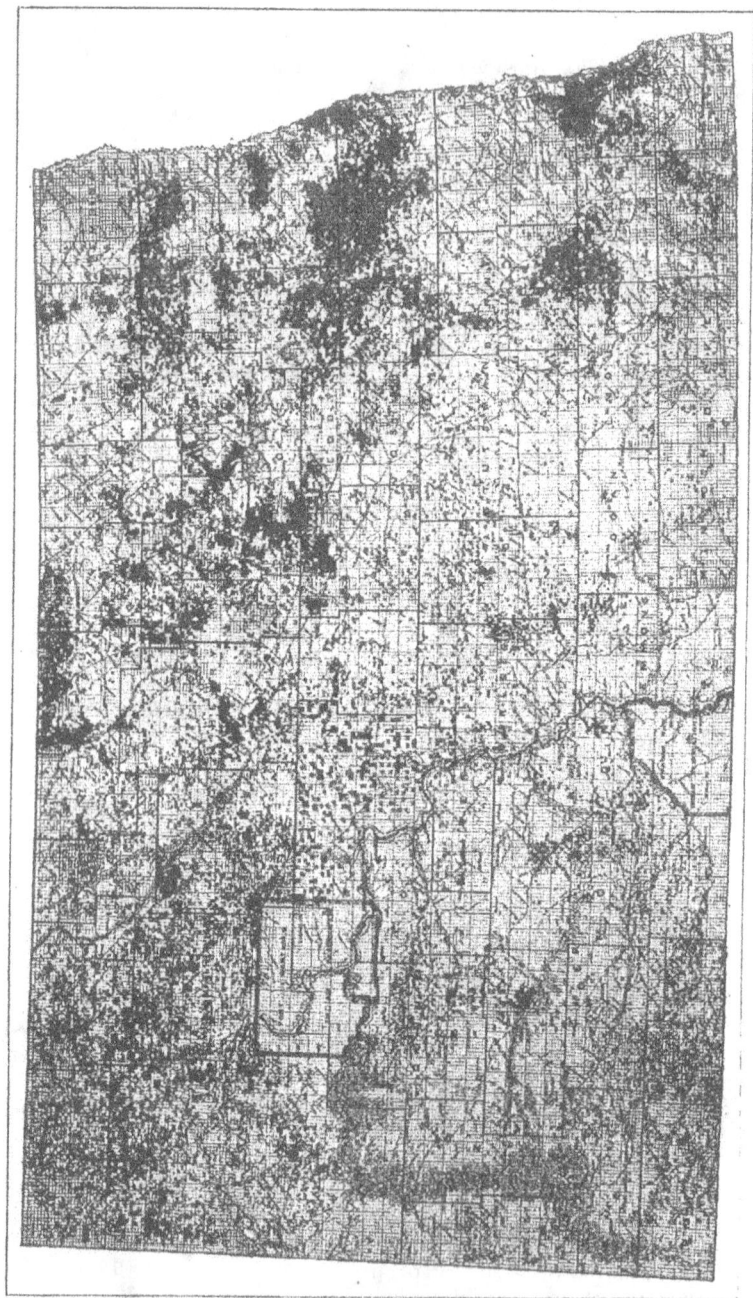

Norwegian Farms in North Dakota, 1914. Prepared by Alfred Gabrielsen. Loaned by Normanden Publ. Co.
Shaded portions are Norwegian Farms.

here as an editor. On this happy exploring trip to North Dakota he came by steamboat from La Crosse to St. Paul; from St. Paul to St. Cloud he journeyed by rail; from St Cloud to Alexandria, on horseback. So far the journey had consumed 17 days. At Alexandria he obtained an ox team and food sufficient for a month. He set out and reached as far as Georgetown, Marshall County, Minnesota, returning at the end of three weeks. He now wrote his first epistle to the readers of "Nordisk Folkeblad," Minneapolis. Again he set out, this time for Ft. Abercrombie, Richland County, North Dakota, and was absent a whole month. As a direct result of the letters that he wrote about the Red River,

Concordia College, Moorhead, Minnesota, Dr. J. A. Aasgaard, President
The Norwegian College of the Red River Valley

letters that were published in many papers here and in Norway, there was an eager rush of Norwegian farmers toward the Red River Valley and a quickening of immigration. The number of Norwegian immigrants leaped from 3,216 in 1870 to 9,418 in 1871, 11,421 in 1872 and 16,247 in 1873.

Many of these immigrants had the Red River Valley in mind as their objective. On the Minnesota side, Clay County received its first Norwegian settlers in 1869, Wilkin and Becker Counties in 1870; Norman and Polk Counties in 1871; Marshall in 1878; Kittson in 1879. On the Dakota side, Richland and Cass Counties were settled in 1870; Traill and Steele in 1871; Grand Forks in 1872; Walsh in 1878. The financial crisis of 1873, due chiefly to excessive railroad building, put a damper on immigration, and the terrible grasshopper plague of 1875-1877 held the line of the settlers so that they did not attempt to go farther west than the first tier of counties just mentioned. Beginning with 1877, the

Norwegians added Barnes County to their possessions. Then in rapid succession came Ransom and Griggs (1878), Nelson, Sargent and Dickey (1880), Morton (1881), Stutsman, Ramsey and Rolette (1882), Bottineau, Benson, Eddy, Foster, and Mercer (1883), and so on, steadily advancing for 30 years until the whole state lay at their feet.

This state in 1909 produced 116,781,886 bushels of wheat, 18.5% of the total crop in the U. S., and the Red River Valley discovered by the old and faithful spy, Paul Hjelm Hansen, has appropriately been entitled the "Bread Basket of the World." It is quite significant of the democratic character and native fitness to become American sitizens that Hjelm Hansen so readily became converted from an avowed enemy of America to an enthusiastic friend. At 60 a man's character is pretty well established and he finds it difficult to make adjustments. Hjelm Hansen, the Norwegian patriot, did not have to make many adjustments to become an ardent American. In recognition of his services a large bronze memorial has been placed in the Library of the Minnesota Historical Society at St. Paul. Though Hansen had been a very active and useful man during the ten years he labored in Minneapolis, he was already well-nigh forgotten. He had edited "Norsk Maanedstidende," "Nordisk Folkeblad," and "Minnesota Skandinav." His letters on the Red River Valley were published in Norway under the title "Om Nord Amerika" (About North America). In 1878 he had published a "Business Directory of

Paul Hjelm Hansen

Norwegian Deaconess Hospital, Grafton, North Dakota

Scandinavians in Minnesota." All worn out by a life of ceaseless activity he died at the home of his friend, Dr. Chr. Grønvold, at Holden, Goodhue County, May 5, 1881, and was buried at Aspelund, hard by. Still he was practically forgotten until the Norwegian-Danish Press Association advocated this bronze memorial. North Dakota will no doubt also do justice to his memory.

The Norwegians did not really seek land in Montana to any great extent before the eighties, nineties and the first decade of the twentieth century. Still, in 1890, every *Montana, 1863* county in Montana had Norwegian settlers. The Census for 1880 lists 174 Norwegians born in Norway. Martin T. Grande settled at Lennep, Meager County, in 1877. He entered the territory by way of Wyoming. Sheep-raising was his occupation, and Helena, the nearest town, was 140 miles distant. The first Norwegian in the state was Anton M. Holter, called the "First Citizen of Montana," who arrived in 1863.

Montana is an empire larger than Norway and Denmark combined. In 1920 the population was only 548,889, or 3.8 to the square mile. Minnesota has 29.5 per square mile; Massachusetts has 479.2. In 1870 the total population was 20,595, most of them newly arrived. Montana, as the name indicates, is a mountainous country, a high plateau with tremendous ridges and vast plains. It has been the paradise of the rancher and cowboy. Said the president of the State University at an after-dinner speech: "I represent a state that has more cows that give less milk, that has longer rivers and less water, that has loftier points of view and fewer things to see, than any other state in the Union." In 1860 this vast territory was occupied by wandering Indians, and the only civilized dwellers were fur-traders and Catholic priests of the lonely Canadian missions. The gold discoveries in 1861 at Alder Gulch, yielding $25,000,000.00 of gold dust in a few months, drew an army of adventurers from all over the world. Most of them were from the Confederate States, and the state has been a Democratic stronghold ever since. It was made a territory in 1864 and a state in 1889. In the early mining days Montana was the Wild West, such as the movies depict, where robbery and murder are of hourly occurrence. Here, in 1876, the Indians made a last stand, and in the fight General Geo. A. Custer and his troops were annihilated to the last man. Since the era of farming and railway-building set in, line after line of rails has been built, thousands upon thousands of farms have been cultivated, and homes, schools, churches, villages, factories, libraries, have dotted the erstwhile lone land. The scenic wonders of Montana now draw tourists from afar. Here is located the insurpassable

C. A. Naeseth, A. M.   C. M. Christianson, Pd.M.   I. F. Grose, A. M.
  English, Luther   Education, Augustana   English, St. Olaf

national parks, Glacier Park and the Yellowstone Park, the latter
being just across the line in Wyoming. The slogan: "See America
First," was invented by Jim Hill, the late president of the Great
Northern, to boost the Glacier National Park.

When Governor R. B. Smith of Montana was asked to send
to the Omaha Exposition a picture of Montana's most representative pioneer he sent a bronze medallion of A. M. Holter with
the legend, "The First Citizen of Montana." Who was Holter?
He was a Norwegian. Born June 29, 1831, at Moss, Østfold,
Norway, he emigrated in 1854 and came to Decorah, Iowa, by
way of Quebec. At Rock Island his party had been quarantined
on account of cholera. He took his trunk, carried it on his back
until he sighted a boat and thus escaped. He was a carpenter.
The wages were only $1.00 a day at best. He hired out for
$20.00 a month, then invested his savings in land and had saved
$3,000.00 by the end of the first year. The panic of 1857 took
his every cent. He made exploring trips to Missouri, western
Iowa and northern Minnesota more than ten years before Hjelm
Hansen electrified his countrymen. In 1859 he lay sick of malarial
and brain fever. In 1860, together with his brother, Martin M.,
he set out for the land of Pike's Peak, now Colorado. In 1863
he decided to go to the gold fields of Montana, not as a miner,

  Olav Lee, A. M.   J. L. Nydahl, A. B.   J. H. Blegen, A. B.
  Latin, St. Olaf   Science, Augsburg   Greek, Augsburg

Nils Flaten, Ph. D.
Spanish, St. Olaf

E. D. Busby, A.M.
Mathematics, Augsburg

C. A. Mellby, Ph.D.
Economics, St. Olaf

but as a manufacturer of mining supplies. He loaded an ox cart with the machinery for a saw mill, and, with a man by the name of Evanson as a companion, he started the long march through the trackless wilderness and across well-nigh impassable ridges and gulches. But he came through in spite of deep snow and wild countryside. He built his mill and sold his lumber at fabulous prices. He became one of the richest and most enterprising men in the state. In 1907 he was president of the A. M. Holter Hardware Company and 15 other larger mercantile establishments, mines, banks, land agencies, lumbering concerns, and development companies. He was also a director of 32 other important agricultural, mining, manufacturing, transportation and commercial companies. He was a multi-millionaire, whose industries stretched from coast to coast. The waves of the Pacific splashed against his forests in western Oregon at the same time that the foam of the Atlantic dashed against his copper works at Bridgeport, Connecticut. He found time to do church work and serve his town (Helena) as alderman and mayor, and his state, though Democratic, elected him Republican member of the legislature and railroad commissioner. He was president of the Montana Pioneer Association for many years, and held other

P. G. Schmidt, A.M.
Mathematics, St. Olaf

A. M. Rovelstad, Ph.D.
Latin, Luther

O. A. Tingelstad, Ph.D.
Philosophy, Luther

offices of trust. In the days of highway robbery and vigilantes
he was often in danger of life and limb, but he outwitted his
pursuers, escaped their bullets, and lived to a ripe old age. He
died in 1921. His son Norman has the degree of M. E. from
Columbia University, is president of his father's hardware company and other enterprises, and is a director of the Federal
Reserve Bank, Minneapolis. His wife is Florence Jeffries, and
he is a member of the Episcopalian Church.

It is hard to tell whether Idaho became an American possession as a part of the Louisiana Purchase of 1803 or as a section
Idaho, 1876
of the Oregon Country which in 1846 was
ceded to the United States by Great Britain.
The first white men in Idaho were the Lewis
and Clark exploring party in 1805. For another fifty years, after
their visit, the rich valleys of Idaho lay in mountain-walled solitude. Gold was discovered in 1860 on the Oro-Fino Creek, and
the pristine solitude was broken by the fighting of the rough
miners and the war-whoops of the disturbed Indians. Idaho became a territory in 1863; a state, in 1890. In area it is of the size
of Minnesota; in density of population it has only 5.2 per square
mile (1920). It is the twelfth American commonwealth in size,
being larger than New England, but in density of population it is
43rd. The population of Idaho in 1920 was considerably less than
that of the city of Milwaukee. The climate varies greatly. Per-
petual snows of mountain-walls look down on lovely temperate
valleys. The sunshiny days number 250 a year. The soil yields
abundant crops of grain and fruit, and grass for grazing summer
and winter. The mines are rich in precious metals. The railroads
—Great Northern, Northern Pacific, Union Pacific and Chicago,
Milwaukee and Puget Sound—have brought the remotest corners
of the state in touch with the whole sisterhood of states.

Tønnes Møller, according to the researches of Martin Ulvestad, that great chronicler of pioneer events, was the first Norwegian to find his way to Idaho. He came from Wisconsin and
settled at Genesee, Lotah County, in 1876. That same year he
was joined by other Norwegian settlers; John Tetly, from Levanger; Ditlef and Hans Smith, from Manger; Knud Bergquam,
from Sogn; Hans Tvedt, from Lindaas, Nordhordland; and many
others. Their chief industry was raising wheat. Wages were 50
cents a day. The nearest town, Lewistown, was 20 miles away.

It will be seen that two migratory streams have reached the
far western states. The main stream was slow acoming, because
it deposited the Norwegians all along the line
Washington, 1847
until the country was fairly well filled up. In
1834 it had reached La Salle County, Illinois.

In 1840 it had reached a line running diagonally northeast and southwest 100 miles farther west. In 1850 this line was removed another 100 miles west; in 1860 another 100 miles; in 1870, yet another 100 miles; and so forth, about 100 miles for each decade up to 1880. After that more than 200 miles was covered per decade. Now, this slow and steady movement would not have reached Washington in time for the Norse-American Centennial, unless there had been some artificial quickening. The railroads came to the rescue. They lifted the newcomer clear across Montana and Idaho into Washington. This happened right along in the '70s, '80s and '90s.

The other stream was small, but reached Washington before there was any Norwegian settlement in Minnesota. Martin Zakarias Tofteson landed at Oak Harbor, Widbye Island, Island County, in 1847. He was a native of Levanger, Norway, who had sailed on an English ship to New Orleans, and then, in company with a Swiss he had started to journey across the great American desert on horseback. The Swiss deserted him. He continued his fatiguing march alone. He awoke one morning to find his horse gone. In the distance he sighted smoke and proceeded to discover who lived there. It was an Indian band, and there was his horse in their camp. He was permitted to get on the horse's back, but then he set off on a gallop with his animal. They set out in pursuit, but did not overtake him. He reached California a year before gold was discovered there. In Washington he became a ranchman. Wahkiakum County was settled in 1863 by John Ericksen, a Stavanger man, from California. Also John P. Nassa, Ole Svorkmo, and others. Lewis County was occupied in 1863 by Harold Hansen and William Johansen, also from California. Skagit County received a Trønder by the name of Hanson in 1869, by way of British Columbia. Whatcom and Pierce Counties were settled in 1870; Snohomish in 1874; Kitsap and Clark in 1875; King County in 1876; Chelan, Douglas and San Juan Counties in 1884; Spokane County in 1886; Skamania, Chehalis and Stevens Counties in 1889; and every county had its quota of Norwegians in 1890.

Washington is a great state, and is destined to be a truly mighty Norwegian-American province. In 1789, the first year of our national republic, Captain Robert Gray came to Washington on his sloop, the "Lady Washington," to trade with the Indians for furs. Gray's Harbor is named after him. He called the great river that he discovered Columbia in honor of one of his ships. In 1805, Lewis and Clark descended the Columbia and wintered on the coast. Together with Oregon and Idaho, Washington lay in the territory held in dispute by England and the United States. The dispute was settled by arbitration in 1846 and the 49th parallel was made the northern boundary of Washington and the United States as far east as Lake Superior. Washington became a territory in 1853, and a state in 1889. Warmed by the Japan Current, the climate is equably warm and moist. They have only two seasons in Washington—rainy in winter, dry in summer. Roses bloom in Seattle in December and pansies blossom in Walla Walla in January. Peach flowers open in February, while the eternal snows of Mt. Tacoma sparkle in the summer sun. Wheat farms and apple orchards occupy a large share of the work of the citizenry of the state. The mining of coal and iron will make Washington the Pennsylvania of the West. The pine forests are the densest in the world, with the possible exception of Oregon. The trees are 200 feet tall and 20 feet thick. The fisheries are far in excess of those of any other state except Massachusetts. In 1915 Washington's output was 158,983,478 pounds, valued at $5,317,080. Most of the Washington fishermen are Norwegians.

A century ago five powerful nations—Spain, France, Russia, England and the United States—laid claim to Oregon and the Oregon Country. Since 1846 it has been a part of the United States, without any dispute as to rights. The country was unsettled. It had been visited by the American explorers Lewis and Clarke in 1805 and a settlement had been made at Astoria in 1811. These American undertakings were the main argument for the right of America to own the land. The part of the disputed territory now known as Oregon was in itself an empire, twice the size of England, rich in natural resources, but empty of people. The majestic Columbia River was called by the Indians Oregon, whence the name of the whole section.

Oregon, 1872

> Where rolls the Oregon, and hears no sound
> Save its own dashing.

In 1836 Dr. Marcus Whitman, perceiving that Oregon was on the point of being lost to the United States on account of the lack of settlers, tried to prevent this disaster. He rode to Missouri on horseback and managed to get a party of men to go and make settlements. He proceeded on to Washington, D. C., and urged upon President Tyler and Daniel Webster that Oregon was worth saving for the Union. Webster thought that Oregon was so "far off that it could never be governed by the United States" and that a delegate to Congress "could not reach Washington until a year after the expiration of his term." Oregon became a territory in 1845; a state, in 1859. Like Washington it is a land of dismal forests and fruitful soil, with rich yields of gold and silver and large deposits of iron and coal. The capital city is Salem; the commercial metropolis is Portland. Portland is the world's greatest lumber manufacturing city. It handles one-sixth of the lumber in the United States. Portland is down grade from every one of the 250,000 square miles forming the Columbia basin. Freight does not have to climb into Portland—it rolls.

Into this fairy land the Norwegians began to come as early as 1872. P. K. Johnson, from Stjørdalen, Norway, was the first arrival. He settled at Silverton, which to this day boasts of a strong Norwegian contingency. No less than 20 Norwegian Lutheran pastors have at some time been stationed there—O. R. Sletten, N. J. Ellestad, C. M. Nødtvedt, J. C. Reinertsen, O. J. Olsen, H. M. Mason, H. Hjertaas, I. Lium, J. S. Sneve, J. C. Roseland, W. H. Sjovangen, A. O. Dolven, N. Pedersen, A. O. White, Geo. Henriksen, J. B. Byberg, J. O. Arevik, B. A. Borrevik, J. A. Stavney and Leif H. Awes. Oscar A. Tingelstad, noted professor of philosophy and education at Luther College, hails from Silverton.

Tennessee is chosen to illustrate the attempts of the Norwegians to find a home in Dixieland. Tennessee was one of the first states west of the Appalachian Mountains to be settled. It was made a state in 1796 without previous territorial organization. It is a land of cotton and tobacco, of hogs and mules. Both lumbering and mining bring large monetary returns to its inhabitants.

Tennessee, 1887

Tennessee had 14 foreign-born Norwegians in 1860; 37 in 1870; 25 in 1880; 41 in 1890; 141 in 1900; 89 in 1910; and 63 in 1920. In 1910 the number of Norwegians of the second generation was 153; in 1900, 131. The largest Norwegian settlement in the state, according to the census, is that at Lawrenceburg, Lawrence County, in south central Tennessee. The first Norwegian to settle here was Lars Syverson, from Drangedal, who came to these parts in 1887. In 1910 this settlement consisted of 14 born in Norway and their 11 children. Though small, the settlement, in true viking fashion, managed to have two congregations—for a season. O. S. Skattebøl organized the Zion Norwegian Lutheran Church at Lawrenceburg in 1894 and had 184 members. This points to the fact that there were more Norwegians in Lawrence County than the census reveals.

The Zion Church was served by P. J. Fadnes in 1898-1904 and had 102 members. In 1904-1908 J. C. T. Moses led them through this earthly wilderness toward the Promised Land. In

1910, for want of a pastor and on account of an exodus, only 24 remained on the congregational books. The other congregation was served by a United Norwegian Lutheran pastor, said to have come down from Frankfort, Morgan County. At Frankfort the pastors have been: Simon J. Nummedal, 1893-1894; P. T. Stensaas, 1896-1897; Hagbart Engh, 1899-1902; C. K. Helland, 1902-1908; T. O. Juve, 1908-1913; Th. M. Bakke, 1924———, with Deer Lodge as postoffice. Frankfort reported 72 members in 1896; 64 in 1907. Juve was born in Telemarken. He had migrated in 1852. Was a graduate of Luther College, Iowa, and Concordia Seminary, Missouri. Had been a teacher, pastor and member of the Wisconsin Legislature. Was a farmer at Lancing, Tennessee, 1895-1913, principal of the high school at Lancing, 1895-1896. He wrote once that he felt lonesome in the South and wished himself back to the Northwest where Norwegian is the language of the streets. He died in 1913, way down south in Dixie. Bakke is a graduate of St. Olaf College and the United Church Seminary. He has been a pastor on the plains of Minnesota and in the woods of Wisconsin. He has broken the Bread of Life to his countrymen on the outstations of Alberta to the North; he now is ministering to their spiritual wants in the mountain fastnesses of the South.

Maine is chosen to represent the states of the East. Maine is called the Pine Tree State from the fact that mast pine, an evergreen of towering height, is the pride of its vast forests. In 1652 Massachusetts began to govern it as a district, but in 1820 it was set off as a state without any previous independent territorial organization. The climate is cold and bracing. It is a land of variable winds and seafogs. Lumbering and ship-building, fishing, farming, maritime trade, are the chief occupations. Portland is the largest city, once the home of Longfellow, the poet. Longfellow was no mean student of Norse language and literature and had spent a year of study in the Scandinavian lands. His "Saga of King Olaf" is concrete proof of his interest in the land of the Northmen. This book has no doubt inspired one of our young Norwegian-Americans, Gustav Melby, a Baptist preacher, to pen the beautiful drama, "Saga of King St. Olaf."

Maine, 1872

Maine has a few place names of Scandinavian origin. Thus, in Oxford County, there is a town called Denmark, another town called Norway, and a lake called Norway Lake. But these places have received their names rather because there were no Scandinavians there than because the county was Scandinavian. William Berry Lapham, in his "Centennial History of Norway, Oxford County, Maine" (1886), discusses the improbability of the name having been chosen because of the presence of Norwegians in that town. And concerning the discussion as to whether the Viking Norwegians ever visited Maine, he says: "Whether it be true or not that the rude Northmen were the discoverers of this continent, is of little consequence, as they left no lasting monuments of their occupancy, laid no claim to the lands discovered, and if they occupied for a short time territory along the coast, they accomplished thereby nothing in the interest or direction of human progress."

Lapham's opinion may be matched by that of O. J. Kvale in the "Congressional Record," March 10, 1925: "Norse sagas and early histories carry reports of Viking trips to Vinland, the name the first explorers gave to America. They came in part to obtain lumber, which was not to be procured in Greenland; they tell of efforts to colonize, of the Indian natives, trade with them, battles with them . . . . Adam of Bremen, who died in 1076, a year after he had completed a book on North European Christianity, which included historical and geographic facts regarding all the countries he mentions, tells of Norway, Sweden, Denmark, Iceland, Greenland, and then tells of Vinland, the new land to the west. His book was authentic; it was widely circulated in his day and after. . . . . Surely Columbus, one of the learned men of his day, well educated and informed, would have known of this book and its contents. Furthermore, Columbus, a geographer and a navigator, had sailed many seas. There is indisputable evidence, contained in letters written by his son Ferdinand, that Columbus visited Iceland in February, 1477. There everyone was familiar with reports of the Norse expeditions to the wonderful land to the southwest—Vinland. He also visited the cloister in Huelva, Spain, in 1484; and his son again tells of the conversation word for word, between his father and the monks, in which Columbus convinced the monks of his certain knowledge of a land to the west . . . . His dogged determination in the face of threatened mutiny of his crew, bears this out. Columbus did not conjecture; he did not hope; he knew. The evidence which he possessed of a land to the west was supplied to him by the descendants of the very people who had themselves discovered the land of promise."

Maine had 12 Norwegians, foreign-born, in 1850; 27 in 1860; 58 in 1870; 99 in 1880; 311 in 1890; 509 in 1900; 580 in 1910; 581 in 1920. In 1890 every county but one had some foreign-born Norwegians; Cumberland had 171; York had 29; Penobscot, 22; Aroostook, 18; etc. In 1910, 433 of the Norwegians were urban; 147, rural. The first Lutheran Church of Portland was organized by N. J. Ellestad, August 24, 1874, with 150 members, of whom 80 were Norwegians. In 1914 this congregation had 300 mem-

Celia Oakland   N. E. Glasoe   Mrs. Julia Christianson,
Sunday School teacher, Parochial School teacher   Ph.D.,
        57 years   61 years   Author of S. S. books

bers, of whom 250 were Norwegians. The pastors since 1880
have been: K. G. Faegre, 1800-1884; G. A. T. Rygh, 1884-1889;
K. O. Storli, 1890-1900; Wm. Williamson, 1900-1902; M. K.
Hartmann, 1903-1904; C. L. Rachie, 1904-1906; K. O. Storli,
1906-1912; Wm. M. Pettersen, 1912-1915; Anders Bersagel,
1915———. Dr. Martin Andrew Nordgaard, now of St. Olaf College, was an instructor in mathematics at the University of
Maine, 1913-1916.

John Cabot, a Venetian in the employ of England, discovered
the North American continent at Cape Breton in 1497. Five
                centuries earlier the Norsemen had cruised
Canada, 1862   along the Canadian shores. Jacques Cartier
                made voyages of exploration to Canada in
1534-1543, on the basis of which France claimed the land and
called it New France. In 1608 Champlain was appointed the first
governor and he founded Quebec as his capital city. Ottawa is
now the capital. In 1620 the population of Canada was 20 white
persons. Indians and Eskimos were not enumerated. Nova Scotia,
or Acadia, as it was also called, was claimed by England, and,
in the struggle for supremacy between the two rival nations, Nova

J. O. Jøssendal   Olav Refsdal   K. O. Løkensgaard
Author of Reader   Author of Reader   Author of Readers, etc.

Svein Strand
Advocate of Parochial
Schools

L. P. Thorkveen
Friend of Parochial
and Sunday Schools

J. N. Andersen
Advocate of Sunday
Schools

Scotia exchanged masters several times before its cession to England in 1763. In 1763, as a result of the French and Indian War, all Canada was ceded to England. In 1755 a great number of the French inhabitants of Acadia were deported and dispersed among the English colonies, many finally reaching Louisiana. Longfellow's sad but beautiful story, "Evangeline," is an incident in this deportation. This is Longfellow's appeal:

Ye who believe in affection that hopes, and endures, and is patient,
Ye who believe in the beauty and strength of woman's devotion,
List to a Tale of Love in Acadie, home of the happy.

The population of Canada in 1706 was 16,417; in 1806, 355,718; in 1916, about 6,200,000.

Since the creation of the Dominion of Canada in 1867, decennial censuses have been taken in 1871, 1881, 1891, 1901, 1911 and 1921. New Foundland is not a part of the Dominion. There are 9 provinces and two territories:

Prince Edward Island, Nova Scotia, New Brunswick, Quebec, Ontario, Manitoba, Saskatchewan, Alberta and British Columbia.

Yukon Territory and Northwest Territory.

Carl Raugland
Author of Handbooks
Sunday School Teacher

H. P. Grimsby
Author of Graded
System

Gabriel Fedde
Author of Handbooks
Sunday School Teacher

Laur. Larsen, D.D. (56)   C. K. Preus (23)   O. L. Olson, Ph.D. (30)

The population at the first dominion census (1871) showed that at that time the ratio between the British and the French was as two to one. In detail the British had 60.55 per cent; the French, 31.07 per cent; and other races 8.38 per cent. Since the English and French are both dominant races, the country is bilingual. The government reports are issued in French and English.

Since it became a dominion Canada has had a spectacular expansion. It began rairoad construction in 1836. Its first transcontinental line was completed in 1885. The Canadian Pacific Railroad contracted to build this line for the consideration of $25,000,000.00 and 25,000,000 acres of land. The last spike on the main line was driven November 7, 1885. This road and other intercolonial and transcontinental rairoads have opened up the country, and a vigorous and generous policy of securing immigrants has peopled the wide domain of Canada with an industrious, prosperous and happy people.

Captain Jens Munk came to Canada in 1619 and wintered in the Hudson Bay. Captain John Svendsen settled at Bury, Quebec, in 1857. Gaspe was the first Norwegian settlement in Canada. Gaspe is the name of a county forming the south bank of the St. Lawrence River, right at its mouth. There is now also a town by that name; also a bay and a cape. Two Trønders, fisher-

Th. N. Mohn (25)   J. N. Kildahl, D.D.   L. W. Boe, D.D., LL.D.
                          (21)   (21)

College Presidents, with Years of Service

Edw. W. Schmidt (37)   D. G. Ristad (18)   J. A. Aasgaard, D.D. (15)

men at Lofoten, had come to Montreal in 1859. Canada resolved to start a Norwegian colony at Gaspe, and these two, Peter and Ludvig Brandt, accepted the offer of the government and became the first settlers in Gaspe, in 1860. In July, 1861, a ship landed their brother Fredrik and his family and mother; also Didrik Nilsen and wife, Karen Brun and son Nils Christian Brun, besides a girl passenger—Ovidia Olsen. N. C. Brun was a cousin of the Brandts. In the historical magazine "Symra," H. R. Holand and N. C. Brun give each a vivid account of the fearful experiences with hunger and cold in this forsaken and weather-beaten spot. Canadian officials employed a Norwegian, Christopher Kloster by name, to act as immigration commissioner. Kloster was a brother of the great Norwegian temperance reformer, Asbjørn Kloster; he was active and successful. Soon other boats arrived with precious boatloads of hopeful Norwegians.

There were about 30 families living in Brun's neighborhood and 70 families scattered along the coast for 30 or 40 miles. They came there to make their living as fishermen. But the coast was so steep that it was impossible to land. Where a landing could be made the land was already taken by Frenchmen. The Norwegians had to accept homesteads of 100 acres each, situated in the deep, primeval forests. They started to make lumber, but had no market. They had no towns or stores, no place to sell

P. M. Glasoe, Ph.D. (24)   H. S. Hilleboe (31)   A. G. Tuve (29)

College Presidents, with Years of Service

or buy a thing. They had little money and the market price for flour was $20.00 a barrel. Starvation and despair walked hand in hand. Kloster had taken their money to buy food, but he did not return for many months. Waiting time is long. Here it was also desperate. When Kloster did return, he had with him only a portion of his intended purchase. Brun had a cow, but had to carry hay five miles through the woods to feed her. They secured some corn and ground it in a handmill that some one had sense enough to take along from Norway. This mill was busy grinding for the colony day and night, each one taking his turn to grind. Those who lived through the winter took the first steamboat that docked at Gaspe. When they reached Montreal they met Kloster and demanded in no mistakable language to know why he had not come to their support. He had invested the money in lead mines. They met also Rev. Abraham Jacobson, who had been sent by the Norwegian Synod to meet the incoming immigrants at Montreal and give them advice and aid and a Godspeed on their way to the States. The immigrant missionary was needed possibly more then than now. The author's mother came by way of Quebec. She and her party could not understand the directions given by the functionary in charge. He swore fearfully and took a rawhide, beat them into a cattle car and then sealed it. The newcomers were thus shipped across Ontario as "dumb, driven cattle." The N. C. Brun of Gaspe fame later became a distinguished pastor in the Norwegian Conference and the United Lutheran Church.

5. Churches, 1860-1890

By this time a new generation of Norwegians are in command. The ranks of the original Sloopers are pretty well thinned out. Their children are in command of the ship. The fathers came to America and became Americans by choice. Though good Americans in every sense, yet they remained Norwegians to the end. They could not change their nature any more than the Ethiopian can change his skin, or the leopard his spots. They were more at home with the Norwegian language than the English. The Norwegian land and its scenery, the home in which they had lived and its surroundings, the laws and their lawmakers over there, the customs, ideals, culture, all had a peculiarly sweet and sacred charm altogether different to them from the things here in America.

"This," says Kristian Prestgard, poet-editor of "Decorah Posten," "does not prevent them from becoming as good Americans as ever trod the earth. It was for the purpose of becoming Americans that they left all that was dear to them, and came here. They did not come like tourists on a visit, or like students, to return after a short stay. They came of their own choice to build their homes here and to become Americans. No other group of citizens has sacrificed so much to become Americans as these immigrants. Through their work and their achievements they are united to America by the strongest ties. But through their memories they are united to Norway. This is the peculiar position of the immigrant, his tragedy." There is a tragedy, thinks Prestgard, enacted in the heart and life of every immigrant. The parting was tragic. Parting is sweet sorrow, bitter sweet. The building of the new home was tragic. It must have something about it to remind him of the old home over there; it was the holy of holies. The enstrangement from the children was tragic: They did not seem to understand when he spoke about the land of his birth. The death of the wife was tragic. She and he had sprung from the same root, had breathed the same national atmosphere, had roamed about in the same surroundings, had sung the same songs, and had cherished the same thoughts; she alone could understand when he asked: "Do you remember?" Her death brought him only sadness and an increased feeling of loneliness. His visit to the homeland was tragic. He did not find what he sought. "And what did he seek? Without knowing it, he was in reality seeking his own youth; and he did not find it. He found nothing of what he sought. Most of his old friends were resting in the churchyard, where he could read their names on the gravestones. The people he met were strangers to him. Everything was changed. But he did not realize that he himself had changed most of all. The picture of the old home district which he had carried in his soul for forty years did not seem real. It was false. This was not his home district, his home, or his people . . . . Poor, stripped of every illusion, he hastened back to Christiania, where he took passage on the first steamer going to America. Neither steamer nor railway train could carry him back fast enough."

The men and women of the second generation are Norwegian-Americans in the truest sense. They did not have this silent, all-consuming, tragic sorrow with regard to the land of their fathers. Norway was never their home. America has always been their home. But they have learned to understand more than their immigrant fathers imagined they would or could and to feel a deep and a true love for things Norwegian. They spoke both languages with the same ease and perfection. They understood too, that the Norwegian heritage can not be transplanted to American soil without much sacrificing labor. They must prepare the soil and plant the seed, they must keep out the weeds and have sufficient rain and shine. The second generation has, therefore, realized very keenly the necessity of working to transplant the culture and religion of the fathers to their own children.

It was especially in the field of religion that they appreciated the heritage of the fathers and worked for its perpetuation. The second period ushers in a most vigorous era of church work. Congregations, synods, schools, missions, publications, charities, societies, all seem to be inspired by the need of work:

> Work through the morning hours,
> Work for the night is coming.

This period witnessed also a most intense loyalty to purity of doctrine. In the midst of a babel of sects there must needs be many heresies. They could not all be in the right. Some of these heresies might easily creep into the teachings and beliefs of the Lutheran Church unless the watchmen watched. And then there was the temperamental divisions—the high church, low church and broad church groups. The churchmen in every synod were keyed up to wage a stiff fight for what they thought was right according to God's Word. They all wanted to be Lutherans, and Lutherans only, of the purest dye. They felt that ordinarily it was a shame and a sin to have controversy, but when it came to correcting a wrong or defending a truth, it would be a shame and a sin not to have a controversy. The doctrinal battles were, on the whole, carried on in a commendable manner. There was relatively very little personal enmity. On the whole, the disputants conducted themselves in a respectable manner. They regarded one another as earnest Christian seekers after the truth. If they could not come to an agreement, they said so and parted company. They tried hard to unite their forces on the basis of unity of doctrine. They prayed fervently in the words of the General Prayer in their liturgy: "Unite us and make us strong." The discussions surely brought large spiritual returns. They increased the interest in Christian doctrine in an age of doctrinal indifference and heresy. They made the second generation a race of Bible readers and seekers after truth. They saved the Norwegian Lutherans from being swallowed up by the sects. If the ideal life for a Norwegian-American is to live the dual life of a Norwegian-American, the doctrinal discussions promoted this state, and never before or since has the Norwegian-American been so Norwegian-American as during this Norwegian-American period.

The first 35 years of Norwegian history in America had produced 38 Lutheran pastors. This second period of 30 years produced 614. Arranged by synods the new accessions year by year are as follows on p. 257:

Pastors, 1860-1890

As representatives of these synods a list of 140 are selected almost at random (See Appendix). Brief sketches of them and photographs can be found in "Norsk Lutherske Prester i Amerika," commonly called simply "Prestekalenderen." The average length of service for these 140 men was 37.8 years.

ORDINATIONS OF NORWEGIAN LUTHERAN PASTORS, 1861-1890

Year	Eielsen	Norwegian	Scandinavian Augustana	Norwegian Augustana	Conference	Hauge	Anti-Missouri	United	Total
1861	1	3	2	..	..	..	..	..	6
1862	0	2	2	..	..	..	..	..	4
1863	1	4	..	..	..	..	..	..	5
1864	1	2	1	..	..	..	..	..	4
1865	0	3	2	..	..	..	..	..	5
1866	0	7	2	..	..	..	..	..	9
1867	0	5	4	..	..	..	..	..	9
1868	2	3	5	..	..	..	..	..	10
1869	3	12	2	..	..	..	..	..	17
1870	3	6	..	2	5	..	..	..	16
1861-1870	11	47	20	2	5	..	..	..	85
1871	1	3	..	2	7	..	..	..	13
1872	3	13	..	1	8	..	..	..	25
1873	3	13	..	2	2	..	..	..	20
1874	1	14	..	1	14	..	..	..	30
1875	2	15	..	..	6	..	..	..	23
1876	..	15	..	1	1	..	..	..	17
1877	..	6	..	..	4	1	..	..	11
1878	..	16	..	2	3	2	..	..	23
1879	..	14	..	2	2	..	..	..	18
1880	..	7	..	3	3	1	..	..	14
1871-1880	10	116	..	14	50	4	..	..	194
1881	2	14	..	1	9	3	..	..	29
1882	..	18	..	..	7	1	..	..	26
1883	1	20	..	3	6	4	..	..	34
1884	1	16	..	2	5	7	..	..	31
1885	..	15	..	4	4	5	1	..	29
1886	1	4	..	2	12	3	7	..	29
1887	..	13	..	1	9	7	12	..	42
1888	1	7	..	1	9	6	14	..	38
1889	1	10	..	3	7	5	9	..	35
1890	..	12	..	..	..	6	..	24	42
1881-1890	7	129	..	17	68	47	43	24	335
1861-1870	11	47	20	2	5	..	..	..	85
1871-1880	10	116	..	14	50	4	..	..	194
1881-1890	7	129	..	17	68	47	43	24	335
1861-1890	28	292	20	33	123	51	43	24	614

In the period 1825-1859 157 congregations had been organized and 12 other preaching stations had been maintained. In the period 1860-1889, 2,272 new congregations were organized and 176 extra preaching places were listed. By decades the growth in congregations and preaching places was as follows:

Congregations, 1860-1890

Decade	New Congregations	New Preaching Stations
1860-1869...................	255	13
1870-1879...................	935	54
1880-1889...................	1082	109
1860-1889...................	2272	176

These are all new congregations located as a rule in new settlements that had no congregations before. In some cases the doctrinal controversies split old congregations and congregational organizations were thereby multiplied. In many communities there were both Norwegian Synod (Missourian) and Anti-Missourian congregations, or Norwegian Synod and Conference or Augustana congregations. Many of the congregations existed only a year or two, or perhaps five, ten or fifteen years, and then dissolved. On account of the great mortality among the congregations the actual number of the congregations during this period is considerably less than the total number organized.

In the '40s congregational work was attempted only in Illinois and Wisconsin. In the '50s new congregations were created in Iowa, Minnesota, Missouri and Texas. In the '60s Indiana, Kansas, Michigan, New Jersey, New York and South Dakota were added to the church states. In the '70s there was the further addition of California, Idaho, Maine, Maryland, Nebraska, North Dakota, Ohio, Oregon, Pennsylvania, Vermont, Washington, Manitoba, Ontario and Quebec. In the '80s the home missionaries entered Colorado, Massachusetts, Montana, New Hampshire, Rhode Island and Wyoming. In all 29 states and 3 provinces had been covered by the Norwegian Lutheran pastors. They usually had three or more congregations each. The pastor would live near one congregation and then serve two or three or more congregations from 10 to 100 miles distant. He would also look around for Norwegian settlements and try to organize more congregations. At times he would be burdened with a dozen or more congregations before the mission board could find a man to come out and help him.

Never have the Norwegian-Americans lived through such hard times as during the '70s. There was the money panic, and to this was added failure of crops and the grass-hopper plague. It never rains but it pours. But these great trials did not hinder the work of the Church. Quite the contrary, as in the days of Israel. Never has the Norwegian people been more churchly than during the '70s. The growth of the congregations was truly remarkable; the attendance and the contributions were such as to please both God and man. The total of 144 pastors in 1873 increased to 310 in 1883; the 587 congregations in 1873 increased to 1,185 in 1883; the 108,694 members in 1873 grew to an army of 193,776 in 1883.

There were only three Norwegian Lutheran synods in the field in 1860—the Eielsen, the Norwegian and the Scandinavian Augustana. In June, 1870, the Scandinavian Augustana was disrupted. A Swedish Augustana was organized to take care of its Swedish members and a Norwegian Augustana was created to look after the Norwegians. In August, 1870, there was a division in the Norwegian Augustana, which added another synod to our list—

Synods, 1860—1890

John E. Haugen
Pharm.D., Manager
St. Paul Hospital

Julius C. Hallum
President Fairview
Hospital

Alfred O. Fonkalsrud,
Ph.D., Consultant
Hospital Service

the Norwegian-Danish Conference. In 1875, the Eielsen people went to work and revised their constitution. The reorganized synod was called the Hauge Norwegian Evangelical Lutheran Synod in America. Eielsen was not able to see the need of making the changes and continued the old organization under the old constitution. In 1886, the Anti-Missourian wing of the Norwegian Synod withdrew from the parent body, and marshalled its forces under the name Anti-Missourian Brotherhood. In 1890, the Anti-Missourian Brotherhood, the Norwegian Augustana and the Conference merged their forces and became the United Norwegian Lutheran Church.

The Eielsen Synod depended for its supply of ministers on the converted laymen who are gifted with power to preach. Eleven such men were discovered during the '60s and prevailed on to accept a call as ambassadors in Christ's stead. This synod made two more attempts to solve the school problem. A preparatory school for ministers was begun at Cambridge, Wisconsin, in 1865 and continued three years under the principalship of Andreas

P. Aaserød. The second venture was at Chicago. Trinity Church on North Peoria Street had secured an energetic and ambitious pastor in J. Z. Torgerson. His congregation offered to build a church so as to accommodate both a congregation and a school. The offer was accepted and the corner stone of the new structure was laid August 27, 1871, on which occasion Elling Eielsen delivered the main address. Thus began Hauge College and Eielsen Seminary, as the school was named. Classes began at once. Torgerson was the president of the school. The great Chicago fire which occurred that fall made it hard for the Chicago people to carry out their promises. Torgerson tried for seven wearisome years to maintain the school, and then gave it up, as the

| Ingeborg Sponland
Sister Superior,
Chicago | Lena Nelson
Sister Superior,
Minneapolis | Lena Brechlin
Sister Superior,
Brooklyn |

Eielsen Synod was not back of him. They wanted a school at Red Wing.

The Norwegian Augustana Synod was organized mainly on account of the language question. The Scandinavian Augustana was not thriving as much as its Norwegian founders had expected. The theological candidates from Norway all went over to the Norwegian Synod; the lay preachers were heading into the Eielsen. The students did not want to go to the Illinois State University, for that was felt to be too much of an American institution and would not fit them for the Norwegian ministry. The Augustana College and Seminary was felt to be too Swedish. A Norwegian supply professor—Johan Olsen—was appointed in 1867; a regular Norwegian professor—August Weenaas—was secured in 1868. He suggested that the Norwegians separate from the Swedes—there could be two schools within the one synod. This was granted. The Norwegian Augustana located at Marshall, Wisconsin, in 1869, and, on motion by O. J. Hatlestad it was renamed Augsburg—the German name for Augustana.

The Swedish Augustana College remained at Paxton, to which place it had been moved from Chicago, in 1863. Since 1872 the Swedish Augustana has been situated at Rock Island. It now owns buildings, grounds and endowments valued at over $1,000,000 and has over one thousand students in attendance. The Norwegian Augustana is now, in 1925, represented by the Augustana College and Normal at Sioux Falls, South Dakota, the Augsburg Seminary, Minneapolis, the Canton Lutheran Normal and a part of the Luther Theological Seminary, St. Paul. In 1870, the Norwegians proposed one more change, namely, that they should establish an Augustana Synod independent of the Swedes. This was granted and the Norwegian Augustana Synod came into being in June, 1870, at Andover, Illinois.

The Norwegian-Danish Conference was organized in August, 1870, by a number of Augustana pastors in conference with C. L. Clausen, who had in 1868 forsaken the Norwegian Synod on

Group of Nurses, Good Samaritan Hospital, Rugby, North Dakota

account of an old resolution (1862) on the slavery question. The occasion for the conference was the coming of B. B. Gjeldaker to America, a candidate from the Norwegian University. Gjeldaker somehow had not applied for admission to the Norwegian Synod. Johan Olsen and August Weenaas were also graduates of Christiania, so there was now no necessity for uniting with the Norwegian Synod. It was suggested: Why not start a new synod with a different name? This was done—the name chosen was Conference, Norwegian-Danish Conference, so as to gather the scattered Danes along with the Norwegians. The Norwegian Augustana was also entitled Norwegian-Danish and for the same reason. In 1869 the Swedes of the Augustana Synod had 46 pastors; the Norwegians, only 19. Twelve of the 19 went along in the making of the new synod, and only 7 remained in the Norwegian Augustana. The Augustana never fully recovered from this blow. It claimed the school at Marshall, and forbade Weenaas the use of its buildings. Weenaas, nothing daunted, turned his own residence into a seminary, until, in 1872, Augsburg Seminary was removed to its new quarters at Minneapolis. There Father Ole Paulson was on hand to welcome teachers and students. The Conference was fortunate in getting strong leaders into its school and chief offices—Weenaas, Sven Oftedal, Georg Sverdrup, Gjermund Hoyme, and others. Oftedal and Sverdrup were university graduates from Christiania and fully as able in debate and strategy as their opponents in the rival synods. They carried on an aggressive fight, attacking with broadsides the weak points in "Wisconsinismen," as they termed the marks of peculiarity in the Norwegian Synod. Oftedal had been here hardly a year when he issued his famous "Aaben Erklæring" (Open Declaration), which he threw into the camp of the Norwegian Synod like a bomb shell. He and Sverdrup paid more attention to polity than to doctrine and established a consciousness of there being a great difference in polity between the synods and the Conference. The congregations in the Conference had greater freedom than in the synods, said they. They began also to develop the idea of "living congregations" as opposed to the "dead congregations" of the synods. Naturally, the Conference as a body could not keep pace with Sverdrup and Oftedal, and two parties arose —the New (Nye Retning) championing the Augsburg professors, and the Old (Gamle Retning), opposing them. J. A. Bergh, N. C. Brun and N. E. Bøe are well-known names in the "Gamle Retning."

The Hauge Synod was a re-organization of the Eielsen and dates its origin from 1846 instead of 1876. The Eielsen Synod still writes 1846 as the year of its genesis.

The Anti-Missourian Brotherhood was a child of doctrinal strife. During the '50s there was strife between Eielsen and the Norwegian Synod; during the '60s, between Augustana and the Norwegian Synod; during the '70s, between the Conference and the Norwegian Synod; and during the '80s, between the Anti-Missourians and the Norwegian Synod. This last strife was a civil war and by far the most intense ever waged by Norwegians anywhere in any cause. The war had raged among the Germans, especially between the Missouri and the Joint Ohio Synod, before the Norwegians were drawn into it. Professor F. A. Schmidt, a German, professor at Luther Seminary, Madison, Wisconsin, and Professor Ole B. Asperheim, a Norwegian, professor at Concordia Seminary, Springfield, Illinois, may be said to have brought the Norwegian Synod into the fray. These men were Anti-Missourians. They accused Missouri of Calvinism;

Missouri charged them with Synergism. To save the Norwegian Synod from a threatened division, the membership in the Synodical Conference was given up, in 1883. In 1884, Dr. U. V. Koren wrote a "Redegjørelse," in which he stated in the form of theses the position of the Norwegian Synod, in favor of Missouri. It was signed by 87 pastors and professors. Drs. F. A. Schmidt and M. O. Bøckman, in 1886, were chosen by the Anti-Missourians to start a new seminary —the Lutheran Divinity School, at Northfield, Minnesota. St. Olaf's School, at that place, was made a complete college—St. Olaf College —and was promised the support of the new body.

Gjermund Hoyme,
Church Statesman

The last of the synods to be founded during this period is the United Norwegian Lutheran Church of America. It was founded June 13, 1890, at Minneapolis, Minnesota. And the event is of so great importance that it easily marks an epoch, not only in Norwegian Lutheran church history, but also in the history of the Norwegians without regard to church connections. In fact, it is the beginning of a movement in church history which has great possibilities in store.

The United Norwegian Lutheran Church was a union of three competing Norwegian Lutheran synods, sprung from the same Mother Church, with the same doctrines and rituals, the same language and customs. They differed only in temperamental

E. J. Homme
the Norwegian Francke

Homme's Orphanage (1881)

matters and minor practices. Some had been brought up in a
high church atmosphere; some in low church; just now they were
all broad church organizations. Several free conferences were
called—St. Ansgar, 1881; Roland, 1882; Holden, 1883; Gol,
1884; Chicago, 1885; Kenyon, 1886; Willmar, 1887; Baldwin,
1888; Scandinavia, 1888—for the purpose of discussing the doctrinal basis. They found that they were in hearty agreement on
all the essentials and mostly everything else beside. They decided
to combine their camps, for in unity there is strength. And so,
on June 13, 1890, the men of Augustana met at Augsburg Semi-

Canton Normal School, 1920— John N. Brown, President
(Former Augustana College, 1884-1918)

nary and ratified the proposed constitution of a United Church;
the Anti-Missourians met in St. Paul's of the Hauge Synod and
voted for the new constitution; and the Conference people assembled at Trinity Church and accepted the constitution. This
done, the three groups met in joint session at Trinity Church.
The Conference men took places in the rear. The Anti-Missourians came marching to the front, at which the assembly burst
forth into a hymn of praise: "God's Word Is Our Great Heritage." Then the Augustana delegation entered in stately proces-
sion, during which another song: "Praise to Thee and Adoration,"
pealed forth from a thousand thankful hearts. Thereupon the
convention united in the "Te Deum," prayer and confession and
another hymn of praise, "Min Sjæl, min Sjæl, lov Herren" (My

Soul, Now Praise Thy Maker). After this the United Norwegian Lutheran Church of America was formally organized. Gjermund Hoyme of the Conference was elected president; L. M. Biørn of the Anti-Missourian Brotherhood, vice president; J. N. Kildahl of the Anti-Missourians, secretary; Hon. Lars Swenson of the Conference, treasurer. Later, in 1894 (1894-1917), J. C. Roseland of the Augustana served as secretary of the United Church.

In the evening a festive gathering was held at the Coliseum, which had seating room for five thousand people. It was filled to overflowing. The atmosphere was filled with joy and thanksgiving: "The Lord hath done great things for us; whereof we are glad" (Ps. 126:3). At the annual conventions of the United Church from 1890 to 1917 the attendance ranged from 3,000 to 15,000. The United Norwegian Lutheran Church was the first merger of Norwegian Lutheran synods in America. It was the first merger of any Lutheran synods in America, at which the merging bodies became extinct. It was the first merger of its kind among all the denominations of the United States. The tendency in the United States is to talk about union, but to keep on multiplying denominations and organizations. In the United States Religious Census for 1890 143 distinct religious bodies are listed; in 1906, 186 religious bodies; and in 1916, 202.

The growth of the synods from 1860 to 1890 can be seen from this table:

PASTORS, 1860-1890

Synod	1860	1870	1880	1890
Eielsen	3	14	3	8
Norwegian	17	60	155	138
Scandinavian Augustana	9	65	..	..
Norwegian Augustana	..	9	24	28
Conference	..	14	60	115
Hauge	..	..	18	66
*Anti-Missourian	..	..	78	98
United Norwegian	..	..	..	241

*Figures from 1886.

The synods increased from a total of 144 pastors in 1873 to 310 in 1883; from 587 congregations in 1873 to 1,185 in 1883; from 108,694 members in 1873 to 193,766 in 1883. The Norwegian population increased from 1880 to 1890 125 per cent; the membership in the synods increased only 67 per cent. Still many new congregations were organized—approximately 600, and about 600 new pastors were secured. The largest congregation was the one at Scandinavia, Wisconsin, having 1,530 members; the smallest was at Juanita, Nebraska, having only 3 members. Ac-

cording to the United States Census for 1890 the congregations
of the Norwegian Synod, Hauge Synod and the United Church
were distributed as follows:

CONGREGATIONS, 1890

State	Norwegian Synod	Hauge Synod	United Church	Total
California	3	0	0	3
Colorado	1	0	0	1
Idaho	1	0	0	0
Illinois	14	10	27	51
Indiana	2	1	0	3
Iowa	49	17	113	179
Kansas	1	1	7	9
Maine	0	0	2	2
Maryland	0	0	1	1
Massachusetts	2	0	0	2
Michigan	14	1	27	42
Minnesota	164	55	405	624
Missouri	2	0	1	3
Montana	3	0	2	5
Nebraska	21	8	13	42
New Hampshire	0	0	1	1
New Jersey	1	0	0	1
New York	5	0	1	6
North Dakota	53	16	162	231
Ohio	4	0	0	4
Oregon	3	0	5	8
South Dakota	46	36	148	230
Texas	4	0	0	4
Washington	1	2	19	22
Wisconsin	95	28	187	310
Total.................	489	175	1122	1786

The Norwegian Synod in 1890 owned 275 church edifices and
182 halls for church services, with a total valuation of $806,825.00;
the Hauge Synod owned 100 churches and 75 halls, valued at
$214,395.00; the United Church owned 669 churches and 393
halls, valued at $1,544,455.00.

In 1853 the Norwegian Synod had 38 congregations and seven
pastors; in 1862 over 100 congregations and 20 pastors, of whom
two were also professors. The congregations were small, but
widely scattered over the prairies, and the road to the church,
school house, log hut or sod cellar, where services were held, was
pretty long for the average church goer. The roads were poor
at the best, and the conveyances were heavy and slow. Rev. B. J.
Muus walked from Goodhue County to Stearns County, Minnesota, with a satchel on his back. The air line distance was 100
miles; the actual route taken was over 250. The "Big Woods"
lay between him and his destination, almost impassable. Rivers,
swamps and lakes beset his path. Muus swam the streams and

walked around the lakes and swamps, burrowed his way through the woods and reached Meeker, Kandiyohi and Stearns. There he organized new congregations, baptized a large number of children, confirmed several groups of overgrown youth, and promised to find some one to send them as pastor. Part of the route on the plains he covered in an oxcart, as in the accompanying picture sketched by Eben E. Lawson of Willmar.

In 1872 the Eielsen Synod had 17 pastors; the Norwegian Augustana had 8; the Conference had 36; the Norwegian Synod had 74—total 125. The pastors of the Norwegian Synod served 335 congregations and 77,415 souls; the pastors of the Confer-

A Crow River Farmer and B. J. Muus Rounding up the Settlers, 1861

ence had 121 congregations and 16,409 souls. Augustana and Eielsen pastors had together about 100 congregations and 10,000 members. There was a gain of 400 congregations during the decade. The line of Norwegian congregations was far-flung, and extended from New York to California, from Canada to Texas.

With regard to the Danes in the Norwegian synods, the Norwegian-Danish Augustana Synod never had a single Danish pastor on its roster. The Norwegian-Danish Conference had a total of 11 foreign-born Danes in the ministry—Anton M. Andersen (ordained 1874); Hans Peder Berthelsen (1879); Gotlieb B. Christiansen (1881); Claus L. Clausen (1843); Adam Dan (1871); Hans Hansen (1874); Niels Madsen (1874); Anders Rasmussen (1883); M. C. H. Rohe (1877); Hans M. Thorup

(1872); and Peter J. Østergaard (1884). The Danes withdrew from the Conference in order to form a Danish Synod. In 1884 they organized the Danish Evangelical Lutheran Church Association. In 1896 they united with another Danish body, the Danish Evangelical Lutheran Church in America, and organized the United Danish Lutheran Church, still in operation, with headquarters at Blair, Nebraska. The Norwegian Synod, while never making a bid for the support of the Danes, in 1903 could boast of 24 Danish pastors and twice that number of Danish congregations. Among the Danish names are: Johannes N. Andersen (ordained 1895); Hans Peter Berthelsen (1894); Johannes R. Birkelund (1897); Peter P. Blicher (1906); Paul Borup (1898); Peter N. M. Carlson (1899); Severin E. S. Meisel (1893); Nils Pedersen (1877); Emil J. Petersen (1879); Christian Falck (1903); Hemming H. Frost (1894); Lars P. Hansen (1894); Søren Hansen (1882); Anders K. Henriksen (1908); Anders H. Jensen (1898); Eskild P. Jensen (1871); Frederik C. M. Jensen (1883); Lars P. Jensen (1884); Jens Johansen (1880); Anders Larsen (1878); Lauritz P. Lund (1909); Svend G. A. Marckmann (1910); Julius C. Møhl (1891); Carl J. O. Nielsen (1901); Hans C. Olsen (1895); Lauritz Rasmussen (1908); Harold W. Sørensen (1902); Ditlev W. Turnøe (1908); Jens D. Wein (1904); Anders O. White (1903); and Markus F. Wiese (1869). The Hauge Synod has in Martin J. Westphal (1890) a good representative of the Danes. The United Church numbered among its clergy such Danes as Christian H. Hjortholm (1896), Niels A. Stubkjær (1893), Nils P. Thorp (1897) and Nils Juel Holm (1907). Nils J. Thomasberg (1893) and James Falk (1918), at one time of the Lutheran Free Church, are Danes; so also Lars C. Pedersen of the Lutheran Brethren Synod (1914).

Of pastors from other nationalities may be mentioned: Alfred E. Backman (1877), Heinrich Thurunen (1885) and William Williamson (1887), born in Finland. Alfred Picard (1908) is a native of France. John Bjarnason (1884), Hans B. Thorgrimsen (1882) and Paul Thorlakson (1875) hailed from Iceland. Rudolf H. Gurland (1893), Emanuel N. Heimann (1903), Theodor C. Meyersohn (1881) and John Resnick (1899) were Russian Jews. Frederick H. Carlson (1869), Karl O. Eliasen (1910), Martin Engen (1893), Anders J. Hulteng (1887), Carl W. Landahl (1896), Gøran Norbeck (1885), Nicholaus Okerlund (1902), Olof Olson (1906), Gustav Rast (1891), Johan O. Seleen (1871), Johannes Telleen (1907), Gustav Westerlund (1887) and Albert Wihlborg (1892), were born in Sweden. Hans P. Duborg (1860), Claus H. Fechtenburg (1897), Max F. Mommsen (1909), Peter Mortensen (1887), Carl Otte (1882), Friedrich A. Schmidt (1861), Villads B. Skov (1889) and Hans J. Wein look to Germany as their native land. Paul Werber (1882) was a Galician Jew. Gabriel N. Isolany (1893), Christian Pedersen (1908), Ludvig C. C. Pedersen (1899) and Eugene A. Rateaver (1911) came from Madagascar. Heinrich Otte (1896) came from Natal; Christopher U. Faye (1912), from Zululand. Sigurd Folkestad (1909) was born in England of Norwegian parentage.

6. EDUCATION, 1860-1890

This period witnessed a great activity in the building of church schools. The public schools taught everything except the cultural heritage of the immigrant races and the Chris-
Aim tian religion. Private schools had existed in this land for three hundred years, while public schools were yet in their infancy in 1860. The state universities are younger than most of the church colleges surrounding them. The University of Illinois dates from 1867; the University of Wisconsin, from 1848; the University of Iowa, from 1855; the University of Minnesota, from 1869. Harvard was founded in 1634; Yale, in 1701. The first American high school was established in Boston in 1821. There were only 64 public high schools in 1850, but that same year there were 6,085 private high schools, or church academies. The situation is, of course, quite different in 1925. In 1915 there were 12,003 public high schools, and only 2,203 private high schools. It was quite natural for the Norwegian pioneers to want to build higher schools. They knew that knowledge is power. They wanted to give their national heritage and their Lutheran faith to their children. The public schools could not teach the Christian religion if they would, and they would not teach the culture of the immigrants if they could. So they proceeded to build church schools.

From 1860 to 1870 these schools were founded and maintained:

By Eielsen Synod:
    a. Eielsen Seminary, Cambridge, Wisconsin, 1865-1868.
    b. Hauge College and Eielsen Seminary, Chicago, Illinois, 1861-1878.
By Norwegian Synod:
    c. Concordia Seminary, St. Louis, Missouri (jointly with Missouri) 1859-1874.
    d. Luther College, Halfway Creek, Wisconsin, 1861-1862; Decorah, Iowa, 1862——.
    e. Holden Academy, Aspelund, Minnesota, 1869-1874.
    f. St. Olaf College, Northfield, Minnesota, 1874——.
    g. Concordia Seminary, Illinois, 1874-1876.
    h. Luther Seminary, Madison, Wisconsin, 1876-1889; Robbinsdale, Minnesota, 1889-1899; St. Paul, Minnesota, 1899-1917.
    i. Monona Academy, Madison, Wisconsin, 1876-1881.
    j. Coon Valley Lutheran High School, Coon Valley, Wis., 1878-1879.
    k. Franklin School, Mayville, North Dakota, 1878-1880.
    l. Willmar Seminary, Willmar, Minnesota, 1883-1919.

 m. Gran Boarding School, Mayville, North Dakota, 1880-1889.
 n. Bode Academy, Bode, Iowa, 1887-1903.
 o. Stoughton Academy, Stoughton, Wisconsin, 1888-1900.
 p. Lutheran Normal School, Sioux Falls, South Dakota, 1888-1918.
 q. Luther Academy, Albert Lea, Minnesota, 1888——.
 r. Aaberg Academy, Devils Lake, North Dakota, 1888-1903.
 s. Bruflat Academy, Portland, North Dakota, 1889-1918.
By Scandinavian Augustana Synod:
 t. Augustana College and Theological Seminary, Chicago, Illinois.
  1860-1863; Paxton, Illinois, 1863-1869. (Continued under Norwegian Augustana Synod).
By Norwegian Augustana Synod:
 u. Augsburg Seminary, Marshall, Wisconsin, 1869-1870.
 t. Augustana College and Seminary (Marshall Classical School), Marshall, Wisconsin, 1870-1881.
 t. Augustana College and Seminary, Beloit, Iowa, 1881-1884.
 t. Augustana College, Canton, South Dakota, 1884-1918.
 t. Augustana College and Normal, Sioux Falls, S. Dak., 1918-....
 v. Salem Seminary, Springfield, Iowa, 1876-1878.
 w. Augustana Seminary, Beloit, Iowa, 1884-1890.
  Philadephia Seminary also used, Philadelphia, Pennsylvania.
By Norwegian-Danish Conference:
 u. Augsburg Seminary, Marshall, Wisconsin, 1870-1872 (From Norwegian Augustana).
 u. Augsburg Seminary, Minneapolis, Minnesota, 1872-....
 x. St. Ansgar Seminary, St. Ansgar, Iowa, 1878-1910.
 y. Norwegian Lutheran Deaconess Home, Brooklyn, N. Y., 1883-....
 z. Norwegian Lutheran Deaconess Home, Minneapolis, Minnesota, 1889-....
By Hauge Synod:
 æ. Red Wing Seminary, Red Wing, Minnesota, 1879-....
By Anti-Missourian Brotherhood:
 f. St. Olaf College, Northfield, Minnesota (From Norwegian Synod).
 ø. Lutheran Divinity School, Northfield, Minnesota, 1886-1890.
 aa. Wittenberg Normal School, Wittenberg, Wisconsin, 1887-1890.
  Capital University also used, Columbus, Ohio, 1873-1890.

a. *Eielsen Seminary*

The Eielsen Synod was somewhat afraid of higher learning, but clearly saw the need of some training in secular and religous

Higher Schools

branches. Eielsen Seminary was intended to be an academy and seminary combined in a two or three years' course. Andreas P. Aaserød (1823-1907) was a "seminarist" from Norway and had had eight years of experience as a parochial teacher. The attendance was about 20 each year. Aaserød became a pastor at Badger, Iowa, 1871-1878. Then he farmed, 1878-1882. He closed his career as a music teacher at Portland, Oregon, 1891-1907.

b. *Hauge College and Eielsen Seminary*

This was the most auspicious of the school enterprises of the Eielsen Synod. The president of the school, John Z. Torgerson, had attended Lawrence University, 1860-1863, Illinois State University, 1863-1865, and Chicago University, 1865-1867. As colporteur for the Chicago Bible Society, 1867-1869, he had visited 15,000 homes. As pastor of Trinity Congregation from 1869 to 1905 he is said to have officiated at 15,000 marriages. But the times were hard. Torgerson and Eielsen did not agree. Torgerson left the Eielsen Synod in 1876 and soon afterward the school closed for want of support.

G. O. Brohough (44)   H. H. Elstad (39)   O. O. Stageberg (29)

A. K. Feroe (28)   G. H. Gilbertson (26)   H. T. Ytterboe (22)

c. *Concordia Seminary*

This was the school of the German Missourians. A very thorough school. The professors lectured in Latin as readily as in German. The students had to have a mastery of both of these languages. Laur. Larsen was the first Norwegian teacher at Concordia, 1859-1861. F. A. Schmidt represented the Norwegian Synod at Concordia, 1872-1876, as professor of theology. 138 Norwegians have graduated from the school with the degree of C. T. (Candidate in Theology). Concordia has given the degree of Doctor of Divinity (honoris causa) to U. V. Koren, 1903, Laur. Larsen, 1903, H. G. Stub, 1913, and Joh. T. Ylvisaker, 1914. Concordia Seminary was founded in 1839. From 1839 to 1922 it graduated 2,641 men for the ministry. It has upward of 400 students each year and is the largest theological school in the land, if not in the world.

d. *Luther College*

The beginnings of Luther College were humble. It was started in a parsonage at Halfway Creek, Wisconsin, with 16 students in attendance and two instructors—Rev. Laur. Larsen and Rev. F. A. Schmidt. It had been planned by the Norwegian Synod pastors, graduates of the University of Christiania, to be a university fully as good as the university where they had been trained, and for 20 years it was frequently referred to as "The University." The times were very difficult. The panic of 1857 had left its marks. The Civil War was raging. The most pressing needs were met by the aid which Concordia Seminary was furnishing. But Concordia was down in Missouri, a slave state, and this placed the school between the fighting lines. The connection with Concordia was not broken by the war, and it was not until 1876 that the Norwegian Synod founded its own seminary.

The Synod felt the need of a preparatory school and decided to begin in 1861, despite the war. It was not a university. It began as a six-year gymnasium, leading to the A. B. degree. It was a classical school. College classes were added as fast as students who could take such work were developed. The first graduating class was turned out in 1866, the members of which were: R. B. Anderson (1846——), J. E. Berg (1842-1905), G. Erdahl (1840-1914), T. O. Juve (1840-1913), L. J. Markhus (1842-1885), Ellef Olsen (1841——) and H. G. Stub (1849——).

The second school year opened in Decorah, Iowa, in the St. Cloud Hotel. The first college building was completed in 1865 at a cost of $75,576.23. The site for the school had been chosen by U. V. Koren. The task of raising so large a sum as $75,000.00 in the dark days of the Civil War can hardly be appreciated now. Eggs were six cents a dozen, butter five to ten cents per pound. The markets were far away, the roads to town were wretched. Money had no stable value, everything to be bought in town was way up in price. In 1860 the Norwegian Synod had only 7,500 baptized members. In 1865, not much over 15,000. But they raised the money gladly and promptly. And when they dedicated their building they met up over 6,000 strong.

Among the things deposited in the corner-stone was an historical sketch of the Norwegian Synod. The following words from the sketch state specifically the aim of Luther College, but also reflect the general aim of all the schools of the Norwegian Lutherans:

"Emigrated Norwegians, Lutheran Christians living in Wisconsin, Iowa, Minnesota and Illinois, united in erecting this building to educate teachers of the Church, through whose ministry,

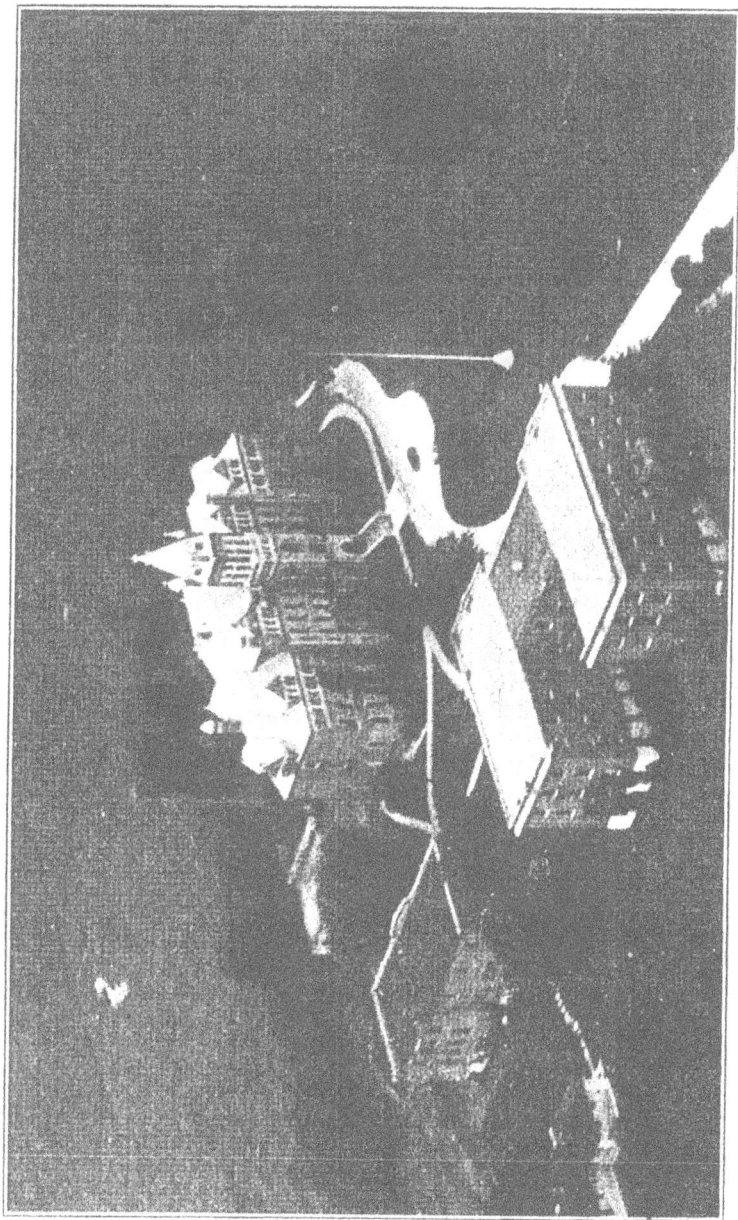

An Airplane View of Luther College, Southwest Corner

Taken by Prof. George Henriksen

by the grace of our Lord, the saving truth of the Gospel in Word and Sacraments might be preserved for their descendants unadulterated according to the doctrine of the Evangelical Lutheran Church as set forth in the Unaltered Augsburg Confession. The Lord grant this. Amen."

Luther College has made good. It stands in the front rank of American colleges with regard to scholarship and is an accredited school. It has graduated (1866-1924) 861 men with the A. B., 358 of whom have been ordained as clergymen in the Norwegian Lutheran Church; 195 other students have become clergymen without having attained to the bachelor's degree. Its property is now valued at over $1,000,000.00. Laur. Larsen was president 1861-1902; C. K. Preus, 1902-1921; Oscar L. Olson, 1921———.

e. *Holden Academy*

Founded by B. J. Muus at his parsonage, Holden, Minnesota, as a preparatory school. Muus encouraged his best confirmation pupils to go to school. An unusually large number of the leaders among the Norwegian people have come from his congregations and from the parishes of other pastors who followed his example in leading the young. Holden Academy was discontinued to make way for St. Olaf's School.

f. *St. Olaf College*

St. Olaf College was founded November 6, 1874, at Northfield, Minnesota, under the name St. Olaf's School. It was the first co-educational school in the Norwegian Church. It remained an academy until 1886, when it was extended upward as a college. That year it became the college of the Anti-Missourian Brotherhood. In 1890 it became the college of the United Norwegian Lutheran Church. In 1894 it was placed on its own resources, and, but for the heroic labors of H. T. Ytterboe, it might have entirely collapsed. In 1899 it again received the support of the United Church and has since made great advances. Harald Thorson, one of the founders of the school and a true friend of it until his dying hour, bequeathed to it at various times a total of about $1,000,000.00. The school now has a faculty of about 75 and a student body of nearly 1,000. For lack of room it has to limit its attendance. The academy was discontinued in 1917. From 1890 to 1924 it graduated 1,090 men and 603 women, a total of 1,693. In 1924 314 were employed as clergymen and missionaries; 778 as teachers; 152 were employed in other professions; 449 were engaged in other occupations. Th. N. Mohn was the first president, 1874-1899; J. N. Kildahl, the second, 1899-1914; L. A. Vigness, the third, 1914-1918; and L. W. Boe, the fourth, 1918———.

Old Main, St. Olaf College, 1876

New Science Hall, St. Olaf College, 1925

g. *Concordia Seminary*

Concordia Seminary is the practical seminary of Missouri. It was founded in 1846 at Ft. Wayne, Indiana. In 1874, when the Missouri Synod purchased the Illinois State University school property, it was moved to Springfield, Illinois. It was conducted for such theological students as did not have a full college preparation. In 1874 the Norwegian practical students began to attend there. In 1875 Ole Bugge Asperheim, a graduate from the University of Christiania, became the representative of the Norwegian Synod on the faculty of the school. He was transferred to Luther Seminary, Madison, Wisconsin, in 1876. Concordia graduated seven men into the Norwegian ministry. The school is in a flourishing condition. In 1922 it had a total of 1,540 alumni, an attendance of 147 studying for the ministry, and several substantial buildings at its disposal.

h. *Luther Seminary*

The Norwegian Synod established its own seminary in 1876, at Madison, Wisconsin. It never came to Decorah, as was first the intention when"The University" was being planned. Luther Seminary was located at Robbinsdale, Minnesota, in 1889, in a suitable building erected for it. This school plant was destroyed by fire in 1894, and the school sought temporary quarters in a hotel. A new, modern school building was made ready for use in 1899, at a cost of over $100,000.00. It was situated within St. Paul, at Hamline, Minnesota. In 1917, due to the merger of the Norwegian Synod, the Hauge Synod and the United Church into a new synod, the Norwegian Lutheran Church, the three seminaries of these church bodies were also merged into one— Luther Theological Seminary, St. Paul. The Hamline building of Luther Seminary and the theological plant of the United Church Seminary at St. Anthony Park were both used during 1917-1918; but since then the Hamline building has been used by the Miller Lutheran Bible School. The teachers at Luther Seminary, 1876-1917, were: O. B. Asperheim, 1876-1878; K. K. Bjørgo, 1881-1882; O. E. Brandt, 1897-1917; J. B. Frich, 1888-1902; B. A. Harstad, 1889-1890, 1910-1911; Elling Hove, 1902-1917; W. M. H. Petersen, 1894-1899; F. A. Schmidt, 1876-1886; H. G. Stub, 1878-1896, 1900-1917; and Joh. T. Ylvisaker, 1879-1918. From 1876 to 1915 451 ministers were trained at this school.

i. *Monona Academy*

A co-educational school, with an attendance from 41 to 79. It occupied the buildings of the defunct orphanage that had been sold to the Norwegian Synod for $18,000.00. The school was discontinued in 1881 for lack of suitable quarters. J. J. Anderson, formerly president of Augustana College, was the president of the school.

j. *Coon Valley Lutheran High School*

Founded by Hagbart Engh, a graduate of Luther College. He conducted the school one year, 1878-1879, and then accepted a position at Monona Academy.

k. *Franklin School*

Franklin School was conducted in Rev. Bjug A. Harstad's parsonage, about 7 miles southeast of Mayville, North Dakota. Harstad proposed to two of his friends, Stephen H. Hustvedt and Jens Mehus, both Luther College boys, that they start a school for confirmed youth of Traill County. He would furnish his residence as a school house if they would be content with the tuition fee from the pupils. The agreement was made. The attendance was about 55 each year. The school was in session only two years.

l. *Willmar Seminary*

Willmar Seminary was at one time one of the largest and most popular high schools in the state of Minnesota. It started in 1883 with 116 students. In 1891 it had 371. Its president, Hans S. Hilleboe, was considered one of the best school men in the state. He was, in addition to busy tasks as executive and teacher, often called on to lecture on educational and temperance subjects. He was a fine orator and a dangerous enemy of the saloon. The high schools and the War ended its days of usefulness. 7,110 students were in attendance from 1883 to 1919. The school property was largely the gift of the two brothers Lars O. Thorpe and Mikkel O. Thorpe. Hans S. Hilleboe was connected with the school, 1884-1899, 1904-1907; J. C. Jansrud, 1894-1905; Oscar K. Omlie, 1895-1904; Alfred C. Pederson, 1910-1919; Albert Struxness, 1896-1897, 1906-1918; Jonetta Thorpe, 1911-1919; and S. O. Tjosvold, 1893-03. 65 other teachers have also taught at Willmar for a shorter term.

m. *Gran Boarding School*

This is also the creation of B. Harstad, that great friend of church schools for youth of high school age. Gran was started in 1885 and was in operation until 1891. This school was held in the church building of the Gran Congregation one-half mile south of Harstad's parsonage. The first two years A. Ingberg and T. C. Sattra were teachers. Sattra was the housefather; Mrs. Sattra, the mother. There were up to 85 in attendance. On Friday evening they went home to their folks, and on Sunday they came back to church services and school.

n. *Bode Academy*

Erected in 1887 by the Bode Norwegian Lutheran Congregation as a high school for the youth of the vicinity. It was conducted eight years by the congregation. The attendance varied from 40 to 100. It was found that the building used by the school was too small and the drain on the congregation too great, hence the congregation voted to discontinue the school. Enthusiasts for the cause kept the work agoing another stretch of 7 years, and then it was quietly laid to rest, in 1902. It had a total of 800 students. Among the teachers may be mentioned: John E. Granrud, 1889-1890; Celia Gullixson, 1890, 1895-1896; Andrew C. Kirkeberg, 1891-1894; Lars O. Lillegaard, 1889-1896; O. L. Olson, 1893-1895. The building was later converted into a public school house.

o. *Stoughton Academy*

Stoughton is one of the strongest Norwegian communities in America. K. A. Kasberg planted a school there in 1888. In 1894, an association of Norwegian Synod men came to his aid. In 1899 it received the full backing of the Synod, but on March 25, 1900, fire destroyed the building. The building was restored, and the school was run for a while as a business college by non-Lutherans. During the 12 years of its existence it had a total attendance of 2,124 young men and women.

p. *Lutheran Normal School*

The Lutheran Normal School opened October 1, 1889, with a faculty of three teachers and 52 students. The Norwegian settlers of this country had long felt the need of a Norwegian-American normal school, which could train teachers both for common and parochial schools. For a number of years, 1865-1885, Luther College maintained a normal school department for training men parochial teachers. The attendance was never large—12 in 1883, 10 in 1884, 8 in 1885. The department was discontinued in 1886, and reestablished at Sioux Falls in 1889 as a normal school. The total attendance from 1889 to 1918 was 4,197; the actual number of persons in attendance was 2,200. Nearly 750 have been teachers in the parochial and common schools; 28 have later entered the ministry. In 1918 Augustana College of Canton and the Sioux Falls Normal were united under the name Augustana College and Normal. The presidents of the Sioux Falls Normal have been: Rev. Amund Mikkelsen, 1889-1892, 1896-1908; Rev. S. C. N. Peterson, 1892-1893; Rev. H. B. Hustvedt, 1893-1896; Rev. Z. J. Ordal, 1908-1917; Professor H. S. Hilleboe, 1917-1920; Dr. Charles Orrin Solberg, 1920———.

q. *Luther Academy*

Another child of faith in the Christian education of the young. The presidents of Luther Academy have been:

Hon. L. S. Swenson, 1888-1897, now United States minister to Norway.

Rev. E. I. Strom, 1897-1902, now pastor, Watson, Minnesota.

Professor Martin L. Ullensvang, 1902-1903.

Rev. J. E. Thoen, 1903-1914, now pastor, Oklee, Minnesota.

Professor Sigurd S. Reque, 1914-1919, now professor of French, Luther College.

Professor Kalmar J. Jacobson, 1919-1921, now Augustana College.

Luther Academy, J. O. Tweten, President

Professor Eli A. Jensen, 1921-1924, now busines smanager, Wittenberg College.

Rev. Jacob O. Tweten, 1922———, Albert Lea, Minnesota.

The school had an attendance of 4,970—2,590 boys and 2,380 girls during the years 1888-1923, an average of 142 each year, 74 boys and 68 girls.

r. *Aaberg Academy*

Aaberg Academy was organized as a private enterprise by Rev. Ole H. Aaberg, pastor among the Norwegian Lutheran pioneers of Ramsey, Benson, Rolette, Bottineau and Ward counties, North Dakota. A religious junior academy for newly confirmed and other youth. Aaberg built a school house costing $2,000.00. The school had a Norwegian department, 1888-1903, and an English department, 1891-1903. It was conducted only in the winter months, yearly, but had no graduates. Ole H. Aaberg, Albert Hesla and Stener Svennungsen are numbered among the teachers.

s. *Bruflat Academy*

A few lines from the 1915 catalog of the Bruflat Academy: "Bruflat Academy was founded in 1889. It had its origin in the desire of the Norwegian Lutherans of Rev. B. Harstad's congregations to provide better parochial school facilities than could be had by means of the usual parochial schools held at various times of the year in each of the congregations of this charge. Some three years before a boarding school had been organized at Gran Church, about seven miles southeast of Mayville, North Dakota. This school soon proved too small for the whole charge, and being located at the extreme eastern part of the settlements, four of the congregations, lying farther in the west, decided to organize a similar school of their own at Portland. As it was necessary to build anyway, it was suggested to erect a larger building than was needed for the parochial school only, and thus make room for an academy to be maintained in connection with the parochial school . . . . A great deal of credit is due to the early settlers for their courage in undertaking the task of establishing a school of this character, always difficult under the most favorable circumstances, and certainly a tremendous undertaking in a comparatively new country and with small resources. The one man who seems to have had the clearest vision, and the courage and enthusiasm to inspire the rest was Rev. B. Harstad, whose portrait we present in this issue (of the catalog). Let the knowledge and remembrance of the sacrifices that the pioneers made for the cause of higher Christian education inspire the rising generation to do their share in aiding Bruflat Academy to fulfil its mission." The younger generation to whom this appeal was addressed inherited much wealth from their pioneer fathers and live in a day when money can more easily be made; still they allowed Bruflat to die. It died in 1918. 2,354 boys and girls of high school age received a Christian education at Bruflat. The principals of Bruflat were:

Professor John G. Halland, 1889-1892, state superintendent of schools, North Dakota, 1897-1901.

Rev. John O. Tingelstad, 1892-1900, now professor of Scandinavian, University of North Dakota.

Professor Knut M. Hagestad, 1899-1904, now high school instructor, Santa Cruz, California.

Professor Alfred C. Pederson, 1904-1906, now superintendent, Argyle, Minnesota.

Professor T. E. Thompson, 1906-1908, high school teacher, Chicago, Illinois.

Professor A. T. Felland, 1908-1911, 1916-1918, principal, Benson County Agricultural School, North Dakota.

Professor Martinus C. Johnshøy, 1911-1912, pastor, Starbuck, Minnesota.

Professor Erick J. Onstad, 1913-1916, attorney, Madison, Wisconsin.

t. *Augustana College and Theological Seminary*

This school has been on wheels. The idea of the school was conceived at the Illinois State University, Springfield. It was established at Chicago in 1860 and was moved to Paxton in 1863, being then the school for the Swedes and the Norwegians of the Scandinavian Augustana Synod. In 1869, the Norwegian students

Augustana College and Normal, Dr. Charles O. Solberg, President

and their professor—A. Weenaas—were moved to Marshall, Wisconsin, where a building had been purchased to accommodate the school. The Norwegian Augustana congregations lay to the south and especially to the west of Marshall, so it was generally agreed that Marshall was not a good location for it. Through the energetic work of Hon. James M. Wahl the school was moved to Beloit, Iowa, in 1881. In 1884, the college was separated from the Seminary and moved to Canton, South Dakota, then a rival town of Beloit on the opposite side of the Big Sioux River. Canton furnished the Naylor House as a school building on condition that the school would stay in Canton 10 years. Under the able management of President Anthony G. Tuve the college at Canton grew large and strong. In 1918 it had 324 students and had had for 14 years an average of 250 a year, men and women.

It had a total enrollment of 6,990 from 1860 to 1918. The powers that were decided in 1918 to put the school on wheels again. They rolled it up to Sioux Falls, where it is now happily united in lawful wedlock with the Lutheran Normal. The presidents of Augustana have been: Rev. L. P. Esbjørn, 1860-1863; Rev. T. N. Hasselquist, 1863-1869; Rev. A. Weenaas, 1869-1870; Professor J. J. Anderson, 1870-1874; Professor Dorman, 1874-1876; Professor Fred S. Huntington, 1876-1877; Professor J. W. Dennison, 1877-1881; Hon. J. M. Wahl, 1881; Professor M. D. Miller, 1881-1889; Rev. C. S. Salvesen, 1889-1890; Professor A. G. Tuve, 1890-1916; Dr. Paul M. Glasoe, 1916-1918; Professor H. S. Hilleboe, 1918-1920; Dr. C. O. Solberg, 1920———. At Marshall it was commonly called the Marshall Classical Academy.

Main Building, Augsburg Seminary. George Sverdrup, Jr., President

u. *Augsburg Seminary*

Augsburg Seminary dates its existence from the time that the Norwegian professor (A. Weenaas) and his students left Paxton in 1869 and settled down at Marshall. The school was called Augsburg by synodical resolution. Now, as already related, Augsburg became the school of the Norwegian-Danish Conference. In 1872 it was located permanently at Minneapolis, where it stands today in a thriving condition. From 1870 to 1890 it was the seminary of the Conference; from 1890 to 1893 of the United Church; and since 1893, of the Lutheran Free Church. It has always been a strong school, with strong personalities at its head. The names Sverdrup and Oftedal are some of the best known and most respected names in Norwegian-American history.

The presidents of the school have been: A. Weenaas, 1869-1874; Georg Sverdrup, 1874-1907; Sven Oftedal, 1907-1909; George Sverdrup, Jr., 1909——. Theologians at Augsburg holding full professorships: August Weenaas, 1869-1876; Sven Oftedal, 1873-1904; S. R. Gunnersen, 1874-1883; Georg Sverdrup, 1874-1907; B. B. Gjeldaker, 1876-1877; M. O. Bøckman, 1890-1893; F. A. Schmidt, 1890-1893; E. G. Lund, 1891-1893; H. A. Urseth, 1899-1909; Andreas Helland, 1905——; George Sverdrup, 1908——; J. O. Evjen, 1909-1919; E. P. Harbo, 1909——; Lars Lillehei, 1920——. College professors of long standing: J. H. Blegen, 1885-1916; Theo. S. Reimestad, 1885-1900; Wilhelm M. Petter-

Ole G. Felland   J. C. M. Hanson   Karl T. Jacobsen
Libr., St. Olaf College   Librarian, U. of Chicago   Libr., Luther College

sen, 1886-1910; J. J. Nydahl, 1891——; H. N. Hendrickson, 1900——; S. O. Severson, 1904-1915; Wm. Mills, 1907-1919; P. A. Sveeggen, 1915——; R. B. Nell, 1916-1924. The aim of the school was to meet the demands of our Lutheran immigrants for earnest, consecrated ministers of the Gospel. But if this aim was to be attained the very foundations of the school would have to be a true, living Christianity, Lutheran profession, and a close allegiance with the congregations. The school has therefore stressed conversion, prayer meetings, and other manifestations of Christian life, as well as careful and prayerful study of God's Word. The total number of students (men), from 1869 to 1923, was 6,988. The school has a four-year academy, a four-year college and a three-year theological seminary. It has been the most successful of the colleges in getting its college men to study theology. From 1869 to 1914 348 of its graduates became pastors. 54 per cent of its college graduates have taken up the study of theology. Since 1922 the school has been co-educational.

v. *Salem Seminary*

Started by Rev. David Lysnes, pastor at Springfield, Iowa, six miles south of Decorah, in his parsonage. Lysnes was a profound Bible student and a pietist, akin to the great mystics of medieval history. He was a very earnest and inspiring preacher and teacher, and fortunate were those who sat at his feet. The Springfield congregation has given a number of good men to the Church—Abraham Jacobson, K. Salvesen, Iver Andreassen, A. E. Erikson, K. O. Lomen, C. S. Salvesen, and Olaf Lysnes, all ministers, and Professor A. G. Tuve, president of Augustana College, 1889-1916. The Salem Seminary did not have a large attendance. It was moved to Marshall in 1878, and from that time it was called Augustana Seminary. Rev. C. J. Roseland of Philadelphia is one of the Salem boys.

w. *Augustana Seminary*

Augustana College and Seminary came to Beloit, Iowa, in 1881. In 1884, Augustana College was detached from the Seminary and moved to Canton. The Seminary kept right on at Beloit until 1890, when the Augustana Synod voted to merge the seminary with the Augsburg. Professor K. O. Lomen, a graduate of Marshall, Thiel College, and Philadelphia Seminary, died January 1, 1890; Professor Lysnes, August, 11, 1890. They were the whole faculty at Augustana in 1890.

x. *Red Wing Seminary*

Red Wing Seminary is now one of the leading college preparatory schools of the Norwegian Lutheran Church of America. The equipment of the institution at Red Wing, Goodhue County, Minnesota, includes a pro-seminary (pro-theological) department, a school of commerce, a Bible school, and a school of music and dramatic art. It has a faculty of twelve members. In 1879 the Red Wing Seminary became the successor of the Red Wing Collegiate Institute, an independent institution which in 1871 erected the present Sande Hall, now a dormitory for boys. In the early '80s Sumner Hall, now used as a woman's dormitory, was added. The seminary opened in 1879 with two departments: an academy with a four-year course and a divinity school with a three-year course. One of the first teachers, G. O. Brohough, Ph. D., is still a member of the faculty. The owner of the school was the Hauge Norwegian Lutheran Synod, an organization which in 1917 united with two other Norwegian Lutheran synods to form the Norwegian Lutheran Church of America. In 1899 an expansion toward a junior college began, and by 1910 the school had a senior college department, graduating in the year its first class to receive the A. B. degree. Because of the church union in 1917 the theological department was moved to Luther Seminary in St. Paul, and the college department to St. Olaf College. At the same time various other departments as indicated above were either added or enlarged. The present main building, a very fine structure of pressed brick, was built in 1903. The school has a fine heating plant, a hospital, and a residence for the president.

The number of students annually in attendance varies from 150 to 200. During the last few years co-education has been in force. The school has distinguished alumni organized into an active alumni association. The following educators have been presidents of the institution: The Rev. Ingvald Eisteinsen, 1879-1881 (acting); Rev. August Weenaas, 1882-1885; Rev. J. N. Kildahl, 1885-1886 (acting); Rev. M. G. Hanson, 1886-1887 (acting); Rev. O. S. Meland, 1887-1889; H. H. Bergsland, 1889-1897; Rev. M. G. Hanson, 1897-1910; Edward W. Schmidt, 1910-1918;

Red Wing Seminary, H. E. Jorgensen, President

Rev. M. J. Wick, 1918-1920; Herman E. Jorgensen, 1920——. Of the many able teachers who have taught at the seminary seven deserve special mention for long and efficient service. They are: G. O. Brohough, 1879——; H. H. Elstad, 1887——; C. R. Hill, 1887-1895; Julius Boraas, 1895-1900; E. O. Ringtsad, 1900-1917; George H. Ellingson, 1908-1917; O. O. Stageberg, 1908——. The names of Hans Markusen Sande, Ole Ellingson and Rev. Østen Hanson should be mentioned as the original purchasers of the old Main Building, in 1878. This involved an expenditure of $10,000.00 and was an act of foresight and courage on their part which deserves to live on in fond memory. Total attendance, 1879-1923, 6,127. Pastors trained at Red Wing, 1879-1914, 177.

y. *Lutheran Divinity School*

The seminary of the Anti-Missourians, 1886-1890. Dr. M. O. Bøckman and Dr. F. A. Schmidt, professors. 29 men were graduated. The school merged with Augsburg Seminary in 1890.

z. *Wittenberg Normal School*

Rev. E. J. Homme had established at Wittenberg an orphanage, an old people's home, a printing press, a Sunday school paper, a young people's paper, an almanac, etc. He wanted also a school. Wittenberg Normal School was established as the training school for teachers within the Anti-Missourian Brotherhood. Two exceptionally good teachers were secured—Knute O. Løkensgaard and Peter J. Eikeland. The school was in session three years (1882-90) and had an attendance of 35, 41 and 50 boys and girls.

Herman W. Sheel	William Paul Sihler	Frederick Zilliox
40 years	35 years	30 years
Chemistry	Greek	Commerce

Three German Professors at Norwegian Colleges

æ. *St. Ansgar Seminary*

St. Ansgar Seminary was a great school in its day, 1878-1910. The history of St. Ansgar dates from October 1, 1878, when Professor Halsten S. Houg, a teacher at Augsburg Seminary, encouraged by Revs. Johan Olsen and B. B. Gjeldaker, opened a private high school in two vacant rooms in the public school building of St. Ansgar. The school continued here for two years, and then the two following years it was conducted in two rooms above one of the down-town stores. In 1882 Professor Houg had secured the backing of the St. Ansgar Circuit of the Conference and a suitable building was erected for his school. In 1890, Knute O. Løkensgaard and P. J. Eikeland of the Wittenberg Normal were added to the faculty, making six teachers. The general aim of the school was "to give to young men and women an opportunity of acquiring a thorough, practical education on a Christian foundation." The total attendance at the school was 2,868. It had 56 teachers. The presidents were as follows:

Halsten S. Houg, 1878-1890, later county auditor, Mitchell County, Iowa.

Knute O. Løkensgaard, 1890-1893, president elect, Gale College.

Knut Gjerset, Ph. D., 1893-1895, now professor of history, Luther College.

John Olaf Sethre, A. M., 1895-1898. Deceased.

L. J. Sigurd Olsen, 1898-1901, pastor, Minneapolis, Minnesota.

John P. Tandberg, 1901-03, pastor, Weldon, Saskatchewan.

Matias R. Odegaard, 1903-1905 (teacher, St. Ansgar, 1893-1910), Sioux Falls, South Dakota.

Ivar Ramseth, 1905-1907, now pastor, Luther Valley, Wis.

George T. W. Mohn, 1907-1908, now business manager, Mohn Printing Company, Northfield, Minnesota.

Carl C. Swain, Ph. D., 1908-1910, president, Mayville State Normal School.

a. *Baptist*

From 1884 to 1913 the Norwegian and Danish Baptists conducted the Dano-Norwegian Baptist Seminary at Morgan Park, Chicago. The school had organic connection *Reformed Schools* with the University of Chicago and its Divinity School, which is Baptist. The first head of the Morgan Park school was a Dane, N. P. Jensen, 1884-1895. His first associate was a Norwegian, Edward Olsen, Ph. D., who had been professor of Greek at the University of Chicago, 1875-1885. In 1887 Dr. Olsen was elevated to the presidency of the University of South Dakota. He lost his life on a visit to his brother, the merchant prince, S. E. Olsen of Minneapolis, in the Tribune fire, November 30, 1889. Another Norwegian, Dr. Henrik Gundersen, took Olsen's place at the seminary in 1887 and

Northern Baptist Seminary

he became the dean of the school in 1895 upon the death of Dean Jensen. He has been assisted by a Norwegian, C. J. Olsen, and a Dane, Dr. Nils S. Lawdahl. In the first 20 years of its existence 170 men were in attendance, many of whom are now in the ministry in Norway, Denmark, America and foreign mission fields. In 1910 the Norwegians organized a General Conference and in 1913 they established a Norwegian Seminary, which, since 1921, has been in affiliation with the Northern Baptist Theological Seminary, Chicago. Dr. Gundersen continues as the dean of the school and professor of New Testament Greek.

In the 1924 catalog of this school it is stated that there are about 2,000,000 Norwegians in America. "To give this people the Gospel, free from human inventions and admixtures, is both a duty and a privilege for us as Baptists. The progress, however, of our Baptist work among them, has been somewhat hampered on account of the strong attachment of the Norwegians to the Lutheran Sacramentalism in which salvation is connected with outward forms and conveyed through them. There are about 2,000 Norwegian Baptists in the United States and Canada and 40 churches. They have formed an organization called the Norwegian

J. H. Johnson   A. Haagensen   T. Ottman Firing

Norwegian Methodist Divines

Baptist Conference of America, for the promotion of the welfare of the churches connected with it and for the spread of the Gospel."

b. *Congregationalist*

In proportion to their numbers the Congregationalists spend more money on educational and missionary work than perhaps any other denomination in the world. The Mayflower people who landed at Plymouth Rock in 1620 were Congregationalists. They developed great strength in New England and have wielded a tremendous influence throughout the whole country in all fields of thought and endeavor. Being Separatists, they naturally were interested in the early Norwegians, of whom many were Dissenters. There was a Norwegian Congregational church organized in connection with the Tabernacle Church in Chicago in the early '80s and one in Tacoma, Washington, a little later. The present system of Norwegian Congregational congregations had its beginning as a result of the work originating in the Chicago Theological Seminary, which was opened to Scandinavian students in 1884, with Rev. P. C. Trandberg as their teacher. Trandberg was a Danish Lutheran, who had been a dissenter in his native land, and had established there The Danish Evangelical Free Church. He was on the faculty of the Congregational School until 1890 and then withdrew in order to found a new school, The Evangelical Lutheran Free Church Seminary, Chicago. This seminary he conducted until 1894. He died in 1896. In 1885 R. A. Jernberg, a graduate of Yale, became Trandberg's assistant. Dr. Jernberg was a professor at the Dano-Norwegian Institute of the Chicago Theological Seminary, 1885-1916, and at its successor, Union Theological College, Chicago, 1916-1923. He was the founder of the church paper "Evangelisten" and its editor ten years, 1889-1899. Rev. O. C. Grauer has been an associate professor in the Seminary. During its first 20 years of work the school had 123 Norwegian and Danish students, of whom 52 completed the full course. Six of these eventually came back into the Lutheran Church. From 1887 to 1915 21 of the graduates of this Congregational school sought admission to the ministerial ranks of the Norwegian Lutherans.

c. *Methodist*

The Norwegian-Danish Theological Seminary at Evanston, Illinois, dates from 1870, when three Norwegian Methodist pastors—Andrew Haagensen, John Henry Johnson and P. H. Rye, all Norwegians, and two laymen—Ole Wigdal and O. M. Oren, resolved that Carl Schou, then a student at Northwestern University, should start a school for those who desired to enter the Norwegian-Danish Methodist ministry. C. B. Willerup succeeded Schou in 1873, and after him came B. Johannesen, Marcus Nilsen and Martin Hansen in turn. In 1886 Nels Edward Simonsen, A.M., D.D., was elected president of the seminary. He was connected with the school as president and teacher over 30 years. I. Ottman Firing is in charge of the school at present. H. P. Bergh, John O. Hall, Tobias Foss, Herbert Hansen, Carl W. Schevenius, T. H. Loberg and Asbjørn Smedstad

Methodist Theological Seminary, Evanston, Illinois

have been on the teaching staff at various times. The school was chartered in 1875 and obtained its own building in 1889. It has close relations with the Garrett Biblical Institute and Northwestern University. From 1870 to 1905 the school graduated about 45 ministers.

d. *Quaker*

The Norwegian Quakers, according to Ulvestad, maintained a school at LeGrand, Marshall County, Iowa, for a number of years. Ole T. Sawyer was the principal. The attendance ranged from 20 to 25.

a. *Valder Business College and Normal School*

Founded in 1888 by Charles H. Valder, teacher of penmanship at Luther. The first year he sent out 12,000 catalogs to country youth and they came by scores. Sub-
Private Schools   sequently he had up to 400 students a year. The growth of the public high schools gradually diminished his attendance. He had 10,000 students in all and 900 graduates. He died in 1922, and his school closed down in 1923.

b. *Albion Academy*

In 1889 Peter Hendrickson, at one time professor of Latin at Beloit College and editor of "Skandinaven," bought the Albion Academy property and re-opened the school in 1890. The attendance the first year was over 100—boys and girls. In 1900 Hendrickson sold his school to a corporation composed of sixteen Norwegian Lutheran congregations of the Norwegian Synod, and the school took a new lease of life in the fall of 1901 under the name H. A. Preus Academy, which a few years later was changed back to Albion Academy. In 1918 it closed its doors for good.

Albion Academy was an old school, founded in 1854 by the Seventh Day Baptist Church, under the leadership of Dr. C. R. Head. The people of the Seventh Day faith had that year organized two academies ten miles apart—Milton Academy at Milton, and Albion Academy at Albion. These schools are only four years younger than the University of Wisconsin and nine years older than the oldest public high school in that state. They had a fairly good attendance. R. B. Anderson was added to the faculty of Albion in 1866 as teacher of languages, and the attendance rose by leaps and bounds. Anderson was a Norwegian and attracted the Norwegians from the neighboring Koshkonong settlements. Milton also appointed a Norwegian teacher, Edwin E. Evenson. He secured a number of students from Edgerton and Stoughton. The most outstanding of these is the well known Dr. Anthony Rud, Chicago, whose son, Anthony M. Rud, is the author of a novel, "The Second Generation." Ludwig Kumlien, son of Thure Kumlien, the noted naturalist, was on the Milton faculty, 1889-1902. R. B. Anderson's work attracted the attention of Madison educators, and in 1869 he was asked to take a position at the University of Wisconsin. Anderson is the first Norwegian to hold a professorship of Scandinavian at an American university. K. A. Kasberg was a teacher at Albion in 1884-1888. Owing to the growth of the high schools, the Baptists found that they could not keep two schools going and offered Albion for sale. Professor Hendrickson bought it.

In the list of its graduates are such names as Senator Knute Nelson of Minnesota; Governor Alva Adams of Colorado; Hon.

O. A. Buslett   H. H. Boyesen   Kr. Janson

Early Literary Men

C. V. Bardeen, judge of the Supreme Court of Wisconsin; Dr. J. F. A. Pyre, professor of English, University of Wisconsin.

In 1901 Albion Academy became a church school, having been transferred to an association consisting of 16 Norwegian Lutheran congregations of that vicinity. D. G. Ristad (1901-1904), Theo. R. Ringøen (1904-1914), and Torger C. Torgerson (1914-1918), were the presidents.

In its last published catalog, 1917, the last message of this school to the Church which supported it and the world which tolerated it, we read: "While the Church recognizes the great work done by our free public schools, it nevertheless laments the fact that the spiritual nature of the student must of necessity in these schools be more or less ignored in order to conform to the laws of our free Republic. Our church schools then fill a gap in the American plan which every fair-minded citizen will be forced to admit. What the twentieth century needs more than anything else is, men and women of Christian faith and character, true to their convictions and ideals, honest and upright in all things. That is the type of men and women a Christian school always aims to develop. Having this aim, our church schools ought to commend themselves to all who have the highest interest of the young at heart."

c. *Wraamann's Academy*

Wilhelm W. Wraamann studied at Luther College, 1868-1869, taught at St. Ansgar Academy and Augsburg Seminary, and served as county superintendent of schools, Hennepin County, Minnesota, 1886-1888. He established in 1890, a private high school, known as Wraamann's Academy, which he was able to conduct until 1897. The school was located in South Minneapolis, but was kept in different buildings according to the attendance. H. Borglund, a Swede, was the most important assistant. The strength of the school was built on Professor Wraamann's great popularity as a teacher. The last year the attendance dwindled down to 26 and the school closed. Wraamann was the author of a textbook on learning English, "Praktisk Lærebog i Engelsk."

The number of Norwegians seeking a college education was on the increase. At the Norwegian Lutheran colleges the total attendance of college students in 1860 was *Graduate Work* 0; in 1870 it was 36; in 1880 it was 131; and in 1890 it was 145. A number of these were encouraged to do postgraduate work at standard universities, and others felt the urge from within to get more wisdom and win scholastic degrees. Luther College, famed for its thorough classical scholarship, took the lead. Sixteen of her graduates won the Master of Arts degree between 1883 and 1890. in the '70s there were only two Norwegians who attained to the Doctor of Philosophy degree. From 1881 to 1890 there were six who graduated with this degree. From 1891 to 1900 there were 15; from 1901 to 1910, 26; from 1911 to 1920, 43. From 1877 to 1925 at least 112 Norwegian-Americans became Ph.D.'s. A list of these doctors will be found in the Appendix. It is probably not complete. The following won their doctorate during this period:

Anton B. Sander, Luther College, A.B., 1874; Yale, Ph.D., 1877.

Magnus C. Ihlseng, A.B., 1875, Ph.D., 1879.

Thorstein B. Veblen, Carleton, A.B., 1880; Yale, Ph.D., 1884.

Albert E. Egge, Luther, A.B., 1879; Johns Hopkins, Ph.D., 1887.

Andrew Fossum, Luther, A.B., 1882; Johns Hopkins, Ph.D., 1887.

Ole Edward Hagen, Wisconsin, A.B., 1882; Leipzig, Ph.D., 1890.

Joseph S. Schefloe, Luther, 1885; Johns Hopkins, Ph.D., 1890.

Agnes M. Wergeland, Nissen, A.B., 1878; Zurich, Ph.D., 1890.

Sander was the first Ph.D. He was a teacher at Flushing for one year, 1877-1878, and at Luther College for one year, 1878-1879. His subjects were Hebrew, Greek, Latin and German. He died young—only 30 years old. Ihlseng has been instructor at Pennsylvania State College and Brooklyn Polytechnic Institute and is a civil engineer in the employ of the New York Central. Veblen has been professor of economics at the universities of Chicago, Leland Stanford and Missouri and the New School for Social Research, New York. He has written ten or more scholarly books on economic and social problems and is considered one of the world's greatest authorities in his field. Egge was an English philologist and teacher at St. Olaf, University of Iowa, State College of Washington and Willamette University. He died in 1919.

Andrew B. Sander   Agnes M. Wergeland   Andrew Fossum

Andrew Fossum has been a teacher of Greek and French at St. Olaf, Park Region and Concordia Colleges and has written on the Greek theater and Norse discovery of America. He has been a wonderful pedagog in Greek. Hagen was a professor of languages at the University of South Dakota, 1891-1901. Schefloe was a professor of Romance languages at Johns Hopkins. Miss Wergeland was a professor of history at the University of Wyoming. She has written two volumes of poetry and other books. She was the first Norwegian woman in the world to receive a Ph.D.

7. Publications, 1860-1890

This country guarantees to its citizens freedom of speech and freedom of press. The Norwegians early made use of their

The Press

privilege and right to use the press. From 1860 to 1890 they established no less than 169 journals—91 news and political papers, 25 cultural and reform, 35 Lutheran religious and 18 non-Lutheran religious. A list of these periodicals will be found in the Appendix.

The aim of the newspapers was to chronicle the news of Nor-

way and America and as much of the rest of the world as would
be of special interest to the Norwegian readers. These papers
introduced the Norwegian immigrants to the ideals and practices
of the Americans, recounted the best news of the Norwegian
settlements and kept the Norwegians here in touch with the course
of events in their former home land. They contain hundreds and
thousands of little poems written by the immigrants, expressing
in lyric lines their love for the land they forsook as well as their
loyalty to the land they had of their own free will sworn allegiance
to. They give first hand glimpses of the Norwegians at work in

B. Anundsen   Gustav Amlund   John Anderson

Pioneer Founders of Publishing Houses that Bear Their Names

home and school, in church and state, on the broad prairies and
in the busy marts. It is indeed sad to think that most of these
papers have been destroyed, and of some of them there is not a
single copy left in any historical depository.

> Only a newspaper! Quick read, quick lost,
> Who sums the treasure that it carries hence?
> Torn, trampled under feet, who counts thy cost,
> Star-eyed Intelligence?

It may be that the books penned by theNorwegian immigrants
and their children during this period, 1860-1890, cannot be called
immortal. The pioneers were as yet too busy
Books   with the work of clearing the ground and
building the foundations of home, school,
church, state, industry, society, to find time to write artistic literature, belles lettres. What books they did write, were written as a
rule to meet some practical requirements, to satisfy some deep-
felt want.

a. *Theological Works*

Next to their homes and their work the pioneers were concerned about their religion. They had to be supplied with Bibles,
hymn books, catechisms, postils and other Christian literature.

There was no attempt by the Lutherans to write anything in the field of Biblical theology, such as commentaries and introduction. Most of the books were written by clergymen. One bibliography enumerates 115 books by Norwegian Lutheran pastors, 1860-1890, —26 in dogmatic theology, 38 in historical theology, and 51 in practical theology. In dogmatic theology there was considerable writing on the subject of Predestination by such men as: N. Amlund, A. Bredesen, O. N. Fosmark, H. Halvorsen, U. V. Koren, J. I. Krohn, I. G. Monson, P. A. Rasmussen, F. A. Schmidt and H. G. Stub. A. H. Gjevre wrote on the Sabbath, O. Juul and O. J. Norby wrote on Baptism, A. Wright wrote on Redemption, N. T. Ylvisaker wrote on the Gospel and Absolution. The doctrines of the sects were analyzed by

Dean C. P. Lommen   Dr. H. P. K. Agersborg   J. A. O. Larsen, A.M.
Biology, U. of S. Dak.   Zoology, Jas. Millikin U.   History, U. of Wash.

O. L. Kirkeberg and I. G. Monson; the religion of the lodges, by J. B. Frich and H. G. Stub. In historical theology the ground covered was general church history, the history of the synods, the story of the colleges, personal memoirs. Among the historians were such writers as: O. B. Asperheim, J. A. Bergh, S. R. Gunnersen, S. M. Krogness, H. A. Preus, A. Weenaas, M. Shirley, J. T. Ylvisaker and J. C. Roseland. In practical theology E. K. Thuland, a "Norsk Læsebog," 3 volumes (1882); B. J. I. Muus, "Til Mine Konfirmander" (1890); K. L. Lundeby, "Fra Missionsmarken i Dakota" (1884); J. A. Bergh, "Hans Egede" (1886); K. B. Birkeland, "Missionens Betydning for den Kristne Menighed" (1888); Georg Sverdrup, "Diakonissegjerningen" (1888); N. T. Ylvisaker, "Seks Prædikener" (1876); F. E. Wulfsberg, "Prædikener over Kirkeaarets Evangelier" (1888); D. Lysnes, "Scrivers Sjæleskat" (1874); J. M. Eggen, "Forlovelsen" (1889); M. P. Ruh, "Guds Evige Pagt" (1874); C. O. Brøhaugh, "Børnenes Harpe" (1879); M. F. Gjertsen, "Hjemlandssange" (1887); J. P. Gjertsen, "Missionssange for Israel" (1881); G. Hoyme and L. Lund, "Harpen" (1878-88); E. Jensen, "Børneharpen" (1883); "Scandinavian Songs" (1890), "Koral-

Thorvald Gulbrandsen

Gunnar Lund

J. J. Fuhr

bog" (1880); Isaac Jenson, "Nogle Aandelige Sange" (1860); T. S. Reimestad, "Afholdssange" (1888); O. Waldeland, "Missionssalmer" (1888); M. F. Wiese, "Lidt Salmehistorie" (1879); A. Wright, "Turtelduen" (1877); P. G. Østby, "Sangbog for Børn" (1885).

Of religious books by non-Lutherans mention may be made of the works of Andrew Haagensen and J. H. Johnson, Methodist pastors, and Kristofer Janson, Unitarian pastor. Haagensen was editor of the Methodist church paper "Missionæren," 1870-1877, of the church organ "Den Kristelige Talsmand," 1880-1884, 1890-1897. He was author of a "trenchant volume entitled 'Methodism and Lutheranism Compared'; also 'The Norwegian and Danish Mission History' and an illustrated Bible history, all in the Norwegian language." J. H. Johnson issued a volume of sermons, "Opvækkelses Prædikener," in 1880. Kr. Janson (1841-1917) had been a poet, novelist and school teacher in Gudbrandsdalen, Norway. In 1879 and 1880 he made a visit to the United States. In 1881 he returned to become pastor of a Norwegian Unitarian congregation at Minneapolis. While here, he kept up his remarkably productive literary ac-

A. N. Rygg

P. O. Thorson

Carl G. O. Hansen

Publishers and Editors

tivity. Among his writings were: "Salmer og Sange for Kirke og Hjem," 1883; "Jesus-Sangene," 1893; "Lys og Frihed: Prædikener," 1892; "Har Ortodoxien Ret?" He published a Unitarian paper, "Saamanden," and several novels dealing with Norwegian-American life. Unitarianism did not make very strong appeals to the Norwegians. Janson himself drifted over to Spiritualism, and the Unitarian congregations he founded have faded away with the exception of one, on Mt. Pisgah, at Hanska, Minnesota, served by Amandus Norman. Janson returned to Norway in 1894. The Norwegian Congregationalists published a hymnal that has been quite extensively used in some of the Norwegian Lutheran churches of Chicago.

b. *Poetry and Fiction*

The oldest piece of poetry written by a Norwegian-American was composed for a Fourth of July celebration on the good ship Ægir in 1837. The poet was Ole Rynning. The poem struck the keynote for two or more generations of sweet singers of Norwegian birth and descent —a love of two countries. It was entitled "Til Norge" (To Norway). The second stanza has been rendered, in free translation, by Theodore C. Blegen as follows:

Wm. Ager

Hans A. Foss

Kr. Prestgard

Wm. M. Pettersen

Jon Norstog

Peer O. Strømme

Poets and Novelists

Iver A. Hain

N. N. Rönning

K. C. Holter

A. M. Sundheim

Though Destiny, as Leif and Bjørn,
    Call Northern son to alien West,
Yet will his heart in memory turn
    To native mountains loved the best,
As longs the heart of a lone son
    To his loved home once more to come.

It is believed that the first Norwegian-American who seriously took up the task of writing literature was Hjalmar Hjort Boyesen. He was born in Norway in 1848 and died in New York in 1895. He immigrated to America in 1868 and was assistant editor of the Norwegian paper "Fremad," Chicago, in 1868-1871. Thereupon he obtained a position as teacher of German at Urban University, Ohio, 1871-1874; at Cornell University, 1874-1880; and at Columbia University, 1880-1895. His first book was the novel "Gunnar," a story of Norway. His first volume of poetry was "Idyls of Norway and Other Poems," 1882.

The Father of Norwegian-American Literature is Ole A. Buslett. He was born in Gausdal, Norway, May 28, 1855. Came to Northland, Waupaca County, Wisconsin, in 1868. Has been a farmer, merchant, postmaster, justice of peace, member of the legislature, editor and author. His writings are a battle for the best in Norwegian-American life. His own life was very honest and noble. On May 17, 1909, when he was at Madison, the state legislature adjourned to hear him give a Seventeenth of May oration in the capitol. His writings have appeared in a great variety of periodicals. In January, 1922, he began a magazine, "Buslett's," in which he aimed to reprint these articles in 30 issues. But he died, June 5, 1924, before this goal was reached. His first book was a story, "Fram," which appeared in 1882. The next year he published two poems in book form, "Skaars Skjæbne" and "Oistein og Nora," pioneer tales in verse; also a history of the Fifteenth Wisconsin Regiment, enlarged and re-issued in 1893. These were succeeded by a six-act drama, "De To Veivisere," in 1885; "Digte og Sange," in 1889; a tragedy, "Et Dødens Tegn," and a comedy, "Snip-snap-snude." Most of his writings are in prose, not poetry. Other Norwegian poets in the '80s are Edvard Larssen ("Politiske Røvere," 1885), John Benson ("Ved Gry og Kveld," 1889), and Wilhelm M. Pettersen ("Digte," 1890).

Boyesen was the first Norwegian to publish a novel in English. It seems that Andreas Wright was the first to publish a story in Norwegian. His allegory, "Gjenløser blandt Syndere," was set up, printed and bound in 1881 in the Wright parsonage at Rushford, Minnesota, by Wright and his daughter Anna, who is now a ward school principal at Minneapolis (Jackson and Clay Schools). In 1882 Buslett published his story "Fram" and Kristofer Janson his collection of historical stories, "Vore Bedsteforældre." Two other writers of fiction appeared— Hans A. Foss and Bernt Askevold.

Boyesen's novels were all in English —"Gunnar," 1874; "Norseman's Pilgrimage," 1875; "Tales from Two Hemispheres," 1876; "Falconberg," 1878; "Against Heavy Odds," 1880; "Ilka on the Hill Top," 1881; "Queen Titania," 1882; "A Daughter of the Philistines," 1883; "Norseland Tales," 1884; "A Daring Fiction," 1885; "The Modern Vikings," 1887. Buslett's tales are in Norwegian—"Rolf Hagen," 1893; "Sagastolen," 1900; "Folkefærd og Dumfærd," 1908; "Glans-om-sol," 1911. Kr. Janson's chief aim seemed to be to undo the work of the Norwegian Synod pastors, nevertheless his stories are very interesting— "Præriens Saga," 1885; "Vildrose," 1887; "Et Arbeidsdyr," 1889; "Bag Gardinet," 1890; and others. His wife, Drude Krog Janson, published in 1887 a novel entitled "En Ung Pige"; in 1888

Rasmus Malmin

Peder Tangjerd

Thore Eggen

J. M. Sundheim

Four Editors of Lutheraneren

she had another novel ready, "Ensomhed," and in 1894, yet another, "En Saloonkeepers Datter." Another woman writer, Ingrid-Berrum, made quite a success with her idyllic "Familien paa Stjerneklip," published late in the '80s. H. A. Foss is a newspaper man. He has edited "Nordmanden," Grand Forks, and "Nye Normanden," Minneapolis, and other journals. Born in 1851, he emigrated from Norway in 1878. He taught school and worked as a farm hand. In the winter of 1884 he wrote his "Husmandsgutten," which he published first as a serial in "Decorah Posten." The story was popular. It increased the subscription list of "Decorah Posten" by 6,000 new subscribers in one winter. It is still a good seller in book form. In 1885 he wrote "Kristine." Later he wrote "Livet i Vesterheimen," "Hvide Slaver," and "Den Amerikanske Saloon." The last mentioned book has been

Amandus Norman   Dr. R. A. Jernberg   Dr. Henrik Gundersen
Unitarian   Congregationalist   Baptist

translated into English by J. J. Skørdalsvold and bears the title, "Tobias, a Story of the Northwest." It is perhaps Foss's best work. Askevold's "Familien paa Skovsæt," "I de Gamles Sted," "Et Barns Død" and "Trang Vei" are worthy stories by a worthy pastor.

c. *Other Books*

Books cover many fields besides theology, poetry and fiction, but not many of these were cultivated during this period. Boyesen tried his hand at history and literary criticism. His "Story of Norway" (1876) is found in public school and private libraries generally; it was written 1,000 years after the Norsemen discovered Greenland (America). His standard book on "Goethe and Schiller" (1879) has been translated into German, Norwegian and Russian. His work on Ibsen (1893) was sold out within ten years—cannot now be had at any price. His "Essays on Scandinavian Literature" (1895) is a work of the first order. Knud Henderson was the first Norwegian in America to teach Norwegian singing school and the first to write a "Koralbog" (Choral book) and instruction books for playing and singing

J. Dorrum   O. E. Rølvaag   J. A. Holvik

Professors of Norwegian

(1865). Emil J. Petersen wrote a text book in shorthand in 1886, and H. Roalkvam wrote a text book in catechetics in 1881. These were forerunners to a many-sided literary activity in the Third Period, 1890-1925, when the Norwegians have become thoroughly acclimatized and have leisure to write.

8. Miscellaneous Matters

A number of other interesting and vital topics belong to the history of this period, such as, occupations, publishing houses, foreign missions, home missions, charitable institutions, associations, science and art, home life, public life, representative men and women, relative place and influence, but space does not permit any discussion at all. "The half has never yet been told." Some day these noble deeds of the Norwegians in America will be adequately written up. And many of them will live in the memory of the nation.

> For the good deed, through the ages
> Living in historic pages,
> Brighter grows and gleams immortal,
> Unconsumed by moth or rust.

F. L. Tronsdal   Taaraand Vik   Julius J. Hopperstad

Book and Subscription Agents

Laurits Selmer Swenson
Minister of the U. S. to Norway

Helmer H. Bryn
Minister of Norway to the U. S.

CHAPTER VII

AMERICAN PERIOD, 1890-1925

The third period of the century that we are reviewing may be called the American Period. It begins around the year 1890 and occupies 35 years of time. In this period we shall find that the Norwegians in America are far more American than Norwegian and that they are assuming positions of trust and influence in state and nation as though they were to the manor born. In 1925, at least five of the 48 governors of the United States happen to be Norwegian and a sixth governor is Norwegian in his remote ancestry. In the Norwegian Period, no Norwegian could ever have reached the governor's chair. Such things do not happen. In the Norwegian-American Period, it might have happened, but it didn't. In the American Period, there is no reason why it should not happen to a man of Norwegian descent as well as to a descendant of Irish or English forebears. The Norwegians in this period are in every way native to the American soil just as their fathers before them were born and bred in America. They are Americans all, even if one-half of them still can speak Norwegian and are familiar with Norwegian culture. They are 100 per cent Americans even if they all nourish kindly thoughts of the land of the North that gave birth to their grandsires.

It can be truly said even of the immigrant, theNorwegian of

the Norwegian Period, if you please, that he, too, can be 100 per cent American, notwithstanding all the unjust things which have been said to the contrary during the recent War and since. Speaking on this point, Kristian Prestgard very aptly remarks: "Lately much has been spoken and written about this matter, but the amount of nonsense which has been uttered reveals an astonishing ignorance of the difficult position of the immigrant. I do not refer merely to the hysterical absurdity to which we were treated during the war. But even highly cultivated and intelligent men and women have talked away about these things without thinking. Even former President Roosevelt, who was such

First Norwegian Church Built in Washington,
at Stanwood, 1878, Destroyed by Fire, 1892

a master in coining striking phrases, said once that it was just as impossible to love two countries at the same time, as to be faithful to two women. Now, I am sure that I am in no way an exception when I state that I have loved two women at the same time, and that, as far as I know, I have been faithful to both. One of them was my mother; the other, my wife. It has never occurred to me that I loved my wife less because I also loved my mother, and I am sure that President Roosevelt would have said the same. But without thinking he coined a phrase that has done great harm."

Now, if it can be said of an immigrant that he can be 100 per cent American and still be deeply attached to the land he forsook, it surely ought to be true of the Norwegians of the third, fourth, fifth and sixth generations born on American soil and carefully nurtured in American ideals. The American-born Norwegians would love America even if they had never been taught to do so. It is natural for a man to love his native land, as natural as for him to care for his kith and kin.

Breathes there the man with soul so dead,
Who never to himself hath said,
This is my own, my native land!
Whose heart hath ne'er within him burned,
As home his footsteps he hath turned,
From wandering on a foreign strand!

1. Historical Background, 1890-1925

Modern civilization, through railroads and telegraphs, through steamships and cable-grams, through airplanes and radio, tends to draw mankind closer together in under-
Europe   standing and sympathy and unity of purpose.
It should make it easier to understand the Gospel message that all men are brothers. But, sad to say, national rivalries and antipathies have been developing alongside the growth in internationalism. The countries of Europe have been promoting patriotism at any cost, deifying their own flags, and engaging in a mad race to get ahead of their neighbors in the amount of land possessions and the ability to fight. America has been just as imprudent as the European powers. When Roosevelt visited Norway, he addressed the Norwegian Storthing. "If you want peace," said he, "prepare for war. Prepare so well that they will not dare to touch you."

Meanwhile, the nations of Europe had been pursuing a policy of intense national expansion. They built up their countries internally and then looked around for colonies to annex. Germany was most aggressive in her industrial and commercial work, rapidly gaining on England, which had held the lead for a century. There was a good deal of war talk and much preparing for war. Carnegie endowed a Peace Palace and kept a Peace Tribunal at the Hague, but the commissioners who were sent there returned home only to find that their countries were going into militarism and navalism worse than ever. Carnegie wrote strong tracts to prove that we could never again have a war because we were so highly civilized and had so much commercially at stake, but he let his factories construct warships and manufacture ammunition. The nations were afraid of one another in spite of the influences toward internationalism. Germany, Austria and Italy in 1882 formed a Triple Alliance to go to each other's assistance in case of need. France and Russia promptly made a Dual Alliance, in 1884, and England joined them informally in a Triple Entente. So the great powers of Europe were aligned in these two hostile bands. They had sown the wind and in due season they reaped the whirlwind.

During the intense race for national improvement from 1890 to 1914, when the war broke out, times were very good in Germany and England, and the emigration was reduced very materially. In the decade 1881-1890, 1,452,970 Germans came to

America, while in the decade 1891-1900, only 543,922 arrived here, and in 1901-1910, only 341,498. The falling off of English emigrants was also great. Now the War is over, leaving so much wreckage in its trail, many would naturally like to get away from all their war debts and sorrows, and start anew here in America. Our immigration which was much reduced during the war, would be larger in volume than ever before. But there are at least two factors which have kept the Central Europeans at home: They have been too poor to come, and we limited the number of those who may enter.

Norway was one of the few countries that did not enter the World war. Like the rest of Scandinavia, Norway maintained

Norway

its neutrality throughout those terrible years, 1914-1918. On the whole Norway fared well during the war and has made much material progress since 1890. The greatest event in this period is the peaceful negotiation with Sweden and the house of Oscar II, which resulted in the separation of Norway from Sweden, in 1905. Norway was an independent nation before the separation, but since the separation this fact does not have to be asserted and proved in season and out of season. The country has witnessed a phenomenal industrial growth since 1905. There have been hard times, especially since the War. The newer arrivals from Norway are as a rule city bred people and they prefer to settle in the cities.

In the United States, since 1890, Benjamin Harrison (1889-1893), Grover Cleveland (1893-1897), William McKinley (1897-

America

1901), Theodore Roosevelt (1901-1909), William H. Taft (1909-1913), Woodrow Wilson (1913-1921), Warren G. Harding (1921-1923). and Calvin Coolidge (1923——) have been elected to the presidency of the country. Vast changes have taken place during the 35 years here marked off.

Under Harrison the McKinley Protective Tariff (1890) was passed. By means of this law the trusts of the United States have been protected at the expense of the consumer, and a fine crop of millionaires was produced. Roosevelt was made a civil service commissioner in 1890, and he was able to rally fresh enthusiasm about him in the hope of getting reforms in an "orgy of spoils."

Under Cleveland the Columbian Exposition was held in Chicago in 1893. The attendance was 27,000,000. The fair brought the world to Chicago and Chicago to the world.

The world went Columbus-mad. A secret order, the Knights of Columbus, was organized in 1882 within the Roman Catholic Church, and a Columbus Day as a legal holiday was inaugurated in many states. The references to Leif Erikson in the school histories were weeded out of most of them. Men sneered at the idea that the Viking could have crossed the ocean in an open boat. Spain decided to make three ships exactly like the three of Columbus fame and they were towed to America by a man-of-war. The pride of the Norseman, Magnus Andersen, was hurt. He would vindicate the historical name and fame of his native land on the seas. He made an exact replica of the Viking ship found at Gogstad, and with eleven men sailed over to the United States without the aid of anything except a small sail and twelve pairs of oars plied by twelve pairs of stout arms. They left Bergen May 1, 1893, and reached New London, Vinland, June 13, after 44 days' sailing,—"with Jesus in the boat," as F. T. Bullen says in his book "With Christ at Sea."

Norway did not take any notice of the deed of Captain Magnus Andersen until 25 years later, and then not until Captain

The Viking Boat, 1893　　　　Rasmus E. Rasmussen

Andersen himself had given an anniversary dinner to the survivors of the expedition. America was for the moment very enthusiastic about the success of the venture and greeted the boat as it sailed up to the Chicago Exposition Grounds with the booming of cannon. The American historians paid no attention to the feat and gradually eliminated from the American consciousness the story of the Norsemen five centuries before the coming of Columbus. A student at Luther College, high school trained, said to his teacher: "The story of the Norse voyages is a myth. You believe it because you want to." Although Andersen's boat is on exhibition at Lincoln Park, Chicago, the possibility and probability of the Viking voyages is generally scoffed at. A man convinced against his will, is of the same opinion still. History is made to order, and it is hard to recast it. One of the twelve who rowed over in 1893, Rasmus E. Rasmussen, fell in love with America and finally made it his home. He became a slum missionary in Brooklyn and like Hercules cleaned out abodes of the Devil in Hamilton Avenue. He exchanged his sailor's togs for the pastor's frock. He died in 1912 as a Lutheran pastor at Cox, South Dakota. His son, Elias, was a pastor in Chicago, 1914-1921, and since 1921 he has been located at Windom, Minnesota.

The financial panic of 1893-1896 hit the country under Cleveland. There was a revolt of the West. Coxey's Army marched on to Washington. For many years the farmers had been organizing themselves under various names, to discuss matters belonging to their occupation and interests. They organized the People's Party and demanded many reforms that were sorely needed. They agreed with the Democrats in thinking that the free coinage of silver at the ratio of sixteen to one would be a cure for the panic and voted for William Jennings Bryan for president. Bryan was then a young man, whose marvellous speech "The Cross of Gold," won him instantaneously national recognition and the presidential

Norwegian Lutheran Deaconess Home, Brooklyn, N. Y.
C. O. Pedersen, Rector, Mathilde Gravdahl, Supt. of Nurses

nomination. His progressive views and noble life have endeared him to the Norwegians, even when they have felt that it would be more practical to vote for a Republican candidate. McKinley advocated a full dinner pail a la Mark Hanna on the gold standard basis, and won the election.

During McKinley's presidency the Spanish-American War was fought, and since then America has been obliged to have an imperialistic policy.

Under Roosevelt there was some attempt made to curb the trusts. He advocated the conservation of natural resources—forests, coal, oil, gas, parks. He got the Panama Canal built, though not completed before 1914.

During Taft's peaceful reign Marconi succeeded in sending wireless messages through the air and the Wright brothers took the lead in inventing ships that could navigate the air.

Wilson "kept us out of the War" during his first term and

brought us into it as soon as he was re-elected. The entrance of America seemed to have been the most decisive factor in ending the War. The American effort includes 4,000,000 men drafted, $21,850,000,000.00 spent, and 50,572 deaths in action. Another bumper crop of millionaires was produced by the War, an increase of nearly 300 per cent. The number who had a net income of $50,000.00 and over in 1918 was 43,037; 67 of these had a personal income of $1,000,000.00 and over.

Harding called the country back to normalcy again and Coolidge is doing his best to keep down the taxes.

This period has been one of great advances in almost all material lines. The best prairie lands have all been taken, and people are flocking to the cities. The farmer may think that he has not received his just share of the labor of his hands, still he lives in a modern house, and drives his Ford or Buick as proudly as his town brother. The changes in town life are just as noticeable as are those in the country. Houses and streets are better. Candles and oil lamps are replaced by gas jets and electric lamps. Pianos and victrolas are a thousand times more common than spinning wheels. Schools provide ample education for everybody. The daily news is delivered free to the farmer as to the townsman. Libraries freely dispense the best books and magazines. Industrial workers have reduced the hours of labor from 16 to 8 hours per day and have increased the minimum wage. Child labor is restricted. Immigration is checked by a network of "verbotens."

A number of successful expositions, national in scope, have been held, each one adding a chapter to the story of amazing progress in the United States. The Chicago Fair in 1893 was a world's fair and one of the most impressive. In many ways the succeeding fairs have even surpassed the great Columbian. In 1895 the Atlanta Exposition, in 1898 the Omaha, in 1901 the Buffalo, in 1904 the St. Louis, in 1905 the Lewis and Clark at Portland, in 1907 the Jamestown, in 1909 the Alaska-Yukon, in 1915 the Panama-Pacific at San Francisco and San Diego, in 1920 the Plymouth, in 1921 the America's Making at New York, each has tried to tell from some point of view the most up-to-date story of progress, the like of which the pioneer fathers never dreamt. Cleng Peerson's dream has been realized, thirty, sixty, a hundred fold. Soli Deo gloria. And "God is able to do exceeding abundantly above all that we ask and think" (Eph. 3:20).

2. Norwegian Immigration, 1891-1924

The census figures for emigration from Norway and immigration to the United States never agree. The discrepancies during this period vary from 2 in 1907 to 4,005 in 1905. The

Norwegian statistics include all who leave Norway for any foreign lands—United States, Canada, Australia, etc. And yet the Norwegian statistics are often considerably smaller than the actual number of Norwegians registered at the American ports of entry. For example, in 1908 Norway lost by emigration 8,497, but we gained by immigration of Norwegians 12,412 and Canada gained approximately 2,000 that year. That is, 5,915 more people are recorded as having arrived in the United States and Canada from Norway than actually left Norway. In 1909 the United States received only 12,627 of the 16,152 who emigrated from Norway. The comparative tables are given herewith.

COMPARATIVE IMMIGRATION TABLES

Year	U. S. Immigration Statistics	Norway Emigration Statistics	Discrepancy U. S. Larger	Smaller
1891	12,568	13,341	....	773
1892	14,325	17,049	....	2,724
1893	15,515	18,778	....	3,263
1894	9,111	5,642	3,469	....
1895	7,581	6,207	1,374	....
1896	8,885	6,679	2,306	....
1897	5,842	4,669	1,173	....
1898	4,938	4,859	79	....
1899	6,705	6,699	6	....
1900	9,575	10,931	....	1,356
1891-1900	95,045	94,854	8,307	8,116
1901	12,248	12,745	....	497
1902	17,484	20,343	....	2,859
1903	24,461	26,784	....	2,323
1904	22,808	22,264	544	....
1905	25,064	21,059	4,005	....
1906	21,730	21,967	....	237
1907	22,133	22,135	....	2
1908	12,412	8,497	3,915	....
1909	12,627	16,152	....	3,525
1910	17,538	18,912	....	1,374
1901-1910	188,505	190,858	8,464	10,817
1891-1910	283,550	285,712	16,771	18,933
1891-1918	343,503	339,220	25,151	20,968

These comparative figures show, in the 27-year period, 1891-1918, a discrepancy of 4,283 in favor of the United States. That is, the United States has received 4,283 more Norwegians than emigrated from Norway. These must have, like the famous Sloop baby, Margaret Allen Larsen, been born on the passage across! In 1911 Canada made a census of the birthplace of her people. Also the same in 1921. In 1911 14,354 of the Canadian citizens were born in Norway; in 1921, 68,856. Some of these may have come into Canada by way of the States, but not all of them.

The census statistics for Norway in this period are therefore manifestly too small.

It should be noted that the immigration from Norway as well as from other countries fluctuates with the business cycle. When times are hard in America, immigration is slight; when times are good, immigration is heavy. Good times over there keeps people at home. Hard times brings them to us. Hunger breaks down stone walls. Money makes the mare go.

3. NORWEGIAN POPULATION, 1890-1925

A question often asked, but never answered satisfactorily, is: How many Norwegians are there in America? It is hard to answer for several reasons:

Madison Normal School, E. R. Rorem, President

(1) The census lists only two generations of Norwegians—those born in Norway, who came here as immigrants (1st generation) and their children born here (2nd generation). The census counts all children born af native-born parents as Americans.

(2) In the case of mixed marriages no inquiry is made beyond the 1st generation. Mixed marriages are on the increase among all the generations. Thus, in the earlier periods practically all Norwegian men were married to Norwegian women and vice versa. In 1890 0.16 per cent of the marriages—only one out of 600—among the immigrants were mixed—Norwegian husband and Swedish wife, Danish husband and Norwegian wife, etc. In 1910 the number of mixed marriages among the 1st generation had increased to 8.4 per cent; in 1920, to 11.2 per cent. In 1890, 11.1 per cent of the Norwegians born here secured a help-meet from some other nationality; in 1900, 22.9 per cent; in 1910, 28.6 per cent; and in 1920, 33.8 per cent. In the third generation the tendency to secure a spouse from some other race is still greater, and in the fourth, fifth, and sixth generations marriage

with a Norwegian is the exception, not the rule. Very few of the Slooper descendants have married Norwegians. None of the 57 descendants of Lars Larson has married a Norwegian; only one of the 36 descendants of Ole Johnson had a Norwegian mate. The blood of a dozen nationalities flows in the veins of the Rosdails; B. F. Stangland has been in the public eye of New York and Rochester for 50 years, but nobody knew that he was a Norwegian until the other day when he was mentioned in an article on the Sloopers by Mrs. Anna Danielson Parker of Kendall. His mother was an American and all the rest of the Stanglands have married outside of the Norwegian race. It is impossible to estimate correctly how many persons have a Norse strain.

The white population in 1820 was 7,866,297. If we use two as the multiplier on the number representing the 1st two generations of immigrant population, which is approximately the same as the total immigration during the century, then we shall still have a balance of over 22,000,000 whites to account for. They can be accounted for by supposing that while the immigrants have doubled their numbers, the 7,866,297 who lived in this country in 1820, have trebled their numbers. Three times 7,866,297 equals 23,598,891. This was the size of the old colonial stock in 1920. Even C. S. Burr, who is particularly biased toward the Anglo-Saxons, in his "America's Race Heritage," does not call for a much larger figure than this. He says that 25,046,962 is a fair approximation in the year 1920 for the descendants of the Old Immigration, that is, the white population of 1820.

(3) The census depends for its correctness on the completeness and accuracy of the returns. It was not popular after the War to have been born in a foreign land or to be of foreign descent other than British. Looking at the census returns, one is forced to think at least that there must have been some pretty tall lying during the taking of the census.

But people want to know how many Norwegians there are in America, and so many guesses have been ventured, ranging from 1,000,000 to 5,000,000. The two following methods are given as being fairly scientific and reasonably accurate:

In 1920 the foreign white stock in the United States numbered 36,398,958, made up of 13,712,754 foreign-born and 22,686,204 native born of foreign-born parentage. Since *Method of* 1820 the immigration to the United States *Multipliers* has been very heavy. During the 100 years from 1820-1919 the white immigrants totaled 31,200,103. The immigrants raise large families. Counting the immigrant parents who came as the 1st generation, then from three to six generations have lived in this country. Some of the Norwegian Slooper families, for example, have six generations.

The census accounts for only the first two generations. On the basis of individual studies of families, it is reasonable to suppose that the census returns for the two generations can be multiplied by two as a general average multiplier. For the newer races —Russians, Italians, Austrians—this multiplier is too high; for the older races—English, Irish,German—this is too small. For the Norwegians it is just right. They have been coming the whole century and belong rather to the Old Immigration than the New. Now, two times 1,023,225, the census statistics of Norwegians for 1920 equals 2,046,445, an estimate of Norwegians in 1920.

Another way is to estimate the number of Norwegians in the third, fourth, fifth and sixth generations of each census and add these numbers to the census returns. The estimate must be based on a fixed reasonable *Method of* standard, as, for example, five children to each *Generations* Norwegian family. Adopting this standard, one arrives at the following conclusion:

NORWEGIAN POPULATION BY GENERATIONS

First Generation (Census)

Year	Norwegians	Year	Norwegians
1830	100	1880	181,729
1840	1,000	1890	322,665
1850	12,678	1900	338,426
1860	43,995	1910	403,858
1870	114,246	1920	362,174

Second Generation (Census)

Year	Norwegians	Year	Norwegians
1830	5	1880	109,037
1840	100	1890	273,466
1850	1,902	1900	449,410
1860	10,999	1910	575,241
1870	45,698	1920	661,174

Third Generation (Estimate)

Year	Norwegians	Year	Norwegians
1850	2	1890	48,651
1860	64	1900	167,912
1870	1,261	1910	446,202
1880	9,503	1920	989,711

Fourth Generation (Estimate)

Year	Norwegians	Year	Norwegians
1870	11	1900	6,136
1880	32	1910	36,250
1890	673	1920	151,613

Fifth Generation (Estimate)

Year	Norwegians	Year	Norwegians
1890	0	1910	370
1900	17	1920	3,714

Sixth Generation (Estimate)

Year	Norwegians	Year	Norwegians
1910	0	1920	12

Total Norwegians

Year	1st Gen.	2nd Gen.	3rd Gen.	4th Gen.	5th Gen.	6th Gen.	Total
1830......	100	5	....	....	....	....	105
1840......	1,000	100	....	....	....	....	1,100
1850......	12,678	1,902	2	....	....	....	14,582
1860......	43,995	10,999	64	....	....	....	55,058
1870......	114,246	45,698	1,261	1	....	....	161,206
1880......	181,246	109,037	9,503	32	....	....	300,301
1890......	322,665	273,466	48,651	673	....	....	645,455
1900......	338,426	449,410	167,912	6,136	17	....	961,901
1910......	403,858	575,241	446,202	36,250	370	....	1,561,921
1920......	362,051	661,174	989,711	151,613	3,794	12	2,168,355

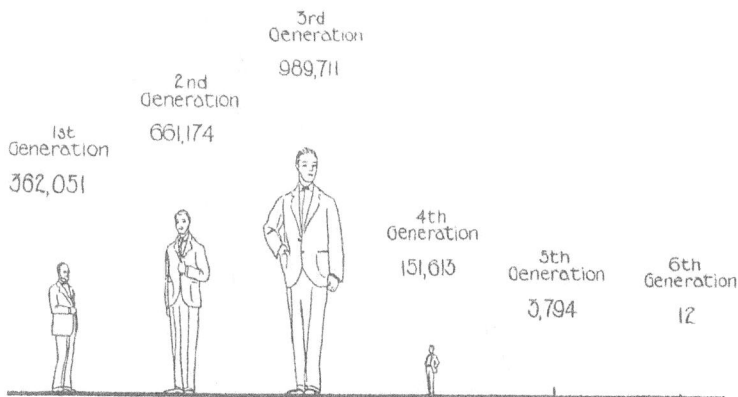

3rd Generation 989,711

2nd Generation 661,174

1st Generation 362,051

4th Generation 151,613

5th Generation 3,794

6th Generation 12

Norwegians in America, 1920, By Generations

The increase of the white population in the United States has varied from 35.8 per cent in 1790-1800 to 16.0 per cent in 1910-1920. If the normal increase of the Norwegians is 20.0 per cent for a decade or 2 per cent per year, then in the years 1920-1925 they will have increased 10 per cent, or 216,835. The total Norwegians in 1925 is then 2,385,290. This makes no allowance for intermixture of races. Allowing for those who are partly Norwegian, the total will far exceed the 2,500,000 mark.

Ragnvald Jønsberg, chief of the Statistical Central Bureau of Norway, has published a similar calculation, which the writer did not come across until he had made his own. Jønsberg allows for only five generations and keeps down his total in 1920 to 1,532,000—362,000 (1st), 597,000 (2nd), 450,000 (3rd), 120,000 (4th), 30,000 (5th). The writer has found 25 Rosdails belonging to the sixth generation. O. E. Rølvaag made a canvass of the St. Olaf students and found the third generation largest, in harmony with the above estimate.

The Distribution of the Norwegians, 1910

4. NORWEGIAN SETTLEMENTS, 1890-1925

In this third period there have been several movements of the Norwegians into the western counties of North Dakota and South Dakota and the northern counties of Wisconsin and Minnesota; into all the counties of Montana, Idaho and Washington and other parts of the Far West; clear up into remotest Alaska and far down into the Sunny South—Virginia, Tennessee, Alabama, Florida, etc.; and, last, but not least, into Canada—Manitoba, Saskatchewan, Alberta and British Columbia.

On page 315 is a map showing where the Norwegians lived in 1910, in the United States and Canada. This map indicates by shading the density of the larger settlements. The heaviest shading shows the greatest Norwegian population. In the other counties the

Norwegian Land in Central Alberta, 1904

census population of the first and second generations are given for the United States, and for Canada the census· population of Norwegians born in Norway is multiplied by four. About 50 per cent of the Norwegians living in Canada were born in the United States and are therefore not listed in the Canadian census as Norwegians, but as Americans. Foreign-born Norwegians plus their children, plus the Norwegians counted as Americans, make a number three or four times the census figures.

The map shows that the Norwegians are found in 1949 out of 2938 counties of the United States and in 164 out of 218 provincial districts of Canada—in 66.3 per cent of the American counties, 75.2 per cent of the Canadian districts. In the most northeastern corner of Quebec—Rimouski Provincial District (county) —they located four foreign-born Norwegians in 1911. In the most southeastern corner of Florida—Dade County—in 1910 10

R. Rogstad (26)　　　　N. J. Hong (25)　　　　Hans Allen (22)

Norwegians were found. Way down in San Diego County, California, to the southwest, the census reports have discovered 339 Norwegians. Far up to the northwest in the remotest regions of British Columbia lies Comox-Atlin Provincial District, with 3,644 Norwegians. There are 3,156 counties and districts (counties) in America. Norwegians of the first generation have found their way into 2,113 of them. They are rovers and pioneers as of old.

A census of the Scandinavian pioneers of Alberta was taken in 1904. The accompanying map of the land holdings by Norwegians in Central Alberta was made at that time. The pioneer days of Alberta were pioneer days, with the hardships and privations incident to such conditions. Excepting for the C. P. (Canadian Pacific Railroad) crossing Lower Alberta and sending a sideline up to Edmonton, the country had no railroads. Many of the farmers had 100 to 150 miles to town. There were few roads, and they were abominable. Central Alberta was full of woods and swamps and lakes, and it sometimes took a whole day to cross a creek with a wagon.

A man had been to Edmonton to get a load of provisions. It took two weeks to go to town. When he came within 14 miles

H. S. Houg (21)　　　　J. P. Fossum (18)　　　　Carl Tyssen (17)

Academy Principals, with Years of Service

O. O. Løkensgaard (16)   A. H. Solheim (14)   K. O. Eittreim (14)

of his home, while crossing a stream his wagon tipped over, and his flour, sugar and other supplies were gone in the twinkling of an eye. A Galician woman chanced to be there when he was crossing. She stopped. Out there one could travel a whole day and not see a human being, therefore any kind of person, Norwegian, Galician, Indian or what-not, was a precious sight to behold. This woman understood the cost and sacrifice represented by the overturned load, so she stripped off some clothes and dived into the icy waters and fetched up sack after sack and package upon package. The Norwegian said "Thank you" and "Mange tak," in as many languages and gestures as he could invent, and bade goodbye with the feeling that "these foreigners" are not all bad anyhow.

Out there in the wilderness was a little store surrounded by marsh and fen. The storekeeper related that in the early spring his place is situated in the midst of a lake. "Do you then have any trade in the spring?" "Certainly. Why, the first day that I discovered that I had located in a lake, two women came to my store in the afternoon. I asked them if they had a boat. They said no. I asked how they had come across. They said they had

C. B. Helgen (14)   A. O. B. Molldrem (13) H. E. Jorgensen (12)

Academy Principals, with Years of Service

H. A. Ustrud, S. Dak.   J. G. Halland, N. Dak.   C. G. Lawrence, S. Dak.
State Superintendents of Schools

waded. I asked how they escaped getting wet. They said: 'We carried our clothes and shoes over our heads.'"

Such was pioneer life in 1904. And these pioneers lived in log cabins and sod cellars as their fathers had done in South Dakota and their grandfathers in Wisconsin. Their farm tools were not quite as primitive. Still, some of the settlers were obliged to use primitive tools. Hakon C. Norlie made his own wagon and plow. He made even the hinges and knobs on the door of his house, and everything that he made was very well done.

The horses and cattle imported from the States died of swamp fever, and much sickness raged among the settlers too. A little girl broke her arm in several places. It happened in early March when the country resembled a vast lake. It happened on a cold, rainy day. Her father picked her up and carried her in the dead of night on a pony's back to the home of a country doctor 15 miles away. He was happy when he found the doctor at home. The pioneer doctor, like the pioneer pastor and store keeper, has gladdened many a soul.

The Norwegian people in Alberta felt keenly the loss of their wonted church services. They began to organize Sunday Schools,

J. A. Widtsoe, Ph.D., LL.D. Aven Nelson, Ph.D.   Edward Olsen, Ph.D.
Pres., U. of Utah   Pres., U. of Wyo.   Pres., U. of S. Dak.

Gertrude M. Hilleboe,
A. M.
Dean, St. Olaf College

Elsa Ueland
Pres., Carson College

Beatrice Olson, A. M.
Dean U. of N. Dak.

ladies' aids and congregations. They made use of their best lay preachers to expound the Word unto them and sent for regularly ordained pastors to come over and help them. As soon as they could—scarcely ten years after they had begun to settle in Alberta —, they founded a college in their midst—Camrose College— at Camrose, now a thriving town of 1,892 people. In 1904 there was no town there at all.

Many of the Norwegian names end in "son"—"Anderson," "Johnson," etc. These are good names, but the Alberta land officials found trouble in keeping track of the many "sons." So they recommended that the names in "son" be changed—not to Smith and Jones, but to Norwegian place names—Groven, Ekland, Ostrom, Kjøsness, Bjerke, Levang, etc. Near Camrose lived a Norwegian. Before going over to this man's farm, the census enumerator asked about him, his name, and the like. "Well, his name had been Sørenson," said the informant, "but he has followed the custom here of changing it." "And what is his name now?" "His name now? It is Olson," was the reply.

J. O. Evjen, Ph. D.
Pres., Mayville Normal

V. O. Skyberg, A. M.
Gallaudet College

C. C. Swain, Ph. D.
Pres., Mayville Normal

Manitoba is the most easterly of the prairie provinces of
Canada and the first to be rated as a province. It is in area four
times as large as Iowa, having 231,926 square
Manitoba   miles of land and 19,906 square miles of water
surface. It is twice the size of the British
Isles. It became a province in 1870. It is typically an agricultural
country, especially on the southern plains. Lake Winnipeg is
situated in the heart of the province and abounds in fish. East
and north of this lake the country is rough and covered with
woods. Copper mining and lumbering are as yet infant industries
which are bound to grow to lusty manhood. Winnipeg, the capital,
had a population of 241, in 1871; 7,985, in 1881; 25,639 in 1891;
42,340, in 1901; 136,035, in 1911; and 179,087, in 1921. It is
the third largest city in the Dominion, being surpassed only by
Montreal and Toronto.

The provincial government of Manitoba resembles that of
Saskatchewan and Alberta. There is a lieutenant governor, appointed by the government at Ottawa. He holds office five years.
He is assisted by a cabinet, consisting of a minister of public
works, an attorney general, a minister of agriculture, a provincial
treasurer and a provincial secretary. In local matters there is
much self-government, as in the United States, but the laws are
more strictly obeyed and enforced. Laws in Canada seem to be
meant to be observed.

The Norwegians are said to have made their first settlement
in Manitoba in 1887, at Brown, near the Dakota line. B. O. Holo,
of Sogn, came to Brown from Pembina County, North Dakota.
Holo was a veteran of the Civil War and well acquainted with
pioneer hardships. Jacob Spangelo, Nils O. Vigen, Ole B. Nelson,
Knud Halvorsen, Gisle K. Gundersen, Halvor Halvorsen, Thore
Halvorsen, and Lars H. Lien are other first settlers mentioned
by Martin Ulvestad in his great work "Nordmændene i Amerika"
(The Norwegians in America). These first settlers established a
post office called Nummedal, in honor of the district in Norway
from which most of them hailed.

The Norwegian foreign-born population of the provincial
districts of Manitoba for 1911 and 1921 was as follows:

District	1911	1921	Dirtrict	1911	1921
Brandon	33	114	Winnipeg Centre	405	489
Dauphin	144	159	Winnipeg North	...	183
Lisgar	49	221	Winnipeg South	...	246
MacDonald	273	132	Neepawa	...	84
Marquette	150	517	Nelson	...	165
Portage la Prairie	19	197	Springfield	...	239
Provencher	118	452			
Selkirk	203	905		1434	4203
Souris	40	100			

Camrose College

J. J. Akre
Pres. Norw. Luth.
Church, Canada

Martha Østensø
Winnipeg
Winner of $13,500.00
Literary Prize

Henrik Voldal
Founder of Det Norske
Selskab and For
Fædrearven

Outlook College

Manitoba has been the favorite province of the Icelanders. Vilhjalmur Stefansson, the artic explorer, recently voted the most distinguished alumnus of the University of North Dakota, was born in the Icelandic settlement of Arnes in Manitoba. Martha Østensø, the Norwegian girl who in 1924 won the $13,500.00 "Pictorial Review" Prize for the best novel (the Curtis Brown Prize), was born in Bergen, Norway, but had her training at the University of Manitoba. There were 1,500 contestants for the prize, but she won out. Her plot is taken from a little Icelandic settlement in Manitoba. Her story, "Wild Geese," will be filmed.

Icelandic immigration to America began in 1870. The first company settled in Milwaukee, Wisconsin. Rev. Jon Bjarnason, D.D., an Icelander, educated in Iceland, came to the United States in 1873, was engaged as a professor at Luther College 1874-1875, was editor of "Budstikken," Minneapolis, 1875-1877, and then he moved to Ny Island, a little settlement of Icelanders on the shores of Lake Winnipeg. Rev. Paul Thorlaksson of the Norwegian Synod organized the Vidalius, Flotsbygd, Gudbrands, Hallgrims and Winnipeg congregations in 1876. T. K. Thorvilson, J. P. Øien, T. Castberg, A. H. Bergford, Otto Lock, S. G. Nelson, A. O. B. Molldrem, L. M. Skunes, R. Bogstad, J. K. Lerohl, O. H. Haugen, G. A. Søvde, Olof Olson, A. O. Breivik, S. O. Vangstad, H. H. Hagen, J. J. Akre, are some of the Norwegian Lutheran pastors who have brought the Good News to the Norwegians of Manitoba. 29 Norwegian congregations have been established. Rev. R. O. Sigmond is a Norwegian pastor, formerly of Staten Island, N. Y., now on the faculty of Jon Bjarnason Academy, Winnipeg.

Saskatchewan is a province situated right west of Manitoba, and of nearly the same size—242,808 square miles of land and 8,892 of water. It became a province in 1905.

Saskatchewan   The country consists for the most part of open rolling prairie at an average altitude of 1,500 feet above sea level, while in the north it assumes a more broken aspect, and is abundantly watered by lakes and rivers and rich in coal and timber resources. The south is almost treeless. Saskatchewan is the greatest wheat producing state in America. In 1921 it had over 12,000,000 acres sown to wheat, one-sixth as great an acreage as the total wheat fields of the United States, and its wheat yield is 18% of the total of that of the United States, and of better quality, No. 1 hard. Norwegian farmers are scattered all over the Saskatchewan plains and take the lead in wheat raising.

The total number of Norwegians in Saskatchewan in 1911 was 7,625 born in Norway; in 1921 it was 31,438. It would have been larger but for the World War, in which Canada made such heroic sacrifices. Saskatchewan is the most Norwegian of the Canadian provinces. If we count all the Norwegians from the States as well as from Norway, and of all generations, then Saskatchewan in 1921 must have had from 100,000 to 125,000 of them. The first Norwegian settlement, according to Ulvestad, was Glen Mary, about 40 miles from Prince Albert. It was made by Christian and Ole Bøe, from Solør, Norway. Carl C. Larsen, from Hønefos, Tollef Knøntvedt, from Numnedal, and Carl Hovdeby, from Kongsberg, Norway, joined this first colony; also others. In 1903 Rev. H. C. Holm, of the United Norwegian Lutheran Church, then mission superintendent, organized at Norden a congregation, and S. H. Njaa became the first pastor, 1903-1908, followed by H. O. Grønlid, 1908-1914, and T. Thompson, 1914. Christian

N. A. Grevstad
Ex-Minister to Uruguay
and Paraguay

L. S. Reque
Consul General to
Rotterdam

Roald Amundsen
Discoverer of Northwest
Passage and South Pole

Bøe, Ole Orvedal, Carl Larsen, Jørgen Svenkesen, M. Jacobsen, Iver Nelson, Carl Thompson, M. Breimon, J. Petersen, Iver Nesheim, Hans Thompson, O. Hamre were among the first officers of the congregation. In 1903 they paid a salary of $30.00 per year, in 1914 they had raised it to $75.00. Their first church cost $1,200.00. The oldest congregation in the province is the Saskatchewan First Norwegian Lutheran Congregation, situated 10 miles southwest of Langham, Eagle Creek, P. D., organized in September, 1903. H. Jensson was the first pastor, followed by O. J. Hungness, K. O. Eliassen, O. J. J. Tollerud, and others.

The pastor at Shell Brook and Prince Albert, 1910-1913, and at Mistawasis, 1913——, is Sigfried Wessel, born and bred in the glamor of Oslo, capital city of Norway, an officer in the Norwegian Army, an excellent pianist and a composer of piano music, yet freely and faithfully sharing the trials of the prairie pioneers. It is said of his young bride that when she stepped across the threshold of his shanty she could not hold back her tears. The change was so great—from the cultured homes of Oslo to a miserable shack in the wilderness of Saskatchewan.

Norwegian Lutheran Congregations in Alberta, 1915

The Norwegian Lutherans in the period 1903-1916 established 224 congregations and 98 preaching stations in Saskatchewan, the work of the home missions. Many faithful men of the type of Wessel, Njaa and the other pastors alluded to above, have alongside of their farmer friends up there been "sowing in the morning, sowing seeds of kindness, sowing in the noontide, and the dewy eve." The Norwegian Lutherans erected Outlook College in 1916. Hjalmar O. Grønlid, A.B., C.T., was the first president. He joined the colors during the War, serving as chaplain with the rank of captain. He is now located at Trinity Church, Brooklyn, N. Y. as Rev. Sven O. Sigmond's first assistant.

Alberta is a trifle larger than its sister to the east, Saskatchewan. It has 252,925 square miles of land and 2,360 of water. It is larger than Germany and Bulgaria together.
Alberta Formerly almost exclusively a ranching country, it has now become a great grain, lumber and coal producing region. It yields enormous crops of wheat, oats, barley, rye, flax and potatoes. The southern part is an open prairie, suitable for winter and summer grazing and all sorts of grain farming. The middle and northern portions are covered with a belt of forests, with open patches here and there. The south is dry, has little rain and few streams. The middle and northern sections have more rain and many streams and lakes. The climate loses some of its severity by the presence of the warm Chinook winds from the west. The Rockies on the western border rise to a height of over 15,000 feet. Coal beds crop out of the hills; coal mines can be unearthed by digging a cellar. Alberta is said to possess a trillion tons of coal, 87 per cent of the coal fields of Canada. It has also gold and gas in great store. Here, too, the Norseman has built himself a kingdom.

Calgary was the first district in Alberta to receive Norwegian settlers. Bernt Thorp, Conrad Anderson and a dozen other men from Oslo, Fredrikstad and Farsund, Norway, came to Calgary in 1880 and made their home among the Indians and Canadian halfbreeds. New Norway was organized in 1893 in central Alberta by Even O. Olstad of Hedemarken, Gulik Iverson of Nummedal, and Peder O. Haukedal of Ringerike, Norway. New Norway was soon reinforced by settlers from the States, especially South Dakota, and it became a prosperous community. It is very beautifully located. Seminarist Peder O. Olufson, schoolmaster from Bangor, South Dakota, was the first parochial teacher at New Norway, and, if he is not dead, he no doubt still plies his beloved profession. H. C. Wik (1901-1902), C. M. Nødtvedt (1903-1907) were the first pastors in New Norway.

Not far from New Norway Jacob M. Støle settled down, coming up from North Dakota. One of his sons is Dr. Michael J. Stolee, formerly missionary at Ft. Dauphin, Madagascar, and now professor of missions at Luther Theological Seminary. Another son of Jacob Støle is Rev. Haakon J. Stolee, superintendent of Coeur d'Alene Old People's Home, Idaho. Rev. Hans Mosby, of Torquay, Saskatchewan, is also from this vicinity.

A few miles to the north of New Norway lies Bardo, or Northern, on beautiful Beaver Lake. This place was founded in 1894 by men from Bardo, Nordland, Norway. The first settlers included P. B. Anderson, son of the pioneer Hauge missionary, Rev. Bersvend Anderson, who was the first Hauge pastor in the Red River Valley (1878-1894), and the first Lutheran pastor in

Alberta (1894-1918), a man whose whole life as a sailor, farmer and pastor was spent in doing good to others. He came to Bardo in 1894 and organized the Bardo Congregation in 1895. In 1897 the congregation had 67 members. A son of the congregation is the Rev. Albert Anderson, Fancheng, Honan, China. In 1916 Alberta had 159 Norwegian Lutheran congregations and 20 preaching places extra. It had a college at Camrose and an old people's home at Bawlf. Rev. N. R. T. Braa is the superintendent of the home. Rev. A. H. Solheim is president of the college. A bi-lingual church paper, *Hyrden* (The Shepherd), is edited by Rev. Knute O. Løkensgaard, of Edberg, Alberta.

Norwegian Lutheran Deaconess Home, Chicago, Ill.

British Columbia lies in the far west on the coast and bordering Alaska. It is, next to the province of Quebec in the far east, the largest of the Canadian provinces. It has **British Columbia** 353,416 square miles of land area and 2,410 square miles of lakes. It is as large as the United Kingdom, Norway and Italy together. The many islands along the Pacific coast, notably Vancouver Island with an area of 13,500 square miles, belong to the province and are remarkable for their temperate climate and abundant natural resources. In some respects British Columbia is the most favored part of Canada. Within its boundaries are reproduced almost all the varied climates of the Dominion and almost every natural feature and resource. The mineral and lumber wealth of British Columbia is simply fabulous; the fishing and agriculture possibilities are stupendous. The mountain scenery is the wildest and vastest in North America. Mt. Fairweather is 15,287 feet. British Columbia became a province in 1866.

Says the chronicler Martin Ulvestad: "The first Norwegian to become a permanent resident of British Columbia, as far as we know, is the Hon. Hans Helgeson, who has lived in the neighborhood of Victoria since 1860. He is a well known and influential man, a fact that is proved also by the circumstance that he has

Norwegian Lutheran Deaconess Home, Minneapolis, Minn.

been a member of the British Columbia Legislature." The first Norwegian settlement, near Matsqui and Aldersgrove, New Minster, was organized in 1884, by John L. Broe, from Fayette County, Iowa. He was soon joined by John L. Wilson, a Stavanger man, and others.

The Census for 1911 reported 3,732 Norwegians born in Norway located within British Columbia; in 1921 there were 6,570—4,084 men, 2,486 women, pretty evenly divided throughout the 13 provincial districts of the province. The actual Norwegian population is three or four times as large as the number born in Norway. In 1916 there were 20 Norwegian Lutheran congregations in the province, all located in Vancouver and Westminster districts near the Washington boundary. There the Norwegians have lived longest and closest together.

The chief settlements are in Vancouver and New Westminster provinces, where some 15 congregations had been organized between 1890 and 1916. The Norwegian Synod had 7 congregations; the United Church had also 7; the Lutheran Free Church had 2. There was a Free Church congregation at Hagensborg, Comox Atlin, a United Church congregation at Waldo, Kotenay, and a Hauge Synod congregation at Pauce Coupe in the Peace River country of Yale-Cariboo. Rev. H. N. Rønning, brother of Editor N. N. Rønning, of Minneapolis, and formerly a missionary in Central China, was the pastor at Peace River from 1908 to 1917. Among the pastors who have worked in British Columbia are: G. M. Aasheim, A. O. Bjerke, O. Borge, K. O. Eliassen, E. A. Ericksen, O. J. Eriksen, C. Forthun, L. C. Foss, E. A. Hage, O. Hagoes, G. N. Isolany, E. O. Lane, C. J. Olsen, O. J. Ordal, A. C. Quale, P. O. Qualen, H. O. Sageng, B. O. Sand, C. T. Saugstad, W. N. Sjovangen, M. Skonhovd, M. C. Stensen, H. O. Thormodsgaard, S. R. Tollefsen.

A word should be said about the extension of the Norwegian settlements to Alaska, farthest northwest. The Norwegians are scattered over Alaska from Petersburg to *Alaska* Nome. The city of Petersburg was named after a Norwegian, Peter Thams Buschmann, who in 1891 with wife and nine children left Norway and settled in Tacoma, Washington. He put in the first salmon trap at Lummi Island, Puget Sound, in 1892, a location that soon sold for $90,000.00. In 1894 he moved to Alaska, as he figured that Alaska was the future fishing country. And his judgment was correct. Alaska's fisheries in 1923 yielded over one-half as much as the 48 states of the Union together—$38,678,825.00 for Alaska and $76,326,000.00 for the United States excluding Alaska. Buschmann started a cannery, and later on more canneries. On his homestead a town grew up, named Petersburg in his honor. It is a Norwegian town. Nome, too, is quite a Norwegian town. One of its leading citizens is Judge G. J. Lomen, a Decorah boy, formerly an attorney in Minneapolis, since 1900 a resident of Alaska. He is one of the great promoters of the reindeer industry, which supplies the American markets with venison. He controls a herd of 30,000 animals. The Alaskan reindeer were imported from Norway through the kindly offices of Hon. R. B. Anderson, United States minister to Denmark, 1884-1888.

The Dane, Vitus Bering, explored Alaska for Russia in 1741. Siberian fur-hunters exploited the land for nearly a century, killing off the Eskimo natives as well as the polar bears. Russian missionaries began to work among the natives in 1818. In 1867 the

United States purchased the land for $7,200,000.00, or less than one-half cent per acre. The area is 531,000 square miles. It is over twice the size of Texas, nearly ten times the area of Iowa. In 1920 the population was 55,036—27,883 whites, 26,558 Indians (Eskimos) and 595 of other races. There are 11,597 foreign-born whites in Alaska. 2,169 of these were born in Norway, 1,687 in Sweden, and 371 in Denmark, that is, 37.6 per cent of the foreign-born whites were born in Scandinavia. Many of the Scandinavians in Alaska were born in Canada and the United States, so that over 50 per cent of the whites are Scandinavians. About 25 per cent of the whites in Alaska are of Norwegian blood.

The United States Government asked the Norwegian Synod in 1893 for a competent teacher at the Government School at Port Clarence, Alaska. Rev. T. L. Brevig was sent. He occupied this post four years and preached the Gospel to his countrymen, besides the Lapps and Eskimos on the side. He returned to the States and prevailed on the Synod to start a mission among the Eskimos at Teller and neighboring points—Agiopak, Mary's Igloo, Council, Nook, Cape Wolly, Grantly Harbor. An orphanage was built at Teller—the Mrs. T. L. Brevig Eskimo Orphanage, which now harbors 35 Eskimo orphans. Schools were set in operation, running eight months a year. The sick were cared for. In 1908 D. R. Tørnoe relieved him; in 1910 H. M. Tjernagel took Tørnoe's place. In 1913 Brevig returned to the task. In 1917 Olaf Fosso was sent to Teller and C. K. Malmin to Igloo. Fosso returned to Minnesota in 1920 and Malmin in 1921. Elmer H. Dahle went into the breaches from 1921 to 1924. There have been a number of women assistants, as: Sisters Agnes Nostdahl (Mrs. John Reed) and Sister Anna Huseth, Miss J. Enestvedt and Mrs. T. L. Brevig. Leonard Soologuak, an Eskimo, attended Red Wing Seminary two years to prepare himself for work among his people.

Finally, a word should be said about the extension of the Norwegian settlements to Florida, farthest southeast. Florida was the

Florida

first region of North America to be colonized by Europeans and is one of the last to be colonized by Norwegians. Like Maine in the northeast, Florida has a post office called Norway (Gadsden County), but no Norwegian lives there. Ponce de Leon landed in Florida in 1513 in search of the water of life. In 1565 Menendez massacred the French colony at Ft. Caroline, leaving the grim inscription on their hanging bodies: "Not as to Frenchmen, but as to Lutherans." In 1568 De Gourgues's expedition captured the Spanish fort on the St. John's and hanged the garrison: "Not as to Spaniards, but as to traitors, thieves and murderers." In 1819 Florida was obtained by the United States. It

Senator M. N. Johnson
Senator Reed Smoot   Senator Asle J. Grønna

became a territory in 1821; a state, in 1845. It is a land of lumbering and fishing, cotton and corn, tobacco, rice, sugar cane, oranges, bananas, lemons and limes, grapes and grape fruit. Palm Beach is the Nation's most exclusive winter resort.

There have been foreign-born Norwegians in Florida at every census—17 in 1850; 11 in 1860; 16 in 1870; 79 in 1880; 179 in 1890; 235 in 1900; 304 in 1910; 610 in 1920. The favorite haunts of Norwegians in Florida are: Pensacola, with 129 foreign-born in 1920; Jacksonville, with 48; Miami, with 38; Tampa, with 31; Palm Beach had 31 and Dade County had 59. In St. Lucie County Norwegian congregations were organized at Oslo and Viking in 1914. H. O. Helseth and A. L. Stowell of the Lutheran Free Church have been the pastors. The Norway Seamen's Mission keeps a pastor at Pensacola.

Floridans have made several attempts to induce Norwegians to settle down there. A typical example is that of the Kissimmee project of 1893-1895. The Henry Disston Saw Company, Philadelphia, owned large tracts of land in Central Florida, which they wanted disposed of to the mutual advantage of good settlers

Senator H. O. Bursum   Senator H. Shipstead   Nils P. Haugen
                                                      Congressman

Kittel Halvorson   Haldor E. Boen   Herman B. Dahle

and themselves. They erected sugar mills and other conveniences for the settlers. They sent Norwegian agents out to paint the glories of the Florida climate and resources to the Norwegian farmers of South Dakota suffering, as they were, from winter blizzards and summer droughts. In the year 1893 there was a great exodus of farmers from Dakota to Kissimmee and Narcoossee, Osceola County. Among these settlers were John and Perry Juel, brothers; Ole H. and Hakon C. Norlie, father and son; M. J. Aus and Shulson, brothers-in-law; Rev. Ole E. Hofstad and many others. They settled to the south of Lake Tohopekaliga at Narcoossee. They built themselves bungalows and planted orange groves. They enjoyed the climate and urged all their friends to leave the North and come to beautiful Florida. each man to live under his own fig tree and date palm. Here grew the best oranges in the world, 50 varieties. Everything was lovely—until the frost came and killed their orange crop. They had no immediate prospects as farmers. Wages was only 50 cents per day. Times were hard. They were in the midst of the Cleveland Panic. They asked their friends in Dakota to send them

(Copyright)   (Copyright, Harris & Ewing)   (Copyright, Harris & Ewing)
Gilbert N. Haugen   Halvor Steenerson   A. J. Volstead

Congressmen of Norwegian Descent

John M. Nelson   Sydney Anderson   Henry T. Helgesen

money to keep them alive and to enable them to come back. So they all came back, after a two years' sojourn in the land of "cotton and cohn." Sometimes now they long for the magnolia blossoms and the live oaks, the razor back hogs and the drowsy alligators, the friendly southern neighbors and the happy darkies, and they sing:

> I wish I was in de land ob cotton,
> Old times dar am not forgotten.

Or, still better:

> Way down upon de Suwanee Ribber,
> Far, far away.

Visiting Narcoossee in 1921, the writer asked a storekeeper what he thought of the South Dakota settlers. "Those foreigners were fine," he replied. "Why call them foreigners?" "They spoke a foreign language." "Why call them fine?" "They paid their debts." "Why do you suppose they did that?" "They were brought up that way." Floridans still welcome Norwegians to settle in their midst. The Norwegians are considered first class settlers.

(*Copyright, Harris & Ewing*)   (*Copyright, Clinedinst*)

Chester B. Van Dyke   Harold Knutson   C. A. Christopherson

Congressmen of Norwegian Descent

(Copyright, Hoff)   *(Copyright, Harris & Ewing)*

Alger B. Burtness   M. A. Michaelson   William Williamson

5. Steamship Lines

Robert Fulton was ahead of his time when he made his experiment on the Hudson with his steamboat, the Clermont. The usefulness of the invention was not appreciated. Still, he slowly convinced the skeptical world that it was possible to apply steam power to transportation by water. One of the first shipping men to realize the practical advantages of steamboats over sailing ships was Samuel Cunard, a Halifax ship owner. In 1838 Cunard sailed for England to raise the necessary capital for starting a steamship company. In 1840 he launched the Britannia, which was 207 feet long and registered 1,154 tons. The first trip of his boat was begun on July 4, 1840. The event assumed international importance. When the boat anchored at Boston, Cunard was the embarrassed recipient of no fewer than 1873 dinner invitations during his first twenty-four hours' sojourn in that place. He had a good deal of powerful opposition, especially from the competing Collins Line. Still he went on with his program, and the Cunard Line has grown to become one of the greatest in the world. The largest Cunarder in commission in 1880 was the

(Copyright, Edmonston)   Knud Wefald   August H. Andresen
O. J. Kvale

Congressmen of Norwegian Descent

Gallia, of 4,880 tons, four times the tonnage of the Britannia.
The Saxonia in 1900 displaced 14,027 tons, 12 times as much as
Britannia. The Berengaria in 1920 had a tonnage of 52,000, forty-
five times the size of the Britannia. Among the well known vessels
of this line are the Aquitania, 901 feet long, 97 feet wide, and 60,-
000 horsepower; the Mauretania, 790 feet long, 88 feet wide, and
67,000 horsepower. The Cunard Line has swallowed up minor
lines such as the Anchor and the Donaldson, both of which, as
well as the Cunard itself, have been instrumental in transporting

Stavangerfjord of the Norwegian-America Line

thousands of Norwegians to America. Commodore Vanderbilt,
one of the mighty organizers of the Cunard Line, was of remote
Norwegian ancestry.

A Norwegian Steamship Company was organized a little over
a decade ago. It bears the name Norwegian-America Line. Besides a whole fleet of freight boats, it has had two boats—Ber-
gensfjord and Stavangerfjord, looking after the passenger traffic.
They are of large tonnage and modern in every respect. In the
twelve years, from 1913 to 1924 inclusive, The Norwegian-America Line carried 120,586 passengers westward and 82,077 easward,
a total of 202,663. Magnus Swenson is the president of the Norwegian-America Line Agency, Inc., with residence in Madison and
offices in New York. "His life," says "The Wisconsin Engi-

neer," for April, 1918, "should serve as an inspiration to all present and future engineers. If the details of his varied experiences could be written, they would read more like a romance than a chapter from real life." He was born April 12, 1854, at Langesund, Norway. In 1868 he left his native land in a sailing vessel bound for America. The voyage was long and tempestuous. It lasted twelve weeks, during which time 22 of the 60 passengers died of starvation and exhaustion. The ship finally landed at the island of Anticosti at the mouth of the St. Lawrence River. The ship was towed to Quebec. There was not a friend to meet him. A thunder storm was raging such as Magnus had never seen or heard in Norway. He was a stranger in a strange land, but he made his way to Wisconsin, secured employment in a blacksmith shop belonging to the Chicago and Northwestern Railway at Janesville, Wisconsin. He made up his mind to go to school and become an engineer. He sent for a catalog of the University of Wisconsin, and came to Madison to attend Commencement, but to his surprise, he learned that Commencement was the end of the school year, not the beginning of it. Four years later, he took his Bachelor's degree. In 1883 the university gave him the M. S. degree; in 1899, an honorary M. E., and in 1921, an honorary LL.D.

He was instructor in chemistry at his alma mater, 1880-1883. The United States Department of Agriculture offered a prize of $2,500.00 for the best paper on making sugar. This prize Magnus Swenson won, and with it came an offer of the management of a sugar factory in Texas. He made many improvements in sugar machinery and processes. In 1886-1905 he was a chemical engineer and manufacturer at Fort Scott, Kansas, and Chicago. In 1906-1915 he constructed hydro-electric plants of the Southern Wisconsin Power Company at Kilbourn and the Wisconsin River Power Co., at Prairie du Sac, being president and general manager of both companies. These plants, next to Keokuk are the largest in the West. Since 1905 he has been first vice president of the Central Wisconsin Trust Company and since 1919 vice pres. of the First Nat. Bank, Madison. Since 1920 he has been chief executive director of the Norw.-Am. Line Agency. He has held many civic offices of trust, such as: President of the Board of Regents of the University of Wisconsin; chairman of the Wisconsin Capital Commission; chairman, State Council of Defence; Federal Food Administrator for Wisconsin, and chief of Mission for Northern Europe, American Relief Administration. He has received the John Scott medal in recognition of his services. The King of Norway has created him a Knight of St. Olav. The president of Finland has decorated him with the White Rose and Star of Finland. America has bestowed on him the United States Liberty Service medal. The "Wisconsin

Engineer" says: "Mr. Swenson possesses those qualities that go to make up a sturdy and loyal citizenship. He loves America and never tires of speaking of her as the land of opportunity for those who have vision, and are not afraid of hard work." The "People's Favorite Magazine" for February, 1921, has an article about him by Walter A. O'Meara, which calls attention to his motto: "Save the Waste." His whole life has been spent saving for others, whether the waste be in dollars, power, or lives. "He was the pioneer in what has become almost a national passion—efficiency. Out of the industrial scrap heap he has extracted a fortune."

The "North Star" for October, 1919, quotes from a Copenhagen paper concerning Swenson. Here are a few lines taken

| Ole Nilsen | G. T. Lee | John Peterson |

Editors of Lutheran Periodicals

almost at random: "A pessimistic Swedish observer once said that Scandinavians who emigrated to America became the slaves of the Anglo-Saxons. Magnus Swenson is decidedly of another opinion; he holds that the descendants of these immigrants will be among America's leaders. . . . . Magnus Swenson represents the plain, democratic America. . . . . We are pleased to have had him with us. His great nation wishes to win the confidence and good will of all nations; by being represented by such men as Magnus Swenson it will succeed in this effort."

6. RAILROADS

No history of America could proceed far without some mention of "the iron rails." The development of the Mississippi Valley and the Far West of Lower Canada and the Prairie Provinces, could be followed step by step if there were such a thing as the diary of the railroads intersecting these parts.

Some of the railroads that have been of great service to the Norwegians in their work of building the West should receive a passing recognition here. Between New York and Chicago the Baltimore and Ohio, Erie, Pennsylvania, Wabash, and, last but not least, the New York Central, are most conspicuous. Between Chicago and the Northwest the following have sometimes gone ahead of, or usually followed upon, the heels of the Norwegian settlers: Chicago, Milwaukee and St. Paul, Chicago and Northwestern, Chicago, Burlington and Quincy, Chicago Great Western, Chicago, Rock Island and Pacific Chicago, St. Paul, Minneapolis and Omaha, Illinois Central, Minneapolis and St. Louis, Great Northern, Northern Pacific, and the Minneapolis, St. Paul and Sault Ste. Marie. In the Southwest the Union Pacific, Southern Pacific and the Atchison, Topeka and Santa Fe have received most patronage. In Canada the great roads are the Canadian Pacific and the Canadian National Railways, the latter including the Grand Trunk and Canadian Northern systems.

H. M. Sæterlie   Dr. J. R. Birkelund   C. S. B. Hoel
Sec'y Foreign Missions Sec'y Foreign Missions   Sec'y Home Missions

The first of the railroads heading for the West was the Baltimore and Ohio, organized in 1827 to offset the activity in Pennsylvania and New York in finding a speedy and cheap route to the West. In 1828 the work of construction began; in 1830 the road was opened a distance of 15 miles. The cars were drawn by horses. In 1831 four 3 1-2-ton engines were ordered. In 1854 the line was extended as far as Chicago. The eastern road most used by Norwegians was the New York Central. It was begun in 1828 as the Hudson and Mohawk Railroad. On August 9, 1831, it ran its first train, drawn by the famous locomotive "DeWitt Clinton," and this event marks the beginning of steam railroading in America. This historic locomotive and train now stand at the outer edge of the east gallery of the Grand Central Terminal in New York City, where it can be plainly seen from any point in the concourse. The Hudson and Mohawk was but a tiny, short road. A number of other little roads were constructed. In 1843, it took a dozen of these together to make a line from Albany to Buffalo. The fast express that year made this run in 30 hours. Now it takes about 5 hours and 55 minutes. In 1854 a number of other little roads had been built, connecting up with Chicago. The New York Central as it is now organized, includes what was originally 315 separate companies. It has 6,899 miles of main line. It reaches directly 162 cities having over 10,000 people, and serves 50.3 per cent of the population of the United States. It carries 70 per cent of the passenger traffic between New York and Chicago. It used 79,600 tons of steel rails in one year (1923) just for repairs in the lines east of Buffalo alone, and 1,646,100 new ties to replace those worn out in the same region. The leading spirit in the creation of this great railway system, the greatest in the world, was Commodore Cornelius Vanderbilt, who is generally considered the first outstanding genius in the railroad world. Vanderbilt was a descend-

The DeWitt Clinton: New York Central's
First Locomotive, 1831

ant of the Dutchman Jan Arentzen Van der Bilt, who settled in New Amsterdam and married the Norwegian maid Anneken Hendricks, from Bergen, Feb. 6, 1650. This girl at that time owned a farm on which New York's mightiest sky scrapers now stand. Wall Street is in the heart of it.

The Wabash Railroad was the first railroad in Illinois, having laid its first rail in 1838. Now it has 2,473 miles of track stretching from Omaha and Kansas City to Buffalo. 87 years of service.

The present Illinois Central Railroad comprises more than 130 separate railroads that have been joined by purchase or lease to the original Illinois Central, which was chartered in 1851 and built in 1852-1856. It was then only 705.5 miles long; now, in 1925, it has 6,220 miles extending from Chicago to New Orleans on the south, and from Chicago to Omaha, Sioux City and Sioux Falls on the west and Minneapolis on the north. In the two decades 1850 to 1870 the number of acres under cultivation in Illinois increased from 5,000,000 to 19,000,000. In 1867 the Illinois Central began its expansion westward into Iowa. It pierced the heart of the great agricultural country of north central Iowa, and the part it played in shaping the early agriculture, industry, commerce and trade in Illinois it also had in Iowa between 1867 and 1880. It has done its share in solidifying the economic interests of the North and the South, the East and the West. The Illinois Central ranks 14th in mileage and 4th in amount of freight traffic handled annually.

The Rock Island is also a combination of many former roads. It was first known as the Mississippi and Missouri Railroad Co., and secured its right of way in 1852-1853. A charter

Twentieth Century Limited: "The Greatest
Train in the World"
(*From "Shipper and Carrier," Sept.,* 1921)

was granted permitting a bridge to be built across the Mississippi at Rock Island, and the bridge was built, a wooden structure 1,582 feet long, glistening white by day and standing by night like a monster spider, resting on five stone piers. It was dedicated Sept. 1, 1854, by James Grant, speaker of the House of Representatives of Iowa. Fourteen days after the crossing of the first train, the bridge was hit by a boat, and boat and bridge were burned. The Bridge Co. was sued and an attempt was made to prohibit the reconstruction of the bridge on the ground that it was an obstruction. Abraham Lincoln appeared as the attorney for the railroad and won the case. In 1866 the road was incorporated as the Chicago, Rock Island and Pacific Railroad Co. In 1852 it had 40 miles of road in one state; in 1862 it had 444 miles in 3 states; in 1872 it had 1,298 miles in 4 states; in 1882 it had 2,216 miles in 4 states; in 1892 it had 5,229 miles in 10 states; in 1902 it had 6,351 miles in 12 states; in 1912 it had 7,309 miles in 13 states; and in 1922 it had 7,961 miles in 13 states.

It runs eight main tracks from Chicago to the Mississippi, carrying mighty locomotives—power units of 300, 400 or 500 tons' weight each.

The Chicago, Milwaukee and St. Paul Railway is the second longest system in the United States. Like other large railways, it began with a consolidation of numerous small railroads. A study of the industrial map of the United States in connection with a map of this road, discloses that along its lines is produced every kind of mineral taken from the soil of the United States; every variety of lumber milled in the country may be found along the company's lines; and its farms and factories, its cities and marts, portray a most astounding variety and vigor of progress. The road began in 1863 with a track of less than 300 miles and its mileage on Dec. 31, 1922, was 11,032, with tracks stretching from Chicago to Seattle, and criss-crossing back and forth throughout the great Northwest. This road, possibly more than any other, penetrates the Norwegian settlements. It has the largest engine in the world and the longest stretch of electrified road, 440 miles across the Rockies and 209 miles across the Cascades.

The Chicago Great Western dates back to 1886, when the Old Mason City and Fort Dodge line was built. From this line and the Iowa and Pacific, started in 1870, the present Chicago Great Western, or Maple Leaf Route, has been built. It has the shortest track between Chicago and Minneapolis, Minneapolis and Kansas City. The traveling public calls it the "friendly line." The Chicago and Northwestern is an old line with 8,463 miles of track. One of the Northwestern passenger trains between Chicago and Minneapolis in 1925 was named "The Viking." Closely affiliated with this road is the Omaha Road with 1,749 miles in operation. The Minneapolis and St. Louis has 1,650 miles and the Burlington has 9,401. The Northern Pacific has 6,669 miles, the Northern has 8,254, and the Soo has 8,254, and the Soo has 4,396.

James J. Hill is the great name connected with the Great Northern Road. He obtained control also of The Northern Pacific and the Burlington, competitors of the Great Northern. He came to St. Paul from Canada in 1856, an 18-year-old boy of Scotch-Irish parentage, said to have been not so very remotely also of Norse strain. He worked in steamboat offices at St. Paul, 1856-1865; was in business for himself, 1865-1870; established the Red River Transportation Co. between St. Paul and Winnipeg, 1870; organized the St. Paul, Minneapolis and Manitoba Railway, 1878; reorganized this company into the Great Northern, 1890, extended it from St. Paul to Puget Sound, served as its president, 1893-1907, its chairman, 1907-1916. Owned and directed steamship lines, banks, iron mines, steel mills, scientific farm stations, and many other industries throughout the United

States. He was one of the greatest empire builders and was voted the First Citizen of Minnesota. A philanthropist, he gave large gifts to church schools. In 1903 he gave $50,000.00 to the Luther College Endowment Fund; in 1915 he gave $50,000.00 to the St. Olaf College Endowment Fund. He affiliated with the Roman Catholic Church. Dr. Egil Boeckmann is married to one of his daughters. Dr. Egil is one of the best foot ball stars Minnesota has had and a son of Dr. Eduard Boeckmann, illustrious Norwegian surgeon.

California was admitted as a state in 1850, and a plan was inaugurated to bind her firmly to the Union by a great railroad, built at national cost. By 1856 the people began to demand it, and in that year the Republican party, and in 1860 both the Republican and Democratic parties, pledged themselves to build one. Two companies were chartered. One, the Union Pacific, was to begin at Omaha and build westward; the other, the Central Pacific, was to begin at Sacramento and build eastward until the two met. The roads received aid from the Government to the extent of $55,076,000.00 plus every odd numbered section in a strip of public land twenty miles wide along its entire length. The roads met on May 10th, 1869, thus making the first transcontinental system. In 1924 the Union Pacific operated 3,709 miles. The Santa Fe road runs in a southwesterly direction from Chicago to Kansas and Galveston, Texas, to Albuquerque, New Mexico, and west to Los Angeles and San Francisco. The Santa Fe is the fifth largest railway in the United States in mileage, operating 8,957 miles of track. The largest railroad in the United States is the Southern Pacific with 11,119 miles.

The Southern Pacific takes us farthest south. It starts at New Orleans and follows the southern boundary of the United States as far as California, then it proceeds north as far as Portland, Oregon. The trip to California by any transcontinental route is fascinating. Not least the one over the Southern Pacific. You cross great mountain ranges, and pass through sections made famous by the colorful exploits of hardy pioneers. Here are stately snow-capped peaks; here are rich valleys. A desert which is strange and beautiful contrasts with gardens of rare blossoms from all the world. Green, rolling foot-hills and vast, fearful forests. Wide sandy beaches throw back the long breakers, rocky headlands battle the thundering surf, in the solitude of the mountains lie charming camps. Down by the deep blue sea are gay and giddy multitudes. Imperial Valley, Salton Sea, San Jacinta, Mt. Lowe, Yosemite Valley, Mount Shasta, beauty spots of nature of surpassing charm. This is the lure of California.

The first Canadian railway was constructed in 1836, between St. Johns, Quebec, and LaPrairie. It was 16 miles long and was operated by horses. In 1850 Canada had 66 miles of railway; in 1860, 2,065; in 1870, 2,617; in 1880, 7,194; in 1890, 13,151; in 1900, 17,657; in 1910, 24,731; and in 1920, 39,384. The railway era in Canada may be said to have begun in 1851 when an act was passed providing for the construction of the Grand Trunk Railway between Montreal and Toronto. In 1871 the terms under which British Columbia entered the confederation pledged the Dominion of Canada to commence the Pacific railway within two years and complete it within ten years. As a matter of fact, the main line was not completed before 1885. The Canadian Pacific is the longest railroad in America, having 13,350 miles to

Lars Swenson   Lars O. Thorpe   Halle Steensland

Financiers and Philanthropists

its credit. A second transcontinental railway, the Canadian Northern, was begun in 1896. In 1921 this road had 9,717 miles of single track. These two railroads were instrumental in opening up the prairie provinces and bringing hundreds of thousands of immigrants from Europe and the United States into Canada. The Grand Trunk began to look with envy at the large and increasing revenue drawn by the Canadian Pacific from the great Northwest. In 1902, therefore, this road submitted to the Dominion Government a plan to construct a third transcontinental—the Grand Trunk Pacific. The original Grand Trunk had 3,589 miles of single track, and the Grand Trunk Pacific has 2,743. The World War checked immigration and reduced the income of these railroads so that they got into dire financial difficulties. Ultimately the Dominion Government had to take over all the Canadian Northern and Grand Trunk properties. In 1923 these two roads were amalgamated and together with some other Canadian government roads now constitute the Canadian National Railways. In 1921 the total length was 20,738 miles.

Many Norwegians have risen to prominence in the railroad world, some as railroad commissioners working for the state, others as railroad officials working for the railroads. Typical of the officials of the railways are the building and economy engineers, such as Olaf Hoff of the New York Central and O. L. Lindrew of the Illinois Central.

John L. Erdall, born June 5, 1863, at Deerfield, Wisconsin, a graduate of the University of Wisconsin (A. B., 1885; LL.B., 1887), was a lawyer at Madison, 1887-1901; district attorney; asst. attorney general, Wisconsin, 1895-1899. In 1901 he became asst. general attorney for the Chicago Great Western, with office at St. Paul; in 1908 he became general attorney of the Soo, and in 1922 he was promoted to the office of general solicitor, with office in Minneapolis. His son Arthur is assistant solicitor for the Milwaukee Road.

Commodore Vanderbilt   Gerhard M. Dahl   Hauman G. Haugan

Captains of Industry: Railroad Builders

Hauman G. Haugan was the comptroller of the Chicago, Milwaukee and St. Paul, with offices at Chicago, 1901-1921. Haugan was born November 7, 1840, at Oslo, and died in Chicago in 1921 at the age of 81. He came to the United States in 1858. Became a store clerk, then a bank clerk, then cashier. In 1870 he was made paymaster and auditor of the Southern Minnesota Railroad. When this road was purchased, in 1880, by the Chicago, Milwaukee and St. Paul he moved to Milwaukee and became private secretary of Sir W. C. Van Horne of this road. He next served as land commissioner including the placing, naming and developing of many new towns. In 1884 he became a member of Haugan and Lindgren, bankers; he was a director and controlling factor in the State Bank of Chicago, one of the great Norwegian banks of America. He was one of the founders of the Norwegian Chamber of Commerce and the Norwegian-America Line. He worked hard for the Mindegave (Memorial Gift) to Norway in 1914. Fostered at the Christiania Orphanage, he remembered this institution with gifts of money from time to time, including $5,000.00 in his will.

The street railways have also had in their employ Norwegian talent. As, for example, Nils Marcus Thygeson, who was the general counsel for the Twin City Traction Lines. Tygeson was a law graduate of Wisconsin, 1887. Gerhard Melvin Dahl, a son of Rev. Theodore Dahl, D.D., former president of the United Norwegian Lutheran Church, is the chairman of the Brooklyn-Manhattan Transit Corporation, the largest street railway system in the world. Mr. Dahl is a law graduate of Wisconsin, 1896, and an A.M., 1921. In 1912-1917 he was vice president of the Electric Bond and Share Co., New York; in 1917-1923, vice president of the Chase National Bank; since 1923, partner in Hayden-Stone and Co. He is a director of the Alabama Power Co., the Alabama Traction, Light and Power Co., the American Foreign Banking Corporation, the Electrical Utilities Corporation, the Lehigh Power Securities Corporation, the Philadelphia Co., the Chase National Bank, the New Orleans Public Service, Inc., the Pierce Arrow Motor Car Co., the Williamsburg Power Plant Corporation, the Nassau Electric Railroad Co., the Duquesne Light Co., New York Rapid Transit Corporation, etc. He has been decorated by the Emperor of Japan with the Order of the Rising Sun. The companies of which he is chairman or director have a total valuation running up into the billions.

The Norwegian farmers have started building several railroads, which later have become integral parts of larger systems. One of the promoters of Norwegian railroad building is Julius Rosholt. Born at Scandinavia, Wis., August 27, 1854, trained at the Oshkosh State Normal, he became a high school superintendent. In 1881 he moved to Mayville, N. D., and settled down as a farmer. In 1885 he was induced to take shares in a bank. In 1887 he organized the Mayville National Bank, and later he did likewise at Hatton, Aneta, Sharon, Lawton, Edmore, Hampden, Willow City, Omemee, Westhope, Sawyer, Ryder, Hunter, Maddock, and Donnybrook, all in North Dakota; Halstad and Hendrum in Minnesota; Homestead in Montana; Waupaca in Wisconsin; and Rosholt in South Dakota. In 1906 he began his career as a railroad builder. He built the Hill City Railroad which connects with the Great Northern at Swan River, Minn., and this road he sold to the Armour Co., Chicago. In 1912 he built a 90-mile line for the farmers of Roberts and Marshall counties, S. D., and sold it to the Soo. It cost the farmers only 62.5 cents per acre, and "it is no wonder," says Harriet E. Clark in "Scandinavia," June, 1924, "that Mr. Rosholt is held in high esteem by the farmers residing along that line." The War stopped his building of railroads. He has land investments as far north as Prince Albert, Sarsk., and rice fields in Texas and Louisiana.

7. OCCUPATIONS, 1890-1925

The whole earth bears impress of the law of work. It is a very busy place. The ground on which we walk, the air above and the waters beneath us, all teem with busy life. As Coleridge says:

> All nature seems at work; slugs leave their lair,
> The bees are stirring—birds are on the wing,
> And Winter, slumbering in the open air,
> Wears on his smiling face the dream of Spring.

The Norwegians who came to America and their descendants have been workers. They came here to work; they teach their children the dignity of labor in any honest calling. They enjoy their work. Most of them settled on the farm; and though one-half of them still live on the farm they are not like Markham's "Man with the Hoe":

> Bowed with the weight of centuries he leans
> Upon his hoe and gazes upon the ground;
> The emptiness of ages in his face,
> And on his back the burden of the world.
> Who made him dead to rapture and despair,
> A thing that grieves not and that never hopes,
> Stolid and stunned, a brother to the ox?

Not so the Norwegian. He came here as a free man, sprung from a free race that has never known bondage, the most independent and individualistic people that history knows about. He came here because this was a free country after his own heart and because he would have the privilege of carving a home and an empire out of the wilderness. His heart was full of sadness at parting with beloved land and people across the sea, but it was filled with gladness that he had a great work to do here and that God was near him with His blessing. So he rejoiced at his task, like Mackey's "Miller of the Dee":

> There dwelt a miller hale and bold
>   Beside the River Dee;
> He worked and sang from morn till night,
>   No lark more blithe than he;
> And this the burden of his song
>   Forever used to be—
> "I envy nobody; no, not I,
>   And nobody envies me."

The question of occupation is a very important one, and state and national government officials, social workers and students of domestic economy, are making one investigation in this field after another. A few of these will be briefly summarized.

Prior to 1850 no effort was made to obtain a census of the occupations of the people, although in 1820 and in 1840 the number of persons engaged in certain general classes *Census of 1890* of occupations was called for. At the census of 1850 an inquiry was made on the population schedule as to the occupations of free males over 15 years of age, and 323 occupations were listed alphabetically, but without any details as to age or nationality. In 1860 a list of 584 occupations was compiled, with census returns. At the census of 1870 occupations were tabulated for all persons 10 years of age and over, and subdivided by sex, age and nationality, and classified under four general heads—agriculture, manufacturing and mechanical and mining industries, trade and transportation, professional and personal service. There were 338 occupations designated. In 1880 the occupations were reduced to 265 classes, and the number of separate nationalities was much reduced. In the 1890 census the occupational list is reduced to 218, and several other changes are made. The census reports are hard to use satisfactorily, because no two are alike in plan. The 1890 Report contains 98 pages of summary and 500 pages of tables on occupations. The statistics of Norway are combined with those of Sweden. Two tables are herewith submitted:

OCCUPATIONS OF FOREIGN-BORN NORWEGIANS

All Foreign-born

Occupations	1880 Number	1880 %	1890 Number	1890 %
Agriculture, fisheries, mining	99,615	48.17	182,519	37.93
Manufacturing and mechanical pursuits	36,299	17.66	112,851	23.45
Trade and transportation	15,789	8.06	43,848	9.34
Domestic and personal service	51,592	25.10	135,213	28.10
Professional and public service	2,081	1.01	5,665	1.18
All occupations	205,376	100.00	480,096	100.00

Foreign-born Norwegian Males

	1880 Number	1880 %	1890 Number	1890 %
Agriculture, fisheries, mining	98,983	54.37	179,076	44.15
Manufacturing and mechanical pursuits	33,040	18.15	102,871	25.37
Trade and transportation	15,789	8.67	43,484	10.81
Domestic and personal service	32,415	17.80	74,882	18.46
Professional and public service	1,832	1.01	4,910	1.21
All occupations	182,059	100.00	405,223	100.00

Foreign-born Norwegian Females

	1880 Number	1880 %	1890 Number	1890 %
Agriculture, fisheries, mining	632	2.69	3,443	4.55
Manufacturing and mechanical pursuits	3,259	13.89	9,980	13.20
Trade and transportation	149	0.64	1,102	1.46
Domestic and personal service	19,177	81.72	60,331	79.79
Professional and public service	249	1.06	755	1.00
All occupations	23,466	100.00	75,611	100.00

In the following statement the total number of persons in each sex is distributed according to the principal occupations in 1890. The data have to do with the foreign-born Swedes and Norwegians only. In 1890 there were six foreign-born Swedes in America to every four foreign-born Norwegians.

PRINCIPAL OCCUPATIONS

Occupations	Males Number	%	Females Number	%
Farmers, planters, overseers	110,013	27.12	3,097	4.10
Laborers (not specified)	60,637	14.95	....	....
Agricultural laborers	45,206	11.14	....	....
Carpenters and joiners	21,758	5.36	....	....
Miners and quarrymen	14,869	3.66	....	....
Steam railroad employes	11,057	2.72	....	....
Saw and planing mill employes	9,817	2.42	....	....
Iron, steel and other metal workers	8,253	2.03	....	....
Tailors and tailoresses	7,217	1.78	1,211	1.60
Dressmakers	....	....	3,930	5.21
Merchants and dealers	7,168	1.77	....	....
Painters, glaziers, varnishers	6,004	1.48	....	....
Blacksmiths and wheelwrights	5,473	1.35	....	....
Boatmen, canalmen, pilots, sailors	5,320	1.31	....	....
Draymen, hackmen, teamsters, etc.	5,272	1.30	....	....
Clerks, copyists, stenographers	5,041	1.24	....	....
Lumbermen, raftsmen, wood choppers	4,945	1.22	....	....
Machinists	4,732	1.17	....	....
Boatmen, canalmen, pilots, sailors	4,692	1.16	....	....
Brick and stone masons	4,582	1.13	....	....
Servants	4,401	1.08	53,644	71.04
Laundresses	....	....	3,066	4.06
Cabinet makers, upholsterers	2,992	0.74	....	....
Salesmen	2,225	0.55	....	....
Wood workers (not otherwise specified)	2,201	0.54	....	....
Engineers, firemen (not locomotive)	2,189	0.54	....	....
Cotton, woolen, textile mill operatives	2,095	0.52	1,460	1.93
Seamstresses	....	....	1,915	2.54
Marble and stone cutters	1,784	0.44	....	....
Housekeepers, stewardesses	....	....	1,785	2.36
Restaurant and saloon keepers	1,767	0.44	....	....
Brick and tile makers	1,508	0.37	....	....
Agents (claim, commission, insurance, etc.)	1,141	0.34	....	....
Clergymen	1,305	0.32	....	....
Foremen, overseers	1,298	0.32	....	....
Bartenders	1,174	0.29	....	....
Messengers, packers, porters, etc.	1,162	0.29	....	....
Watchmen, policemen, detectives	1,128	0.28	....	....
Leather curriers, dressers, tanners	1,118	0.28	....	....
Hostlers, livery stable keepers	1,013	0.25	....	....
Other occupations	33,120	8.10	5,402	7.16
All occupations	405,677	100.00	75,510	100.00

The Immigration Commission was created by Congress in 1907. Its object was to make full inquiry into the subject of immigration. The "Reports of the Immigration Commission" make up a series of 40 volumes of detailed information on the immigration from 1820 to 1910, the emigration condition in Europe, the immigrant races, immigrants in industries, immigrants in cities, education, crime, insanity, distribution of immigrants, etc. There are several volumes on the immigrant in industries. The following is a digest of these reports with regard to the Norwegians of the 1st and 2nd generations.

Immigration Commission, 1910

Male Breadwinners, 1900

Occupation	Norwegians 1st generation	Per cent	Norwegians 2nd generation	Per cent
Agricultural pursuits	85,093	49.9	53,942	63.0
Mining	2,180	1.3	416	0.5
Manufacturing and mechanical pursuits	37,413	21.8	9,071	11.1
Transportation	5,191	3.0	2,207	2.4
Trade	12,961	7.5	6,372	7.3
Domestic and personal service	21,973	12.8	8,228	9 6
Clerical service	3,198	2.0	3,514	3.9
Professional and public service	2,997	1.8	1,914	2.2
All occupations	171,006	100.0	85,658	100.0

Female Breadwinners, 1900

Occupation	Norwegians 1st generation	Per cent	Norwegians 2nd generation	Per cent
Agricultural pursuits	3,169	13.8	962	3.8
Mining	....	....	....	....
Manufacturing and mechanical pursuits	3,522	15.4	4,564	18.2
Transportation	....	....	....	....
Trade	125	0.5	44	0 2
Domestic and personal service	14,649	64.0	14,172	56.5
Clerical service	831	3.7	2,408	9.6
Professional and public service	600	2.6	2,931	11.7
All occupations	22,986	100.0	25,082	100.0

These tables are self-explanatory and are worthy of much meditation. They show what occupations each generation prefers. They show the relation between the 1st and the 2nd generation, between men and women breadwinners. They do not show what standing the Norwegians have among the races of America, nor do they show what per cent of Norwegians are breadwinners. The following table presents these facts with respect to farming:

American Farmers, 1900

Rank 1st Generation	Nationality	1st generation	Per cent	2nd generation	Per cent	Rank 2nd Generation
1	Norwegian	85,093	49.8	53,942	63.0	1
2	Danish	34,951	42.3	11,622	50.3	2
3	Swiss	22,831	37.8	14,597	42.0	6
4	Swedish	89,806	30.2	29,067	43.1	3.5
5	Bohemian	22,857	32.0	13,997	42.8	5
6	German	348,265	27.3	426,910	28.6	9
7	French	11,355	22.1	14,845	26.9	10
8	English Canadian	41,659	21.8	54,992	30.9	7
9	Scotch	23,710	18.3	27,111	43.1	3.5
10	English	79,340	18.1	117,760	26.6	11
11	French Canadian	22,850	13.6	21,109	22.1	15
12	Irish	97,454	13.6	179,499	16.5	16
13	Polish	19,256	10.5	6,236	24.0	14
14	Russian	19,490	10.2	4,284	29.3	8
15	Austrian	12,314	8.0	3,812	26.1	12
16	Italian	16,614	6.0	1,613	9.5	18
17	Hungarian	2,854	3.2	371	9.6	17
18	Other races	84,370	24.5	89,823	25.0	13
	All races	1,034,176	21.2	1,071,590	25.9	

The census figures indicate that 21.2 per cent, or more than one-fifth, of the foreign-born have gone to work on the farm, and that the percentage in the second generation has increased to 25.9, or more than one-fourth. It should be said that the increase is really not in the per cent of farmers, but in the per cent of farm laborers. It should be noted that some of the nationalities are represented by very small numbers in the second generation as compared with the first. This is true of the Austrians, Hungarians, Italians, Poles and Russians. It results from the fact that the immigration of these people is of comparatively recent origin, so that the second generation in 1890 consisted principally of children, few of whom were old enough to take up an occupation in 1890. Finally, it should be noted that the Norwegians are far in the lead in agriculture. The Norwegian farmer is unique. Long may he live! Greatly may he thrive!

The average size of the Norwegian farms in 1920 was 240 acres over against 180 acres for the country at large. The average price of land in the Northwest where the Norwegians live was $25,518.00 in 1920 over against $12,084.00 for the country at large. That is, the land in the Northwest is more than twice as valuable as the average for the whole country. The Norwegians in Iowa own the best land in that state, averaging nearly $40,000.00

per farm. In Wisconsin they have the best land. In Minnesota, the Dakotas, Montana, the same. Only 15 per cent of the Norwegians are tenants in Iowa, as over against 41 per cent of the state as a whole. In the adjoining states the same condition prevails. The Norwegian farmers have been making America.

Rev. H. C. Holm, Eagle Grove, Iowa, president of the Iowa District of the Norwegian Lutheran Church, happened to be in Washington once while Theodore Roosevelt was in office. He called on President Roosevelt to pay his respects. Now, Holm is a very imposing looking man. Six feet tall, large-boned, weighing easily 250 pounds, with open, kindly face, deep, expressive voice that can carry a half mile or more. In short, a manly man, sure to delight the Rough Rider Roosevelt. These two men looked at each other in mutual admiration and clasped hands long and vigorously. "So you are a Norwegian," said Teddie. "Yes, sir," answered Holm, "and it looks as if we Norwegians are going to rule the land at last." "What do you mean, sir?" asked the President in surprise, as he withdrew his fist. "Mean? I mean that we Norwegians are buying up the land and raising the children, and the future of America is ours." "Shake again," said Roosevelt.

In 1901 Martin Ulvestad published his "Norge i Amerika med Kart" (Norway in America with Map). In this work he lists 64,682 Norwegians by name, and gives *Martin Ulvestad:* their occupation and post office. On the basis *1901* of his researches he concludes that in that year 64 per cent of the Norwegians were engaged in farming, 18 per cent worked in towns and cities, 7 per cent were occupied on the water as sailors, etc., 6 per cent were lumbermen, 3 per cent miners, and 2 per cent fishermen. A recount of the names, however, gives the following occupational distribution:

NORWEGIANS IN THE OCCUPATIONS

Occupation	Representative Men	Per cent
Agriculture	41,533	64.2
Mining	56	0.1
Manufacturing and mechanical pursuits	2,108	3.2
Trade	7,289	11.3
Transportation	322	0.5
Domestic and personal service	7,878	12.2
Professional and public service	5,496	8.5
All occupations	64,682	100 0

Volume IV of the Census of 1920 is devoted exclusively to occupations. It deals with the enumeration and classification of occupations, the number and sex of occupied persons, color, nativity, parentage, age, marital condition, etc., of the people who work, but it does not give any information about nationality. People are interested to know how many Norwegians are in this and that occupation, how many are physicians, clergymen, druggists, hold public office, and the like. With the help of this census report and other data an estimate can be made.

Census of 1920

This report shows the number and proportion of males and females 10 years of age and over engaged in gainful occupations. It is 78.2 per cent of the men and 21.1 per cent of the women. In the 1890 Report it is shown that the per cent of Norwegians engaged in gainful occupations was 4.5 per cent greater than the average for the whole country. Let us then assume that 80 per cent of the Norwegian men are breadwinners and 20 per cent of the women.

Volume II of the Census Report for 1920 gives the distribution as to ages. 21.7 per cent of the people are under 10 years of age; 78.3 per cent are 10 years and over. The total Norwegian population in 1925 is approximately 2,500,000, 1,250,000 males, 1,250,000 females. 78 per cent of the males is 975,000; 78 per cent of the women is 975,000. 80 per cent of the males 10 years and over are at work—80 per cent of 975,000 is 780,000; 20 per cent of the females 10 years and over are at work—20 per cent of 975,000 is 195,000. 780,000 Norwegian men and 195,000 Norwegian women at work.

Volume IV of the 1920 Report shows, furthermore, the per cent of males and females in total persons 10 years of age and over in each general division of occupations. Thus:

PER CENT AND SEX OF OCCUPIED AMERICANS, 1920

No.	Occupation	Per cent male	Per cent female
1.	Agriculture, forestry, animal husbandry ...	29.8	12.7
2.	Mining	3.3	0.0
3.	Manufacturing and mechanical pursuits ...	33.0	22.5
4.	Transportation	8.6	2.5
5.	Trade	10.8	7.8
6.	Domestic and personal service	3.7	25.6
7.	Clerical service	5.1	16.7
8.	Professional service	3.4	11.9
9.	Public service	2.3	0.3
	All occupations	100.0	100.0

If the Norwegians were just typical Americans the above percentages could be applied to them. Thus, 29.8 per cent of the

men would be on the farm; 12.7 of the women. But they are
not typical in many respects. Nearly one-half of them are on
the farm, and in that regard they are not typical, for only 29.8
per cent of the breadwinners of the whole country are engaged
in farming. The following is an estimate of the per cent and
sex of the Norwegians who work for a living.

PER CENT AND SEX OF OCCUPIED NORWEGIANS, 1920

No.	Occupation	Per cent male	Per cent female
1.	Agriculture, forestry, animal husbandry ...	45.0	5.8
2.	Mining ...	1.0	0.0
3.	Manufacturing and mechanical pursuits ..	25.0	20.0
4.	Transportation	5.5	2.0
5.	Trade	10.0	5.0
6.	Domestic and personal service	5.0	35.0
7.	Clerical service	4.0	20.0
8.	Professional service	3.5	12.0
9.	Public service	1.0	0.2
	All occupations	100.0	100.0

Applying these percentages to the Norwegians in 1925, we can
arrive at a fair estimate of the number of men and women of
Norwegian blood engaged in gainful occupations, to wit:

NUMBER AND SEX OF OCCUPIED NORWEGIANS, 1925

No.	Occupation	Men at work	Women at work	Total
1.	Agriculture, forestry, animal husbandry	351,000	11,310	362,310
2.	Mining	7,800	....	7,800
3.	Manufacturing and mechanical pursuits	195,000	39,000	234,000
4.	Transportation	42,900	3,900	46,800
5.	Trade	78,000	9,750	87,750
6.	Domestic and personal service	39,000	68,250	107,250
7.	Clerical service	31,200	39,000	70,200
8.	Pofessional service	27,300	23,400	50,700
9.	Public service	7,800	390	8,190
	All occupations	780,000	195,000	975,000

The Norwegians in America in 1925 are nearly as strong
numerically as the state of Minnesota. On that account it will
be profitable to compare the estimated distribution of workers
among the Norwegians with the actual occupational distribution
in the state of Minnesota in 1920.

NORWEGIANS AND MINNESOTANS COMPARED

No.	Occupation	Minnesotans		Norwegians	
		Male	Female	Male	Female
	Total population	1,245,537	1,141,588	1,250,000	1,250,000
	Population 10 years and over ..	986,877	890,255	975,000	975,000
1.	Agriculture, forestry, animal husbandry	298,258	9,618	351,000	11,310
2.	Mining	14,975	19	7,800	....
3.	Manufacturing and mechanical pursuits	180,607	23,395	195,000	39,000
4.	Transportation	64,977	5,315	42,900	3,900
5.	Trade	87,761	16,670	78,000	9,750
6.	Domestic and personal service	25,482	44,638	39,000	68,250
7.	Clerical service	35,360	32,842	31,200	39,000
8.	Professional service	24,307	31,175	27,300	23,400
9.	Public service	11,220	554	7,800	390
	All occupations	742,947	164,226	780,000	195,000

Each of the general groups of occupations has many subdivisions. Agriculture, for example, in the 1920 Census was subdivided into 46 divisions and subdivisions. Fishing was classified under farming. Mining had 19 groups. Manufacturing and mechanical pursuits had 290 groups; transportation, 77; trade, 96; domestic and personal service, 47; clerical service, 15; professional service, 52; and public service, 23 classes. Thus under Professional Service the actors and showmen are by themselves, the architects, artists, authors and editors, chemists, clergymen, college presidents and professors, other teachers, dentists, designers, draftsmen, inventors, lawyers, judges, justices, musicians, osteopaths, physicians and surgeons, veterinary surgeons, trained nurses, photographers, technical engineers (civil, electrical, mechanical and mining), are each by themselves. Also various other professional and semi-professional services are marked off into special classes. There are Norwegians in every one of these occupations. Little by little they are becoming more and more like the typical American. They are entering all the vocations and professions. The Norwegians number now about 2 per cent of the population of the United States. Except in farming, a man can strike a pretty good estimate of how many Norwegians are engaged in any particular line of work, by finding the census figures as to the number of workers engaged in that field and then multiplying by 2 per cent. The answer will be the number of Norwegians engaged in that field. Thus, how many Norwegians are in the ministry? The Census for 1920 says there were 127,270 clergymen in the United States. 2 per cent of

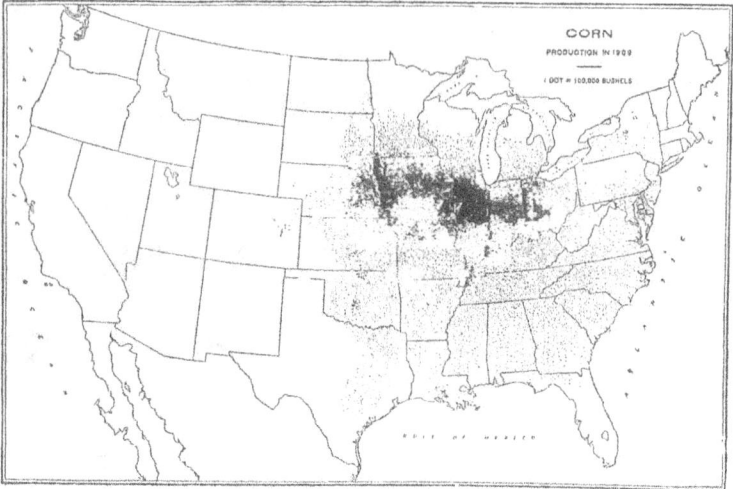

Corn Production in 1909

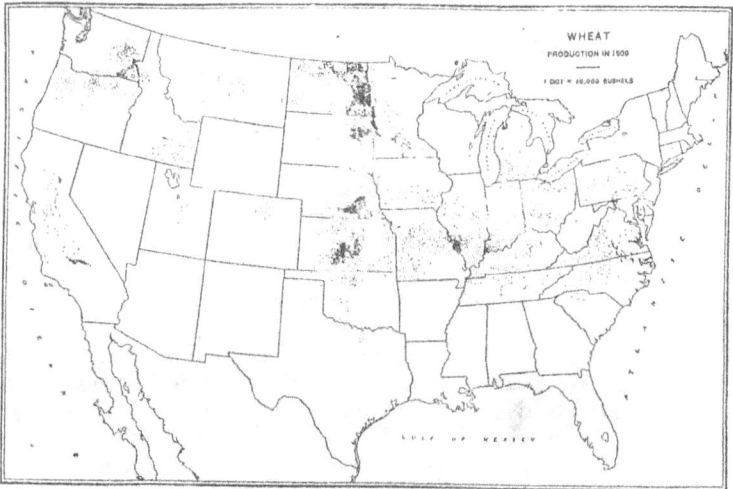

Wheat Production in 1909

The Norwegians Live in the Food Producing Belt:
They Head the List as Farmers

(From "Statistical Atlas of the United States: 1914")

127,270 is 2,545. The Norwegian Lutherans had 1,554 clergy-men in 1921, and there were many Norwegian pastors in the Reformed denominations. 2 per cent of the physicians is 2,900—hence, 2,900 Norwegian doctors in America. 2 per cent of the civil engineers is 1,292—about 1.292 Norwegian civil engineers. And so on down the whole list of occupations.

It would be pleasant and profitable to make a study of any of these groups of workers. The present writer has made such studies of the Norwegian Lutheran pastors—see "Norsk Luther-ske Prester i Amerika, 1843-1915," a Who's Who of 1,929 pastors in the Norwegian Lutheran synods. He has also made a similar book about the teachers in the higher schools of these synods—

†Hon. Osmund J. Wing   Anton E. Anderson   †Fingar G. Enger

Successful Farmers, Generous Givers, Influential Citizens

the "School Calendar, 1824-1924," a Who's Who of 3,600 teach-ers. Hans Jervell has written a few small books about the farmers of North Dakota—"North Dakota," and "Nordmænd og Norske Hjem i Amerika." Jervell has also published a book written by T. A. Høverstad entitled "The Norwegian Farmers of the United States." These books are very inspirational, but altogether too brief. Now, will some one write about the fishers and miners, the manufacturers and artisans, the transportation by water and by land, the bankers and storekeepers, the doctors and lawyers, the artists and musicians, and so forth? A study of the lives of these men in the many occupations will make us appreciate what they have done in the making of America.

8. Churches, 1890-1925

The Church is still the most conservative, as it is also the most inspiring, influence in the world. The Norwegian Lutheran Church, including all its branches, has been the strongest spokes-man and the hardest worker in the matter of preserving the Nor-wegian language and culture among the Norwegians in America,

Hans Gerhard Stub

and yet, in spite of the weighty influence and earnest labor of the Church, the Norwegian people in America during this period have been dropping the use of Norwegian to such an alarming extent that about 50 per cent of them do not even understand the spoken language. Many erstwhile Norwegian congregations have passed over to the exclusive use of English.

In "Religious Bodies: 1906," a United States Census report, the Norwegian synods had only 21 English congregations out of a total of 2,639, less than one per cent using English only; but 674, or 25 per cent, used both English and Norwegian. In "Religious Bodies: 1916," the Norwegian synods had advanced to 200 congregations using English only. 200 out of 3,161 is 6.3 per cent;

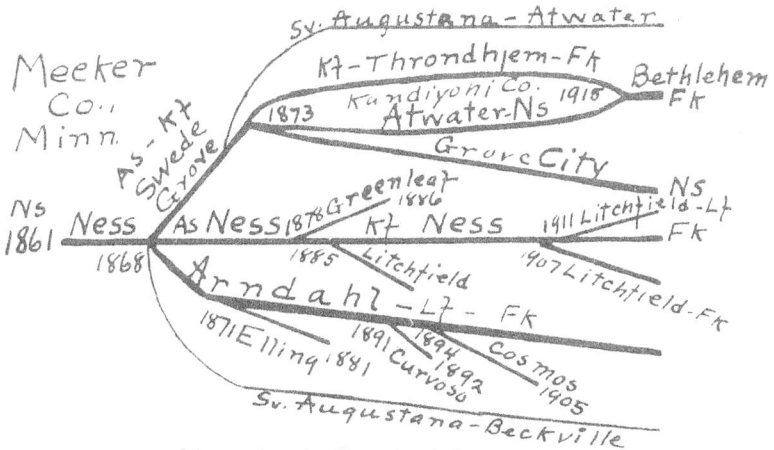

Illustrating the Growth of Congregations

1,598, or over 50 per cent, were bilingual at public services. The progress toward English can be summarized in the following table:

ENGLISH IN THE NORWEGIAN LUTHERAN SYNODS

Church work	1905	1910	1915	1920	1924
Sermons	5%	13%	22%	34%	47%
Catechizations	18%	27%	27%	49%	73%
Sunday School pupils ...	17%	21%	27%	75%	89%

This rapid departure from the bi-lingual standard to the use of English only is one of many proofs that the Norwegian people are fast becoming Americanized, and that this period can be called the American Period of their story. In reality they are much more Americanized in language and sentiments than these church statistics show. The large number of nominal Lutherans who do not belong to any congregation are more Americanized as a rule than the church members, not in the sense of being better Americans, but in the sense of having sloughed off their best

Norwegian culture. The homes, the schools, the street, all favor the use of English now. Said an old Norwegian grandma as she was down town shopping: "Ay tank ay gaa to de movies tode." Said another old lady at her side: "Ja, ve do dat, end dan ve gaa to da chørch end hev aas sahm kaffe." Some of these good old dames can not speak English, and they will not speak Norwegian. It is the American Period.

The Norwegian Lutheran synods trained and ordained about 1,700 new ministers of the Gospel during the years 1891-1925.

Pastors, 1890-1925 The exact figures for the first three decades are as follows:

ORDINATIONS, 1891-1900

Year	Eielsen Synod	Norwegian Synod	Hauge Synod	United Church	Lutheran Free Church	Lutheran Brethren	Total
1891........	0	17	3	29	..	..	49
1892........	0	22	2	19	..	..	43
1893........	2	16	3	23	2	..	46
1894........	0	11	5	13	2	..	31
1895........	0	17	6	10	8	..	41
1896........	0	14	9	26	11	..	60
1897........	0	12	7	14	9	..	42
1898........	0	17	6	16	8	..	47
1899........	0	7	6	15	12	1	41
1900........	0	14	6	19	8	..	47
1891-1900........	2	147	53	184	60	1	447

ORDINATIONS, 1901-1910

Year	Eielsen Synod	Norwegian Synod	Hauge Synod	United Church	Lutheran Free Church	Lutheran Brethren	Total
1901........	0	14	7	17	7	0	45
1902........	0	21	6	15	8	1	51
1903........	1	18	9	22	15	0	65
1904........	1	10	4	16	12	0	43
1905........	0	14	11	24	6	0	55
1906........	0	21	4	30	3	0	58
1907........	0	14	12	23	3	2	54
1908........	0	19	5	22	9	1	56
1909........	0	18	11	22	5	3	59
1910........	1	16	6	30	6	1	60
1901-1910........	3	165	75	221	74	8	546

ORDINATIONS, 1911-1916

Year	Eielsen Synod	Norwegian Synod	Hauge Synod	United Church	Lutheran Free Church	Lutheran Brethren	Total
1911........	0	12	9	18	6	0	45
1912........	0	20	9	20	6	3	58
1913........	0	11	7	36	11	2	67
1914........	0	13	4	30	8	1	56
1915........	0	16	3	23	9	6	61
1916........	1	10	6	32	9	3	61
1911-1916........	1	82	38	159	49	15	344

	Eielsen Synod	Norwegian Synod	Hauge Synod	United Church	Free Church	Lutheran Brethren	Norwegian Lutheran	Norwegian Synod	Total
1917	0	..	..	..	7	4	35	0	46
1918	1	..	..	..	7	1	32	0	41
1919	1	..	..	..	7	0	32	0	40
1920	0	..	..	..	4	2	37	0	43
1917-1920	2	..	..	..	25	7	136	0	170

The building of new congregations during this period almost kept pace with the planting of new settlements. The United Nor-

Congregations, 1890-1925

wegian Church at its first meeting issued a protest to the Reformed denominations against their proselyting, and organized itself to do vigorous home mission work. It appointed able secretaries and superintendents and aimed to send out into the new fields every year the best pick from its seminary. The home mission superintendents were: N. J. Ellestad, 1891-1900;

GROWTH OF THE NORWEGIAN LUTHERAN CHURCH

(Figures indicate number of congregation by decades)

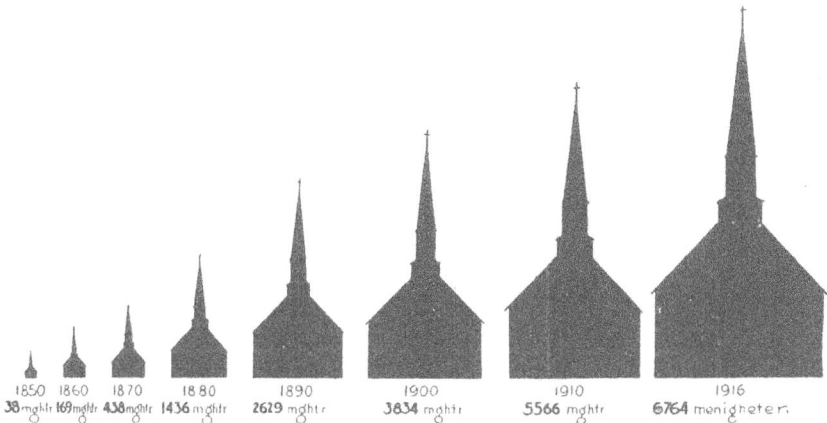

| 1850 | 1860 | 1870 | 1880 | 1890 | 1900 | 1910 | 1916 |
| 38 mghtr | 169 mghtr | 438 mghtr | 1436 mghtr | 2629 mghtr | 3634 mghtr | 5566 mghtr | 6764 menigheter |

H. C. Holm, 1900-1906; O. Glasøe, 1906-1914; and G. A. Larsen, 1914-1917. The other synods were also up and doing and in many places outdistanced the United Church in the race. Then came the World War and the merger of three of the synods in 1917—the Hauge Synod, the Norwegian Synod and the United Church becoming the Norwegian Lutheran Church. On account of financial straits accompanying the War the synods have been forced to adopt a policy of retrenchment, and fewer congregations have therefore been established. Due to the merger of the three synods into a new synod, there have been similar mergers of competing congregations. At least 130 such congregational mergers have been recorded by Secretary N. J. Løhre of the Norwegian Lutheran Church.

From 1825 to 1916 a total of 6,764 congregations and preaching places were established by the Norwegian Lutherans—5,811 congregations and 953 preaching places. The total for the century no doubt reached the 7,500 mark. About one-half of these are still maintained. A comparison of the three periods shows that the church work of the third period is by no means to be despised:

CONGREGATIONAL GROWTH

Period	No. of New Pastors	No. of New Congregations	No. of New Preaching Places	Total Preaching Stations	New Congs. per Preacher
1825-1860.........	38	157	12	169	4.5
1860-1890.........	614	2282	178	2460	4.0
1890-1916.........	1337	3372	763	4135	3.1
1916-1925...... Est.	363	439	297	736	2.0
1890-1925...... Est.	1700	3811	1060	4871	2.8
1825-1925...... Est.	2352	6250	1250	7500	3.2

A few attempts have been made to tell the story of the Norwegian Lutheran congregations. Considerable information about the congregations are found in the various county histories of the Northwest. Individual congregations are briefly sketched in several of the narratives about the Norwegian people in America, as, for example, in A. E. Strand's "History of the Norwegians in Illinois" (1905) and E. M. Stensrud's "Lutheran Church and California" (1916). "Norske Settlementer og Menigheter i Benton, Sherburne og Mille Lacs Countier" (1903), by P. Langseth, A. Larsgaard and R. J. Meland, is a brief account of these three Minnesota counties. The most exhaustive survey of the congregations is, outside of the annual reports of the synods, the two volume work entitled "Norsk Lutherske Menigheter i Amerika, 1843-1916" (2,212 pages). It was compiled and edited by O. M. Norlie, assisted by T. O. Tolo, D. Kvaase, K. A. Kasberg, C. M. Hallanger, E. M. Stensrud, L. C. Jacobson, A. M. Arntzen, A. L. Wiek and L. Lillehei. It is based on first-hand information obtained by means of questionnaires, correspondence, visitations, annual reports, etc. The editor mailed out 50,700 letters of inquiry in compiling the material. A number of the older congregations have celebrated their 25th, 50th, 60th, 75th, or 80th anniversary, and some of them have published souvenirs in honor of the event. A list of representative souvenirs is printed in the Appendix.

Four new Norwegian Lutheran synods came into being during this period—The Lutheran Free Church, The Lutheran Brethren, The Norwegian Lutheran Church of America, **Synods, 1890-1925** and The Norwegian Synod of the American Evangelical Lutheran Church.

The Joint Norwegian Synod—United Church Union Committee (Standing, from left to right: J. E. Jørgensen, P. Tangjerd, R. Malmin, O. G. U. Siljan, I. D. Ylvisaker, S. Gunderson, N. N. Boe, G. T. Lee, G. Rasmussen, M. H. Hegge, J. Nordby, H. Engh. Siljan host, not a member).

a. *The Lutheran Free Church*

From 1893 to 1897 this body was known as the Friends of Augsburg. Augsburg Seminary, founded in 1869, became the seminary of the Conference, 1870-1890, and of the United Norwegian Church in the 1890 merger. Now there was, as related before, within the Conference two factions, not disagreeing on points of doctrine, but rather as to the aims in the education of the ministry and the anatomy of the local congregation. The controversy was carried into the United Church, in the effort of the United Church to obtain control of Augsburg Seminary. The controversy finally resulted in the expulsion in 1893 of a number

Knute Nelson, Minn.
1892-95

A. E. Lee, S. D.
1896-00

C. N. Herreid, S. D.
1900-04

of congregations and pastors who took sides with Professors Ofte-dal and Sverdrup, the leaders of the minority fight. The expelled congregations and pastors called themselves the Friends of Augsburg, and since 1897 they have borne the name the Lutheran Free Church. Augsburg Seminary is their theological school. "Folkebladet" is their church organ. Their slogan is congregational polity and the free congregation, hence the name Free Church. The Free Church is active in publication, education, foreign missions, home missions and charity work. Rev. E. E. Gynild, Willmar, Minnesota, is the present president; Rev. Johan Mattson, Minneapolis, secretary; Rev. J. H. Blegen, Minneapolis, treasurer.

b. *The Lutheran Brethren*

The Lutheran Brethren, known also as the Church of the Lutheran Brethren, was organized in Milwaukee, 1900, with five congregations as a nucleus. The members of this synod felt that they could not enter any of the other Norwegian bodies, owing to disapproval of their practice in the acceptance of new members,

J. O. Davidson, Wis.
1906-11

Peter Norbeck, S. D.
1917-21

John J. Blaine, Wis.
1921—

State Governors of Norwegian Parentage

R. A. Nestos, N. D. (*Copyright, Lee Bros.*) Theodore Christianson,
1921-25 J. A. O. Preus, Minn. Minn. 1925—
1921-25

church discipline, confirmation and a few other matters. Only believers are admitted as members of Lutheran Brethren congregations and they are in theory allowed to remain only as long as their life and conduct are in accordance with this Christian profession. Church discipline is rigidly enforced. In 1903, the Lutheran Brethren built their first and only school—the Lutheran Bible School, located at Wahpeton, N. D., 1903-1918, Grand Forks, North Dakota, 1918——. Rev. E. M. Broen has been president of this school since its beginning. The synod has never been large in numbers—in 1919, only 10 pastors serving 27 small congregations. But it is extraordinarily plucky and active. In 1925 six of its 27 ordained workmen are on the foreign mission fields —in China and West Africa. There is probably no church body in America that gives more per capita to the support of synodical enterprises than this little synod. In 1907 the individual contributions of the Lutheran Brethren averaged $35.76 per baptized member; in 1916, $34.00 per head; in 1919, $40.00. The church organ is "Broderbaandet," edited by R. S. Gjerde. The president is Rev. Erik H. Gunhus, Minneapolis. M. E. Sletta, Coopers-

John E. Erickson, Mont. Carl Gunderson, S. D. Arthur G. Sorlie, N. D.
1925— 1925— 1925—
State Governors of Norwegian Parentage

town, North Dakota, is vice president; G. Stengien, Mayville, North Dakota, is secretary; Otto Rood, Minneapolis, is treasurer.

c. *The Norwegian Lutheran Church of America*

The movement so auspiciously begun in 1890 toward union of different Lutheran synods, resulted in the organization of the Norwegian Lutheran Church of America, June 9, 1917. In 1905 the Hauge Synod took up the question of union. The Norwegian Synod and the United Church responded cordially; the Lutheran Free Church expressed its sympathy, but, on account of its polity, could not as a body enter the proposed union. Committees were appointed which, during the years 1905-1912, met and came to

G. Smedal
Sec'y, Pensions

H. B. Kildahl
Sec'y, Charities

L. A. Vigness
Sec'y, Education

doctrinal agreement on the questions which had separated them—absolution and lay preaching (1906), the call and conversion (1908), and predestination (1912). These Committees were made up of the presidents of the respective synods and their theological faculties. These committees laid the foundation for the new work of the new committees which in 1912 crowned the work of negotiation. On February 22, 1912, the Norwegian Synod and United Church union committees held a joint session at Madison, Wisconsin, and came to agreement on predestination. The news of the Madison Agreement was almost too good to be true. Men doubted it. A strong minority in the Norwegian Synod, under the leadership of C. K. Preus and I. B. Torrison, demanded certain additions and footnotes to the pacificatory document. Their request was granted in the so-called Austin Agreement, made at Austin, Minnesota, 1917. There was a strong minority also in the Hauge Synod, but through the efforts of M. O. Wee and others this minority was won over for the union, after their reasonable doubts had been removed and their requests had been satisfactorily met. At this, practically everybody was satisfied that doctrinal agreement had been reached, and steps were taken to unite the Norwegian Synod, the Hauge Synod and the United Church. This being the Quadri-centennial year of the Reformation (1517-1917), men thought a good deal about a united Lutherdom and longed for the union of the Norwegian church bodies. At the time of the union the Hauge Synod had 120 pastors serving congregations; the Norwegian Synod had 355; the United Church had 556; a total of 1,031. Hauge had 389 congregations; the Norwegian Synod had 1,119; the United Church had 1,799; a total of 3,307. Hauge had a membership of 39,737; the Norwegian Synod had 150,455; the United Church had 280,668; a total of 470,860. A small handful of pastors thought the union too hasty, and therefore did not join the new body. Then came the War; hard times and general

| G. A. Gullixson | Erik H. Gunhus | S. M. Stenby |
| (Norw.) | (Brethren) | (Eielsen) |

Presidents of smaller Synods

discontent everywhere. Still, the Norwegian Lutheran Church has easily weathered the storms, though tested in every beam and seam.

The present officers are: Dr. H. G. Stub, president; Dr. J. A. Aasgaard, vice president; Rev. N. J. Løhre, secretary; Mr. Erik Waldeland, treasurer. The Norwegian Lutheran Church is divided geographically into nine districts and it has, in addition, an English Association, which is ranked with the districts. The presidents of these divisions are: Rev. J. Nordby, Eastern District; Rev. I. T. Aastad, Northern Minnesota; Rev. C. J. Eastvold, Southern Minnesota; Rev. H. C. Holm, Iowa; Rev. N. Bøe, South Dakota; Rev. I. D. Ylvisaker, North Dakota; Rev. A. M. Skindlov, Rocky Mountain; Rev. J. A. E. Naess, Pacific; Rev. J. J. Akre, Canada District; Dr. G. A. T. Rygh, English Association. The Norwegian Church is provided with good working boards, committees and societies. The secretaries of the main boards are as follows: Olaf Lysnes, Publication; Olaf Guldseth, Book Mission; Dr. Jacob Tanner, Elementary Christian Education; L. A. Vigness, Education (Higher); H. M. Sæterlie and

Dr. J. R. Birkelund, Foreign Missions; C. S. B. Hoel, Home Missions; H. B. Kildahl, Charities; G. Smedal, Pensions; M. E. Waldeland, Transportation; Joseph Estrem and H. O. Shurson, Trustees. *Lutheraneren,* edited by Dr. Jacob Tanner and Rev. Rasmus Malmin, is the Norwegian organ of this body, and *Lutheran Church Herald,* edited by Rev. G. T. Lee, is the English official organ. "Teologisk Tidsskrift" (R. Malmin, editor) is a theological magazine; "Our Young People" (John Peterson, editor) is a paper for youth. The budget for synodical expenses amounts to about $1,500,000.00 a year.

d. *The Norwegian Synod of the American Evangelical Lutheran Church*

This synod was organized in 1918 by those pastors and congregations that, on account of conscientious scruples or for other reasons, did not want to join the Norwegian Lutheran Church. They maintain that the Madison Agreement and the merger were too hasty, and that indifferentism, unionism and hierarchy prevail in the Norwegian Lutheran Church. Their aim is to defend and to desseminate the old truths as they see them. In 1922 they had 32 pastors, 46 congregations and 6,737 souls. They have been made members of the Synodical Conference and make use of its schools. Rev. B. A. Harstad, of Parkland, Washington, was the first president of the Norwegian Synod. The present incumbent is Rev. George Gullixson, of Chicago, Illinois.

Just how many Norwegians are members of non-Lutheran bodies no one can at present say for sure. Just how many are worshipping in Norwegian is on record in the **Non-Lutheran** census reports and in the annual reports of **Bodies** these organizations. The notices in the census reports are, of course, very inadequate, all too brief. The work that these organizations are doing is in many ways pioneer work and is the occasion of many a story of sacrifice and suffering. Here also is many a flower that blooms unseen.

a. *United States Census,* 1906

The following table shows the denominations using Norwegian in their church services. The table is found in "Religious Bodies, 1906."

DENOMINATIONS USING NORWEGIAN

Denominations	Congregations	Communicant Membership
Adventist	14	374
Baptist	41	1,889
Brethren	1	26
Congregationalist	9	790
Disciples	1	58
Independent	16	1,072
Methodist	125	7,032
Presbyterian	2	36
Quaker	4	246
Salvationist	4	120
Swedish Mission	3	42
Theosophical	1	27
Unitarian	4	452
Total Non-Lutheran	225	12,164
Missouri Synod	1	80
United Norwegian	1,133	180,566
Hauge Synod	256	32,277
Eielsen Synod	25	983
Norwegian Synod	875	104,556
Lutheran Free Church	319	26,864
Lutheran Brethren	16	482
Total Lutheran	2,625	345,808
Grand Total	2,850	357,072

This table shows that in 1906 there were 2,849 congregations that reported that they were working among the Norwegians, that 7.9 per cent of these congregations were non-Lutheran, and 92.1 per cent were Lutheran. It shows furthermore that these congregations were caring for 357,892 Norwegians holding communicant membership, of which 96.6 per cent was Lutheran, 3.4 per cent was not. The communicant membership is about 60 per cent of the baptized membership.

b. *United States Census,* 1916

In "Religious Bodies: 1916" the situation is as follows:

DENOMINATIONS USING NORWEGIAN

Denominations	Congregations	Communicant Membership
Adventist	22	863
Assembly of God	1	300
Baptist	39	1,799
Brethren	2	20
Congregational	12	614
Independent	8	422
Methodist	119	6,699
Moravian	1	159
Presbyterian	1	12
Quaker	1	92
Swedish Mission	4	128
Unitarian	2	400
Total Non-Lutheran	212	11,508

Denominations	Congregations	Communicant Membership
Hauge Synod	263	23,221
Norwegian Synod	894	107,010
United Norwegian	1,371	171,595
Joint Ohio Synod	1	104
Eielsen Synod	19	1,163
Immanuel Synod	1	80
Lutheran Free Church	356	27,011
Apostolic Finnish	1	275
Lutheran Brethren	20	850
Total Lutheran	2,926	331,309
Grand Total	3,138	342,817

This table shows that in 1916 there were 3,137 congregations using the Norwegian language; 225, or 6.7 per cent, were Non-Lutheran and 2,925, or 93.3 per cent were Lutheran. Of the communicant members 96.7 were Lutherans, 3.3 per cent were Non-Lutherans.

c. *Canadian Census*, 1921

In Canada a religious census is taken at every regular census. Each man is asked what church he belongs to or prefers. The results of this kind of census taking is as follows:

CANADA RELIGIOUS CENSUS

Year	Population	Church Membership	Unspecified	Per cent Members
1891	4,833,239	4,752,972	80,267	98.3
1901	5,371,315	5,328,093	43,222	99.2
1911	7,206,643	7,174,490	32,390	99.5
1921	8,788,483	8,769,129	19,354	99.8

From this table we see that practically everybody in Canada reckons himself an adherent, if not a member, of some Christian Church.

Now, with regard to the Lutherans of Canada there is a great discrepancy between the census returns and the returns made by the Lutheran synods. G. L. Kieffer has shown that the census figures are more than four times as large as the membership lists of the congregations. That is to say, there are many Lutherans in Canada who have come from Lutheran lands and homes and regard themselves as Lutherans, but they have not joined any Lutheran congregation as yet.

The same condition no doubt holds good here. Of the 2,500,000 Norwegians in the United States, nearly all of them might reasonably be supposed to want to be called adherents of the Lutheran faith, but barely 500,000 are members of Lutheran congregations in 1925. Possibly four times that number would be classified as Lutherans if the United States followed the example of Canada and found out from each man at the census taking what religion he confessed. The religious census of the United States makes inquiry only into the communicant membership of the congregations. This will be seen from the following table:

UNITED STATES RELIGIOUS CENSUS

Year	Population	Church Membership	Unchurched	Per cent Members
1890......	62,947,714	20,612,806	42,334,908	32.7
1900......	75,994,575	27,700,804	48,293,771	36.4
1906......	84,562,000	32,936,445	51,625,555	38.9
1910......	91,972,266	34,517,877	57,454,389	37.5
1916......	102,431,000	41,936,854	60,494,146	40.9
1920......	105,710,620	42,140,807	63,569,723	39.8

The figures for 1900 are from the "Independent"; those for 1910 and 1920 have been compiled by H. K. Carroll; those for 1890, 1906 and 1916 are from the Federal Census. They all show that less than one-half of the population in the United States as listed on the books of the congregations. But the situation here is no doubt similar to that in Canada, namely, that if a census were taken of the faith of the individuals nearly everybody would belong to some denomination. In that event the number of Norwegian Lutherans would be much increased, possibly to 2,000,000.

d. *Baptists*

Concerning the Norwegian Baptists Dr. Henrik Gundersen writes: "There are in the United States and Canada 30 Norwegian churches with a membership aggregating about 2,000 members having the right to vote. But this number does not give the real number of Norwegian Baptists, as we confidently assume that there are just as many Norwegian Baptists in the American churches as those who belong to churches of the Norwegian Conference. Instances have occurred where whole churches, having been so much Americanized that they found it to their advantage to reorganize themselves as American churches. The Norwegian Baptists belonging to the General Conference contribute to their own local work about $30,000.00 per year, and more than $20,000.00 for missions and benevolence. They have church property valued at $152,000.00 with a debt of $10,000.00. In the Sunday Schools there are enrolled 1,500 children with 180 teachers. The Conference publishes a weekly paper, 'Missionæren,' and there is a book store conducted by the Conference at 3232 W. Wrightwood Avenue, Chicago. The Conference officers are: Rev. O. Larson, Minneapolis, president; Rev. J. Rovik-Larson, Eau

Claire, vice president; Rev. T. Knudsen, La Crosse, treasurer and secretary; Rev. O. Breding, Minneapolis, general missionary. Among ministers who should be remembered for efficient work are: J. B. Smith, N. K. Larson, C. W. Finwall, L. J. Anderson."

As an illustration of what up-hill work it is to start a Baptist congregation among the Norwegian Lutherans let us take the case of the Norwegian Baptist congregation at Decorah, as described by Dr. N. S. Lawdahl in his book, "De Danske Baptisters Historie i Amerika." At the conference meeting held at Newell in 1896 this thought was uppermost in the minds of the Baptists: "Iowa's 60,000 Norwegians for Christ." A missionary was chosen, Brother L. J. Andersen, of North Dakota, and the field was assigned, Decorah, the seat of Luther College, the capital city of the Norwegian Synod, the most stalwart of the Norwegian Lutheran synods. Andersen came and worked with zeal. There were six Norwegians in Decorah who had already joined the American Baptist congregation in town. These six, together with Anderson and wife, organized the Norwegian Baptist Congregation of Decorah in February, 1897. Andersen labored here three years and baptized four adult converts. In 1900 Brother Anderson reports that "God had given him also four souls in Calmar." He relates that he had tried to get an entrance into the territory of Glenwood, eight miles east of Decorah, and complains: "The doors and the hearts were closed against us, so that we scarcely got shelter on New Year's eve at 9:15 p. m." Martin Nielsen relieved Andersen in 1901, but met with the same hardness of heart. With tears he testified before his conference that he had been denied even water for himself and his beast as he went from farmstead to farmstead witnessing about his Master. Nielsen thought it was best to leave this citadel of prejudice and church forms to its fate. It were better to go to the heathen. So, in 1903, after six years of hard labor this field was abandoned.

e. *Methodists*

The annual report for 1924 of the Norwegian-Danish Methodist Conference is authority for the information herewith presented:

METHODIST PROGRESS

Work	1880	1890	1900	1910	1920
Pastors	24	48	66	56	62
Congregations	43	70	91	94	81
Members	2,266	3,902	4,640	4,984	5,356
Sunday School Pupils	848	2,799	3,378	3,035	5,132

The value of churches in 1924 was $586,000.00 and of parsonages, $181,200.00. Salaries for 1924 were $62,151.00 and gifts to charity amounted to $31,354.00. Between 1880 and 1924 31 pastors had gone to their reward. Of the 47 pastors in service in 1924 32 were born in Norway, 6 in Denmark, 2 in Sweden and 7 in America.

The first Norwegian Methodist congregation was that among the Sloopers at Norway, Illinois. Harry M. Peterson, the pastor now in charge, and H. T. Haagensen, Lutheran pastor at Stavanger, Illinois, have furnished the following roster of Methodist pastors for the period 1860-1925.

METHODIST PASTORS, NORWAY, ILLINOIS

Pastor	Term	Pastor	Term
Carlson, Erick	1860-1862	Danielson, H.	1891-1893
Westergren, W. O.	1862-1863	Peterson, J. J.	1893-1896
Lindquist, L.	1863-1866	Rosness, A. W.	1896-1897
Gundersen, Ole	1865-1866	Johnson, C. J.	1897-1898
Eckstrand, John H.	1866-1869	Hanson, Carl W.	1898-1902
Knutson, J. M.	1869-1872	Josephsen, C. H.	1902-1903
Hanson, C.	1872-1873	Hanson, Carl W.	1903-1905
Jensen, P.	1873-1876	Andersen, Arnt	1905-1907
Johanson, B.	1876-1877	Helliksen, David	1907-1908
Sanaker, Otto	1877-1880	Levin, Richard	1908
Wierson, O. A.	1880-1882	Hanson, Carl W.	1908-1909
Erickson, F. W.	1882-1883	Hofstad, Ottar	1909-1912
Tollefson, J. C.	1883-1885	Bagne, O. J.	1912-1916
Hanson, Eliot	1885-1886	Firing, O. T.	1916-1919
Munson, H. C.	1886-1887	Rohrsaff, O.	1919-1920
Jacobson, J. A.	1887-1888	Egeland, M.	1920-1922
Erickson, Andrew	1888-1889	Pedersen, C. E.	1922-1924
Pedersen, A. C.	1889-1891	Peterson, Harry M.	1924-----

In 1859 a church was built, 26x40 feet, at a cost of $1,500.00. During Sanaker's pastorate it was moved to Norway, where it now stands, remodeled. An addition to the main frame was built on; also a tower.

f. *Reformed Influence*

The influence of the Reformed denominations is no doubt much larger than the statistics of their church work in Norwegian would indicate. When Dr. Frederick Lynch visited Scandinavia in 1922 he found the church work there of a good Lutheran type and wrote in the "Christian Work," of which he is editor, that "Methodists and Baptists are looked upon as interlopers, and the people can not understand why they have come, and wonder why America sends them and Adventist and Pentecostal Brethren and other groups."

It is a part of history to record how these two large and distinctive church groups have lived together and influenced each other.

The Norwegian Lutherans believe that they have the Christian religion the way the Bible presents it in its truth and purity;

Lutheran Ladies' Seminary, Red Wing, Minn.
1894-20

*Some
Norwegian
Lutheran
Academies*

Pacific Academy, Parkland, Wash.
O. J. Ordal, President

*You May
Bend the
Sapling,
But Not
the Tree*

Park Region Luther College, Fergus Falls, Minn.
E. Wulfsberg, President

*Some
Norwegian
Homes
for the
Aged*

Aftenro Old People's Home,
Duluth, Minn.

New Building, Homme Old People's Home
Wittenberg, Wis.

*Cast Me
Not Off
in the
Time
of Old Age*

Norwegian Christian Home for Aged
Brooklyn, N. Y.

they therefore resent the idea that the Reformed churches should treat them as a foreign mission field that is shrouded in darkness. In its report for 1907 the Norwegian-Danish Conference does not deign to admit that the Lutheran churches in the Northwest can take care of the Scandinavians. There were 7,773 Lutheran congregations here, but they were all ignored as of no account. In the annual minutes of the Norwegian-Danish Baptist Church for 1908, it is reported that they have 300,000 people of their nationality in Minnesota. The report reads: "Therefore our privileges are great and our responsibilities stretch equally far. Others do not know our people's characteristics, and, therefore, we must win them." In 1921, at the Baptist convention held in Des Moines, a Baptist professor from Norway said: "The Norwegians discovered America. I ask the Baptists of America to come to Norway to discover the greatest missionary field in the world." His speech met with a round of applause. The Norwegians resent the idea that they are "heathens," "350 times as criminal as the native population of America," as a Methodist paper, "The Vanguard" (St. Louis), once put it. The charge is not true. The Census Report on Crime for 1904 shows that one out of 6,404 native-born Americans was in prison, but only one out of 13,139 of the immigrants of Scandinavia and Germany, Lutheran lands. The Norwegians were three times as moral and law-abiding as the average American citizen.

The influence of the Reformed churches on the Norwegians is not very great in this "foreign mission" work. It is greatest in an indirect way. Perhaps greatest through its books and papers. Thousands upon thousands of Reformed books are sold in the Lutheran book stores and occupy places of honor in the book shelves of pastors and lay people and are studied in the Lutheran schools. The Lutheran papers freely clip stories from the Reformed papers and portray the progress within the Reformed camps, with many a word of sympathy and appreciation. About 80 per cent of the material in the English Lutheran hymnals is from Reformed sources, and over 90 per cent of the songs sung in Sunday School are the compositions of Reformed poets and musicians. Much of the work of the Lutheran Church—in the Sunday School, at the expense of the parochial school, in the Bible school movement, in the young people's Luther leagues, in missionary, evangelistic and other church work, is clearly influenced by Reformed models.

Whether or not the Norwegian Lutherans are exerting a beneficent counter influence on their Reformed friends is harder to say. The Reformed will not buy Lutheran books or use Lutheran hymns or copy Lutheran ways to any great extent. The Lutheran Church has a message for the world, especially in a day like ours, when Modernism under many forms—Materialism, Spiritism, Evolution, Rationalism, etc.—lifts its horrid head. Concerning the Lutheran Church, the "New Reformation," a Reformed paper, says (November, 1924): "The Lutherans so far as we have been able to detect, know of no divided ranks. The Church named after the Hero of Worms is compact and solid for the Christ of God."

9. EDUCATION, 1890-1925

The fact that the Norwegian people of America have now entered the American stage of their sojourn is very forcibly brought out in the story of their schools. Never before have patriotic Norwegians and consecrated Lutheran Christians pleaded so eloquently for the support of the Norwegian schools, and never have they been maintained with so much difficulty.

The period started with practically every Norwegian believing in the whole school system as an absolute necessity—parochial schools for the children, academies for the youth, and colleges for young manhood and womanhood, besides the theological seminary for the training of ministers and missionaries, normal schools for the training of parochial teachers and deaconess homes for the training of deaconesses. In the faith of the fathers they founded a number of academies and colleges in the first half of this period, and, up to 1907, the attendance at these schools was steadily on the increase year by year.

But, beginning with 1907, the attendance has gradually declined and one precious school after another has given up the ghost and is no more. The Norwegian academies are going. A wind has passed over them, and they are gone; and the place where they stood shall know them no more. Such seems to be the sad educational tale of the American Period. They prospered nicely as long as the Norwegians were Norwegian-Americans, but they were starved out for want of students and other support as soon as the Norwegians became Americans. As Americans the Norwegians prefer to give their undivided support to the American school system. The American public schools are free, publicly controlled, tax-supported and non-sectarian. The system extends from the kindergarten to the university. It teaches everything except the cultural heritage of the immigrant and the Christian religion. It often blots out that heritage and robs one of his Christian faith.

The Academy

The friends of Christianity argue that the church academy is needed. The history of the Norwegian Lutherans cannot be fully understood except in the light of the views these Norwegians hold with regard to education. They hold as to the academy that

✝ ✝ ✝ ✝ ✝ ✝

Luther
Hospital,
Eau Claire,
Wisconsin

*

Millie A.
Jacobson,
Supt.

F. L. Trønsdal,
Fin. Sec'y

✝ ✝ ✝ ✝ ✝ ✝

✝ ✝ ✝ ✝ ✝ ✝

St. Paul
Hospital,
St. Paul,
Minnesota

*

J. E. Haugen,
Manager

H. G. Stub,
President

✝ ✝ ✝ ✝ ✝ ✝

✝ ✝ ✝ ✝ ✝ ✝ ✝

Fairview
Hospital,
Minneapolis,
Minnesota

*

O. S. Meland,
Rector

Jos. G. Norby,
Supt.

J. C. Hallum,
President

✝ ✝ ✝ ✝ ✝ ✝

it is needed in the American Period more than ever before. It is needed especially in early and middle youth, the high school age. Early and middle youth is the time of greatest bodily growth, and of greatest mental, moral and religious development. It is the age of confirmation, conversion, choice and character formation. It is the age of beginning religious indifference, skepticism and criminality. Nearly all are confirmed at this time of life. Over 80 per cent of the registered conversions are of people under 20 years of age. Choice of occupation is made in four cases out of five in the high school age. Character is best molded in early youth, for then there is greater plasticity than at any time

Why Destroy the Main Supports of Christian Training?

later in life. You may bend the sapling, but not the tree. Strike while the iron is hot. Most criminals get their start at this early age. All need moral and religious instruction of the right kind at this time. The public schools do not give, can not give, this instruction. Only a true Christian instruction can create a Christian conscience and faith, in short, a Christian character. Only the Christian academy can satisfy this inherent need. The homes, Sunday Schools and churches are not supplying this instruction adequately. Secular instruction alone during these four crucial years, especially if anti-Christian, which sometimes happens, is harmful to conscience and faith and conduct. The secular schools, by their very secular nature, not to speak of their anti-Christian spirit in many places, are de-Christianizing the land, no matter how much some of them try not to do so.

The Norwegian Lutheran academy has reached more Norwegian boys and girls than any other church school, and it has reached them at a more crucial time. It has furnished a preparatory training for theological study of nearly all the Norwegian pastors during the 75 year period, 1850-1925, while the colleges have trained only 27 per cent. The Norwegian Lutheran pastors have not been reared in the high schools and universities. If they had been, but few of them would have entered the humble but holy calling of the Gospel ministry in the Norwegian synods. The religious and national heritage of the Norwegians can not be transmitted through the public schools, for the only nationalism that the public schools will tolerate is that of America, and Eng-

Agnes M. Kittilsby
Principal, Unity School,
China

Anna E. Bagstad
Pacific University,
Oregon

Anna W. Wright
Principal, Clay School,
Minneapolis

land as the Mother Country. And the only religion that can legally be taught in the public schools is that of the Christian example of the teachers, which is often present and far-reaching in its influence, and yet not strong enough to counteract the steady trend toward secularization and religious indifference which secularization gives rise to. The system tends to weaken the distinctively Lutheran and Norwegian character of the Norwegians, to erase and efface these from their consciousness, to rob them of their heritage, which should be theirs for ever, and which should be their cultural contribution to America.

The Norwegian Lutherans founded 38 new schools during this period. Twenty of these are still alive, 18 have been discontinued.

New Schools Twenty-two were academies, of which one (Concordia) has become a college, and another (Park Region) was a college for a few years, but went back to the academy grade. Six of the academies have had to become junior colleges in order to keep alive.

Following is a list of the schools founded during this period:

School	Location	Years	Total Attendance	Synod
Concordia College	Moorhead, Minnesota	1891-....	11,111	United
Grand Forks College	Grand Forks, North Dakota	1891-1894	297	United
Lutheran Normal	Madison, Minnesota	1892-....	3,961	United
Park Region College	Fergus Falls, Minnesota	1892-....	5,934	Norwegian
Scandinavia Academy (now Central Wisconsin College)	Scandinavia, Wisconsin	1893-....	2,703	United
Mt. Horeb Academy	Mt. Horeb, Wisconsin	1893-1898	302	United
United Church Seminary	Minneapolis, Minnesota	1893-1917	2,124	United
Bethania College	Poulsbo, Washington	1894-1896	68	Free Church
Glenwood Academy	Glenwood, Minnesota	1894-1911	2,335	Norwegian
Pacific Academy	Parkland, Washington	1894-1917		
Lutheran Ladies' Seminary	Red Wing, Minnesota	1920-....	3,527	Norwegian
Jewell College	Jewell, Iowa	1894-1920	4,129	Norwegian
		1894-1918		
Pleasant View College	Ottawa, Illinois	1919-1922	4,069	Hauge
Norwegian Deaconess	Chicago, Illinois	1896-....	3,354	United
Clifton College	Clifton, Texas	1897-1900	471	United
Northwestern Bible School	Belgrade, Minnesota	1901-....	1,435	Norwegian
Grand Forks College	Grand Forks, North Dakota	1897-1901	70	Free Church
Albion Academy	Albion, Wisconsin	1900-1910	1,708	Norwegian
Gale College	Galesville, Wisconsin	1901-1918	999	Norwegian
Wittenberg Academy	Wittenberg, Wisconsin	1901-....	1,903	Norwegian
		1901-1913	1,357	Norwegian

School	Location	Years	Number	Affiliation
Northwestern Mission School	Grand Forks, North Dakota	1901-1903	30	Free Church
Wartburg Bible School	Belgrade, Minnesota	1901-1902		
Lutheran Bible School	Alexandria, Minnesota	1902-1906	70	Free Church
	Wahpeton, North Dakota	1903-1918	1,538	Brethren
Waldorf College	Forest City, Iowa	1903-....	5,617	United
Bethania College	Everett, Washington	1904-1917	732	Free Church
Oak Grove Ladies' Seminary	Fargo, North Dakota	1906-....	1,712	Free Church
Spokane College	Spokane, Washington	1907-....	1,994	United
Columbia College	Everett, Washington	1909-1919	751	United
Northwestern College	Velva, North Dakota	1910-1912	142	Norwegian
Camrose College	Camrose, Alberta	1911-....	1,006	United
Lutheran Bible School	Minneapolis, Minnesota	1916-1920	28	Eielsen
Outlook College	Outlook, Saskatchewan	1916-....	592	United
Luther Theological Seminary	St. Paul, Minnesota	1917-....	687	Norwegian
Lutheran Bible School	Chicago, Illinois	1917-....	3,500	Inter-synodical
Luth. Sunday School Institute	St. Paul, Minnesota	1919-1921	40	Norwegian
Luth. Miss. Training School	Minneapolis, Minnesota	1919-....	150	Inter-synodical
Canton Lutheran Normal	Canton, South Dakota	1920-....	844	Norwegian
Willmar Bible School	Willmar, Minnesota	1921-....	163	Free Church

38 schools (statistics up to 1922) 71,453

In addition to these new schools several of the older schools kept on functioning during a part or all of this period. Eight of these schools have been forced to the wall, and eight are still on duty, namely, the four colleges—Augsburg, Augustana, Luther, and St. Olaf, besides Luther Academy, Red Wing Seminary, and two deaconess schools.

Old Schools

Aaberg Academy 1888-1903
Augsburg Seminary .... 1869-....
Augustana College .... 1860-....
Bode Academy 1887-1902
Bruflat Academy 1889-1918
Luther Academy .... 1888-....
Luther College .... 1861-....
Luther Seminary 1876-1917
Lutheran Normal School 1889-1918
Lutheran Deaconess, Brooklyn ..... 1883-....
Lutheran Deaconess, Minneapolis .. 1889-....
Red Wing Seminary .... 1879-....
St. Ansgar Seminary 1878-1910
St. Olaf College .... 1874-....
Stoughton Academy 1888-1900
Willmar Seminary 1883-1919

Clifton Junior College, Carl Tyssen, President

From 1852 to 1922 the Norwegian higher schools have had a combined enrollment of about 150,000 students—7,000 at the theological seminaries, 20,000 at the colleges, 120,000 at the academies and normal schools, and 3,000 at the deaconess homes and Bible schools. As some students stay at the same school three or four, nay, even seven or eight years, the actual attendance of persons is considerably smaller. The combined enrollment at Luther College from 1861-1922, for instance, was 10,250, but the actual number of names was only 3,554. A careful estimate of the actual number of Norwegians who have attended the Norwegian higher schools arrives at the following result: Total,

Location of Norwegian Lutheran Schools. (Not on the map: Bruflat, Clifton, Brooklyn.)

72,000, 43,000 men and 29,000 women, 60 per cent men, 40 per cent women. There have been 2,400 at the theological seminaries; 6,000 at the colleges; 61,000 at the academies and normal schools; and 2,000 at the deaconess and Bible schools. That is, 3.3 per cent have studied theology; 9.2 per cent have been at college; 84.7 per cent have been taking secondary studies at academy or normal schools, and 2.8 per cent have been in attendance at deaconess homes or Bible schools. Over 80 per cent of these students are still alive.

The following tables illustrate and summarize the attendance at the Norwegian Lutheran schools by decades:

ATTENDANCE AT NORWEGIAN LUTHERAN SCHOOLS

Year	Academy	College	Seminary	Special	Total
1852.............	8	0	0	0	8
1862.............	41	4	10	0	55
1872.............	244	51	40	0	355
1882.............	388	121	89	0	598
1892.............	2,089	165	117	197	2,568
1902.............	2,864	335	159	531	3,889
1907.............	3,906	428	159	730	5,223
1912.............	3,249	572	179	669	4,669
1922.............	2,037	1,378	117	1,889	5.421

TOTAL ATTENDANCE AT NORWEGIAN LUTHERAN SCHOOLS

Decade	Academy	College	Seminary	Special	Total
1852-1861........	122	10	30	0	162
1862-1871........	1,130	242	218	0	1,590
1872-1881........	3,514	971	604	0	5,089
1882-1891........	10,384	1,243	1,022	400	13,049
1892-1901........	23,245	2,543	1,404	3,987	31,089
1902-1911........	32,407	4,083	1,621	6,621	44,732
1912-1921........	27,263	8,889	1,357	9,392	46,901
1852-1921........	98,065	17,981	6,256	20,310	142,612
Per cent........	69.0	12.6	4.3	14.1	100.0

By special schools are here meant deaconess schools, normal schools, ladies' seminaries, business schools and Bible schools. These are nearly all of secondary school grade, though they can not be strictly classified as academies.

The Lutheran Church is an educational church. She believes in the Christian training of the young, for childhood and youth *Other Lutheran Schools* are the most plastic and impressionable periods of life. "As the twig is bent, so the tree is inclined." "Train up the child the way he should go, and when he is old he will not depart from it." Her best leaders have advocated Christian education; her best members have been active in promoting schools of every sort that will make for knowledge of the Lord and His will. There are therefore many plans on foot to further Chris-

Attendance

Year	Academy	College	Seminary	Special	Total
1852	0	0	0	0	0
1862	41	4	10	0	55
1872	244	51	40	0	335
1882	300	121	89	0	598
1892	2009	165	117	197	2560
1902	2864	335	159	551	3909
1912	3249	372	179	669	4069
1922	2037	1378	117	1889	5421

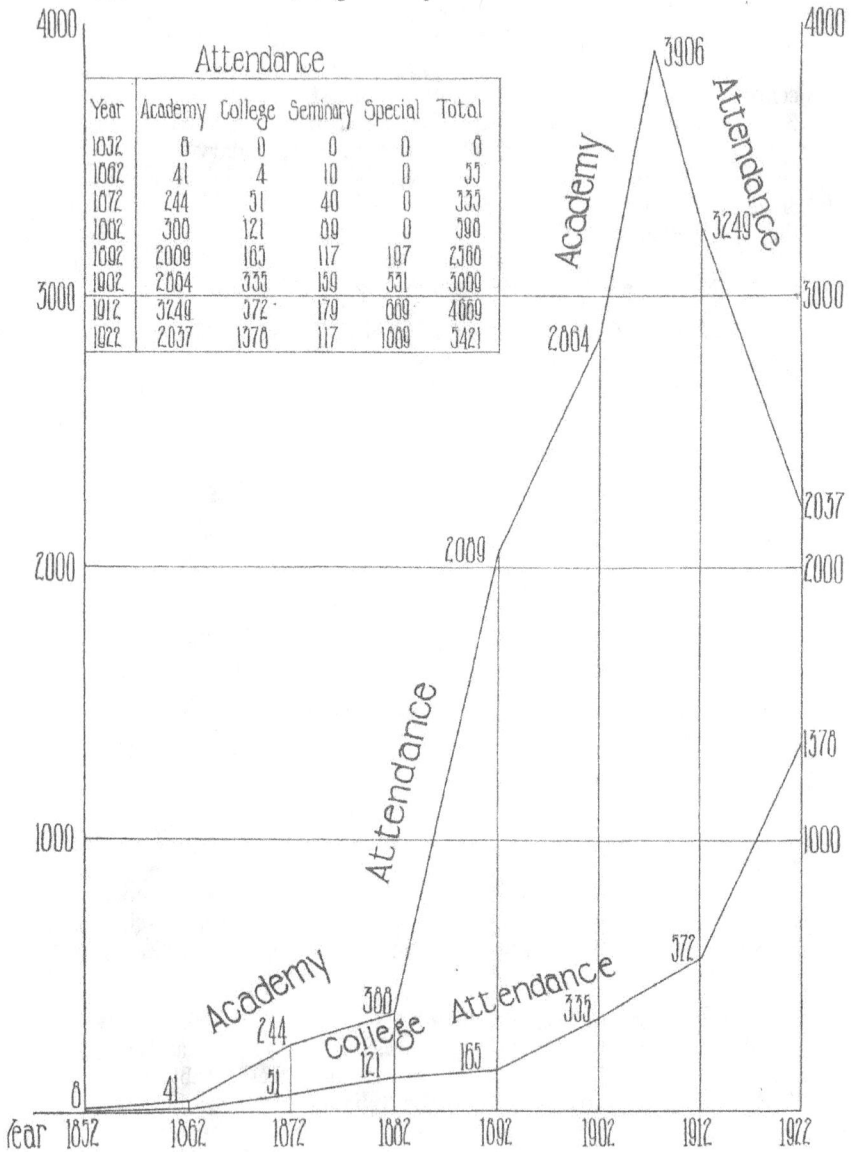

Attendance at Norwegian Lutheran Schools

tian education. In elementary education there are still men like
Svein Strand and Knute O. Løkensgaard, to plead for the old-time
parochial school, or vacation religious school. J. N. Andersen and
H. P. Grimsby are examples of men who work for the Sunday
School—how to utilize it and improve it. G. M. Bruce, L. P.
Thorkveen and Jacob Tanner have conducted Sunday School in-
stitutes. Orlando Ingvoldstad, A. B. Anderson and Marius Dixen
have established Bible schools. F. A. Schaffnit and C. K. Solberg
have been spokesmen for inner mission training, and Olaf Guldseth and H. B. Kildahl have been pioneers in making the deaconess
school understood. John Peterson and Gustav Amlund are typical
of those who try to teach through the Sunday School and parochial
school papers. N. M. Ylvisaker is promoting the Christian training
of the youth in the congregations through the Luther League. The
academies, colleges, seminaries and normal schools are active as
never before in teaching religion pure and undefiled.

a. *Lutheran Colleges*

The language, literature and history of Norway are taught
at all the academies, colleges and normal schools of the Norwegians. At Luther College the chief instruc-
Norwegian Studies   tors in Norwegian have been: Thrond Bothne,
1876-1882; Gisle Bothne, 1885-1907; Knut
Gjerset, 1907-1923; Ingebret Dorrum, 1923——. At St. Olaf
College, Th. N. Mohn, 1874-1899; P. J. Eikeland, 1900-1921;
and Ole E. Rølvaag, 1906——, are best known. John S. Nordgaard taught Norwegian at Augustana College from 1897 to 1923;
Carl E. Nordberg was Norse instructor at Augsburg Seminary
and St. Olaf; John H. Blegen, at Augsburg, 1885-1916; J. L.
Nydahl, at Augsburg, 1891-1920; J. L. Holvik, at Waldorf College, 1912-1919, and at Concordia College, 1923——. Eikeland,
Rølvaag and Holvik have written a number of grammars, dictionaries, readers, handbooks and other text books for the study
of Norwegian.

b. *State Universities*

The study of Norwegian and other Scandinavian languages
has also been pursued at a number of American universities and
colleges—New York University was the first to offer courses in
Scandinavian—in 1858. Paul G. Sinding, a Dane, was the instructor. The University of Wisconsin, in 1869 instituted courses
in Scandinavian, with R. B. Anderson in charge. He is the first
Norwegian to teach Norwegian at a state university. Cornell University that same year installed William Fiske as teacher in Old
Norse. Columbia began in 1880, Northwestern in 1882, Minnesota in 1884, Johns Hopkins in 1885, Indiana in 1885, Nebraska

in 1886, Harvard and Michigan in 1888, Yale in 1889; Bryn Mawr in 1890, North Dakota in 1891, South Dakota and California in 1892, Chicago in 1893, Leland Stanford and Princeton in 1894, Pennsylvania in 1895, Iowa in 1900, Kansas in 1902, Illinois in 1904, Washington University, Seattle, and Washington University, St. Louis, in 1912, Oregon in 1912, Utah in 1914, Smith in 1920, Texas in 1921, Colorado in 1922, Pennsylvania in 1923. Wellesley, Western Reserve, Ohio, Fargo and other schools have given courses in Scandinavian, both ancient and modern, language and literature. Minnesota has, of course, the largest attendance in the Scandinavian classes. Gisle Bothne is the head of the department and professor of Norwegian. Andrew A. Stomberg is professor of Swedish, succeeding Dr. John S. Carlson.

Dr. T. R. Running,	Dr. J. E. Granrud	Dr. L. M. Larson
Mathematics	Latin	History
University of Michigan	Univ. of Minnesota	University of Illinois

Some State University Scholars

Among Norwegians teaching Norwegian at state schools are: R. B. Anderson at Wisconsin, 1869-1884; Julius E. Olson at Wisconsin, 1884——. Olaus J. Breda, 1884-1898, and Gisle Bothne, 1907——, at Minnesota; George T. Flom, 1900-1909, and Henning Larsen, 1900——, at Iowa; George T. Flom, 1909——, at Illinois; Ole E. Hagen, 1892-1901, John R. Lavik, 1903-1906, Tollef B. Thompson, 1906-1918, at South Dakota; George T. Rygh, 1891-1895, Carl J. Rollefson, 1898-1903, and John O. Tingelstad, 1900——, at North Dakota; Olaus Dahl, 1891-1895, at Yale, and 1895-1897, at Chicago; Agnes M. Wergeland, 1896-1907, at Chicago; O. J. P. Widtsoe, 1920——, at Utah. These professors have all made good as teachers, lecturers, writers, exponents of Scandinavian culture, and scholarly representatives of the Norwegian people. They have not always been appreciated, and one reason for the lack of appreciation is, that their colleagues on the university faculties have had little or no acquaintance with the Scandinavian North, its language, literature, history, science and fine arts. The professor longest in the service is Julius E. Olson of Wisconsin. He has built up a strong Scandinavian department against many odds, and the appreciation which is voiced in the following letter from Dean C. F. Smith of the Graduate School at Wisconsin is well earned. The occasion for the letter was a public lecture that Olson had delivered on the poet Wergeland.

"My dear Professor Olson: I did not get over my stirring of spirit quickly last night, but lay awake a long time. I knew before that you were a good speaker, but I did not know till last night that you were one of the very chief interpreters of poetry in our midst, though I did know that you loved it. With a grateful heart I thanked God on my knees last night for what the evening seemed to open up for me. When you are discouraged, remember that it took fifteen years to win your way completely into my heart and judgment. You were here all the time, and I might have found it out long ago, but I didn't know, or hadn't taken the trouble. I beg your pardon . . . . I understand better now why more and more students want your lecture courses in Norse literature.   CHARLES FORSTER SMITH."

A complete list of the teachers and courses in Scandinavian at American universities has been compiled by Dr. Flom in "Iowa Studies in Language and Literature" (May, 1907) and "Skandinaven: Almanak og Kalender, 1925."

c. *High Schools*

During the years 1906-1910 Dr. J. N. Lenker and others began a campaign for the study of Scandinavian in the high schools and common schools of the Northwest. Lenker pleaded in writing and lectures for a three-language education—the language of the land, the language of the immigrant homes, and a language for professional purposes. A few common school districts introduced Norwegian, but only a few. In 1910 the high schools of Minneapolis were ready to try the experiment of offer-

Thrond Bothne   Maren Michelet   P. J. Eikeland, Litt D.
Luther College   Mpls. South High   St. Olaf College

Inspiring Teachers of Norwegian

United Church Seminary (now Luther Theological Seminary), in 1914
Dr. M. O. Bøckman, President

ing Norwegian and Swedish alongside of German and French.
And why should they not? Norwegian and Swedish are just as
good languages as are German and French. Norwegians and
Swedes outnumber the German and French in Minnesota and
surely have the right to get the kind of school subjects they want
their children to study, seeing that they are paying their share
of the taxes. Thus they reasoned.

Chicago Luther Bible School
Orlando Ingvoldstad, Founder and President

In 1917, after seven years of pioneer work, Miss Maren Michelet was able to report that she had sent out questionnaires to 168 high schools that were giving instruction in Scandinavian, and had received 73 replies. 43 schools, in seven states—Minnesota, North Dakota, Iowa, Wisconsin, Illinois, South Dakota, and Washington—gave instruction in Norwegian to 1,380 scholars, and 20 schools in 3 states—Minnesota, Illinois and Nebraska—gave instruction in Swedish to 918 scholars. The intense anti-foreign spirit during the World War checked the good work considerably. There was an almost insane hostility toward every foreign language, resulting in the abandonment of many Scandinavian classes. Since the armistice it has been very hard to get the interest in Scandinavian studies re-awakened. Dr. J. N. Lenker is as enthusiastic as ever, and Miss Michelet is still at her post, at South High, Minneapolis. Dr. Lenker is German-Scotch-Irish but his better half is Norwegian. He claims that the Scotch-Irish in him is of the Old Norse strain from Edinburgh. Mrs. Lenker, before her marriage, was Nora Cecilia Walstead, for many years president of the Walsh County Normal and Agricultural School in North Dakota and state rural supervisor of schools in California. This happy pair has a daughter, appropriately named Lutherin Lenker, in view of the fact that Lenker has been a translator of Luther into English and the author of "Lutherans in All Lands." Miss Michelet is the first teacher of Norwegian in any public high school in the United States. She is the author of a text book for high schools—"First Year Norse," which has run six editions already. She has edited Dr. Agnes M. Wergeland's works and written much on modern language instruction. Minneapolis is still the center of the agitation for the study of Norwegian in the high schools. The teachers in this subject in 1925 are: Maren Michelet, South High; A. C. Erdahl, Central High; E. Pauline Farseth, North High; and B. O. Eggen, Roosevelt High.

In 1915 the population of the United States was 100,725,000. The total enrollment in all schools, elementary and higher, was 23,113,931, or 22.9 per cent of the total population. *Norwegians in the Nation's Schools* 6.4 per cent of the school population attended high schools, 1.0 per cent attended colleges and universities, .7 per cent attended professional schools. Of the 565 standard American colleges and universities 92, or 16 per cent, were public institutions, tax-supported and controlled; 473 were private schools, founded and supported by some church or privately endowed. There are professors and instructors of Norwegian stock at more than 100 of these higher institutions. In the Appendix will be found a list of 50 universities and 50 colleges employing Norwegians and the names of a few of the Norwegian instructors in their faculties, together with their scholastic degree, principal subject and years of tenure. Of the 752,055 teachers in the elementary schools, about 2 per cent were Norwegian—an army of 15,000 school ma'ams.

Occasionally a Norwegian rises to the highest positions of trust in the teaching world. At least three men have occupied the office of state superintendent of public schools:

John G. Halland, superintendent North Dakota, 1897-1901.

Hans Andrias Ustrud, superintendent South Dakota, 1906-1910.

Garl Gustavus Lawrence, superintendent South Dakota, 1910-1914.

A number have been at the head of state universities, agricul-

R. B. Anderson, LL.D.   Julius E. Olson, B.L.   George T. Flom, Ph.D.
Univ. of Wisconsin   Univ. of Wisconsin   Univ. of Illinois
1869-1884   1884—   1909—

Famous Professors of Norwegian at State Universities

tural schools, normal colleges and other higher institutions of learning, as, for example:

Edward Olsen, Ph.D., president, University of South Dakota, 1887-1889.

Aven Nelson, Ph.D., president, University of Wyoming, 1912-1922.

John Andreas Widtsoe, Ph.D., LL.D., president, University of Utah, 1916-1921; also president, Utah Agricultural College, 1907-1916.

Ludvig Hektoen, M.D., Sc.D., LL.D., director, McCormick Institute for Infectious Diseases, 1902——.

Conrad George Selvig, A.M., president, Crookston North Western School of Agriculture, 1910——.

Harold Waldstein Foght, Ph.D., president, Aberdeen Northern Normal and Industrial, 1919——.

Carl Gustavus Lawrence, A.M., president, Springfield Normal, 1919——.

John O. Evjen, Ph.D., president, Mayville Normal, 1919-1923.
Carl C. Swain, Ph.D., president, Mayville Normal, 1923——.
Joseph Wist, A.B., president, Honolulu Normal.

Elsa Ueland, A.M., president, Carson College, Flourtown, Pa.

A considerable number are deans and departmental heads of great institutions. Of deans we have an example in Alfred Owre, M.D., D.M.D., C.M., dean of the College of Dentistry, University of Minnesota, 1905——. Other examples: Christian Peter Lommen, B.S., dean of College of Medicine, University of South Dakota, 1891——; M. Beatrice Olson, A.M., dean of women, University of North Dakota, 1922——; Frank Morton Erickson, A.M., dean of Ripon College, 1909-1914; Francis E. Peterson, A.M., director of extension work, Honolulu, 1924——.

| J. S. Nordgaard | George Sverdrup | J. U. Xavier |
| Augustana College | Pres., Augsburg Sem. | Pacific College |

During the first period (1825-1860) there was one private school—the Tank, at Green Bay, Wisconsin. During the second period (1860-1890) there were three private *Private Schools* schools—the Valder Business College and Normal School, Decorah, Iowa, (1888-1922), the Albion Academy, Albion, Wisconsin (1890-1900), and the Wraaman Academy, Minneapolis (1890-1897). During the third period (1890-1925), there have been at least 14 private schools. These are:

Mankato Commercial College, Mankato, Minnesota, 1891——.

Crookston Commercial College, Crookston, Minn., 1895——.

Humboldt College, Humboldt, Iowa, 1895-1914; Minneapolis, 1914——.

North Star Normal School, Minneapolis, Minn., 1895-1898(?).

Minnesota Normal and Business College, Minneapolis, Minnesota, 1898-1900.

Ronnei's Business College, Devils Lake, N. Dak., 1902-1906.

Skørdalsvold Night School, Minneapolis, Minn., 1902-1912.

Aaker Business College, Fargo, North Dakota, 1902-1923.

Norway Lake Domestic Science School, Norway Lake, Minnesota, 1904-1907(?).

Aaker Business College, Grand Forks, N. Dak., 1915——.

Elbow Lake Business College, Elbow Lake, Minn., 1902-03(?)

Monson Institute of Music, Brooklyn, New York.

Quam Practical Business College, Minneapolis, 1917—.

American Business College, Grand Forks, North Dakota, 1924.

The Mankato Commercial College was founded by J. R. Brandrup, who has been a teacher at the school and its president ever since 1891. It has had a good attendance and has given

L. J. Monson
Monson Inst. of Music

O. J. Hanson
Am. Bus. College

Hans H. Aaker
Aaker Bus. College

an excellent business instruction to thousands of young people. Brandrup was a teacher at Luther Academy 1889-1891.

The Crookston Commercial College was started by M. L. Tuve and Gabriel Loftfjeld in 1895. The attendance was so encouraging that they decided in 1896 to move to Minneapolis. The school continued under new managers. J. C. Sathre was president from 1896 to 1922. He was an M.S. from Valparaiso, an LL.B. from Minnesota. He was president of the Northwestern Commercial Schools Association, the Men and Religion Forward Movement, the Social Service League, etc. He died in 1922. There were six teachers and about 150 students annually. The school is continued under the management of E. M. Sathre, president; F. M. Sathre, vice president, and K. S. Sathre, secretary.

Humboldt College, Humboldt, Iowa, was started early in the '70s as a Unitarian school, but discontinued through lack of support. In the spring of 1895 Jens P. Peterson, commercial teacher at Jewell College, and his brother-in-law, August Leonard Ronell, register of deeds at Vermilion, South Dakota, re-opened the school on condition that the citizens of Humboldt would donate the property. The school opened in October, 1895, with only 30 students, but it had a hundred before the year closed. The available cash was only 87 cents, but yet it was found necessary to erect a dormitory—West Hall—in 1896. To make a long story short, inside of five years the school had four buildings and an attendance of more than 200 students taking work in sixteen departments. It was paying its expenses, although the tuition was only $33.00 for 40 weeks. The students came from ten different states, but most of them were from Humboldt and neighboring counties. Then like a bolt from a clear sky came the announcement that the college was to be assessed $40,000.00. In vain did Professor Peterson call the attention of the Board of Equalization to the fact that this was the only school of its kind in the

Mrs. Ida Picard   J. N. Brown   Mrs. Lena Dahl

Luther League and Missionary Leaders

state that was taxed. Plans were immediately taken to remove the school to some more favorable state. In 1914 the college buildings and eight acres of the campus were traded for Red River land, and the remaining 72 acres were sold for cash. The school then moved to Minneapolis, where it is now located on Washington Avenue, at Seven Corners, and is being conducted as a very successful business college. The school has done noble work. Among its graduates are such men as: A. O. Hauge, now president of the Iowa Trust and Savings Bank, Des Moines; Hans Flo, head of the Discount Department of the Federal Reserve Bank of Salt Lake City; John Lakness, manager of the Rocky Mt. Telegraph and Telephone Co., Ontario, Oregon; Bert L. Stringer, president of the Erie Business College; A. D. Cromwell, commissioner of education, Porto Rico, now professor of agriculture, West Chester Normal, Pennsylvania, was one of the most faithful of the teachers, 1896-1912. The staff of teachers numbered from 15 to 25 each year. Peterson is an unusually able business man, executive and teacher. Like so many other Norwegians in the '80s, he had received his college training and educational ideals at the Northern Indiana Normal School, now known as Valparaiso University. His wife, née Elizabeth Everson, has been a teacher at his school for 30 years. She took third prize in artistic shorthand in the Teachers' Blackboard Contest, conducted by the Order of Gregg Artists, 1917; took highest prize in the fifth annual contest, winning over 2,100 contestants from 41 states and countries, in 1919; took first prize in America, second in the world, in contests for school clubs on the "Gregg Writer," 1923. In 1924 one of her pupils, Minnie Mozeng, took first prize in world contest in which more than 8,000 contestants took part. Professor Peterson and wife can be found in the school room every school day of the year, summer and winter. A. L. Ronell has been a farmer at Minot, North Dakota, since 1906.

The North Star Normal was started in 1895 and conducted a

Humboldt College, J. P. Peterson, President

few years in the former Norw. Y. M. C. A. building at 1900 Riverside Avenue, Minneapolis. A. H. Faroe was the principal and E. M. Schelde assisted. A very promising start was made; but Professor Faroe died and Schelde laid down the work, removing to Austin, Minnesota.

The Minnesota Normal and Business College was conducted at 1700 E. Franklin Avenue, Minneapolis, 1898-1900, by M. L. Tuve and Gabriel Loftfjeld.

S. P. Ronnei conducted the Ronnei Business College at Devils Lake, North Dakota, 1902-1906. He had two assistant teachers and about 30 students. Ronnei has taught at Forest City, Iowa, 1897-1898; Jewell College, 1898-1900; Scandinavia Academy, 1906-1907; Buena Vista College, 1908; Sioux City, 1909-1914; Augsburg Seminary, 1915-1916; Osakis, Minnesota, 1917-1918; Willmar Seminary, 1918-1919; Grinnell, Iowa, 1919-1920; Augustana College, 1920-...... He is the author of the "Ronnei System of Business," 1913-1917.

Johannes J. Skørdalsvold maintained the Skørdalsvold Night School from 1902-1912, at first in the Nazareth Church, and later in a little school house of his own. English was the main subject taught. It happened that young people came to the school in the evening of the very day on which they arrived from Norway. The whole number of persons doing work at the school was about 1,500. Among the teachers were Samuel Garborg, a brother of the poet Arne Garborg, Amandus Norman, Inga Dahl and Thorwald Nelson. The school closed because the city offered the same grade of work free of charge. Skørdalsvold received his A.B. at Augsburg Seminary in 1881 and a B.L. at the University of Minnesota in 1888. He studied at the University of Berlin in

J. J. Skørdalsvold   Mrs. Elizabeth Peterson   J. P. Peterson

1889-1890. He was a teacher 22 years. Since 1918 he has been a proofreader at Augsburg Publishing House. Since 1881 he has been a newspaper reporter and correspondent, translator, editor, writer of poems, stories and magazine articles. The poem, "To Our Real Heroes," on page 512, is from his versatile pen. He has been a consistent temperance advocate and pacifist all his life and at all times a friend of the people in every political and social issue. He is a heavy stockholder and secretary of the Fremad Publishing Co., Eau Claire ("Reform"). His son Magne, student at the Minnesota Agricultural College, is the champion turner in the Middle West. His daughter Jennie, trained at Minneapolis, Chicago and New York, is one of the sweetest singers. His daughter Sigrid is dietitian and teacher at the Norwegian Daconess Hospital, Minneapolis, and has a knack for pulling her scholars through at the state examinations. His son, Peter Skurdalsvold, has three scholastic degrees, B.S., LL.B. and C.E. He is employed in the Schedule Department of the Twin City Rapid Transit Co. And Professor Skørdalsvold, as well as his wife, née Anne Romundstad, resembles Ibsen's "Terje Viken" in this that:

> On land or in sea, no quarrel he'd seek,
> From him, none of harm need fear.

Aaker's Business College, Fargo, North Dakota, was named after its founder, Hans H. Aaker. Professor Aaker, trained at Luther College and Valparaiso, has taught at Willmar Seminary, 1883-1888; Concordia College, 1891-1902; Aaker's College, Fargo, 1902-1923; Aaker's College, Grand Forks, 1907----. He has been mayor of Moorhead, candidate for Congress in Minnesota and for governor of the state of North Dakota; he has also run for congress in North Dakota as a Progressive. He was president of Concordia College, 1893-1902, and is one of the leading citizens of the Northwest.

The American Business College is a continuation of the Aaker's in Fargo. Oscar J. Hanson has taught business subjects

Upper row: Mrs. O. S. Reigstad, Mrs. H. B. Kildahl, Mrs. O. S. Meland
Lower row: Mrs. Edw. Johnson, Mrs. G. T. Rygh,
Mrs. I. D. Ylvisaker (President)
Miss Mathilde Rasmussen, Mrs. Jos. O. Estrem

at Crookston, Grand Forks and Concordia College 18 years. He bought Aaker's College in Fargo in 1918 and conducted it successfully for five years under the name Fargo Business College. He sold it in 1922 and started the Hanson Funeral Homes in Fargo and Grand Forks. As the school did not seem to flourish, Hanson bought it back. He has 400 students. He now runs three establishments and is a vigorous church worker besides, being also president of the Luther League of North Dakota.

A hundred higher schools in a hundred years! That is the mark reached by the Norwegians in America. Forty-one of these are still alive and in good health. Sixty-three *100 Schools* of them were founded by the Norwegian Lutherans alone, 12 by the Norwegian Lutherans in conjunction with other Lutheran nationalities—Germans,

Swedes, Danes. Seven were founded by Norwegian Methodists, Baptists, Congregationalists and Quakers. Eighteen were private ventures. The Norwegian Lutherans still maintain 26 alone and four in connection with other synods; the Reformed bodies have four; there are seven privately-owned schools still a-running.

Thirty-three of the schools were first located in Minnesota; 18 in Wisconsin; 12 in North Dakota; 13 in Illinois; 9 in Iowa; 4 in Washington; 3 in New York; 2 in South Dakota; and 1 each in Texas, Pennsylvania, Ohio, Missouri, Alberta and Saskatchewan. Several schools have moved to new localities with the moving population—Augustana moved from Illinois to Wisconsin, and from Wisconsin to Iowa, and from Iowa to South Dakota. Augsburg and Luther Seminary moved from Wisconsin to Minnesota; Bethania moved from Poulsbo to Everett, Washington; Lutheran Bible School moved from Wahpeton to Grand Forks, North Dakota; Augustana moved from Canton to Sioux Falls, South Dakota.

Augustana is the oldest school still in existence and holds the record for moving. Under Dr. C. O. Solberg's presidency it is taking rank as a leading college in South Dakota. Luther College is the next oldest and holds the record for conservatism and

Rev. L. C. Johnson and His Three Hand-written Bibles (Copied by himself — Norwegian Bible, 1,147 pages; English Bible, 1,032 pages; and German Bible).

wide-reaching influence. Dr. O. L. Olson is a worthy successor of Larsen and Preus. Augsburg Seminary is the third oldest, and is the oldest theological seminary and the most urgent in stressing the need of living converted, Christian lives. George Sverdrup, the president, is one of the best Hebrew scholars among the Norwegians. He has studied in the Holy Land. St. Olaf is the fourth oldest, was the first to establish co-education, is the largest and most modern. Dr. L. W. Boe's organizing talent will bring this school up to the highest standards of efficiency. Luther and St. Olaf are meeting all the requirements of the North Central Association of Universities and Colleges and are fully accredited; Augustana, Concordia and Augsburg are trying hard to meet the standards.

The youngest schools of the Norwegian Lutherans are the Bible schools—Chicago, 1917; Minneapolis, 1919; Miller, 1920; and Willmar, 1921. Although the idea of teaching the Bible to the children and youth goes back to the pioneer fathers and Martin Luther, the founder of their church, still the plan of these modern Bible schools is really borrowed from the Reformed denominations, especially from the Bible school leaders, Wm. Dwight Moody of Chicago, Reuben A. Torrey of Los Angeles and John Campbell White of New York. The movement itself is very commendable, for it emphasizes more Bible study and daily Bible reading, in short, back to the Bible as the only source and

Marius Dixen   Orlando Ingvoldstad   A. B. Anderson

rule of faith and works. Many Lutheran educators are hoping that all the Lutheran higher schools will give more attention to the reading and study of the Bible at first hand, while not neglecting the study of the catechism, Bible history, church history and other religious courses. Orlando Ingvoldstad, a student of White, is the founder and dean of the Chicago Lutheran Bible School. He has a good faculty and reaches out to upwards of 1,500 a year. The school has acquired property to the value of $400,000.00, free-will gifts. F. A. Schaffnit and J. A. O. Stub, D.D., are the founders of the Minneapolis Missionary Training School. C. K. Solberg is the president. The school is supported by the Lutheran Inner Mission Society of Minnesota and its chief aim is to train inner mission and parish workers. Samuel Miller, a Swedish Lutheran, is the founder and dean of the Lutheran Bible Institute, St. Paul. He is assisted by Dr. C. J. Sodergren, formerly a professor of theology at Augustana Seminary; A. B. Anderson, a pupil of Torrey's; Odd Gornitzka, a former Norwegian pastor at Seattle; and others. The management of the school does not solicit funds, but lays the case before the Lord, and He has so far furnished the necessary money. Marius Dixen, a graduate of Augsburg, is the dean at Willmar, assisted by Dr. B. P. Farness and others. God bless the Christian schools!

10. PUBLICATIONS, 1890-1925

The literary productivity of the Norwegians in America during the third period as far outstrips that of the second as the second surpassed the first. The writer made *The Press* a survey of the Norwegian periodicals in 1918 for Professor Rob. E. Park of the University of Chicago and the Carnegie Foundation. He listed 458 periodicals, distributed as follows:

PERIODICALS ACCORDING TO PERIODS

Periods	Secular	Cultural	Lutheran	Non-Luth.	Total
1847-1860	8	1	2	0	11
1860-1890	91	25	35	18	169
1890-1917	96	69	104	9	278
1847-1917	195	95	141	27	458

The list was not complete. A complete list in 1925 would bring the total up to 500 or more. This does not include the many local congregational papers or the county and city papers in English edited by Norwegians.

The increase in book production is even more significant than that of journalism. In the first period there was only one original book written here and printed here in America, namely, Krug's veterinary manual (1859). Eielsen's translation of the Catechism (1841) was published here and also reprints of a dozen Norwegian books. In the second period there were at least 115 Lutheran theological works and surely as many other books by Norwegians, as over 90 per cent of the books printed are secular. In the third period it has been estimated that the Norwegians have published approximately 3.500 books, or an average of 100 per year. In 1921, according to "Publishers' Weekly," January 28, 1922, the United States published 8,329 new books, or one book to every 12,600 inhabitants, and Norway published 949 new books, or one book to every 2,635 inhabitants. The Norwegians in Norway are, then, nearly five times as productive in book writing as the people of America. If the Norwegians of America maintain the average pace of book writing in America, they will produce 166 books a year. The estimate of 100, based on incomplete bibliographies, is, then, perhaps not too high.

The Norwegian periodicals have been classified as to place of publication, yar of beginning, year of discontinuation and circulation.

PLACE OF PUBLICATION OF PERIODICALS

State	Number of Periodicals Begun	Number of Periodicals Discontinued	Number Existing in 1917
California	9	7	2
Colorado	1	1	0
Illinois	61	50	11
Iowa	39	32	7
Massachusetts	1	1	0
Michigan	5	5	0
Minnesota	153	94	59
Montana	3	3	0
Nebraska	3	1	2
New Jersey	2	2	0
New York	22	17	5
North Dakota	41	35	6
Oregon	2	1	1
South Dakota	13	8	5
Texas	1	0	1
Utah	5	4	1
Washington	34	28	6
Wisconsin	58	51	7
Wyoming	2	2	0
British Columbia	1	0	1
Manitoba	2	1	1
Total	**458**	**343**	**115**

As to number of papers begun in any one year there was 1 accredited to 1850, 0 to 1860, 10 to 1870, 7 to 1880, 22 to 1890, 11 to 1900, 13 to 1910. As to number of papers discontinued in any one year, 1850 had 2, 1860 had 1, 1870 had 8, 1880 had 7; 1890 had 20, 1900 had 5, 1910 had 8. As to the age of the Norwegian papers in 1918:

AGE OF NORWEGIAN PAPERS

165 were 1 year old or less	10 were from 26 to 30 years
292 were 5 years old or less	9 were from 31 to 35 years
68 were from 6 to 10 years	4 were from 36 to 40 years
28 were from 11 to 15 years	9 were from 41 to 45 years
18 were from 16 to 20 years	3 were from 46 to 50 years
15 were from 21 to 25 years	2 were 50 years or more

The two papers over 50 years were "Skandinaven," Chicago, and "Ved Arnen," Decorah, both established in 1866. If we could reckon "Lutheraneren" with all its antecedents as one paper, then on the Conference side it dates back to 1870 ("Lutheraneren"); on the Hauge Synod side it dates back to 1869 ("Budbæreren"); on the Augustana side it dates back to 1866 ("Den Norske Lutheraner"); and on the Norwegian Synod side it dates back to 1851 ("Maanedstidende"). "Minneapolis Tidende" can also claim old age as it is a consolidation of several smaller papers of long ago.

As to circulation it was found that Minnesota had 185,000 subscribers to some Norwegian paper; North Dakota had 120,000; Wisconsin, 85,000; Iowa, 40,000; South Dakota, 35,000; Illinois,

H. O. Shurson
Sec'y, Trustee, N. L. C.

Joseph O. Estrem
Auditor, N. L. C.

M. E. Waldeland
Chm., Transportation

30,000; Washington, 30,000; New York, 10,000; California, 10,000; Michigan, 5,000; and Canada, 15,000; all other states, 50,000; total, 615,000. "Decorah Posten" led with 42,478 subscribers; "Minneapolis Tidende" had 33,505; "Lutheraneren," 32,193; "Washington Posten," 11,600; "Normanden," 8,375. Ayer's "Directory" reported 17,000 for "Skandinaven" in 1917; 28,000 for "Barnevennen"; 7,250 for "Duluth Skandinav"; 12,250 for "Sønner af Norge"; 15,000 for "Ungdommens Ven"; 13,000 for "Visergutten"; 19,000 for "Luthersk Børneblad"; etc. 89 per cent of the papers started have been in Norwegian only; 6 per cent have been in Norwegian and English; 5 per cent have been in English only.

The Norwegian Press, both secular and religious, has done nobly and deserves general support and appreciation. May it live and increase in strength and influence. As Shakespeare says in "Henry IV":

> And tidings do I bring, and happy joys,
> And golden times, and happy news of price.

Or, as Joseph Story put it in the Motto of the "Salem Register":

> Here shall the Press the People's right maintain,
> Unawed by influence and unbribed by gain.
> Here Patriot Truth her glorious precepts draw,
> Pledged to Religion, Liberty and Law.

Olaf Guldseth
Sec'y, Book Mission

J. Tanner, S.T.D.
Sec'y Elem. Christian
Education

Olaf Lysnes
Sec'y, Publication

During the first period (1825-1860), the Norwegians in America did not produce much literature because they were too busy making their living and getting their *Poetry and Fiction* bearings. What they did produce was largely the result of that innate and irresponsible craving for self-expression: "gjennem arbeidets gang en digtende trang," to use Bjørnson's happy phrase. That is, they simply had to write, work or no work. In a large measure this was true also of the second period (1860-1890), but in the third period (1890-1925), the Norwegians are pretty thoroughly Americanized, are in good circumstances, and have time to devote to literary pursuits. More of the young people go off to school to get a higher education. They take a greater variety of courses of study, and train themselves for every kind of profession and trade. They buy more books and papers, and read more than their fathers and grandfathers did, although it can not be truly said that they read more thoughtfully. The tiny brooklet of literature which trickled down through the Norwegian settlements of the first period swelled into a respectable brook in the second period, and now, in the third period, has become a mighty river fed by many streams, turning the wheels of industry, carrying the ships of commerce, purifying, refreshing and invigorating the lives of men. In this great republic there is also a republic of letters in which each one has freedom to speak up; there is an avenue to glory, possibly, at least an opportunity to influence one's fellow-men through letters. The Norwegians have been cultivating practically all the fields of literature during this period,—newspaper writing, books on all subjects, pamphlets and tracts, in English and in Norwegian.

The following poets, fifty in number, have during this period put on the market one or more volumes each, of Norwegian verse: Wm. Ager, B. Askevold, J. B. Baumann, J. A. Berven, Johs. S. Bothne, Laura Bratager, O. O. Brecke, C. O. Bruflodt, Ulrikka F. Gustav Melby, David Svennungsen and Ola J. Saervold are Sigurd Folkestad, Oscar Gundersen, Johannes Haarvei, John Hegg, L. Heiberg, O. S. Hervin, Anna M. Holter, Gjermund Hoyme, Johannes Høifjeld, O. J. Hustoft, Knut Kjøs, U. V. Koren, Olav Kringen, Thorleif Larsen, Ludvig Lima, Otto Lock, N. N. Minne, J. Mortensen, Anders Neppelberg, Jon Norstog, Johan Olsen, Johan Ovren, Palma Pederson, Franklin Petersen, Wilhelm M. Pettersen, Kristian Prestgard, J. Rasmussen, Olav Refsdal, R. O. Reine, D. G. Ristad, K. K. Rudie, P. Smedsrud, O. S. Sneve, C. K. Solberg, Peer O. Strømme, Knut M. O. Teigen and Agnes M. Wergeland. Anna Emilia Bagstad, Th. M. Bakke, Gustav Melby, David Svennungsen and Ola J. Saervold, are among the few who have published volumes of English verse.

Selecting fifty of the books of Norwegian verse, the writer

Jørgen Nordby
Eastern District

I. T. Aastad
N. Minn. District

C. J. Eastvold
S. Minn. District

found that quantitatively they contain 6,180 pages, or 123.6 pages to the book. Jon Norstog was the author of seven of these volumes, totaling 2,345 pages. Sigurd Folkestad had written three of the books, a total of 345 pages. Agnes M. Wergeland had written two of the books, 435 pages. The output of these three authors, then, comprised more than one-half of the pile examined. Qualitatively, these three are among the best Norwegian-American writers of poetry. Of the same rank in excellence some would place J. B. Baumann, Wilhelm M. Pettersen, D. G. Ristad, C. K. Solberg, C. O. Solberg, G. T. Rygh, J. J. Skørdalsvold, Knut M. O. Teigen and Peer O. Strømme. Johannes Høifjeld is a very promising writer, also. Jon Norstog stands head and shoulders above all the other Norwegian-American writers. He is Ibsenesque. He writes mainly in the Telemarken dialect. For that reason his books are not as popular as they deserve to be and do not find a great sale, but they are wonderful books. Their themes are Biblical. The workmanship is astounding. His first book, "Moses," published in 1914, was a drama in five acts, 531 pages. The second one, "Natten," 1917, a drama in five acts, had 135 pages. The third book, "Israel," 1917, a drama in twelve acts,

L. C. Foss
Pacific District

A. M. Skindlov
Rocky Mt. District

J. A. E. Naess
Pacific District

District Presidents of Norwegian Lutheran Church

' N. J. Løhre   Erik Waldeland   G. T. Rygh, Litt.D.
Sec'y, Norw. Luth. Ch. Treas., Norw. Luth. Ch. Pres., English Assoc.

comprises 885 pages. The fourth book, "Joseph," was an epic
poem of 135 pages, issued in 1918. The fifth book, "Tone," 1920,
a drama of 270 pages. The sixth, "King Saul," 1920, a drama of
208 pages; and the seventh "King David," 1923, 181 pages; also
"Kain," a drama, said to be a very large work. The work of
Norstog is more remarkable in view of the fact that he is
a farmer and that he not only writes his books, but he sets the
type, prints them and binds them with his own hands. His
wife is Inga Bredesen, a daughter of the pioneer pastor of
Stoughton, Adolf Bredesen. She has an A.M. from the University
of Wisconsin, is a former fellow of the American-Scandinavian
Foundation, and has been teacher of Norwegian in the Minneapolis
Central High School.

Ola J. Saervold, in 1894, while a student at Luther College,
published an epic poem, "Erling," which gave promise of much
good poetry from his pen. Saervold, unfortunately, did not continue the work of writing poetry. He became a journalist and
lecturer. He returned to his home at Strandvik, Norway, in 1899,
and took up the work of running his father's farm according to
American farming methods. He was somewhat disappointed at

H. C. Holm   I. D. Ylvisaker   N. N. Bøe
Iowa District   N. Dak. District   S. Dak. District

District Presidents of Norwegian Lutheran Church

the results, and returned to America. He is now a globe trotter, journalist and lecturer. Gustav Melby is the most prolific and successful of the Norwegians writing poetry in English. His first book, "The Seamless Robe," is a collection of lyrics appearing in 1914. The next one, entitled "King St. Olaf," is a drama in five acts, published in 1916. Number three "The Lost Chimes, and Other Poems," is a fine bouquet of lyrics, 1918. The fourth volume, "Twilight," is a collection of lyrics from 1921. Success to thee, Rev. Gustav Melby!

A large number of people have written occasional verse, and the Norwegian-American Press is pretty well dotted with short poems of this kind. Here are:

> Roses red and violets blue
> And all the sweetest flowers that in the forest grew.

And yet, many of them are destined like the wild rose to blush unseen, unless some lover of poetry takes the time to gather them into appropriate volumes, such as, Kristian Prestgard's "Norske Kvad" and Ludvig Lima's "Norsk-Amerikanske Digte i Udvalg," or, could not each one who has been writing occasional verse, collect what he himself has written, such as Peer Strømme fortunately did with his fugitive poems before he died? Strømme's little volume, "Digte," contains only 84 pages, but is worth its weight in gold, being the best selection of poems from the long literary career of this remarkable man. Strømme was the Mark Twain among the Norwegians, and, though his life was full of hard knocks, he was always the optimist, and his poems reflect the struggle between light and darkness in his own life, but, as Dryden says, in his "Art of Poetry":

> Happy, who in his verse can gently steer
> From grave to light, from pleasant to severe.

Fiction has the same place among the Norwegians as among the rest of mankind. It is the most popular style of writing ever invented. Story telling has always been popular and the desire is deep-rooted in all of us to hear some new thing, and to tell again something deserving remembrance. By fiction is here meant any story, short or long, true or false, real or imaginary, romantic, realistic, naturalistic, idealistic. The Norwegian writers have not plunged headlong into fiction writing. The modern novel and the short story are relatively quite recent types of literature, although story telling is as old as the race itself. The Norwegians seem to have hesitated in taking up this new form. During this period, however, a goodly number of them have been trying their hands at novel writing, and it is quite easy to list at least 100 names of Norwegians who have published works of fiction. Here are fifty names: Wm. Ager, A. E. Anderson, J. W. Arctander, B. Aske-vold, B. Aslagsson, J. A. Bergh, H. Bottelson, Laura Bratager,

Ulrikka F. Bruun, O. A. Buslett, Dorthea Dahl, Lena Dahl, P. C. Danielson, Hans A. Foss, M. Falk Gjertsen, G. T. Hagen, Haldor J. Hanson, Thor Helgesen, Albert Houeland, Ole Hustoft, Simon Johnson, H. B. Kildahl, J. N. Kildahl, Gunnar Kleven, Olav Kringen, A. P. Lea, John O. Lie, Otto Lock, F. Lunde, J. E. Løbeck, H. Løvik, A. H. Mason, E. L. Mengshoel, Jon Norstog, Torkel Oftelie, O. O. Odegaard, O. Br. Olsen, Palma Pederson, Franklin Petersen, Olav Refsdal, Jacob Rivedal, Sigv. Rødvik, O. E. Rølvaag, N. N. Rønning, Ole Shefveland, Peer O. Strømme, K. M. O. Teigen, T. K. Thorvilson, D. J. O. Westheim, J. B. Wist.

Ole E. Hofstad   Nels N. Tøsseland   S. O. Simundsen

(Hofstad baptized, Tøsseland confirmed, Simundsen married the author)

The author took down from his shelves 100 volumes written by 84 Norwegian-American novelists. These books had a sum total of 17,908 pages, or 179 pages per book. They were all in Norwegian. In the front rank of these Norwegian writers, he would place Waldemar Ager, Hans A. Foss, Simon Johnson, O. E. Rølvaag, N. N. Rønning, Peer O. Strømme, Knut M. O. Teigen, and J. B. Wist. The two Kildahls never really tried to write stories. They are theologians and churchmen busy with a multiplicity of duties, but they have done everything well that they have attempted to do, including, of course, their one attempt to tell something in story form. J. N. Kildahl's "Naar Jesus Kommer ind i Huset," has been one of the most widely read books published by a Norwegian, as popular as Peer Strømme's "Hvorledes Halvor Blev Prest." Kildahl's book has been translated into English and bears the title "When Jesus Enters the Home." H. B. Kildahl's book, "His Workshop," is not quite so pretentious, but makes good reading. If the popularity of a person is to be judged by the character of editorials written about him during his life and at his death, and by the number of poems which at his death are lovingly placed like floral emblems upon his coffin, then it is quite evident that no Norwegian-American has been more beloved than was Dr. John Nathan Kildahl.

This period bore a fruitful harvest in religious literature in both languages. At least a thousand important books in most branches of theology were written by Nor-*Religious Books* wegian - Americans. Quite extensive bibliographics of these can be found in O. M. Norlie's "Norsk Lutherske Prester i Amerika, 1843-1915," "Lutheran World Almanac for 1922," and "Cumulative Catalog of Lutheran Books in the English Language."

T. O. Tolo
A country pastor
Locust, Iowa

H. B. Thorgrimsen
An Icelandic pastor
among the Norwe-
gians, N. Dak.

O. S. Reigstad
A city pastor
Minneapolis, Minn.

There has been considerable activity in all departments of thought. A few illustrations will suffice: In *biology,* including botany and zoology, are such writers as Hanna *Secular Books* C. Aase, H. T. K. Agersborg, I. E. Melhus, J. P. Munson, Aven Nelson, P. O. Okkelberg, C. O. Rosendahl and Leonhard Stejneger.

In *physics* such names as H. A. Erikson and L. O. Gröndahl.

In *chemistry*: Edward X. Anderson, E. O. Ellingson, P. M. Glasøe, L. M. Henderson, C. M. Knutson, J. C. Olsen and F. W. Woll.

In *astronomy*: John A. Anderson.

In *geology*: Thomas M. Dale, F. W. Sardeson and Knud Throndsen.

In *ethnology*: F. I. Monsen.

In *physiology*: Ole O. Stoland.

In *medicine*: Ludvig Hektoen, F. Voss Mohn, Carl M. Roan, M. N. Voldeng.

In *dentistry*: Alfred Owre and Erling Thoen.

In *agriculture*: Peter Hendrickson, T. A. Hoverstad, James Johnson, Carl W. Larson, J. A. Widtsoe.

In *business*: S. P. Ronnei and Harry R. Tosdal.

In *military science and life*: Alfred Wm. Bjørnstad and Granville Gutterson.

In *law*: John W. Arctander, Henry Gjertsen and Lauritz Vold.

In *sociology*: H. C. Anderson, B. A. Arneson, J. E. Granrud, A. Furuseth, Ole Hanson, A. J. Lien, M. Mikkelsen, R. S. Saby, Chas E. Stangeland, T. K. Urdahl and Thorstein Veblen.

In *temperance*: Gustav Eide, H. A. Foss, B. B. Haugan, J. L. Nydahl, Elias Rachie, J. J. Skørdalsvold and Andreas Wright.

In *library science*: Thorstein Jahr and Thorvald Solberg.

In *art and architecture*: Olaf Glasøe, J. E. Granrud, Michael Mikkelsen and A. M. Sundheim.

In *travels*: J. A. Berven, K. B. Birkeland, P. O. Langseth and W. M. Pettersen.

In *philology*: A. R. Anderson, L. I. Bredvold, A. E. Egge, P. J. Eikeland, Nils Flaten, George T. Flom, Andrew Fossum, L. O. Fossum, Knut Gjerset, S. N. Hagen, J. A. Holvik, Thorleif O. Homme, Maren Michelet, O. M. Norlie, J. A. Ness, O. M. Peterson, O. E. Rølvaag and A. M. Rovelstad.

In *literary criticism*: S. B. Hustvedt, Hanna Astrup Larsen, Henning Larsen, O. M. Norlie, Julius E. Olson, Oscar L. Olson, M. B. Ruud.

In *domestic science*: Lilla Frich.

In *engineering*: M. C. Ihlseng and Peder Lobben.

In *mathematics*: J. O. Eiesland, Hans Dalaker, Peter Field, Peder Lobben, Martin A. Nordgaard, A. L. Nelson, Theodore R. Running, Oswald Veblen and Edvard Skille.

In *statistics*: Carl G. O. Hansen, John Hjellum, John Koren, O. M. Norlie and Oscar H. Reinholt.

In *education*: David A. Anderson, David E. Berg, H. W. Foght, Martin Hegland, Andreas Helland, C. B. Larson, Knut Løkensgaard, O. M. Norlie, Sven Strand, O. A. Tingelstad and L. A. Vigness.

In *musical theory and history*: Maja Bang Hoehn, F. Melius Christiansen, John Dahle, Knud Henderson, Erik Jensen, O. M. Norlie, Peter H. P. Rydning.

In *history*: W. I. Brandt, H. W. Elson, B. J. Hovde, M. L. Hansen, Paul Knaplund, Laurence Marcellus Larson, Bert L. Wick.

In *Norwegian history*: R. B. Anderson, A. O. Barton, Theodore Blegen, Juul Dieserud, John O. Evjen, A. O. Fonkalsrud, Andrew Fossum, Knut Gjerset, John O. Hall, Carl G. O. Hansen, Einar Hilsen, J. Hjellum, H. R. Holand, J. O. Hougen, T. A. Høverstad, P. P. Iverslie, Thorstein Jahr, Hans Jervell, J. S. Johnson, O. S. Johnson, P. O. Langseth, Gabriel Loftfjeld, A. E. Norman, O. M. Norlie, Halvor Skavlan, Harry Sundby-Hansen, A. M. Sundheim, Knut Takla, Martin Ulvestad, Andrew A. Veblen and J. U. Pedersen.

In *Norwegian church history*: J. A. Bergh, Adolph Bredesen, N. C. Brun, K. O. Eittreim, John O. Evjen, Halvor Halvorsen, Andreas Helland, O. M. Norlie, E. M. Stensrud and K. B. Birkeland.

In *psychology*: Julius Boraas, E. M. Broen, C. D. Larson and O. M. Norlie.

Lack of space prevents any adequate story of the publication houses. The Augsburg Publishing House is the largest, but a dozen or score of other concerns are just as **Publishing** worthy of honorable mention, as: The Luther-**Houses** an Free Church Book Concern (since 1920 called the Lutheran Free Church Book Concern), the K. C. Holter Publishing Co. (1890-1923), the Christian Literature Co., the Lutheran Publishing House, the Waisenhus Press, the John Anderson Publishing Co., the John G. Mohn Publishing Co., the J. J. Fuhr Publishing Co., the Norrøna Publishing Co., the Hauge Synod Book Department, and many others.

Augsburg Publishing House, Minneapolis

A few remarks about Augsburg Publishing House will indicate the character of the work of most of these concerns. Back of its foundation is the belief in the power of the written word, especially the Bible. Almost every synod, society and institution feels the need of an official organ, reports, periodicals, books, pictures, etc., and with this need comes the demand for a printing house.

Augsburg Publishing House was incorporated in 1890 and was the printery of the United Norwegian Church. It was a union of two older establishments—from Northfield and Minneapolis, and a third, at Rushford, ceased also to exist through this union. The managers of Augsburg have been: Lars Swenson, 1890-1904; Erik Waldeland, 1904-1917; A. M. Sundheim, 1917——. The House employs about 100 men and women in its offices and shops, and is also the headquarters for the officials and boards of the synod that operates it, since 1917 the Norwegian Lutheran Church. It is a very busy place day and night and the center of the Norwegian Church. It is no doubt the most important spot in the Norway of America. In 1914 it was said in the Jubilee book of the United Norwegian Church that the output of Augsburg every week varied from 50,000 to 100,000 pounds of printed matter. It is the most productive Norwegian printing shop in the world. In 1890 its net valuation was $16,404.97; in 1913, $208,776.48; and in 1925, $465,731.94. In 1891 its net profits were $2,399.54; in 1913, $22,948.26; in 1924, $29,677.45. Its total income in 1900 was $56,892.87; in 1919 it was

$512,599.31—$189,913.92 for books, $221,786.30 for job work, and $100,899.09 for papers. It is rated by Dun as a concern conservatively worth more than $1,000,000.00 and has Dun's highest rating as to credit. Several have been connected with the institution over 20 years: A. M. Sundheim and J. A. Anderson, 35 years; Erik Waldeland and Alfred C. Haugen, 27 years; Oscar C. Fremo and Nels Johnson, 23 years. The following are heads of departments:

A. M. Sundheim, manager, 1890—; P. A. Hovland, printing manager, 1924—; A. J. Anderson, mgr. book department, 1890

J. A. Bergh	Theodore C. Blegen	L. Lillehei
Hospital Missionary	Professor of History	Theologian and
and Historian	and Librarian	Author

(1884)—; Einar Josephsen, mgr. advertising dept., 1920—; O. C. Fremo, office mgr., 1902—; R. Skabo, circulation mgr., 1924—; Ed. Bergum, shipping mgr., 1915—; George Lindstrom, billing mgr., 1908—; H. G. Meyer, composing room mgr., 1923—; A. Bergsøbrenden, chief Norwegian proofreader; J. J. Skørdalsvold, chief English proofreader; Fred Carlson, press mgr.; W. E. Taylor, folding mgr.; Phil. Greffin, binding mgr.; Lawrence Johnson, paper stock mgr., 1916—; Nels Johnson mailing mgr.

A. M. Sundheim was born in Valdres, Norway, Oct. 25, 1861. Came to America in 1878. In 1879 he entered the printing world. Was publisher at Madison, Wis., and San Francisco, Cal. In 1890 he became asst. manager at Augsburg; in 1917, manager. He has been treasurer and president of the Valdris Samband, the Lutheran Publishing House Managers' Assn.; treasurer of the Norwegian-Danish Press Assn., the Mindegaven Assn., and the General Council of Bygdelags. He has been a good member of Bethlehem Cong., Minneapolis, having held many offices of trust. Every task in his hands is handled conscientiously. He has been found faithful in little things and in great. He has wide cultural interests, as is shown, for example, by the Christmas annual, "Jul i Vesterheimen," which he has edited since 1911. There have been 100 attempts to establish a Norwegian cultural magazine in America and nearly all have failed through lack of support. Sundheim, with his stubborn perseverance, keen business sense and fine artistic taste, has made "Jul i Vesterheimen" an international event. He is a lover of the out-door life, and there are few wild spots in North America that he has not seen. On May 22, 1925, two of his children, Marcus and Borghild, were elected members of the Phi Beta Kappa at the University of Minnesota, the highest scholastic honors conferred by the University. His oldest daughter, Marie, also attained to this distinction. As a friend he is faithful and true.

N. N. Rønning, the manager of the Christian Literature Co., was born May 17, 1870, in Telemarken, Norway. Emigrated, 1887. Started to go to school at Faribault. They looked him over and put him in the kindergarten. The 17-year-old boy was tall and the teacher did not know what to do with his legs. After due consultation with her superintendent she promoted Nels to 1st grade. He was brighter than he looked, so he kept on advancing a grade a day until he reached the high school. When spring arrived he was in the senior class. He has the distinction of having completed nine grades in one year, and of becoming president of the senior class and licking the biggest bully of the school. He is a Master of Arts from the University of Minnesota, has been editor of Holter's publications since 1899 and also business manager. Is interested in Sunday schools, Luther leagues, foreign missions, evangelization, charity work, etc. A wide awake man, a great force for good. His "Experiences of a Newcomer," "Bare for Moro," "Abraham Lincoln" and "Gutten fra Norge" are samples from his fruitful, brilliant pen.

Waldemar Ager, editor of "Reform," has found time to conduct the Sigvald Qvale Norwegian declamatory contests. Mrs. Anna Qvale established a legacy for such contests, in memory of her son. Over 200 contests have been held.

It is considered an honor to write a good book; it should be considered an honor to go out and sell it as a book agent. The general public does not give the book agent
Book Agents a very glad hand and the Norwegian people have been slow in trying to sell their wares through agents. They even hesitate to place their books and papers in their own city and school libraries.

Augsburg Publishing House is the largest publishing house of the Norwegian people and the biggest publishing plant in Minneapolis, and yet it is a question whether the Minneapolis City Library has a single book published by this great house by and about Norwegians. It is largely the fault of the Norwegians themselves who are a modest people, and do not demand that their literature be placed in public libraries. Canton, S. Dak., is a strong Norwegian community, no finer in the state. The City Library was presented with 103 volumes of Norwegian classics. The Library refused to accept books in the Norwegian language —year 1920. The Norwegians meekly acquiesced. They make up 80 per cent of the population in that town. Occasionally, some Norwegian man or woman feels the call to become an agent canvassing books and papers. It is part of the work of the Church to do so, it is a noble and needed calling. This history has pictures of three such agents—F. L. Trønsdal, Julius J. Hopperstad and Taaraand Vik. Trønsdal was trained as a lawyer, but saw the

| G. B. Wollan | J. E. Løbeck | T. C. Wollan |
| Journalist | Bible Teacher | Mathematician |

need of getting Bibles into every home, so he has dedicated his life to this work—and temperance speaking. Hopperstad, a refined poet and choir director, spent 40 years of his life as circulation manager of "Decorah Posten" and "Lutheraneren." Taaraand Vik, a parochial school ma'am, is an exceptional agent. She secured 1,172 new subscriptions to church papers and sold 2,435 "Menighetskalenders" (a $10.00 work) in 1918-1922, while working only part time. G. O. Oudal, Minneapolis, has the largest second hand theological book store in America, if not in the world. Theological works in all languages.

A few years ago, when Harding's speech at the funeral of the unknown soldier was heard by wireless in San Francisco, the people marvelled. Now the novelty has worn off, for nearly everybody has his radio. But radio is just as marvellous today as if it were new. So it is with the printed word. That, too, is a sort of radio, and thousands of years ago, books flashed the greatest messages around the world and across the centuries. Books are more wonderful than radio or movie or phonograph. The moving pictures of the past are thrown upon the screen of our minds through books. The sweetest rhythms of long ago are sung to our inner ear.

11. Foreign Missions, 1890-1925

The Norwegian Lutherans have never been anxious to proselyte among other Christian denominations. They have, however,

• Dr. T. R. Chow and Family,
Kioshan, China
*A Christian
Daughters Seem As Good to Him
As Sons*

distinguished themselves for their missionary zeal among those who do not have the Gospel. Leif Erikson was sent to Greenland by King Olaf Trygvasson to Christianize it, and he succeeded. Except for this work which had to be performed, he might have become a permanent settler in Vinland, which he discovered. Hans Egede came to Greenland in 1721 as a missionary, 72 years b e f o r e William Carey, the Baptist, went as a missionary to India. The oldest Protestant mission in the world was the Norwegian mission among the Lapps, begun while Luther was still in the heat of the battle for a more Biblical religion and a more Christian order of things. The Norwegian Missionary Society, organized in 1842, is one of the most successful missionary organizations in the world.

The Fields

The Norwegian Lutherans of America began to support foreign m i s sions almost as s o o n as t h e y w e r e organized into synods. P. A. Rasmussen announces in his "Kirkelig Tidende" (Church Times) for April, 1859, that he had received $118.00 in 1857 and $223.02 in 1858, which he had forwarded to the Hermannsburg and Leipzig Mission societies. The synods did not at first have their own foreign mission fields. They supported societies already existing. The Norwegian Synod aided

Abraham, the Malagasy, Reading
His Bible

the Norwegian Missionary Society in Madagascar and Zululand, and the Missouri Synod in its work among the Indians and Negroes. The Augustana Synod sent its contributions to the General Council East India missions. The Conference aided the Norwegian Missionary Society, and this caused the Norwegian Synod to withdraw its support and align itself with the Schreuder Mission in Zululand and Natal. In 1878 a Jewish mission society was founded by J. P. Gjertsen and Sven Rud Gunnersen, called the Zion Society for Israel. It began work in Egypt and Palestine, but especially in Russia and the United States. The United

Norwegian Mission Church at Manambaro, Madasgascar

Church in 1892, and the Lutheran Free Church in 1895, secured their own mission fields in southern Madagascar. The Norwegian-American China Society was organized in 1890, and a few years later its fields in Honan and Hupeh were taken over by the Hauge Synod and the United Church. The Lutheran Brethren established themselves in Honan in 1902; the Norwegian Synod, in 1912; and the Lutheran Free Church, in 1914. The Santal Mission of the Northern Churches, which had been begun by Børresen and Skrefsrud in Santalistan, India, in 1867, began to receive weighty support from the Norwegian Lutherans of the United Church and the Free Church, especially after 1893, when a Santal Committee was elected to represent the United States. The Norwegian Synod began work among the American Indians of Wisconsin in 1884; the Eielsen Synod began in 1893. The Norwegian Synod sent its first missionary to the Eskimos of Alaska in 1894.

From 1891 to 1901 the Norwegian Synod kept a missionary stationed at Salt Lake City to win back the Mormons to Lutheranism. Three attempts have been made to start a mission in the Near East—in 1878 at Jerusalem, by the Zion Society for Israel; in 1895 to 1909, at Urmia, Persia, by the Chaldean Mission Society; in 1910 at Soujboulak, Kurdistan, by the Evangelical Lutheran Orient Mission Society. Since 1915 the Sudan Mission Society has labored zealously for the planting of the Gospel in Madagascar, Zululand and Natal, South Africa, and the Sudan, West Africa. The Jewish work is still conducted by the Zion Society. The Norwegian Lutheran Church has assigned the work among the Eskimos, Indians and Negroes to its Home Mission Board.

Erik A. Søvik   Daniel Nelson   O. R. Wold, D. D.

Foreign Missionaries to China

P. A. Rasmussen, Laur. Larsen, Ole Waldeland, John P. Gjertsen, Sven R. Gunnersen stand among the first Norwegian-American exponents of foreign missions. **Mission Leaders** Hans Martin Sæterlie has served longest as secretary of the Foreign Mission Board —since 1904. He has written several books on missions—"Til Guds Riges Fremme" (1910), "Madagaskar" (1912), "The Foreign Missions of the United Church. 1890-1915" (1917). He has edited two mission papers (1895-1904) and has furnished the church papers with news of the foreign mission work for 30 years. Another prominent mission promoter is the Rev. J. R. Birkelund, M.D., who has been an emissary and secretary of the Board of Foreign Missions of the Norwegian Church since 1917. He was born in Denmark, has been a missionary in Japan (1892-1897, 1900-1902), a home missionary in Chicago (1891-1892) and Wisconsin (1902-1905), a city missionary in Chicago (1905-1917), and a mission inspector in China (1912-1913). Lars Lund, Elroy, Wisconsin, was the treasurer of the foreign missions of the Conference, 1881-1890, of the United Church 1890-1917, and of the Zion Society, 1881-1924. Peder Tangjerd was a good friend of the missions and mission treasurer of the Norwegian Lutheran

Church 1917-1923. Professor Georg Sverdrup started the Madagascar mission movement among the Norwegian-Americans. He supported it with great energy through the mission paper "Gasseren." John H. Blegen, professor at Augsburg, has been treasurer of the foreign missions of the Lutheran Free Church and also of the Santal Committee since 1893. He has edited "Santalmissionæren" since 1897 and is the author of a history of the Zion Society for Israel (1903) and a bird's-eye-view account of the world fields white unto harvest—"Al Verden for Kristus" (1910). Professor Andreas A. Helland, of Augsburg Seminary, has been the secretary of the Lutheran Board of Missions of the Lutheran Free Church since 1907 and has written valuable contributions about the Madagascar missions. Lars Lillehei has taught missions at Wahpeton, Grand Forks and Augsburg and has writ-

M. A. Pedersen   T. L. Brevig   M. J. Stolee
Bihar, India   Teller, Alaska   Ft. Dauphin, Mad.

ten a mission book entitled "Arbeidere in Vingaarden" (Workers in the Vineyard), 1912. Michael J. Stolee was a missionary and superintendent at Ft. Dauphin, Madagascar, 1901-1909, and has been a professor of missions at the United Church Seminary, St. Paul, 1911-1917, and Luther Theological Seminary, 1917-..... Mrs. T. H. Dahl founded the Women's Missionary Federation and Mrs. I. D. Ylvisaker is now at the head of this very useful organization. These are but a few of hundreds and thousands of mission friends in the Norwegian Lutheran synods, who are working and praying:

> Savior, sprinkle many nations,
> Fruitful let Thy sorrows be!
> By Thy pains and consolations
> Draw the gentiles unto Thee!

The statistics of the foreign missions are vibrant with life. The small sums of the '50s and '60s represent great sacrifices and much love on the part of the pioneer givers. There has been a happy increase in the general and special knowledge churchmen have of missions, in the number who give and the average annual

Expenditures

donations. In the period 1868-1872, the Norwegian Synod contributed $4,015.22, or about 2 cents by each baptized member yearly; in the period 1918-1922, the Norwegian Lutheran Church contributed $1,653,196.17 to its own fields in China, Madagascar and South Africa, or about 80 cents annually per capita. In 1922 the Norwegian Lutheran Church reported an income of $449,245.00 for foreign missions; the Lutheran Free Church reported $39,807.00; the Lutheran Brethren, $12,927.00; these three synods, a total of $501,979.00. If we add the Eielsen and Norwegian Synods, the Santal, Orient and Sudan missions and the Zion Society, the sum total will amount to over $600,000.00, or $1.25 per baptized person for foreign missions. Add to this the work done by the Norwegian Methodists, Baptists, Congregationalists and members of other Reformed branches, and the sum will become quite respectable.

The expenditure brings good returns. The converts were few and far between at first. The Norwegian Missionary Society labored in Zululand from 1842 to 1858—

Results

16 long years—before it was able to report a single convert. But the news of this one Baptism—of the Zulu maiden Umatendwase—inspired M. B. Landstad to write the well-known Norwegian hymn "Opløft dit Syn." Similarly, the work of the Norwegian-American missionaries in China, Madagascar and elsewhere at first was rather meagre in converts. But in 1922 the Norwegian Lutheran Church alone had 2,997 converts who had been baptized that year, 392 who had been confirmed, 11,825 who had communed, and a total membership of 36,071, served by 71 ordained missionaries from the Norwegian Church in the United States, assisted by 8 unordained men, 57 single women missionaries and 67 married women. There were 960 native men preachers and teachers and 208 native women workers. There were 26 main stations and 272 out-stations. The work had steadily advanced—the missionaries had advanced upon their knees. They had lived through the Boxer Raid and the World War in China, the French persecution and the Malagasy rebellion in Madagascar. The Gospel has triumphed; the doors are now open.

Mention should be made of a few of the earliest missionaries sent out from the Norwegians in the United States. The following

Early Mission Heroes

ing table does not include the men sent out from Norway, but supported by the Norwegians in America, such as: Nils Astrup (1883), Hans J. S. Astrup (1884), Carl

Døving (1883), and Carl S. Otte (1882), of the Norwegian Missionary Society in South Africa.

Missionaries	Years	Lands	Synods
Hogstad, Johan Peter ...	1887-1911	Madagascar	Conference United Church Free Church United Church
Tou, Erik H.	1889-1903	Madagascar	Conference United Church Free Church
Isolany, Gabriel N.	1893-1901	Madagascar	United Church
Sanders, Ole B.	1893-1902	Madagascar	United Church
Pedersen, P. A. G.	1893-1900	Madagascar	Free Church
Halvorson, Peter C.	1896-1914	Madagascar	United Church
Høigaard, Jonas R.	1896-1901	Madagascar	Free Church
Skaar, Johannes J.	1896-1902	Madagascar	United Church
Nestegaard, Ole S., Jr. ...	1890-1902	Hupeh and Mongolia	China Society
Nelson, Daniel	1890-....	Honan	China Society United Church Norwegian Church
Netland, Sigvald	1890-1896	Honan	China Society
Rønning, Halvor N.	1891-1908	Hupeh	China Society
Landahl, Carl W.	1896-....	Hupeh Honan	Hauge Synod Norwegian Church
Stokke, Knut S.	1896-1921	Honan	United Church Norwegian Church
Wold, Oscar R., D.D. ...	1898-....	Hupeh	Hauge Synod Norwegian Church

Theodor C. Meyersohn was the first missionary among the Jews. He worked in Egypt and Palestine, 1881-1882, and in Russia, 1882-1913. Another Jewish missionary was Dr. Rudolf

A Group of Preachers in Zululand

H. Gurland, missionary at Odessa, Russia, 1896-1905, author of "I Tvende Verdener" and other mission tales. Jewish missionaries in America include the following: Paul Werber, Baltimore, 1882-1896; E. N. Heimann, Chicago, 1894-1918; Isadore Schwartz, Chicago, 1918-....; Johan A. Eliassen, Chicago, 1907-1921; Anders H. Gjevre, New York, 1900-1903, Minneapolis, 1913-....; John Resnick, Minneapolis, 1917-1924; Ole Waldeland, emissary, 1895-1903; John J. Breidablik, emissary, 1903-1913. C. K. Solberg is the president of the Zion Society for Israel. The Norwegians have not forgotten the Jews, as the chief butler forgot Joseph in the prison. The mission among the Jews is in places very successful. The work of Gurland in Russia, for example, bears comparison with that of the New Testament times.

R. H. Gurland   Axel Jacobson   A. H. Gjevre
Jewish Missionary   Indian Missionary   Jewish Missionary

Tollef L. Brevig was the first missionary to the Eskimos (1894). Erik O. Mørstad was missionary to the Indians at Wittenberg, Wis., 1884-1886, and to the Indians at Carter, Wis., 1893-1915. The work is continued at Wittenberg by Axel Jacobson, 1888——, and at Carter and Soperton by Louis Adolf Dokken, 1913——. The Pottawattomie Tribe among which Dokken works is anxious to hear the Gospel. Nils J. Bakke, a Norwegian, was preacher and teacher among the Negroes of the South, 1877-1920. Osa A. Lawrence, a Negro preacher, joined the Norwegian Lutheran Church and worked for a year (1923-1924) among the colored people of Minneapolis. The Eskimo, Indian and Negro missions are now under the home mission board.

Nor have the Norwegians forgotten the Mohammedans. They are of all non-Christians the nearest to the Christian faith and the most hostile. However, even they submit to the beloved yoke of Christ. In 1895 Nestorius George Malech, an archdeacon in the Old Evangelical Apostolic Church of the East, commonly called the Nestorian Church, prevailed on Norwegian Lutherans to support him as a missionary at Urmia, Persia. In 1898-1899 Mons O. Wee was sent by the friends of this cause to investigate conditions in Persia. In his book "Fra Undersøgelsesreisen" (1900) he reported unfavorably concerning this mission but, nevertheless, it was continued until 1909, when Ludvig O. Fossum, Ph.D., after a three years' experience as missionary in Urmia also advised that the mission be not supported. Dr. Fossum thereupon turned his attention to the Mohammedans. He offered his services to the Evangelical Lutheran Orient Mission Society and became a missionary among the Mohammedans at Soujboulak, Kurdistan, Persia, in 1911. Dr. Fossum was a linguistic genius truly exceptional. He learned a language or dialect almost without effort. He created the written language of Kurdistan. He wrote grammars, dictionaries and school books, translated Luther's catechism, Christian hymns and the New Testament into Kurdish. His wonderfully romantic and noble career would fill a book in the relating, a book that would hold a creditable place in any series of stories about missionary heroes. Fossum died October 10, 1920, 41 years of age, but his work will go on. The boards of foreign missions report that they have more candidates, men and women, who are willing to go to the foreign mission fields than their funds permit them to send. The day of the Viking raids is past and gone; the day of the pioneer settlement is no more; but the sons of the Vikings ought to do well as missionaries (Ps. 110:3).

> Up! the ripening fields ye see,
> Mighty shall the harvest be;
> But the reapers still are few,
> Great the work they have to do.

12. HOME MISSIONS, 1890-1925

By home missions in general is meant the gathering and establishing of congregations in the home land, and the aiding of these congregations in securing pastors and **General** teachers. Historically, it has worked this way, that each mission group after organizing itself into congregations and synods, began to help the immigrant brethren of the same nationality, also to organize themselves into congregations and to secure pastors and teachers. The Germans took care of the scattered Germans, the Swedes did likewise for the Swedes, the Norwegians for the Norwegians, and so on. The first congregational work was carried on exclusively in the mother tongue of the immigrant. Later on, after these people had become somewhat anglicized, they began slowly to use English at the church services and to reach out to bring into the fold men of other nationalities who were unchurched. The synods using foreign languages most exclusively have sought to build up their constituency from the immigrants of their own nationality and their children. The synods now using English predominatingly seek to win for their denomination the unchurched and the unconverted people from all nations and classes about them.

The term home missions is used also to designate the work among people of non-Christian races within our own land. The *Special* missions among the Eskimos of Alaska, the Indians of Wisconsin, and the Negroes, were formerly rated as foreign mission work, but are now more properly classified as home mission work.

West 9.1%

East 8.5%

South 1.1%

Canada 3.7%

Northwest 77.4%

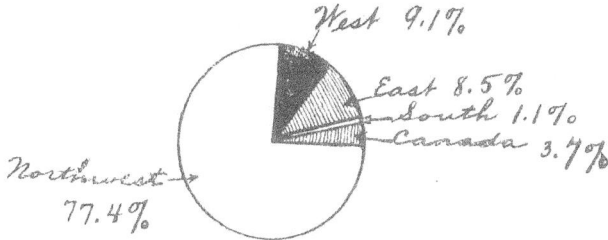

Distribution of Norwegians by Sections, 1906

The Jewish missions within this country as carried on by the Zion Society and supported by the Norwegian synods, can be thought of as home mission work, being in the home country. The home mission board also has charge of a great deal of work which more properly belongs to the inner missions.

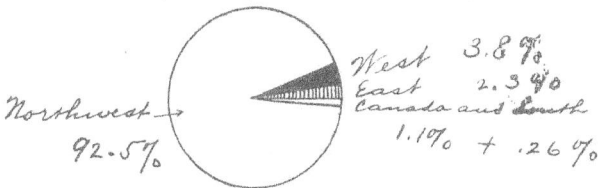

Northwest 92.5%

West 3.8%

East 2.3%

Canada and South

1.1% + .26%

Distribution of Norwegian Lutherans by Sections, 1906

As examples of this work may be mentioned: Evangelistic work, city mission work, slum missions and settlements, camp missions, hospital missions, university missions, work for soldiers and sailors, prison and reformatory mission work, Bible and tract distribution work among the blind, deaf and epileptics, seamen's missions, immigrant missions, and the like. Much, and sometimes all, of this work is now being done by home mission boards, although the attempt is made from time to time to shift it over to inner mission boards and charity workers.

The home missions among the Norwegians go back almost to the beginning of synodical work. Home mission work was, of *Organization* course, extensively performed by every pioneer pastor, but the work was not organized under committees and boards before the

Oluf Glasøe
Supt. Home Missions

Ole M. Anderson
Evangelist

Ole L. Kirkeberg
Advocate of Norse
Culture

synods were established. These committees and boards would look over the field, select competent men to go out and organize congregations and raise funds to pay the home mission pastors. Of the 7,500 Norwegian Lutheran congregations which have been established in the United States, no doubt at least 7,000 have been established under the direction of home mission committees and boards. The difference between a committee and a board is not neces-sarily great and often not very clear. In general, it may be said that a board has greater responsibility and is more carefully chosen and permanently organized. Beginning with 1890, the United Norwe-gian Church immediately planned a vigorous home mission work and appoint-ed a home mission super-intendent, whose sole duty was to travel over the whole field, organize con-gregations, find workers and direct the work. The following men ably filled this position in the United Church: N. J. Ellestad, 1891-1900; H. C. Holm, 1901-1906; Oluf Glasøe, 1906-1914; G. A. Larsen, 1914-1917.

Bethesda Slum Mission, Brooklyn, N. Y.
It Cleaned Out the Slum

The work increased to such an extent that in 1904 it was found necessary in the United Church to appoint a salaried secretary for the joint foreign and home mission board. The work of this office increased by leaps and bounds, and in 1910 two paid secretaries were elected, one for the foreign mission board and one for the home mission board. H. M. Sæterlie served as secretary for the joint board. Olaf Guldseth was secretary for the home mission board of the United Church from 1910-1917. Carl Severin Berthinius Hoel has been secretary of the home mission board of the Norwegian Lutheran Church since 1917. The Nor-

A class of Indians just confirmed, Wittenberg, Wis.

wegian Lutheran Church does not maintain the office of mission superintendent. In lieu thereof it has nine district presidents and nine district home mission committees looking after the home missions in their respective districts. There is also an English Association taking charge of the English interests and the establishment of English Lutheran congregations. B. J. Rothnem is the missionary among the state institutions for deaf and dumb at Sioux Falls; H. O. Bjørlie has a similar position at Faribault, Minn.; P. C. Birkelo is in charge of the immigration mission at the Norway House, 92 Columbia Heights, Brooklyn, N. Y. In 1867 the Norwegian Synod had established a seamen's mission in New York. C. S. E. Everson was pastor for the Seamen's Mission, 1876-1878, and a member of the immigration committee, 1888-1917. Emil J. Petersen was immigration missionary in New York City, 1889-1919. The United Church appointed Tobias

A Memorial to Fugleskjel at St. Olaf College

Ole O. Fugleskjel

A soldier of Uncle Sam and a soldier of the Cross. Born July 10, 1868, in Freeborn Co., graduate of St. Olaf College, 1894, and of the United Church Seminary, 1909. Had been a soldier in the U. S. Army. Became a pastor in 1909 and froze to death Dec. 6, 1909, in the woods near Clementson, Minn., while on his way to a preaching appointment. He was found sitting down with the open Bible in his hands.

In the Cross of Christ I glory . . . .

Tjørnhom immigrant missionary at Ellis Island, 1906-1910. In his wake Christen Westermoe, T. A. Lillehei and Iver Tharaldsen have met the newcomers at Ellis Island. Seamen's Missions have been maintained at San Francisco, Seattle, Boston, Philadelphia and Galveston for many years. In San Francisco the work was organized by C. M. Hvistendahl, 1870-1875; L. A. K. Carlsen took charge in 1875-1879 while serving Our Savior's Scandinavian Church. He preached to the sailors one thousand times, distributed many thousand tracts, papers and books, visited thousands of ships and sick sailors. The pastors following him have been: O. N. Grønsberg, 1890-1900; A. H. Lange, 1890-1896, 1900-1902; L. A. K. Carlsen, 1902-1912; T. C. Satra, 1912-1913; E. S. Belgum, 1913-1914; and O. N. Grønsberg, 1913—. From 1902 to 1912 this mission was visited by 175,000 Norwegian sailors. It distributed 80,000 letters and over one million dollars in money.

The Seattle Seamen's Mission is now conducted by E. B. Slettedahl; the Galveston Mission, by Johan Olsen; the Boston Mission, by Oddmund Nielsen; the Philadelphia Mission was in charge of A. W. Hvistendahl, 1907-14. The Seamen's Mission of Norway conducts mission of Norway coteaoinnuod sion stations in Philadelphia, Baltimore, New York, Mobile, Pensacola and New Orleans. Secretary C. S. B. Hoel has a number of evangelists at work, notably: H. N. Rønning, T. Tjørnhom, E. L. Scotvold and Johan Olsen. The home mission work in Alaska among Norwegians is now in charge of John Flint, Petersburg, and C. K. Malmin, Ketchikan; among the Eskimos it is conducted by the three deaconesses Anna Huseth, Mabel Lien and Magdalene Kleppe besides Leonard Sulooguak. The Indian mission at Wittenberg is conducted by Axel Jacobson, superintendent, and T. M. Rykken, pastor.

Meet Miss Eskimo

The smaller synods—Lutheran Free Church, Norwegian Synod, Lutheran Brethren, Eielsen Synod—are actively engaged in home mission work, as are also the Methodists, Baptists and Congregationalists. The Congregationalists, known as the Norwegian-Danish Evangelical Free Congregations in America, have established a mission loan fund of $100,000.00 for the purpose of church extension. Since 1884 they have grown from nothing to a group of 60 congregations, chiefly in the large cities, with a printing press in Chicago, a Bible school, including academy, seminary, business and music courses, at Minneapolis, an orphanage at Fort Lee, N. J., and another in Chicago, a large share in the Scandinavian Alliance Mission, which has an annual budget of $120,000.00 and labors in China, Africa and South America, besides Denmark and Norway.

The contributions to the home missions in the early decades of the church work were rather small owing to lack of systematic organization. In 1868-1872 the Norwegian Synod raised only $2,878.46 for this *Expenditures* cause. Most of the home mission work was performed by the individual pastors without any record being made at the central office. From 1873 to 1882 the Norwegian Synod collected $26,000.00, the Conference, $6,000.00, and the Augustana Synod, $3,000.00 for home missions. In 1920 the Norwegian Luth. Church contributed $263,989.00 to home missions; in 1922, $263,998.00. In 1922 the Lutheran Free Church home mission budget was $46,000.00; that of the Eielsen Synod was $2,280.00.

There is, as stated before, a great discrepancy between the number of Norwegian Lutherans on the church books and the actual number of Norwegian Lutheran adherents. This fact has been brought out by *Literature* the Canadian census and other studies. O. M. Norlie published in 1909 a statistical study entitled "The United Church Home Missions." In 1919 he edited Oluf Glasøe's "Omsorg for Sine Egne" (Care for One's Own). Of the many who have written on the home mission situation in the church periodicals, no one has written more instructingly and inspiringly than Supt. Glasøe. In this day of rapid Americanization and religious indifference such home mission literature has been of great guiding influence both to boards and officers and the rank and file of congregational supporters.

13. Charities, 1890-1925

Charities, or inner missions, is an organized effort to promote the spiritual and bodily welfare of the destitute and the indifferent who are, at least nominally, within the church. Chris-

tianity is a missionary religion. Christ, its founder, commanded
His disciples to preach the Gospel to every creature and to be His
witnesses. He Himself set the example. The Church has ever
since had its work to do and Christians gladly follow in His footsteps, not least in emulating His works of mercy.

Human needs are so multitudinous, human labor is so diversified, therefore it has been found expedient also to organize the
work of charity according to some sort of classification. There
is the care of children, for example, through orphanages, home
finding societies, day nurseries, slum schools, kindergarten, country holidays for the city poor children, etc. There is the care of
the aged through old people's homes, rest homes, relief funds and
pensions. There is the care of the sick through hospitals, institutions for defectives, convalescent homes, deaconess work, volun-

J. A. Wang	A. Oefstedal	N. A. Stubkjær
Supt., Homme	Rector, Chicago	Supt., M. Luther
Orphanage	Deaconess Home	Orphanage

teer work, flower missions. There is the care of the stranger
through hospices, immigrant missions and homes, diaspora missions, seamen's missions and homes, river and canal boat missions,
employment bureaus, shelters for homeless, tramps, etc. There is
the saving of the lost through juvenile courts, Magdalene homes,
temperance work. There is the care of family through colonization efforts, building aids, housing reforms, temporary loans.
There is the work of training charity workers, deacons and deaconesses, Bible readers and teachers, colporteurs, evening schools
for working men and women. There is last, but not least, the
work of evangelization through regular evangelistic sermons, tent
missions, slum missions and settlements, midnight missions, camp,
railroad and factory missions, hospital missions, university missions, work among soldiers and sailors, prisoners and reformatory
inmates, Bible and tract distribution, colportage, free libraries and
reading rooms, mission by posters and pictures, Sabbath observance, and the like. Charity work is not only almsgiving. It
is concerned with teaching the Gospel and to this adds the labor

of Christian love wherever sin has left its tracks, or is likely to do so, in order to relieve, renew and prevent. It uses the Word and the Work as its two hands of service.

The Norwegians, both Lutheran and Reformed, have been laboring in this field, even before they organized their first congregation. Christian charity affects even the state so that it relieves the Church of much of its load of helping the pauper, the defective and the sick. The first Norwegian to organize charity work institutionally was Even J. Homme, who, in 1881, laid out the town of Wittenberg, Wisconsin, and there in the wild woods founded the Homme institutions according to the spirit of Wichern

Rev. and Mrs. A. Vatne
(In charge of Sarepta Old People's
Home, Sauk Center, Minn., of the
Lutheran Brethren)

and the plan of Francke. He built up one branch of this work after another—an orphans' home, an old people's home, a normal school and academy, a printing press, Sunday school and young people's papers, books, almanacs, tracts. From that day the work has expanded to include every kind of charity work mentioned in the classification above. In the Norwegian Lutheran Church the budget for charities in 1922 was $451,671.00, or $1.05 per member. A good deal of money raised does not pass through the synodical budget, not even through the treasury of an institution, the left hand does not know what the right hand doeth in a great deal of this charity work. If we add the local to the synodical charities then the annual benevolences of the Norwegian people will surely amount to respectable sums beyond the million dollar mark.

The charities of the Norwegian Lutheran Church of America for 1922, based on incomplete returns, were as follows:

Institutions	Employees	Inmates	Property	Income
Orphanages	85	820	$972,180	$370,495
Home Finding	17	313	24,023	17,467
Hospitals	625	54,749	3,673,232	956,231
Hospices	10	6,991	166,500	15,911
Homes for Aged	65	576	971,544	259,322
Total	802	63,449	$5,807,479	$1,619,426

The charities of the other Norwegian synods, and the independent institutions added to the above will bring the total for the year nearly up to $2,000,000.

Rescue Mission, Minneapolis

Rescue the Perishing

✝ ✝ ✝ ✝

✝ ✝ ✝ ✝

Matt. 28:19

Luke 5:5

Lutheran Bible School, Grand Forks, N. D.

✝ ✝ ✝ ✝

Suffer the little children to come unto Me

✝ ✝ ✝ ✝

Lake Park Orphanage, Lake Park, Minn.

The chief charitable institutions of the Norwegians are as follows:

DEACONESS HOMES

No.	Name	Place	Year	Head
1.	Norwegian Lutheran	Brooklyn	1883	C. O. Pederson
2.	Norwegian Lutheran	Minneapolis	1889	E. Berntsen
3.	Norwegian Lutheran	Chicago	1896	A. Oefstedal
4.	Norwegian Methodist	Chicago	1910	Fredrik Ring

(Nos. 1-3 are Lutheran; No. 4 is Methodist)

CHILDREN'S HOMES

1 Homme, Wittenberg, Wis., 1881, J. A. Wang
2 M. Luther, Stoughton, Wis., 1889, N. A. Stubkjær
3 Beloit, Beloit, Ia., 1890, T. T. Thompson
4 Lake Park, Lake Park, Minn., 1895, L. J. A. Jahren
5 Bethesda, Beresford, S. D., 1896, John O. Johnson
6 Wild Rice, Twin Valley, Minn., 1898, N. O. Skauge
7 Parkland, Everett, Wash., 1900, H. H. Holte
8 Coeur d'Alene, Coeur d'Alene, Ida, 1923, H. J. Stolee
9 Martha-Maria, Poulsbo, Wash., 1891, J. L. Bestul
10 Bethesda, Willmar, Minn., 1905, Johan Mattson
11 Norw. Lutheran, Edison Park, Ill., 1898, Martha Bakke
12 Children's, Brooklyn, 1915, N. M. Jorgensen
13 Christian Orphans', Fort Lee, N. J.
14 Lydia, Chicago, Ill.

Nos. 1—8 are conducted by the Norwegian Lutheran Church. They had 881 children in 1924. This synod has also an orphanage at Teller, Alaska, for Eskimo children, and two day nurseries and kindergartens, at Brooklyn and Chicago, with 13,535 children. Nos. 9—10 belong to the Lutheran Free Church; Nos. 11—12 are independent, supported by Lutherans; Nos. 13 and 14 belong to the Norwegian Congregationalists.

Home Finding

The Norwegian Lutheran Church has a Home Finding Department which placed 247 children during 1924, and over 1900 children since 1917, in Christian homes for adoption. It placed

Lauritz Larsen,
D.D., S.T.D., L.L.D.
Pres., National Luth.
Council, 1920-22

Rev. J. C. Roseland,
Philadephia,
Pres., Knights of
Leif the Discoverer

J. A. O. Stub, D.D.
Sec'y, National Luth.
Council for Soldiers'
and Sailors' Welfare

169 children in 67 boarding homes, where they are kept at a price until called for. It has seven juvenile court attendants, 15 city and hospital missions, with 24 workers in 15 cities. Rev. Helge Høverstad first advocated the plan of placing children in homes rather than in orphanages. Rev. H. B. Kildahl is the secretary of the board of charities of the Norwegian Lutheran Church.

Rescue Homes

The Norwegian Lutheran Church has three rescue homes for girls—Minneapolis, Fargo and Sioux Falls. In 1924 these cared for 242 adults and 216 infants.

HOSPICES AND INNS

1 Seamen's Home, Boston, Mass., 1911, O. Nielsen
2 Luth. Home of Mercy, San Francisco, Cal., 1921, Bertha J. Bragstad
3 Seamen's Mission, San Francisco, Cal., 1870, Ole Grønsberg
4 Norway House, Brooklyn, N. Y., 1923, P. C. Birkelo
5 Seamen's Mission, Seattle, Wash., 1907, E. B. Slettedahl
6 Seamen's Mission, Galveston, Tex., 1910, Johan Olsen
7 Norw. Emigrant Mission, New York, N. Y., 1865, Iver Tharaldsen
8 Siloah Scand. Mission, Seattle, Wash., 1907, R. J. Berge
9 Luther Home, Minneapolis, Minn., 1904, F. A. Schaffnit
10 Hospice for Young Women, Minneapolis, Minn., 1918, F. A. Schaffnit
11 Scand. Sailors' Temp. House, Brooklyn, N. Y.
12 Girls' Home, Evanston, Ill.
13 Girls' Home, Seattle, Wash.
14 Girls' Home, Los Angeles, Cal.
15 Seamen's Mission, Brooklyn, N. Y.
16 Seamen's Mission, San Francisco, Cal.
17 Young W. Christian Home, Brooklyn, N. Y.
18 Young W. Christian Home, Chicago, Ill.
19 Norw. Mission House, Boston, Mass.
20 Salem Y. M. Mission House, Chicago, Ill.

Nos. 1—11 are Lutheran; Nos. 12—16 are Methodist; Nos. 17—20 are Congregationalist.

Sec'y Gustav Eide
Minnesota Total
Abstinence Assoc.

Mrs. Ulrikka F. Bruun
Temperance and
Settlement Worker

Hon. E. E. Løbeck
Temperance Orator
and Senator

Martin Norstad   N. M. Ylvisaker   J. C. K. Preus
Dr. Martin Hegland

Executive Board of Young People's Luther League

HOSPITALS

1. Deaconess (Luth.), Chicago, Ill., 1896, A. Oefstedal
2. Deaconess (M. E.), Chicago, Ill., 1907, Emma Linderud
3. Norwegian-American (Indep.), Chicago, Ill., 1896,
4. Central Iowa, Story City, Ia., 1914, I. T. Heggen
5. St. Luke's, Mason City, Ia., 1920, O. L. N. Wigdahl
6. Ft. Dodge, Ft. Dodge, Ia., 1924, S. A. Berge
7. Bethesda, Crookston, Minn., 1898, Anna M. Førlie
8. Dawson Surgical, Dawson, Minn., 1915, G. S. Froiland
9. Deaconess, Minneapolis, Minn., 1889, Marie Folkvard
10. Ebenezer, Madison, Minn., 1902, Otto Mostrom
11. Fairview, Minneapolis, Minn., 1916, Gina Aaserud
12. St. Luke's, Fergus Falls, Minn., 1903, Margaret Fjelde
13. St. Olaf's, Austin, Minn., 1896, Belle S. Anderson
14. St. Paul, St. Paul, Minn., 1901, J. E. Haugen
15. Deaconess, Brooklyn, N. Y., 1883, C. O. Pedersen
16. Deaconess, Grafton, N. D., 1904, Naema Johnson
17. Deaconess, Grand Forks, N. D., 1899, Amund Othmo
18. Deaconess, Northwood, N. D., 1902, Mildred Olsen
19. St. Luke's, Fargo, N. D., 1908, A. O. Fonkalsrud
20. Minot, Minot, N. D., 1923,
21. Wittenberg, Williston, N. D., 1911, Albert Johansen
22. Luther, Watertown, S. D., 1915, N. O. Spilde
23. Lutheran, Sioux Falls, S. D., 1894
24. Moe, Sioux Falls, S. D., 1917, Frances Moe
25. Luther, Eau Claire, Wis., 1907, F. L. Trønsdal
26. Lutheran, La Crosse, Wis., 1899, J. Mutschmann
27. Lutheran, Los Angeles, Cal., 1924, Mr. Norswing
28. Good Samaritan, Rugby, N. D., 1910, Josephine Stennes

All except No. 2 are Lutherans. Defunct hospitals, such as Zumbrota and Thomas Consumptive, not listed. Hospitals in foreign mission fields, such as Kioshan, Honan, not listed. The Norwegian Lutheran hospitals for 1922 had 625 employees, 54,749 patients, property valued at about $4,000,000.00 and an income and outlay of about $1,000,000.00. From 10 per cent to 40 per cent of the work is charity work. "Be ye therefore merciful," is the spirit that inspires the majority of hospital workers.

HOMES FOR THE AGED

 1 Homme, Wittenberg, Wis., 1882, R. P. Washotten
 2 Skaalen, Stoughton, Wis., 1900, B. J. Larsen
 3 Josephine, Stanwood, Wash., 1908, Mrs. John J. Jacobson
 4 Bethesda, Beresford, S. D., 1910, John O. Johnson
 5 Central Iowa, Story City, Ia., 1913, A. C. Molstre
 6 Aase Haugen, Haugenville, Ia., 1914, O. E. Schmidt
 7 Glenwood, Glenwood, Minn., 1914, H. J. Stormo
 8 Coeur d'Alene, Couer d'Alene, 1920, H. J. Stolee
 9 Bethany, Bawlf, Alta., 1922, N. R. T. Braa
10 Bethesda, Willmar, Minn., 1898, Johan Mattson
11 Ebenezer, Poulsbo, Wash., 1908, Ingebrigt Tollefsen
12 Sarepta, Sauk Center, Minn., 1910, A. Vatne
13 Elim, Minneapolis, Minn., 1914, J. A. Jacobsen
14 Norwood Park, Chicago, Ill., 1896, Camilla Andersen
15 Norw. Christian, Brooklyn, N. Y., 1902, Erick Ericksen
16 Northwood, Northwood, N. D., 1910, S. H. Njaa
17 Lyngblomsten, St. Paul, Minn., 1912, Johanne Larson
18 Ebenezer, Minneapolis, Minn., 1916, Julia Ekern
19 Scandinavian, Mliwaukee, Wis., 1918, P. Langbach
20 Aftenro, Duluth, Minn., 1921, Mrs. I. N. Sodahl

Extinct homes not included. Nos. 1-9 belong to the Norwegian Lutheran Church; had 383 inmates in 1924. Nos. 10-11 belong to the Lutheran Free Church; No. 12, to the Lutheran Brethren; No. 13, to the Norwegian-Danish Methodist Church. No. 14-20 are independent, but get most of their support from the Norwegian Lutheran Church.

14. SOCIETIES

Societies, as here used, are any free-will associations organized for the purpose of furthering some cause. In this sense societies are usually a selective group and labor for love in order that others, as well as they themselves, may reap a rich harvest. To them much of the progress of the world is due, and their history makes interesting and edifying reading.

There have been formed many societies among the Norwegians and of many kinds. On account of limited space the societies are regretfully dismissed, except that a few remarks will be made about the "Bygdelags," through whose efforts the Norse-American Centennial is being planned. This celebration will be held at the Minnesota State Fair Grounds, St. Paul, June 6-9, 1925.

A Multitude of Societies

Pictures are submitted of some of the officers of the Norse-American Centennial Committee, namely: Prof. Gisle Bothne, president; Mr. S. H. Holstad, managing director; Dr. Knut Gjerset, chairman of the Committee on Exhibits.

The Norse-American Centennial Committee, with headquarters at the New Nicollet Hotel, Washington Ave. South, Minneapolis, has under their direction a whole army of committees, with a membership of 4,000, who are working day and night to make the Norse-American Centennial a World's Fair not easy to forget. Bothne is the head of the Scandinavian Department at the University of Minnesota, a man of great abilities and international fame. Holstad is the president of the S. H. Holstad Coffee Co., a man of unusual executive ability, optimism and tenacity of purpose. Gjerset is the scholarly historian of the Norwegian people and the curator of the pioneer museum at Decorah. The names of other members of the central organization of the Norse-American Centennial are given herewith.

NORSE-AMERICAN CENTENNIAL COMMITTEE

GISLE BOTHNE, *President*   TRYGVE OAS, *Treasurer*
N. T. MOEN, *1st Vice-President*   A. UELAND, *Counsel*
A. C. FLOAN, *2nd Vice-President*
J. A. HOLVIK, *Secretary*   S. H. HOLSTAD, *Managing Director*

MEN

Program Committee
  B. E. BERGESEN, *Chairman*
  H. ASKELAND, *Secretary*
  CARL D. KOLSET
  O. H. SLETTEN
  H. K. MADSEN

Budget Committee
  JOS. G. NORBY, *Chairman*
  OSCAR J. THORPE
  O. I. HERTSGAARD

Committee on Finance
  E. G. QUAMME, *Chairman*
  L. W. GORDER, *Vice-Chairman*

Publicity Committee
  OSCAR ARNESON, *Chairman*
  GUSTAV B. WOLLAN, *Director*

Transportation Committee
  O. P. B. JACOBSON, *Chairman*
  HERMAN MUELLER
  LEE KUEMPEL
  M. E. WALDELAND
  ARTHUR L. JOHNSTON

Committee on Athletics
  ARNOLD C. OSS, *Chairman*

Committee on Exhibits
  KNUT GJERSET, *Chairman*
  OLAF M. NORLIE
  THEODORE C. BLEGEN

WOMEN

WOMEN'S AUXILIARY
Executive Committee
  MISS ELISA PAULINE FARSETH, *Chairman*
  MRS. J. E. HAUGEN, *Vice Chm.*
  MRS. WILLIAM O. STORLIE *Sec.*
  MRS. MANLEY FOSSEEN
  MRS. GILBERT GUTTERSEN

Hospital Committee
  MRS. SOPHIA WETTELAND *Chairman*

Reception Committee
  MRS. GISLE BOTHNE *Chairman*

Committee on Concessions
  MRS. J. O. LEE, *Chairman*

Committee on Exhibits
  MISS HERBORG REQUE *Chairman*
  MRS. BERTHA DAHL LAWS *Vice-Chairman*
  DR. INGEBORG RASMUSSEN

Program Committee
MRS. A. C. FLOAN, *Chairman*
MISS GUNHILD OFTEDAL
Vice Chairman

MRS. LAURA BRATAGER, *Sec.*
MRS. AMANDA ANDERSON
MISS GEORGINA LOMMEN

Pictures are also submitted of three temperance leaders in view of the fact that the Norwegian-Americans have been a temperate people and have been voting for the prohibition cause. It was not by mere chance that the Eighteenth Amendment to the Constitution of the United States was written by a Norwegian—A. J. Volstead. There are some two million others like unto him in the Norwegian phalanx. The pictures chosen are of the Honorable Engebrit E. Løbeck, Mrs. Ulrikka Feldtman Bruun and Gustav Eide. Løbeck spent a long life speaking the temperance cause, writing about it, and making laws in the state capitol in support of it. Mrs. Bruun built Harmony Hall in the slums of Chicago, established a Hope Mission, lifted the drunkards out of the gutter, saved the girls from lives of shame, organized kindergartens, published a temperance periodical, wrote poems, song books, and novels against strong drink, stumped several states—truly a noblewoman. Gustav Eide, for about 30 years identified with the Minnesota Total Abstinence Association and the Association for Our Country's Welfare, and serving as a secretary since 1902, being J. J. Skørdalsvold's successor to this important and difficult post.

Gustav Eide blir aldrig lei det.

In addition to these three temperance workers out of a host of over 300 societies we select three leaders—J. A. O. Stub, D.D., Lauritz Larsen, D.D., S.T., LL.D., and Jens C. Roseland. Dr. Stub was secretary of the National Commission for Soldiers' and Sailors' Welfare during the World War. As pastor of the Central Lutheran Church, Minneapolis, he has in the short space of five years built up in a dying church community a very strong Lutheran congregation. He is about to build a new $300,000 church. Dr. Larsen was elected secretary of the National Lutheran Council in 1918 and president in 1920. The National Lutheran Council under his direction gathered and distributed over 2,500,000 pounds of clothing and $2,500,000.00 for temporal relief and reconstruction of church work in 17 European lands and many foreign mission fields. In the work of his office it became his duty twice to visit the devastated lands of Europe, and, on the return from his second trip, which had proved very strenuous, he took sick with the flu and died. He was a great and noble executive, a tall, strong man of handsome appearance and gentle manners. Rev. J. C. Roseland is the president of the Knights and Dames of Leif, the Discoverer. He is a Norwegian Lutheran pastor at Philadelphia and Washington, D. C. Has been secretary of the Augustana Synod and the United Church. Is an author, an "Israelite without guile."

A "bygdelag" is a society composed of natives from a "bygd," that is, some particular settlement or group of settlements in Norway and of their descendants in this country. Thus, the Valdris Lag is a society of men and women from Valdres, Norway, and their children born here. The members of Telelaget hail from Telemarken; the members of Stavangerlaget came from Stavanger City and County.

Norwegian Bygdelags

The objects of the bygdelags are various: (1) To re-unite relatives and friends who lived close together in Norway, but are scattered far and wide in this land; (2) To foster and preserve

Andrew A. Veblen   Thomas Lajord   Torkel Oftelie

the traditions and memories of the ancestral home localities; (3) To collect and publish historical and biographical information both regarding immigrants to America who came from the district which the "lag" represents and also their descendants; (4) To collect charitable and memorial gifts to be given to their ancestral community. Veblen, in his "Valdris Book," styles the lags "For-auld-lange-syne-societies," but explains that they are much more than that. Since they began their course in 1899 they have printed at least 25,000 pages of biographical and historical material about their members. They have built a large number of hospitals, asylums, and rescue ships, established endowments to help the poor and sick, and in other ways given concrete demonstration of their good will to the land of their birth. The lag movement is unique. No other people seems to have taken part in it. The nearest approach to it in this country is the annual reunion in California of the natives of this or that state, as, for example, former citizens of Iowa meeting once a year at a picnic in Los Angeles.

a. *Valdris Samband*

The honor of starting the bygdelag movement no doubt belongs to Thomas Lajord. Lajord was born Feb. 26, 1842, in Vang, Valdres, and came to America in 1870. He worked for

21 years as a farmhand, parochial school teacher and precentor, until 1891, when he moved to Alexandria, Minnesota, and got an appointment in a furniture factory. His salary as teacher was a dollar a day, but he did very good work. Through his friend, Senator Knute Nelson, he was appointed an inspector of weights and grain. Later, he became Senator Nelson's private secretary at Washington. He died June 7, 1906. On Feb. 2, 1899, Lajord wrote an Open Letter in "Nordvesten," St. Paul, addressed to the Valdrises of the Twin Cities. Couldn't these good people

Mons O. Wee
Theological Professor

Hans Jervell
Historian

Engebret M. Broen
Bible School President

have a reunion some time that spring? The letter started a discussion. A picnic-reunion was held in Minneapolis, June, 1899, at which Lajord presided. There were songs and speeches, feasting and games, besides informal visiting between long-separated fellow-dalesmen. The Valdris dialect was much in evidence.

The Bygdelag Movement Had Begun

A similar meeting was held in 1900. In 1901 a permanent society was organized, called Valdris Samband. Andrew A. Veblen, professor of physics at the University of Iowa, was the first president-elect. He was succeeded in 1920 by Andrias M. Sundheim, manager of the Augsburg Publishing House. In 1924, Dr. John E. Haugen, manager of the St. Paul Hospital, was elected to this office. In 1903 President Veblen and the secretary of the Valdris Samband, Dr. J. S. Johnson, began the publication of a quarterly, bearing the name "Valdris Helsing," as an organ of the lag.

In 1910 this magazine was enlarged and made a monthly and bore the name "Samband." It was discontinued in 1917. In 1920 Veblen published "The Valdris Book," telling the story of the lag movement and the Valdris Samband. A. M. Sundheim issued a historical year book in 1922 and an illustrated quarterly magazine, "Samband," in 1924. This society has published over

7,000 pages of historical matter about the Valdreses. Now there are 35 other similar societies representing other valleys and districts of Norway, besides a number of division lags. This happy, thriving brood gladly look up to the Valdris Samband as the mother of them all.

The little seed sown by Mr. Lajord has become a mighty tree in the shadow of whose noble branches Norsemen of every clan, from every nook of this land, congregate and relax from toil.

As soon as the Valdris Society got well under way a number of similar organizations sprang up to represent the Norwegian people of this or that community in Norway. The order in which these societies were founded is as follows:

(2)	1907	Telelaget	(22)		Sundalslaget
(3)		Hallinglaget	(23)		Hardangerlaget
(4)	1908	Numedalslaget	(24)		Søndhordlandlaget
(5)		Gudbrandsdalslaget	(25)	1912	Vinger, Odalen & Eidskog
(6)		Trønderlaget			Samlag
(7)		Nordlandslaget	(26)		Søndfjordlaget
(8)		Sognalaget	(27)	1913	Romdalslaget
(9)	1909	Selbulaget	(28)		Kristianialaget
(10)		Vosselaget	(29)		Nordhordlandlaget
(11)		Sætesdalslaget	(30)		Hurdalslaget
(12)		Nordfjordlaget	(31)	1915	Smaalenslaget
(13)	1910	Landinglaget	(32)		Ringerikeslaget
(14)		Totninglaget	(33)		Kongsberglaget
(15)		Østerdølslaget	(34)		Mjøsenlaget
(16)		Søndmørslaget	(35)	1920	Opdalslaget
(17)		Hadelandslaget	(36)	1911	Iowa Telelag
(18)		Solunglaget	(37)		Wisconsin Telelag
(19)		Stavangerlaget	(38)	1912	Bandak Telelag
(20)	1911	Tinnsjølaget	(39)	1911	Twin City Stavangerlag
(21)		Sigdalslaget	(40)	1912	West Coast Numedalslag
			(41)		Minneapolis Trønderlag

b. *Telelaget*

Editor A. A. Trovaten, of "Fram," Fargo, North Dakota, was the originator of the Telelag. In 1914 this association had 1,600 members. It has published since 1909 a little magazine in the Telemarken dialect. The name of the magazine is "Telesoga." The articles are all from the pen of Torkel Oftelie, the most prolific collector and writer of lag history in America. The presidents of Telelaget have been: Bendik Bondahl, 1907-1908; A. A. Trovaten, 1909-1919; Hans Samuelson, 1919-1922; J. O. Saeter, 1922—.

Among the representative men from Telemarken may be mentioned: B. Anundsen, founder of "Decorah Posten," the largest Norwegian paper in the world; O. Andrewson, pioneer pastor, Wisconsin; H. H. Bergsland, professor of theology, Red Wing Sem.; Halvor Bjørnson, pastor, president of "For Fædrearven"; Herbjørn Gausta, noted artist; Osmund Gunderson, tobacco farmer and merchant, Stoughton, Wisconsin; Torjus and Saamund Hemmestvedt, Ada, Minnesota, holding world-records in ski jumping; Østen Hanson, pastor and synodical president, with four sons in the ministry; E. J. Homme, the Norwegian Francke, founder of the Wittenberg charitable institutions; J. O. Hougland, Montevideo, Minnesota, statesman; Samuel G. Iverson, state auditor of Minnesota, 1903-1915; Isaac Johnson, Methodist pastor; K. O. Lundeberg, field missionary; Th. N. Mohn, president of St. Olaf College, 1874-1899; T. G. Mandt, inventor and wagon manufacturer; A. E. Rice, lieutenant-governor of Minnesota, 1887-1891; N. N. Rønning, editor of "Familiens Magasin" and "The Friend," and manager of The Christian Literature Co., Minneapolis; O. G. U. Siljan, Lutheran pastor, Madison, Wisconsin; C. K. Solberg, president of Missionary Training School, Minneapolis; Peer O. Strømme, world traveler and journalist, poet and novelist, preacher, teacher and politician; A. K. Strand, successful farmer and county treasurer, Norman County, Minnesota; Halvor Steenerson, Minnesota congressman, 1903-1923. Governor Carl Gunderson of South Dakota is a Telemarking.

c. *Hallinglaget*

Hallinglaget held its first "stevne" (meeting) at Walcott, North Dakota, in 1907, at the suggestion of Halvor Ulsaker of that place. The first president was Dr. Olaf Th. Sherping, Fergus Falls, Minnesota, who served eight years. The second president was S. O. Olstad, piano dealer of Minneapolis, who served for three years. The present president is Prof. Knute Løkensgaard, Edberg, Alta., who has served since 1918. The membership is 1,000. In 1914 this lag sent a gift of $20,000.00 to Hallingdal, Norway, as a fund for the benefit of the "worthy" poor, the interest alone to be distributed from year to year. The fund is administered by the local government of the valley. Hallinglaget has since 1912 been publishing a quarterly called "Hallingen," which has a circulation of about 1,200. Rev. Ole Nilsen, Grand Forks, North Dakota, is the editor.

The following are fairly representative of the Hallings: Ole H. Halvorson, Litchfield, Minnesota; C. O. Livedalen, Traill County, North Dakota, and Ole O. Thormodsgaard, Hudson, South Dakota, all leading farmers; Jørgen Kvarve, of Houston County, Minnesota, is said to be the first Norwegian in Minnesota to take a seat in the legislature; K. K. Finseth was a representative from Goodhue County in 1868; S. G. Gilbertson was the first Norwegian in Iowa to hold the position of state treasurer, 1901-1907; G. N. Haugen has been a congressman from Iowa since 1899 and is chairman of the Committee on Agriculture; Asle G. Grønna was a congressman from North Dakota, 1905-1911, and a U. S. Senator, 1911-1921, and is said to have made a million dollars in farming; Lars Swenson was the treasurer of the United Church and the Hennepin County Court House Commission and manager of the Augsburg Publishing House, 1890-1904; O. S. Swenson was the warden of the South Dakota Penitentiary; Lauritz S. Swenson has been minister to Denmark, Switzerland and Norway, besides a teacher and a banker; A. Weenaas was the first president of Augsburg Seminary; H. Allen was the first president of Lutheran Ladies' Seminary; Ole Nestegaard was the first Norwegian missionary to China; Ole Løkensgaard was the first president of the Madison Normal School; O. T. Rikansrud is a Lutheran pastor, having served in Texas; H. S. Houg was a great teacher and so was Svein Strand; B. K. Savre is the editor of the Glenwood "Herald"; B. J. Rothnem is a missionary to the deaf and dumb and the winner of the prize for the best cantata for the Norse-American Centennial; Tollef Sanderson is a trusted banker at Harmony, Minnesota; Dr. Eric O. Giere is the surgeon-in-chief of the St. Paul Hospital, St. Paul, with one brother and a son in the ministry, and many near relatives in the learned professions; Ole O. Otterdokken fell at the Battle of Gettysburg, defending the Union cause; O. H. Sletten has been president of the Lutheran Free Church; and Rev. Martin Halling is, of course, a Halling, and a goad pastor.

d. *Other "Lags"*

Since 1912 the following have been added to the list of lags: (42) Agderlaget; (43) Bergenslaget; (44) Haugesundlaget; (45) Nerstrandslaget, and (46) Viktnalaget.

In addition to these associations of natives from a particular valley and their descendants, a few family groups have organized themselves into permanent societies for the purpose of meeting annually to promote acquaintance and intercourse among the respective members and to write their saga. The Aaker Family and the Tollefsrude Family are examples of this very interesting and worthy movement. The Solberg Family, Holden, Minn., and the Waldeland Family, St. Ansgar, Iowa, have published genealogical books. A number of extensive biographies and autobiographies have appeared—R. B. Anderson, J. N. Kildahl, Ole Paulson, Ole Juul and C. K. Preus. The present writer made family trees of the C. K. Preus Family, going back on the father's side, as far as Abraham Preus, 1650, and on the mother's (Hjort) side to 1525. He discovered interconnections with 621 other families in Norway and America. Some of the lags are emphasizing the importance of holding on to the land and sticking to the soil. Others call attention to the value of keeping the old Norwegian names intact and of getting more place names on the American map. In 1911 only 18 out of 886 of the postoffices in North Dakota had a Norwegian name. No state and no large city has ever been named after the Norsemen. In 1856 the Norwegians

Ole J. Glasøe   John P. Johnson   John Juel

came to Meeker County, Minnesota. They were the first settlers there and called their town Ness, because they came from Ness in Hallingdal. The town was called Ness by the railroad when it came, and Ness was a good enough name for all time. But some Americans came and said: "This will never do. Let's get an English name." The Norwegians meekly yielded and Ness became Litchfield (which means in Old English graveyard). In New York, in the winter of 1924-1925, the Norwegians asked for a Leif Erikson Square, and got it.

The story of the "Bygdelags" is of far-reaching interest. It is curtailed here for want of room.

15. CULTURAL AND PROFESSIONAL PURSUITS

Of the cultural and professional pursuits of the Norwegians in America brief mention will be made of a few inventors, architects, engineers, musicians, painters, sculptors, doctors, dentists, and lawyers. Norwegian culture is, of course, represented also by the preachers, teachers, writers, publishers, missionaries, charity workers, society promoters, athletes, public service men, etc., discussed elsewhere in the book. It should be understood that the following is not a catalog or inventory of names and deeds in the fields surveyed. The subject invites further study.

Walker says in his "Making of the Nation": "Agriculture was the chief occupation in the United States at the achievement of independence . . . . Of two sons of the same mother, one became a lawyer, perhaps a judge, or went down to the city and became a merchant, or gave himself to political affairs and became a governor or a member of Congress. The other stayed upon the ancestral homestead, or made a new one for himself and his children out of the public domain further west, remaining

Norwegian Inventors

through his life a plain, hard-working farmer. . . . There was then no other country in the world, there is now no considerable country where equal mental alertness has been applied to soil as to trade and industry."

Walker goes on to show that the saying "necessity is the mother of invention," is better illustrated here than in any other land. "Invention is a normal function of the American brain. The American invents as the Greek chiseled, as the Venetian painted, as the modern Italian sings."

A Stoughton Wagon

In this feature of Americanism the Norwegians have from the start been like unto their English brethren, and they have helped in no small measure to improve the known tools of husbandry and to invent new ones. The axe, the spade, the shovel, the plow, the wagon, the thresher, and a hundred and one other implements have been improved in their hands, so that these tools have become marvels of combined efficiency, lightness and strength.

The T. G. Mandt and Stoughton wagons and sleds, for example, have never been excelled. T. G. Mandt invented these and manufactured them. The Vea Brothers and the Moline Plow Co. continued to manufacture them after his death.

John P. Johnson (Moen), Litchfield, Minn., invented the first twine binder, or self binder, in 1877. His patent was infringed upon, his rights stolen.

Ole J. Glasøe, a blacksmith at Lanesboro, Minn., early saw the need of a plow that would run lighter, and invented the first sulky plow

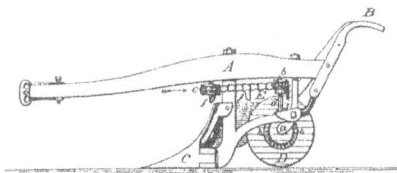

The First Sulky Plow

in the world. The number of his patent is 164,727, dated June 22, 1875. He began to manufacture the sulky plow, and so did other concerns. He had no money to carry on lawsuits, and so his patent did not protect his rights.

John Juel, Canton, S. D., a farmer and thresher, found that he could no longer feed his machine by hand, so he invented a self feeder and started a factory at Larchwood, Ia. His patent number was 474,254, granted May 3, 1892, the first self feeder in the world. He soon learned that other factories were making use of his models, but he was unable to check the infringements.

Then, somehow his factory was set on fire, and he ceased to manufacture.

John O. Ulberg had been a contractor and builder from 1890 to 1905, farmer and brick manufacturer, Mott, N. D., 1905-19, and experimenting with rotary engines since 1919. He has spent 20 years planning a rotary engine. In 1914 he visited the Patent Office at Washington, D. C., and found 3,086 patents of rotary engines ahead of him, but not one of them used his principle. He is president of Ulberg and Sons Rotary Engine Co., Sioux Falls.

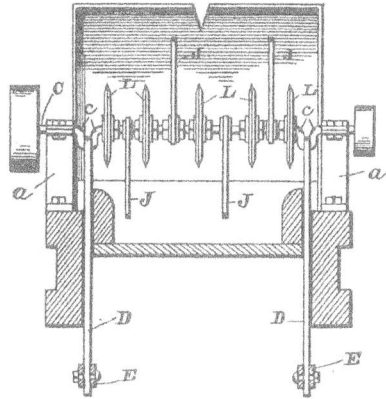

The Juel Self Feeder, Front View

Beecher says that "he that invents a tool or a machine augments the power of man and the well-being of mankind." The inventors just mentioned have surely contributed to the welfare of humanity, and while in this life they received no material rewards for their foresight and sacrifice. It is said of a man that he asked his fellowmen for bread, and they gave him a stone—when he was dead. It is earnestly to be hoped that the world will eventually reward these inventors of machinery of such universal and far-reaching value with proper monuments of stone.

It has been estimated that the Norwegians have produced 33,000 inventions in the United States. In the table below will be found 33 of these chosen to show their variety and practicality.

L. O. Grondahl   C. E. Tharaldsen   J. O. Ulberg

Some Early and More Recent Inventors

NORWEGIAN INVENTORS

Name	Place	Invention
Aasen, Mr.	Stoughton, Wis.	Sleeping masks
Bonhus, C. Alfred	Minneapolis, Minn.	Furnace heat regulator
Borge, John	New York, N. Y.	Incinerator
†Cappelen, F. W.	Minneapolis, Minn.	Reduction plant
Cappelen-Smith, E. A.	New York, N. Y.	Copper extracting methods
Dahl, Knut	San Francisco, Cal.	U. S. Navy oil burner
Danielson, Mr.	Cannon Falls, Minn.	"Never-Wiggle" ironing board
Evenrude, Ole	Milwaukee, Wis.	Evenrude marine motor
Flood, Eyvind	Boston, Mass.	Milling machinery
†Gisholt (Johnson), J. A.	Madison, Wis.	Simplematic lathe
†Glasøe, Ole J.	Lanesboro, Minn.	First sulky plow
Grøndahl, L. O.	Pittsburgh, Pa.	Railway signaling apparatus
Guettler, H. W.	Chicago, Ill.	Barking drum
Heidenreich, E. L.	Chicago, Ill.	Grain elevator
Himle, Th.	Spokane, Wash.	Life preserver
†Hoff, Olaf	Montclair, N. J.	Subaqueous railroad tunnel
†Johnson, J. P.	Litchfield, Minn.	First self binder
Juel, John	Canton, S. D.	First self feeder
Langemo, Edward	Minneapolis, Minn.	Threshing machine
Loss, Henrick V.	Philadelphia, Pa.	First rolled steel railway car wheels
†Mandt, T. G.	Stoughton, Wis.	Mandt wagon
Monson, George S.	St. Paul, Minn.	Instrument for reproducing movement of human jaws
Nordtop, Gullick	Millet, Alta.	Automatic power engine
Olsen, Tinius	Philadelphia, Pa.	Testing machine
Olson, Carsten F.	Brooklyn, N. Y.	Instrument of precision (for detecting position of ships at sea)
Pihlfeldt, Thos. G.	Chicago, Ill.	Jack knife bridge
†Rigness, John	Norse, Tex.	Disk harrow (1850)
Ruud, Edwin	Pittsburgh, Pa.	Automatic bake oven
Sageng, H. O.	Milaca, Minn.	Combination engine-thresher
Skille, Edvard	Drummond, Wis.	Metrical calendar
Tharaldsen, C. E.	Evanston, Ill.	Micro-dissecting machine
Ulberg, John O.	Sioux Falls, S. D.	Rotary engine
Wigtel, Carl	New York, N. Y.	Hydraulic machinery

†Deceased

A remark or two about these inventions is surely in order. J. A. Johnson (Gisholt), the inventor, is the founder of the Gisholt Manufacturing Company, Madison, Wisconsin, which has for over 50 years been making high grade farm implements and machine making machinery. The Simplematic, for example, is a simplex highly productive lathe which meets the need for a simple automatic machine capable of taking a number of cuts on a variety of chucking and between-centers work. L. O. Grondahl's Railway signaling apparatus (Patents No. 1,503,316, 1,503,317 and

1,503,318) uses photo-electric and other light sensitive means of actuating automatic signals for the control of traffic on railways. As director of research for the Union Switch and Signal Co., Swissvale, Pennsylvania, Dr. Grondahl has invented a number of other electrical devices, as: A focus indicator for headlights (Patent No. 1,414,125), a system of submarine detection in alternating magnetic fields. He has several patents pending. He is an authority on box photometers, pneumophonographs and other things electric. Th. Himle's life preserver was devised by Pastor Himle during the World War. So many people were being drowned by the submarines, and this set him to thinking. He made a life-saving outfit which provided air, food and electric light. It is easy to put on, and when once on, it will take a man right to the surface. Rev. Th. Himle had been a medical and clerical missionary in China, 1895-1909, and was a pastor at Santa Rosa, California, when he invented this life saver. He is now an evangelist and has been in the spiritual life-saving business all his working life. Gulick Nordtop is an Alberta farmer who has applied the principles of the clock and automatic elevator to engines and has made an automatic power engine that runs without fuel, steam, electricity, gas or oil. The Philadelphian, Tinius Olsen, won gold medals on his testing machines as early as the Philadelphia Centennial of 1876. The Texan, John Rigness, invented a disk harrow as early as 1850. Edvard

Th. Himle and His Life Saving Outfit

Skille came to America as a 15-year old boy and at once secured a job in a Wisconsin saw mill. He rose from position to position until he became a log scaler, a position that called for considerable mathematical knowledge. He became a student of higher mathematics all by himself and profoundly efficient. He discovered a method of trisecting an angle, a feat that had never before been performed, and invented a log marker by which he could divide an angle into any required part. And, finally, he devised a Metrical Calendar in which he applies the decimal system to the year. Astronomers and mathematicians regard the work, both as to originality and accuracy, as truly remarkable. Conrad E. Tharaldsen is a professor of zoology at Northwestern University. He has invented a parafin oven and a micro-vivisection apparatus.

In connection with inventions may be mentioned a few who

have devised efficiency methods. Thus: Carl G. Barth, Philadelphia, is the inventor of a system of efficiency in industrial management. John E. Haugen, St. Paul, is the inventor of a plan of hospital bookkeeping which is used generally even in New York. O. M. Norlie, together with G. L. Kieffer, New York, has devised the minimum parochial blanks of the National Lutheran Council and many statistical blanks for institutions, departmental agencies and societies, no doubt the simplest, most systematic and fullest church statistical blanks in the world. Magnus Swenson has invented methods of saving in manufacturing sugar and other products. E. A. Cappelen-Smith has invented methods of smelting copper. J. C. M. Hanson is one of the chief authors of the Library of Congress System of cataloguing.

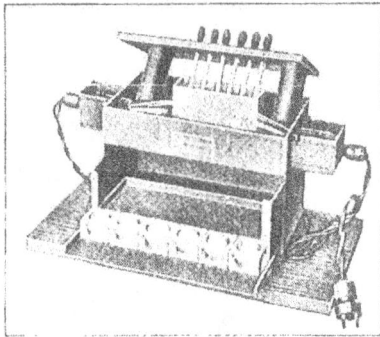

Tharaldsen's Parafin Oven

U. S. Senator Norbeck was the champion well-digger of South Dakota before he went into politics. He didn't like the way they were drilling with the machines then in use so he invented a combination drilling machine and pump.

T. Alvasaker, Chicago, "who is thoroughly conversant with Norse church architecture as well as Lutheran architecture in general," has contributed designs I-XII in Glasoe's "Church Designs" (1917). Of course Alvasaker is an expert in other architectural fields, too.

Norwegian Architects

Kort Berle, New York, shared with his business partner, Gunvald Aus, the responsibilities and honors of designing and erecting the Woolworth Building, the tallest of its kind in the world, on Broadway, near City Hall Park, New York. Cass Gilbert was the chief architect.

John Engebretsen, San Diego, Norwegian consul, is the leading street contractor and builder in his city.

John A. Gade, New York, a high standard architect, has practiced his profession in the great metropolis. He has been knighted by Norwegian, Danish, Swedish, Belgian and Italian potentates and given the Navy Cross by the U. S. A. He is the author of "Book Plates, Old and New" (1898), "Cathedrals of Spain" (1911), etc.

Nils I. Edward Mohn, St. Paul, oldest son of Thorbjørn N.

Mohn, first president of St. Olaf College, is an architect, with offices at 596 Endicott Bulding, St. Paul, Minnesota.

Olaf Thorshov, of the Long and Thorshov Co., Minneapolis, has erected many of the tallest buildings of Minneapolis.

Olav M. Topp has for 40 years been building some of the largest skyscrapers and churches of Pittsburgh. Topp is at the top of his profession.

Rear Admiral Peter C. Asserson (1839-06), in the U. S. Navy, 1862-06, was a civil engineer and builder of dry docks at Norfolk, Brooklyn, etc. "The Army and Navy Journal," *Engineers* December 8, 1906, calls him the "greatest authority in America on dry docks." He was from Ekersund. Came here in 1859. Had four sons, two sons-in-law, and 5 grandsons in the U. S. army and navy. One of his sons-in-law, Wm. B. Fletcher, is a rear admiral. The other son-in-law, Lieut. Frank A. Spicer, is descended from Kjerulf, the Norwegian musician.

Nils F. Ambursen, New York, consulting hydraulic engineer, inventor of the Ambursen dam. Otto J. Andreason, New York, designing and estimating engineer, for many years with the world famous Wm. Barclay Parsons. Gunvald Aus, New York, consulting engineer, designer of steel frame for the Woolworth Building, the "Cathedral of Commerce," the world's highest building. Builder of the United States Custom House, the monumental and artistic structure facing Bowling Green, New York City, and several other important structures, as: U. S. Post Office, New York, Essex Court House, Newark, Armory Building, New York, Union Central Life Insurance Co's Building, Cincinnati. He was construction engineer of the Phoenix Bridge Co., 1888-1894; chief engineer of the U. S. Treasury, 1894-1900.

K. Baetzman, Chicago, engineer in large steel plant. A. Berg, Patterson, chemical engineer and expert in silk dyeing.

Gustav Bergendahl, Einar Bergendahl, and Carl Bergendahl, brothers, Chicago, engineers and builders. Einar Bergendahl built the bridge between Philadelphia and Camden, the largest in the United States. Ole Berger, New York, paper mill engineer. A. A. Boedtker, Chicago, builder of exhibit buildings, Columbian Exposition, and railroad engineer. John Borge, New York, engineer, identified with the manufacture of incinerators. John S. Braune, New York, consulting engineer.

Frederick W. Cappelen, Minneapolis, engineer, with Northern Pacific Railroad, in Montana, city engineer, 1886-1821, builder of city filtration plant, the Northern Pacific bridge and the Cappelen Bridge crossing the Mississippi at the foot of Franklin Avenue. This has the largest concrete span in the world. He also built the bridge at Third Avenue, Minneapolis, and the new Cedar Avenue bridge, which is to be one of the finest in America, is to be built according to his specifications. E. A. Cappelen-Smith, New York, chemical and hydro-metallurgical engineer and copper mining expert, winner of gold medal of the Mining and Metallurgical Society of America and member of the Guggenheim Corporation. H. L. Christie, Pittsburgh, engineer with American Bridge Co. for many years. Gustav L. Clausen, Chicago, civil engineer and superintendent of sewers of Chicago. Mr. Clausen planned the towns of Pullman and Hyde Park and has planned the sewer systems of many cities. H. Claussen, engineer with E. P. Allis Co., Milwaukee.

Knut Dahl, San Francisco, is engineer of the Union Iron Works of that city. Sverre Damm, New York, engineer in direct

The Cappelen Bridge

charge of subway construction, New York, for 25 years. Viggo Drewson, New York, a leading chemical engineer and a recognized authority on paper manufacture. J. A. Dyblie, for years the chief engineer of the Anaconda Mining Company, Montana. At present, chief engineer Illinois Steel Company's Works, Joliet, Illinois.

Eyvind Flood, Boston, mining engineer and inventor.

Berge B. Furre, New York, subway engineer.

Joachim G. Gaiver, Pittsburgh, civil engineer, designer of exhibit buildings at Chicago, 1893, bridge engineer. Herbert W. Guettler, Chicago, paper mill engineer, inventor of Guettler Barking Drum, an improved device for removing bark from logs.

E. Lee Heidenreich, the foremost engineer in the world of reinforced concrete construction, inventor of modern type of grain elevators. J. Heyerdahl-Hansen, San Francisco, is president of the Diesel Engine Company. Olaf Hoff, Montclair, N. J., consulting engineer, inventor of new method of laying tunnels, builder of the New York Central tunnel under the Detroit River and several tunnels under the Harlem River. Hoff died in New York City, December 23, 1924. About 30 years ago Hoff built a belt line railroad bridge across the Mississippi, near Eleventh Avenue South, Minneapolis. The bridge was built from both sides toward the center. Everything was so carefully designed that when the last pieces met, the bolts shipped into their places without any filing or fitting of any sort. This marvel of engineering astounded the technical world. N. N. Rønning had a thrilling account of this wonderful man in the April number of "The Friend." 1925. Hoff arrived in New York in 1879, a 20-year-old Norwegian newcomer, his breast pocket containing a diploma from the Polytechnic Institute at Copenhagen, and his heart throbbing with the ambition to make his mark in this land of wonderful engineering feats. He started at the bottom in a fitting-up shop. Soon he was an engineer with the Mexican Central Railway, and shortly after that the locating engineer of the line. He lived several years in Minneapolis and took a leading part in the

The Woolworth Building, a product of Norwegian Engineering and Architectural Science

Lutheran church work. He built a bridge across the Mississippi at St. Paul. In 1910 he took charge of the bridge work of the New York Central and, in four years, constructed over 400 bridges. Last year he built the Castleton Bridge for this railroad. His brother, J. H. Hoff, is the chief engineer for the American Bridge Co. at Chicago. Leonhard Holmboe, Chicago, has designed and built one of the largest steel plants in America, and has been in the service of the Illinois Steel Co. since 1870. Christian and Severin Holt are engineers and inventors. Christian Holt has specialized in river locks and has worked for the U. S. A. Severin Holt has specialized in farm machinery and has worked for the McCormick Co., now the International Harvester Co. One of his inventions is the Holt Cream Separator. Norman B. Holter is a mechanical engineer. He is the son and successor of the illustrious Anton M. Holter, Helena, Montana.

Axel Olaf Ihlseng, Brooklyn, N. Y., is a zinc mining engineer, operating in Colorado, Missouri, Mexico, Kansas and Oklahoma. M. Rude Jacobsen, Brooklyn, is a tunnel making expert. D. S. Jensen is a prominent paper mill engineer of New York.

Halfdan Lee, Pittsburgh, is an engineer in the coke manufacturing industry. His brother, Leif Lee, is the chief engineer at a large steel plant, Youngstown, Ohio. O. L. Lindrew, Chicago, was a farmer boy at Jefferson Prairie, Wisconsin. He became a fireman on the Illinois Central in 1886, an engineer in 1890, trans-

Olaf Hoff
New Jersey

Edward Mohn
Minnesota

Ingvald Rosok
Arizona

portation inspector and expert on fuel conservation for the Illinois Central system in 1912.

Guttorm Miller, New York, has for over 20 years been connected with subway engineering and other big construction enterprises.

A. B. Neumann, Chicago, is the designer and builder of the largest steel plant in America, possibly in the world, the United States Steel Corporation plant at Gary, Indiana. He planned and laid out the City of Gary. He built the plant of the American Rolling Co. at Middletown, Ohio, and the seamless tube plants for the Pittsburgh Steel Products Co.

Alf Otto is the builder of the five-mile long bridge across the Savannah. He was born at Oslo in 1881.

J. P. Paulson, San Francisco, is the chief engineer of the C. H. Moore Iron Works of that city. Thomas Pihlfeldt, Chicago, is a noted bridge engineer, chief engineer of bridges for Chicago, inventor of the Pihlfeldt-Ericsson, or Chicago type, of jack-knife bridges.

Oscar H. Reinholt, San Diego, is a mining engineer. Was a geographer in the Philippine Forestry Bureau, superintendent U. S. army coal mines, with U. S. Bureau of Mines, consulting petroleum engineer, with Treasury Department, valuation engineer of natural resources, awarded bronze and silver medals, St. Louis, and gold medal, San Diego, for mineral exhibit; geologist, teacher of Spanish, author of "Statistical Handbook," "Treasures and Tragedies of Oildom," associate editor, "U. S. Treasury Manual of the Oil and Gas Industry."

Ingvald Rosok, Bisbee, Arizona, is an electrical and mining engineer in charge of electric light plants, ice-making factories and other enterprises. He is mayor of his city and operates oil wells in California on the side. Edwin Ruud, Pittsburgh, where the anvil blows never cease and the smoke always hangs over the city. Inventor of the Westinghouse gas engine, automatic bake ovens, dual fire control services, president of the Edwin Ruud Manufacturing Company.

Frederick Schaefer, Pittsburgh, is an engineer, inventor and manufacturer of mechanical devices in use on railroads. A member of the Norwegian Society of Pittsburgh, which has 30 members, most of them engineers. Eugene Schou, New York, is structural engineer for the board of education of the metropolis, and has for years superintended the construction of the city's numerous school buildings. Benjamin Franklin Stangland, Slooper, is a mechanical engineer. He was in the employ of the Fairbanks Co., Chicago, 1873-1877; with Howard and Morse, New York, since 1879; has designed many ventilating plants in large buildings. Charter member of American Society of Heating and Ventilating Engineers.

Magnus Swenson, Madison, is a chemical and hydraulic engineer, the greatest authority on sugar manufacturing and a world exponent of economy in manufacturing and the saving of waste.

Halsten J. Thorkelson, E. Orange, N. J., is a mechanical engineer. Took his M. E. at the University of Wisconsin, 1901. Was draftsman 7 years, superintendent, J. I. Case Plow Works, Racine, 1901-1902, professor of steam engineering, University of Wisconsin, 1902-1914; business manager of same, 1913-1921; now connected with the General Education Board, New York.

T. D. Yensen, Pittsburgh, is the chief of the Westinghouse Chemical Laboratory.

P. G. Zwilgmeyer, a former city engineer of Seattle, and at present a civil engineer in the employ of the Northern Pacific Railroad, is a profound student of theology according to scientific methods, but (sic!) in childlike, orthodox faith. His treatises on Luther, Pascal, Paul's Relation to the Classics, Bible Introduction, are masterpieces.

Norway has produced a host of musicians, many of them of far fame, as, for example: Ole Bull, M. B. Landstad, Halfdan Kjerulf, Otto Winter-Hjelm, Johan S.
Musicians   Svendsen, Richard Nordraak, Edvard Grieg,
Johan Selmer, Christian Cappelen and Ole
Olsen. These men wrote the musical composition distinctly peculiar to Norway, and yet of universal charm, for music is a universal language. As Longfellow says in his "Outre-mer":
"Music is the universal language of mankind," and Pollak says in
his "Course of Time":

> He touched his harp, and nations heard, entranced,
> As some vast river of unfailing source,
> Rapid, exhaustless, deep, his numbers flowed,
> And opened new fountains in the human heart.

The Norwegian musicians have made an important contribution to the world's music, a contribution different in many respects from that of the other races, but yet harmonizing with and
enriching the grand orchestra and chorus of the nations. It
stands to reason that the sons and daughters of Norway who came
to America would carry with them a love for the Norwegian
songs and melodies, which meant so much to them over there.
And this they did.

This heritage is treasured in the Norwegian home. Mother
sings her babies to sleep with the Old Country lullabies. Father
and mother and children, too, all unite their voices in prayer and
praise and thanksgiving at meals and evening devotions. At
prayer meetings and Sunday services each one takes part in the
congregational singing of the Lutheran chorals, with their measured rhythm and deep devotional content, as well as in the lighter
hymns and spiritual songs. In the parochial school and confirmation instruction the best hymns and tunes are learned by heart.
Many of the older people whose sight has become dimmed by
years, can recite hundreds of stanzas by heart; in fact, it is nothing unusual to find Norwegians who know their whole hymn-
book by heart. In the congregational choirs, Luther leagues, and
singing societies vocal music is fostered.

Much attention has been paid by the Lutherans to the publication of suitable song books for congregations, young people's
societies, children, choirs and special occasions. The early newcomers took along with them in their traveling box, copies of
Balle's "Evangelisk-Kristelige Salmebog" (1797), Guldberg's
(1778), Kingo's (edition 1819), Harboe and Guldberg's (edition
1823). In 1854 two editions of the Harboe and Guldberg hymn
books were published by the pioneer settlers, one printed by Ole
Andrewson at Norway, Ill., having 784 pages, and the other
printed by the Scandinavian Press Association at Inmansville.

Wis., having 648 pages. The Norwegian Synod published in 1870 a hymnal called "Synodens Salmebog," revised in 1903. The United Church together with the Hauge Synod published in 1893 a revision of Landstad (1869), and added 96 hymns, making 730 instead of 634. Hagen's "Salmetoner" was issued in 1915. The Norwegian Synod in 1898 published "Christian Hymns," a hymnal for the congregation and Sunday School. That same year the United Church issued the "Church and Sunday School Hymnal." Of the 309 hymns in the "Christian Hymns," and of the 316 hymns in the "Church and Sunday School Hymnal," about 40 per cent were taken from Lutheran sources, the remaining 60 per cent chiefly from the Reformed. From 1908 to 1913 a special committee of 12 men from the Norwegian Synod, the United Church and the Hauge Synod compiled the "Lutheran

John Dahle   Carlo A. Sperati   F. Melius Christiansen

Professors of Music

Hymnary." It has 618 hymns, of which 7 per cent are taken from the pre-Reformation times, 40 per cent from Lutheran lands, and 53 per cent from Reformed sources. The aim in these congregational books, as in the books for children and youth, is to select only the best as to doctrine, poetry and music. In the creation of the "Lutheran Hymnary Junior," which was published in 1916 as a Sunday school book jointly by the three Norwegian Synods which amalgamated in 1917, no less than 20,000 hymns were tried out. From this rich treasury 164 songs were chosen. The best seller is "Concordia," by Bersagel, Bøe and Sigmond.

Among the compilers and editors of hymnals for children may be mentioned: Erik Jensen, who published 16 song books (1878-1898); C. O. Brøhaugh (1879); P. G. Østby (1885); D. G. Ristad (1897); N. B. Thvedt and O. M. Norlie (1911); A. Bersagel, V. E. Bøe and S. O. Sigmond (1915); D. G. Ristad, M. O. Wee, L. C. Jacobson, L. P. Thorkveen and O. M. Norlie (1916). The following have published song books for youth: S. Krogness (1858); J. H. Myhre (1874); M. F. Gjertsen (1877); A. Wright (1877); G. Hoyme and L. Lund (1878-

1888); C. O. Brøhaugh (1879); A. Nelson (1881); J. P. Gjertsen (1881); T. S. Reimestad (1888); O. Waldeland (1888); T. S. Reimestad and M. F. Gjertsen (1897); O. M. Anderson (1898); K. B. Birkeland (1898); E. Jensen (1899); L. O. and O. M. Anderson (1913); O. H. Sletten (1914). The books for the congregation and for the Sunday school children already mentioned also contain hymns and songs suitable for youth. The pedagogical principle in Lutheran hymn book making is this: That children should be taught what they ought to sing and would like to sing when they grow up, and the best is not too good for the children. Therefore a nucleus of the finest hymns are taught at the start, around which are gathered during youth and maturity larger clusters of the best hymns and tunes from all lands.

A number of excellent choral and choir books have been issued. Knud Henderson, born in 1835 in Voss, emigrated 1849, a wagon painter by trade, studied music under Root, Chant, and Wemmerstad in Chicago. He became an organist and music teacher, and was the first Norwegian in America to organize a singing school. He published the first Norwegian book of chorals in America in 1865, of which over 25,000 copies have been sold. He has also published a volume of national songs, text books for the "salmodikon," and other music books. He was married in 1868 and moved to a farm near Cambridge, Wis. Though 90 years of age, he is in good trim. Erik Jensen in 1880 published a "Koralbog"; and Olaf Glasøe in 1889 revised Lindeman's "Koralbog." K. C. Holter published "Frydetoner" (I-III) in 1893-1900, the book that has had the widest circulation among Norwegian choir singers. E. Jensen published "Scandinavian Songs" (1890), "Klokketoner" (1896), and "Sangbog for Kirkekor" (1896). L. P. Thorkveen published "Kirkesange for Blandet Kor" (1905). Together with Glasoe he published the widely used book, "Korsange" (1903). The most productive and influential of the choir book publishers are John Dahle and F. Melius Christiansen. Dahle's "Sangbog for Mandsforeninger" (1891), "Fram" (1898), "Sangbog for Kirkekor" (1908), "Nordisk Sangalbum" (1909), "Jubilate" (1900), are wonderful treasuries of song, Christiansen's "Kor og Kvartet Sange," "Korsangeren" (1901), "Sangerhefte," "Sanggudstjeneste," "Song Service," "Nationale Sange," "Lette Lyriske Sange," "Fifty Famous Hymns," various cantatas, and, particularly, the "St. Olaf Choir Series" (I-V), easily belong to the first order of music. The work of T. S. Reimestad, author of "Sangalbum" (1914), a series of hymns with music of his own composition or interpretation, is also a valuable contribution to music. Alfred Paulsen, of Chicago, has published many valuable compositions for piano, organ and voice. We venture to say that when his "Naar fjordene blaaner" (When the Fjords Are Like Violets

Blue) is forgotten by Norsemen it will be because the last Norseman will have become so thoroughly Americanized as to have forgotten his own origin. This song will never die.

Instruction in music is given at every Norwegian school, and music is a fixed part of the daily chapel exercises. The most conspicuous example of vocal training performed by these schools, is no doubt the St. Olaf Choir. Eugene E. Simpson, having heard this choir sing in New York, of his own initiative, wrote a history of it (1921), a book of 192 pages. This choir has sung in all the principal cities of the United States and in many of the great cities of Europe. It has sung before presidents and kings and the best musical critics of the world, and everywhere the enthusiasm is as flattering as it is spontaneous, with never a dissenting note from the keenest critics. "The Sun" (Pittsburgh), remarks: "This organization of fifty young voices sang Bach motets, chorales, double choruses, Mendelssohn and Gretchaninoff works with an ease that was simply staggering." The "Washington Herald" says: "Their work is an exposition of choral singing which is probably without equal." The "Ohio State Journal" (Columbus) said: "As a whole the program was an amazing commentary on the life of real music. From the opening number, Luther's favorite hymn, 'A Mighty Fortress,' it continued number after number, all the work of masters of the earlier days of the Protestant faith. Memorial Hall was the only place where this music would have seemed fitting. This little group of men and women from the small Minnesota college in Northfield dominated the great building and filled it with song until the very rafters rang with their hosannas." Some Negroes who attended the concert at St. Louis said that they thought the angels from Heaven had come down to earth to sing. Says the "Akron Press": "The atmosphere created by the choir was marvelous—organ-like tones, pure in quality, a unit in expression, made a direct appeal to the heart. The entire program was a refreshment, an inspiration and a power. It was a sermon in music, and through the poetic forms one felt that God surely spoke." Hundreds of quotations of this sort from the pens of men like Karl Nissen, Johannes Haarklou, Herman Devries, Hubbard, Moore, Gaul, Keeble, Aldrich, Sanborn, Harry Sundby-Hansen, Carl G. O. Hansen, Pierre Key, Gabriel, Krebhiel, Rogers, all critics of the first class in Norway and America, can be given. Suffice it to say that the St. Olaf Choir is the more remarkable in view of the fact that its members are most of them boys and girls from the farms and with little or no musical training. It should be noted that this choir sings "a capella."

The Norwegian schools pay much attention to instrumental instruction, piano, organ, violin, orchestra and band. Luther College Band is unquestionably the most famous Norwegian col-

Top Row: 1. A. K. Eittreim; 2 O. C. Ferguson; 3. T. O. Kvamme; 4. W. O. Rindahl; 5. K. N. Roe; 6. H. B. Bestul; 7. C. B. Nervig; 8. A. W. Jørgenson; 9. O. A. Jordahl; 10. G. O. Westby; 11. T. Arnevik; 12. A. C. Huselid; 13. J. W. Opheim; 14. A. W. Wellner; 15. W. L. Eittreim; 16. L. H. Woldum.

Middle Row: 1. R. O. Stoskopf; 2. I. W. Lane; 3. E. J. Ordal; 4. J. G. Westby; 5. K. L. Norlie; 6. M. A. Elvebak; 7. I. R. Berg; 8. S. I. Sanderson; 9. A. W. Sorenson; 10. P. G. Hoel; 11. G. T. Norswing; 12. O. T. Torrison; 13. R. O. Akre; 14. C. E. Lucky; 15. M. S. Dahl.

Bottom Row: 1. C. Vittori Sperati; 2. E. Ravndal; 3. J. A. Peterson; 4. L. A. Suby; 5. M. A. Eistad; 6. O. M. Jordahl; 7. H. R. Gregerson; 8. W. W. Korsrud; 9. I. O. Brendsel; 10. Carlo A. Sperati; 11. K. O. Kiland; 12. S. J. Fardal; 13. O. T. Olsen; 14. A. A. Hendrickson; 15. N. Duckstad; 16. M. T. Jenson; 17. S. R. Sperati; 18. O. C. Sand; 19. H. L. Larsgaard. Suby, Sanderson, Kvamme and Larsgaard in male quartet.

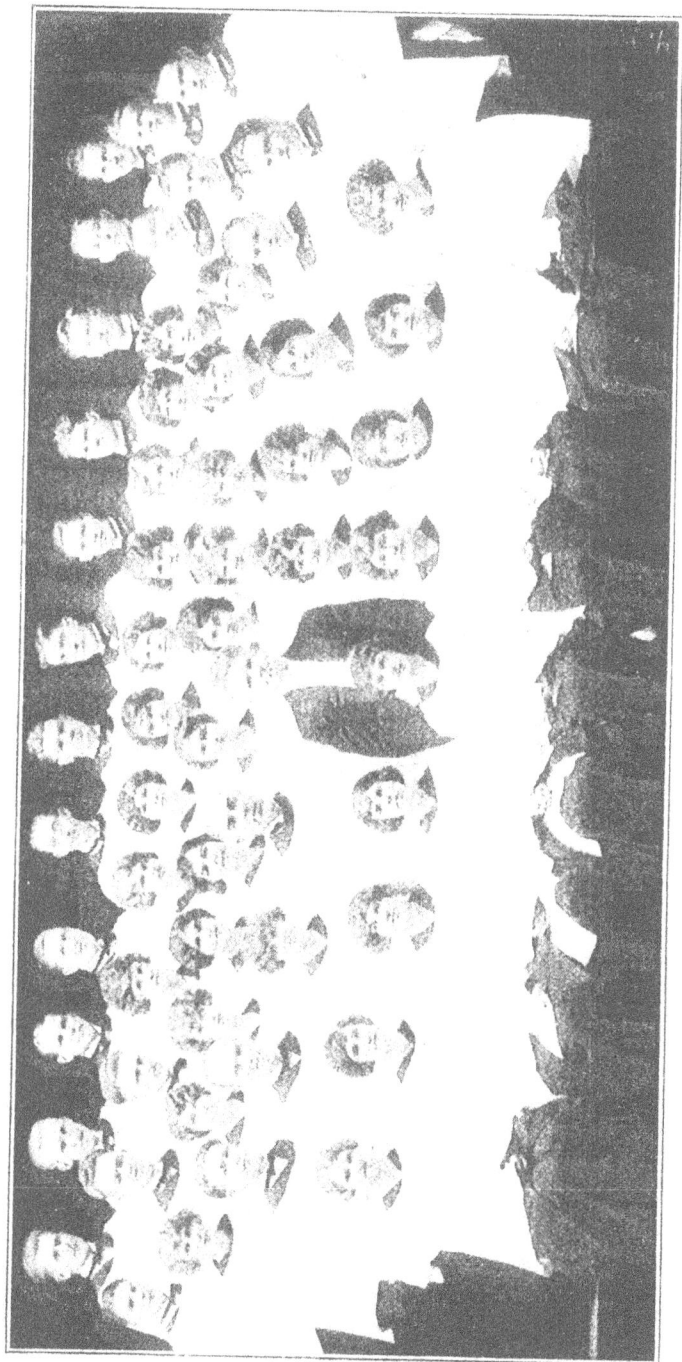

Top Row: G. Malmin, K. Onsgaard, H. Halvorsen, W. Furgeson, C. Kittleson, T. Groth, M. Soelberg, G. Thompson, O. Christiansen, O. Hagen, E. Rossing, S. Pederson. *Second Row from Top:* C. Nestande, O. Grinder, A. Snesrud, Luella Thygeson, Alda Rice, Audrey Armstrong, Ruby Benson, Ella Hjertaas, Gladys Grindeland, Elvira Osterberg, Alvira Haasarud, Viola Benson, O. Rossing, L. Tallakson. *Third Row from Top:* Bernice Armstrong, Solveig Magelssen, Irene Helgen, Marion Landahl, Sylvina Sundahl, Lillian Landahl, Nellie Hoyem, Borghild Julsrud, Ella Johnson, Anna Njaa, Anette Hoidahl, M. Lyders, O. Strand. *Fourth Row from Top:* G. Paulsrud, R. Benson, Gladys Wold, P. G. Schmidt, F. M. Christiansen, Esther Erickson, Arndis Lundberg, Alma Olson, G. Guidseth, O. Westlie. *Front Row:* Alphild Boe, Ellen Kjos, Anita Hanson, Gertrude Schmidt, Gertrude Boe-Overby, Alice Giere, Sara Magelssen, Georgia Drexler. *Not on the Picture:* Arvid Romstad, Martha Byholt.

lege band in America, although St. Olaf, in the person of John A. Bergh, has developed a college band of remarkable efficiency. The two chief names in the history of Luther College Band are Haldor J. Hanson and Carlo Alberto Sperati. When Professor Hanson was at Luther he increased the membership of the band from a baker's dozen to fifty-three. He increased with characteristic energy the Musical Library and founded the Musical Union. He created a magnificent orchestra, and the Choral Union which presents annually some of the greatest of the sacred oratorios and cantatas. He organized the Luther College Museum and collected many thousand articles of great value. When he left Luther, he became the proprietor of the Northern Book and Music Co., Chicago.

His successor, Prof. Sperati, comes from a musical family. His parents were musical; his children are musical. His father, an Italian musician, married a Danish girl and finally settled at Christiania, where he was a church organist and musical director of brilliant and solid worth, and famed from Turin to Trondhjem. The boy Carlo learned to play the violin, piano and organ, but was especially good on the drums. At the Tivoli Gardens, Copenhagen, he played before the crowned heads and in Christiania he received a beautiful set of studs from the dowager Queen Josephine. He attended a navigation school and sailed the seven seas. On one occasion when his boat stopped at Havana, he went on shore and stepped into a fine hotel. A piano was standing there with the paid musicians resting for the moment from their task. One of his companions said, "Sperati, you go and play us a tune on the piano." The musicians beckoned him to try it, smiling to themselves at the thought of this sailor lad playing on the piano. But their smiles were soon changed to wonder and amazement as he played by heart with exquisite technique the masterpieces of Italy, Germany and Norway. The room was soon filled with enchanted listeners, and after an hour or two of playing in which there was absolute quiet, the delighted audience rushed up to him to give him their heartfelt thanks.

Through his life as a sailor Sperati had a burning desire to study theology and through the instrumentality of Sister Elizabeth Fedde, he was led to go to Luther College and later to Luther Seminary, after which he went into the Norwegian ministry at Bellingham, 1891-1894, Parkland, 1894-1895, Tacoma, 1895-1905. He became instructor in music at Pacific Academy in 1894 and director of choirs all along Puget Sound. He was the first choir director of the Norwegian Singers of the Pacific Coast and held the position 13 years, 1903-1916. Rudolf Moeller, the composer, is now president of this association. In 1905 he came to Luther College, and has won distinction as choir director and musical instructor of national and international repute. In

Haldor J. Hanson   Theo. S. Reimestad   Peter H. P. Rydning

Musicians, Composers, Teachers, Directors

1914 the climax of band tours was achieved when the band represented Luther College and Norwegian-American culture in the field of music at the hundredth anniversary of Norway's independence. A total of 127 concerts were played besides, no doubt, an equal number of special short concerts and serenades. Ten different countries and six capital cities, namely: Washington, Christiania, Copenhagen, Berlin, Paris and London, were visited. There were sixty band members on the Norway tour, besides seven others. The press notices concerning Prof. Sperati and the Luther College Concert Band everywhere have been highly favorable. The three following are illustrative: "This band is without doubt one of the finest amateur organizations in the world today, and has played in every city of note in the United States and several foreign countries."—"Daily Avalanche," Glenwood Springs, Colo. "Mr. Sperati is a masterly leader, and the baton in his hands becomes a wand to sway his men at will. He has a crisp, clean-cut style of directing, and is absolutely reliable; and this, combined with a refined musical temperament, profound understanding of his art and command of his men, can produce but one result, success."—"Everett Morning Tribune," Everett, Washington. "That this able and well disciplined corps is master of things of sterling artistic value, was shown by their rendition of Grieg's 'Peer Gynt Suite' and Liszt's 'Second Hungarian Rhapsody,' which was artistically and effectively played."—"Verdens Gang," Oslo, Norway.

In addition to the musical organizations which flourish in the Norwegian schools and congregations, there are a number of other musical associations, local, state and national. There is a Choral Union of the choirs in the Norwegian Lutheran Church. Dr. Paul M. Glasoe is the president. There is an association of men's choirs which includes a large number of strong local organizations. Male chorus singing is one of the most unique contributions of Norwegians to American song. The first male

O. M. Oleson
Ft. Dodge, Iowa

Alfred Paulsen,
Chicago, Ill.

J. Arndt Bergh
Northfield, Minn.

Far-famed Musicians

chorus established by the Norwegians in America was organized
at Granddad Bluff, La Crosse, June 1, 1869, by C. R. Jackwitz.
It was called the "Normanna Choir." Hauman G. Haugan,
noted Chicago banker and railroad promoter, was the first president. Emil Berg was the first instructor. The writer's father,
Ole H. Norlie, from Lillehammer, Norway, was along organizing
it. A few years later he helped organize a similar organization
in Sioux City, and in 1891 the "Fram Singing Society," also of
Sioux City, and he was a member of the United Scandinavian
Singers of America who sang so sweetly at the Columbian Exposition in 1893. A great number of these societies have sprung
up here and there. Some of them have had only a short existence,
others are still virile, as, for example: Luren, Gauken and Grieg,
in Winneshiek County, Iowa. Luren was organized in Decorah
in 1874, and celebrated its fifty-first anniversary March
17, 1825. The annual song conventions (sangerfest) of the Norwegian male choirs are indeed most impressive and win from
the American public of every nationality unstinted praise. The
Norwegian Singing Association of America, organized in 1892, has
at present 32 choirs in its membership, located in six states. The
association publishes a musical monthly, "Sangerhilsen," edited
by Th. F. Hamann, the secretary, 4009 Harriet Avenue, Minneapolis. The president is H. L. Oftedahl, Chicago; A. C. Floan,
St. Paul, is vice president; Th. F. Hamann, Minneapolis, is secretary; Anton O. Sætrang, Chicago, treasurer; Fred. Wick, Sioux
City, and I. N. Sødahl, Duluth, the choir directors. O. M. Oleson, Ft. Dodge, is the honorary president. Oleson is a druggist.
He is a man of many interests outside of his professional work.
He has given his city a very beautiful park called the Oleson
Park, has donated $35,000.00 to the Lutheran Hospital there, and
has for many years given an annual prize of $50.00 for the best
literary production in Norwegian and $100.00 for the best musi-

cal composition by a Norwegian. He is himself a splendid musician and director, and the author of a number of standard compositions, as: "In Flanders Field."

Aside from Christiansen, Dahle, Reimestad, Paulsen, and Oleson, there have been a cheerful number of composers bearing Norwegian names. J. Rode Jacobson has been a very successful composer. In 1920 he was awarded the first prize of $100.00 by the Norwegian Singers' Society of America for his composition "Valkyrien," which was sung by a male chorus of 700 voices at the Duluth convention in 1920. Again, in 1925, he won the first prize for his cantata in honor of the Norse-American Centennial. He has written "Berceuse," "Foraarsjubel," "Vær snil mot mor," "Lek paa engen," "September Rose," and others. His organ teacher was Peter Lindeman of Christiania. He is a graduate of the Conservatory of Christiania, and has studied under famous masters at Berlin. He is the organist and musical director of Christ Lutheran Church, Chicago, conducts a music school and lectures on missions and music. Another Norwegian-American composer is Signe Lund. In 1917 she competed with 600 other composers and won the prize of $500.00 awarded by the National Arts Club of New York for the best American war song, entitled, "The Road to France." She composed the music for "Du Land," which was written for the Norwegian Singers' Association and sung by them at the

Signe Lund

Sangerfest in Fargo, 1912. She wrote the text and music to "Mor Norge," dedicated to the Minnesota Singers who visited Norway in 1923. Lives now at Oslo.

Among the music directors not already mentioned the following are representatives: P. H. P. Rydning, United Church Seminary; Erick Oulie, Minneapolis Orchestra and Choir; Henrich M. Gunnersen, church organist, composer and director, Minneapolis; Paul Harold Ensrud, Red Wing Seminary, Concordia College and the University of Michigan; Oscar I. Hertsgaard, Concordia College and Minneapolis; L. Josephine Wright, Mayville Normal School; Emil Biørn, painter, sculptor, musician and choir director par excellence, Chicago; Christian Sinding, Eastman School of Music, Rochester; Ole Windingstad, New York City; Alf. Klingenberg, Eastman School; Oscar R. Overby, Concordia College, Park Region College, St. Olaf College; Oscar Lyders, Waldorf College; Carl R. Youngdahl, Augustana College; Martin Bjornson, Oak Grove Seminary; Edith Quist, Concordia College; Harry Anderson, Augsburg Seminary; Jo (Philip)

Troniz, Dallas, Texas, Conservatory, Hollywood, California; Mr. Lindtner, choir director Scandinavian Singing Association, Chicago, and organist, San Francisco; Frederick Wick, Sioux City, Ia.

The following stand in the front rank among the singers: Andrew J. Boe, Vigleik E. Bøe, C. N. Engelstad, Erik Bye, Oscar A. Grønseth, Mus. D., Ralph Hammer, Christian Mathiesen, H. B. Thorgrimsen, Albert Arveschou, Theodor S. Reimestad, Mr. Norskou, Carsten Woll and Paul G. Schmidt. Among the women singers of note are: Adelaide Hjertaas Roe, Mabel Jacobs, Gertrude Boe-Overby, Dikka Bothne, Hannah Christensen-Dorrum, Carolyn Jacobson-Moe, Alice C. Jacobson-Arneson, Blanche Wollan-Rovelstad, Jennie Skurdalsvold, Sofie Hammer-M o e l l e r, Madame Bergljot Aalrud Tillisch, and Olive Fremstad, an operatic star of the first magnitude.

Of instrumental soloists the number is legion: Andrew Onstad is a remarkable clarinetist and band director; Marie Elizabeth Toohey is a violinist and orchestra leader at Augustana College. She is a graduate of Leipzig Conservatory of Music. Hilma Louise Wright-Drake is an expert on the piano; so also are Lulu Glimme, Mathilde Finseth-Roseland. Hjalmar Rabe, of Chicago, has the distinction of being one of the foremost trombone players in America. He is a member of the Chicago Symphony Orchestra. Maja Bang, daughter of Bishop Bang, is a violinist in New York. Her book, "Violin Methods," is used by 40.000 teachers of violin. In 1922 she married Baron Hoehn. Nils Rein is a good violinist. Adolf Olsen, Minneapolis, as a violinist and director, is in great demand. Vittorio Sperati plays the Xylophone with remarkable technique. Pearl Gran won the $1,650.00 prize in piano playing at the Cosmopolitan School of Music, Chicago, May 19, 1925. George Markhus is a manufacturer of good violins. Knute Reindahl is also a violin maker and president of the Violin Makers' Association of America.

Most famous of Norwegian-American musicians was Ole Bull, the man who first introduced Norwegian Music to the American public. Auber Forestier says of him in "The Norway Music Album": "When the young artist sallied forth into the world with his violin, in 1829, the word Norway scarcely existed in the European vocabulary; but he carried with him the name of his Fatherland, that poor little beginner among nations, and during his long and brilliant career he glorified it wherever he won triumphs for his own name. He never forgot to consider himself a representative of Norway, wherever he went he talked of his native land, her people, her mountains, her fjords, her wonderful natural grandeur, and played her folk-music in the highest circles of Europe in the presence of kings and emperors. When the home people became aware that he thus carried about with him what no one else would have ventured to bring forward, and that it found favor among those whom the world honored, courage was infused into them. Ole Bull gave his native land self-confidence—the noblest gift he could have made it."

The urge of self-expression within the Norwegian group has at times taken the form of painting and sculpture. Among the

Painters

Norwegian painters are: Herbjørn Gausta, Arne Berger, August Klagstad, Sarah Kirkeberg-Raugland, Olaf M. Brauner, Jonas Lie, Emil Biørn, Sigurd Schow, Lars Haukanes, Alexander Grinager, Brynjulf Strandenæs and Amanda Bloom-Zainoff. Gausta studied in Italy, Germany and Norway and lived and labored as a bachelor in solitude in Minneapolis. He made many hundred paintings of men, and pictures from life. The pictures "The Lay Preaching" and "Grace before Meat," in this book are copied from two of his masterpieces. Arne Berger is a very good portrait and altar painter. His portraits of Thomas Lajord and O. P. Holman, for example, are masterpieces. His studio is at Minneapolis. Sigvart Sieverts has won a national prize by his painting "A Snow Stormy Day." He painted the "Restaurationen" reproduced in this book on page 121. Klagstad worked in portrait studios of Chicago, Brooklyn and Boston for eight years. He had a studio at Marinette, Wisconsin, where altar paintings and portraits were the principal products of his brush. In 1915 he moved to Minneapolis, where he specializes in altar paintings. Among the outstanding portraits by him are: Martin Luther, Bjørnstjerne Bjørnson, James J. Hill, T. H. Dahl, Agnes Mellby and Judge J. W. Stone. Mrs. Raugland was an excellent altar picture painter. Brauner is head of the Department of Fine Arts at Cornell University. His father was a wood engraver. He has won several fine art prizes. Lie is a nephew of Jonas Lie, the distinguished novelist of the same name. Harry Sundby-Hansen says of Lie: "Few painters of any immigrant group have achieved the fame that Mr. Lie has. His subjects show great versatility. He depicts the storm, the thunder cloud, snow covered hills and rocks, dark, half hidden rivers and forest streams, fishing boats and a great variety of other subjects. Jonas Lie has painted New York as perhaps no other artist. Prosaic things like city streets and bridges he has interpreted in color, and he presents them to the onlooker in pictures of rare artistic beauty. He has painted the Panama Canal during construction operations, and these paintings are declared by critics to be a color-epic to labor. Pictures by Jonas Lie hang in the Carnegie Institute, Pittsburgh, in the Luxembourg Gallery, Paris, and in many clubs and public institutions in Europe and America." Emil Biørn is not only a versatile painter but a versatile artist in all respects. He is a sculptor, poet and musician. Concerning him Olaf Huseby says in "Den Nye Heimen:" "Director Emil Biørn is the idol of every singer, an excellent director, an artist by profession, wonderful as a man. Lives in

H. Gausta
Portrait Painter

Jens O. Grøndahl
Author of
"America, My Country"

A. Klagstad
Altar Painter

Chicago; was born in Christiania." Schow is well known for his excellent color works. Haukanes is a painter of Hardanger landscapes. One of these pictures hangs in the Minneapolis Institute of Art; another, in the Chicago-Norwegian Club. In 1923 he became teacher of art at the Academy of Arts in Winnipeg, Manitoba. Grinager is a Minnesota man who does "fine work in landscapes with babbling brooks and sunsets, rich in lights and shadows." Strandenæs excels as an illustrator. One of his Liberty Loan Campaign posters was considered remarkable. Mrs. Zainoff was a young painter of much promise, an exponent of the modern realistic school. Her specialty was landscape work with high color effects. She died March 4, 1925. How many of the pictures by these and other Norwegian artists will live on, it is impossible to say, but it is safe to conclude with Hawthorne, that: "One picture in a thousand, perhaps, ought to live in the applause of mankind, from generation to generation until the colors fade and blacken out of sight, or the canvas rot entirely away" ("Marble Faun").

As representatives of the sculptors, Jacob Fjelde easily is in the front rank. He had his studio in Minneapolis. The Ole Bull Statue in Loring Park is a sample of his *Sculptors* handiwork. His son, Paul Fjelde, with studio in New York, has modeled the Colonel Hans C. Heg monument which is this year to be raised in Madison, Wisconsin. Dr. Herman O. Fjelde, physician at Abercrombie, North Dakota, 1897, and Fargo, 1912, was a builder of monuments. He took the lead among his countrymen in having a memorial erected at the Agricultural College in Fargo to the memory of Bjørnson, also one of Wergeland, at Fargo, and later one in honor of Rolf Ganger. An Ibsen monument was raised at Wahpeton through his hardy work. At Moorhead the monuments commemorating Ivar Aasen and Hans Nielsen Hauge, which stand on the Concordia Campus, are the result of his indefatigable toil and insuppressible idealism. He believed that the sight of these memorials would be an inspiration to his people to live more noble lives, and to treasure the inheritance of the land of their pioneer fathers. Hendrik Christian Andersen studied art and architecture at Boston, Paris, Naples and Rome. His principal works as sculptor are: "Fountain of Life," "Fountain of Immortality," "Jacob Wrestling with the Angels," "Study of an Athlete," busts and medallions and portraits of Pope Benedictus XV. He is the founder of the World Conscience Society, and author of a book entitled "Creation of a World Center of Communication," in two volumes. Christian Schiøtt is a pianist employed by the Cahill's Telharmonic Music Company of New York, and a sculptor, having his studio with the Society of Independent Artists, Waldorf-Astoria. Among his works is a bust of the tennis queen, Molla Bjurstedt-Mallory. Sigurd Neandross, Ridgefield, New Jersey, has won great distinction by his works of sculpture, notably, "The Kiss," "The Egyptian Widow" and "The Song of the Sea." Trygve Hammer, New York, "has done good work in stone, wood, and copper, and has endeavored to awaken an interest in Norwegian wood carving and ornamentation. He is a director of the Society of Independent Artists and has exhibited in the Society's annual exhibits in New York." Prof. E. Kr. Johnsen, Luther Theological Seminary, was an expert wood carver, and Professor M. O. Bøckman, D.D., president of Luther Theological Seminary, paints landscapes remarkably well. Gilbert P. Riswold, born of Norwegian immigrant parents on a farm near Baltic, South Dakota, located now at Chicago, is a sculptor of unusual promise. His statue of Stephen A. Douglas, standing in front of the State House in Springfield, is declared by critics to be one of the finest works of art in America. This work was accepted in a competition participated in by more than

75 artists, including several of America's leading sculptors. In his hands:

> The stone unhewn and cold
> Becomes a living mould,
> The more the marble wastes
> The more the statue grows.

On the basis that the Norwegians in America comprise 2 per cent of the population and have produced 2 per cent of the medical men, there are 2,900 Norwegian physicians and surgeons in America, also 100 osteopaths, 270 veterinary surgeons, 1,125 dentists, besides 2,982 nurses. Most of these settle down in Norwegian communities, but they are found also in the remotest sections of the land practising their profession.

Doctors

Ludvig Hektoen   Ingeborg Rasmussen   Thrond Stabo

Illustrious Norwegian Physicians

The greater number of the Norwegian pioneer doctors had their training at the University of Christiania. The alumni directory of the University covering the first 70 years of its work mentions about 70 of the medical graduates who emigrated to America. Such names as the following are more or less familiar to those who are acquainted with the pioneer settlements: Hans Christian Brandt (1814-88), graduated 1838, emigrated 1840, chief residence Kansas City, Mo. Eduard Boeckman (1849-..), class of 1867, emigrated 1886, St. Paul. Eye specialist. He has twice been honored by his Alma Mater with honorary degrees—the M. D. in 1882 and the Ph. D. in 1911; the King of Norway in 1911 knighted him Commander of the Order of St. Olav. Berent Martin Behrens (1843-11), class of 1868, came to America in 1882, located in Chicago. Christian Christensen (1852-——), class of 1879; emigrated 1888; surgeon at La Crosse Lutheran Hospital. Johan Dundas (Dass) came to Wisconsin in 1847, returned to Norway and came back in 1850, locating at Cambridge. Born in 1812 in Norway; died in 1883 at Madison, Wis. Anders Daae

(1852-24), Christiania, M.D., 1878; to America, 1880, Chicago.
Johan Andreas de Besche (1855—), M. D., 1883, emigrated
1884, Milwaukee; he returned to Norway in 1913. He is the author of the Wisconsin law requiring certificate of good health as
a requisite for marriage. Adolf Gundersen, M. D., 1890; surgeon,
La Crosse Lutheran Hospital, 1891—; president, Security Savings Bank. Søren Johan Hanssen (1820-?), Christiania, 1855,
to Koshkonong, Wis., 1856; in the Fifteenth Wisconsin Regiment;
author of "Orthodoxi og Kristendom," 1865. Jacob Hvoslef
(1865—), M. D., 1891, professor of orthopedic surgery, Hamline University, practising physician in Minneapolis and at
International Falls. Jens Andreas Holmboe (1827-76), M. D.,
1853; emigrated, 1863; leper specialist. Knut O. Hoegh (1844-
—), M. D., 1869; La Crosse, 1869-88; Minneapolis, 1888—.

Eduard Boeckmann,
M.D., Ph.D.
St. Paul

Anna Sigmond,
D.H.
New York

Carl M. Roan.
M.D.
Minneapolis

Professor at Hamline University for many years. Michael Iversen (1861—), M. D., 1890, Stoughton, Wis., 1891—. Johan
Balthazar Meyer (1851-18), M. D., 1877, Chicago, 1884-18, lung
specialist. Bernhard J. Madsen, Chicago and Cambridge, 1851.
Henrik H. Nissen (1864—), Albert Lea and Minneapolis, 1889
—; specialist in eye, ear, nose and throat. Johan A. R. Nanne-
stad; Madison, 1891, Canton, 1895, Bricelyn, 1901, and Albert
Lea, 1906. Axel C. Rosenkrantz (1844-17), M. D., 1869; emigrated, 1873. Karl Ferdinand Sandberg (1855—); to America,
1882, professor of gynecology, Jenner Medical College. Theodor
A. Schytte (1812-2), M. D., 1840; lived in America five years,
1843-48; wrote on his return to Norway a handbook for emigrants,
published in Swedish at Stockholm in 1849: "Vägledning för
Emigranter." Tonnes A. Thams (1848-12), Fargo, 1884—.
Thomas D. Warloe, (1867-23), Chicago. Also a musician. Trond
Stabo (1870—), Spring Grove, 1895, Decorah, 1906—. Norwegian vice consul, president of Luther College Board of Trustees.

Not less conspicuous, able, or conscientious than their Chris-
tiania-trained brethren are the Norwegian doctors educated in

America. Perhaps first among these in recognized standing in the scientific world is Ludvig Hektoen, pathologist. Born at Westby, Wis., July 2, 1863; trained at Luther College, College of Physicians and Surgeons and Rush, Chicago, with graduate study at Upsala, Prague and Berlin, head professor of pathology and morbid anatomy at Rush and University of Chicago and director of McCormick Institute for Infectious Diseases, etc. The University of Christiania gave him an honorary M. D. in 1911; the University of Michigan created him Sc. D. in 1912, the University of Wisconsin likewise in 1916. He is an author and editor.

Of other authors may be mentioned Dr. Carl M. Roan (1878--), Minneapolis, who has written a practical hand book for the average man—"Sygdom, Sundhet og Velvære" (Sickness, Health and Happiness). He has contributed health talks to "Familiens Magasin" since 1913. He has taught at the Minneapolis Deaconess Training School for Nurses, has been treasurer of the Lutheran Free Church, and has been a promoter of every good cause within his circle. Fred. Voss Mohn (1856--), Los Angeles, winner in a prize contest on the "Therapy of Vaginal Diseases" (1912), is the editor of a health magazine, "För Doktoren Kommer."

Albert C. Amundson (1855-1919), Cambridge, wrote a household medical book in Norwegian. Herman O. Fjelde (1866-1918), a graduate of Minnesota, practised medicine at Abercrombie and Fargo, and erected statues in honor of great Norwegians—Rolf Ganger, Wergeland, Hauge, Aasen, Bjørnson, Ibsen. Irenaeus E. Krohn (1867--), Black River Falls, Wisconsin, built up a Norwegian museum as a side line. Jacob Wright Magelssen (1843--), a Rush graduate, has practised at Koshkonong and Rushford, Minnesota, since 1866. Dr. Jonas Rein Nilsen(1845--), Brooklyn, is a professor of gynecology at the Postgraduate Medical School, Brooklyn. Gerhard S. C. H. Paoli (1815-1898) was a professor at Women's Medical College, Chicago. Separated fusel-oil from alcohol. Got gold medal at World's Exposition in New York, 1853; built a fusel-oil distillery, Chicago, and organized the Blaney-Pool Co. Niles T. Quales (1831-1914), a graduate of Copenhagen and Rush, a veteran of the Civil War, a promotor of charitable institutions at Chicago, a professor,at Tabitha, Deaconess Hospital, city physician, etc.

Ingeborg Rasmussen (1858--), M. D., Northwestern, 1892, has practised medicine in Chicago; has been with the Rush Medical Dispensary, Mary Thompson Hospital, Norwegian-American Tabitha Hospital. Is a member of Women's Medical Society, Women's Press Association, Women's City Club., etc., and since 1911 one of the editors of "Skandinaven." She has received a gold medal from King Haakon VII in recognition of her services to humanity. Valborg Sogn (1858-16) has been professor of gynecology at Northwestern University and the Tabitha Hospital. Haldor Sneve is professor of mental diseases. C. P. Lommen is dean of the College of Medicine, University of South Dakota. M. N. Voldeng, M. D., LL. D., has been professor at Drake University, the superintendent of the State Insane Hospital at Cherokee, Ia., and is director of the Colony of Epileptics at Woodward, Iowa.

This list is already continued beyond the capacity of this little volume. But just one more word: A Norwegian center like Minneapolis and Saint Paul is a real mecca for Norwegian doctors and sick folk. Here are names such as: E. O. Giere, Eduard and Egil Boeckmann, the Bessesens, A. F. Bratrud, Ivar Sivertsen, N. H. Scheldrup, H. Lysne, C. A. Fjeldstad, Kr. Egilsrud, Hendrick Nissen, G. Bjornstad, H. Sneve, C. M. Oberg, Harold Pederson, R. J. Petersen, Oscar Owre, A. G. Wethall, Carl M. Roan, A. C. Tingdale, and many others.

George S. Monson, dentist, St. Paul, is the inventor of an instrument for reproducing the movements of the human jaw and
Dentists founder of the Monson Clinic Club. Alfred Owre is dean of the Dental College at the University of Minnesota. Erling Thoen is a professor of dental anatomy at the University of Iowa. Anna Sigmond of New York is a professor of dental hygiene at Statens Tannlæge Institut, University of Christiania.

Mankind has been concerned about law and order ever since the first family. Every branch of government is concerned about
Lawyers law and order. Men everywhere recognize the authority of certain laws as fundamentally right, with binding force in consequence. Man has the faculty of conscience, and society is a moral institution with moral ends. Therefore Kant, the philosopher, says:

Aad J. Vinje			Herman L. Ekern			Elias Rachie, Ph.D.
Chief Justice, Wis.		Attorney General, Wis.		Lawyer, Minneapolis

Two things I contemplate with ceaseless awe:
The stars of heaven and man's sense of Law.

Now, the Norwegians have given their best contribution to American law and order in just this thing, that they have kept close to their native conscience and also to the clearer teachings of God's Word. They have, therefore, on the one hand insisted on their personal freedom and, on the other hand, their duty to obey just laws. They have shown the same independence here as in times of yore when they were the freest people in Europe. They have taken law-making and law enforcement seriously. As legislators they have tried to make just laws; as citizens they have tried to obey the laws, even if they were oppressive. Some of the best laws of state and nation have been written on the statute books by Norwegian-Americans. The Volstead Law, for example.

Theodore Wold   Victor F. Lawson   Harald Thorson

Great Bankers

There have been many good Norwegian-American lawyers, justices and judges. John W. Arctander, LL.D., a man who seldom lost a case. He was a criminal lawyer. The picture shows him assuming one of his favorite poses before a jury. He wrote several books—a practical handbook of Minnesota law, a story of his conversion, a story of W. Duncan of Metlakatla, the "Apostle of Alaska," and a novel, "Guilty." His "Apostle of Alaska" won him a gold medal for the best book at the Portland Exposition. Elias Rachie is a good lawyer, located at Minneapolis. He is said to have taken more degrees at the University of Minnesota than any other alumnus of the school, including B.L., A.M., Ph.D. and LL.B. Herman L. Ekern is a graduate of the University of Wisconsin. He has been a specialist in insurance and is now the attorney general of Wisconsin. Aad J. Vinje is a chief justice of Wisconsin, A. M. Christianson is chief justice of North Dakota, and Frank Anderson held a similar position in South Dakota.

There have been several district judges, as: Aad J. Vinje, Gullick Risjord and George Thompson in Wisconsin; Albert W. Johnson (1909—, I. M. Olson (1906—), G. E. Qvale (1897),

Lewis S. Nelson (1911—), Andrew Grindeland (1903—), Norman E. Pederson and Gunnar H. Nordbye of Minnesota; Edward Engerud, Harrison A. Bronson and A. T. Cole of North Dakota; and Frank Anderson and William Williamson of South Dakota.

Of county and city judges there have been quite a number. As, for example, among the city judges: N. T. Moen, Fergus Falls; H. C. Ryen, Moorhead; Martin Berger, Sioux Falls; J. C. Gilbertson, Eau Claire; Erick L. Vinje, Duluth; J. M. Arntsen, Tacoma; C. M. Nielsen, Salt Lake City; Manley L. Fosseen, Minneapolis; and Oscar M. Torrison, Chicago. Judge Torrison talks just enough Hebrew to hold the Jewish vote in his precinct. Andreas Ueland is a well known ex-probate judge and attorney in Minneapolis. Judge L. K. Haskill has held his job since 1901.

August D. Reymert, the first Norwegian to enter state politics, became a federal judge in Arizona. Lucius J. M. Malmin was federal judge in Illinois and Gudbrand J. Lomen is a federal judge at Nome, Alaska. As judges the Norwegians have been eminently fair, too fair to suit some people.

The Norwegians are engaged in every kind of honorable work and are making good all along the line. It is refreshing, thrilling, inspiring to trace the steps of these men from the depths of the valley to the mountain peaks of success. Lack of space forbids any further discussion. We present pictures of three men who have done very well: Harald Thorson, Victor F. Lawson and Theodore Wold, all three bankers. Harald Thorson established a chain of banks throughout the Red River Valley and left an estate of over $1,000,000.00. He helped to found St. Olaf College and remembered it with gifts from time to time—in all about $1,000,000.00. Victor F. Lawson, the publisher of the "Chicago Daily News," is the founder of the Postal Savings Banks in America. Theodore Wold was trained by Harald Thorson. He became president of the Scandinavian-American Bank, Minneapolis, in 1910, governor of the Federal Reserve Bank, 1914, and first vice president of the Northwestern National Bank, Minneapolis, 1921.

Dr. John W. Arctander

16. Sports and Athletics

The race, like the child, demands play and recreation. All work and no play makes Jack a dull boy. Play gives strength and skill, and, in the form of athletic contests and sports, through victory and defeat, it has great educational values and wholesome, refining, uplifting effects. It calms the passions, strengthens the will, arrests insubordination, crime, vice and physical decline. It relieves distraction from study and protracted labor of other sorts, tones up the body, makes the heart glad, drives away sorrow, tempers a man's estimate of himself and his fellows, creates sportsmanship and good will. It is one of the creators of well-balanced manhood and womanhood, and, as Horace Mann says: "One former is worth 100 reformers." Or, as old Samuel Johnson says: "I am a great friend to public amusements, for they keep people from vice." Play keeps the race young, keeps the individual young. Men grow old because they stop playing.

Nels Nelson
World Champion on Skis

The Norwegians are toilers, but not slaves to toil. From time immemorial they have taken time off to play and to care for their bodies. They are a clean and vigorous race. The name of their Saturday in Modern Norwegian is "lørdag," in Old Norse "laugardagr," and it means bathday. On that day, their custom was to take hot baths, a good old custom that still flourishes. And, moreover, they took their weekly, or even daily, dip in the

THE MINNEAPOLIS SKY-LINE, 1875

cold waters of the sea, winter as well as summer, a custom which even now has not entirely died out. They rejoice in feats of daring, strength and skill, such as, sailing and skiing.

In this country, it is especially in the ski sport that they have distinguished themselves, and that to such a degree that they are *Skiing* in a class by themselves. Nearly all the amateur and professional ski champions have been Norwegians. Skiing is the king of winter sports. It takes one out into the open. Combined in skiing are the pleasures of both hiking and snowshoeing, and in addition there is the thrill of coasting. Surely sport with such exhilaration, putting roses on cheeks of young and old and giving vigor to all, can be called healthful. A number of ski clubs have been organized. The first one is believed to be Dovre, organized at Eau Claire, Wisconsin, in 1886. The next year clubs were estab-

Hakon C. Norlie and His Home-made Cart

lished at Minneapolis, St. Paul, Stillwater, La Crosse and Stoughton. Since then they have been planted all over America from Maine to Washington and from Denver to Edmonton. In 1904, at the instigation of the Ishpeming Club, a National Ski Association was formed. Carl Tellefsen, Ishpeming, was the first president; Aksel H. Holter, Ashland, Wisconsin, was the first secretary. The officers in 1925 are: Oscar T. Oyaas, Superior, Wisconsin, president; K. Rieber, Canton, South Dakota, vice president; Gustave E. Lindboe, Chicago, secretary; Olaf Thompson, Lanesboro, Minnesota, treasurer. The National Ski Association now includes 30 local clubs and has 20,000 members. There are more clubs outside the national organization than within it.

Since 1916 there have been national tournaments every year except 1919, and, of course, many local contests. The national ski champions have been as follows on the next page:

THE MINNEAPOLIS SKY-LINE, 1900

AMATEUR SKI CHAMPIONS

Year	Place	Champion	Address
1916	Glenwood, Minnesota	Andrew Olson	Iola, Wisconsin
1917	St. Paul, Minnesota	Ludvig Hoiby	Northfield, Minnesota
1918	Chicago, Illinois	Sverre Hendrickson	Duluth, Minnesota
1920	Chippewa Falls, Wisconsin	Sverre Hendrickson	Superior, Wisconsin
1921	Denver, Colorado	Einar Jensen	Chicago, Illinois
1922	Chicago, Illinois	Ragnar Omtvedt	Chicago, Illinois
1923	Minneapolis, Minnesota	Anders Haugen	Minneapolis, Minnesota

PROFESSIONAL SKI CHAMPIONS

Year	Place	Champion	Address
1916	Glenwood, Minnesota	Henry Hall	Ishpeming, Michigan
1917	St. Paul, Minnesota	Ragnar Omtvedt	Chicago, Illinois
1918	Chicago, Illinois	Lars Haugen	Chippewa, Falls, Wisconsin
1920	Chippewa Falls, Wisconsin	Anders Haugen	Steamboat Springs, Colorado
1921	Denver, Colorado	Carl Howelsen	Steamboat Springs, Colorado
1922	Chicago, Illinois	Lars Haugen	Steamboat Springs, Colorado

RECENT WORLD'S RECORDS

Year	Place	Champion	Record
1917	Steamboat Springs, Colorado	Henry Hall	203 feet
1919	Dillon, Colorado	Anders Haugen	213 feet
1920	Dillon, Colorado	Anders Haugen	214 feet
1921	Revelstoke, British Columbia	Henry Hall	229 feet
1923	Steamboat Springs, Colorado	Hans Hansen	210 feet
1924	Revelstoke, British Columbia	Nels Nelson	240 feet

All in the last table were professionals except Hans Hansen. All in all three tables used Northland skis made by the Northland Ski Manufacturing Co., St. Paul, except Nels Nelson. C. A. Lund, president of this company, is a native of Norway and has been actively interested in skiing since boyhood. He personally knows most skiers of prominence and has the satisfaction of seeing them ski and win on Northlands.

Athletics has held an honored place at all the Norwegian colleges and nearly all the academies. In the early days the boys *College Sports* found exercise and enjoyment in running, jumping, wrestling, weight lifting and hiking. Baseball dates back to the beginning of school life, and during the last 20-30 years football, basketball,

S. S. Reque   Knute Rockne   E. B. Anderson

Champion Coaches

tennis, soccer, golf, turning, track, military drill and gymnastic instruction have also made claim on the time and energy of the students. Modern gymnasiums are being provided at all the colleges and several of the academies. Athletic associations have been started at all the stronger institutions. Letter societies for those who have won unusual distinction in athletics and forensics, illustrate the efforts of the students to maintain high standards and enthusiasm. Competent coaches and athletic directors are being provided, and a high grade of instruction and sportsmanship is being inculcated.

Luther College, for example, is a classical school of the first rank, which has stressed honest, thorough scholarship. Says C. F. Sanders, in the "Educational Review" (March, 1923): "Luther College has a record of which she may without offense have a high sense of becoming pride. She has done a great work." And James F. Conover, writing in the "Iowa Magazine" for February, 1923, says: "Luther College, with its cluster of imposing buildings and wonderfully beautiful campus situated on a high eminence overlooking the Upper Iowa River, today is an educational institution of national reputation." Nevertheless, Luther College is just as jealous of its athletic honor and fame as it is of its scholastic standing. It is a school for men, with "mens sana in corpore sano" (a sound mind in a sound body), as one of its golden rules. Wm. P. Sihler and Oscar L. Olson were the first promoters of the remarkable success in baseball at Luther College. Arthur Laudell was elected coach in 1917; Styrk Sigurd Reque, in 1919. Luther played its first intercollegiate baseball game with St. Olaf College, May 17, 1891, and won. St. Olaf played on the Luther grounds May 17, 1925, and won, 2 to 0. In the nine innings not a St. Olaf man hit the ball, Luther made only two hits. St. Olaf has always been Luther's most interesting and feared rival in baseball and other contests, a foeman worthy of his steel. In baseball Luther has so far been on top. In the 30 years, 1891-1921, there have been 36 Luther-St. Olaf games. Luther tied once, lost ten times and won 25. From 1891 to 1921 Luther has played 41 colleges and universities, tied five times, lost 87 times and won 128 times—40.5 per cent lost, 59.5 per cent won. Football coaches at Luther have been: Walter Jewell, 1919, a former Iowa University tackle; Oscar M. Solem, 1920, a former Minnesota University end tackle; Ivan Doseff, 1921-1922, a former Chicago University all-Western honor man; Franklin C. Cappon, 1923-1924, a former Michigan University, all-American honor man; also last, but not least, Orlando W. Qualley, 1920—, and S. S. Reque, athletic director, 1925—. Instructors in military drill have been: Peter S. Reque, 1865; Brigadier General Christian Brandt, 1876; O. B. Overn, 1917. An S. A. T. C. unit was maintained by the War Department of the U. S., 1918, with Lieuts. H. H. Fisher and Allen C. Grundy in charge; an R. O. T. C. was established in 1919 and discontinued in 1920. Instructors in turning at Luther have been: Carlo Alberto Sperati, 1886; Dr. Ole Boe, 1907; Francis E. Peterson, 1921; William Johnson, 1924. In 1909, the first year Luther took part in the Iowa State Gymnastic Meet, the team was awarded the championship. Luther made 256.4 points to 47.2 for Iowa University. Wm. P. Sihler and Gisle Bothne laid out the first tennis court at Luther and played the first game. Many championship teams have since been developed at Luther. David Nelson, Rhodes scholar and captain in the World War, coaches tennis in addition to his duties as instructor at the college. The interest in athletics acquired at Luther as a rule stays by a man the rest of his days. Gynther Storaasli, L.C., '11, was a chaplain. On a Sunday morning he preached a good, earnest sermon to the soldier boys, then had his dinner, entered his flying ship and landed near a place where the boys were playing ball. They insisted on that he should try his hand at pitching. He pitched and won the game. He had learned the trick at Luther.

At St. Olaf College the athletic spirit is as good as at Luther and the laurels won are as brilliant. Guided by Endre B. Anderson as coach and Dr. Edward R. Cooke as physical director, St. Olaf boys keep in good trim and keep Luther and other doughty rivals at bay. Augustana College and Concordia College are likewise up and doing, with a heart for any fate. The co-educational schools provide also adequate physical training and athletic sports for the girls.

In connection with football it is interesting to note that Knute Rockne, coach at the great Catholic university, Notre Dame, since 1914, is a Norwegian and a Lutheran. He was an all-American end in football in 1913. Inter-collegiate football is the most sensational of American sports. Gatherings between 50,000 and 100,000 spectators are not uncommon. Rockne has been able to develop every year some of the top-notch teams in America that draw immense crowds. He reached the pinnacle of his fame in 1924 when, after defeating Lombard, Wabash, West Point (Army), Princeton, Georgia Tech., Wisconsin, Northwestern and Carnegie Tech., and having his team conceded the strongest in the East, he went out West and defeated Leland Stanford, the strongest team out there. Rockne is a double cousin of S. S. Reque, baseball coach at Luther College. There are only five Norwegian colleges in America, but nearly 500 other colleges, state and private. A large number of Norwegians attend these state and private schools and distinguish themselves there as athletes. At the University of Minnesota, for example, there have been many football stars of Norse blood, such as Oscar M. Solem, Trygve Johnsen, Erling Platou, Arne Oas, Arnold C. Oss, Egil Boeckmann, and many others. Magne Skursdalsvold, a senior in the Agricultural College of the University of Minnesota, has twice been awarded gold medals by the Western Intercollegiate Gymnastics, Wrestling and Fencing Association: Parallel bars, 1924, first prize; tumbling, 1925, tied for first place. He is a son of J. J. Skørsdalsvold. In the Metropolitan Association meet held in New York in 1919 the Norwegian Turning Association of Brooklyn ("Turn og Idrætsforening") won with 45 points against 13 for the National Turnverein and 11 for the New York Turnverein. The first, second and third prizes on horizontal bars, horse and parallel bars, went to three Norwegians—Peter Hoe, Bjarne Jørgensen and Thorvald Hansen. Klaus Olsen has since 1887 conducted at San Francisco the Olsen Gymnastic and Medico-Mechanical Institute, and, thanks to practising what he preaches, he is 70 years young.

Norwegians have been making good records in a number of other sports. In sailing, swimming, diving, jumping, walking,

Miscellaneous Records skating, boxing, wrestling, tennis, shooting, dog-running and other events.

Sir Thomas Lipton, owner of the famous Lipton Teas, is also the owner of the racing yacht Shamrock. Every year since 1899 he has entered the international cup races hoping to win the America's Cup. The American yachts which have defended this cup have as a rule been manned by Scandinavian tars. Thus, in the race between the American yacht Resolute and the English yacht Shamrock, July 20, 1920, the whole crew of the Resolute was made up of Scandinavians—22 Norwegians, 7 Swedes and 1 Dane. The master of the defender was Captain Chris Christensen, of Brooklyn, a Norwegian. His boat won. "No man," says Carl G. O. Hansen in "Norwegian Immigrant Contributions to

Henry Ordemann   Sybil Bauer   Gustav Stearns

America's Making," "no man knows the vagaries and whims of the wind and weather along the Atlantic Coast better than he." Hansen adds: "Many of the racing captains of the Atlantic ports are Americans of Norwegian birth. The racing master of the New York Yacht Club since 1874 is Louis W. Blix from Sandefjord, Norway."

Miss Sybil Bauer, Chicago, a junior at Northwestern University and member of the First Lutheran Church, Chicago, is the daughter of Carl Bauer, manufacturer of parlor furniture frames, a Norwegian. Miss Bauer, born in 1903, at the age of 18 became both indoor and outdoor national champion swimmer. In 1924 she won the Olympic backstroke championship at Paris. She is the holder of all women's world's records at backstroke, from 50 yards to 440 yards. She also broke the men's record for 440 yards—the first time in the history of athletics. In the 100 meter backstroke she has set a world's record at 1 minute, 23 1-5 seconds.

L. Jensen, Brooklyn, won the championship in diving at the Madison Square Garden, New York, in 1921. O. M. Norlie during the '90s made standing broad jumps 11 feet 6 inches probably

1,000 times. This is over one-inch better than the highest national and international championship records. Joseph Bredsteen, while a student at the University of Wisconsin in 1901, won all walking matches. Orrin Markhus, St. Paul, is the best fancy skater in America. Axel Paulsen, the international champion skater, made the United States his home in 1888-1890 and took part in many races. Oscar Mathiesen, Oslo, who first won international fame at Davos, Switzerland, in 1906-1907, lived in the United States a couple of years and met several of the best skaters in this country. He defeated Bobby McClean of Chicago and was declared the champion skater of the world. Arthur Staff, national champion skater, is a Chicago boy, born of Norwegian parents. His prowess and skill were developed by the old Sleipner Athletic Club, which now is called the Norwegian-American Athletic Association of Chicago.

Molla Bjurstedt Mallory in Action

In wrestling, Henry Ordemann was the all-American Champion two years, 1910-1912. He learned the blacksmith's trade. Came to America in 1903 and worked as a blacksmith four years at the Mandt Wagon Works, Stoughton, Wisconsin. He is now a real estate man at Minneapolis. He began to wrestle and has defeated over 100 able men on the mat. He has also wrestled the greatest wrestling champions of the day, as: Yussiss Maumouth, the Turk, in 1909; Stanley Zbyszko, the Pole, in 1910; George Hackensmith, the Russian, in 1911. These three men defeated him, but not without a struggle. He held the Turk one hour and 13 minutes and is the only man who ever got behind his back. He threw the Pole once out of three times. He withstood the Terrible Russian two hours and 37 minutes. He has defeated such notables as: Dr. Benjamin Roller, Charles Cutler, Fred Bell, Gus Westergaard, Joe Stechler. He was a personal friend and disciple of Frank Gotch, the world champion, who refereed at the Chicago contest in which Ordemann came out victor over 30 contestants and was declared by Gotch to be the rightful holder of the American championship. His hold is half-Nelson and crotch, or toe hold. Aurid Mevik is the amateur champion boxer in New York, and Harry Martinsen and Eddie Christensen are veterans and victors in many fistic encounters. Ingrid Solfeng is acclaimed on Broadway, New York, as one of the most marvelous fancy dancers in the history of the stage. She spends some of her time as a movie star at Holywood, California.

A very unusual photograph on file in the archives of the Government in Washington. It was taken by an official U. S. Signal Corps photographer who was sent up to the front with instructions to take some photographs of activities in the front line trenches. He was not allowed to develop these pictures during the war but had to send the films sealed to Paris. The picture shows Captain-Chaplain Gustav Stearns, 127th Inf. 32nd Div. A.E.F. conducting a church service between the trenches in the Haute-Alsace trench sector in the spring of 1918. All were ordered to wear steel helmets and gas masks constantly while in this area. The gas mask is seen at the chaplain's side. This is not a posed picture but was taken without the chaplain's knowledge while he was preaching. A few days later he was wounded by enemy shrapnel.

Mrs. Molla Bjurstedt Mallory, "Marvelous Molla," has the best record for tennis playing of any woman in America. She was born in Oslo and baptized Anna Margrethe. She was trained as a teacher of gymnastics and a masseuse. She came to Canada in 1914 and worked as a governess. She assisted in the Red Cross by knitting sweaters and doing embroidery, at both of which she was an adept. In 1915 she competed for the indoor tennis championship at New York, and won. That same year she won the women's national outdoor championship. This honor she has captured seven times, four times oftener than any other woman. She published in the "New York Sun" a series of articles on Tennis which have been re-issued in book form. In 1919 she married Franklin L. Mallory, of Philadelphia, a widower.

During the World War many Norwegians distinguished themselves as good marksmen. Sergeant Olav Gunheim, of Canby, Minnesota, won fourth place as sharpshooter, in a contest against 1,300 riflemen in the American Expeditionary Forces. He was awarded a gold medal from the hands of General Pershing. Trygve Mordt, New York, with Uncle Sam's navy four years, won the distinction of being the best all-around athlete among the blue-jackets.

In this same connection may be mentioned some of the brave soldiers who received some recognition for gallantry in action. The Congressional Medal of Honor, the highest distinction awarded to an American soldier, was given to four Norwegian-Americans, namely, Corporal Birger Loman, Sergeant Reidar Waaler, Privates Nels Tidemand Wold and Johannes S. Andersen. Waaler holds three American medals, three French medals, also English and Belgian decorations. Loman is said to be the most decorated soldier in the American army. He has medals from America, England, Belgium, France, Italy and Montenegro. On one occasion he captured without assistance 140 German soldiers, including Major Henneman, the first German officer captured during the War. All alone, on another occasion, he captured a machine gun and a cannon. At another time he crawled up to No Man's Land and over it clear into the German trenches and returned with a prisoner of war. Not satisfied with this exploit he crossed over again and came back with 25 captives. He is a painter by professsion and lives at 1451 N. La Salle St., Chicago. He was born in Bergen.

One of the bravest men in the American army was Gustav Stearns, chaplain with the rank of captain in the 127th Infantry, 32nd Division of the A. E. F. He was on duty and in engagements in the Haute-Alsace trench sector, the Aisne-Marne offensive (the second Battle of the Marne) and the Oisne-Aisne offensive (the Battle of Juvigny). He was wounded by enemy shrapnel at Badricourt, France. July 12, 1918, but continued on duty after being bandaged. He was cited by General Pershing for "gallantry in action near Juvigny, Sept. 1, 1918, in burying the dead under heavy shell fire." He was authorized to wear the "Silver Citation Star" and the "Silver Wound Button." On Jan. 1, 1925, he was promoted to chaplain with rank of major, with federal recognition in the National Guard and Officers' Reserve Corps, and is the only chaplain in Wisconsin to receive this rank. Stearns was born at New Richland, Minnesota, of parents who came from Norway. Halvor K. Stearns, the father, came from

Numedal; Bergitte Sevats, the mother, came from Hallingdal. These two married and had 13 children, of whom Gustav is the only boy living. In these pioneer days Halvor Stearns could not send his boy to college, but one of the girls, Sophia, now Mrs. Benson, of Washington, went into business and put Gustav Stearns and sister, Kaia, through St. Olaf College. Stearns worked his way through the United Church Seminary and became, in 1899, a pastor in Milwaukee, and is today no doubt the best known and most beloved pastor in that city. He is the author of a book of letters written to his congregations when he was in the army, entitled "From Army Camps and Battlefields" (1919). Three editions have been sold out. Stearns is perhaps the most enthusiastic and original baseball rooter that ever attended St. Olaf.

The Dog Team in Alaska

In the famous dog races of Canada, Norwegian drivers have often come out victorious. Also in far distant Alaska, that great and almost unknown country far beyond the Arctic Circle, the dog races awaken a keen enthusiasm common to true sportsmen of all times and places. The dog race is the national sport of Alaska. At Nome, Alaska, in 1908, the Nome Kennel Club was organized with Albert Fink, a Norwegian, as president. This club has developed a most splendid type of racing dog, which has won the praises of the two great Arctic explorers, Roald Amundsen and Vilhjalmur Stefansson, both of whom have bowed knee with the dog-worshippers at Nome. At Nome the All Alaska Sweepstakes Dog Races were established as the great annual athletic event, and Leonard Seppala, a Norwegian, has been the winner. He was born at Lyngenfjord in 1877 and settled in Alaska in 1900. Every second white man in Alaska is a Scandinavian; every fourth Caucasian is a Norwegian. Seppala came to find gold and spent his first winter alone at Seward

Peninsula. It was a terrible experience. The cold was intense, 72 degrees below, and he froze his feet. He was on the point of starving to death and set out to find some human habitation. He found a hut snowed in, but the lonely occupant was dead. The hungry hounds ate the dead man up. By the help of his dogs Seppala got back to civilization. He hired out to Jafet Linde-berg, president of the Pioneer Mining Co., the Norwegian company which first discovered gold at Nome. In 1914 he entered his first race. In 1915 he won the 408-mile race in 78 hours. In 1919 he made the world record in the Borden Marathon, making 26 miles in 1 hour and 50 seconds. In 1915 his wife was crowned the Carnival Queen of Nome. In 1917 the "Nome Daily Nugget" contained a poem entitled, "Seppala Drives to Win," written by the Northland poetess Esther Darling. The occasion was, not a race for laurels, but to save the life of Bobby Brown, which was fast ebbing away.

> There's a race on the trail into Candle,
> With a Nome Sweepstakes team in the game
> Hear the rhythm and beat of the pattering feet
> Of the dogs that have earned them a name!
> But this contest is not for a record;
> Neither cup nor a purse is the goal,
> For Seppala is bent and his mind is intent
> On racing with death for a soul.

Seppala won. Enough said.

The daily press and the magazines in February, 1925, contained screaming headlines and long columns of news about the men who brought the serum to Nome and saved the town from being wiped out by epidemic. Who were these men? Norwegians—Gunnar Kasson (Kaasen) og Leonard Seppala.

17. Public Service

The Norwegians are good voters. They go to the polls. They vote for principles and good men. They are independent in their thinking and their balloting. They can be fooled but not bought. They are modest and patient and do not clamor for office. They do not hold their fair share of public offices, not in any state or community. North Dakota, for example, is a strong Norwegian state, but it never had a Norwegian governor before 1921. A small handful of Scotchmen ran the state for years and years, and to a large extent do so yet. In the little town of Stoughton, Wisconsin, 80 per cent of the population was of Norwegian extraction, but the whole school board was run by a dozen or so of English families. Some one said something which hurt the pride of the Norwegians, and at the next election the whole school board was made up of Norwegians. In Minnesota, the Norwegians showed what they can do if they want to, when they

elected Henrik Shipstead United States Senator in place of Frank
B. Kellogg. Kellogg was strong. He is strong still. He has
just come back from the Court of St. James where he was the
U. S. Ambassador, and now he is the President's secretary of
state. But he was defeated by Dr. Shipstead, because the Norwegians were dissatisfied with the War and its results. Shipstead's campaign manager was only a slip of a girl, Miss
Karen Andersen by name. Shipstead represented the despised
Farmer-Labor Party and had the powerful dailies and the monied
interests squarely against him, yet he won by a handsome margin,
83,539 more votes than Kellogg, the Republican candidate, 201,748
more than Anna D. Olesen, the Democratic candidate.

In Strand's "History of the Norwegians of Illinois" an account is given of the principal offices held by Norwegians in
Miller, Mission and Adams townships of
La Salle County   La Salle County, Illinois, the second home
of the Sloopers. Mission Township was organ-
ized in 1850. The first justice of the peace in Mission was
Lars Larson, and its first constable was Nels Nelson. Strand's
list includes 125 names from Mission Township; 50 from Miller
and 140 for Adams. Ovee (Aave) Rosdail (Rosedal) was collector in 1852. Peter C. Nelson was constable in 1852; collector,
1856; commissioner of highways, 1859-1860; collector, 1863;
commissioner of highways, 1864-1872; assessor and collector,
1874; assessor, 1877-1879-1880; collector, 1881-1885; assessor,
1886-1888. B. Thompson, Nels Nelson and J. A. Quam had one
office or another throughout the '60s, '70s, '80s, '90s and beyond.
In Miller Township, organized in 1876 by the influence of Nels
Nelson, Jr., had Norwegians in office every year from its organization. Among the office holders are Nels Nelson, Lars
Heyer, Lars Fruland and Austin Heyer. The man who held the
greatest variety of offices and longest, in Adams Township, was
A. A. Klove. Klove was a Sunday school superintendent for 50
years. He helped to organize the Scandinavian Augustana Synod
in 1860; The Norwegian Augustana Synod in 1870; and the
United Church in 1890. He was a synodical treasurer from 1860
to 1890; a member of the board of trustees, 1890-1899. He was
the secretary of the Adams branch of the American Bible Society
30 years. He served as assessor, justice of the peace, supervisor,
notary public, etc., from 1860 to 1899, the year of his death. He
lived on a farm near Leland.

Alfred Søderstrøm's "Minneapolis Minnen: Kulturhistorisk
Axplockning" (1899), gives a brief summary of Scandinavians
holding office in Minneapolis. The list in-
Minneapolis   cludes the following Norwegians:

NORWEGIANS IN OFFICE IN MINNEAPOLIS, 1871-1899

Term	Name	Office	Party
1870	Rice, A. E.	Senate	Republican
1871-1877	Johnson, Geo. H.	Sheriff	Republican
1874-1876	Edsten, A. H.	City Council	Republican
1876-1886	Oftedal, Sven	Board of Education	Republican
1877	Johnson, Geo. H.	House of Rep.	Republican
1878-1888	Haugan, A. C.	City Council	Republican
1878-1879	Karl Bendeke	City Council	Democrat
1879-1881	Tharaldsen, Andrew	House of Rep.	Republican
1881-1883	Ueland, Andrew	Court Commissioner	Republican
1883-1887	Ueland, Andrew	Judge of Probate	Republican
1885-1895	Oftedal, Sven	Bd. Public Library	Republican
1885-1886	Swenson, Lars	City Council	Republican
1885	Byorum, Ole	House of Rep.	Republican
1886-1888	Wraamann, W. W.	County Supt. Schools	Democrat
1887-1891	Dahl, Peter M.	County Surveyor	Republican
1887-....	Swenson, Lars	Court House Com.	Republican
		Senate	Republican
1887-1889	Ellingson, Severt	House of Repr.	Republican
1888-1894	Haugan, A. C.	Park Board	Republican
1889-1899	Olson, S. E.	Governor's Staff	Republican
1889	Husher, F. A.	House of Rep.	Republican
1889-1891	Enstad, C. P.	City Council	Republican
1889-1891	Ellingsen, Chris	City Council	Republican
1889-1893	Blichfeldt, John A.	City Council	Republican
1889-1891	Flaten, O. P.	City Council	Republican
1889-1901	Gjertsen, M. Falk	County Supt. Schools	Republican
1889-....	Askeland, Halvor	Asst. Public Librarian	Republican
1889-....	Heiberg, Kristian	Asst. Public Librarian	Republican
1889-1899	Reese, Chas. M.	State Weighmaster	Republican
1889-1891	Gjertsen, N. H.	Board of Police Commissioner	Republican
1890-1894	Jaeger, Luth.	Board of Education	Democrat
1890-1894	Husher, F. A.	U. S. Consul, Port Stanley	Republican
1891-1893	Kortgaard, Kristian	City Treasurer	Democrat
1891-1893	Peterson, H. O.	County Treasurer	Democrat
1891-1899	Schwartz, Fred A.	City Council	Democrat
1891-1903	Rand, Lars M.	City Council	Democrat
1893-1897	Haugan, A. C.	City Treasurer	Democrat
1893-1899	Cappelen, F. W.	City Engineer	Democrat
1895-1897	Dahl, Peter M.	County Surveyor	Republican
1895-1897	Ellingsen, Chris.	House of Rep.	Republican
1895-1897	Dahl, J. F.	House of Rep.	Republican
1895-1897	Gjertsen, M. Falk	Bd. Public Library	Republican
1897-1899	Simonson, Hans	House of Rep.	Republican
1897-1899	Peterson, James	County Attorney	Republican
1899-1901	Megaarden, Phil.	Sheriff	Republican
1899	Owrie, Lars	Asst. Supt. Poorhouse	Democrat

The combined service of these 46 positions amounted to 211 years for the 30-year period, or seven offices each year. Since 1899 the Norwegians have naturally done even better than the record shown above, gotten more and higher offices, but by no means their proportionate share.

From these two illustrations, La Salle and Minneapolis, it can be seen that the Norwegians are taking some part in the local government, county and city. The number of men who have held such positions reaches up into the thousands.

City and County Offices Ulvestad, in his "Norge i Amerika" (1901), concludes that he has found 593 postmasters, 116 county commissioners, 113 justices of the peace, 105 county registers of deeds, 94 members of the legislature (1898-1901), 77 postal clerks, 63 sheriffs, 61 county treasurers, 47 clerks of court, 46 aldermen, 43 county auditors, 31 mayors of larger cities, 31 notary publics, 27 county clerks, 27 county superintendents of schools, 24 judges, 20 police chiefs, 20 coron-

Ole Hanson
Seattle, Wash.

Storm Bull
Madison, Wis.

A. G. Bonhus
Valley City, N. D.

City Mayors

ers, 19 school board members, 25 city clerks, 13 city treasurers, 13 tax collectors, 13 fire captains, 12 fire wardens, 10 street commissioners of large cities, and 5 presidents of city school boards. In all, 1,648 offices, most of them held in the year 1900. The actual number of city and county positions occupied by Norwegians was no doubt much in excess of this number. In 1920 there were 770,400 of the citizens of the United States engaged in public service occupations. Over one-half of these were in the service of cities and counties. If the Norwegians in America comprise 2 per cent of the population, and if they hold 2 per cent of the offices, then there were some 15,000 Norwegian individuals in public service, over one-half of whom would be in city and county public positions. If they held only 1 per cent of the public offices, they would still have nearly 8,000 public service positions.

The first Norwegian to run for the office of governor was Adolph Biermann. He was born in Oslo, Norway; came to Olm-
State Offices sted County, Minnesota, in 1862; was a soldier in the Union Army, and was chosen county auditor three times. In 1882 he was nominated for Congress on the Democratic ticket, but was defeated. In 1883 the Democrats nominated him for governor. He would have been elected but for the activity of Knute Nelson. In 1885 Biermann was appointed internal revenue collector for Minnesota. In 1890 he was elected state auditor, and reelected in 1892. From 1892 until his death, in 1914, he lived on his farm near Rochester.

Capt. Canute Matson Lieut. Joseph M. Johnson Alderman Peter J. Pryts
Sheriff, Cook Co., Ill.   Chicago, Ill.   Minneapolis, Minn.

The first Norwegian to become the governor of an American commonwealth was Knute Nelson. Nelson was born in Voss, Norway, Feb. 2, 1843. He came to the United States in 1849 at the age of six. His father having died when Knute was three years old, he was reared in poverty. His mother conceived the idea of improving the opportunity for her boy by coming to America. She arrived in New York penniless. She borrowed enough money from friends to gain admission at Castle Garden. She sat there weeping in her loneliness and trouble amidst the great throng of immigrants from every land. The little boy tried to comfort her, saying: "Do not weep, Mother, when I grow up I shall be next to the king." They went to Chicago, where young Knute sold papers on the street. When he was eight years of age, they moved to Deerfield, Wisconsin, where they secured a piece of land. He attended district school and Albion Academy. At the outbreak of the Civil War, he enlisted as a private. In 1863, at the siege of Port Hudson, he was wounded and lay all day on the field exposed to fire from both sides. He studied law with Senator W. Vilas at Madison and was admitted to the bar. In 1867 he ran for the office of assemblyman and was elected. In

1871 he moved to Alexandria, Minnesota, and married Ida G. Nelson. That fall he was elected county attorney. In 1875 he became a state senator; in 1883, a congressman; in 1892, governor of Minnesota; in 1895, United States senator. He was "next to the king." He held political office continuously from 1867 to the day of his death, April 28, 1923. During the 28 years he was in the Senate, he was considered one of the hardest workers in Washington and one of the most respected and influential of the members of the Upper House. He was chairman of the Committee of Commerce for some years, and also the Judiciary Committee. His secretary and friend, ex-Governor Jacob A. O. Preus, pays tribute to the old stalwart senator in part as follows: "Senator Nelson's strongest characteristic was his simplicity. In order to understand his life, you have but to proceed to his farm and his home in Alexandria, and view it as it there stands, a home in the future to be utilized as an Old Folks' Home, a simple farm home. . . . . His home in Washington was a modest three-story building, old and simple in appearance. I doubt that the furniture in this residence could be sold for $400.00. When I listed his jewelry in his inventory I listed one watch. It was presented to him just after he was inaugurated governor in 1893. He had a little old silver watch which his friends considered too shabby for a governor, and they therefore presented him with a gold one on which was engraved 'From your Norwegian and Swedish friends.'"

The complete roster of Norwegians who have become governors numbers twelve men, fourteen if we add the two Whitfields who have been governors of Mississippi. Concerning the present governor of Mississippi, Henry Lewis Whitfield, Mr. Gaius Whitfield of Macon, Mississippi, writes: "There were two brothers who went from Norway to Normandy, and from there went to England with William the Conqueror. They fought in the Battle of Hastings, and after William ascended the English throne, they settled in Lancashire. Some of their descendants came to Virginia in the Colonial days, but soon after moved to North Carolina. There were several of them in the Continental Army. Some of them moved to Alabama and Mississippi about 1825 to 1830. The present governor of Mississippi, who is the second Governor Whitfield of Mississippi, is of the third generation of the family in this state. There are two different coats of arms in the family that show the name spelt Hvitfeldt." The governor himself says: "I believe the name Whitfield was formerly Whitfeld and is probably Norwegian. I have never heard, however, that I was of Norwegian extraction. I rather think that my people were English." His descent, therefore, from the Norsemen, is at best quite remote, and he is consequently not included in the following roster of Norse governors:

AMERICAN GOVERNORS OF NORWEGIAN DESCENT

Name	State	Term	Party
Nelson, Knute	Minnesota	1892-1895	Republican
Preus, Jacob Aall O. ...	Minnesota	1921-1925	Republican
Christianson, Theo.	Minnesota	1925-....	Republican
Lee, Andrew E.	South Dakota	1896-1900	Populist
Herreid, Chas. N.	South Dakota	1900-1904	Republican
Norbeck, Peter	South Dakota	1917-1921	Republican
Gunderson, Carl	South Dakota	1925-....	Republican
Davidson, James O.	Wisconsin	1906-1911	Republican
Blaine, John J.	Wisconsin	1921-....	Republican
Nestos, Ragnvald A. ...	North Dakota	1921-1925	Republican
Sorlie, Arthur G.	North Dakota	1925-....	Republican
Erickson, John E.	Montana	1925-....	Democrat

It should be noted that Peter Norbeck's father was a Swede —Gøran Norbeck, born in Sweden. He moved to Norway in 1854 and became a preacher there. He was a pastor in the Norwegian church, Hauge Synod, in South Dakota, 1885-1900. The father of John J. Blaine was not a Norwegian. His mother was Elizabeth Johnson Brunstad by name. She emigrated from Hadeland, Norway, in 1867. Both Nelson and Nestos were born in Norway, both at Voss. Quite a number of Norwegians have run for the governorship but have been defeated.

A case in point: Joseph S. Anderson ran strong on the Republican ticket in 1924 for the governorship of Iowa, but was defeated at the primaries. In North Dakota there were three tickets, each one headed by a Norwegian candidate for governor. This same thing occured in South Dakota in the campaign of 1895. There were three candidates for the governorship, and all three were Norwegians.

Carl G. O. Hansen has published an interesting and comprehensive history of the Norwegian people in America during the past century which has been running as a serial in "Minneapolis Tidende." In chapter 29 of this serial he gives a good account of Norwegians who have held high positions in public office below that of governor. On the basis of his information, checked by the legislative manuals and blue books of the northwestern states, the following names are given. The list is not complete.

LIEUTENANT-GOVERNORS OF NORWEGIAN DESCENT

Name	State	Term
Davidson, James O.	Wisconsin	1903-1906
Dahl, C. M.	Wisconsin	
Rice, A. E.	Minnesota	1887-1891
Frankson, Thomas	Minnesota	1917-1921
Herreid, Charles N.	South Dakota	1893-1896
Norbeck, Peter	South Dakota	1915-1916
Gunderson, Carl	South Dakota	1921-1924
Kraabel, A. T.	North Dakota	1913-1914
		1917-1918

SECRETARIES OF STATE OF NORWEGIAN DESCENT

Name	State	Term
Warner, Hans B.	Wisconsin	1878-1882
Irgens, John S.	Minnesota	1876-1880
Brown, Frederick P.	Minnesota	1891-1895
Ringsrud, A. O.	South Dakota	1889-1892
Thorson, Thomas	South Dakota	1893-1896
Berg, O. C.	South Dakota	1901-1903
Flittie, John	North Dakota	1889-1892
Dahl, Christian M.	North Dakota	1893-1896
Hoff, O. P.	Oregon	1920-....

STATE TREASURERS OF NORWEGIAN DESCENT

Name	State	Term
Peterson, Sewell A.	Wisconsin	1899-1903
Davidson, James O.	Wisconsin	1903-1904
Dahl, Andrew H.	Wisconsin	1907-1913
Kittelson, Charles	Minnesota	1880-1887
Gilbertsen, Gilbert S.	Iowa	1900-1907
Johnson, George G.	South Dakota	1909-1912
Helgerson, G. H.	South Dakota	1917-1919
Nomland, Knud J.	North Dakota	1893-1894
Peterson, Albert	North Dakota	1905-1908
Olson, Gunder	North Dakota	1911-1914
Steen, John	North Dakota	1915-1918
Olson, Olbert A.	North Dakota	1919-1920

STATE AUDITORS OF NORWEGIAN DESCENT

Name	State	Term
Biermann, Adolf	Minnesota	1891-1895
Iverson, Samuel G.	Minnesota	1903-1915
Preus, Jacob A. O.	Minnesota	1915-1921
Anderson, H. B. (?)	South Dakota	1911-1914
Jorgenson, Carl O. (?)	North Dakota	1913-1916
Clausen, C. W.	Washington	....-....

ATTORNEY GENERALS OF NORWEGIAN DESCENT

Name	State	Term
Blaine, John J.	Wisconsin	1919-1921
Ekern, Herman L.	Wisconsin	1923-
Frich, Carl N.	North Dakota	1903-1906
Linde, Henry	North Dakota	1915-1916

STATE SCHOOL SUPERINTENDENTS OF NORWEGIAN DESCENT

Name	State	Term
Ustrud, H. A.	South Dakota	1907-1911
Lawrence, C. G.	South Dakota	1911-1914
Halland, J. G.	North Dakota	1907-1910

RAILROAD COMMISSIONERS OF NORWEGIAN DESCENT

Name	State	Term
Haugen, Nils P.	Wisconsin	1882-1887
Peterson, Atley P.	Wisconsin	1887-1901
Erickson, Halford (?)	Wisconsin	1905-1916
Ringdal, P. M.	Minnesota	1899-1901
Jacobson, O. P. B.	Minnesota	1914-....
Rasmussen, Nells P. (?)	North Dakota	1893-1894
Erickson, Henry	North Dakota	1899-1900
Christianson, John	North Dakota	1905-1906
Stafne, Erick	North Dakota	1907-1908
Anderson, O. P. N.	North Dakota	1909-1916
Johnson, M. P.	North Dakota	1917-1918
Aandahl, S. J.	North Dakota	1917-1920

(5) NATIONAL OFFICIALS

CONGRESSMEN OF NORWEGIAN DESCENT

Name	State	Term	Party
Nelson, Knute	Minnesota	1883-1889	Republican
Haugen, Nils P.	Wisconsin	1887-1895	Republican
Halvorson, Kittel	Minnesota	1890-1892	Prohibitionist
Johnson, Martin	North Dakota	1890-1898	Republican
Boen, Haldor E.	Minnesota	1892-1894	Populist
Dahle, Herman B.	Wisconsin	1898-1902	Republican
Haugen, Gilbert N.	Iowa	1899-....	Republican
Steenerson, Haldor	Minnesota	1903-1921	Republican
Volstead, Andrew J.	Minnesota	1903-1921	Republican
Grønna, Asle	North Dakota	1905-1911	Republican
Nelson, John Mandt	Wisconsin	1906-1919	Republican
		1921-....	
Anderson, Sydney	Minnesota	1911-1925	Republican
Helgesen, Henry T.	North Dakota	1911-....	Republican
Van Dyke, Carl Chester	Minnesota	1915-1919	Democrat
Knutson, Harold	Minnesota	1917-....	Republican
Christopherson, Chas. A.	South Dakota	1919-....	Republican
Burtness, Olger B.	North Dakota	1921-....	Republican
Michaelson, M. Alfred	Illinois	1921-....	Republican
Williamson, William	South Dakota	1921-....	Republican
Kvale, Ole J.	Minnesota	1923-....	Farmer-Labor
Wefald, Knud	Minnesota	1923-....	Republican
Andresen, August H.	Minnesota	1925-....	Republican

These congressmen have made good. They have been honest and democratic. Nils P. Haugen is one of the greatest tax experts in America. He has been the tax commissioner in Wisconsin, 1901-1921, counsel for the tax commission in Montana, president of the National Tax Association. He was one of the first to advocate income tax. Gilbert N. Haugen is the chairman of the Committee on Agriculture in the House and is the author of the Haugen Packer and Stockyards Act, the Butter Standards Act, the Bee Act, the Anti-Profiteering Act, and a large number of other bills supporting the farmers and consumers. Andrew J. Volstead wrote the Volstead Act for federal prohibition and his good name has thereby at once been blasphemed in the gutter and praised from the housetops as one of the greatest benefactors of mankind in his day. He is the author of the Farmers' Cooperative Marketing Act and other bills. John Mandt Nelson is a Christian gentleman, an Israelite in whom there is no guile, who ably represents one of the most progressive states in the Union, the home of LaFollette and the Progressive Party. Sydney Anderson is a half Swede, and a credit to both nationalities. He has been chairman of the National Agriculture Conference, 1922; the National Wheat Conference, 1923; and since 1923 he has been president of the Wheat Council of the U. S. Van-Dyke is the only Democrat among these Norsemen. His father was of Dutch origin, his mother of Norwegian—Bertha Solum. He was a Spanish-American war veteran and was interested in the railway mail service. Harold Knutson is the Republican whip in the House, chairman of the Committee on Pensions. Ole J. Kvale is a Norwegian Lutheran pastor. In Congress his clear ringing voice is often heard, and with increasing respect. To him belongs the honor of having secured from the House the passage of a bill authorizing the issuing of 2,000,000 stamps commemorative of the Norse-American Centennial and of 40,000 silver medals. The stamps are of two denominations—two cents and five. The two cent stamp with the Sloop Restaurationen on it is black and red—the ship is black, the border and legends are red. The five-cent stamp is black and blue, with similar arrangement, except that the ship is flanked on the left by the Norse flag and on the right by the American Stars and Stripes. They were planned by Mr. Eidsness, a Norwegian in charge of the Stamp Division.

UNITED STATES SENATORS OF NORWEGIAN DESCENT

Name	State	Term	Party
Nelson, Knute	Minnesota	1895-1923	Republican
Smoot, Reed	Utah	1903-....	Republican
Johnson, Martin	North Dakota	1909-1910	Republican
Grønna, Asle J.	North Dakota	1911-1921	Republican
Bursum, Holm O.	New Mexico	1921-....	Republican
Norbeck, Peter	South Dakota	1921-....	Republican
Shipstead, Henrik	Minnesota	1923-....	Farmer-Labor

Reed Smoot is a half-Norwegian. His father was Abraham Owen Smoot; his mother, Anne K. Mauretz, a Norwegian. He has been a woolen manufacturer, merchant and banker. He is one of the apostles of the Mormon faith. He is the chairman of the Public Buildings Commission at Washington and vice-chairman of the World War Foreign Debt Commission. Holm O. Bursum was born at Fort Dodge, Iowa, of Norwegian parents. He has been a resident of New Mexico since 1881 and is engaged in stock raising. He was chairman of the Republican Territorial Central Committee, 1905-1911, Republican floor leader of the Constitutional Convention, 1910. Peter Norbeck was a South Dakota farmer. When he was 25 years of age he began well drilling and developed the largest and most successful firm in this line in the state—the Norbeck and Nicholson Co., Platte, South Dakota. When he turned to politics he found success awaiting him also there. Henrik Shipstead was a dentist at Glenwood. His neighbors wanted him as mayor. He made a good mayor. They wanted him to go to the state legislature. He went. Then he ran for governor and was defeated. He hitched his wagon to a star and announced his candidacy for the U. S. Senate. He won.

Juul Dieserud, Librarian   Thorvald Solberg   Thorstein Jahr, Librarian
Library of Congress   Register of Copyright   Library of Congress

A few Norwegians have been chosen to represent the United States in foreign lands. Rasmus Bjørn Anderson was the first to attain to this honor. He was appointed by President Cleveland as U. S. minister to Denmark, 1885-1889. "The Life Story of R. B. Anderson," written by A. O. Barton on the basis of conversations with Prof. Anderson, tells the tale of this ministry and the high points of interest in this great man's busy life. Lauritz Selmer Swenson was appointed U. S. minister to Denmark in 1897-1905 by Presidents McKinley and Roosevelt. In 1909 he was appointed to Switzerland; in 1911 to Norway. In 1913 he came back to America to take charge of his banking affairs. He was vice president of the Union State Bank, Minneapolis, 1905-1910; president of the Mercantile State Bank, 1915—. President Harding appointed him to Norway in 1921, and he again accepted. He has the finest U. S. Legation House in Europe and is much beloved. Like R. B. Anderson he is a graduate of Luther College. Swenson was principal of Luther Academy, 1889-1897. He was appointed by President Taft to represent the United States at the Spitzbergen Conference, Christiania, 1913. He is the president of the Scandinavian Art Society of America. Another Norwegian-American diplomat is Nicolay A. Grevstad, who was United States minister to Uruguay and Paraguay, 1911-1917, with headquarters at Montevideo. He came to America as a newcomer in 1883, served on the editorial staff of the "Minneapolis Journal" and the "Minneapolis Tribune" until 1900. He edited the "Minneapolis Times," 1900-1901, "Skandinaven," 1901-1911. Since his return from South America he has been a member of the Minnesota Safety Commission and of the General Publicity Service, Chicago. John Allyne Gade, New York architect and banker, was a naval attache at the U. S. Legation, Copenhagen, 1917-1919; member of the Baltic Mission to Lithuania, Latvia and Esthonia, and represented the United States in these new states, 1919. Gabriel Bie Ravndal was editor of the "Sioux Falls Ekko" and the president of the Scandinavian Singers' Association. Then, in 1898, he was called by Uncle Sam to take a consulship at Beirut, Syria. He staid there until 1905, then he was transferred to Dawson, Alaska. In 1906-1910 he was consul general at Beirut, and at Constantinople, Turkey, 1910-1915. During the war he was in charge of the consular interests of England, France, Italy, Servia, Russia, Montenegro, Switzerland. Was appointed consul general at St. Nazare, France, 1917, at Nantes, 1918. Invited to appear before the American Peace Mission, 1919. Appointed U. S. commercial and consul general, Constantinople, 1920. Member of many Oriental societies, president of the Beirut Relief Committee. His son, Christian M. Ravndal, has been in the consular service four years, stationed at Vienna and Frankfort. He has been promoted eight times in two years. Olaf Ravndal, another son, holds high and responsible positions with the American Express Co., having served in New York, Athens and Constantinople. These two young men are Luther College graduates, 1920. Lars S. Reque, professor of Latin and French at Luther College for 38 years, was U. S. general consul at Rotterdam, Holland, 1893-1897. James Adolph Ostrand was born in Trondhjem, Norway, in 1872. Came to Minnesota, 1892. Became a lawyer. Was made judge of Court of Land Registration, Philippines, 1909-1911; judge, district court, 1911-1914; chief judge, Manila Court, 1911-1914; judge, district court, 1914-1920; chief justice, appellate court, Santo Domingo, 1920-1921; associate justice, supreme court, P. I., 1921——. Wm. C. Magelssen has been the U. S. consul at Melbourne, Australia; John Schroeder, at Costa Rica; Otto O. Boyesen, at Gothenburg; Robert S. Bergh, at Gothenburg; and B. M. Rasmussen, at Stavanger.

There are quite a number of Norwegians holding office in Washington, the capital city. Washington has 236,027 men and women classified as breadwinners, and 16,070 of these hold public service positions. The Norwegian contribution to this vast concourse of employes is but as a drop in a bucket. Still that drop is of good quality. Major Oscar N. Solbert is the assistant in charge of public buildings and grounds, Department of War. Michael L. Eidsness is the superintendent of stamps, Post Office Department. A. H. Hoiland is the disbursing clerk, Navy Department. Carl W. Larson is the chief of the Bureau of Dairying, Agriculture Department; E. W. Nelson is the chief biologist of the Biological Survey; A. T. Larson is the chief of the Synthetic Ammonia Research Laboratory; Laura A. Thompson is the librarian of the Department of Labor; Emma Lundberg is the director of the Social Service Division of the Children's Bureau; Mary Anderson and Agnes L. Peterson are in charge of the Women's Bureau. Leonhard Stejneger is the head curator of the National Museum of the Smithsonian Institution. Torstein Jahr is a cataloguer and reviser and expert on Scandinavian at the Library of Congress; Juul Dieserud is also employed as an expert reviser in the Catalog Divison. J. C. M. Hanson, since 1910 associate director of the libraries at the University of Chicago, was the chief of the Catalog Division at the Library of Congress. 1897-1910, and the one who founded the present Library of Congress Catalog System. Karl T. Jacobsen, since 1920 librarian at Luther College, was a cataloguer at the Library of Congress, 1907-1911, a classifier at the University of Chicago, 1911-1920. Jahr, Hanson and Jacobsen, three of the most expert librarians in the United States, are all Luther College graduates. Thorvald Solberg has been the register of copyright since 1897. He has taken active part in efforts to secure international copyrights. The president's body guard is headed by Major Seibert, a Norwegian. The Norwegians have respect for constituted authority and obey the laws of the land. They pray every Sunday in their churches and in many of their daily prayers: "Protect and bless Thy servants, the President of the United States, the Governor of this commonwealth, our judges and magistrates, and all others in authority."

This book is provided with pictures of the governors, senators and congressmen of Norwegian-American stock. Also a few pictures to illustrate the hundreds and thousands in city and county, state and national public service. Of city and county service six were chosen—Andrew G. Bonhus, mayor Valley City, North Dakota; Storm Bull, mayor of Madison, Wisconsin; Ole Hanson, mayor of Seattle, Washington; Peter J. Pryts, Minneapolis alderman; Joseph M. Johnson, Chicago lieutenant of police; Canute R. Matson, Cook County sheriff. Bonhus is a Republican and checked a lot of grafting, waste and booze traffic while in office. A St. Olaf College graduate and a law graduate from the Uni-

versity of Minnesota, he established a plumbing company together
with his brothers, C. Alfred and Arthur M. At present he is in
the hardware business in Minneapolis. Bull was a Democrat and
a professor of steam engineering at the University of Wisconsin,
1879-1907. He was a brother of Ole Bull, the violinist. Hanson
is a Democrat. He is a self-made man. Studied law and was
admitted to the bar in Wisconsin. Settled in Seattle and engaged
in real estate. Sponsor for many good laws in the Washington
Legislature. Elected mayor in 1918 and became nationally prominent by prompt and decisive measures in meeting and overcom-
ing a general strike, Feb. 1, 1919. Author of "Americanism vs.
Bolshevism." Is now a real estate man in Los Angeles, California. Peter Pryts is a carpenter by trade and a Socialist in
politics. Is a good man, with a typically Norwegian high sense
of law and right. Joseph M. Johnson is distantly related to Ole
Johnson, the Slooper, and is perhaps the man in the world most
interested in the Sloopers. He was born July 4, 1865, on the
John Rosdail estate, Miller Twp., La Salle County, Illinois. Took
his B. S. at Valparaiso in 1892. Taught school at Stavanger and
elsewhere four years. Became a patrolman in Chicago, 1896;
a sergeant, 1906; a lieutenant, 1912, in charge of S. Green and
85th Street Station, 10th District. He has kept a dairy for
20 years. Colonel Canute Ragnvald Matson was born at Voss
in 1843. Left for America in 1849. Attended Albion Academy.
Was Knute Nelson's room mate at school. Studied law and became a soldier in the 13th Wisconsin Infantry. Was superintendent of Lincoln Park Substation, Chicago, 1866-1886; sheriff
of Cook County, 1886-1890, the first sheriff to hold a four-year
term. Also justice of the peace and coroner. Married Isabella,
daughter of Rev. Ole Andrewson, of Jefferson Prairie, Wisconsin. She was president of the School Children's Aid Society
and founder and president of the Lutheran Women's League of
Chicago. Matson attained much prominence during the Hay-
market riot. He would have become governor of Illinois had
not one of his prisoners once escaped, through no fault of Matson's.

Of men of state and national positions three Jacobsons were
chosen to represent the state. Every major office in this land
could be manned by Norwegian Jocobsons. As to the three whose
pictures are presented, Jacob N. Jacobson is a banker at Hills,
and a member of the Minnesota Legislature. He has been treasurer of the National organization of the Young People's Luther
League since 1909. Jacob F. Jacobson, "Honest Jake," of Madison, Minn., has put more good laws on the statute books of Minnesota than perhaps any other man. He was a strong candidate for
governor, but was defeated by the unjust slogan of his enemies:
"He eats pie with a knife." O. P. B. Jacobson is one of nature's

noblemen. He is the conscientious and fearless railroad commissioner, with a heart big enough to encompass Norwegian interests
as well as American. He is president of the Norwegian Society
of America. During the World War his loyalty to this country
was characteristically expressed in a speech in which he mentioned
that 13 of his sons and nephews were at the front. With intense
earnestness he declared: "Ve must vin the wictory!"

Of the Washington group the photos of Thorstein Jahr,
Thorvald Solberg and Juul Dieserud are printed. No apologies
are offered. They are good men.

Jacob F. Jacobson   Jacob N. Jacobson   O. P. B. Jacobson
Senator, Minn.   Representative, Minn.   R. R. Com., Minn.

The Norwegians are not as a class seekers after office. If
they had come from the official classes in Norway instead of
from the farming and fishing population, they would have forged
to the front more rapidly than they have done, not in the matter
of doing good work and being good citizens, but in regard to
getting offices and becoming prominent. When they do seek office, they have to overcome the handicap of nationality. The so-
called Americans are a proud race and jealous of their Anglo-
Saxon institutions. They do not quickly step aside and say to the
other races: "Say, come here. Let us give you an office as president of our university, governor of our state and president of the
United States." The wonder is, that so many Norwegians have
gotten office at all. It is not a mere co-incidence that this year
there are five Norwegian governors in the United States. They
have deserved it. Joseph Anderson should also have been elected
governor of Iowa—he deserved it. They are able to hold any
office in the gift of this great and good land. As Oley Nelson,
of Slater, Iowa, the grand old Civil War veteran, said in his speech
at the Norway Centennial, 1914: "I may be reasonably pardoned
if I, at my age, say that I have an idea that even I could make a
fairly good president of the United States, for what the country
needs is a chief executive who is from the common people, sensible and honest, and these qualities I hope that I have. And one

thing I am very sure of, and that is, that Mrs. Oley Nelson, my wife, would make an excellent First Lady of the Land, the occupant of the White House." The Norwegians, it must be remembered, are in race, language, history, culture, institutions and genius, of all nationalities most like the English, and therefore, they have proven the quickest to assimilate with the American stock. They are quicker to become naturalized in fact as well as in name than even the English, who cling longingly to their British ways. This is the strength and, at the same time, the greatest weakness of the Norwegians. They become Americans so fast that they forget at times to take along with them their cultural heritage, which should help to strengthen and broaden American life and institutions. Best of all the good things they have, is their Christian faith and their moral earnestness. This makes men of them, courageous, gentle, simple, thoughtful, independent, obedient, thrifty, generous, loyal, enduring, manly, Christian men. The country at all times needs such men. As the poet sings:

> Give us men!
> Men from every rank,
> Fresh and free and frank,
> Men of thought and reading,
> Men of light and leading,
> Men of loyal breeding,
> National welfare speeding.
> Men of faith and not of faction,
> Men of lofty aim in action—
> Give us men!—I say again:
>   Give us men!
>
>   Give us men!
> Strong and stalwart ones,
> Men whom highest hope inspires,
> Men whom purest honor fires,
> Men who trample self beneath them,
> Men who make their country wreathe them,
>   As her noble sons,
>   Worthy of their sires.
> Men who never shame their mothers,
> Men who never fail their brothers,
> True, however false are others—
> Give us men!—I say again,
>   Give us men!
>
>   Give us men!
> Men who, when the tempest gathers,
> Grasp the standard of their fathers,
>   In the thickest of the fight.
> Men who strike for homes and altar,
> (Let the coward cringe and falter)
>   God defend the right.
> True as truth, though lorn and lonely,
> Tender as the brave are only—
> Men who tread where saints have trod,
> Men for Country, Right and God—
> Give us men!—I say again, again,
>   Give us men!

18. Patriotism

The patriotism of the Norwegian-American can not very well be challenged. During the Civil War nine per cent of the Norwegians took up arms as volunteer soldiers; in the World War six per cent of the Norwegians went with the American colors while only four per cent of the population at large were mustered into service. In times of peace the Norwegians obey the law and work hard for the upbuilding of the land. They do it with the vim and vigor of youth, with the love which Jacob had for Rachel. He worked seven years for her, but they seemed as so many days "for the love he had to her."

The opening poem, "America, My Country," by Jens Kristian Grøndahl, editor of the "Red Wing Daily Republican," is a spontaneous and sincere expression of the average, sane Norwegian-American, whether war-horse or pacifist. Grøndahl is a man of peace and of principle. When he was in the State Legislature of Minnesota he would not accept railroad passes, because he did not believe that a legislator should do so. His stand started a movement which has since resulted in laws in many states regulating passes and, finally, a national law prohibiting passes. He has written numerous poems expressing his high idealism and their practical application. The poem "America, My Country," was read in Congress during the War and adopted for schools by the educational departments of six states.

A large number of other writers have written patriotic poems addressed to America or its flag. Nels Bergan wrote a poem entitled "Our Land," and received a letter of thanks from President Woodrow Wilson in person. Here is a cluster of beautiful national poems with America as the theme:

Songs to America

Askeland, Hallvard: "Vinlands Sang"
Garborg, Samuel: "Fjerde Juli Sang"
Guldseth, Olaf: "Norsk-amerikanernes Sang"
Heitmann, John: "This Land of Ours"
Norstog, Jon: "Amerika, eg takker deg."
Teigen, Knut M. O.: "Old Glory"
Wergeland, Agnes M.: "America Magna"

As Ristad sings in "The Pioneer":

I love this mighty land of God—
My fathers' home and mine,—
Where honest labor proudly trod
In peaceful battle-line.
From Maine and to the Golden Gate
Is flung our free and fair estate
Upon the shining sod.

The Norwegians in Canada are not a whit different from their kinsmen in the States, except that they love Canada instead of the United States and are loyal citizens with might and main up there. Their poets are laboring to express this devotion in lyric strains. As in the following song to Canada in Norwegian dialect by R. B.:

CANADA

Aa nei, so fagert eit solskins-ver,
Aa nei! aa nei! so vakkert her er.
Her eig vi heime baad' du og eg.
Canada! Canada! Land fyr meg.

Her rudde far min seg grund og gard,
so ryggen vart bøygd, næven vart hard.
Han sleit og stridde fyr meg og deg.
Canada! Canada! Land fyr meg.

Sjaa deg 'kring, skal du sjaa kor det gror,
det bryter og veks, der far min for.
Alt dette stræv var fyr meg og deg.
Canada! Canada! Land fyr meg.

Mor mi var med, ho sveittad og sleit,
taara turkad, um nokot var leit.
Ho vølte og stelte um meg og deg.
Canada! Canada! Land fyr meg.

Naar far var sliten og tung i sind,
mor mi strauk lindt hans skjeggute kind.
Dei lyftad samen, — eg saag det eg.
Canada! Canada! Land fyr meg.

Høgsæte-stolpar fraa Noreg var,
sætt vart i stova i fars sin gard.
Alt gjort i stann fyr meg og deg.
Canada! Canada! Land fyr meg.

Canada ligg her fagert og stort,
venter at sonen nokot fær gjort.
Canada roper paa meg og deg.
Canada! Canada! Land fyr meg.

The Norwegians in Canada, as in the United States, have not forgotten Norway, and their love for that far-off country of their own birth, perhaps, or that of their sires, has not grown cold.

In his poem "Emigranten" (The Emigrant) Franklin Petersen expresses the wish that he may always be poor and unfavored if America should cause him to despise his original home. Thus, in the Norwegian:

EMIGRANTEN

Norge, o Norge! nei aldrig jeg finder
land jeg kan elske saa barnligt som dig.
Norge, o Norge! din krans av smaa minder
bliver et lys paa min mørkeste vei.
— Gid i Amerika jeg fattig maa vandre,
gid ingen lykke maa løfte mig frem,
dersom den kunde mit sind saa forandre,
at jeg ringeagter mit fattige hjem.

Many are the poems that have been penned by Norwegian immigrants in memory of the dear land they forsook, and poets of the stock born and bred under the starry flag sing songs to Norway. Thus, Dr. Knut M. O. Teigen, whose poem graces page 4 of this book, was born here, and Dr. C. O. Solberg, author of a tribute, "To Norway," is a grandson of the Ole K. Nattesta that first settled Rock County, Wisconsin. Listen to Solberg, who, by the way, is as patriotic an American as ever trod United States soil:

> Thou land of the North, rudely riven and thrust,
> Where the waves of the ocean forever will rush;
> Whose people the noise of the bottomless deep
> At morning awakens, sobs at even to sleep!
>
> By the sheen of the fjord thou hast mothered us well,
> Where the croon of the pine on our infancy fell;
> By the glint of the sun on the tall mountain crag
> Thou has lighted our youth to the high deeds of eld.
>
> Round the graves of our fathers the gray cliffs arise,
> And they shelter the tomb where the warrior lies,
> While the requiem sung by the storms on the sea
> In our souls unforgotten, eternal, shall be.
>
> All we ask in the stress of the battles that are,
> When a beckoning fate leads to regions afar,
> Is the dent on the shield, is the sword flame that won,
> Ere the mold over us as on them shall be dun.
>
> Like the stone that has sheltered the wild mountain flower,
> Whose fragrance and charm are its tenderest dower,
> The love that we yield thee still firmly shall trace,
> The dream thou hast lit in the heart of the race.
>
> O thou land of the North, rudely riven and thrust,
> Where the waves of the ocean forever shall rush,
> Whose people the noise of the bottomless deep
> At morning awakens, sobs at even to sleep.

In similar strain are the following national lyrics by Norwegian-Americans:

Songs to Norway

Anonymous: "Jeg hilser dig Norge"
Askevold, Bernt: "Normandens Hjemlaengsel"
Baumann, Julius B.: "Syttende Mai"
Melby, Gustav: "We are not ashamed of our heritage"
Sneve, O. S.: "Broder, Bring en Hilsen over"
Solberg, C. K.: "Bedstemor Norge"

The Norwegians of America delight in celebrating the Seventeenth of May by speech and song, in athletic contests and games. It is Norway's Fourth of July, her Independence Day. A Two Rivers local paper in 1899 carried the news item: "The two Norwegians in town held a mass meeting, called for the purpose of making arrangements for the annual Seventeenth of May Celebration in this town." These Seventeenth of May celebrations remind the Norseman of his wonderful past as a free man and keys him up, not only for the Fourth of July celebration, but for his daily walk as a free American citizen.

Norwegian-Americans frequently visit the old home land and bring with them to the dear ones across the sea greetings such as the following from the inspired pen of O. S. Sneve:

TO NORWAY

Broder! bring en hilsen over
til vor fælles gamle mor,
naar du over vandets vover
styrer nu mot høie Nord.
Naar du lægger ut fra havnen,
kommer ut paa selve "myren,"
stil dig forut tæt ved stavnen,
utkik hold paa hele turen.
Naar saa hist i horisonten,
der hvor hav og himmel mødes,
der hvor morgenrøden fødes,
dukker op av bølgeskummet
hvit i toppen, grøn i fronten,
træder ind i himmelrummet,
stiger frem i al sin vælde
Norges fjelde,
graa av ælde,
vil du da dit hoved hælde,
i vort sted en taare fælde,
sagte melde.

at vi stunder, stunder, stunder,
gaar og grunder,
sukker, sørger,
ofte spørger:
Faar vi aldrig mer den glæde,
Norges jordbund at betræde?
Hvor i glade ungdomsaar
først vi stammet "Fader vor,"
hvor vor ømme mor os lærte:
"Bøie Gud mit unge hjerte,"
medens elvens sus i dalen,
bjelders klang og gjøkens galen.
skogen, lien,
bækken, stien,
slog sig ned i fantasien,
holder endnu til derinde.
og som aldrig nogensinde
helt forsvinder,
— — — fagre minder.

Jim Hill gave $50,000.00 to St. Olaf College and $50,000.00 to Luther College. Dr. Babcock has written two of the best books about Norwegians. Dr. Lenker praises the Norwegians from the house-tops in facts and figures. Babcock and Lenker speak Norwegian. Many other Americans have learned the language. Senator Robert Lafollette speaks Sogning.

J. N. Lenker
Statistician

K. C. Babcock
Professor

J. J. Hill
Railroader

19. THE NORWEGIAN HOME

The home is the most important and fundamental institution in society viewed from almost any angle—language, morals, religion, education, work, amusement, thrift, generosity, ambition, patriotism, etc. God save the home! It was instituted in Paradise, and, in spite of man's fall, God in His infinite goodness and wisdom has let man keep and maintain this institution down through the ages. The vexing problems of society are all solved in the home, particularly the Christian home:

> When Jesus enters meek and lowly,
> To fill the home with sweetest peace,
> When hearts have felt His blessing holy
> And found from sin complete release,
> Then light and calm within shall reign,
> And hearts divided love again.

The influence of a Christian home is well illustrated in the study of the pastor's home. Luther in 1525, 400 years ago, by his

Maren Wasboe Iverson (1822-1924), Kenyon, Minn., Knitting.

Took care of Rev. J. A. Bergh at his Baptism. Wove him a carpet when she was 100 years old.

marriage, restored to the consciousness of the world the place of the home in society. Since his day clergymen of all denominations except the Roman Catholic have had the privilege of establishing homes, and their homes have as a rule felt the influence of Christianity more than the average home. What has been the result? The result has been that the parsonages have furnished a larger percentage of ministers and other church workers than any other source. But that is not all. Every general encyclopedia shows that the sons of clergymen distinguish themselves relatively in greater numbers than men from any other profession. Just one citation—There is one preacher to every 327 breadwinners, but there is one famous preacher's son to every eight distinguished Americans. From 16 per cent to 20 per cent of the great men in the world are preachers' sons. Even among the millionaires over 30 per cent are preachers' sons. The reason is plain: The Christian instruction and example of the home have left their impress for good and the fact that the parsonage is the center of a community, at least the place where all the most vital interests of life are discussed and settled right, in the light of God's Word, makes the pastor's home, with all its poverty and self-denial, the best place in the world for getting a start towards a career both good and great.

The Norwegians are lovers of home. The divorce problem does not really as yet affect their lives as a people. God forbid that it ever should do so. The Norwegian pioneer dugout, sod cellar or log hut was very primitive—one little room, without even a floor or a board roof. It was not a house, but it was a home. There Father was high priest, leading in prayer and devotion, and Mother was prophetess, teaching her young the Word of God. If he was king and master, she was as truly queen and mistress.

In the "Decorah Posten," beginning with the issue for Jan. 20, 1925, there has been a series of weekly articles on the Norwegian pioneer home, entitled "Den gamle stova" (The Old Living Room).

The series is of remarkable historical and sociological value, as each writer describes his own home and the life that was lived there. The writers of these articles are:

No.	Writer	Title	Bygd	Date	
1.	Tolo, T. O.	Den Gamle Stova	Hardanger	Jan.	20
2.	Ristad, D. G.	Den Gamle Stuu	Overhalden	Jan.	27
3.	Njus, L. J.	Den Gamle Stova	Sogn	Feb.	3
4.	Rølvaag, O. E.	Den Gamle Stua	Helgeland	Feb.	6
5.	Braatelien, G. T.	Den Gamle Stua	Sigdal	Feb.	10
6.	Kolset, Carl D.	Den Gamle Stua		Feb.	17
7.	Dørrum, I.	Den Gamle Stogo	Opdal	Feb.	24
8.	Knaplund, Paul	Den Gamle Stuo	Nordland	March	3
9.	Bredeson, Kristjan	Den Gamle Stugua	Solør	March	10
				March	17
10.	Oftelie, Torkel	Den Gamle Stoga	Telemarken	March	24
11.	Kirkeberg, O. L.	Den Gamle Stogo	Valdres	April	7
12.	Møst, S. O.	Den Gamle Stuo	Nordmøre	April	14
	Flotten, Ole J.	Den Gamle Stuu	Østerdalen	April	14
13.	Jordahl, D. C.	Den Gamle Stuo	Nordmøre	April	21
14.	Grandfør, Mrs. Anna	Den Gamle Stova	Søndmøre	April	28
15.	Lien, O. H.	Den Gamle Stoga	Borte	May	5

One of the most beautiful Norwegian homes, characteristic of Norwegian faithfulness, is that of Ole Anderson and wife, née Mary Katterud, of Decorah. She was born at Lier, Norway, March 22, 1837. Came to Muskego in 1842. When Jenny Lind, the Swedish singer, was here, she established scholarships for Scandinavians at various schools. There was such a scholarship in connection with the Platteville Academy. Mary Katterud was given that scholarship in 1853 and became a public school teacher near Decorah in 1854. Ole Anderson courted this fine, sensible school ma'am and they became engaged. Then the Civil War

broke out and he enlisted as a soldier with rank of lieutenant. He
returned alive, but a cripple for life. He released his betrothed
from the engagement, but she felt that he needed her now, if ever.
So they were married, and both lived to a very ripe old age. She
died April 23, 1918; he a few years before her. Not having any
children of their own, they adopted and reared two orphan girls.
The noble mutual life of Ole Anderson and wife inspired John

Grace Before Meat

Hegg, Sr., to write a poem in their honor. Their life contains
material for a good novel or film. It has been a powerful influence in wide-reaching circles.

It can not exactly be said of the Norwegian mother, as it has
been said of the Irish, that she wants at least one of her sons to
become a pastor. But there are cases among the Norwegians
where several of the sons have become pastors. Thus: P. A.
Rasmussen raised up four sons as preachers; so also Østen Hanson. In the case of the merchant Osul Torrison, Manitowoc,
Wis., he had a large family of whom one, Isaac B. Torrison, became a pastor (Waco, Chicago, Decorah); another, Oscar M.
Torrison, became a lawyer and judge (Elbow Lake, Chicago), and
a third, George A., became a physician and professor of medicine
at Rush (Chicago).

One of the most unique Norwegian families is that of Dr. Johannes T. Ylvisaker, professor of theology at Luther Seminary, 1879-1917. Below is a picture of the widow, with nine of her ten children. She has had seven sons and three daugh-

The Johs. T. Ylvisaker Family
Nils M., Lauritz S., Sigurd C., Olaf S.
Gudrun O., Mrs. Kristi, Inga M.
J. Wilhelm, Carl B., Ragnvald S.

ters. The seven sons graduated from Luther College, and six of them from Luther Seminary; the three daughters graduated from the Lutheran Ladies' Seminary, and two married ministers; all the children have taken post graduate work; all have engaged in church work. The names of the children are given herewith:

THE YLVISAKER CHILDREN

No.	Name	Year of Birth	Luther College Graduate	Luther Seminary Graduate	Present Occupation
1.†	Tora L.	1878	....	....	Mrs. Rev. N. A. Larsen
2.	Olaf S.	1880	1899	1906	Treasurer, St. Paul Hospital
3.	Nils M.	1882	1902	1906	Exec. Sec'y. Y.P.L.L.
4.	Sigurd C.	1884	1903	1907	Ph.D., Pastor, Madison, Wis.
5.	Inga Marie	1886	....	....	Mrs. Rev. C. S.Thorpe, Minneapolis
6.	Lauritz S.	1889	1910	1914	M.D., St. Paul Hospital Staff
7.	Gudrun O.	1892	....	....	Organist, Christ Church, St. Paul
8.	Carl B.	1896	1917	1920	Pastor, Northwood, Ia.
9.	Ragnvald S.	1898	1920	....	Medical Student
10.	J. Wilhelm	1900	1921	1925	Candidate of Theology

†Deceased

The reader's attention is called especially to the picture of the family saying grace before meat (p. 505). The picture is a reprint of Herbjørn Gausta's painting in "Jul i Vesterheimen," 1911. The appearance of the dining room in the homes of the Norwegians has changed. Our dining rooms are quite modern and look exactly like those of our American neighbors. But the custom of giving thanks before and after a meal still remains. This devotional period may be quite brief, as, by the offering up of a simple prayer by one member of the family or all in unison, or each one in turn. Or, it may consist of the reading of Scripture or out of some postil followed by a song by the whole family. The writer has taken part in such devotions every day of his life and considers it to be one of the greatest legacies he received from his parents and one of the best contributions that Norway can give to America. America as such does not say grace before meat, and apparently wants to break down this good practice of the Norsemen. On one occasion Rev. B. J. Muus sat down at a restaurant table to eat. But first of all he said grace. "Do they all do it that way where you come from?" asked a bystander mockingly. "All except the hogs," was his blunt reply.

Norwegian hospitality reaches out to every wayfarer who asks for shelter. Norwegian generosity shares the last bite of bread with the hungry, the last rag with the naked.

AMERIKA

Amerika, eg takker deg
for det høgsyn du gav meg,
for det frisyn du gav meg!
Eg vil vera med aa bygja deg
med staal i di jord,
med varde-eld fraa dine tindar!

("Dedicatum" in "Fraa Audni.")

MEMBERS CENTENNIAL COMMITTEE

The Women's Auxiliary of the Norse-American Centennial

Mrs. Gilbert Guttersen (nee Pettersen), Mrs. Wm. O. Storlie (nee Nelson),
Miss Elisa Pauline Farseth, Mrs. J. E. Haugen (nee Norlie),
Mrs. Manley Fosseen (nee Jorgens)

| Gisle Bothne | S. H. Holstad | Knut Gjerset |
| General President | Managing Director | Chairman Com. Exhibits |

20. Adieu

This brief story of the Norwegians in America must draw to a close. The author has barely scratched the surface, and the soil is rich for other historians to cultivate. The Norwegians have received freely from America, but they have also given freely. They discovered this land first. They came in goodly numbers and there are as many Norwegians in the United States and Canada as in Norway itself. They raise large families. They cling to the soil in larger measure than any other race. They are frontiersmen and pioneers, brave and resourceful. They are honest toilers, often cheated out of their rights, but never discouraged. They are God-fearing churchmen and good citizens, chaste, temperate, conscientious, respectful of law and order. They are sound educators, emphasizing home training in childhood and youth, and the fear of the Lord as the beginning of wisdom. They are ennobling writers and preachers without fear of man. They are zealous foreign missionaries and active home missionaries, like Joseph seeking their brethren. They are large-hearted charity workers and hospitable almost to a fault. They engage in a many-sided and far-reaching cooperation and can teach all mankind the spirit of brotherhood and mutual helpfulness. They are lovers of home and invite Jesus to be their Guest. They are staunch defenders of law and land, but feel no shame in loving also the little land from which they sprang. They are men and women of sturdy Christian character, and one of their daily songs, which nearly every Norwegian knows by heart, is:

> On my heart imprint Thine image,
> Blessed Jesus, King of Grace,
> That life's riches, cares and pleasures,
> Have no power Thee to efface.

The author has been interested in this subject for a long time. He began writing this book December 1, 1924, and being busy with his work as teacher, he has been hard crowded in getting the History ready in time for the Norse American Centennial. He had to submit the first draft to the printer long before he saw the end of the book. Naturally, if he had had more time he could have readjusted the place and space of the material in considerable measure. He regrets very much that he has had to omit many sections of the book, including all the valuable appendices and bibliographies, besides many photographs and graphs. And now that the book is ready, he is reminded of Bjørnstjerne Bjørnson's words:

> Norrønafolket, det vil fare,
> det vil føre kraft til andre.

> (The Norsemen like to go abroad,
> They like to bring strength to others).

A number of kind friends not mentioned on page 7 should be given personal mention for valuable aid rendered. The author wishes at this belated time and out-of-the-way place to mention especially the following who assisted him generously:

Theodore C. Blegen, St. Paul, Minn.; A. Ragnv. Bræklin, Bergen, Norway; Elias Rasmussen, Windom, Minn; Henrietta C. Pryts, Minneapolis; I. Tollefsen, Poulsbo, Wash.; Gilbert O. Oudal, Minneapolis; J. A. Wang, Wittenberg, Wis.; John J. Wang, Crookston, Minn.; Th. Rasmussen, Portland, Ore.; F. J. Trønsdal, Eau Claire, Wis.; L. W. Boe, Northfield, Minn.; Otto Hansen, Minneapolis; Ulrikka F. Bruun, Chicago, Ill.; Arthur Ager and J. E. Haugen, Minneapolis; Mrs. Frances W. Anderson, Decorah; Carl Teisberg, Minneapolis; Hjalmar Rued Holand.

J. A. Thorsen	C. F. Hjermstad	H. N. Hendrickson
Byron, Minn.	Red Wing, Minn.	Augsburg Seminary
Pastor	Trustee	Professor

On the eve of the Norse-American Centennial the Norwegians are as happy as a bride going to meet her bridegroom. They are thankful to God for this good land (Deut. 8:7-10) and are tuning their harps to sing in jubilee chorus:

Praise to the Lord, Who doth prosper thy work and defend thee;
Surely His goodness and mercy here daily attend thee;
Ponder anew
What the Almighty can do
If with His love He befriend thee.

We close our book with a Norwegian Telemarking poem by H. B. Kildahl, urging the Norsemen to be true to their heritage, followed by a poem written shortly after the World War, by J. J. Skørdalsvold, in which he thanks the real heroes who held the Norsemen's ideals up before them in the heat of the strife, through poverty and want and to riches abounding.

TO OUR REAL HEROES

It brings relief
In such an age as ours—
An age of cant
And mock-heroic deeds
To look around for heroes
Worthy of the name

Not far we need to go
To find them
The Norseland preachers
In our western wilds
Have left a saga
More bright and fair to see
Than Minnesota's
Indian-Summer skies

Some of you were at home
In Greece and Rome of old,
While others knew
But little of the world
Save Canaan and
Your native mountains
With their vales and fjords.
But all of you went out
With this in mind:

To serve your Master
And to help your fellow-men.

In every neighborhood
Were hungering souls
That openly or secretly
Received your message
With thankfulness and holy joy.

How lonesome and how sad
The older ones would feel,
Because their childhood church
Was out of reach!
And yet the younger ones
Were far worse off—
Cut loose from all restraints
Of settled life,
Adrift where each man's will
Was law unto itself.

To such you came
As saving angels from above,
To save imperiled souls
Ere they were lost and damned.

No flood too deep,
No plain too vast,
No sun too fierce,
No storm too wild
When you set out to preach
"The Word of God."

Few men can clearly see
What you have done.
Much less reward
A service so immense
But let me, tho belated,
Join the host of those
Who wish to thank you,
With hearts aglow,
For what you did for us.

And now I wish that what
Remains of me beyond
The veil of death,
The wreck of worlds,
The trump of doom
May meet and thank you
Evermore
For bringing help from heaven
To a failing soul.

J. J. Skordalsvold

Supplement

BY

OLAF MORGAN NORLIE

Contents

MINNEAPOLIS, MINN.
AUGSBURG PUBLISHING HOUSE
1926

Printed in U. S. A.

I. ADDITIONS

P. 103—Middle.—Add: Caption under pictures: Paulson—Pioneer Pastor; Bjørgo—President Minnesota District of Norwegian Synod; Harbo, Professor, Augsburg Seminary.

P. 148—Middle—Add: Pennsylvania, 1 settlement. Total, 16 states, 111 settlements. Grand total, 111 settlements.

P. 168—Bottom—Add: West Koshkonong was dedicated December 19, 1844; East Koshkonong, January 31, 1845; and Muskego, March 13, 1845.

P. 170—Middle—Add: Caption under picture: Prairie Fire Threatening.

P. 271—Middle—Add: Caption under pictures: Academy Teachers.

P. 300—Bottom—Add: R. B. Anderson published in 1874 his "America Not Discovered by Columbus"; in 1875, "Norse Mythology"; in 1877, "Viking Tales from the North"; in 1888, "The Younger Edda." During the '80s he translated Bjørnson's novels and Horne's "History of Literature," edited "Heimskringla" and, together with Auber Forestier issued "Norway Music Album" (1881). He shares with Boyesen the honor of being the first Norwegian to write extensively in English.

P. 396—Middle—Add: Caption under picture: Women's Missionary Federation Officials, 1925.

The Women's Missionary Federation of the Norwegian Lutheran Church of America was founded June 12, 1917, three days after the Norwegian Lutheran Church was organized. Mrs. T. H. Dahl was the first president; Mrs. I. D. Ylvisaker, Fargo, N. D., is the present president. Miss Mathilde Rasmussen, Minneapolis, is vice president; Mrs. George T. Rygh, Minneapolis, is recording secretary; Mrs. Edward Johnson, Mankato, is corresponding secretary; Mrs. Joseph O. Estrem, Minneapolis, is treasurer. Corresponding to the nine Districts into which the Norwegian Lutheran Church is divided, the Women's Missionary Federation has nine branches. In 1923 there were 2,636 local societies, with a combined membership of 57,159 and a number of societies whose membership was not included. The Federation held 137 circuit meetings during 1925. It works for foreign and home missions, charities and Christian schools within the Church body to which it belongs, cooperating with the respective boards of the Church. By far the greatest portion of the money raised by the societies is turned into the congregational and synodical treasuries without being accredited to the Women's Missionary Federation at all. The actual amount raised by these local societies of women for all purposes no doubt exceeds the million dollar mark every year. The amounts officially reported by the Federation are as follows: In 1920, $50,087.39; in 1921, $74,941.61; in 1922, $75,835.86; in 1923 (8 months), $59,572.26; in 1924, $85,524.79; in 1925, $102,191.11. The Federation publishes an annual report, a missionary program manual and other literature. It has built a number of cottages for missionaries at home on furlough and two high schools for girls in China, one at Sinyang, Honan, and the other at Fancheng, Hupeh. It has donated a sum for a memorial chapel in memory of Sister Caroline Thompson on the field that she served in Madagascar. The Federation holds triennial conventions. District conventions are held every year in which the national body does not convene. Circuit meetings are held oftener. Woman holds a noble place in the Norwegian Lutheran Church.

P. 406—Top—Add: James A. Peterson under novelists.

P. 406—Middle—Add: Caption under pictures: Pastors from the Rank and File.

P. 408—Top—Add: In temperance: Wm. Ager, O. B. Olson, Henry Wærdahl, K. T. Stabeck, T. K. Thorvilson, Ulrikka F. Bruun, E. E.

Løbeck, O. S. Sneve.
> P. 408—Middle—Add: In education: Anne Emilie Poulssen.
> P. 430—Bottom—Add: Stub also president of the Sudan Mission and of the Lutheran Brotherhood of America.
> P. 432—Young people's societies are excellent training schools in Christian experience and church work. They take hold of a person in the most critical time of his life. They lead young men and women into a deeper knowledge of the Word of God, urge them to accept Christ as their Savior and make a bold profession of their choice, to consecrate their lives to the active service of God, to walk every day as the children of light. The Young People's Luther League of the Norwegian Lutheran Church came into being in June, 1917. It aims to "quicken the spiritual life among its members, to promote the study of the Bible and the history, confessions and activities of the Lutheran Church, and to assist the pastor and the congregation in the spiritual care of the young." It holds triennial conventions. The attendance at Red Wing, in 1919, was 15,000, from 700 societies; at La Crosse, in 1922, it was 18,000, from 1.295 societies; at Minneapolis, in 1925, it was 15,000 from 1,971 societies. Total membership, 100,000. Money raised, 1922-1925, $33,145. Money expended, $12,000 for Soldiers and Sailors' Relief; $9,014 for Church Extension; $4,502 for Foreign Missions in China and Madagascar; $1,469 for Mission at Untunjambili, Natal; also a hospital in Madagascar; $14,100 for Scholarship Fund at Theological Seminary. The "Lutheran Church Herald" is the official organ. Reports and pamphlets are issued: "Senior Luther League," "Junior Luther League," "Life Worth While" (book), "Forward with Christ" (book), "Convention Song Book" (25,000 sold). Dr. Martin Hegland is president; Martin Norstad is vice president; J. C. K. Preus is secretary; N. M. Ylvisaker is executive secretary; and S. R. Torgerson, Joice, Ia., is treasurer, succeeding Jacob N. Jacobson.

> *How beautiful is youth! how bright it gleams*
> *With its illusions, aspirations, dreams!*
> *Book of Beginnings, Story without End,*
> *Each maid a heroine, and each man a friend.*

The Norwegian Lutheran Federation for Young People in America (Norsk Lutherske Landsforbund for Ungdom i Amerika) was organized at Chicago in 1920. It aims to introduce Norwegian newcomers to America, particularly to Lutheran church work, also to aid in mission work, especially among sailors and fishermen, as in Alaska, Seattle and Brooklyn. "Norsk Ungdom" is the official organ, of which Prof. M. O. Wee is editor. M. O. Wee was the organizer of the Federation and its president from 1920 to 1925; the present incumbent is P. E. Ericksen, Chicago. The Federation has one or more local societies in Brooklyn, New York City, Detroit, Chicago, Madison, Sioux City, St. Paul, Minneapolis, Seattle, Ketchikan and Petersburg, besides several rural societies.
> P. 433—Middle—Add after Ebenezer, Mpls.: John H. Field is the soul and mainstay of this institution.
> P. 435—Middle—Add: Hope Mission, organized by Mrs. Bruun October 1, 1888, was the first Scandinavian city mission in Chicago. Within a block of its first location, 73 West Indiana Street, were 70 saloons and the headquarters of the Milwaukee Brewers' Association. It later moved to 166 North Halsted Street, then to Milwaukee Avenue near by, and finally, in 1901, to Harmony Hall, where it remained until 1913. Since the Harmony Hall has belonged to the Presbyterian Board of Home Missions and has been a gathering place for Italians about the Word of God. Mrs. Bruun in 1889 organized a Prohibition Club and the first Scandinavian W. C. T. U. in America. In her Hope Mission she maintained daily services, a reading room, a five cent lunch counter, free lodging and

an employment bureau. On May 19, 1900, she opened at 329 West Erie Street a Scandinavian Working Girls' Home and Employment Bureau, called Bethany Home. In 1925 her W. C. T. U. celebrated its 36th anniversary.

P. 435—Temperance Societies—The Norwegians are a temperate people. This is the testimony of all the authorities. For example, Deets Pickett says in his "Encyclopedia of Temperance, Prohibition and Public Morals" (1917, p. 306) : "Of all countries in Europe, Norway is, next to Finland, the one with the least amount of intoxicating liquor used." As far back as 1854 Norway adopted local option and during the World War national prohibition; but unfortunately, by application of financial pressure, since the War France has forced Norway to permit the importation of wines against her will. According to Josiah Strong's "Social Progress" (1906, p. 231), Norway consumed less spirits per capita than any other country in Europe except Russia. In this period, covering 15 years, Norway consumed 5.50 gallons per capita of wine, beer and alcohol, Russia consumed 3.18 gallons, the United States 14.07 gallons, Germany 28.50 gallons, Great Britain 32.74 gallons, France 32.98 gallons and Belgium 46.78 gallons. The Norwegians in America, like their kinsmen across the sea, are a temperate people, as can be seen from the fact that Norwegian settlements have, as a rule, been among the first to secure local option, county option and state prohibition. Andrew Volstead, the author of the Eighteenth Amendment to the Constitution of the United States (the Prohibition Amendment), is a Norwegian-American, who for eighteen years represented a bone-dry Norwegian congressional district.

Nevertheless, there has been much hard drinking among the Norwegians, too, both farmers and townsfolk, and the American saloon has blighted many a Norwegian home and has dragged many a promising youth into the gutter. And there has been much hard work to introduce temperance among the Norwegians. Wm. Ager ventures to say in his "Afholdsfolkets Festskrift" (1914, p. 5), that the Norwegians of America, as a people, have accomplished more towards temperance, in proportion to their numbers, than any other race in the land, not excepting even the Americans of English descent.

Probably the first Norwegian to work with might and main against the direct evil, was Elling Eielsen, who began to preach temperance in La Salle County, Illinois, in 1839. The first Norwegian church paper in America was "Maanedstidende," and this paper contained in its second number, April, 1851, a strong plea for temperance, written by Rev. A. C. Preus. In the December issue, 1851, this paper announces that temperance societies have been organized in eight congregations—Muskego, Yorkville, Koshkonong, Bluemount, Dodgeville, Skoponong, Hartprairie and Sugar Creek, all in Wisconsin. Wilhelm Wærenskjold organized a Norwegian temperance society in Texas in 1853. Since then there have been many hundred temperance societies organized within the Norwegian congregations, and the pastors have, in recent years, almost to a man lined up against the saloon. Many of the pastors may be reckoned in the front rank of prohibition speakers; as, for example, B. B. Haugan, T. K. Thorvilson, Jens I. Lønne, Ole Løkensgaard, Andreas Wright, K. B. Birkeland, Edward Brekhus, T. H. Dahl, G. Hoyme, C. K. Holter, M. Falk Gjertsen, J. Mueller Eggen, Ole Paulson, Hans Caspersen, Adolf Bredesen, H. G. Stub and J. H. Brønø.

Perhaps the most influential church institution in the temperance fight has been Augsburg Seminary. This school has been a storm center in prohibition work, and has trained a large number of pastors who have been radically opposed to the saloon. On its faculty have been some of the leading anti-saloon heroes among the Norwegian people, such as Georg Sverdrup, Sven Oftedal, Th. S. Reimestad and J. L. Nydahl. In the latter part of the eighties Professor Reimestad was at the head of the Augsburg Quartet, which "sang the temperance cause into thousands of hearts."

"The Total Abstinence Congress," a joint committee representing the state associations, provided scientific lectures on the drink problem. From 1898 to 1917 there were 18 regular classes (at Augsburg Seminary, Madison Normal, Belgrade, Eau Claire and Elbow Lake). Certificates were given to 205 persons (mostly men) who had attended about 20 lectures. Afterwards about 50 of the men became ministers. With the exception of one year, J. J. Skørdalsvold was at the head of this work. Neither those who conducted this work nor the speakers got as much as one cent for their trouble.

Much of the temperance work, and perhaps the boldest and most effective, has been performed by lay workers and temperance societies not connected with the Church. One of the first and most notable of these lay workers was Lauritz Carlson of Chicago. He had been a drunkard and had suffered much, but had been saved as a brand from the fire. He *could* talk temperance, his main theme being: "Carlson, the slave, and Carlson, the freedman." He organized in Chicago, in 1876, a temperance society called Harmony, and built a temperance hall called Harmony Hall, in which he preached prohibition until his death, in 1893. Here Ulrikka F. Bruun signed the pledge in June, 1877, Ole Br. Olson in 1879 and Wm. Ager, in 1887. Olson became the first founder and editor of a Norwegian temperance paper in America, namely: "Afholds-Bladet," Chicago, 1882-1888. In 1888 he became editor of "Arbeideren," Eau Claire. In 1890 these two papers were merged under a new name —"Reform," Eau Claire, which has since been the chief Norwegian temperance organ in America. Ager became connected with "Reform" in 1892, and has been its editor since the death of Olson, in 1903. Ager has been the most prolific of the Norwegian prohibition scribes. Olson was a dramatic speaker of unusual power; Ager is a speaker of unusual wit and point.

Following the example of Carlson in Chicago, the friends of prohibition established similar temperance societies here and there throughout the Norwegian settlements. These, in turn, organized themselves into state societies. Thus the Minnesota Total Abstinence Association was founded in 1885, and a similar organization was created for Dakota Territory that same year. In 1888 the Wisconsin Temperance Society was organized; in 1894 the South Dakota, in 1896 the North Dakota, in 1904 the Pacific. In 1905 the National Temperance Union was founded. In 1921 the Minnesota Association reorganized under the name The Society for Our Country's Welfare and the platform of the Society was widened so as to include not only work for personal temperance; but also law enforcement, world peace, Sabbath observance, the dance, immoral movies and other social evils. In 1887 it was estimated that these temperance societies had a membership of 5,000. The Minnesota Society has at times had a membership of 8,000. In addition to these associations, there are also a number of Norwegian Good Templar lodges and Norwegian Women's Christian Temperance Union local units. In 1896 there were 220 local Good Templar lodges, with a membership of 17,000, and about 20,000 Scandinavians were members of the English Good Templars. These associations have taken a leading part in the battle for local option and a saloonless nation.

It was no easy task to be a temperance speaker in the early days. The churches were seldom opened to temperance speakers. Even some of the Norwegian pastors were hostile to the movement. The speakers were often rotten-egged and otherwise abused; the pay was small; but the cause was great, and the zeal of the temperance speakers was marvelous. Among the pioneers in this field may be mentioned the fol-

Dorthea Dahl   Mrs. Laura Bratager   Clara Olson

A. M. Arntzen   C. K. Solberg   J. A. Ottesen

John Benson   Simon Johnson   N. T. Moen

Abram Markoe   Helge Rogness   James Cox Markoe

lowing: H. H. Aaker, Mrs. Anna Qvale Anderson Fergestad, T. J. Anderson, H. Askeland, A. Berge, Mrs. Ulrikka Feldtman Bruun, Lauritz Carlson, T. A. Dahl, Gustav Eide, Swen Ellingsen, John Engelsen, Alfred Engelstad, J. E. N. Figved, H. A. Foss, T. J. Frøiland, Alfred Gabrielsen, A. G. Gjevre, Albert Hansen, G. T. Hagen, Arne P. Haugen, Martin Haugen, J. F. Heiberg, Sven Heskin, H. S. Hilleboe, J. S. Holland, Torger Hov, Knut Johnson, Kjetil Knudsen, P. Langbach, Chr. Larsen, A. H. Lindelie, E. E. Løbeck, N. T. Moen, J. L. Nydahl, Tarral Olsen, Bertheus Olson, Lars Øvre, Henry Paulson, M. G. Peterson, Wilhelm Pettersen, Elias Rachie, Th. S. Reimestad, Miss Lavine Rokke, Ole Rosendahl, H. P. Rud, N. G. Rude, Ole O. Sageng, Andrew S. Sather. T. O. Skaar, J. J. Skørdalsvold, O. S. Sneve, Edwin P. Stubson, Miss Petrine Thorsen, F. L. Trønsdal, P. I. Williams and C. O. Winger.

The Norwegian temperance literature is quite extensive and pictures clearly the great crusade against strong drink. The following works are representative:

PERIODICALS

"Afholds-Basunen"	....Hillsboro, N. D.	1887-96	J. Lønne, editor
"Afholds-Bladet"	......Chicago, Ill.	1882-88	O. Br. Olson
"Afholdsvennen"	......Chicago, Ill.	1894-98	P. A. Olson
"Dakota-Bladet"	.......Portland, N. D.	1886-87	H. A. Foss
"Det Hvide Baand"	....Chicago, Ill.	1907-17(?)	Ulrikka F. Bruun
"Feltraabet"	..........Minneapolis, Minn.	1886-89	H. Askeland
"Folkets Røst"	........Hillsboro, N. D.	1886-87	L. P. Brevig
"Folkets Vel"	........Minneapolis, Minn.	1907-19	Gustav Eide
"Hjemmets Værn"	....Spokane, Wash.	1891-92(?)	— — —
"Lyngblomsten"	......Eau Claire, Wis.	1908-14(?)	O. Refsdal
"Reform"	...........Eau Claire, Wis.	1890—	Wm. Ager
"Templarbladet"	......Chicago, Ill.	1890-96(?)	Marius Hansen

Also "Folkebladet" (Minneapolis), "Normanden" (Grand Forks), "Fram" (Fargo), and "Den Skandinaviske Goodtemplar" (Swedish-Norwegian, Minneapolis) have been enlisted in the temperance work.

HISTORY

Ager, Wm.	"Mindeblade om Ole Br. Olson"	1903
Ager, Wm.	"Afholdsfolkets Festskrift"	1914
Eide, Gustav	"Aarbog for Minn. Totalafholdsselskab"	1902-19
Foss, H. A., Johnson, Simon, and Olson, B.	"Trediveaarskrigen mod Drikkeondet"	1922
Nydahl, J. L.	"Afholdssagens Historie"	1896
Rachie, Elias	"The Temperance Crusade"	1908
Wærdahl, Henry	"Illinois Norske Goodtemplarers Historie"	1909

TREATISES AND TRACTS

Ager, Wm.	"Afholdssmuler"	1901
Eide, Gustav	"Aarbog," an annual.	
Haugan, B. B.	"Den Gutten"	1924
Heiberg, L.	"Brogede Blade" (No. 8)	1893
Hoyme, Gjermund	"Saloonen"	
Olson, Ole Br.	"Haandbog for Afholdsvenner"	1885
Stabeck, K. T.	"Alkoholens Fysiologiske og Pathologiske Indflydelse paa Menneskelivet"	1885
Sumstad, M. O.	"Afholdsforedrag"	1912
Thorvilson, T. K.	"Drikkeondet"	1896

STORIES

Ager, Wm.	"Paa Drikkeondets Konto"	1894
Ager, Wm.	"I Strømmen"	1899
Ager, Wm.	"Fortællinger for Eyvind"	1905
Ager, Wm.	"Fortællinger og Skisser"	1913
Ager, Wm.	"Ny Samling Fortællinger og Skisser"	1921
Bruun, Ulrikka F.	"Fiendens Faldgruber"	1884
Eide, Gustav	"Skitser, Fortællinger og Digte"	1909
Foss, H. A.	"Den Amerikanske Saloon"	1889
Janson, Drude Krog	"En Saloonkeepers Datter"	1889

Janson, Kr.	"Præriens Saga"	1885
Johnson, Simon	"Et Geni"	1907
Kildahl, J. N.	"Naar Jesus Kommer ind i Huset"	1906
Kildahl, J. N.	"When Jesus Enters the Home"	1917
Løbeck, E. E.	"Billeder fra Dødens Dal"	1899
Lock, Otto	"Syndens Sold"	1910
Lunde, Fr.	"Døgnfluer"	1908
Mason, A. H.	"I Ørneskyggen"	1907
Omann, Chr.	"Drukken og Ædru"	1886
Skørdalsvold, J. J.	"Tobias" (translation of Foss above)	1899
Wright, Andreas	"Skaal"	1894

POETRY

Bruun, Ulrikka F.	"Sange, Digte og Rim"	1919
Bruun, Ulrikka F.	"Den Syngende Evangelist"	1909
Løbeck, E. E.	"Forglemmigei"	
Reimestad, Th. S.	"Afholdssange"	1888
Reimestad, Th. S.	"Kampmelodier"	1892
Sneve, O. S.	"Samlede Sange og Digte"	1912

P. 435—It is difficult to say just how many societies have been founded by Norwegian-Americans. In 1914 Carl G. O. Hansen wrote a brief sketch of 650 societies (in J. B. Wist's "Norsk-amerikanernes Festskrift," 266-291). But his list is not complete and it includes a number of local or subordinate societies. If we include the ladies' aids, young people's societies, choirs, brotherhoods, girls' societies, boys' associations, mission bands, hospital units and other organizations in each of the 7,500 Norwegian congregations, past and present, the number 650 is manifestly too small. Hansen estimates the total membership of the societies of his list to be about 60,000. The membership of the church choirs almost reaches this number; that of the Young People's Luther League of the Norwegian Lutheran Church or of the Women's Missionary Federation, far surpasses the total membership of all these secular societies together.

These societies are of many kinds—publication, education, foreign missions, home missions, charities, politics, labor, professions, sport, social, literary, musical, art, theatrical, insurance, temperance, statistical, historical, national, cultural. Most of them are open; a few are secret lodges. This is an age of societies, and there is perhaps not a Norwegian community of any size that does not have one or more of these Norwegian associations at work in its midst. A few lines were devoted above to the temperance work of the Norwegians, and now a few more lines will tell about some of the attempts to organize the Norwegian people about their general cultural heritage and their history.

The first Scandinavian society in America was the Scandinavian Society of Philadelphia, dating from 1769, of which George Washington was a member and honorary president. The first president of this association was Capt. Abram Markoe, whose picture and the picture of whose great-grandson, Dr. James Cox Markoe, of St. Paul, Minn., are published in this supplement. Abram was born in the Danish West Indies, July 2, 1727, and died at Philadelphia, August 28, 1806. His son John was born in 1781, died in 1837. His grandson William was born in 1820, died in 1916. His great-grandson, James Cox, was born August 13, 1856. Abram Markoe organized a Philadelphia Company of which he became captain. This company served as Washington's body-guard on his way to Lexington. Markoe made the first flag of 13 stripes, in six colors, which he presented in 1775 to his company, the Philadelphia Light-Horse, and it was carried by that troop in the War of the Revolution. A picture of this flag, minus the colors, is reproduced here, because it came from the first Scandinavian Society in America and because it was the first forerunner to the "Stars and Stripes."

Local cultural societies, sometimes Scandinavian like the Philadelphia Society, but more often simply Norwegian, sprang up quite soon after the Norwegians had obtained a foothold here. Boston had a Norwegian

Society as early as 1853 and organized a Norumbega Society in 1889.
New York, Cleveland, Chicago, Milwaukee, Madison, La Crosse, Decorah,
Sioux City, Minneapolis, St. Paul, Fargo, Grand Forks, Spokane, Seattle,
San Francisco, all have had some local societies. New York City had 50
Norwegian secular societies in 1914; Chicago had 34 in 1913. The New
York societies are federated under the name Det Norske Nationalforbund.
Such unions exist also in Chicago and Seattle. Some of these societies

STANDARD PRESENTED BY CAPTAIN MARKOE IN 1775 TO THE PHILADELPHIA LIGHT-HORSE
AND CARRIED BY THAT TROOP IN THE WAR OF THE REVOLUTION.

present stated programs of excellent merit and are famous far beyond
their local habitation. "Yggdrasil" of Madison and "Symra" of Decorah,
for example, are internationally known.

It has been said that the fact that so many Norwegian societies are
springing up in the American Period (1890-1925) is due to the Norwegian-Americans' being more Norwegian than their fathers. Such is not
the case. These societies are being organized by those who are interested
in their Norwegian heritage; and they are trying to save this heritage
for the coming generations. As John G. Mohn put it in founding the

"Norwegian American": "We wish to impress upon the growing generation of Norwegian-Americans the best interests that have characterized the generation now passing away."

"Det Norske Selskab i Amerika" (The Norwegian Society in America) was founded January 28, 1903, at Minneapolis. Among its members have been the ablest and most self-sacrificing champions of Norwegian culture. B. Anundsen, Gisle Bothne and O. P. B. Jacobson have served as presidents. Most active of all in the interests of this society is without question Waldemar Ager of Eau Claire, the secretary of "Det Norske Selskab" and editor of its quarterly publication, "Kvartalskrift." This magazine has compiled much valuable material in the field of Norwegian-American history. The Society has promoted the introduction of the study of Norwegian in public high schools. It has superintended the erection of monumemts to the memory of illustrious Norwegians, the

Dr. George A.   Judge Oscar M.   Rev. Isaac B.
Three Torrison Brothers (see page 505)

most recent being that of Colonel Hans C. Heg, at Madison, Wis. It has conducted Sigvald Qvale Norwegian Declamatory Contests, at which silver and gold medals are awarded to the winners. Waldemar Ager was born at Fredrikstad, Norway, in 1869. He came to Chicago in 1886, signed the temperance pledge at the age of 17, and ever since has been one of the best temperance apostles of any time or clime. He learned the book binding trade in the employ of "Norden" and edited "Templarbladet" in his spare hours. In 1892 he came to Eau Claire to assist Ole Br. Olson with the management and publication of "Reform." He has been the business manager and treasurer of Fremad Publishing Company, which publishes "Reform," and the editor of this weekly since 1903, one of the best editorial writers in the land. In his "free" hours he has also edited "Kvartalskrift," written many books, and travelled up and down the country speaking against the American saloon and for the Norwegian culture. He is a Good Templar, a Son of Norway and a Knight of St. Olav.

The "Normandsforbundet" (Norsemen's Union) was organized in 1907. It is international in its relations, and its list of members is a good index of Norwegian world activities. It has 285 local units, totaling 45,000 members, plus 6,000 individual members. These 51,000 members are scattered over Norway, the United States, Canada, Australia, Africa, South America and Asia. The mission of this Association is to maintain a bond of friendship and brotherhood between individuals and branches of the Norwegian race throughout the world, and thus to keep up a close connection between their various adopted homes and Norway. The Union has in many cases acted as the advance guard of commercial, banking and shipping enterprises by spreading information about Norsemen and their ways and their works in the world, especially through the medium of the monthly magazine "Nordmandsforbundet," and "Nord-

Solheim, Consul E. H. Hobe's Summer Home at Bald Eagle, Minn.
(For nearly forty years Consul Hobe's spacious house has been a welcome home to visitors from abroad, and the scene of many happy gatherings of his countrymen in America)

mænd Jorden Rundt," a weekly paper devoted to the interests of the emigrants (S. C. Hammer's "Norway Year Book," 1924, p. 467-469).

The American-Scandinavian Foundation dates from 1908, and owes its origin to the bequest of $600,000.00 by Niels Paulsen, a rich New York Dane. The Foundation secures the exchange of professors and students between the universities of Scandinavia and America. Twenty selected graduate students from American schools are every year sent across to Denmark, Norway and Sweden, each one receiving a scholarship of $1,000.00; a similar number from the Scandinavian lands come here to study. Thus, Scandinavia and America are brought closer together by scholastic ties. The Foundation publishes the "American-Scandinavian Review," and a series of translations of "Scandinavian Classics." Henry Goddard Leach was the secretary of the Foundation, 1912-1921; James Creese has held this position since 1921.

The Society for the Advancement of Scandinavian Study, organized in 1911, aims to advance the teaching of the languages, literature and culture of the Scandinavian North in this country. It is a national

Mrs. Guri Endresen   Mrs. Mable Quam Stevens   Mrs. Diderikke Brandt

Lauritz Carlson   D. C. Jordahl   Ole Br. Olson

G. B. Ravndal   G. J. Lomen   E. H. Hobe

Gilbert P. Risvold   Andrew Furuseth   E. O. Wesley

organization, but its members are drawn also from Canada, Europe and elsewhere. At the annual gatherings, held at some college or university, scholarly papers are read and plans are worked out for the furtherance of the cause for which the Society stands. The Society has worked for the introduction of the study of the Scandinavian languages into the schools of this country and the preparation of adequate text books for this instruction. It publishes a quarterly—"Scandinavian Studies and Notes." Joseph Alexis, professor of Scandinavian at the University of Nebraska, is the secretary of the Society. Among the other leaders in the organization are: Kemp Malone, A. M. Sturtevant, Chester N. Gould, Lee M. Hollander, George T. Flom, Julius Olson, Henning Larsen, M. B. Ruud, Gisle Bothne, Maren Michelet, Ingebrigt Lillehei, L. M. Larson, Julius Mauritzon, A. Louis Elmquist, Halldor Hermansson and O. E. Rølvaag.

"For Fædrearven" (For the Heritage) was started at Eau Claire, Wis., in 1919, and formally organized at Crookston, Minn., May 16, 1920. As the name of the Society indicates, the aim was to awaken a deeper love for the Norwegian heritage—language, literature, history, religion, music, art, customs, culture, to teach these spiritual values to the children and youth, in the home and the school, to strengthen the family ties and social feelings, and to build a bridge between Norway and America. The Society seeks to realize these aims by a constant agitation in the press, by public lectures, literary programs, conventions, publications, the organization of local societies, and other reasonable means. The founder of the Society was Henrik Voldal, whose zeal for Northern culture was as heroic as his knowledge of things Norwegian was profound. He became the first president of "For Fædrearven," and upon his death in December, 1920, he was succeeded by H. Bjornson, who has been reelected annually to this office. O. E. Rølvaag is secretary and Gustav Amlund is treasurer.

The Order of the Knights and Dames of Leif the Discoverer states in its Constitution, adopted on Leif Erikson Day, September 29, 1923: "The Order shall have but one object, namely, that of working for the general recognition of the historical fact that America was discovered by the Norsemen already in the year 1000 A. D." (See page 100 of this History.) This Society was organized under the auspices of the Ushers' League of the Norwegian Trinity Church, Philadelphia. Annual meetings are held by the Order every September 29th, and local Leif Erikson celebrations on that day are encouraged. The Order has already obtained foothold in eight states. Jens C. Roseland is the president, 4238 Parkside Ave., Philadelphia; Leon Schov is secretary; Louis H. Christenson, treasurer.

The descendants of the Sloopers held a special Norse-American Centennial at Ottawa, Ill., September 6-7, 1925, which they advertised as the Home-Coming of the Sloopers. Ottawa is the county seat of La Salle County, and La Salle County is the first permanent home of the Sloopers in America. The Ottawa celebration put on a rich program and published a souvenir book, edited by H. T. Haagenson. Here was organized September 7, 1925, a national society of the Sloopers, modelled after the Society of the Mayflower Descendants. A constitution was adopted which reads in part as follows: "1. Name—The Sloopers: A society of the Descendants of the Norwegian people who came to America in the sloop 'Restaurationen,' leaving Stavanger, Norway, July 4, 1825, and arriving at New York, N. Y., October 9, that same year. 2. Objects—(1) To honor the memory of the Sloopers of 1825, and to perpetuate to a remote posterity the story of their spirit and deeds. (2) To promote the publication of the history of the Sloopers as a group, and of the individual families thereof, and to discover and publish any other original matter in regard to the Sloopers and their descendants. (3) To authenticate, preserve and mark historical spots made memorable by Slooper associations.

(4) To maintain a museum collection of articles having belonged to the original Sloopers and their descendants, or, otherwise illustrating their history. (5) To acquaint the present day descendants of the Sloopers with one another, through such means as the publication of literature and the holding of conventions having literary and social programs. (6) To promote the interests that are common to the Society as a whole, which is a federal body, and to any section thereof, such as, state and family organizations, within the federal body. 3. Membership—The members of this Society shall be lineal descendants of the Sloopers who came in 1825, and the spouses of such members." A "Who's Who" of the Sloopers is being prepared. Articles that came over on this Sloop are being gathered into one place. The future will tell whether the Sloopers can parallel the Mayflower people in making and writing history. J. A. Quam, Sheridan,

Rev. C. S. B. Hoel   Rev. O. S. Reigstad
Dr. G. M. Bruce   Rev. R. Malmin   Dr. G. T. Rygh
Centennial Committee of the Norwegian Lutheran Church of America

Ill., was elected the first president of the Sloopers. John Arthur Quam was born on a farm near Norway, Ill., May 24, 1854. His father, Ole A. Quam, came from Nerstrand, Norway, in 1843. Graduated from the Fowler Institute at Newark, J. A. Quam entered the mercantile business at Sheridan in 1875, later taking up banking. He is now the president of the Farmers' and Merchants' State Bank of Sheridan. He has held many town offices and has been prominent in the Methodist Church. In 1875 he married Amelia Nelson, a daughter of Peter C. Nelson, who was a son of Cornelius Nelson Hersdal, the Slooper. Mrs. Quam was a third-genera-tion Slooper, a great niece of Cleng Peerson, the Pathfinder. She died

October 30, 1925. J. A. Quam's children—Mrs. Mable Stevens, Mrs. Vida Bernard and Mrs. Hila Campbell—are of the fourth generation. His grandchildren—Hugh Quam Stevens, Ethel Bernard, and James, Gwendolin, Joyce, Maxine, Richard and Hugh Nelson Campbell—are of the fifth generation. His great-grandchildren—Stuart and Elise Stevens—are of the sixth generation of Sloopers.

The Norwegian-American Historical Association was organized October 6, 1925, at St. Olaf College, Northfield, Minn., with 116 charter members. The purpose of the Historical Association is to collect and preserve relics and records which may throw light on the life and activity of people of Norwegian birth or descent in America. "For this purpose the Association shall help to develop and maintain Norwegian-American historical archives and a museum. It will encourage and promote Norwegian-American historical research and literary work by publishing a periodical, monographs and other works." The need of this Association is apparent and its task is Herculean. The Norwegians have been in America a century, since the coming of the Sloopers (in 1825), and a thousand years, since the discovery of Greenland (in 876). They have been making history, but not writing it. They know only the outline of their own history, and their neighbors of course know less about them. The Association invites its members to serious study.

In his address held in St. Paul at the Norse-American Centennial June 8, 1925, President Coolidge commended the Norwegians for their interest in their own past and for commemorating the coming of the Sloop. Said the President: "It is a good thing that anniversaries such as this are so widely commemorated. The next few years will be filled with a continuing succession of similar occasions. I wish that every one of them might be so impressively celebrated, that all Americans would be moved to study the history which each one represents. I can think of no effort that would produce so much inspiration to high and intelligent patriotism. Occasions of this nature bring to our attention whole regions of the past that would otherwise remain unexplored, tend to be forgotten even by scholars, and pass entirely from the public mind. These incentives to special examination of particular historical phases teach us better to understand our country and our countrymen. Anyone who will study the institutions and people of America will come more and more to admire them. One reason that moved me to accept the cordial invitations to come here today was the hope of directing some measure of national attention to the absorbingly interesting subject of the social backgrounds of our country. The making of such a country is not to be told in any mere category of dates, battles, political evolutions and partisan controversies. Back of all these, which are too often the chief material of history, lies the human story of unsung millions of plain people whose names are strangers to public place and fame. Their lives have been replete with quiet, unpretentious, modest but none the less heroic virtues. From these has been composed the sum of that magnificent and wondrous adventure, the making of America. Somewhere in the epic of struggle to subjugate a continent there will be found a philosophy of human relations that the world will greatly prize. If we could seize and fix it, if we could turn it over, examine and understand it, we would have taken a long step toward solving some of the hardest problems of mankind."

The following were elected the first officers of the Norwegian-American Historical Association: D. G. Ristad, president; L. M. Larson, vice president; O. E. Rølvaag, secretary; J. Jørgen Thompson, financial secretary; O. M. Oleson, treasurer; Birger Osland, assistant treasurer; Theo. C. Blegen, Knut Gjerset and Kristian Prestgard, editorial staff; O. M. Oleson, Birger Osland and A. C. Floan, finance board. The chief mover in the organization of the Historical Association was Knut Gjerset, professor of history at Luther College and curator of the Norwegian-

American Historical Museum located there. Gjerset holds a Ph. D. from Heidelberg University (1896) and a Litt. D. from St. Olaf College (1925). He is the author of a "History of the Norwegian People" and a "History of Iceland," both Macmillan publications. He was the chairman of the Norse-American Centennial Exhibit at St. Paul, June 6-9, 1925, which in many respects assumed the proportions of a state, national or world's fair.

P. 441—Middle—Add: Leif Erikson Square is in Brooklyn, on Fourth Avenue, between 66th and 67th Streets.

P. 456—Bottom—Add: Caption under picture: Luther College Concert Band.

P. 457—Bottom—Add: Caption under picture: St. Olaf Choir.

P. 473—Middle—Add: Caption under picture: Vegreville, Alta. Picture illustrates text on page 318.

P. 475—Middle—Add: Caption under pictures: Reque—Luther College; Rockne—Notre Dame University; Anderson—St. Olaf College.

P. 503—Middle—Add line under picture: This Norwegian Grandma Is 100 Years Old Here.

P. 509—Add: Asked to give in a word the Norwegian contribution to America, the author would say: Minnesota. The Norwegian element in the United States is as large as the population of Minnesota. Minnesota is the strongest Norwegian State. Minneapolis is the capital of the Norway in America.

NOTES ON PHOTOS IN SUPPLEMENT

Arntzen, Arnliot Mattias—Page 360. 1857—. Home mission pastor in the Lutheran Free Church, editor of "Minneapolis City Directory," 1894-1904; historian.

Benson, John—Page 299. 1862—. Editor-in-chief of "Skandinaven" since 1899. Author of beautiful lyric collection "Ved Gry og Kveld."

Brandt, Mrs. Diderikke. Wife of Rev. Nils O. Brandt, the first Norwegian pastor to come west of the Mississippi River. She was one of the best known and most beloved of the pioneer women, her work at Luther College, 1865-1882, in particular endearing her to all. Mother of Mrs. Prof. Lars S. Reque, Rev. Realf O. Brandt, Prof. Olaf E. Brandt, John A. Brandt (Hayti, S. D.) and Mrs. Prof. Gisle Bothne.

Bratager, Mrs. Laura R. 1862—. Poetess, novelist, leader in church, charity and cultural activities. Lyngblomsten Society was organized at her home in 1902. This society has built Lyngblomsten Old People's Home, St. Paul. Sunelvslaget was also organized by her, and she has served as president of the lag. Collected $2,000.00 for Sunelvens Old People's Home. One of the founders of a literary club in Minneapolis. Gathered $4,000.00 for "Mindegaven" in 1914. Editor of "Døtre af Norge" and president of the Order of Daughters of Norway. Has written much for the periodicals and has published three books: "Digte og Smaafortællinger," "Før og Nu," and "Over Hav og Land." Lecturer, singer. Mother of five. See pages 402, 405, 435.

Carlson, Laurits. First lay temperance speaker and organizer. Builder of Harmony Hall, Chicago.

Dahl, Dorthea. Born in Norway, lives in Moscow, Idaho. Wonderful short story writer. Winner of literary prize. Author of "Fra Hverdagslivet," "Returning Home," "Byen paa Berget," etc. See page 406.

Endresen, Mrs Guri. Heroine of Kandiyohi County in Sioux Indian War, 1862. The State of Minnesota has erected a monument to her memory. See "North Star," December, 1920.

Furuseth, Andrew. 1854—. President International Seamen's Union of America since 1908, official secretary of Seamen's Union of the Pacific. Recognized as an authority on the American merchant marine. Home at San Francisco. See page 408.

Hanson, Karl, 1883—. Graduate of Luther College, 1908. Fine example of great band of Norwegian-Americans in public high school work. Principal, Bode Parochial School, 1908-10; principal, Story City High School, 1910-12; superintendent, Roland, Ia., 1921-1922; supt., Tama, Ia., 1922—. Instrumental in introducing the first week-day religious schools in connection with the public schools in the state of Iowa (at Roland). As secretary of the Board of Elementary Christian Education of N.L.C. in Iowa, very influential as institute conductor.

Hobe, Engebreth Hagbarth, 1860—. Trained in Arendal and Copenhagen. Came to America in 1883. Banker at Boyd, Minn. With "Nordvesten," St. Paul. To Denmark in 1886. Returned in 1887. Real estate and lumber prince. Built a railroad to his forests, also two towns—Brantwood and Knox Mills, Wis. Vice consul for Sweden and Norway 1891-1905; consul for Norway, 1905—. Chief American promoter of Norwegian America Line. He owns a 360 acre farm and a beautiful summer home—Solheim—at Bald Eagle, Minn. Hundreds of Scandinavian notables, including Prince Aksel of Denmark (1919), have been entertained at his hospitable board. He is active in the work of St. Paul Hospital, the Sons of Norway, the Norsemen's Union and other enterprises.

H. G. Leach   J. A. Quam   Arne Kildal

Together with his wife he made a trip around the world, which has been accounted for in Mrs. Hobe's well-written book "Reisebeskrivelser." He became a Knight of St. Olav in 1902, a Commander in 1916.

Johnson, Simon. Born in Gudbrandsdalen, Norway, came to North Dakota at an early age. Won the "Norske Selskap" literary prize in 1912. Is the Novelist of the Prairies. His books are: "Et Geni," "Lonea," "I et nyt Rige" (translated by C. O. Solberg under the title "From Fjord to Prairie"), "Fire Fortællinger," "Fallitten paa Braastad" and "Frihetens Hjem." See page 406.

Jordahl, Daniel C., 1864—. Lutheran pastor, 1892—, now located at Ridgeway, Iowa. Shorthand writer, former synodical secretary, president of Board of Publication. Poet. See page 504.

Kildal, Arne, 1885—. Trained at University of Christiania and New York Library Training School. In Library of Congress, 1907-10, librarian at Bergen, 1910-20; official press agent for Norway in America, 1920-25; secretary of Nordmandsforbundet, 1925—. Promoter. Author.

Leach, Henry Goddard—Page 37. 1880—. Ph.D. from Harvard University, 1908. Author of "Scandinavia of the Scandinavians," 1915; "Angevin Britain and Scandinavia," 1923. Editor of "American-Scandinavian Review," "Scandinavian Classics" and "Scandinavian Monographs," and secretary of American Scandinavian Foundation, 1912-1921. Curator of Scandinavian Collection, Harvard, 1921-1923. Editor of the "Forum," 1923—.

Lomen, Gudbrand J.—Pages 328, 471. 1854—. Judge at Nome, Alaska. Mayor of Nome, 1917-19. Promoter of reindeer industry.

Markoe, Abram—Page 71. 1727-1806. Dane. Lutheran. Friend of Washington. First president of the first Scandinavian Society in America.

Markoe, James Cox, 1856—. Great grandson of Abram Markoe, St. Paul physician. Has a complete record of the Markoes back to Denmark and France. Loaned picture of first flag. His father an Episcopalian pastor who later became a Roman Catholic priest.

Moen, Nels T. —Pages 431, 471. Graduate of Red Wing Seminary and University of Minnesota. Lawyer, 1893—; also probate judge and county attorney, Norman Co., Minn., 1893-08; municipal judge, Fergus Falls, 1911-16; member of Minn. State Legislature, 1916—; president of Østerdalslaget, 1910—; vice president of Norse-American Centennial, 1924-25; president of Council of Bygdelags, 1925—; visited Norway as member of "Amerika Kor," 1914; editor of "Fergus Falls Ugeblad," 1911—; temperance orator; had three sons in World War.

Norlie. O. M., 1876—. Photo put in here at the request of the Centennial Committee.

Olson, Clara. Has been secretary to ten governors of New Mexico.

Karl Hanson   H. J. Thorkelson   O. M. Norlie

Governor Miguel A. Otero calls her the "best informed public official in New Mexico." He speaks of her "admirable, sound judgment, discretion, unselfishness and loyalty, consideration, politeness and kindness to everyone alike, no matter whether rich or poor, Democrat or Republican."

Olson, Ole Brunshus—Page 406. Born in Oslo, Norway, in 1857, and came to Chicago at the age of twenty. Having had a fine school training, he drifted into newspaper work, and during the last twenty years of his life he devoted his best thoughts, day and night, to the cause of total abstinence and prohibition. His eloquence was sweetly persuasive, and his personal amiability paved his way into the hearts of all kinds of people. For Brunshus he wrote Br., which was interpreted "Broder" (brother) by the common people. This seemed so fitting that it clung to him to his very last. The influence of this poor, unpretentious man became great. "Ole Broder Olson" was the apostle of love among the Norse-American anti-drink champions.

Ottesen, Jacob Aall—Pages 169, 195, 196, 200, 201, 206. One of the best known of the early pastors trained at the University of Christiania. Said to be the most learned theologian of the early days.

Quam, John Arthur—Pages 132, 484. Biography on page 527.

Ravndal, Gabriel Bie—Page 494. 1865—. Consul-general at Constantinople, 1910—. Has been stationed also at Beirut, Syria, (1898-1905), Dawson, Yukon, (1905-1906), Beirut again (1906-1910). President of

Beirut Relief Commission, 1909; founder of Constantinople Red Cross. Has many decorations.

Risvold, Gilbert P.—Pages 465-466. One of the most famous of Norwegian-American sculptors.

Roe, Herman. 1886—. Publisher, "Northfield News; secretary, Minnesota Editorial Association; vice-president, National Editorial Association; secretary, Minnesota Republican Central Committee; president, Minnesota State Agricultural Society. Home, Northfield, Minn.

Roe, Louis I. 1860—. Merchant, manufacturer, banker, Stanley, Wis. Has held many public and church offices. Father of eleven children, nine living, of whom seven are graduates of St. Olaf College.

Roe, Ludvig I. Publisher, "Montevideo News" and "Thief River Falls Tribune"; past commander, Minnesota State Dept., American Legion; member several committees, National American Legion. Home, Montevideo, Minn.

Rogness, Helge. 1874—. Farmer and stock raiser near Hudson, S. D. Member of South Dakota State Legislature, 1918-1922.

Solberg, Carl K.—Pages 385, 398, 402, 403, 419, 439, 504. 1872—. Lutheran pastor. Former president of Zion Society, president of the Inner

Herman Roe   Louis I. Roe   Ludvig I. Roe
Father Roe and Two Sons

Mission Society of Minnesota, and of the Minneapolis Missionary Training School. Poet.

Stevens, Mable. 1876-1922. Daughter of J. A. Quam, great granddaughter of Cleng Peerson. Graduate of Chicago Training School for City, Home and Foreign Missions, Columbia and Soper Schools of Oratory. National organizer of the Women's Home Missionary Society of the Methodist Church. Principal of the Iowa Bible Training School, Des Moines, 3 years. Ordained in 1917 as minister in the Congregational Church, serving as state evangelist in Florida. Made two trips to Europe, Palestine, Egypt, etc. Chautauqua lecturer, 4 years. Had 84 lectures which she gave by heart.

Thorkelson, Halsten Joseph—Page 451. 1875—. A graduate of the University of Wisconsin. Later professor there in steam engineering (1902-1914), then business manager of the University (1914-1921). Secretary of General Education Board (Rockefeller), New York, 1921—. Author of "Air Compression and Transmission." Presbyterian.

Wesley, E. O. 1863—. A grading contractor in Sioux City and street commissioner. In 1911 he laid the first concrete pavement that could stand heavy traffic, which made him nationally known. He invented the Cary Expansion Joint No. 2 to put in between the sections of the pavement, now sold all over the world. He was too busy to think of patenting this device used in steel bridges, iron constructions, walls exposed to open air, etc. A good churchman, too.

Follinglo Orchestra

This is the "Follinglo Orchestra." Its members all belong to the Tjernagel family living on farms east of Story City, Iowa, brothers and their children. The musicians meet in the music room on the Peder Tjernagel farm. All pieces of furniture in this room except the piano and the organ were made by Mr. Peder Tjernagel (the cellist) from black walnut grown on the farm. The seats of the chairs have the shape of violin-bodies, the backs that of the antique lyre. The music desks are carved in Old Norse design. The large music cabinet contains drawers for music by Bach, Beethoven, Mozart, Mendelssohn, Grieg, Tschaikowsky and others, besides a special drawer for operas. The Tjernagel brothers have named the orchestra after their mother who came from Follinglo, Valders, Norway. Their father came from a farm north of Haugesund, Norway. This family has meant much to the musical life of Story City and vicinity.

First row (sitting) from left: M. Rosnes, Past President; T. O. Gilbert,
President; L. Stavnheim, Secretary
Second row: J. O. Engesather, Treasurer; J. N. Berg, Attorney; L. A.
Anderson, Actuary; O. Erichsen, Trustee
Standing: Olaf I. Rove, Trustee; H. J. Anderson, Trustee;
Arne Richstad, Vice President

SUPREME BOARD, SONS OF NORWAY

The fraternal benefit society Sønner af Norge (Sons of Norway) had
its foundation laid by a mutual benefit society which was organized in
North Minneapolis January 16, 1895, with 18 charter members. Three
years later it was decided to establish a fraternal order as soon as three
lodges had been organized. The third lodge was organized April 24, 1900,
and on June 29, 1900, the first supreme lodge meeting was opened. The
total membership of the three lodges was then 312. Since then the
Order has had a steady growth. It has now some 250 lodges and a membership of 21,000. It has been admitted into 15 states and also has some
lodges in British Columbia and Alberta, Can. It has paid death benefits
to the amount of $360,000 and some $400,000 has been paid for sick benefits
by the subordinate lodges. Sons of Norway writes life insurance in
amounts from $250 to $10,000 on a single life. The insurance business is
based on the American Mortality Table, and the valuation of its certificates as per December 31, 1924, showed a reserve of 129.37 per cent.
Since 1918 both men and women of Norwegian birth or descent are admitted to membership. The assets of the society are at present some
$750.000.(L. Stavnheim in "Norse-American Centennial Souvenir," p. 57.)

The coming of the Sloop "Restaurationen" in 1825 was appropriately commemorated in 1925 by the Norwegians in the United States, Canada and Norway. Besides hundreds of local festivals there were large celebrations at Boston, New York, Chicago, St. Paul, Seattle, Decorah, Grand Forks, Outlook, etc. Ottawa, Ill., had a Homecoming of the Sloopers. The main celebration was held at St. Paul June 6-9, at which President Calvin Coolidge was the most distinguished guest, and his speech was the most notable contribution to the success of the Norse-American Centennial. The attendance by gate tickets was over 225,000. Below the President is addressing a gathering of nearly 100,000.

Extract from the address of President Calvin Coolidge at the Norse-American Centennial, June 8, 1925, St. Paul, Minn.:

"Our America with all that it represents of hope in the world is now and will be what you make it. Its institutions of religious liberty, of educational and economic opportunity, of constitutional rights, of the integrity of the law, are the most precious possessions of the human race. These do not emanate from the government. They come from the consecration of the father, the love of the mother, and the devotion of the children. They are the product of that honest, earnest and tireless effort that goes into the rearing of the family altar and the making of a home of our country. They can have no stronger supporters, no more loyal defenders, than that great body of our citizenship which you represent. When I look upon you and realize what you are and what you have done, I know that in your hands our country is secure. You have laid up your treasure in what America represents, and there will your heart be also. You have given your pledge to the land of the free. The pledge of the Norwegian people has never yet gone unredeemed." This address has been published by Congress as House Document No. 143, 1926.

II. CORRECTIONS

P. 5—Top—1825, not: 1925.
P. 34—Bottom—*Du Chaillu,* not: Dechaillu.
P. 59—Top—1280, not: 1380.
P. 61—Middle—*Jenson,* not: Jensen.
P. 63—Top—*C. N. Gould,* not: G. N. Gould.
P. 64—Middle—*Elwha, Wash.,* not: Elva, Alaska.
P. 74—Top—53.5%, not: 63.5%.
P. 87—Middle—*Hendrick Hudson,* not: Henrik Hudson.
P. 91—Top—*Ellwood,* not: Elwood.
P. 96—Middle—*Erik,* not: Eric.
P. 110—Bottom—*Whigs,* not: Whig.
P. 123—Top—*Slogvig, Knud Anderson,* not: Slogvig, Knud.
P. 128—Bottom—*Three Larson Grandchildren,* not: Three Larson Children.
P. 134—Bottom—*Nobles,* not: Noble.
P. 146—Top—*Ozaukee* County, not: Osaukee County.
P. 146—Middle—*Hennepin* County, not: Ramsey County.
P. 147—Middle—*Redwood* County, not: Red Wood County.
P. 156—Middle—1837, not: 1838.
P. 160—Bottom—*part,* not: Part.
P. 161—Bottom—*James D. Reymert,* not: Johan R. Reymert.
P. 168—Bottom—*Was the second,* not: the first to be dedicated.
P. 169—Bottom—*George T.,* not: J. T.
P. 169—Bottom—*Erdahl,* not: Erdall.
P. 174—Middle—*Professor O. A.,* not: Professor C. A.
P. 186—Middle—*Thorson,* not: Thorsen.
P. 196—Middle—*Ekersund,* not: Egersund.
P. 198—Top—*Poulsbo,* not: Paulsbo.
P. 198—Middle—29 *years,* not: 31 years.
P. 199—Middle—*West Koshkonong,* not: East Koshkonong.
P. 200—Middle—Photo of Biørn occurs also on p. 205. The intention was to insert *J. A. Ottesen's photo* here. See p. 519.
P. 211—Middle—*Jørgen Pedersen,* not: Jørgen Pederson.
P. 213—Middle—*St. Olaf's Congregation,* not: St. Olaf Congregation.
P. 213—Middle—*gives a true account,* not: give a true account.
P. 220—Top—*"palace,"* not: palace.
P. 223—Middle—*Luther,* not: Lutheran.
P. 225—Middle—*See page 226,* not: See Page 215.
P. 227—Heading should be: *The Norwegian-American,* not: Norwegian American.
P. 228—Middle—*Newfoundland,* not New Foundland.
P. 231—Middle—*Go west,* not: Go West.
P. 246—Middle—*Oregon,* 1869, not: Oregon, 1872.
P. 246—Middle—*Clark,* not: Clarke.
P. 247—Top—*as early as* 1869 *or before,* not: as early as 1872.
P. 247—Middle—*C. J. Olsen,* not: O. J. Olsen.
P. 250—Top—*G. T. Rygh,* not: G. A. T. Rygh.
P. 251—Middle—1906, not: 1916.
P. 251—Middle—*Newfoundland,* not: New Foundland.
P. 256—Top—Two lines of verse should be *transposed.*
P. 268—Bottom—*Jon Bjarnason,* not: John Bjarnason.
P. 269—Bottom—b. 1871, not: 1861.
P. 270—Top—1885-1891, not: 1880-1889.
P. 272—Middle—*J. E. Bergh,* not: J. E. Berg.
P. 279—Middle—*business manager,* not: busines smanager.

P. 283—Middle—*J. L. Nydahl,* not: J. J. Nydahl.
P. 284—Bottom—*Luther Theological Seminary,* not: Luther Seminary.
P. 284-287—*Order:* x. St. Ansgar Seminary; y. Brooklyn Norwegian Lutheran Deaconess Home; z. Minneapolis Norwegian Lutheran Deaconess Home; æ. Red Wing Seminary; ø. Lutheran Divinity School; aa. Wittenberg Normal School.

P. 301—Top—*I. Dorrum,* not: J. Dorrum.
P. 302—Heading should be: *The American Period,* not: American Period.

P. 309—Bottom—*Larson,* not: Larsen:
P. 311—Middle—*B. B. Burr,* not: C. S. Burr.
P. 315—Top—314, not: 315.
P. 316—Bottom—*J. E. Fossum,* not: J. P. Fossum.
P. 322—Middle—*Rev. Paul Thorlakson,* not: Rev. Paul Thorlaksson.
P. 323—Top—*Numedal,* not Nummedal.
P. 328—Top—*Kootenay,* not: Kotenay.
P. 329—Middle—*D. R. Tornøe,* not: D. R. Tørnoe.
P. 330—Bottom—*Hamilton Disston,* not: Henry Disston.
P. 331—Middle—*Edward* Shulson, not: Shulson.
P. 332—Bottom—*Carl Chester* Van Dyke, not: Chester B. Van Dyke.
P. 334—Middle—*"Stavangerfjord,"* not: Stavangerfjord.
P. 337—Top—*Pacific, Chicago,* not: Pacific Chicago.
P. 340—Middle—*Omit:* and the Soo has 8,254.
P. 344—Top—*Thygeson,* not: Tygeson.
P. 344—Bottom—*Sask.,* not: Sarsk.
P. 359—Bottom—1901-1906, not: 1900-1906.
P. 365—Middle—*Presidents of Smaller Synods,* not: Presidents of smaller Synods.
P. 365—Bottom—*Dr. G. T. Rygh,* not: Dr. G. A. T. Rygh.
P. 367—Middle 2,850 *congregations,* not: 2,849 congregations.
P. 368—Middle—3,138 *congregations,* not: 3,137 congregations.
P. 370—Middle—*Andersen,* not: Anderson.
P. 371—Middle—*Firing, T. O.,* not: Firing. O. T.
P. 380—Insert—*Lutheran Bible School* in fourth line.
P. 385—Middle—*J. A. Holvik,* not: J. L. Holvik.
P. 387—Middle—*Foster,* not: Forster.
P. 388—Bottom—*Chicago Lutheran Bible School,* not: Chicago Luther Bible School.
P. 388—Bottom—*Founder and Dean,* not: Founder and President.
P. 390—Bottom—*Northwestern,* not: North Western.
P. 391—Middle—*Wraamann's Academy,* not: Wraaman Academy.
P. 392—Top—*Munson,* not: Monson.
P. 392—Middle—*L. J. Munson,* not: L. J. Monson.
P. 395—Bottom—*Deaconess,* not: Daconess.
P. 395—Bottom—*Terje Viken,* not: "Terje Viken."
P. 399—Bottom—*year of beginning,* not: yar of beginning.
P. 401—Top—*Sec'y Trustees,* not: Sec'y. Trustee.
P. 401—Middle—The present circulation of "Skandinaven" is as follows: Semi-weekly issue, 31,459; Daily, 16,672; Sunday, 8,000. Figures on page 401 were for daily issue only.
P. 402—*Omit line* 14 *from bottom,* namely: Gustav Melby, David Svenningsen and Ola J. Saervold are. *Add line: Bruun, O. A. Buslett, C. L. Christensen, K. Dalager, J. Erdahl.*

P. 406—Top—*E. E. Løbeck,* not: J. E. Løbeck.
P. 408—Bottom—*Omit:* Einar Hilsen.
P. 410—Top—*A. J. Anderson,* not: J. A. Anderson.
P. 410—Middle—*Nels Johnson, mailing mgr.,* not: Nels Johnson mailing mgr.

P. 411—Middle—*He has the distinction of having completed thirteen grades,* not: He has the distinction of having completed nine grades.

P. 416—Middle—*M. A. Pederson,* not: Pedersen.

P. 425—Middle.—*Omit:* sion of Norway coteaoinuod.

P. 430—Top—*C. O. Pedersen,* not: C. O. Pederson.

P. 430—Bottom—*Commission for Soldiers',* not: Council for Soldiers'.

P. 432—Bottom—*Knud Norswing,* not: Mr. Norswing.

P. 433—Top—*The American Period,* not: he American Period.

P. 433—Middle—*Coeur d'Alene,* not: Couer d'Alene.

P. 435—Middle—*established Hope Mission in the slums of Chicago, conducted Harmony Hall,* not: built Harmony in the slums of Chicago, established a Hope Mission,

P. 435—Middle—*Og Gustav Eide blir aldrig lei det,* not: Gustav Eide blir aldrig lei det.

P. 435—Middle—*Larsen. S. T. D.,* not: Larsen, S. T.

P. 435—Middle—*Welfare, has served,* not: Welfare, and serving.

P. 437—Middle—*Anders M. Sundheim,* not: Andrias M. Sundheim.

P. 438—Top—*Valdrises,* not: Valdreses.

P. 438—Middle—*Romsdalslaget,* not: Romdalslaget.

P. 439—Bottom—*Gilbert S. Gilbertsen,* not: S. G. Gilbertson.

P. 440—Top—*Laurits S. Swenson,* not: Lauritz S. Swenson.

P. 440—Middle—*Martin Halling is, of course, a Halling, and a good pastor,* not: Martin Halling is, of course, a Halling, and a goad pastor.

P. 440—Bottom—*and on the wife's (Hjort) side,* not: and on the mother's (Hjort) side.

P. 443—Middle—*but while in this life,* not: and while in this life.

P. 443—Bottom—*Some More Recent Inventors,* not: Some Early and More Recent Inventors.

P. 444—Top—*Aasen, Niels,* not: Aasen, Mr.

P. 446—Middle—*Alvsaker,* not: Alvasaker.

P. 452—Top—*Pollok,* not: Pollak.

P. 452—Bottom—*Scandinavian Printing Association,* not: Scandinavian Press Association.

P. 454—Middle—*Glasøe in 1899,* not: Glasøe in 1889.

P. 455—Bottom—*Krehbiel,* not: Krebhiel.

P. 460—Middle—*Norwegian Singers' Association,* not: Norwegian Singing Association.

P. 460—Middle—*March 17, 1925,* not: March 17, 1825.

P. 462—Top—*Anna Christensen,* not: Hannah Christensen.

P. 464—Middle—*Jens K. Grøndahl,* not: Jens O. Grøndahl.

P. 466—Bottom—*Eduard Boeckmann,* not: Eduard Boeckman.

P. 469—Middle—*Henrik Nissen,* not: Hendrick Nissen.

P. 471—Top—*Martin Berge,* not: Martin Berger.

P. 471—Middle—*James D. Reymert,* not: August D. Reymert.

P. 480—Top—*Hollywood,* not: Holywood.

P. 482—Near top—*his congregation,* not: his congregations.

P. 483—Middle—*Kasson (Kaasen) and Leonard Seppala,* not: Kasson (Kaasen) og Leonard Seppala.

P. 485—Bottom—*The combined service of these 45 positions,* not: The combined service of these 46 positions.

P. 487—Top—*Adolf Biermann,* not: Adolph Biermann.

P. 487—Top—*From 1842 until his death,* not: From 1892 until his death.

P. 489—Top—After Sorlie, *Non-Partisan,* not: Republican.

P. 493—Middle—*Laurits Selmer Swenson,* not: Lauritz Selmer Swenson.

P. 494—Middle—*Dawson, Canada.* not: Dawson, Alaska.

P. 495—Middle—*Major Solbert,* not: Major Seibert.

P. 509—Bottom—*but being busy with his work,* not: and being busy with his work.

P. 511—In the fifth stanza, *transpose* first and second lines.

III. TABLE OF CONTENTS

An Appendix to this "History" was originally planned, but was omitted for lack of space. It was to have contained the following statistical tables and lists, all pertaining to the Norwegians in America:

Statistical Tables
1. Immigration.
2. Population.
3. Distribution.
4. Farms.
5. Occupations.
6. Churches.
7. Pastors.
8. School attendance.
9. Pauperism and wealth.
10. Crime and war.

Tabular Lists
1. Institutions (publication, education, charity, etc.)
2. Associations.
3. Newspapers and magazines.
4. Representative churchmen.
5. Teachers of long standing at Norwegian schools.
6. Professors at 100 universities.
7. Doctors of philosophy, science, letters, law, divinity.
8. Norwegians in "Who's Who."
9. Knights of St. Olav.
10. Bibliography and references.

IV. INDEX

www.ingramcontent.com/pod-product-compliance
Lightning Source LLC
Chambersburg PA
CBHW060546280326
41932CB00011B/1410